Encyclopedia
of Sociology

Second Edition

Editorial Board

Encyclopedia of Sociology

Second Edition

VOLUME 5

Edgar F. Borgatta
Editor-in-Chief
University of Washington, Seattle

Rhonda J. V. Montgomery
Managing Editor
University of Kansas, Lawrence

Macmillan Reference USA
an imprint of the Gale Group
New York • Detroit • San Francisco • London • Boston • Woodbridge, CT

Encyclopedia of Sociology
Second Edition

Macmillan Reference USA
an imprint of The Gale Group
1633 Broadway
New York, NY 10019

Library of Congress Catalog in Publication Data
Encyclopedia of Sociology / Edgar F. Borgatta, editor-in-chief, Rhonda Montgomery, managing editor.—2nd ed.
    p. cm.
    Includes bibliographical references and index.
    ISBN 0-02-864853-6 (set: alk paper)—ISBN 0-02-864849-8 (v. 1: alk. paper)—0-02-864850-1 (v. 2)—0-02-864851-X (v. 3)—0-02-864852-8 (v. 4)—0-02-865581-8 (v. 5)
    1. Sociology—Encyclopedias. I. Borgatta, Edgar F., 1924- II. Montgomery, Rhonda J. V.

HM425 .E5 2000
301'.03—dc21
                             00-028402
                               CIP

Printed in the United States of America by the Gale Group
Gale Group and Design is a trademark used herein under license.

Staff

Publisher
Elly Dickason

Project Editors
Timothy Prairie
Pamela Proffitt

Editorial Assistants
Shawn Beall
Wayne Yang

Assistant Manager, Composition
Evi Seoud

Buyer
Rhonda Williams

Senior Art Director
Michelle DiMercurio

SOCIOLOGY AMONG THE SOCIAL SCIENCES

The relationship between sociology and the other social sciences is in reality a relationship between sectors of different disciplines, not between whole disciplines. Sociology is one of the most open disciplines toward other disciplines. This openness is manifested in the citation patterns in academic publications, which allows one to measure the degree of coherence of a discipline, the relationship between specialties within a discipline, and the interactions among disciplines. If specialists in a subdiscipline tend to cite mostly or exclusively specialists in the same subdiscipline and if relatively few authors cite outside their subdiscipline, as a whole the discipline has a low degree of internal coherence. In this case, the real loci of research are the specialties. If, by contrast, a significant proportion of authors cross the borders of their specialties, the discipline as a whole can be considered an integrated territory.

As can be seen in the analytic and alphabetical indices of most compendiums and textbooks, sociology has a weak core. The fragmentation of the discipline into isolated specialties can be seen in most sociological treatises: "We divide up the discipline into a number of topics, each the subject of a chapter. These chapters are minimally integrated" (Calhoun 1992, p. 185). Theoretical sociology is presented as a subfield disconnected from substantive domains: "General sociology has been relegated primarily to introductory textbooks and to a lesser extent to a sort of social theory that most practicing sociologists use but little in their work" (Calhoun 1992, p. 185). For instance, in Smelser (1988), the twenty-two chapters represent autonomous specialties that are only weakly related to each other. Few of the 3,200 authors cited in that work are mentioned in more than one specialty (Dogan 1997). This lack of a consensus among sociologists has been emphasized in a symposium devoted to that book (Calhoun and Land 1989).

In most general works of sociology published in the last two decades, the most frequently cited authors are ancestors, not contemporary sociologists. With exceptions such as Parsons, Merton, Lazarsfeld, and Mills, few mentors belong to the immediately previous generation. Nowadays, sociologists, in their pattern of references, are like children elevated by their grandparents. This cult of the ancestors is surprising, because "following advances in the division of labor and specialization, the works of the classics ceased to be directly useful to an average sociologist. To do correct research in a specialized branch of sociology one does not in fact have to read the works—bulky, often abstruse, and semi-philosophical in nature—written by Marx and Spencer, Simmel and Weber, Mead and Znaniecki. To do such research if suffices to master, on the basis of a possibly recent handbook, the standard techniques and the current theories of the middle range" (Szacki 1982, p. 360).

The fragmentation of sociology can be explained in part by the absence of consensus on a dominant, integrative theory or widely accepted paradigm. If a consensus could be reached among sociologists, it would be that sociology has a small, soft, and old core, that sociology is not a centripetal discipline, and that it expands in all directions.

There is very little communication between the fifty specialized domains recognized by the International Sociological Association (ISA) and between the thirty sectors of the American Sociological Association. If cooperation among the specialized fields is weak or absent, a vivid traffic can be observed between each specialized sociological domain and across disciplinary borders: the specialized group of scholars belonging formally to other disciplines, particularly specialties rooted in social psychology, social demography, social anthropology, social history, social geography, social ecology, some branches of political science, political economy, and sociolinguistics. A double phenomenon appears in the sociological literature of the last two decades: a division of the discipline into noncommunicating specialties and an opening of the disciplinary frontiers to specialties from different disciplines.

Bridges are built over the disciplinary borders. The circulation on these bridges is almost as important as the circulation along the internal arteries of formal sociology. The importance of this "foreign" trade can be measured. In a study covering four decades from 1936 to 1975, it was found that sociologists cited articles in sociology journals 58 percent of the time; political scientists cited scholars from their own discipline only 41 percent of the time; anthropologists referred 51 percent of the time to their colleagues; psychologists referred

73 percent of the time to their own kin, and 79 percent of the economists did the same (Rigney and Barnes 1980, p. 117). These figures indicate that in each social science a significant proportion of theoretical, methodological, and substantive communication has been with other disciplines, with the most open discipline being sociology and the most autonomous being economics.

In an analysis of journals identified as belonging to sociology and economics, there was a significant shift from sociology to "interdisciplinary sociology" and from economics to "interdisciplinary economics" between 1972 and 1987. The criterion for interdisciplinarity was the proportion of cited references in the journals of the respective disciplines (Crane and Small 1992, p. 204–205). An analysis by those authors in terms of clusters of references shows a clear increase in interdisciplinary relationships.

In addition to this the crossing of disciplinary borders, another important trend in the last fifteen years has been the multiplication of new hybrid journals that cross disciplines and specialties. More than 300 hybrid journals in English that concern sociology directly or indirectly have been established in this period, along with many others in French and German. Most of these new journals have a limited circulation and are addressed to readers in highly specialized subfields.

FROM SPECIALIZATION TO FRAGMENTATION TO HYBRIDIZATION

The fragmentation of disciplines is generated by an inevitable and growing process of specialization. All the sciences experience such specialization. As a discipline grows, its practitioners generally become increasingly specialized and inevitably neglect other areas of the discipline. The division of physics into physics and astronomy and the division of chemistry into organic chemistry and physical chemistry are examples in the natural sciences. In the social sciences, what was originally the study of law divided into law and political science; anthropology split into physical anthropology and cultural anthropology; and psychology broke up into psychology, social psychology, psychotherapy, and psychiatry.

Each formal discipline gradually becomes too large and unmanageable for empirical research.

No theory or conceptual framework can encompass the entire territory of sociology. Talcott Parsons was the last one to attempt such a unification, but his ambition was unrealistic (Johnston 1997). Contemporary theories are influential only within their subdisciplines. The process of fragmentation and specialization eventually is followed by a process of recombination of the specialties into new hybrid domains. These recombinations correspond to the logic of multiple and concatenated causality in the social sciences.

The more renowned new hybrid domains hoist their own flags, for instance, political sociology, which is a fusion of sectors from both of its parent disciplines; social psychology, which is already autonomous; political economy, which detaches large sectors from economics and political science and smaller sectors from sociology; and historical sociology, which has revived on both sides of the Atlantic. None of these four subfields were mentioned three decades ago by Smelser (1967). This absence shows the changes that have occurred since then.

It is pointless to lament the fragmentation of sociology or any other social science, because the interaction between specialties in different disciplines is beneficial. All social sciences, sociology in particular, have grown in depth and breadth through exchanges with cognate specialties in other disciplines. What some scholars perceive as dispersion is in reality an expansion of knowledge and an inevitable trend.

In the history of social sciences, the progression from fragmentation to specialization to hybridization has taken one of the following six forms:

1. Division in two parts, or bifurcation. The history of the sciences is a long chain of divisions. One of the oldest, going back to Aristotle, is the separation of philosophy and political theory. One of the most recent is the divorce of cognitive science from traditional psychology.

2. Changing the boundaries of formal disciplines. The growth of specialties at the interstices between disciplines has as a consequence the shrinking of the borders of the parent disciplines. When social psychology became independent, psychol-

ogy lost an enormous territory. One of the borders of economics retracted when political economy was emancipated. Anthropology has seen its frontiers retract as a result of modernization, industrialization, and urbanization; consequently, urban studies expanded. The margins of political science are in perpetual change.

3. Migration of individual scholars from one formal discipline to another or to a new territory. The founders of sociology have moved away from philosophy, such as Durkheim; from history, such as Weber; or from economics, such as Pareto (see Dogan and Pahre 1990).

4. The convergence of two domains in a new hybrid field. One of the most recent examples in medical sciences is the intermingling of fragments of cardiology with fragments of pneumonology. The nomenclature of social sciences is full of such hybrid fields.

5. Outgrowth from the mother discipline for pragmatic reasons, to the point of joining another formal discipline. For instance, sociology of medicine, the most populated sociological subdiscipline, is today located more often in hospitals than in departments of sociology; it has become a problem-solving subdiscipline.

6. Borrowing from neighboring disciplines and exchanging concepts, theories, methods, practices, tools, and substance. This borrowing and lending process is an important route of hybridization. All the social sciences share concepts, theories, and methods. The contribution of sociology to this shared repository is impressive. Sociology has devised and exported many more concepts to neighboring disciplines than have borrowed from it (Dogan 1996). Most theories formulated in a discipline sooner or later spread to other disciplines. The diffusion of theories across disciplinary borders is one of the arguments that could be invoked by those who advocate more interdisciplinary strategies in the social sciences. The borrowing and lending of methods among disciplines have itineraries different from those for the spread of concepts and theories. As contributions of methodology in social sciences, the most productive in strategies and techniques of research were until recently psychology, econometrics, social psychology, and statistics. For concepts and theories, the most creative disciplines are sociology, political science, economics, anthropology, and philosophy.

A distinction must be made between interdisciplinary amalgamation and hybridization through recombination of specialties belonging to different disciplines. A "unified sociology" existed only in the early phase of sociological development. Hybridization of specialties came later, after the maturation of the process of the internal fragmentation of disciplines. The word "interdisciplinary" is misleading when used to describe contemporary trends, because today only specialties overlap, not entire disciplines. The word "hybridization" may seem to be imported from biology, but it has been used by social scientists such as Piaget and Lazarsfeld.

Sociometric studies show that many specialists are more in touch with colleagues in other disciplines than with colleagues in their own disciplines. The "invisible college" described by Robert Merton, Diana Crane, and other sociologists of science is an eminent multispeciality institution because it ensures communication not only from one university to another and across all national borders but also between specialists attached administratively to different disciplines. The networks of cross-disciplinary influence are obliterating the old classification of the social sciences.

RECOMBINATION OF SOCIOLOGICAL SPECIALTIES WITH SPECIALTIES IN OTHER SOCIAL SCIENCES

Sociology has exchanged concepts, theories, methods, practices, and substance most intensively with three other disciplines: political science, history, and economics. The analysis here will focus first on these three disciplines. The well-known dominion of social psychology can be surveyed briefly. The relationships between sociology and social geography have long been difficult and poor. What happens in the absence of intermingling? Other specialties intervene in the empty space, as in case of ecological geography. I have to forgo the overlapping areas between sociology and social anthropology, social demography, ethnology and sociolinguistics, but the comments on the process of fragmentation of disciplines, on multiplication of specialties, and recombination of the specialties in new hybrid fields are also applicable to them.

Relations with Political Science. A double phenomenon can be observed in the relationship between sociology and political science. First, there is weak communication within each of these two disciplines among the multiple specialized fields, an impermeability between the specialized research subfields that belong formally to the same discipline. The disciplines appear like watertight compartments in large ships (Dogan 1997). Typically, there is relatively little scholarly exchange between a student of the American Congress and a specialist in Middle Eastern politics, between a political philosopher and an expert in statistical analysis, and between an Africanist and an expert on welfare states. However most of these scholars are likely to have relationships with cognate specialties in neighboring disciplines. The diversity of methodological schools contributes to the fragmentation of each discipline.

Second, across disciplinary frontiers there is a vivid traffic between special fields or subfields belonging to one discipline and similar or cognate fields in the other discipline. A convincing way to show the importance of these cross-disciplinary bridges is to rank on two columns the fifty research committees of the ISA and the forty committees of the International Political Science Association (IPSA). For each area of research in one discipline there is a homologue in the other discipline: religion, ethnicity, generations, gender, mass communication, elites, socialization, crime, social inequality and so on. To these interminglings should be added theoretical and methodological pairs: All major schools and sects are represented in both disciplines from rationalists to Marxists and from qualitative methods to proponents of quantification.

The relationships between sociology and political science can be observed by counting the proportion of authors belonging to a discipline who cite articles from other disciplines. Such an analysis of footnotes in major journals shows the trade across disciplinary frontiers and the changes in trade routes over time. In terms of import–export balance, political science has borrowed from economics, sociology, and social psychology, and has exported mostly to sociology.

There has been a change in the cross-fertilization of political science. In the 1950s and 1960s, sociology was the major lender to political science, making important contributions such as group theory, political socialization, social cleavages, and systems theory. In the 1970s and 1980s, economics was the major cross-fertilizer of political science, especially with theories of public goods and collective action, game theory, social choice, and international trade theory. Psychology has been a constant exporter to political science and sociology, but at a lower level. In the 1960s, its major contributions came from personality theory and the study of values.

One domain of sociology—political sociology—and one domain of political science—comparative politics—have privileged relations, in some cases achieving a real fusion. In the history of comparative research, there was a privileged moment of cooperation and convergence between political sociology and comparative politics in the 1960s. Between 1958 and 1972, three dozen important books and articles were published that shared three characteristics: comparison by quantification, hybridization, and cumulative knowledge. That combination had never previously been achieved in the history of sociology and political science (Dogan 1994, p. 39). This privileged moment also marks a break with European classical comparisons in the sociological style of Tocqueville, Mill, Marx, Weber, and Pareto.

The alarm over the parochial state of comparative politics after the subjugation of all social sciences during the period of totalitarianism in Europe (Scheuch 1992) and before their renaissance in the United States was raised by Roy Macridis in 1955. At the same time (1954), the Statistical Bureau of the United Nations started to publish "social statistics" on demographic variables, income, standards of living, social mobility, sanitary conditions, nutrition, housing, education, work, and criminality. These sources facilitated the encounter between political sociology and comparative politics.

In 1957, *Reports on the World Social Situation* began to be published by the Department of Economic and Social Affairs of the United Nations. The chapters in these publications in 1961 and

1963 on "the interrelations of social and economic development and the problem of balance" and on "social-economic patterns" are contributions that can be read profitably today by sociologists interested on developmental theories. Lipset's *Political Man* (1959) borrowed from all the social sciences. A year later, Deutsch produced his "manifesto" (Deutsch 1960), followed by a seminal article (Deutsch 1962). Both articles dealt with comparative indicators. The following year an important article by Cutright (1963) was published that appears in retrospect to have been prophetic. In the same year, Arthur Banks and Robert Textor published *A Cross-Polity Survey*, in which the majority of the fifty-seven variables are of direct interest to sociologists. Shortly afterward, the *World Handbook of Political and Social Indicators* by B. Russett et al. discussed seventy-five variables, the majority with sociological significance. In *Comparative Politics* by G. Almond and G. Bingham Powell (1966), several social sciences, particularly sociology and social anthropology, are seen in the background. From that moment on, the field of international comparisons became bifurcated, with both trends being related to political sociology. One road continues with quantitative research, in which contributors constantly use nonpolitical factors in their analyses of the correlates of democracy and transition to democracy. An important contribution comes again from the Development Program of the United Nations, the *Human Development Report* (1990 and after). In this publication, gross national product (GNP) per capita is replaced by a new indicator: purchasing power parity (PPP).

The other road gave priority to sectoral comparisons, for instance, the eight volumes on development published by the Princeton University Press, where politics is most of the time a dependent variable explained by social economic and cultural factors. About a thousand books and articles appear in a selected bibliography of sectoral comparisons published during the last three decades. About half of their authors belong administratively to political science, a quarter belong to sociology, and a quarter are hybrids scholars.

Comparative political sociology does not consist only in cross national analysis. It is also a cross-disciplinary endeavor, because in comparative research one is crossing units (nations) and variables (numerical or nominal). The variables are usually more numerous than the units. The relations between variables are often more important for theoretical explanations than are discoveries of analogies and differences between nations. In comparative political sociology, there is not a single major book that attempts to explain politics strictly by reference to political variables. Of course, the amount of hybridization varies with the subject and the ability of the author to omit what should be implicitly admitted.

More than 200 contemporary European and American scholars have held a joint appointment in the departments of sociology and political science or have moved from one to the other. Some comparativists cannot be locked in only one of these two disciplines.

Historical Sociology and Social History. History is the most heterogeneous discipline in the social sciences, dispersed in time and space. It is divided into a nomothetic part and an ideographic part. The dispute over the role and borders of history, which in France goes back to Durkheim, Simiand (1903), and Seignobos, does not seem to have ended. Three generations later, history has been excluded from the social sciences under the authority of an international institution: It is not numbered among the nomothetic sciences covered in UNESCO's *Main Trends in the Social and Human Sciences*. Historians do not appear to have reacted vigorously to this affront. Indeed some have come to terms with it: "The progress of history in the last fifty years is the result of a series of marriages: with economics, then with demography, even with geography . . . with ethnology, sociology and psychoanalysis. When all is said and done, the new history sees itself as something like an auxiliary science of the other social sciences" (Chaunu 1979, p. 5). This is clearly not the opinion of the other French historians (*Annales* 1989, p. 1323), who are resolutely committed to interdisciplinarity: "History will progress only in the context of interdisciplinarity."

As long as the focus is on the long time span and the comparative approach, there is agreement between Durkheim and Braudel. At a distance of sixty years, using different words, they say much the same thing: "History can be a science only in so far as it compares, and there can be no explanation without comparison . . . Once it starts comparing, history becomes indistinct from sociology" (Durkheim in the first issue of *L'Année Sociologique*

1898). Braudel is just as accommodating: "Where the long time span is concerned, the point is not simply that history and sociology tie in with each other and support each other but rather that they merge into one" (Braudel 1962, p. 93). However, this refers only to the part of history that compares while considering the long time span; other fields of history have very little to do with sociology. Similarly, many sociologists do not need to have recourse to history to resolve the problems with which they are concerned. Durkheim and Braudel would have been more explicit if instead of considering their disciplines as a whole, they had referred clearly to their common territory, which is now called comparative social history or historical sociology. Once it is accepted that history and sociology overlap only in certain areas, the long territorial dispute between history and sociology will become a thing of the past. However, this is only one sector of history brought face to face with a sector of another discipline. Exchanges with economics have thus generated economic history, which is of interest only to enough historians and economists, to provide material for several major journals. Each human activity has its historian, who, in order to perform his or her task, has to hunt in other people's lands.

On the other side of the Atlantic, as soon as their disciplines had begun to fragment, innovative historians and sociologists reached out to one another. Frederick Jackson Turner's study of the American frontier was a marriage of sociology and history with the benediction of geography. Later, sociologists such as Bellah (*Tokugawa Religion*, 1959) and Lipset (*The First New Nation*, 1963) were joined by a new generation of historians, represented by Charles Tilly's *The Vendee* (1964), Barrington Moore's *Social Origins of Dictatorship and Democracy* (1966). This interweaving of sociology and history continues to the present day.

"Most sociologists and historians have no clear understanding of what historical sociology really is" (Aronson 1969, p. 294). Unlike in economics, political science, or linguistics, the distinction is not based on subject matter. Many have attempted to clarify the differences between the two disciplines, leaving no two authors in agreement (see Boudon 1979; Lipset and Hofstadter 1968; Tilly 1981). The reason for the lack of consensus is clear: The remarkable diversity of the historical sociologies, to say nothing that of their parent disciplines, makes any unidimensional characterization of the issue unsatisfactory.

The comparative method is a very useful way to unify general statements of causality of historical events. One of the first to take this path was the French school in the journal *Annales*, which developed an approach to social history that was both sociological and comparative. Marc Bloch was one of the most influential figures in the development of this school both in his programmatic statement *Pour une histoire comparée des sociétés européennes* (1928) and in *La société féodale* (1939–1940). For some historians it is impossible to assess the validity of any causal interpretation on the basis of a single case, making a comparative approach absolutely necessary for useful explanation (Cahnman and Boskoff 1964, p. 7). Comparative history overcomes the fragmentation of specialized (and especially national) history. Examining similar causal processes in two or more specific contexts can illuminate the nature of the causal forces at work and improve one's understanding of the events being studied.

The dialogue between the specific and the general is an important issue explored by many who discuss historical sociology. Along these lines, Burke (1980) isolates two different aspects of the contributions history can make to sociology, one negative and one positive. The negative contribution entails picking away at the edifice constructed by others by showing how a theory does not fit one's society. This entails tests that are hazardous for any theory, but the theories that survive are proved to be of greater value. The positive contribution involves working out from the general to the particular in order to construct a revised general theory. This task is especially valuable because a sociologist's generalizations often appear vacuous to a historian. Historians have invalidated many of the theories of sociologists and political scientists.

When posed in this fashion, the social sciences' insistence on generalization can be helpful for historians. In the words of a sociologist turned historian, "Whatever else they do, the social sciences serve as a giant warehouse of causal theories and concepts involving causal analogies; the problem is to pick one's way through the junk to the solid merchandise" (Tilly 1981, p. 12). When one finds solid ground, a simple application of sociological theory to historical problems can be innovative.

Knapp (1984) suggests that historians can help overcome the inattention to context of most social theory. He argues that one of the major problems in sociological theory is the implicit or explicit *ceteris paribus* (all else being equal) clause. Since all other factors are never the same in the real world, such theories are repeatedly disconfirmed and often appear vacuous: "When sociologists (or political scientists, economists, or anthropologists) decide that concern with theory absolves them from concern with history, their product will not only be irrelevant historically, it will not even be adequate as theory" (Knapp 1984, p. 34). When theories are opened up to allow variation in the *ceteris paribus* clause, they can be applied to specific historical contexts. Historians who are most familiar with the peculiarities of "their" period or country have much to add to social theory in this type of research.

Contrary to what is generally believed, historical sociology sometimes is not based on quantified research. Nonetheless, quantification is so ubiquitous in most social sciences that it is easy for historians to misunderstand the nature of the field. As Tilly points out, "In field after field, the leading edge of the change was some form of quantification. Because of that uniformity, many nonquantitative historians mistook the prow for the whole ship" (Tilly 1981, p. 34). Quantified data are for most sociologists what primary sources are for historians: Some historians cannot resist quoting diaries, and some sociologists cannot resist quantifying. Both kinds of evidence have advantages and disadvantages, and each discipline can gain from making greater use of the kind of evidence most useful to the other.

In addition to a difference in method, history and sociology often are distinguished by their conceptual inventories. There are a number of sociological concepts historians can use to their advantage, such as structure, function, social role, kinship, socialization, deviance, social class and stratification, social mobility, modernization, patrons and clients, and factions. The breadth of this list makes it clear that there is much room for hybridization of subfields across the disciplinary boundaries. For instance the concept of "development" is central in several social sciences (Riggs 1984).

Relations with Eclectic Economics. To discuss the relationship between sociology and economics, it is necessary to distinguish several varieties of economists: econometricians, monodisciplinary monetarist theorists, landless theorists, and eclectic transgressors of borders (a fifth variety, economic historians, has been expelled from the field). The first two varieties have well-known physiognomies. Landless theorists (Rose 1991) are economists who believe that they do not have to deal with nation-states and tend to reduce all countries to a single model. They travel at the level of landless economies. One may assume that the first three varieties are outstanding contributors to scientific knowledge, since so many of them have been awarded Nobel prizes, but here only the last variety has good relations with the other social sciences.

Eclectic economists denounce the reductionism advocated by other economists. Four decades ago, Hayek wrote that "nobody can be a great economist—and I am even tempted to add that the economist who is only an economist is likely to become a nuisance if not a positive danger" (Hayek 1956, p. 463). For the Nobel prize laureate Buchanan, "it becomes increasingly clear that the channels of effective communication do not extend throughout the discipline that we variously call 'economics' and that some 'economists' are able to communicate far more effectively with some scholars in the noneconomic disciplines than with those presumably within their own professional category" (Buchanan 1966, p. 181). Another Nobel prize laureate asked: "Why should economics be interdisciplinary? The answer is, presumably, because otherwise it will make mistakes; the neglect of all but the narrowly economic interactions will lead to false conclusions that could be avoided" (Solow 1970, p. 101). Many economists state that "it is necessary to reduce the use of the clause *ceteris paribus*, to adopt an interdisciplinary approach, that is to say to open economics to multidimensionality" (Bartoli 1991, p. 490).

Economics is also divided, but to a lesser degree than the other social sciences. It has maintained some coherence but has had to pay a high price for this by considerably reducing its field. At one time, economics reached a fork in the path: It could have chosen intellectual expansion and the penetration of other disciplines at the cost of heterogeneity and diversification and at the risk of dispersal (a risk taken by sociology and by political science); it chose instead to remain true to itself, thereby forfeiting vast territories. Many economists consider that the choice of purity, methodological rigor, and hermetic terminology was the right choice.

It is thus clear that self-sufficiency eventually leads to a shrinking of borders, but this does not mean general impoverishment, since the lands abandoned by economists were soon cultivated by others. Those lands now have their own departments, research centers, and professional schools (management, political economy, development science). The position of economics in the constellation of the social sciences today might have been more dominant if so many economists had not withdrawn into monodisciplinarity.

This situation is surprising in that "few classical sociologists have failed to assign a central place in their theories to the relationship between economy and society: from Marx and Weber to Schumpeter, Polanyi, Parsons and Smelser" (Martinelli and Smelser 1990).

If many economists have locked themselves in an ivory tower and allowed whole areas to escape from their scrutiny, other economists have advocated an "imperialistic expansion of economics into the traditional domains of sociology, political science, anthropology, law and social biology" (Hirschleifer 1985, p. 53; Radnitzky and Bernholz 1986). Several of these economists are famous scholars, including several Nobel laureates. A kind of manifesto has been published in *The American Economic Review*:

> It is ultimately impossible to carve off a distinct territory for economics, bordering upon but separated from other social disciplines. Economics interpenetrates them all, and is reciprocally penetrated by them. There is only one social science. What gives economics its imperialist invasive power is that our analytical categories are truly universal in applicability. Thus economics really does constitute the universal grammar of social science. But there is a flip side to this. While scientific work in anthropology and sociology and political science and the like will become increasingly indistinguishable from economics, economists will reciprocally have to become aware of their functions. Ultimately, good economics will also have to be good anthropology and sociology and political science and psychology. (Hirschleifer 1985, p. 53)

This view is anachronistic, but many outstanding economists have succeeded not only in exporting their knowledge to other disciplines but also in invading them with their methods and theories and achieving innovative research. Arrow's *Social Choice and Individual Values* (1951) led mathematically trained economists to apply game theory to a variety of social conflict situations. Several works made such applications, including Anthony Down's *An Economic Theory of Democracy* (1957), Duncan Black's *The Theory of Committees and Elections* (1958), Buchanan and Tullock's *The Calculus of Consent* (1962), Riker's *The Theory of Political Coalitions* (1962), and Olson's *The Logic of Collective Action* (1965). Since then, many social scientists have borrowed ideas and techniques from economists and applied them to the analysis of various processes and situations. The economists were the first in the field because they had a longer tradition of mathematical training and used more abstract and thus more widely applicable concepts. The other social sciences had learned statistics in order to handle the interpretation of their empirical data but were much slower to learn advanced mathematics. In a number of important graduate schools, economists hold joint appointments with other social science departments.

Some economists continue to spread the application of their analytic techniques to outside fields. Becker wrote a book on discrimination and prejudice and in *Treatise on the Family* (1981), applied economic analysis to topics such as the incidence of marriage, divorce, and childbearing. He was awarded the Nobel Prize in Economic Sciences in 1992 for his work applying economics to different areas of human behavior, particularly the family, a traditional stronghold of demography. Gordon Tullock's *The Economics of Non-Human Societies* deals with ants, termites, bees, mole rats, sponges, and slime molds. Many similar examples could be given (Szenberg 1992): "The fields to which the economic approach or perspective has been applied over the last thirty or forty years include politics, sociology, ethnology, law, biology, psychology" (Radnitzky and Bernholz 1986). An examination of recent issues of journals of economic literature shows that some economists explore a wide range of issues. Among these eclectic economists a few who work in another discipline and then return immediately to the home discipline. Intriligator (1991) has presented in a schematic way the patterns of cross-fertilization among the behavioral sciences by identifying concepts and theories developed in economics and adopted by others. He traces in terms of input–output the itinerary of social choice theory, structural models, decision theory, organization theory, bounded rationality, utility theory, game theory, the concept of balance of power, and anomie.

The interactions between economics and political science are deeper than those between economics and sociology. Many economists are better known in political science than in economics, particularly in the domain of political economy. In *A New Handbook of Political Science* (Goodin and Klingemann 1996), the new economic sociology receives great attention, but it is not clear how it is different from the older political economy. This work should be confronted with *Handbook of Economic Sociology* (Smelser and Swedberg 1994). For instance, Offe describes the "asymmetry" between the two disciplines: "Political economists do have an economic theory of institutions and tend to disregard this demarcation line separating spheres. Sociologists have perhaps only the rudiments of a sociological theory of what is going on in markets and firms, while the most ambitious argument that sociologists do have to offer effectively demonstrates that non-economic spheres of society are not only constituted in different ways than the economy, but that the economy itself depends on non-economic spheres" (Offe 1992, p. 687).

Social Psychology. Most sociologists are not involved in the kind of research that interests most psychologists, and vice versa. For the majority of sociologists and the majority of psychologists, their respective territories are clearly separated. Nevertheless, between the two disciplines there is a condominium, social psychology, inhabited by hybrid scholars, some of whom have began their scientific activity in one of the two disciplines while others started as "hybrids." In addition, for many sociologists who are not social psychologists, psychology is the nearest and most important disciplinary neighbor. What Inkeles wrote three decades ago is still valid: "It would not be at all difficult to assemble a set of fifty or one hundred recent articles in social psychology, chosen half from the psychological and half from the sociological jour-nals, which would be so much alike that no one, judging without knowledge of source or author, could with any precision discriminate those written by professional sociologists from those written by psychologists. Several considerations follow from this simple fact. Clearly, the two disciplines cannot be defined in terms of what psychologists and sociologists respectively do, since they so often do the same thing" (Inkeles 1970, p. 404).

The growth of social psychology during the last two generations makes Durkheim's arguments in favor of the supremacy of sociology over psychology irrelevant, along with the old debate about the individual–society dichotomy: "The claim to a principled distinction of sociology from psychology based on the distinction of individual from society is challenged by the substantial attention that at least some sociologists pay to individuals, by difficulties in describing psychology as the study of individuals, and by difficulties in the very conceptual distinction of individual from society" (Calhoun 1992, p. 175). At the early stages of the discipline's postwar history, psychology had been the most cited cognate discipline by sociologists, but during the last two decades, it was partly overtaken by political science and economics. Meanwhile social psychology has become an autonomous discipline.

Relations with Ecological Geography. As a reaction against the exaggerations of the sociologist Huntington (1924), who was criticized by Pitirim Sorokin in 1928, an entire generation of American sociologists was dissuaded from taking geographic factors into consideration. Even today, most sociologists and geographers ignore each other.

Until recently, sociologists neglected environmental and climatic factors, but many prominent hybrid scholars did not remain silent. Lewis noted that: "it is important to identify the reasons why tropical countries have lagged during the last two hundred years in the process of modern economic growth" (Lewis 1955, p. 53). Galbraith wrote: "If one marks off a belt a couple of thousand miles in width encircling the earth at the equator one finds within it no developed countries . . . Everywhere the standard of living is low and the span of human life is short" (Galbraith 1957, p. 39–41). The book published by Kamarck, director of the Economic Development Institute of the World Bank, challenges the common perception of tropical areas.

Trypanosomiasis, carried by the tsetse fly, prevented much of Africa from progressing beyond the subsistence level: "For centuries, by killing transport animals, it abetted the isolation of Tropical Africa from the rest of the world and the isolation of the various African peoples from one another" (Kamarck 1976, p. 38). An area of Africa larger than the United States thus had been denied to cattle (Kamarck 1976, p. 39). Agricultural production in the humid tropics is limited by the condition of the soil, which has become laterite (Kamarck 1976, p. 25). Surveys by the World Health Organization and the World Food Organization estimated that parasitic worms infected over one billion people throughout the tropics and subtropics. Hookworm disease, characterized by anemia, weakness, and fever, infected 500 million in those areas (Kamarck 1976, p. 75).

These ecological factors are confirmed by a considerable amount of research in tropical areas during the last several decades by geologists, geographers, biologists, zoologists, botanists, agronomists, epidemiologists, parasitologists, climatologists, experts of the World Bank and several agencies of the United Nations, and hybrid scientists well versed in tropical agriculture, the exploitation of minerals, and the sanitary conditions in those countries. The situation has improved, according to dozens of reports prepared by international organizations. To explain the economic underdevelopment of tropical Africa and other tropical areas, natural sciences and demography are brought into the picture. Dependency theory may be of some help for Latin America and eastern Europe, though much less so for tropical Africa.

The literature on the ecological parameters of the tropics can be contrasted with the literature on the transfer of flora and fauna from one temperate zone to another. For instance, Crosby's *Ecological Imperialism: The Biological Expansion of Europe 900–1900* (1986), casts new light on the building of American power.

This is an example of what can happen when a discipline neglects an important topic. The vacuum left by the absence of sociological studies of this geographic-ecological-economic issue has been filled by eclectic economists and hybrid ecologists.

Sociologists and geographers have met not in vast "interdisciplinary" work but in a series of individual fields such as urban studies. In the history of this hybrid in the United States, important work came from sociologists in the subfields of "human ecology," geographers influenced by sociologists, and scholars in both disciplines working on spatial statistics. Once a hybrid, urban studies is now a department at many large universities in Europe and the United States.

Urban studies as a quasi-discipline includes subfields that overlap specialties in sociology, geography, and anthropology. It also encompasses architecture, which covers engineering (building design and methods), the natural sciences (climatology, energy conservation), the social sciences (social-physical research), the humanities (history of architecture), and some hybrids of its own (urban planning). Some architects today are well versed in engineering, the natural sciences, the social sciences, and the humanities, as well as urban planning.

Urban studies also has been influenced by economics and economic geography. This hybrid has made its major contribution in the area of location theories for agricultural, industrial, and commercial activities. Communication seems to be much better with geographers and even sociologists than it is with economists, partly because the inductive nature of much of this work makes it difficult to integrate into deductive economic theory.

Other sociologists have drawn from sectors of geography in conjunction with history and economy. Rokkan (1995) has suggested a conceptual framework for comparative political analysis. He weaves together Parsonian pattern variables, the sequence of various kinds of "crises," and the typically Scandinavian notion of center–periphery relations into a geographic schema built around the main Hansa–Rhine–Italy trade routes, the notion of a country's distance from Rome, and whether a state faces seaward or is landbound. This schema is very suggestive not only because it can clarify the different political outcomes in the states of modern Europe but also because it can help one understand why many once-powerful states have disappeared, such as Scotland, Wales, Brittany, Bohemia, Bavaria, and Aragon.

Today, geography's breadth can be seen in the multiplication of hybrid subfields. The discipline now encompasses the subfields of human geography, cultural geography, biogeography, geomorphology, climatology, medical geography, economic geography, political geography, urban geography, environmental science, regional geography, and cartography. Each subfield relates directly to specialties outside the discipline. Different interests have favored closer contacts sometimes with one field and sometimes with another. These outside fields have made some of geography's most important advances.

As a result of all these trends, there is an incredible fragmentation that has made geography span large areas in both the natural and social sciences, with a general tendency to drift from the former to the latter. From studying habitats, geographers have turned to studying societies. Many traditional geographers have become social scientists.

As in other disciplines, interaction has kept geography on the move. Many geographers have developed their method and have penetrated other disciplines to such a degree that they have become specialists in another discipline (geology, hydrology or ethnology) or one sector of another discipline. Such emigration leaves the old core of the discipline empty. At a symposium on the social sciences in Paris in 1982, a geographer asked, "With the progress of the other social sciences, what remains proper to geography? A residual part, or a boring nomenclature?. . . Does geography still have its own domain, or is it a relic . . . of an old division of labor? Has geography an identity and, if so, of what is it made?" (Brunet 1982, pp. 383, 402). As is true for the other social sciences, its identity can be found in hybrid specialties, not in disciplinary unity.

CONCLUSION

The contemporary social sciences have experienced three major trends: rapid expansion, fragmentation of formal disciplines by increasing specialization, and recombination of specialties in new hybrid domains. The social sciences have expanded enormously over the last four decades. During the years 1956–1960, the number of citations in the Social Science Citation Index (SSCI) for all social sciences amounted to 2,400,000. Thirty years later, in the years 1986–1990 the number of articles cited in this thesaurus rose to about 18,000,000, increasing by a factor of 7.5 (SSCI 1994, pp. 61–63).

It is difficult to evaluate the number of articles rooted in sociology or relevant for sociologists even if one can locate the origin of the articles and adopt criteria for what is relevant and what is not. The main difficulty comes from the ambiguity and arbitrariness of the borders of these disciplines. Between one-quarter and one-third of the articles cited by sociologists in the last few decades were written by economists, political scientists, psychologists, historians, geographers, and other social scientists.

In 1994, the SSCI contained almost two million citations involving 400,000 authors from fifteen disciplines and from many countries, an average of five citations per author. Among those citations, between 5 and 8 percent referred to articles written by sociologists. Obviously, no one can master the entire spectrum of sociology. There are no paradigms in the discipline, only partial and contested theories and moving borders. One can succeed in finding one's way in the bibliographical labyrinth because the scientific patrimony is structured in sectors, subdisciplines, areas, fields, subfields, specialties, topics, and niches in spite of the fact that the borders are blurred. This increasing specialization within sociology is the main route of scientific advancement. Some scholars recommend an interdisciplinary approach. Just as some seem to believe that the social sciences can be neatly categorized, many others persist in pursuing interdisciplinarity. That recommendation is not realistic because it overlooks an essential phenomenon in the history of science: specialization through a process of fragmentation.

To understand scientific creativity, another phenomenon is even more important than the expansion of the scientific literature and the increase in specialization: the recombination of specialties into new hybrid domains, a phenomenon called the hybridization of scientific knowledge.

A hybrid scholar is a specialist who crosses the borders of her or his home discipline by integrating into her or his research factors, variables, theories, concepts, methods, and substance generated in other disciplines. Different disciplines may proceed from different foci to examine the same phenomenon. This multidisciplinarity implies a division of territories between disciplines. In contrast, hybridization implies an overlapping of segments of disciplines, a recombination of knowledge in new and specialized fields. Innovation in each discipline depends largely on exchanges with other fields belonging to other disciplines. At the highest levels, most researchers belong to a hybrid subdiscipline. Alternatively, they may belong to a hybrid field or subfield.

An innovative recombination is a blending of fragments of sciences. When old fields grow, they accumulate such masses of material that they split up. Each fragment of the discipline then confronts the fragments of other fields across disciplinary boundaries, losing contact with its siblings in the old discipline. A specialist in urbanization has less in common with a sociologist studying elite recruitment than he or she does with a geographer doing research on the distribution of cities, who in turn has more in common with a colleague in economics analyzing urban income inequality.

Most hybrid specialties and domains recognize their genealogical roots: political economy, social psychology, social geography, historical sociology, genetic demography, psycholinguistics, political anthropology, social ecology, biogeography, and many others. The hybrid specialties branch out in turn, giving rise, to an even larger member of hybrids (Dogan and Pahre 1990, pp. 63–76).

Among the ISA research committees and study groups, about half focus on hybrid specialties. The number of sociologists who work across disciplinary borders is so high that there is more communication between various fields of sociology and their cognates outside the discipline than there is between fields within sociology.

One can find in the literature of each social science, with the possible exception of linguistics and econometrics, complaints about the "lack of core": "The substantive core of the discipline may have dissolved" (Halliday and Janowitz 1992, p. 3). Dozens of similar testimonies could be collected. If so many scholars formulate the same diagnosis, that means that most disciplines are facing a problem of self-identity. However, if one considers that the real world cannot be cut into disciplinary pieces, this issue of disciplinary identity may appear fallacious.

It is difficult or impossible to inquire into the large social phenomena within a strictly monodisciplinary framework. Only by taking a position at the crossroads of many branches of

knowledge can one explain the impact of technological advancement on structural unemployment in western Europe, the proliferation of giant cities in the third world, the economic decline of the United Kingdom and the economic growth of Japan, or how a child learns to speak. Whenever a question of such magnitude is raised, one finds oneself at the intersection of numerous disciplines and specialities. All major issues cross the formal borders of disciplines: war and peace, generational change, the freedom–equality nexus, individualism in advanced societies, and fundamentalism in traditional societies. Most specialists are not located in the so-called core of a discipline. They are in the outer rings, in contact with specialists from other disciplines. They borrow and lend at the frontiers; they are hybrid scholars. The notion of hybridization does not mean "two whole disciplines in a single skull" but a recombination of two or several domains of knowledge originating from different disciplines.

Most classical sociologists were interdisciplinary generalists, but in recent times, cross-disciplinary advancements have been achieved not by generalists but by hybrid specialists. The hybrid specialist today may be in reality a "marginal" scholar in each of the disciplines from which he or she borrows, including his or her original discipline, but such a specialist becomes central to the intersection of two or several disciplines (Dogan 1999).

Today most social scientists admit that the best alternative to the difficulty of experimentation in their disciplines is the comparative method, which is one of the few ways to validate or falsify generalizations in the "soft" sciences. The comparative method is the key to circulation among sciences.

Comparative sociologists and comparative political scientists have developed methods to a greater extent than have workers in other social sciences. One of them wrote: "There is no noncomparative sociological theory. All scientific analyses are a subset of the general set entitled comparitive analysis . . . any generalized statement involving variables implies a comparison" (Levy 1970, p. 100).

Major social phenomena cannot be explained in a strictly monodisciplinary framework or in the absence of a comparative perspective. It is only by taking up a position at the crossroad of various branches of knowledge and simultaneously adopting comparative perspective that social scientists can advance knowledge. The intersections of hybrid specialties and comparative approaches are privileged sites in the social sciences.

REFERENCES

Aronson, Sidney 1969 "Obstacles to a Rapprochement between History and Sociology: A Sociologist's View." In Muzafer Sherif and Caroline Sherif, eds., *Interdisciplinary Relationships in the Social Sciences.* Chicago: Adline.

Aymard, Maurice 1988 "Histoire et Sociologie." In H. Mendras and M. Verret, eds., *Les Champs de la Sociologie Française.* Paris: Colin.

Bartoli, H. 1991 *L'Economie Unidimensionnelle.* Paris: Economica.

Boudon, Raymond 1979 "Sociologie et Histoire: L'analyse Sociologique du Singulier." In *La Logique du Social.* Paris: Hachette.

Braudel, Fernand 1962 "Histoire et Sociologie." In G. Gurvitch, ed., *Traité de Sociologie.* Paris: PUF.

Brunet, Roger 1982 "La Géographie." In *Les Sciences de l'Homme et de la Société en France: La Documentation Française.*

Buchanan, James 1966 "Economics and Its Scientifc Neighbors." In Sherman R. Krupp, ed., *The Structure of Economic Science.* Englewood Cliffs, N.J.: Prentice-Hall.

Burke, Peter 1980 *Sociology and History.* London: Allen & Unwin.

Cahman, Werner, and Alvin Boskoff (eds.) 1964 *Sociology and History and Research.* Free Press.

Calhoun, Craig 1992 "Sociology, Other Disciplines and the Project of a General Understanding of Social Life." In T. C. Halliday and M. Janowitz, eds., *Sociology and Its Publics.* Chicago: University of Chicago Press.

——, and K. C. Land 1989 "Symposium: Smelser's Handbook: An Assessment." *Contemporary Sociology* 18:475–513.

Chaunu, Pierre 1979 "Interview." *Le Courrier du CNRS* 33:5.

Collins, Randall 1986 "Is 1980s Sociology in the Doldrums?" *American Journal of Sociology* 91 (6):1336–1355.

Crane, Diana, and Henry Small 1992 "American Sociology since the Seventies: The Emerging Identity Crisis in the Discipline." In T. C. Halliday and M. Janowitz, eds., *Sociology and Its Publics.* Chicago: University of Chicago Press.

Dogan, Mattei 1994 "Fragmentation of the Social Sciences and Recombination of Specialties." *International Social Science Journal* 139:27–42.

—— 1996 "Political Science and the Other Social Sciences." In R. Goodin and H. D. Klingemann, eds., *A New Handbook of Political Science.* Oxford, U.K.: Oxford University Press.

—— 1997 "The New Social Sciences: Crack in the Disciplinary Walls." *International Social Science Journal.* 153:429–443.

—— 1999 "Marginality." In M. Runco and S. Pritzker, eds., *Encyclopedia of Creativity.* New York: Academic Press.

——, and Robert Pahre 1990 *Creative Marginality, Innovation at the Intersections of Social Sciences.* Boulder, Colo.: Westview.

Galbraith, J. K. 1957 "Conditions for Economic Change in Underdeveloped Countries." *Journal of Farm Economics* 33:255–269.

Gay, David, and Alan R. Waters 1983 "The Interrelationships of Economics with the Social Sciences." *Social Science Journal* 20(3):1–8.

Goodin, Robert E., and Hans-Dieter Klingemann 1996 *A New Handbook of Political Science.* Oxford, U.K.: Oxford University Press.

Halliday, Terence, and Morris Janowitz (eds.) 1992 *Sociology and Its Publics.* Chicago: University of Chicago Press.

Hayek, F. A. 1956 "The Dilemna of Specializtion." In Leonard White, ed., *The State of the Social Sciences.* Chicago: University of Chicago Press.

Hirshleifer, Jack 1985 "The Expanding Domain of Economics." *American Economic Review* 72 (6):53–68.

Huntington, Ellsworth 1924 *Civilization and Climate.* New Haven, Conn.: Yale University Press.

Inkeles, Alex 1970 "Sociological Theory in Relation to Social Psychological Variables." In J. C. McKinney and E. A. Tiryakian, eds., *Theoretical Sociology.* New York: Appleton.

—— 1983 "The Sociological Contribution to Advances in the Social Sciences." *Social Science Journal* 20(3):27–44.

Intriligator, Michael 1985 "Independence among the Behavioral Sciences." *Structural Changes and Economic Dynamics* 1:1–9.

Johnston, Barry U. 1997 "Dominant Intellectual Tradition and the Coherence or Disintegration of the Discipline?" Paper presented at the International Institute of Sociology, Cologne, Germany.

Kamarck, Andrew M. 1976 *The Tropics and Economic Development.* Johns Hopkins University Press for the World Bank.

Klein, Julie Thompson 1996 *Crossing Boundaries.* Charlottesville: University of Virginia Press.

Knapp, Peter 1984 "Can Social Theory Escape from History: View of History in Social Science." *History and Theory* 23(1):34–52.

Kohn, Melvin, L. (ed.) 1989 *Cross-National Research in Sociology*. London: Sage.

Levy, Marion, J. 1970 "Scientific Analysis is a Subset of Comparative Analysis." In John C. McKinney and Edward A. Tiryakian, eds., *Theoretical Sociology*. New York: Appleton.

Lewis, W. A. 1955 *The Theory of Economic Growth*. Allen Unwin.

Lipset, S. M., and R. Hofstadter 1968 *Sociology and History: Methods*. New York: Basic Books.

Martinelli, A., and N. Smelser 1990 "Economic Sociology, Historical Trends and Analytic Issues." *Current Sociology* 38 (2):1–49.

McKinney, John C., and Edward A. Tyriakian eds. 1970 *Theoretical Sociology*. New York: Appleton.

Messer-Davidow, E., D. R. Schumway, and D. J. Sylvan, eds. 1993 *Knowledge: Historical and Critical Studies in Disciplinarity*. Charlottesville: University of Virginia Press.

Offe, Claus 1992 "Political Economy: Sociological Perspectives." In Robert B. Goodin and Hans-Dieter Klingemann, eds., *A New Handbook of Political Sciences*. Oxford, U.K.: Oxford University Press.

Radnitzky, G., and P. Bernholz 1986 *Economic Imperialism: The Economic Approach Outside the Traditional Areas of Economics*. New York: Paragon.

Riggs, Fred W. 1984 "Development." In G. Sartori, ed., *Social Science Concepts: A Systematic Analysis*. Sage.

Rigney, D., and D. Barnes 1980 "Patterns of Interdisciplinary Citation in the Social Sciences." *Social Science Quarterly* 114–127.

Rokkan, Stein 1995 Special issue dedicated to Rokkan's geoeconomic model. *Revue Internationale de Politique Comparée* 2 (1):5–170.

Rose, Richard 1991 "Institutionalizing Professional Political Science in Europe." *Political Studies* 39 (3):446–462.

Scheuch, Erwin, K. 1992 "German Sociology" In E. F. Borgatta and M. L. Borgatta, eds., *Encyclopedia of Sociology*. New York: MacMillan.

Simiand, François 1903 "Méthode historique et science sociale." *Revue de Synthése Historique*.

Smelser, Neil 1967 "Sociology and the Other Social Sciences." In P. Lazarsfeld, H. Sewell, and H. L. Wilensky, eds., *The Uses of Sociology*. New York: Basic Books.

—— ed. 1988 *Handbook of Sociology*. London: Sage.

Smelser, Neil, and Richard Swedberg eds. 1994 *Handbook of Economic Sociology*. Princeton, N.J.: Princeton University Press.

Social Sciences Citations Index, SSCI, Philadelphia Institute for Scientific Information.

Solow, Robert 1970 "Science and Ideology in Economics." *The Public Interest* 21:94–107.

Szacki, Jerzy 1982 "The History of Sociology and Substantive Sociological Theories." In T. Bottomore, S. Nowak, and M. Sokolowska, eds., *Sociology: The State of the Art*. London: Sage.

Szenberg, Michael 1992 *Eminent Economists: Their Life Philosophies*. Cambridge, U.K.: Cambridge University Press.

Tilly, Charles 1981 *As Sociology Meets History*. New York: Academic Press.

—— 1984 *Big Structures, Large Processes, Huge Comparisons*. New York: Russell Sage Foundation.

Turner, R. H. 1991 "The Many Faces of American Sociology: A Discipline in Search of Identity." In D. Easton and C. Schelling, eds., *Divided Knowledges: Across Disciplines, Across Cultures*. Newbury Park, Calif.: Sage.

MATTEI DOGAN

SOCIOLOGY OF EDUCATION

In the broadest perspective, education refers to all efforts to impart knowledge and shape values; hence, it has essentially the same meaning as socialization. However, when sociologists speak of education, they generally use a more specific meaning: the deliberate process, outside the family, by which societies transmit knowledge, values, and norms to prepare young people for adult roles (and, to a lesser extent, prepare adults for new roles). This process acquires institutional status when these activities make instruction the central defining purpose, are differentiated from other social realms, and involve defined roles of teacher and learner (Clark 1968). Schools exemplify this type of institutionalization.

The central insight of the sociology of education is that schools are socially embedded institutions that are crucially shaped by their social environment and crucially shape it. The field encompasses both micro- and macro-sociological concerns in diverse subfields such as stratification, economic development, socialization and the family, organizations, culture, and the sociology of knowledge. To understand modern society, it is essential to understand the role of education. Not only is education a primary agent of socialization and allocation, modern societies have developed formidable ideologies that suggest that education *should* have this defining impact (Meyer 1977).

Durkheim (1977) was the intellectual pioneer in this field, tracing the historical connections between the form and content of schools and larger social forces such as the rise of the bourgeoisie and the trend toward individualism. Largely because the field focuses so intensively on stratification-related issues (e.g., the impact of family background on educational attainment), the larger issues raised by Marx and Weber are readily evident in current scholarship. However, as Dreeben's (1994) historical account indicates, the direct contribution of the discipline's founders to the development of the sociology of education in the United States was minimal; indeed, even the foremost early American sociologists in the field did not decisively shape its development.

In *The Sociology of Teaching*, Waller (1932) examined teaching as an occupational role and school organization as a mechanism of social control. He emphasized the role of the school in the conflict-ridden socialization of the young as well as the interpersonal and organizational mechanisms that furthered students' acceptance of the normative order. Although now recognized as a classic, Waller's analysis stimulated little work for several decades.

Although less focused on education per se, Sorokin (1927) portrayed schools as a key channel of mobility with their own distinctive form of social testing. He argued that increasing opportunities for schooling would stratify the society, not level it. However, Blau and Duncan's (1967) paradigm-setting study of status attainment (see below) did not refer to Sorokin's analysis of education despite their appreciation of his larger concern for the significance of social mobility. Warner's and Hollingshead's community studies considered education integral to community social organization, especially through its connection to the stratification system, but their influence, like that of Waller and Sorokin, was more a matter of suggesting general ideas than of establishing a cumulative research tradition.

As a subfield within the sociological discipline, the sociology of education has been propelled largely by a host of practical, policy-related issues that emerged with the development of the mass educational system. Essentially, research has focused on whether education has delivered on its promise of creating more rational, culturally adapted, and productive individuals and, by extension, a "better" society. The field was particularly energized by the egalitarian concerns of the 1960s: How "fair" is the distribution of opportunity in schools and in the larger society, and how can disparities be reduced? These questions continue to animate the field.

THEORETICAL DEBATES

Much research, even the most policy-oriented, has been grounded, often implicitly, in more general analytic perspectives on the role of education in modern society. The two main orientations are functionalism and conflict theory, though other, less encompassing perspectives also have shaped the field significantly.

Functionalism. In the functionalist view, schools serve the presumed needs of a social order committed to rationality, meritocracy, and democracy. They provide individuals with the necessary cognitive skills and cultural outlook to be successful workers and citizens (Parsons 1959; Dreeben 1968) and provide society with an efficient, fair way of sorting and selecting "talents" so that the most capable can assume the most responsible positions (Clark 1962). Complementing this sociological work is human capital theory in economics, which contends that investment in education enhances individual productivity and aggregate economic growth (Schultz 1961). The criticism in the 1980s that poor schooling had contributed significantly to America's decline in the international economy reflects a popular version of this theoretical orientation.

However, in the 1970s, both the increasing prominence of critical political forces and the accumulated weight of research spurred a theoretical challenge. Important parts of the empirical base of functionalism were questioned: that schools taught productive skills, that mass education had ushered in a meritocratic social order, and that education had furthered social equality. A number of conflict-oriented approaches emerged.

Neo-Marxist Theory. Neo-Marxist scholars have provided the most thorough challenge to the functionalist position. For all the diversity within this conflict theory, the main point is that the organization of schools largely reflects the dictates of the corporate-capitalist economy. In the most noted formulation, Bowles and Gintis (1976) argue that education must fulfill the needs of capitalism: efficiently allocating differently socialized individuals to appropriate slots in the corporate hierarchy, transferring privilege from generation to generation, and accomplishing both while maintaining a semblance of legitimacy. Thus, the changing demands of capitalist production and the power of capitalist elites determine the nature of the educational system.

More recent neo-Marxist scholarship (Willis 1981) emphasized that schools are not only agents of social reproduction but also important sites of resistance to the capitalist order. Many neo-Marxists also have emphasized the "relative autonomy" of the state from economic forces and, correspondingly, the partial responsiveness of schools to demands from subordinate groups (Carnoy and Levin 1985). Other scholars in this general critical tradition have turned in "post-Marxist" directions, emphasizing inequities related to gender and race along with class, but the common, defining point remains that educational inequities reflect and perpetuate the inequities of capitalist society and that oppressed groups have an objective interest in fundamental social transformation (Aronowitz and Giroux 1985). This newer critical approach has developed with relatively little connection to mainstream approaches (i.e, positivistic, often reform-oriented research) despite some similarities in concerns (e.g., student disruptions and challenges to authority in schools) (Davies 1995).

Obviously, neo-Marxists do not share the essentially benign vision of the social order in functionalist thought, but both perspectives view the organization of schooling as "intimately connected with the changing character of work and the larger process of industrialization in modern society" (Hurn 1993, p. 86). These competing perspectives are rooted in similar logical forms of causal argument: To explain educational organization and change, functionalists invoke the "needs" of the society, while neo-Marxists invoke the "needs" of the capitalist order for the same purpose. Critics contend that both perspectives posit

an overly tight, rational link between schools and the economy and concomitantly downplay the institutional autonomy as schools as well as the complexity of political struggles over education (Kingston 1986).

Status Conflict. Arising out of the Weberian tradition, the status conflict approach emphasizes the attempts of various groups—primarily defined by ethnicity, race, and class—to use education as a mechanism to win or maintain privilege (Collins 1979). The evolving structure of the educational system reflects the outcomes of these struggles as groups attempt to control the system for their own benefit. With varying success, status groups use education both to build group cohesion and to restrict entry to desired positions to those certified by "their" schools. However, as lower-status groups seek social mobility by acquiring more educational credentials, enrollments may expand beyond what is technically necessary. In this view, then, the educational system is not necessarily functional to capitalist interests or other imputed system needs.

Consistent with this view, a primary effect of schools, especially at the elite level, is to provide *cultural capital*, of which educational credentials are the main markers (Bourdieu and Passeron 1977). This form of capital refers to the personal style, social outlooks and values, and aesthetic tastes that make a person suitable for socially valued positions. (The point of comparison is *human* capital, an individual's productive, technical skills.) In this perspective, education is rewarded because occupational gatekeepers value particular forms of cultural capital, and thus education is a key mechanism of class and status reproduction.

The Interpretative Tradition. Sociologists in the interpretative tradition view schools as places where meaning is socially constructed through everyday interactions. This tradition incorporates the general orientations of phenomenology, symbolic interactionism, and ethnomethodology. Accordingly, micro-level concerns predominate—for example, what do teachers expect their students to learn, and how do those expectations condition their conduct in class?—and research tends to rely on qualitative techniques. This tradition is unified by a general sense of what kinds of questions to ask (and how to ask them) rather than a set of related theoretical propositions or a body of accumulated findings.

EMPIRICAL STUDIES

The highly selective review of empirical studies that follows focuses on the two key questions in contemporary American sociology of education: (1) How is education involved in the distribution of life chances? (2) How are family status and school characteristics connected to educational attainment and/or academic achievement? With few exceptions, analyses of education in other countries are not considered. The field is dominated by American research, and American sociologists have engaged in relatively little comparative research. Baker (1994) speculates that this lack of a comparative research tradition in the United States reflects both a belief in American "exceptionalism" (for instance, an extreme emphasis on mass access) and a strong focus on micro-level issues that do not necessarily call for comparative research designs.

Schooling and Life Chances. Throughout the twentieth century in all industrial countries, there has been a dramatic upgrading in the occupational structure *and* a dramatic expansion in educational systems. Ever more jobs have come to require academic qualifications, a process that usually is interpreted as being driven by the rationalism and universalism of modernization. In this functionalist perspective, academic skills are presumed to be technically required and meritocratically rewarded, transforming the stratification system so that individual achievements rather than ascriptive characteristics determine life chances.

This interpretation has been subject to empirical test at two levels: (1) the *individual level*—to what extent, absolutely and relatively, does education affect economic attainment? and (2) the *macro level*—to what extent have educational expansion and the increasing significance of schools for occupational attainment increased overall equality of opportunity?

At the first level, as part of the general analysis of *status attainment*, researchers have concentrated on measuring the connection between individuals' schooling and their economic position. Building on Blau and Duncan's (1967) work, researchers have repeatedly documented in multivariate models that education (measured in years of schooling and degree completion) has by far the largest independent impact on adult attainment (Featherman and Hauser 1978; Jencks et al. 1979). By comparison, the net direct effects of family status (usually measured in terms of parental education and occupation) are modest. Indeed, among the college-educated in recent years, higher family status confers no extra advantage at all (Hout 1988).

Earlier in life, however, family status is substantially related to educational attainment. The total effect (direct and indirect) of family status on occupational attainment is therefore substantial, though its impact is mediated very largely through educational attainment. In effect, then, education plays a double-sided role in the stratification process. Education is the great equalizer: It confers largely similar benefits to all regardless of family origins. However, it is also the great reproducer: Higher-status families transmit their position across generations largely through the educational attainment of their children.

The strong connection between schooling and occupational attainment is open to diverse interpretations. Most prominently, human capital theory suggests that education enhances productivity, and because people are paid in accordance with their marginal productivity, the well educated enjoy greater prospects. In favor of this interpretation is the fact that schooling is demonstrably linked to the enhancement of academic competencies (Fischer et al. 1996) and that basic academic skills are substantially correlated with job performance in a wide variety of settings (Hunter 1986).

By contrast, credentials theory portrays the educational institution as a sorting device in which individuals are slotted to particular positions in the occupational hierarchy on the basis of academic credentials, often with little regard for their individual productive capacities. The fact that possessing specific credentials (especially a college degree) has positive career effects, net of both years of schooling and measured academic ability, provides indirect support for this view. That is, there appears to be a "sheepskin effect," so that employers value the degree per se, although people with degrees may have unmeasured productive capacities or dispositions that account for their success (Jencks et al. 1979). Moreover, the credentialist argument is strengthened by the fact that in some elite segments of the labor market, employers primarily recruit graduates of certain prestigious programs and make little effort to discern differences in the academic-based skills of those included in the restricted applicant pool (Kingston and Clawson 1990).

Both views seem to have some merit; indeed, they may be partially complementary. Employers may generally use educational attainment as a low-cost, rough proxy for productive skill, and for certain positions they may favor holders of particular degrees because of their presumed cultural dispositions and the prestige that their presence lends the organization. The relative explanatory power of the human capital and credentialist perspectives may vary across segments of the labor market.

At the macro level, it might be expected that the great expansion of access to education has reduced the impact of family origins on educational attainment, increasing equality of opportunity, but that has proved to be more the exception than the rule. A rigorous thirteen-country comparative study identified two patterns: greater equalization among socioeconomic strata in the Netherlands and Sweden and virtual stability in the rest, including the United States (Shavit and Blossfeld 1993), where the strata have largely maintained their relative positions as average attainment has increased. Thus, the impact of educational policies designed to promote equality appears minimal; even in Sweden and the Netherlands, the trend toward equalization emerged before reforms were introduced.

Socioeconomic Status and Achievement. Given the centrality of educational attainment in the general attainment process, researchers have focused on the substantial relationship between socioeconomic status and educational attainment. (This relationship appears to be stronger in highly developed societies than in developing societies.) The best predictor of educational attainment is academic achievement (i.e., higher grades and test scores); the school system consistently rewards academic performance and in that sense is meritocratic. Regardless of academic performance, children from socially advantaged families have somewhat disproportionate success in moving through the educational system, but the main reason higher-status students have this success is that they achieve better in schools.

The question here is, Why do higher-status students achieve better in schools? Clearly, there is no simple answer. Research has pointed to the following family-related factors, among others:

1. *Material resources.* Richer families can purchase the materials (e.g., books) and experiences that foster intellectual development.

2. *Parental expectations and/or encouragement.* Well-educated parents more actively stress the importance of academic achievement, and their own success through schooling encourages their children to accept that value.

3. *Direct parental involvement in home learning activities.* Higher-status parents are more willing and able to teach academic lessons at home and help with homework.

4. *Verbal and analytic stimulation.* In higher-status families, interactions between parents and children are more likely to promote verbal sophistication and reasoning.

5. *Family structure and parenting style.* The presence of two parents and parenting styles involving warm interactions favor academic achievement, and both factors are related to socioeconomic status (SES).

6. *Parental involvement in schools.* Higher-status parents are better able to interact effectively with teachers and administrators to secure favorable treatment and understand expectations.

7. *Cultural "fit" with schools.* The cultural styles of higher-status students are more compatible with the prevailing norms and values in schools.

8. *Social capital.* Initially Coleman's (1988) idea, this refers to the extent and nature of the connections between parents and children as well as the connections with other family and community members. By providing informational, emotional, and other resources, these connections facilitate adaptions to the demands of schools.

9. *Social context.* Higher-status families are likely to live in communities where other families promote achievement and their children's peers are committed to academic achievement.

10. *Genetic advantage.* Early IQ is related to SES, and intelligence is related to academic performance.

Individually, none of these factors seems to account for a large part of the overall relationship between SES and academic achievement, nor is the relative significance of these factors clear, yet the very length of the list suggests the complexity of the issue. Higher-status students are not all similarly advantaged by each of these factors, and lower-status students are not all similarly disadvantaged by each one. The substantial aggregate relationship between SES and achievement undoubtedly reflects complex interactions among the many home-related contributing causes. As is more thoroughly discussed below, the mediating impact of school resources and practices is much less consequential.

The Racial Gap. The black-white disparity in academic performance remains large despite some notable reductions in recent years, and it is economically significant. A number of researchers have shown that for younger cohorts, the racial disparity in earnings is accounted for very largely by differences in basic academic skills as measured by scores on tests such as Armed Forces Qualifications Test (Farkas 1996).

Why this gap persists is unclear, partly because until recently, sociologists and other social scientists were wary of addressing such a politically explosive issue. Most relevant for the discussion here is the fact this gap cannot be explained by blacks' lesser school resources (see "School Effects," below). Largely drawing on the work of scholars in related fields, the sociological consensus appears to be that the racial disparity does not reflect a *group*-based difference in genetic potential (Jencks and Phillips 1998). (At the individual level, there is undoubtedly some genetic component to IQ among people of all races.) Moreover, this gap cannot be attributed largely to racial differences in economic advantage: Socioeconomic status explains only about a third of it. However, a broader index of family environment, including parental practices, may account for up to two-

thirds of the gap (Phillips et al. 1998). A complete explanation probably will involve many of the factors previously noted in the discussion of the relation between SES and achievement but also include the distinctive cultural barriers that "involuntary minorities" face in many societies (Ogbu 1978) as well as subtle interactional processes within schools.

Racial disparities in educational attainment have declined dramatically. High school graduation rates are now virtually the same, and the remaining disparity in college attendance reflects blacks' lower economic resources, not a distinctive racial barrier.

School Effects. The governmental report *Equality of Educational Opportunity* (Coleman et al. 1966) strongly challenged conventional wisdom about the connections among economic status, schools, and achievement. In doing so, it fundamentally shaped the agenda for further research in this area.

Attempting to identify the characteristics of schools that improve learning, the so-called Coleman Report documented two key points. First, there is a weak relationship between social status and school quality as measured by indicators such as expenditure per pupil, teachers' experience, and class size despite considerable racial segregation. Second, these measures of school quality have very little *overall* effect on school achievement (scores on standardized tests) independent of students' family background. The Coleman Report also showed, however, that school effects were notably larger for black and Hispanic students than they were for whites and Asians. Among the school effects, the racial composition of schools was the most critical: Blacks did somewhat better in integrated schools.

Later research largely validated the main conclusions of the Coleman Report, but also modified them, often by considering more subtle aspects of school quality. For instance, some school resources, including expenditures, seem to enhance achievement, but the predominance of home factors on achievement remains undisputed. In regard to another between-schools effect, Coleman argued for the educational superiority of Catholic schools, an advantage he attributed to their communal caring spirit and high academic expectations for all students. The Coleman Report did not consider such cultural matters or specific educational practices. Much of the post–Coleman Report research focused on within-school effects because gross between-school effects appeared to be relatively minor.

Ability grouping in elementary schools and tracking in high schools have attracted attention, largely as a source of inequalities of academic performance. The premise of these practices is that students differ substantially in academic ability and will learn more if taught with students of similar ability. Although many different practices are grouped under the term "tracking," students in the "top" groups generally receive a more demanding education, with higher expectations, more sophisticated content, and a quicker pace, and are disproportionately from advantaged families. The obvious but not fully settled issue is whether schools "discriminate" in favor of the socially advantaged in making placements. At the high school level, controlling for measures of prior achievement (themselves affected by family factors), higher SES seems to enhance one's chances modestly, though achievement factors are predominant in placement. Blacks are somewhat favored in the process if one controls for prior achievement. At the elementary school level, research is less consistent, though one study indicates that neither test scores nor family background predicts early reading group placement (Pallas et al. 1994).

Another important but not fully settled issue is whether students in certain ability groups or tracks learn more because of their placement. Gamoran (1992) shows that the effects of tracking are conditioned substantially by the characteristics of the tracking system (for example, how much mobility between tracks is allowed) and subject matter. However, by way of gross summary, higher track placement per se generally seems to have a modestly beneficial impact on achievement and also seems to increase students' educational aspirations and self-esteem. However, to exemplify the important exceptions to this generalization, it appears that within-class grouping for elementary school mathematics may help both low and high groups.

Teacher Expectations. It is commonly supposed that differences in teachers' expectations explain at least some of the racial and socioeconomic disparities in academic achievement. The claim is that a self-fulfilling prophecy is at work: Teachers expect less from socially disadvantaged students and treat them accordingly, and therefore these students perform less well in school. Rosenthal and Jacobson's (1968) small-scale experimental study provided the initial impetus for this argument, but follow-up studies in real classrooms suggest that teachers' expectations have little or no effects on later performance.

If the standard for fairness is race neutrality in light of past academic performance, there is little evidence of racial bias in teachers' expectations, but some limited evidence suggests that teachers' beliefs are more consequential for blacks than for whites (Ferguson 1998). More generally, research has not established that socially discriminatory practices in schools significantly explain the link between family and/or racial status and achievement.

Contextual Effects. Not only do students come to school with different backgrounds that affect learning, schools provide students with different social environments that are importantly shaped by the economic and racial composition of the student body. Because peers are so influential in children's and adolescents' lives, the obvious question is whether the social composition of a school affects individual learning beyond the effects attributable to an individual's status characteristics. This issue has had practical significance in light of ongoing public debates about the impact of racial desegregation initiatives.

Evidence about the impact of social context on learning is mixed, but in any case the impact is not large. To the extent that the SES of a student body is consequential, this appears to result from the connection between SES and a positive academic climate in a school. Greater racial integration generally seems to promote black student achievement slightly, but the benefits are more pronounced for black students when they actually have classroom contact with white students rather than just attending a formerly integrated school.

More recent research suggests an important cautionary note about whether integration "works." Entwistle and Alexander (1992), for example, show that on a yearlong basis, in the early grades black students in integrated schools had better reading comprehension than did black students in segregated schools. However, the apparent advantage of integrated schools totally reflects the fact that black students at integrated schools improved more during the summer than did black students at segregated schools. During the school year black students did slightly better in segregated schools. This analysis exemplifies the increasing recognition that a simple conclusion about integration—works versus does not work—is inadequate.

Learning through the Year. As should be evident, a major issue in the sociology of education is separating the effects of the home from the effects of the school. The perplexing finding is that racial and class disparities in achievement in the early grades become substantially greater as students progress through school. Critics have seized on this finding to indict schools for discriminatory practices that exacerbate social inequality.

However, so-called summer learning research suggests a different interpretation (Alexander and Entwistle 1995; Gamoran 1995). Examining the same students' test scores at the beginning and ending of each of several school years, researchers have shown that (1) despite initial disparities, advantaged and disadvantaged groups have roughly similar gains in achievement during the school year but that (2) advantaged students continue to improve during the summer while disadvantaged students stagnate or decline. As the effects of this process accumulate over the years, initial disparities become ever larger. The important implication is that schools neither reduce nor add to the inequalities that are rooted in homes. Schools in effect passively reproduce existing inequalities.

Enhancing Performance. Although crude measures of school resources (e.g., teacher certification levels) appear at most to be weakly related to school achievement, a burgeoning and increasingly sophisticated line of research finds that effective schools can be identified. These schools are marked by strong leadership committed to academically focused goals and order, high academic demands, and frequent practice of academic skills. This research also directs attention to the benefits of an overall communal culture and classroom interactions that stress cooperative efforts between students and teachers (Lee and Croninger 1994). What appears critical is how resources are organizationally applied.

Macro-Level Effects. This article has focused on the experiences of individuals: how education affects life chances and how personal characteristics and school experiences affect learning. The unit of analysis, in other words, is the individual. Research in the field much less commonly takes the society as the unit of analysis: How do societal features shape the nature of the educational system? How do the features of this system affect other societal arrangements? An important example of macroanalysis is the generally limited impact of increasing educational access on equality of opportunity (see "Schooling and Life Chances," above). Perhaps the most studied macro-level topic is the relationship between educational expansion and economic growth.

If the individual economic benefits of education are clear, the impact of educational expansion on economic growth is less certain. The orthodox view in economics is that educational expansion promotes growth. This view follows from human capital theory: People with more schooling get higher pay *because* they are more productive, and if more people get more schooling, they will produce more and get paid more, with the aggregate effect being economic growth. Many sociologists are at least partially skeptical of this idea. Undoubtedly, more educated workers get paid more, but the positive (private) rate of return they enjoy reflects greater productivity only if it is assumed that the labor market is perfectly competitive and in equilibrium. This assumption is at least partly problematic given socially discriminatory employment practices, internal labor markets with seniority rules and restricted job mobility, professional and union restrictions of labor supply, and public sector employment with politically determined pay structures.

Allocation theory—which also is called the credentialing perspective—offers an alternative explanation of the link between education and economic rewards. In brief, employers assume that the more educated, as a group, are *relatively* desirable people to hire (for reasons that may or may not reflect their individual productive capacities); and in turn, how people are ranked in the educational hierarchy becomes linked to how they are ranked in the hierarchy of the *existing* job structure. Educational expansion, then, does not necessarily promote economic growth; it only affects who gets which of the already existing jobs. To the extent that credentialing processes are operative, it is impossible to infer aggregate effects on growth from individual-level data on income.

Given the ambiguous implications of individual income data, the best way to examine the issue is through aggregate, *national*-level studies of how education affects economic growth. The accumulated weight of this research undercuts claims about the large *universal* benefits of more education of all types. Benavot (1992), for example, establishes the following for a large sample of developed and poor countries in the period 1913–1985: Throughout the period, the expansion of primary education promoted growth; the expansion of secondary education had more modest impact, and only during times of worldwide prosperity; and tertiary education tended to *retard* growth at all times. In the United States, moreover, tertiary enrollments have never stimulated growth (Walters and Rubinson, 1983).

However, even if more education is not a universal economic "fix," in certain circumstances particular types of education may stimulate growth in specific sectors. Reviewing single-country times series studies that use an aggregate production function model, Rubinson and Fuller (1992) conclude that education had the greatest beneficial impact when it created the kinds of skills that were suited to an economy's sectoral mix and technological demands. However, a good fit between the educational system and the economy is by no means certain because educational expansion and the actual educational content of schools are so often driven by political processes, not technological demands.

Even if the actual economic impact of education is often less than is commonly supposed, the widespread belief in the general modernizing benefits of education is central to an ideology that permeates the entire world. Indeed, in Meyer's institutionalist perspective (Meyer and Hannan 1979; Meyer 1977), the quest to appear modern has induced later-developing societies to mimic the educational practices of the early modernizers so that many school structures, rituals, and formal curricular contents are remarkably similar throughout the world. In turn, this institutionalized similarity means that on a global basis, certain types of knowledge become defined as relatively significant, the elite and mass positions become defined and legitimated by educational certification, and assumptions about a national culture rest on the existence of mass education. Nevertheless, if education is associated at the individual level with certain democratic values, educational expansion per se does not appear to contribute to the emergence of democratic regimes or state power.

THE REFORMIST PROJECT

Policy debates about education have often been contentious, fueled by larger ideological and political struggles. In conservative times, schools have been pressed to emphasize discipline and social and/or intellectual sorting; conversely, in more liberal times, issues of equality and inclusion have come to the fore. The apparent result is cyclical, pendulum-like swings in policy between, say, an emphasis on common core requirements and highly differentiated curricula.

While differences at the rhetorical level have sometimes been sharp, actual changes in practice in much of the twentieth century have been relatively minor. This reflects the institutionalization of the school, meaning that there is a widespread collective sense of what a "real" school is like (Tyack and Cuban 1995). This institutionalization rests on popular legitimization and the recurrent practices of school administrators and teachers. Concrete practices such as the division of knowledge into particular subject areas, the spatial organization of classrooms, and the separation of students into age-based grades are all part of the "real" school. Educational practices that depart from this pattern have had limited acceptance, for example, open classrooms in the 1970s. The lesson for current reformers is that policies that modify institutionalized practices, not fundamentally challenge them, are more likely to be successful and that the political support of in-the-school educators is critical for success.

Indeed, much policy-oriented research has had a mildly reformist bent, primarily concerned with making existing schools "work better." That has largely — and narrowly—meant producing students with higher scores on standardized tests in the basic academic subject areas. Critics have questioned both the validity of these tests and the desirability of evaluating school "success" in these limited terms alone. Proponents contend that scores on these tests have considerable predictive validity for later school and occupational performance and that their standardized results permit rigorous comparisons across groups and school settings.

The welter of policy-related studies is impossible to summarize here (and the distinction between sociological research and educational research is hardly sharp), but two general types of contributions from sociologists stand out. The first is essentially a debunking contribution: Sociologists have shown what does *not* work despite fervent beliefs to the contrary. The previously discussed Coleman Report is the most prominent example, undercutting the liberal faith of the 1960s that differences in school resources substantially account for racial and socioeconomic differences in academic achievement.

The second contribution is essentially methodological, alerting policymakers to the fact that many apparent school effects may largely or even totally reflect selection biases. That is, if groups of students are subject to different educational practices, are any differences in their performance attributable to the educational practices per se, or are different sorts of students subject to different practices, thus accounting for the association between practice and performance? In recent years, controversies about the efficacy of private and Catholic schools, related to larger debates about school choice plans, have centrally involved the issue of selection bias. In the most sophisticated study, Bryk et al. (1993) demonstrate net positive effects of Catholic schools on academic achievement and show that the gap in achievement between white and minority students is reduced in Catholic schools.

Even with the most sophisticated multilevel, multivariate statistical models, however, sociologists cannot make firm *causal* claims by analyzing survey data. However, by ruling out many potential sources of spuriousness, these analyses can suggest interventions that are likely to have a positive effect. True experiments, which involve the actual manipulation of the treatment and/or practice, are rare. In a state-sponsored experiment in Tennessee, starting in kindergarten, students were randomly assigned to varyingly sized classes (with and without a teacher's aide). The results showed that students, especially minority students, benefited academically from small classes (thirteen to seventeen students) and that the benefits persisted even when the students later moved to larger classes (Finn and Achilles 1990). Prior nonexperimental analyses had shown, across the range of class size in existing schools, that class size had very little or no effect.

Now that it is accepted that schools can make a difference in learning despite the great significance of family-based factors, the research agenda probably will focus on specifying the conditions in which particular school practices are most effective. This will involve analyzing inside-school practices as well as the links between families and schools and between schools and the workplace.

REFERENCES

Alexander, Karl, and Doris Entwistle 1995 "Schools and Children at Risk." In Allan Booth and Judith Dunn, eds., *Family-School Links: How Do They Affect Educational Outcomes?* Hillsdale, N.J.: Erlbaum.

Aronowitz, Stanley, and Henry Giroux 1985 *Education under Siege: The Conservative, Liberal and Radical Debate over Schooling.* South Hadley, Mass.: Bergin and Garvey.

Baker, David 1994 "In Comparative Isolation: Why Comparative Research Has So Little Influence on American Sociology of Education." *Research in Sociology of Education and Socialization* 10:53–70.

Benavot, Aaron 1992 "Educational Expansion and Economic Growth in the Modern World, 1913–1985." In Bruce Fuller and Richard Rubinson, eds., *The Political Construction of Education.* New York: Praeger.

Blau, Peter, and Otis D. Duncan 1967 *The American Occupational Structure.* New York: Wiley.

Bourdieu, Pierre, and Jean-Claude Passeron 1977 *Reproduction in Society, Culture, and Education.* Beverly Hills, Calif.: Sage.

Bowles, Samuel, and Herbert Gintis 1976 *Schooling in Capitalist America.* New York: Basic Books.

Bryk, Anthony, Valerie Lee, and Peter Holland 1993 *Catholic Schools and the Common Good.* Cambridge, Mass.: Harvard University Press.

Carnoy, Martin, and Henry Levin 1985 *Schooling and Work in the Democratic State.* Stanford, Calif.: Stanford University Press.

Clark, Burton 1962 *Educating the Expert Society.* San Francisco: Chandler.

—— 1968. "The Study of Educational Systems." In David L. Sills, ed., *International Encyclopedia of the Social Sciences.* New York: Macmillan and Free Press.

Coleman, James 1988 "Social Capital and the Creation of Human Capital." *American Journal of Sociology* 94(Supplement):S95–S120.

—— Ernst Campbell, Carol Hobson, James McPartland, Alexander Mood, Frederick Weinfeld, and Robert York 1966 *Equality of Educational Opportunity*. Washington, D.C.: U.S. Government Printing Office.

Collins, Randall 1979 *The Credential Society*. New York: Academic Press.

Davies, Scott 1995 "Leaps of Faith: Shifting Currents in Critical Sociology of Education." *American Journal of Sociology* 100(6):1448–1478.

Dreeben, Robert 1968 *On What Is Learned in School*. Reading, Mass.: Addison-Wesley.

—— 1994 "The Sociology of Education: Its Development in the United States." *Research in Sociology of Education and Socialization* 10:7–52.

Durkheim, Émile 1977 *The Evolution of Educational Thought*, trans. Peter Collins. London: Routledge and Kegan Paul.

Entwisle, Doris, and Karl Alexander 1992 "Summer Setback: Race, Poverty, School Composition, and Mathematics Achievement in the First Two Years of School." *American Sociological Review* 59:446–460.

Farkas, George 1996 *Human Capital or Cultural Capital?* New York: Aldine de Gruyter.

Featherman, David, and Robert Hauser 1978 *Opportunity and Change*. New York: Academic Press.

Ferguson, Ronald 1998 "Teachers' Perceptions and Expectations and the Black-White Test Score Gap." In Christopher Jencks and Meredith Phillips, eds., *The Black-White Test Score Gap*. Washington, D.C.: Brookings Institution Press.

Finn, Jeremy and Charles Achilles 1990 "Answers and Questions about Class Size: A Statewide Experiment." *American Educational Research Journal* 27:557–577.

Fischer, Claude, Michael Hout, Martin Sanchez Jankowski, Samuel Lucas, Ann Swidler, and Kim Voss 1996 *Inequality by Design: Cracking the Bell Curve Myth*. Princeton, N.J.: Princeton University Press.

Gamoran, Adam 1992 "The Variable Effects of High School Tracking." *American Sociological Review* 57:812–828.

—— 1995 "Effects of Schooling on Children and Families." In Allan Booth and Judith Dunn, eds., *Family-School Links: How Do They Affect Educational Outcomes*. Hillsdale, N.J.: Erlbaum.

Hout, Michael 1998 "More Universalism, Less Structural Mobility: The American Occupational Structure in the 1980s." *American Journal of Sociology* 93:1358–1400.

Hunter, John 1986 "Cognitive Ability, Cognitive Aptitudes, Job Knowledge, and Job Performance." *Journal of Vocational Behavior* 29(3):340–362.

Hurn, Christopher 1993 *The Limits and Possibilities of Schooling*, 3rd ed. Boston: Allyn and Bacon.

Jencks, Christopher, and Meredith Phillips, eds. 1998 *The Black-White Test Score Gap*. Washington, D.C.: Brookings Institution Press.

—— et al. 1979 *Who Gets Ahead? The Determinants of Economic Success in America*. New York: Basic Books.

Kingston, Paul 1986 "Theory at Risk: Accounting for the Excellence Movement." *Sociological Forum* 1:632–656.

—— and James Clawson 1990 "Getting on the Fast Track: Recruitment at an Elite Business School." In Paul Kingston and Lionel Lewis, eds., *The High Status Track: Studies of Elite Schools and Stratification*. Albany, N.Y.: State University of New York Press.

Lee, Valerie, and Robert Croninger 1994 "The Relative Importance of Home and School for Middle-Grade Students." *American Journal of Education* 102:286–329.

Meyer, John 1977 "The Effects of Education as an Institution." *American Journal of Sociology* 83:55–77.

——, and Michael Hannan, eds. 1979 *National and Political Change, 1950–1970*. Chicago: University of Chicago Press.

Ogbu, John 1978 *Minority Education and Caste: The American System in Cross-Cultural Perspective*. New York: Academic Press.

Pallas, Aaron, Doris Entwisle, Karl Alexander, and M. Francis Stluka 1994 "Ability Group Effects: Instructional, Social or Institutional?" *Sociology of Education* 67:27–46.

Parsons, Talcott 1959 "The School Class as a Social System." *Harvard Educational Review* 29:297–308.

Phillips, Meredith, Jeanne Brooks-Gunn, Greg Duncan, Pamela Klebanov, and Jonathan Crane 1998 "Family Background, Parenting Practices, and the Black-White Test Score Gap." In Christopher Jencks and Meredith Phillips, eds., *The Black-White Test Score Gap*. Washington, D.C.: Brookings Institution Press.

Rosenthal, Robert, and Lenore Jacobson 1968 *Pygmalion in the Classroom*. New York: Holt, Rinehart, and Winston.

Rubinson, Richard, and Bruce Fuller 1992 "Specifying the Effects of Education on National Economic Growth" In B. Fuller and R. Rubinson, eds., *The Political Construction of Education*. New York: Praeger.

Schultz, Theodore 1961 "Investment in Human Capital." *American Economic Review* 51:1–17.

Shavit, Yossi and Hans-Peter Blossfield, eds., 1993 *Persistent Inequality: Changing Educational Attainment in Thirteen Countries*. Boulder, Colo.: Westview Press.

Sorokin, Pitirim 1927 *Social Mobility*. Glencoe, Ill.: Free Press.

Tyack, David, and Larry Cuban 1995 *Tinkering Toward Utopia: A Century of Public School Reform*. Cambridge, Mass.: Harvard University Press.

Waller, Willard 1932 *The Sociology of Teaching*. New York: Wiley.

Walters, Pamela, and Richard Rubinson 1983 "Educational Expansion and Economic Output in the United States." *American Sociological Review* 48:480–493.

Willis, Paul 1981 *Learning to Labor*. New York: Columbia University Press.

PAUL W. KINGSTON

SOCIOLOGY OF ISLAM

Like Christianity and Judaism, Islam is an Abrahamic religion based on prophecy, prophethood, and the revealed text. It began in sixth-century Arabia and spread rapidly to regions outside the Arabian peninsula. A hundred years after Mohammed had declared it a prophetic religion, Islam had spread to almost all the regions of the known civilized world. This early political success and the idea that the divine message for the proper ordering of society is complete and final account for the social pervasiveness of this religion. The first factor inhibits the handing over of spheres of life to nonreligious authority, and the second makes it difficult to offer rival versions of the blueprint. This social pervasiveness makes Islam especially interesting in the sociology of religion (Gellner 1983, p.2).

Islam is the second largest religion, with an estimated 1.2 billion adherents, constituting about 20 percent of the world population in 1998. Approximately 900 million Muslims live in forty-five Muslim-majority countries. Table 1 provides a sociodemographic profile of Muslim countries included in the *World Development Report* published annually by the World Bank. In terms of size, the Islamic world constitutes a significant part of humanity and therefore warrants a sociologically informed understanding and analysis of its religious, social, and political trends. The following topics will be covered in this article: social, ideological, and economic factors in the origins of Islam; Islam and the rise of the modern West; Islam, Muslim society, and social theory; Islam and fundamentalism; the Islamic state; gender issues in Muslim societies; and, Muslim minorities in the West.

SOCIAL FACTORS IN THE ORIGINS OF ISLAM

Social science scholarship in the twentieth century has been influenced by three dominant intellectual traditions: Marxism, Weberian , and functionalism. Their influence has shaped the analytic approach to historical events, resulting in an increasing focus on the relationship between social and economic factors and historical events. The study of Islam and Muslim societies often reflects these influences.

One strand of scholarship has focused on the analysis of various factors in the origins and early development of Islam. A discussion of the economic and social aspects of the origins of Islam provides a test case for a closer investigation of the wider issues raised by the dominant paradigms in sociology. A number of historical studies have dealt with this issue primarily in terms of the diffusion of Jewish and Christian teaching in pre-Islamic Arabia that laid the foundation for the rise of Islam (Torrey 1933; Bell 1926; Kroeber 1948). The aim of these and similar studies has been to identify and understand how certain ideas and cultural elements utilized by Islam derived from preexisting religions or to point to the existence of elements analogous to Islam in other religious traditions in the same general area.

Another scholarly tradition has approached the analysis of the early development of Islam in terms of sociological and anthropological concepts and traces the origins of Islam primarily to the change in social organization in pre-Islamic Meccan society caused by the spread of trade. Wolf (1951) provides an overview of these studies and shows that the tendencies Mohammed brought to fruition were prominent in pre-Islamic Arabia. The spread of commerce and rapid urban development had caused the emergence of classlike groupings from the preceding network of kin relations. This also contributed to the emergence of a divine being specifically linked to the regulation of nonkin relations as the chief deity. These changes created a disjunction between the ideological basis of social organization and the functional social reality and thus spawned disruption and conflict. Islam arose as a moderating religious-

Sociodemographic Profile of Selected Muslim Countries

COUNTRY	Population Millions (1997)	Urban Population (% of total)	GNP Per Capita 1997 $	Life Expectancy (males and females)	Adult Illiteracy Rate (15 years and (males and females)
Indonesia	200	37	1110	63/67	10/22
Pakistan	137	35	490	62/65	50/76
Bangladesh	124	19	270	57/59	51/74
Nigeria	118	41	260	51/55	33/53
Turkey	64	72	3130	62/65	8/28
Iran	63	60	2190	67/68	25/44
Egypt	60	45	1180	64/67	36/61
Sudan	27	25	125(e)	52/55	45/68
Algeria	29	57	1490	68/72	26/51
Morocco	28	53	1250	64/68	41/53
Uzbekistan	24	42	1010	66/72	—
Afghanistan	22	—	—	43/44	55/86
Malaysia	21	55	4680	70/74	11/22
Saudi Arabia	20	84	6790	66/71	29/50
Yemen	16	35	270	54/54	—
Kazakhstan	16	60	1340	60/70	—
Syria	15	53	1150	66/71	14/44
Mali	10	28	260	48/52	61/77
Tunisia	9	63	2090	68/71	21/45
Niger	10	19	200	44/49	79/93
Senegal	9	45	550	49/52	57/77
Guinea	7	31	570	46/47	50/78
Libya	5	—	5100	62/65	14/41
Jordan	4	73	1570	69/72	7/21
Lebanon	4	88	3350	68/71	10/20
Mauritania	2	54	450	52/55	50/74
United Arab Emirates	3	85	17360	74/76	21/20
Oman	2	79	4950	69/73	—
Kuwait	2	—	19420	76/76	20/27
Albania	3	38	750	69/75	—

Table 1

SOURCE: World Bank: *World Development Report 1998/99 and 1997*. New York, Oxford University Press. UNDP, *Human Development Report 1996*. New York; Oxford University Press.

ethical social movement under these social conditions. According to Wolf:

> The religious revolution associated with the name of Mohammed permitted the establishment of an incipient state structure. It replaced allegiance to the kinship unit with allegiance to a state structure, an allegiance phrased in religious terms. It limited the disruptive exercise of kin-based mechanisms of blood feud. It put an end to the extension of ritual kin ties to serve as links between tribes. It based itself instead on the armed force of the faithful as the core of a social order which included both believers and unbelievers. It evolved a rudimentary judicial authority, patterned after the role of the pre-Islamic soothsayer, but possessed of new significance. The limitation of the blood feud permitted war to emerge as a special prerogative of the state power. The state taxed both Muslims and non-Muslims, in ways patterned after pre-Islamic models but to new ends. Finally, it located the center of the state in urban settlements, surrounding the town with a set of religious symbols that served functionally to increase its prestige and role. (1951, pp. 352–353)

In his historical studies of early Islam, Watt (1954, 1955, 1962a, 1962b) also analyzed the economic, social, and ideological aspects of the origins of Islam. His analysis of the economic situation in pre-Islamic Arabia shows that the economic transition from a nomadic to a mercantile economy had resulted in social upheaval and general malaise. He also found a close affinity between the ideology of Islam and the situation that prevailed in early seventh-century Mecca. However, his analysis led him to question the nature and direction of the relationship between Islamic doctrines and the social and economic conditions of pre-Islamic Meccan society. Are doctrines causally dependent on the social order in such a way that they can be deduced from it? Or is the ideology of Islam a creative factor that made a contribution to the course of events? Watt argues that there was nothing inevitable about the development of a world religion from the economic and social circumstances of early seventh-century Mecca. The malaise of the times might have been alleviated without achieving anything of more than transient and local importance. He argues that the formulation of Islamic ideology was a creative response to the situation, not an automatic result of interacting factors.

According to Watt, the creative response of Islamic ideology is reflected in key foundational Koranic ideas such as *Ummah* and *Rasul*. Like other Koranic ideas, these ideas can be connected to earlier Jewish and Christian conceptions as well as to pre-Islamic Arabian ideas, but the Koranic conceptions had a unique new and creative dimension that made them especially relevant to the contemporary Arabian situation. Mere repetitions of current ideas in the Koran would have rendered those ideas devoid of creative novelty, whereas sheer novelty would have made them unintelligible. What the Koran does is take the familiar conceptions and transmute them into something new and original (Watt 1954, p. 172). In this synthesis, the old images are to some extent transformed but retain their power to release the energy of the human psyche. From this perspective, the Koranic conceptions and images of *Ummah* and *Rasul* took on new meanings that were a combination of the old conceptions and additional meanings conferred by the Koran, which was thus able to release the energies of the older images and inaugurate a vigorous new religion. This energy was directed, among other things, toward the establishment of the Islamic state and the unification of Arabia (Watt 1954, pp. 173–4).

Debate about the social factors in the origins of Islam continues (Engineer 1990; Crone 1996). However, it is evident that under the influence of dominant theoretical paradigms in sociology, this debate has provided new insights into the role of social, economic, and cultural factors in shaping the ideology of Islam and the early development of Islamic social formations.

THE "SOCIAL PROJECT" OF ISLAM

Another recent development has been a revival of interest in the "social project" of Islam. The most significant contributions have come from the work of Rahman (1982, 1989), who claims, "A central aim of the Koran is to establish a viable social order on earth that will be just and ethically based" (1989, p. 37). This aim was declared against the backdrop of an Arabian society characterized by polytheism, exploitation of the poor, general neglect of social responsibility, degradation of morals, injustice toward women and the less powerful, and tribalism. The Koran and the genesis of the Muslim community occurred in the light of history and against the social historical background. The Koranic response to specific conditions is the product of a "coherent philosophy" and "attitude toward life" that Rahman calls "the intellectual tradition" of Islam. This tradition was subverted and undermined by an emphasis on literalist interpretations of the Koran by Ulema Islamic scholars. The Islamic scholarship molded by Ulema came to emphasize "minimal Islam", focusing on the "five pillars," and negative and punitive Islam. Islamic scholarship thus became rigid, fossilized, and largely removed from the intellectual tradition of the Koran. Rahman argues that the intellectual tradition of the Koran requires that Koranic thought be dependent on a factual and proper study of social conditions in order to develop Islamic social norms for reforming society (Rahman 1982).

ISLAM AND THE RISE OF THE MODERN WEST

An important strand of historical scholarship has focused on the relationship between Islam and the rise of the modern West. This question was the focus of *Mohammed and Charlemagne* (Pirenne 1939). According to Pirenne, for centuries after the political collapse of the Roman Empire, the economic and social life of western Europe continued to move exclusively to the rhythm of the ancient world. The civilization of Romania had long outlived the Roman Empire in the West. It survived because the economic life based on the Mediterranean had continued to thrive. It was only after the Arab-Muslim conquests of the eastern and southern Mediterranean in the seventh century A.D. that this Mediterranean-wide economy was disrupted by the Islamic conquest. The Arab-Muslim war fleets closed the Mediterranean to shipping in the later seventh century.

Deprived of its Mediterranean-wide horizons, civilized western Europe closed in on itself, and the under-Romanized world of northern Gaul and Germany gained prominence. The Mediterranean Roman Empire in the West was replaced by a western Europe dominated by a northern Frankish aristocracy that gave rise to a society in which wealth was restricted to land. Its rulers, deprived of the wealth generated by trade, had to reward

their followers with grants of land, and thus feudalism was born. The empire of Charlemagne, a northern Germanic empire inconceivable in any previous century, marked the beginning of the Middle Ages. Pirenne shows that by breaking the unity of the Mediterranean, the conquest made by the Arab-Muslim war fleets ruptured Romano-Byzantine economic and cultural domination over western Europe, which was forced to rely on its own material and cultural resources. From this analysis Pirenne draws his famous observation: "It is therefore strictly correct to say that without Mohammed Charlemagne would have been inconceivable" (Pirenne 1939, p. 234).

The Pirenne thesis linked great historical events that have occupied the attention of historians for a long time: the demise of the classical world centered on the Mediterranean and the rise of the empire of Charlemagne. Pirenne demonstrated that these two events, which are central to the rise of the modern West, are linked to the rise of Islam and its expansion to the Mediterranean. Pirenne's well-documented generalizations have attracted praise as well as criticism from historians who are often wary of broad generalizations (see Hodges and Whitehouse 1983).

While Pirenne's thesis attempts to link the rise and development of Islam to the rise of the modern West, paradoxically, equally influential hypothesis postulates instead a "clash of civilizations." This hypothesis, advanced by Samuel Huntington (1993), holds that whereas in the pre–Cold War era military and political conflicts occurred within the Western civilizations, after the end of the Cold War the conflict moved out of its Western phase and its centerpiece became the interaction between the West and non-Western civilizations and among non-Western civilizations. According to Huntington, future conflicts will occur along the fault lines that separate those civilizations. Globalization tends to heighten civilizational identity, and as a result, civilizational differences are difficult to reconcile and override political and economic factors.

Huntington (1993) postulates that the greatest threat of conflict for the West comes from religious fundamentalism, especially Islamic fundamentalism. He sees Islamic fundamentalism as arising from the failures of Muslim countries to achieve political and economic development of their masses. This failure is exacerbated by the demographic structure of the Muslim world, especially the large bulge in the middle of the age pyramid (the youth). Huntington suggests that Muslim countries have a historical propensity toward violence. The domination and hegemony of the West, he claims, will force an alliance between the Confucianist and Islamic civilizations, and that alliance will challenge Western interests, values, and power, resulting in a civilizational clash. Huntington postulates that civilizational conflict will replace ideological and other forms of conflicts in the future. The outcome of this change is that civilizational conflicts will become more intense, violent, and sustained. This thesis was criticized as a new form of Orientalism. Other criticisms have centered on Huntington's assumption of civilizational unity as well as his assumptions about the basis of alliances between Confucianist and Islamic civilizations (Ajami 1993; Ahluwalia and Mayer 1994).

ISLAM, MUSLIM SOCIETY, AND SOCIAL THEORY

Ibn Khaldun and the political sociology of Muslim society. The sociology of Islam primarily refers to the empirical study of Muslim societies. In this respect, it has occupied an important place in the theoretical discourse of a number of theorists from Ibn Khaldun and Weber to Gellner. It is beyond the scope of this article to provide an exhaustive overview of how Muslim society and Islam have been treated in social theory (for studies of the Islamic revolution in Iran, see Shariati 1979; Fischer 1980; Arjonaud 1988). This section will provide a general overview of the subject in the works of four social theorists: Ibn Khaldun, Weber, Gellner, and Geertz.

Ibn Khaldun, an Arab historian and sociologist (1332–1406), is perhaps the most notable theorist of Muslim society. In the prolegomena (introduction) to his monumental work on universal history, he conceived and formulated the most comprehensive synthesis in the human sciences ever achieved by a Muslim thinker. In the prolegomena, among other topics, he probably provided the first modern outline of sociological principles. He defined sociology as "the study of human society in its different forms, the nature and characteristics of each of these forms, and the

laws governing its development" (Khaldun 1992, p. 7). The basic sociological principles he enunciates are as follows:

1. Social phenomena seem to obey laws that while not as absolute as those governing natural phenomena, are sufficiently constant to cause social events to follow regular, well-defined patterns and sequences.

2. These laws operate on masses and cannot be influenced significantly by isolated individuals.

3. Sociological laws can be discovered only by gathering many facts and observing circumstances and sequences through historical records and the observation of present events.

4. Societies are not static. Social forms change and evolve as a result of contact and interaction between different people and classes, population changes, and economic inequality.

5. Sociological laws are not a reflection only of biological impulses or physical factors but also of social forces.

He then applied these principles to the analysis of Muslim societies (Khaldun 1992, p. 8–9).

The core of Ibn Khaldun's sociology is his concept of *Asabiyya* (social solidarity). For Khaldun, society is natural and necessary, since isolated individuals can neither defend themselves against powerful enemies nor satisfy their economic wants. However, individual aggressiveness would make social life impossible unless it was curbed by some sanction. This sanction may be provided by a powerful individual imposing his will on the rest or by social solidarity. The need for a common authority generates the state, which is to society as form is to matter and is inseparable from it. Ibn Khaldun traces the origin of social solidarity to blood and kinship ties. Nevertheless, social solidarity is shaped by the nature and character of social organization. In this lies the genius of his theory of Muslim social formations and circulation of the elite.

The nature of tribal life generates the strongest form of social solidarity and social cohesion, producing social, political, and civic virtues that characterize tribespeople. For Khaldun, leadership exists only through superiority, and superiority only through group feeling. Domination and authority are the rewards for social cohesion. Only those with superior social cohesion succeed in becoming rulers, but a civilization (state-society) consists of tribes and cities. The division of labor is the essence of urban life. It is the key to cities' capacity to supply economic and cultural services that tribespeople are unable to provide for themselves because the tribal ethos spurns specialization. Civilization needs cities to provide economic wealth, which is achieved through specialization and a complex division of labor. Specialization, however, is inherently incompatible with social cohesion and the martial spirit. There emerges a need to provide a new basis for social bonds, and religion becomes the most powerful force in holding together a sedentary people. Scripturalistic and puritanical religion has as a natural affinity with urban life. The combination of religious and tribal solidarity is formidable, and to it Ibn Khaldun attributes the rapid and sweeping conquests of the Muslim Arabs in the seventh century.

The dialectic between the tribe and the city forms the basis of the model of circulation of the elite in society. The Khaldunian model rests on the distinction and contrast between the tribe and the city. Zubiada (1995) has provided a succinct summary of this model:

> Dynasties which have conquered the city and its wealth do so with the militant vigor of their nomadic stock, and the solidarity (asabiyya) of their kinship bonds. In time, the rulers become settled and accustomed to the comforts and luxuries of the city, the branches of their kin develop factional interests and competition over wealth and power which saps solidarity. The cost of their expanding retinue and luxury spending leads to an intensification of the taxation burden on the urban populations and their growing discontent. The growing weakness of the rulers encourages aspiring tribal dynasties, lusting for the city, to organize military campaigns which ultimately topple the rulers and replace them, only to repeat the cycle. (1995, p. 154; see also Turner 1999)

Ibn Khaldun's sociological generalizations about the Muslim social formations of his time can be summarized in the following statements:

1. Nomadic tribes conquer sedentary societies because of their greater cohesiveness.

2. The combination of tribal solidarity and a puritanical scripturalistic urban religion is overwhelming.

3. Conquest tends to be followed by luxury and softening, which lead to decay and annihilation of the ruling dynasty.

These three statements describe the rise and fall of many historical Muslim social formations in the Middle East and North Africa.

Weber, Islam, and Capitalism. Weber's theoretical interest in and interpretation of Islam is related to his exploration of the affinity of faith and modern socioeconomic organizations. Through a comparative study of world religions, Weber formulated *The Protestant Ethic and Spirit of Capitalism* (Weber 1958). In his analysis, Weber demonstrated an elective affinity between certain types of religious ideas and particular types of economic activity. He hypothesized a nexus between Protestant religious beliefs and the development of modern capitalism and used his study of comparative religion to show why modern capitalism could not have emerged in other societies, including Islamic society. Weber saw Islam as a prophetic, this-worldly, salvationist religion with strong connections with other Abrahamic religions and regarded it as a useful test case of his thesis.

Weber argued that rational formal law, autonomous cities, an independent bourgeois class, and political stability were totally absent in Islamic society because of prebendal feudalism and the domination of patrimonial bureaucracy. He also argued that a hedonistic spirit and an accommodating Koranic ethic could not produce salvation anxiety and that asceticism was blocked by two important social groups: the warrior group that was the social carrier of Islam and the Sufi brotherhoods that developed mystical religiosity.

Weber's characterization of Islam has been criticized as "factually wrong" (Turner 1974b, p. 238). Gellner (1983) describes Weber's notion about the affinity between the bourgeoise style of life and religious sobriety and asceticism as "a piece of Judaeo-Protestant ethnocentricism" (Gellner 1983, p. 78). Gellner also challenges Weber's contention that the institutional preconditions of modern capitalism were not restricted to the West but that it was the ideological element (i.e., the Protestant ethic) that provides the crucial differentia, the extra spark that, in conjunction with the required structural preconditions, explains the miracle. According to Gellner, "the differentiae of Islam seem institutional rather than ideological. Ideological parallels to Christianity can be found, but they operate in a contrasted institutional melieu" (1983, p. 6).

Gellner's Theory of Muslim Society. Gellner made some of the most significant contributions to the sociology of Islam over the past three decades. Building on David Hume, Ibn Khaldun, Marshal Hodgson, and others, he provides a model of Muslim society that aspires to a general interpretation of all past and present Muslim societies. In *Muslim Society* (1983) and other writings (Gellner 1969, 1992, 1994), Gellner identifies unvarying features of Muslim societies that make them susceptible to sociological analysis. Building on the work of Ibn Khaldun, he postulates a dialectic between city and tribe, each with its own form of religion. The central and perhaps most important feature of Islam, according to Gellner, is that it was internally divided into the high Islam of scholars and the folk (low) Islam of the people. High Islam is primarily urban, and folk Islam is primarily tribal and rural. Although the boundaries between the two were not sharp but gradual and ambiguous, they nevertheless projected a distinctive tradition.

High Islam is carried by urban scholars recruited largely from the trading bourgeois classes and reflecting the natural tastes and values of urban middle classes. Those values include order, rule observance, sobriety, and learning, along with an aversion to superstition, hysteria, and emotional excess. High Islam stresses the severely monotheistic and nomocractic nature of Islam, is mindful of the prohibition of claims of mediation between God and the individual, and generally is oriented toward puritanism and scripturalism. Folk Islam is superstitious and mediationist. It stresses magic more than learning and ecstasy more than rule observance. Rustics encounter writing mainly in the form of amulets and manipulative magic. Far from avoiding mediation, folk Islam is centered on it. Its most characteristic institution is the saint cult, in which the saint is more often living rather than dead. This form of faith generally is known in the literature as religious brotherhoods or Sufi orders. Urban religion is Weberian (textual and puritanical), and rural and tribal religion is Durkheimian.

Each religious tradition has a place in the social structure. Saint cults are prominent in the tribal or rural countryside and provide invaluable services in rural conditions: mediating between groups, facilitating trade and exchanges, and providing symbolism that allows illiterate rustics believers to identify enthusiastically with a scriptural religion. The folk Islamic tradition, through its ecstatic rituals, provides the poor with an escape from their miserable conditions. High Islam provides the urban population, and to some extent the whole society, with its charter and constitution entrenched by the sacred texts, which can mobilize resistance against an unjust state. The two systems often coexisted in an amiable symbiosis, but a tension remained that would surface from time to time in the form of a puritan revivalist movement to transform folk Islam in the image of high Islam. Gellner argues that in the traditional order Islam may be described as a permanent or recurrent, but ever-reversed, Reformation. In each cycle, the revivalist puritan impulse would in the end yield to the contrary social requirements (Gellner 1994).

Under modern conditions, the pattern of interaction between the two religious traditions has been transformed. The centralization of political power and the ability of the state to rule effectively with modern technology and control over the military and the economy have undermined the social basis of folk Islam. Puritanism and scripturalism have become symbols of urban sophistication and modernity. According to Gellner, this constitutes the basic mechanism of the massive transfer of loyalty from folk Islam to a scripturalist, fundamentalist variant of Islam: "This is the essence of the cultural history of Islam of the last hundred years. What had once been a minority accomplishment or privilege, a form of the faith practised by a cultural elite, has come to define society as a whole" (Gellner 1994, p. 22).

In short, conditions of modernity (mass literacy, urbanization, modern education, and technology) have reinforced the power of scripturalist, puritanical urban Islam and its challenge to secular power; this explains the current rise of Islamic revivalist and fundamentalist movements. The validity of Gellner's model of Muslim society has been challenged in the historical and the modern contexts. It has been criticized for ignoring the different meanings and roles of concepts and entities such as Ulema in different historical contexts and in different societies and instead treating them as sociological or political constants. Modern Islamism, critics argue, is a political ideology and is distinct from anything in Muslim history, which in recent years has become a dominant idiom for the expression of various and sometimes contradictory interests, aspirations, and frustrations (Zubiada 1995). However, even his critics agree that Gellner's model of Muslim society is the most ambitious attempt in modern sociology to identify the internal religious dynamics that play a significant and in certain conditions, critical role in determining the political character and socioreligious trajectories of Muslim societies.

Geertz and the Islamization process. Like Gellner, Geertz has made significant contributions to the sociology of Islam through his anthropological studies, in this case of religious life in Indonesia and Morocco. His work illustrates the modes of incorporation of Islam into already existing and well-developed cultures and shows how those incorporations manifest themselves in the different Islamic traditions that over time come to characterize them. Geertz shows that in the sociocultural and ecological setting of Morocco, the "cultural center" of Islam was developed not in the great cities but in the mobile, aggressive, fluid, and fragmented world of tribes on the periphery. It was out of the tribes that the forming impulses of Islamic civilization in Morocco came and stamped their mentality on future developments. "Islam in Barbary was—and, to a fair extent still is, basically the Islam of saint worship and moral severity, magical power and aggressive piety, and this for all practical purposes is as true in the alleys of Fez and Marrackech as in the expanses of the Atlas or the Sahara" (Geertz 1968, p. 9).

In the tropical heartland of Indonesia, with its productive peasant society and Indic cultural heritage, once Islam was incorporated, it found a distinctive cultural and religious expression. In Indonesia, Islam did not construct a civilization but appropriated it. The Javanese social structure was shaped by a centralized state and a productive and industrious peasantry. The social structure was highly differentiated and developed, and when Islam came, its expression was influenced pro-

foundly by the context. The Indonesian Islamic tradition was malleable, tentative, syncretic, and multivocal. In Morocco and other Middle Eastern societies, Islam was a powerful force for cultural homogeneity, moral consensus and standardization of fundamental beliefs and values. In Indonesia, Islam was a powerful force for cultural diversification and sharply variant and even incompatible worldviews and values.

The gentry, which was acculturated to Indic ritualism and pantheism, developed a subjectivist and illuminationist approach to Islam. The peasantry absorbed Islamic concepts and practices into its folk religion and developed a distinctive contemplative tradition. The trading classes were exposed to Arabian Islam and, because of their greater exposure to the Meccan pilgrimage, cultivated a doctrinal religious tradition. Islam in Indonesia therefore developed as a syncretic and multivocal religious tradition whose expression differed from one sector of the society to another (Geertz 1960, 1968).

Geertz's work, like Gellner's, provides a framework for explaining the diversity of religious traditions in Muslim societies and indeed the existence of religious diversity in all religions. As Geertz observes, "Religious faith, even when it is fed from a common source, is as much a particularising force as a generalizing one, and indeed whatever universality a given religious tradition manages to attain arises from its ability to engage a widening set of individual, even idiosyncratic, conceptions of life and yet somehow sustain and elaborate them all" (Geertz 1968, p. 14). The purpose of this account is to illustrate that Islam occupies an important place in theoretical discourse on modern sociology. As empirical and comparative study of Muslim societies develops, it will provide more opportunities to test and refine some of the existing theoretical propositions as well as develop new ones (see Arjomand 1988; Fischer 1980; Beyer 1994; Irfani 1983).

Islam and Fundamentalism. Fundamentalism emerged in all the major world religions in the last quarter of the twentieth century and gained prominence and influence in the 1990s (Marty and Appleby 1991, 1992, 1993). It is defined as "a distinctive tendency—a habit of mind and a pattern of behaviour—found within modern religious communities and embodied in certain representative individuals and movements. Fundamentalism is, in other words, a religious way of being that manifests itself as a strategy by which beleaguered believers attempt to preserve their distinctive identity as a people or group" (Martin and Appleby 1992, p. 34). Feeling that this identity is at risk, fundamentalists try to fortify it by means of a selective retrieval of doctrines, beliefs, and practices from a sacred past as well as modern times. This renewed religious identity becomes the exclusive and absolute basis for a re-created political and social order. While there are differences between fundamentalist movements in general, their endeavor to establish a "new" political and social order always relies on charismatic and authoritarian leadership. These movements also feature a disciplined inner core of elites and organizations as well as a large population of sympathizers who may be called on in times of need. Fundamentalists often follow a rigorous sociomoral code and have clear strategies to achieve their goals.

Religious fundamentalism is a growing and important part of social change in Muslim countries. Its main goal is to establish the Sharia (Islamic law) as the explicit, comprehensive, and exclusive legal basis of society (Marty and Appleby 1991, 1992; Beinin and Stork 1997; Esposito 1983). Hardly a day passes without a reference to Islamic fundamentalism in the international media. All Muslim societies are affected by it, although there are large differences among them in terms of its presence and power. Is Islamic fundamentalism the inevitable destiny of all Muslim countries, or is it only a part of larger process of social change? Are there certain social, economic, historical, and other preconditions that predispose some Muslim countries more than others to Islamic fundamentalism? Are there different types of Islamic fundamentalism? These and related questions have been posed and explored by several contributors to the Fundamentalism Project of the American Academy of Arts and Sciences (Marty and Appleby 1991). There are three competing theories of Islamic fundamentalism: Watt's (1988) "crisis of self-image," Gellner's (1983) "pattern of distribution of dominant religious traditions," and the "modernization and religious purification" theory advanced by a number of social scientists (Tamney 1980; Hassan 1985; Yap 1980; Rahman 1982).

Crisis of Self-Image. Distilling insights from his works on the history and sociology of Islam,

Watt (1988) has proposed that the principal root of Islamic fundamentalism is the domination of the traditional "Islamic world view" and the corresponding "self-image of Islam" in the thinking of Islamic intellectuals and great masses of ordinary Muslims. According to Watt,

> *the important distinction is between those Muslims who fully accept the traditional world view and want to maintain it intact and those who see that it needs to be corrected in some respects. The former group are fundamentalists . . . while the latter group will be referred to as Liberals.* (1988, p. 2)

Among both groups, many different political movements and attitudes can be found. The Ulema (religious scholars), who are the primary bearers and transmitters of the traditional worldview, are mostly reactionary in the sense that they tend to oppose reforms. Other Islamic intellectuals subscribe to a variety of reformist elements and sometimes are very critical of the Ulema, but the reforms they are interested in are mostly social and political and leave the traditional worldview of Islam unchanged. Watt then identifies important aspects of the traditional worldview: (1) the unchanging static world that is predicated on the complete absence of the idea of development, (2) the finality of Islam, (3) the self-sufficiency of Islam (Watt sees this reflected in the Muslim's conception of knowledge; when a Muslim thinks of knowledge, it is primarily "knowledge for living," whereas when a Westerner thinks of knowledge, it is mainly "knowledge for power"), (4) Islam in history (the widespread belief that Islam will ultimately be triumphant in changing the whole world into *dar-al-Islam* (the sphere of Islam), and (5) the idealization of Muhammed and early Islam, which renders critical and historically objective scholarship highly problematic in the Muslim consciousness and deviation from (1988) idealized and romanticized notions as a heresy and "unthinkable." According to Watt "These features of the Islamic worldview and the corresponding self-image are the basis of Islamic fundamentalism. The support for fundamentalism is embedded in the consciousness, which fully accepts the traditional worldview and wants to maintain it intact."

Patterns of Distribution of Dominant Religious Tradition. Building on the sociological and historical analyses of Muslim society of Ibn Khaldun

(1958), Weber (1964), Hume (1976), Hodgson (1975), and others, Gellner has advanced a theory of Muslim social formation that is based on his conceptualization of "two strands of Islam." One strand is characterized by "scripturalist puritanism" and represented by the Ulema. This is the Islam of the "fundamentalists." The other strand is characterized by a "hierarchical ecstatic mediationist style and is represented by the 'Saints." These two strands have evolved historically as representing two major social structural features of Muslim society: the city and the countryside. Gellner combines these strands of Islam with the political orientation of the elites and proposes a model of Muslim social formations. If one contrasts fundamentalism with laxity along one dimension and social radicalism with traditionalism along another, according to Gellner, one gets four types of Muslim societies or social formations.

The old-style puritanism prevails in areas where a traditional elite survives but is still fairly close to its origin in an Ibn-Khaldunian swing of the pendulum that brought it to power in a fusion of religious enthusiasm and tribal aggression. The new-style puritanism with its elective affinity for social radicalism prevails in areas where colonialism destroyed old elites and a new one elite came from below rather than from the outer wilderness (Gellner 1983, p. 89). An elaboration of Gellner's typology of Islamic social formations is shown in Figure 1.

Modernization and Religious Purification. This theory holds that religious fundamentalism is one of the consequences of the modernization process. Building on studies by Mol (1972) and Folliet (1955), Tamney (1980) proposed that one way in which modern people are different from traditional people is that they practice purer religious styles. The relationship between modernization and religious purity can take two forms. In its general sense, purification is the opposite of syncretism: It is the elimination of religious elements originating in a traditional religion. Purification means the differentiation of religious traditions at the personality level, so that the individual's religious lifestyle reflects one style of tradition. If being modern means that people are more conscious about the history and the internal structures of various religions, modern people can realize the inconsistencies in a syncretic lifestyle, feel uneasy or even insincere, and seek to purify their lives by

deliberately eliminating elements from religious traditions other than their own. Using this conceptualization, Tamney hypothesizes that modernization is associated with religious purification. His empirical examination of this hypothesis in Indonesia tends to support his theory. Studies by Hassan (1984, 1985a, 1985b) and Irfani (1983) provide some support for this theory.

Islamic Militancy: A New Paradigm? Using the current religious, social, and political conditions of Muslim countries as a kind of "natural experiment," the author is conducting a multicountry study to examine the three competing theories of Islamic fundamentalism outlined in the preceding section. Over 4,400 mostly highly educated Muslim respondents have been surveyed. The empirical evidence shows that the heartlands of the Islamic world, from Indonesia to Egypt, are undergoing a religious renaissance. A large majority of the respondents were devoutly religious. If the term "fundamentalism" is defined to mean a high degree of devotional religiosity, these heartlands are becoming fundamentalist (Hassan 1999d). What are the implications of this for Islamic radicalism? Does this mean increasing support for the militant Islamic movements that are agitating to establish their versions of the Islamic state? Would this increase militancy against the groups or countries they regard as enemies of Islam?

Religious devotion appears to be associated with a decline in the support for militant Islamic movements. A large majority of Muslims do not belong to radical Islamic group. In fact, most of the respondents approved of moderate political leaders who are leading political and social movements for democratic and tolerant societies and political cultures. The declining support for radical and militant movements is paradoxically further radicalizing these movements and transforming them into more violent and secretive organizations. The nature and ruthlessness of violence reflect their desire to gain public attention and are symptomatic of their desperation.

The new form of violence is different from the earlier form that was carried out by organizations often with tacit support from political structures. The new militancy appears to be fueled by a sense of desperation and humiliation caused by globalization and the increasing economic, cultural, technological, and military hegemony of the West.

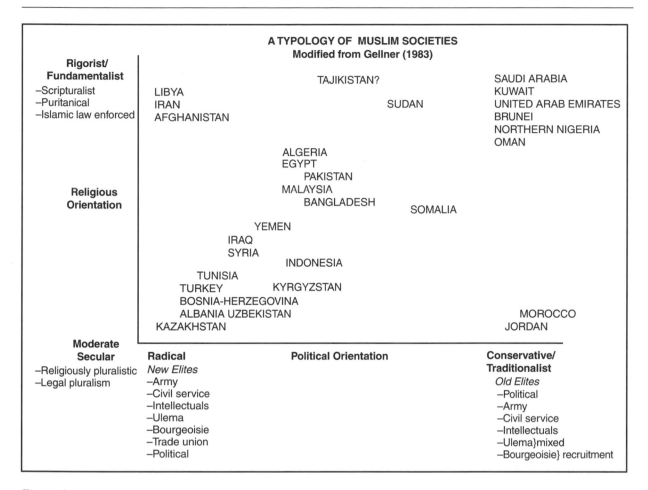

Figure 1

This pattern represents a kind of paradigm shift in the nature, causes, and targets of terrorism carried out by the new militant groups. The old form of militancy attempted to establish the legitimacy of political goals; the new form is guided by religious fanaticism, destruction, and revenge. The old form of militancy identified enemies. The new enemies are ephemeral global conspiracies.

A majority of the respondents regard major Western countries as anti-Islamic. The primary reason for this attitude is not religion, but the perceived indifference and inaction of Western countries toward protecting the Muslim populations of Bosnia-Herzegovina, Palestine, and Chechnya destruction. These views are widely held among the elites. The study provides new insights into the dynamics of the new Islamic militancy. It shows that contrary to the general belief, increasing religiosity in Muslim countries is associated with

political liberalization and diminishing support for militant Islamic groups. The impact of these developments is making the militant movements highly secretive and more violent.

The globalization process is creating a social and cultural hiatus that is affecting the nature and organization of Islamic militancy. The new militancy is not motivated by attitudes toward colonialism and struggles to win the hearts and minds of Muslim populations. Instead, it is fueled by a sense of powerlessness, revenge, and religious fanaticism. The enemy is ephemeral global conspiracies. How Muslim countries and the international community respond to these new developments will have a profound impact on the nature and activities of the new militancy. The solution would require more open and stronger political structures in Muslim countries to legally and politically pursue solutions to the problems posed by the new militancy. It also will require a change in the attitude that increasing religiosity increases support for militancy, when it actually diminishes support for it.

THE ISLAMIC STATE

The relationship between politics and religion in Muslim societies has been a focus of debate among scholars of Islam for most of this century. A commonly stated view of many Western and Muslim scholars is that Islam is not only a religion but also a blueprint for social order and therefore encompasses all domains of life, including law and the state (Maududi 1960, Lewis 1993; Huntington 1993; Rahman 1982; Watt 1988; Pipes 1981; Esposito 1995; Weber 1978; Turner 1974a; Gellner 1983). This view is reinforced by the fact that Islam does not have a church institution, although it does have the institutions of the Ulema, who act as the guardians of the interpretations of the sacred tests, and the Iman Masjid (leaders of the mosques), who lead the mandatory daily prayers in mosques. It is further argued that this characterization sets Islamic societies apart from Western societies built on the separation of state and religious institutions.

After reviewing the evidence on the separation of state and religion in Islamic history, Lapidus (1996) concludes that the history of the Muslim world reveals two main institutional configurations. The undifferentiated state–religion configuration characterized a small number of Middle Eastern societies. This configuration was characteristic of lineage or tribal societies. The historical norm for agrourban Islamic societies was an institutional configuration that recognized the division between the state and religious spheres:

> *Despite the common statement (and the Muslim ideal) that the institutions of state and religion are unified, and that Islam is a total way of life which defines political as well as social and family matters, most Muslim societies did not conform to this ideal, but were built around separate institutions of state and religion. (Lapidus 1996, p. 24)*

Keddie (1994, p. 463) has described the supposed near identity of religion and the state in Islam more as a "pious myth than reality for most of Islamic history." Similar views of Islamic history

have been advanced by others (Zubiada 1989; Sadowski 1997; Ayubi 1991; Sivan 1985).

Historical scholarship indicates that the institutional configurations of Islamic societies can be classified into two types: (1) "differentiated social formations" (societies in which religion and the state occupy different spaces) and (2) "undifferentiated social formations" (societies in which religion and the state are integrated). While a majority of Islamic societies have been and are differentiated social formations, a small but significant number have been and are societies that can be classified as undifferentiated social formations. A common label used in contemporary discourse to refer to undifferentiated Muslim social formations is "the Islamic state."

The empirical evidence shows that religious institutions and religious elites tend to enjoy greater public trust and legitimacy in differentiated compared to undifferentiated Muslim societies. The underlying dynamics that appear to produce this pattern are related to the functional and performance roles of religious institutions (Luhmann 1982; Beyer 1994) and the ability of religious institutions to mobilize public resistance against an authoritarian state that has a deficit of legitimacy in the public mind (Hassan 1999a and 1999b).

GENDER ISSUES IN MUSLIM SOCIETIES

For many Islamic and Western scholars of Islam, the status, role and position of women are important distinguishing features of Muslim societies that, set them apart from their Western counterparts. Many people in the West regard the status of women in Muslim society as symptomatic of their oppression in Islam (Esposito, 1995, p. 5). It is further argued that gender relations in Islam have been shaped primarily by their Arabian origins. While Islam has borne the marks of its Arabian origin throughout its history, in regard to the position held by women in his community, Mohammed was able to introduce profound changes (Levy 1972; Rahman 1966; Ali 1970).

Islam was instrumental in introducing wide-ranging legal-religious enactments to improve the status and position of women in Arabian society and protect them from male excesses. There are numerous Koranic injunctions to give effect to these changes (Ali 1970, pp. 55–59). These injunctions brought about significant improvements in the status of women in a wide range of public and private spheres, but most important, they gave women a full-fledged personality (Rahman 1966).

However, selective literal, noncontextual, and ahistorical interpretations of sacred texts by Islamic scholars over time have shaped the average Muslim's conservative views and attitudes toward women. One of the major dilemmas faced by the nationalist leaders who spearheaded independence movements from Indonesia to Pakistan and Egypt was "woman issue." Their problem was how to respond to the questions raised by women about their role, status, and function in the new independent states. This generated highly emotional and divisive debates between the Islamic scholars and the nationalist leaders that centered on the issues of marriage and family law and the role and status of women in a modern independent Muslim state (see Esposito 1982; Haddad and Esposito 1998).

Notwithstanding strong resistance from Islamicists in several countries, the new nationalist leaders were able to overcome centuries of resistance and introduce modest changes in family and marriage laws. Those changes were introduced within an Islamic framework that did not expressly violate the appropriate Koranic injunctions and Sunnah (Anderson 1976). Those reforms have been criticized and opposed by a majority of Islamic Ulema and their followers, who regard them as violations of Islamic law and commandments as codified in classical Islamic legal texts as well as thinly veiled attempts to find an Islamic justification for an essentially Western approach to issues of interpersonal relations (Haeri 1993; Esposito 1982). This debate between nationalists and Islamicists continues and according to some evidence is becoming an important part of the political agenda of Islamic fundamentalists (Hardacre 1993; Haeri 1993).

Attitudes toward Veiling and Patriarchy: Veiling and seclusion of women and patriarchy have been important features of Islamic societies. In recent years they have attracted much criticism from Muslim and Western feminist scholars. The tradition and custom of veiling in Islam can be attributed to Islamic history, Islamic texts, and the privileged position of males and their control and dominance of positions of power and authority in Muslim society. Veiling and seclusion of women

and their role and function in society also are intertwined with the management of sexuality in Islam (Levy 1972).

Islam recognizes sexual desire as a natural endowment of the human body and enjoins its followers to satisfy and even enjoy sexual needs, providing a framework for doing so enunciated in the sacred texts. Unlike Christianity, Islam does not sanction or idealize celibacy. Over the centuries, the interpretations of sacred texts by the Ulema have led to the development of an institutional framework for the management and satisfaction of human sexuality through the imposition of control over women. As women are seen not only as sexual beings but also as the embodiment of sex, the social framework that has evolved has come to view the woman's body as pudendal. This conceptualization has led to the development and observance of strict dress codes for women, including veiling and seclusion, to prevent them from displaying their bodily charm and beauty (Haeri 1993; Hardacre 1993; Levy 1972).

Other features of the institutional framework arose out of the fact that women were made the principal actors responsible for preserving the sanctity of the family and reproduction. This led to strict injunctions on the types of roles they could play in the public sphere. Strong social and cultural traditions evolved that placed serious obstacles in the way of women seeking to succeed in public roles. Men, in contrast, were assigned all the public roles as providers, protectors, and arbiters, and this reinforced their power in the domestic domain as well. Patriarchal family structures thus became more functionally suitable to the perpetuation of the institutional framework for the satisfaction and management of the family.

That institutional framework and its accompanying normative requirements as they apply to gender roles, dress codes, veiling and seclusion, and patriarchy are by and large universally accepted in Muslim societies, although their observance varies with economic conditions. For most ordinary Muslims, this practice is in keeping with the supremacy of the male over female postulated by the Koran. However, the vagueness of these edicts has given the Ulema greater authority to interpret them as local custom demands. Some Ulema even appear to have invented tradition to bolster their interpretations which may in fact conflict with Koranic statements (Levy 1972; Rahman 1982; Mernissi 1989; Rugh 1984).

As a result of internal and external pressures, the governments of most Islamic countries have initiated reforms to improve the quality of citizenship accorded to Muslim women. These reforms have sought to remove some of the obstacles that have prevented gender equality. While varying in scope and intensity from country to country, these reforms have been initiated in most Muslim countries. Some of the reforms have been successful, and, in some countries, such as Iran and Pakistan, the pendulum has swung to more traditionalist views that have gained favor with the current ruling elites. In general, the reforms are having a positive effect, although obstacles still exist. Those obstacles will continue until the rigid attitudes of the Ulema change or lose significance for the general body of Muslims as a result of the decline of their religious authority.

The empirical evidence about attitudes toward veiling, seclusion, and patriarchy indicates that those attitudes are an outcome of complex processes, including the prevalent social, economic, and political conditions in the country that mediate between the traditional Islamic norms and their practice in the local milieu. The material conditions of the country influence the shaping of attitudes toward these issues more strongly than does traditional Islamic ideology. The empirical evidence also indicates that in Muslim societies where men have experienced greater status loss relative to women as a result of public policies aimed at improving the quality of female citizenship, they appear to have compensated for that loss by developing more conservative attitudes toward women, including veiling, seclusion of women, and patriarchy. The evidence also suggests that paradoxically, Muslim societies, that are more successful in providing women with institutional equality may be more successful in generating more positive attitudes toward traditional Islamic values of patriarchy, veiling, and segregation among women (Hassan 1999c).

MUSLIM MINORITIES

The London-based Institute of Muslim Minority Affairs estimates that about three hundred million Muslims live in one hundred forty-nine non-Muslim states. The institute publishes a biannual journal devoted to studies of Muslim minorities in different countries. With over 100 million Muslims, India is the home of the largest Muslim minority. Over the past fifty years, international labor migration and political upheavals have resulted in increasing Muslim settlement in Europe, Australia, and North America. It is estimated that about 20 million Muslims now reside in Europe. Most of them arrived as immigrants to meet the labor needs of booming west European economies, and their numbers are likely to increase in the future. (Nielsen 1995; Castles 1989).

The Muslim presence in west European countries has raised challenges to both Muslim and European traditions. The evidence shows that on the whole, Muslim communities in European countries are making cultural, social, and religious adjustments to secure their position in society. The host societies are responding by promoting cultural pluralism and containing racism and xenophobic attitudes among some segments of their populations. The cultural interactions between European and Muslim communities is shaping a distinctive European Muslim identity among second-generation Muslims (Nielsen 1995; Gerholm and Lithman 1988).

The Muslim presence in North America, especially in the United States, has been increasing gradually. While there are no reliable statistics on the exact size of the Muslim population in the United States, it is estimated to range from 2 million to 6 million. The American Muslim Council estimates the figure to be around 5.2 million (Duran 1997). Whatever the size, it is a well-established fact that Islam is an important feature of the American religious milieu. Its adherents include American Muslims, who are predominantly of African origin, and more recent immigrants from all over the Muslim world. The most widely known American Muslim group is the Nation of Islam (Gardell 1994). Most of the immigrant Muslims come from south Asian and Middle Eastern countries. They have arrived as skilled and unskilled laborers, students, and refugees from political developments in Muslim countries. The largest concentrations of Muslims are in the metropolitan areas of Los Angeles, New York, and Chicago. Recent sociological studies have focused on acculturation and the tensions Muslim communities experience in adjusting to life in America and how those communities are responding to the competing demands of belonging to a universal Islamic community (*Ummah*) and maintaining their ethnic or national identity. The evidence shows that the majority of American Muslims are not active participants in the organized religious life of mosque or Islamic center, but continue to identify themselves as Muslims in a social setting characterized by prejudice and misunderstanding (Haddad and Smith 1994; Haddad and Lummis 1987). Similar findings have been reported in studies of Muslim communities in Australia (Hassan 1991; Bouma 1994).

The social pervasiveness of Islam in the modern world and the sociopolitical and religious trajectories of contemporary Muslim societies raise important sociological questions. This article has identified some of the questions and issues that make the sociology of Islam a challenging field of social inquiry. Empirical studies of Muslim societies can be a rich source for evaluating the validity of some of the major propositions of social theory that have been formulated in the context of increasingly secular social settings of modern European and North American countries. Through systematic and comparative studies of Muslim societies, modern sociological scholarship can lay the foundations for a more informed understanding of the social reality of the Muslim world.

REFERENCES

Ahluwalia, P., and P. L. Mayer, 1994 "Clash of Civilisations—or Balderdash of Scholars." *Asian Studies Review* 18:129-30.

Ajami Fouad 1993 "The Summarising." *Foreign Affairs* 72(4):2-9.

Ali, Chiragh 1970 "The Position of Women in Aziz Ahmad and E. von Grunebaum, eds., *Muslim Self-Statement in India and Pakistan 1857-1968*. Weisbaden, Germany: Otto Harrassowitz.

Anderson, J. N. D. 1976 *Law Reform in Muslim World*. London: Athlone Press.

Arjomand, Said 1988 *The Turban and the Crown: The Islamic Revolution in Iran*. New York: Oxford University Press.

Ayubi, Nazih N. 1991 *Political Islam: Religion and Politics in the Arab World*. London: Routledge.

Beinin, J., and J. Stork, eds. 1997 *Political Islam, Berkeley:* University of California Press.

Bell, Richard 1926 *The Origins of Islam in Its Christian Environment*. London: Macmillan.

Beyer, Peter 1994 *Religion and Globalization*. London: Sage.

Bouma, Gary D. 1994 *Mosques and Muslim Settlement in Australia*. Canberra, Australia: AGPS.

Castles, S. 1989 *Here for Good: Western Europe's New Ethnic Minorities*. London: Pluto Press.

Crone, Patricia 1996 "The Rise of Islam in the World." In Francis Robinson, ed., *The Cambridge Illustrated History of the Islamic World*. Cambridge, UK: Cambridge University Press.

Duran, Khalid 1997 "Demographic Characteristics of the American Muslim Community." *Islamic Studies* 36(1): 57-76.

Engineer, Asghar Ali 1980 *The Origins and Development of Islam*. Kuala Lumpur: Ikraq.

Esposito, John L. 1982 *Women in Muslim Family Law*. Syracuse, N.Y.: Syracuse University Press.

——, ed. 1983 *Voices of Resurgent Islam*. New York: Oxford University Press.

—— 1995 *The Islamic Threat: Myth or Reality?* New York: Oxford University Press.

Fischer, Michael 1980 *Iran: From Religious Dispute to Revolution*. Cambridge, Mass.: Harvard University Press.

Folliet, Joseph 1955 "The Effects of City Life upon Spiritual Life." In R. Fisher, ed., *The Metropolis in Modern Life*. New York: Doubleday.

Gardell, Mattias 1994 "The Sun of Islam Will Rise in the West: Minister Farrakhan and the Nation of Islam in Latter Days." In Y. Haddad and J. Smith, eds., *Muslim Communities of North America*. New York: State University of New York Press.

Geertz, Clifford 1960 *The Religion of Java*. Chicago: University of Chicago Press.

—— 1968 *Islam Observed: Religious Developments in Morocco and Indonesia*. Chicago: University of Chicago Press.

Gellner, Ernest 1969 *Saints of the Atlas*. London: Weidenfeld & Nicholson.

——, 1983 *Muslim Society*. Cambridge, UK: Cambridge University Press.

—— 1992 *Postmodernism, Reason and Religion*. London: Routledge.

—— 1994 *Conditions of Liberty*. London: Penguin Books.

Gerholm, T. and Y. G. Lithman, eds. 1988 *The New Islamic Presence in Europe*. London: Mansell.

Haddad, Yvonne Y. and John L. Esposito (eds.) 1998 *Islam, Gender and Social Change*. New York: Oxford University Press.

—— and Jane I. Smith (eds.) 1994 *Muslim Communities in North America*. New York: State University of New York Press.

Haddad, Yvonne Y. and A.T. Lummis 1987. *Islamic Values in the United States*. New York: Oxford University Press.

Haeri, Shahla, 1993 "Women and Fundamentalism in Iran and Pakistan." In Martin E. Marty and R. Scott Appleby, eds., *Fundamentalisms and Society*. Chicago: University of Chicago Press.

Hardacre, Helen 1993 "The Impact of Fundamentalisms on Women, the Family and Interpersonal Relations" in Martin E. Marty and R. Scott Appleby, eds. *Fundamentalisms and Society*. Chicago: University of Chicago Press.

Hassan, Riaz 1984 "Iran's Islamic Revolutionaries: Before and After the Revolution." *Third World Quarterly*, 6(3)0675–686

—— 1985a *Islam Dari Konservatism Sampai Fundamentalisme*. Jakarta: Rajawli Press.

—— 1985 "Islamization: An Analysis of Religious, Political and Social Change in Pakistan." *Middle Eastern Studies*, 21(3):263:283.

—— 1987 "Pirs and Politics: Religion, Society and the State in Pakistan." *Asian Survey* 26(5): 552–565

—— 1991 "The Muslim Minority-Majority Relations in Australian Society: A Sociological Analysis." *Journal of Institute of Muslim Minority Affairs* 12(2):285–306.

—— 1999a "Faithlines: Religion, Society and the State in Indonesia and Pakistan." *Islamic Studies* 38(1):45–62.

—— 1999b "Faithlines: Social Structure and Religiosity in Muslim Societies." Working Paper, G. E. Von Grunebaum Center for Near Eastern Studies, University of California of Los Angeles.

—— 1999c. "Attitudes towards Veiling and Patriarchy in Four Muslim Societies." Working Paper, G. E. Von Grunebaum Center For Near Eastern Studies. University of California of Los Angeles.

—— 1999d "The Islamic Ummah: Myth or Reality?" unpublished paper. Department of Sociology, Flinders University of South Australia, Adelaide.

Hodges, Richard, and David Whitehouse, 1983 *Mohammed, Charlemagne and the Origins of Europe*. Ithaca N.Y.: Cornell University Press.

Hodgson, Marshall G. 1975 *The Venture of Islam*. Chicago: University of Chicago Press.

Hume, David 1976 *The Natural History of Religion*. Oxford: Oxford University Press.

Huntington, Samuel P. 1993 *The Clash of Civilizations and the Remaking of World Order*. New York: Simon & Schuster.

Irfani, Suroosh 1983 *Revolutionary Islam in Iran*. London: Zed.

Keddie, Nikki R. 1994 "The Revolt of Islam, 1700 to 1993: Comparative Considerations and Relations to Imperialism." *Comparative Studies in Society and History* 36(3): 463–487.

Khaldun, Ibn 1958 *The Muqaddamah*. London: Rosenthal.

—— 1992 *An Arab Philosophy of History*, trans. and arranged by Charles Issawi. Cairo: American University of Cairo Press.

Kroeber, Alfred 1948 *Anthropology*. New York: Harcourt Brace.

Lapidus, Ira M. 1996 "State and Religion in Islamic Society." *Past and Present* 151:3–27.

Levy, Reuben 1972 *The Social Structure of Islam*. Cambridge, UK: Cambridge University Press.

Lewis B. 1993 *Islam and the West*. New York: Oxford University Press.

Luhmann, Niklas 1982 *The Differentiation of Society*, trans. Stephen Holmas and Charles Lamore. New York: Columbia University Press.

Marty, Martin E. and R. Scott Appleby, eds. 1991 *Fundamentalism Observed*. Chicago: University of Chicago Press.

—— 1993 *Fundamentalism and Society*. Chicago: University of Chicago Press.

—— 1992 *The Glory and the Power: The Fundamentalist Challenge to the Modern World*. Boston: Beacon Press.

Maududi, A. A. 1960 *The Islamic Law and Constitution*. Lahore, Pakistan: Islamic Publications.

Mernissi, Fatimah 1989 *Women and Islam*, trans. by Mary Jo Lakeland. Oxford, UK: Basil Blackwell.

Mol, J. J. 1972 *Western Religion*. The Hague: Mouton.

Nielsen, Jorgen 1995 *Muslims in Western Europe*. Edinburgh, Scotland: Edinburgh University Press.

Pipes, Daniel, 1981. *Slaves, Soldiers and Islam: The Genesis of a Military System*. New Haven, Conn.:Yale University Press.

Pirenne, Henry 1939 *Mohammed and Charlemagne*. London: Barnes and Noble.

Rahman, F. 1966 *Islam*. Chicago: University of Chicago Press.

—— 1982 *Islam and Modernity*. Chicago: University of Chicago Press.——1989 *Major Themes of the Quran*. Minneapolis: Bibliotheca Islamica.

Rugh, Andrea 1984 *Reveal and Conceal: Dress in Contemporary Egypt*. Syracuse, N.Y.: Syracuse University Press.

Sadowski, Yahya 1997 "The New Orientalism and the Democracy Debate." In J. Beinin and J. Stork, eds., *Political Islam*. Berkeley: University of California Press.

Shariati, Ali 1979 *On the Sociology of Islam*. Berkeley, Calif.: Mizan Press.

Sivan, Emmanuel 1985 *Radical Islam: Medieval Theology and Modern Politics*. New Haven, Conn.: Yale University Press.

Tamney, Joseph 1980 "Modernization and Religious Purification: Islam in Indonesia." *Review of Religious Research* 22(2). 208–218

Torrey, Charles 1933 *The Jewish Foundation of Islam*. New York: Jewish Institute.

Turner, Bryan 1974 *Weber and Islam*. London: Routledge & Kegan Paul.

—— 1974 "Islam, Capitalism and the Weber Thesis." *British Journal of Sociology*. 25:230–243.

—— 1999 "The Sociology of Islamic Social Structure." *Sociology* 33:1.

Watt, W. Montgomery 1954 "Economic and Social Aspects of the Origin of Islam." *Islamic Quarterley* 1:90–103.

—— 1955 "Ideal Factors in the Origin of Islam." *Islamic Quarterly*. 2:160–74.

—— 1962a *Mohammed at Mecca*. Oxford: Oxford University Press.

—— 1962b *Mohammed at Medina*. Oxford: Oxford University Press.

—— (1988) *Islamic Fundamentalism and Modernity*. London: Routledge.

Weber Max, 1958 *The Protestant Ethic and the Spirit of Capitalism*, trans. Talcott Parsons. New York: Scribner.

—— 1964 *The Sociology of Religion*, trans. E. Fiscoff. Boston: Beacon.

—— 1978 *Economy and Society*. Geunther Ross and Claus Wittich, eds. Berkeley: University of California Press.

Wolf, Eric R. 1951 "The Social Organization of Mecca and the Origins of Islam." *Southwestern Journal of Anthropology* 7(4): 329–356.

Yap, M. E. 1980 "Contemporary Islamic Revival." *Asian Affairs Journal of the Royal Society for Asian Affairs* 11(2):178–195.

Zubadia, Sami 1989 *Islam, the People and the State*. London: Routledge.

—— 1995 "Is There a Muslim Society? Ernest Gellner's Sociology of Islam." *Economy and Society* 24(2): 151–188.

RIAZ HASSAN

THE SOCIOLOGY OF KNOWLEDGE

The sociology of knowledge as a subdiscipline in sociology deals with the social and group origins of ideas. In its brief history as a field of study, it has included the entire ideational realm (knowledge, ideas, theories, and mentalities), in an attempt to comprehend how that realm is related to particular social and political forces and how the mental life of a group of people arises within the context of the groups and institutions in which those people live and act. More recently, its subject matter has included not only a society's authoritative ideas and formal knowledges but also those which operate in the realm of everyday life: informal knowledges.

The term "sociology of knowledge" (*Wissenssoziologie*) was first used in 1924 and 1925 by Scheler (1874–1928) (Scheler [1924] 1980, 1992) and Mannheim (1893–1947) (Mannheim [1924] 1952). From its inception, it described a field of inquiry closely linked to problems of European philosophy and historicism. In several important respects, this is an accurate description, for the sociology of knowledge reflected the nineteenth-century German philosophical interest in problems surrounding relativism that were linked to the legacies of Karl Marx, Friedrich Nietzsche, and the historicists, whose cultural philosophy of worldviews (*Weltanschauungsphilosophie*) was influential in German social science from the 1890s to the 1930s. Each of these developments was concerned in different ways with the determinate relationship between thought and society, between knowledge and social structure. For Scheler and Mannheim, *Wissenssoziologie* would serve as an empirical and historical method for resolving the intense conflicts of ideologies in Weimar Germany that followed political and social revolutions of the nineteenth and early twentieth centuries and produced warring groups whose battles were manifestly ideational and grounded in conflicting worldviews. Sociology of knowledge would provide a method, outlined in early statements by Scheler and Mannheim, for unmasking the assumptions of political ideologies and indicating their truth content. However much Scheler and Mannheim differed about the nature of truth within relativism, both agreed that truths do not exist apart from historical and social processes. As members of a postwar generation of European intellectuals, they also shared a sense that they were witnessing the gradual disappearance of epistemology and its replacement by the sociology of knowledge as a foundational discipline for all philosophy. As participants in this historical process, they also believed, as did their contemporaries, that intellectuals play a vital role in thought and politics.

The excitement and urgency with which the framers of *Wissenssoziologie* approached the study of the social origins of ideas has been replaced by a widespread acceptance of their premises concerning the social origins of ideas, ideologies, and worldviews. To borrow Weber's term, the sociology of knowledge was "rountinized" into the established structures and practices of modern social science. Many of the positions advanced by Scheler, Mannheim, and other early writers in this field (e.g., in the United States by Florian Znaniecki, C. Wright Mills, and Edward Shils) operate today as working propositions for a range of social scientists as well as for specialists in other disciplines, including the subfields of the history of ideas, social psychology, social studies of science, feminist theory, and cultural studies. Even the urgency, expressed by Mannheim, surrounding the problem of relativism as a "contemporary predicament" has been transformed into a commonplace fact. Today, this is certainly the case in the academic world, whereas in the past, the sociology of knowledge provided the occasion for intense controversies about the postulate of the essential "sociality of mind" (Child 1941).

THE SOCIOLOGY OF KNOWLEDGE: TWO APPROACHES

Partly because of the diffusion of the idea of the social nature of knowledge, the sociology of knowledge has been described as an approach or subdiscipline that has no unified field, but only a series of theoretical works and research agendas. Despite this characterization, the subdiscipline of the sociology of knowledge is a recognized field of endeavor that continues to draw new generations of sociologists. Therefore, one may speak of two ways of introducing the sociology of knowledge: The *broad approach* identifies a range of works in sociology and social theory that examine the social nature of mind and knowledge; the *particular ap-*proach includes the works of specialists the field identified as the sociology of knowledge. Several leading contributors to the sociology of knowledge have provided similar schemes for delineating its subject matter, pointing out that the sociology of knowledge includes both a broad field and a narrow field of studies and that both fields contribute to the sociology of mental and cognitive structures (Remmling 1973; Curtis and Petras 1970; Berger and Luckmann 1966).

The broad approach incorporates a number of works that deal with the relationship of mental life (cognition, consciousness, collective ideas, etc.) and social life (groups, institutions, communities, entire societies). The broad approach treats the sociology of knowledge as a "frame of reference," not a "definite body of theory in its own right" (Curtis and Petras 1970, p.1). Accordingly, the sociology of knowledge is a broad tradition of inquiry, a handing down of key texts and theories, such as theories of the "social determination" of ideas, theories of ideology, the relationship of "real" and "ideal" factors, and the notion of *Weltanschauung*, that are closely linked to the history of sociology. The social theories of Karl Marx, Emile Durkheim, Max Weber, Georg Simmel, and others are studied as classic statements on the relationship of mind, knowledge, and society. This broad approach to the sociology of knowledge has provided not only the basic materials from which particular treatises in the sociology of knowledge have been written (e.g., Stark [1958] 1991; Berger and Luckmann 1966; Gurvitch 1971) but also the materials that have been incorporated into commentaries and edited collections on the sociology of knowledge (Remmling 1973; Curtis and Petras 1970).

In this general sense, the sociology of knowledge is understood as a field that systematizes the leading propositions of the modern social sciences about the social nature of mind. Furthermore, like sociology, the sociology of knowledge constitutes a tradition of inquiry that reflects and shapes the development of modernity. That is, sociology offers a theory of the human mind that is compatible with "our time": The sociology of knowledge "appears as a revision of our way of . . . looking at ourselves and the world. . . . It 'defines' a new 'situation'" (Wolff 1953, p. 618; Wolff cf.1959). Linked as it is to the modernization of consciousness, the sociology of knowledge, broadly conceived, has several distinct national traditions, each focusing on themes characteristic of its own modern intellectual legacies. Therefore, one can speak of French, German, and American traditions of the sociology of knowledge whose roots are based in a Durkheimian "structuralist" legacy, a Marxist or Mannheimian theory of ideology, and a pragmatist theory of mind such as that offered by John Dewey and George Herbert Mead. Each of these national intellectual traditions reflects its particular national and cultural legacies in nineteenth- and twentieth-century modernity; each legacy also can be seen as complementing the sociologies of knowledge of other modern nations, cultures, and civilizations.

A second way of defining the sociology of knowledge considers the field as a particular body of work and examines its origins, development, and future prospects. This approach begins with the original statements of Scheler and Mannheim and proceeds to the later principal works and arguments. The approach also examines major substantive statements made by sociologists identified with its precise subject matter. One of the merits of this approach is that it allows for a critical view of the substantive work in the sociology of knowledge over time and, in keeping with the field's presuppositions about the existential determination of thought (*Seinsgebundenheit*), opens the question of how social theories of knowledge are themselves subject to change and revision over time. In this sense, the sociology of knowledge offers a metatheory through which sociology can examine how its leading concepts and theories arise in response to particular social and political situations. For example, Marx's theory of ideology is closely implicated in particular historical conditions of the industrial capitalist order, and its validity is dependent on particular conditions of social and economic organization, such as the separation and autonomy of economic forces in the social order.

Integral to the sociology of knowledge is a *relative theory of knowledge* from which its own concepts and theories are not excepted. Its methods are critical in the classical sense of the word, for it offers a continuous criticism of what it studies, including its own forms of knowledge and criteria of judgment. With this view in mind, a brief history of its statements and theories offers more than a recounting of its nature and scope. It also draws attention to the reflexive features of all sociological inquiries, particularly the fact that sociology is part of the social reality it studies in that its changing concepts and insights develop out of and address particular social worlds. Sociological theories are neither external nor formal. The brief history of the subfield of the sociology of knowledge that follows is intended to be both a recounting of the leading ideas in this field and a reflexive statement about the social foundations of its theories and presuppositions. The implications that can be drawn from this inquiry are taken up in the conclusion.

A BRIEF SUBSTANTIVE HISTORY

Since its inception in the writings of Scheler and Mannheim, the sociology of knowledge has identified a number of precise ways in which knowledge is socially determined. Scheler's original essays ([1924] 1980) identifying the field of study provoked commentary and debate. His concept of a society's "relatively natural *Weltanschauung*" is still central to cultural sociology, as are his propositions concerning the origins of the modern worldview and its scientific ethos. However, Scheler's importance would be felt decades later (Bershady 1992). It was Mannheim's formulation of the discipline in *Ideology and Utopia* (German edition 1929, English edition 1936) that originally defined the subject matter of the field and continued to do so for years to come. Those who proposed different sociologies of knowledge after its publication defined their positions relative to Mannheim's arguments concerning ideology, utopia, and relationism.

Mannheim's treatise begins with a review and critique of the prevailing and authoritative Marxist theories of ideology (the "particular theory of ideology") and proceeds toward a theory of ideology in the broader sense: the mental structure in its totality as it appears in different currents of thought and across different social groups. This total conception of ideology examines thought on the structural level, allowing the same object to take on different (group) aspects. This understanding of ideology refers to a person's, group's, or society's entire way of conceiving things as it is provided by particular historical and social settings. The "total conception of ideology" defines the subject matter of the sociology of knowledge. Like ideologies, "utopias" arise out of particular social and political conditions, but they are distinguished by their opposition to the prevailing order. Utopias are the embodiment of "wish-images" in collective actions that shatter and transform social worlds partially or entirely. Both concepts form part of Mannheim's theoretical apparatus for a critical but nonevaluative treatment of "ideology" that supersedes the sociohistorical determinism and relativism of Marxism while moving toward a "relationist" notion of truth. The enterprise of the sociology of knowledge examines how collective actions and ideas (ideologies and utopias) emerge out of and are "determined" by the multiple social contexts and positions of their proponents. From an analysis of the various and competing social positions of ideologists and utopians, a kind of "truth" emerges that is grounded in the conditions of intellectual objectivity and detachment from the social conditions that more directly determine ideas. *Ideology and Utopia* established the criteria for a valid knowledge, albeit a *relational* knowledge, of sociohistorical processes. More important, it raised the problems surrounding the historicity of thought and did this within the newly emerging academic discourse of sociology. In the process, this work gave legitimacy to a new set of methodological problems involving the problems of objectivity and truth for the sciences and the humanities.

Despite the many criticisms of *Ideology and Utopia* (particularly Mannheim's attempt to avoid the pitfalls of historical relativism), the work received wide attention and appreciation inside and outside the social sciences, where the problems posed by relativism continued to attract the attention of workers in both the sciences and the humanities. While reviews of the work focused on its failure to overcome relativism and Mannheim's excessive reliance on the Marxist conception of ideology, Mannheim's book provoked discussion and commentary for years (Hughes 1958, p. 420).

In the decades after its publication, *Ideology and Utopia* engaged the leading American social theorists of the period: Merton and Parsons. Merton's two chapters on the sociology of knowledge in his major work (1957) attempt to integrate the social theory of knowledge with his own "structural-functional" theory and demonstrate how other theorists (Marx, Weber, Freud, Durkheim) belong to the broader tradition of the social determination of ideas. In essays by Parsons (1959, 1961), Mannheim's work is criticized and integrated into the approach with which Parsons is identified: the "general theory of action." The contributions of Merton and Parsons were significant, principally with respect to the prevailing functionalist theories of "action," not with respect to advancing the sociology of knowledge. In fact, it could be said that the projects outlined by Scheler and Mannheim, particularly their historical and cultural emphasis, did not conform to the program of formal or "general theory" outlined by Parsons for the functional study of all societies or to Merton's proposal for theories of the "middle range."

This was not the case for their contemporary Stark ([1958] 1991), whose sociology of knowledge attempted to clarify the principal themes in the study of the social determination of ideas and advance its arguments beyond the Marx–Mannheim tradition and its theory of ideology. An émigré for more than half his life and a scholar educated at the universities of Hamburg, Prague, London, and Geneva, Stark was accustomed to move within many mental, linguistic, and moral frameworks. When it is confronted by an almost dizzying array of viewpoints, social existence loses its taken-for-granted quality. As Remmling (1973) has observed, the relationship between social existence and knowledge, which has been the preoccupation of the sociology of knowledge, has always been that of marginal figures and outsiders. This and other traits Stark shared with Scheler and Mannheim. Stark regarded *Wissenssoziologie* as an indispensable method for understanding both the truth of ideas and the history of ideas; truths do not exist apart from the historical and social process. The traditions of German cultural sociology and *Wissenssoziologie* contain the ideals and conventions in which Stark's sociology of knowledge becomes most intelligible. He brought to it judgments concerning the "real" and the "ideal" from Weber's and Simmel's sociology. From Scheler's works in particular, he would find ways of returning to the problem of how to find truths or "ideal values" in the realm of relative social realities or "existential facts."

Stark wrote *The Sociology of Knowledge* to clarify the principal themes of writers, especially sociologists, who had addressed the problem of the social element in thinking. He also intended it to serve as an introduction to the field that would prepare the way for a detailed and comprehensive history of the sociology of knowledge and its most significant ideas, including the theories of ideology of Marx and Mannheim, the philosophical speculations of the neo-Kantians Heinrich Rickert and Max Weber, and the views of the German phenomenological school of the 1920s, especially Scheler. Each of these ideas was vitally important for his project, but Stark's strongest affinity was with Scheler's struggle to reconcile the antithetical claims of idealism and materialism and his view of the sociology of knowledge as the foundation for a knowledge of eternal values.

Stark's sociology of knowledge is directed primarily toward the study of the precise ways in which human experience, through the mediation of knowledges, takes on a conscious and communicable shape. Eventually, Stark intends to direct this inquiry to the problem of truth, a synthesis of the different styles of thought and their limited truths. For either one of these intentions to be realized, he insists that the theory of ideology can have no place within the bounds of the sociology of knowledge. The idea that social influences enter mental life in the form of lies, self-deceptions, and distortions in thinking and are due to class positions and interests has dominated the Marx–Mannheim tradition and its theory of ideology. Stark's contention, shared by many contemporary writers, is that the sociology of knowledge is concerned with the "social determination of knowledge" (a term with a precise meaning of its own), not with the problem of ideology. In fact, this distinction is an indispensable precondition of the sociology of knowledge. It is intended to direct attention to the study of the extent to which all mental life is grounded in conditions that are ineluctably social and historical; it grants to "social determination" a depth that the theory of ideology does not permit, since that theory deals only with errors and misperceptions (Stark [1958] 1991, pp. 50–55). Even more important, in Stark's view, the theory of social determination is entirely compatible with the theory of truth, whereas the theory of ideology is concerned principally with the social conditions of error or false consciousness. While the theory of ideology will always play a vital role in sociology and the history of ideas, it must be relegated to a status outside the principal concerns of the sociology of knowledge.

Stark's project involves building bridges between opposing positions (Mannheim's theory of ideology and Scheler's theory of social determination), what in scholastic philosophy was called a *concordantia discordantium canonum*, a reconciliation of opposing positions of thought. Whether these two traditions are indeed contradictory is not of consequence in grasping Stark's argument in *The Sociology of Knowledge*. Stark's willingness to explore with frankness and according to his own convictions the kind of epistemology that he thought consistent with cultural sociology brought him to a social theory of knowledge that was compatible with both *Verstehen* (lit., understanding) sociology and social phenomenology. This theory also dismissed the relevance of either a simple historical materialist theory or a positivist one. The outcome is a theory of social determination that has moved away from Marx and Mannheim and in the direction of a cultural sociology, one that is consistent with contemporary sociology's interest in the broad range of cultural studies.

Less than a decade after Stark's work appeared, Berger and Luckmann's *The Social Construction of Reality* (1966) advanced a sociology of knowledge that was compatible with the view of sociology as a humanistic discipline and the notion that "human reality" is a "socially constructed reality" (p. 189). These authors broadened the field to include all types of knowledge, including the knowledge of everyday life: "[*T*]he sociology of knowledge must concern itself with whatever passes for 'knowledge' in a society, regardless of the ultimate validity or invalidity (by whatever criteria) of such 'knowledge'" (p. 3). More important, their treatise asked that the sociology of knowledge address how, in the domain of the quotidian, knowledge constitutes social reality, redirecting the traditional theory of social determination of ideas by social realities. What Berger and Luckmann proposed was that knowledge and reality (by which they always mean social reality) exist in a reciprocal or dialectical relationship of mutual constitution. As many have argued, this work placed the sociology of knowledge on an entirely new footing whose focus is the broad range of signifying systems that form and communicate the realm of social realities. Since its publication, the idea of a "constructed reality" has summarized a number of concerns of contemporary writers in the sciences and humanities that may be best described as the problem of meaning and the use of philosophical, literary, and historical approaches to study the social construction of meaning.

The methodological implications of this change in sociology and the sociology of knowledge are noteworthy, since interest in the problem of meaning is linked to a methodological framework that is neither causal nor explanatory (the attitudes expressed by Mannheim's theory of "social determination") but *semiotic*. The semiotic study of culture is directed toward the study of the symbolic and signifying systems through which a social order is communicated and reproduced. These signifying systems and social practices make up a culture and its structures of meaning. According to Geertz (1973, p. 5), one of the principal semiotic theorists, the analysis of knowledge and culture is "not an experimental science in search of law but an interpretive one in search of meaning."

In addition to being a proponent of an interpretive method in the social sciences in the 1960s, Geertz, in his essay "Ideology as a Cultural System" (1964), explicitly criticized the sociology of knowledge (Mannheim and Stark explicitly), arguing that the entire enterprise identified with the twin problems of "ideology" and "truth" should be reformulated as the "sociology of meaning." For Geertz, the sociology of knowledge remained lodged in an older set of presuppositions (principally its use of "ideology") that prevented it from moving toward a nonevaluative understanding of "culture." This and other criticisms at the time effectively redirected sociology in the period of the late 1960s toward what has been described as its "postpositivist" phase (Rabinow and Sullivan 1979, 1987). Ironically, this most recent period of sociology, with its rejection of the classical concerns of the sociology of knowledge, has been described by Robertson (1992) as a "*general* sociology-of-knowledge turn" characterized by a focus on the ideational features of the social world or a resurgence of interest in cultural forms more generally. Put simply, contemporary sociology's turn away from the classical problems and perspectives of the sociology of knowledge occurred precisely at the time when "culture," "knowledge," and "language" became central to sociology.

What has been called "the new sociology of knowledge" (Swidler and Arditi 1994; McCarthy 1996) can be seen as part of this larger movement in the social sciences generally, distinguished by a turn away from materialist theories or theories of social structure and in the direction of semiotic theories that focus on the ways in which a society's multifarious meanings are communicated and reproduced. Hall (1980) has described the theoretical significance of this cultural turn in social science: Its problematic has become closely identified with the problem of the autonomy of cultural practices. The paradign for studying the range of cultural practices has come largely from structuralist theories (Althusser, Levi-Strauss, Barthes). Language is the theoretical and empirical model, one that is neither positivist nor reductionist but interpretive rather than causal.

THE NEW SOCIOLOGY OF KNOWLEDGE

These arguments and others have been made by recent commentators in what has been called the "new sociology of knowledge." In the case of Swidler and Arditi (1994), the new approach examines how specific kinds of social organizations (e.g., the media through which knowledge is preserved, organized, and transmitted) order knowledges rather than examining social locations and group interests. These scholars also examine, in light of new theories of social power and practice (Michel Foucault and Pierre Bourdieu), how knowledges maintain social hierarchies and how techniques of power are simultaneously and historically linked to discursive forms (knowledges). They also argue that newer theories of power, gender, and knowledge depart from the economic, class, and institutional focus of the classical sociology of knowledge.

McCarthy's (1996) theoretical treatise traces changes in three broad national traditions in the sociology of knowledge (German, French, American), delineating the precise ways in which the classical traditions identified with these three national intellectual legacies have moved to models that are linguistically based. McCarthy also points to feminist theories as important contributions to the sociology of knowledge, particularly works in the sociology of science by feminists such as Smith (1987, 1990). These and other changes in sociology are examined against changes in the social location of knowledge and culture today, particularly the predominant role played by systems of mass communication and information technologies. These changes in turn have produced a contemporary culture that is more globally aware, reflexive, and attuned to the operations of culture itself.

CONCLUSION

The brief history of the sociology of knowledge from Mannheim to contemporary sociology lends itself to the type of interpretive scheme that originated with the classical sociology of knowledge, for its principal argument has worked against any formal understanding of either theory or science. Changes in the structures and organizations of social worlds have been functionally related to collective "standpoints" and "perspectives." Sociologists have witnessed the shift, since midcentury, from "social structure" to "culture" as authoritative schemes for describing and interpreting how social knowledges are "socially determined" Clearly, this intellectual shift registers changes in the social landscape of late modernity, where the configurations known to sociology as "economy," "culture," and "social structure" have undergone changes.

Proponents of the new sociology of knowledge and others have documented changes in the industrial societies of the last half century that correspond to the newer "cultural" theories. Neither Swidler and Arditi nor McCarthy claims that the sociology of knowledge as a subfield of sociology has been superseded by newer work in sociology and cultural studies. However, they note that the new sociology of knowledge is not yet a unified field, and their proposals for what constitutes this diffuse field constitute an argument reminiscent of those of the proponents of a broad or diffuse sociology of knowledge discussed above. It would seem that the more "cultural" sociology becomes, the more likely it is that the sociology of knowledge will be seen as a broadly inclusive set of studies rather than a subfield with a distinct subject matter. The subject matter of the sociology of knowledge has undergone significant change: What began as the study of competing and conflicting collective ideas and ideologies has become something more cultural and diffuse. Its subject matter today is both more differentiated and more diffuse and includes the study of "informal knowl-

edge," the knowledge of everyday life. What began as the study of conflicting ideologies has become the study of the unspoken understandings of everyday life, what L Wirth described in his preface to *Ideology and Utopia* as "the most elemental and important facts about a society . . . those that are seldom debated and generally regarded as settled" (1936, p. xxiii). Today these understandings have become the subject matter of sociology and are no longer generally regarded as "settled."

REFERENCES

Berger, Peter, and Thomas Luckmann 1996 *The Social Construction of Reality*. New York: Doubleday.

Bershady, Harold J. 1992 Introduction to Max Scheler, *On Feeling, Knowing, and Valuing*. Chicago: University of Chicago Press.

Child, Arthur 1941 "The Theoretical Possibility of the Sociology of Knowledge." *Ethics* 51:392–418.

Curtis, James E, and John W. Petras 1970 *The Sociology of Knowledge*. New York: Praeger.

Geertz, Clifford. 1964 "Idelogy as a Cultural System." In David E. Apter, ed., *Ideology and Discontent*. New York: Free Press.

—— 1973 *The Interpretation of Cultures*. New York, Basic Books.

Gurvitch, Georges 1971 *The Social Framework of Knowledge*, trans. M. A. Thompson and K. A. Thompson, introductory essay by K. A. Thompson. New York: Harper.

Hall, Stuart. 1980. "Cultural Studies and the Centre: Some Problematics and Problems." In *Culture, Media, Language: Working Papers in Cultural Studies*. London: Hutchinson.

Hughes, H. Stuart 1958 *Consciousness and Society: The Reorientation of European Social Thought 1890–1930*. New York: Vintage.

Mannheim, Karl (1924) 1952 "Historicism." In P. Kecskerneti, ed., *Essays on the Sociology of Knowledge*. New York: Harcourt, Brace & World.

—— (1929) 1936 *Ideology and Utopia*. New York: Harcourt, Brace & World.

McCarthy, E. Doyle 1996 *Knowledge as Culture: The New Sociology of Knowledge*. New York and London: Routledge.

Merton, Robert K. 1957 *Social Theory and Social Structure*. Glencoe, Ill.: Free Press.

Parsons, Talcott 1959 "An Approach to the Sociology of Knowledge." *Transactions of the Fourth World Congress of Sociology* IV:25–49. Louvain: International Sociological Association.

—— 1961 "Culture and the Social System." In T. Parsons, E. Shils, K. P. Naegele, and J. R. Pitts, et al., eds., *Theories of Society*, vol. II. New York: Free Press.

Rabinow, Paul, and William M. Sullivan 1979 *Interpretive Social Science*. Berkeley: University of California Press.

—— 1987 *Interpretive Social Science: A Second Look*. Berkeley: University of California Press.

Remmling, Gunter 1967 *Road to Suspicion: A Study of Modern Mentality and the Sociology of Knowledge*. New York: Appleton-Century-Crofts.

—— 1973 *Towards the Sociology of Knowledge*. London: Routledge & Kegan Paul.

Robertson, Roland 1992 "Cultural Relativity and Social Theory: Werner Stark's *Sociology of Knowledge* Revisited." In E. Leonard, H. Strasser, and K. Westhues, eds., *In Search of Community: Essays in Memory of Werner Stark 1909–1985*. New York: Fordham University Press.

Scheler, Max (1924) 1980 *Problems of a Sociology of Knowledge*, trans. M. S. Frings, ed. and with an introduction by K. W. Stikkers. London: Routledge & Kegan Paul.

—— 1992 *On Feeling, Knowing, and Valuing*. Chicago: University of Chicago Press.

Smith, Dorothy E. 1987 *The Everyday World as Problematic*. Boston: Northeastern University Press.

—— 1990 *The Conceptual Practices of Power: A Feminist Sociology of Knowledge*. Boston: Northeastern University Press.

Stark, Werner (1958) 1991 *The Sociology of Knowledge*, with a new introduction by E. Doyle McCarthy. New Brunswick, N.J.: Transaction.

Swidler, Ann, and Jorge Arditi 1994 "The New Sociology of Knowledge." *Annual Review of Sociology* 20:305–329.

Wirth, Louis 1936 "Preface" in Karl Mannheim, *Ideology and Utopia*. New York: Harcourt, Brace & World.

Wolff, Kurt H. 1953 "A Preliminary Inquiry into the Sociology of Knowledge from the Standpoint of the Study of Man." In *Scritti di Sociologia e Politica in Onore di Luigi Sturzo*. Bologna: Nicola Zanichelli III.

—— 1959 "The Sociology of Knowledge and Sociological Theory." In L. Gross, ed., *Symposium on Sociological Theory*. New York: Harper & Row.

E. DOYLE MCCARTHY

SOCIOLOGY OF LAW

In 1963, the U.S. Supreme Court ruled that in all felony trials the accused must be provided with legal counsel. The case of *Gideon v. Wainwright* (372 U.S. 355, 1963) was widely celebrated as a David and Goliath story of the triumph of the rule of law: An indigent defendant's handwritten petition had persuaded all nine justices of the Supreme Court to provide a nationwide right to counsel (Lewis 1964). Shortly after Gideon's victory, Blumberg (1967) published an empirical case study describing the actual work of criminal defense attorneys. That study suggested that Gideon's case had little relevance to the 90 percent of felony convictions that the prosecution wins not in a courtroom trial but through informal plea bargaining. Moreover, the attorneys to whom the poor were now constitutionally entitled, Blumberg contended, had over the years mutated from trial advocates into bureaucratic cogs whose primary function was to assist the state in processing legal files efficiently.

Blumberg's deconstruction of the legal myth of the centrality of criminal trials and adversarial counsel exemplifies two central features of the sociology of law. First, that field challenges *legal formalism*, the philosophy that the law stands above social life, develops according to its own internal logic, and autonomously constrains or facilitates social interaction. A sociology of law becomes essential once the law's dependence on its social organizational context is recognized (for a defense of legal formalism as a research agenda, see Watson 1985). Blumberg tried to show that the right to legal representation is contingent on the economics of legal services and the networks of dependency that link judges, prosecutors, and defense attorneys in ways that undermine the abstract legal model of the adversarial contest. Second, Blumberg's case rests on observations of legal practice rather than interpretation of the texts of cases and legislation, the stock-in-trade of conventional legal scholarship. As empirical evidence continued to accumulate, Blumberg's (1967) conclusions about the origins, causes, and consequences of plea bargaining were qualified or supplanted; later research suggests that plea bargains may be even more adversarial than trials ever were (Feeley 1997), that the relationship between caseload pressure and plea bargaining is complex (Holmes et al. 1992), and that the real role of the courtroom trial may be independent of its frequency of occurrence because out-of-court negotiations are conducted "in the shadow of the law" (Mnookin and Kornhauser

1979). Blumberg's study and the later work it inspired illustrate how the sociology of law examines empirical evidence to understand how law is created, enforced, and manipulated in the context of social organization.

SOCIOLOGICAL VERSUS JURISPRUDENTIAL PERSPECTIVES ON LAW

The discipline of sociology does not hold a monopoly on efforts to unveil the connections between law and society. In the twentieth century, Roscoe Pound, Jerome Frank, and other legal scholars abandoned legal formalism and created ncw ways to understand the differences between the "law in the books" and the "law in practice" (for a concise overview of both developments, see Hunt 1978). Since the late 1970s, the critical legal studies movement and its variants have emerged as a major competitor to legal formalism in legal research and education (Kelman 1987). For example, Freeman (1978) examines how major Supreme Court decisions on civil rights have shifted the bases for legally defining discrimination from the consequences for the victims to the intentions of the perpetrators. Freeman shows how the law's emphasis on the actor's intention constrains the principle of equal protection and perpetuates inequality. While his conclusions are radical, his method is identical to the legal formalists' practice of textual interpretation (Trubek 1984). Critical legal studies' *doctrinal analysis*—its reliance on interpretation of constitutions, statutes, and judgments—has more affinity with literary criticism than with sociological methodologies based on the observation of events. For an example of this distinction, compare Klare (1978) with Wallace et al. (1988). Sociology of law is distinguished more by its methods than by its theories or subject matter.

SOCIAL ORIGINS OF LAWS

A substantial number of historical case studies (e.g., Hall 1952) have traced the social origins of substantive and procedural law. Sociology enters these investigations with a broader comparative agenda, formulating and assessing general theories of the origin of law. Chambliss's (1964) analysis of six centuries of vagrancy laws as a ruling-class manipulation of criminal law to control labor was a pioneer of contemporary efforts to puruse this line of investigation. Hagan (1980) provides a representative overview of the subsequent sociological analyses of the origins of alcohol and drug prohibition, sexual psychopathology and prostitution laws, and probation. Humphries and Greenberg (1981) produced one of the few sociological efforts showing the relationships among disparate legal changes and linking those changes to their social bases. They explain the diffusion of juvenile courts, probation, parole, and indeterminate sentences in terms of the shift in the political domination of corporate versus competitive capital during the Progressive era. An alternative approach to the study of the creation and diffusion of legal innovation looks to cultural transmission and organizational linkages rather than to underlying economic or social transformations. Grattet et al. (1998) show, for example, how the diffusion of hate crime legislation appears to be influenced by interstate processes of diffusion rather than by local conditions of the economy and society. Soule and Zylan (1997) similarly explore structural and diffusion factors in the reform of Aid to Families with Dependent Children (AFDC) eligibility rules. In terms of both theory and method, the sociology of law offers a rich body of work that reveals the social foundations of change in the law.

SOCIAL STRATIFICATION OF LAW

The most prominent aspect of social structure in sociological investigations of law is stratification. In his early essay *On the Jewish Question*, Marx examined how a legal system that made all litigants equal before the law left them unequal in economic resources and social relationships. Much current research has been devoted to finding new evidence showing how formal legal equality reproduces social hierarchies. Galanter (1974) points out how the organizational properties of the legal system reinforce and in some instances generate inequality. Apart from the extralegal resources they bring to the dispute, repeat players (corporations and career criminals), for example, gain knowledge, skills that are not available, and networks denied to one-shot players. Feeley (1979) found that in a misdemeanor court "the process is the punishment": For the poor, the costs of conviction were minor compared to the costs imposed by the pretrial stages of the process. Shapiro (1990) developed similar insights into the way in which the rules of evidence and organizational priorities of law enforcement bureaucracies create class differences in the punishment of white-collar crime. These studies go beyond the populist notion that the law is like a cobweb that catches the small flies but lets the large bugs go free. Individual resources matter, but sociological research shown how organizational and institutional contexts shape the manner in which equality *before* the law results in inequality *after* the law.

The largest body of research in the field has been devoted to the examination of discriminination in sentencing in criminal courts. Disparities in the type and duration of sanctions vary markedly by class, race, and/or ethnicity, and gender. For example, with 5 percent of the general population, young African-American males account for nearly half the admissions to state prisons. The initial research problem was to determine the extent to which such disparities represent differential involvement in the kinds of crime that lead to more severe sentences or reflect biases in discretionary decision making in the legal system (for a succinct overview of this research, see Walker et al. 1996). The sociologically relevant discoveries of this research include covariation in the extent of discriminatory decision making with social location (see Myers and Talarico 1987).

SOCIAL IMPACT OF LEGAL CHANGE

Brown v. Board of Education (1954) is perhaps the most celebrated Supreme Court decision of the century. It marked the end of over half a century of the Court's acceptance of legalized racial segregation as being consistent with the constitutional requirement for equal protection under the law. It is usually the case one associates with the conviction that law—Supreme Court decisions, in particular—powerfully shapes social change. Less widely recognized is the fact that in the decade after *Brown*, racial segregation in public schools remained virtually unchanged. The sharpest challenge to conventional conceptions of the social impact of law is Rosenberg's (1991) study of the effect of Supreme Court decisions on school desegregation, abortion, reapportionment, and criminal procedure.

While current controversy centers on Rosenberg's thesis, several other research programs address the conditions under which legal reforms engineer social change. Burstein (1985), for example, specifies the contingencies that influenced the impact of civil rights legislation on the economic position of minorities. Horney and Spohn (1991) examine the impact of rape reform laws in six jurisdictions on several indicators of prosecution. The measurable impact of legal reform proved to be limited, because of the response of local court organizations to externally imposed change. Heimer (1995) illustrates that similar complications appear when legal changes are imposed on hospital work groups. Organizational responses occasionally facilitate rather than inhibit change. Edelman et al. (1992), for example, found that personnel departments tend to exaggerate the legal risks of noncompliance in equal-opportunity cases as a way to enhance their power within the corporation.

ORGANIZATIONAL CONTEXTS OF LEGAL PROCEDURES

A public defender explained to Sudnow (1965) that to work in such an office, one has to know the law—and the ropes. Learning about the organizational ropes of courts, police departments, and law offices has been the objective of a large body of contemporary research in the sociology of law.

Albonetti (1987) utilizes organizational theories to explain variation in the decisions of prosecutors to drop cases or reduce charges; apart from the legal evidence, prosecutors' decisions are shaped by extralegal factors that govern their uncertainty about winning a case at trial. Ofshe and Leo (1997) investigate the coercive persuasion that continues to occur in post-Miranda police interrogations. Police investigators generally follow the letter of the Miranda rules while continuing to practice forms of coercive persuasion that induce most suspects to waive their rights and confess.

Many discoveries about procedure turn on the emergence of informal organizational rules and relationships. Sudnow (1965) found that plea bargains were forged in a common currency of offense seriousness that existed apart from the penal code's definitions of crimes and punishments.

Emerson (1969) showed how the legally relevant aspects of a juvenile's offense and career are organizationally transformed into judgments of character, which then become the real bases for determining verdicts and imposing sentences. This work suggests that due process is a variable whose appearance and effects are shaped by organizational contexts (see Dobbin et al. 1988).

THE ROLE OF GENERAL THEORY IN THE SOCIOLOGY OF LAW

The sociology of law can be distinguished from economics, psychology, and other social science enterprises that have law as their subject matter principally in terms of its integration of its investigations with general theories of social structure. The role of general theory becomes apparent, for example, in comparisons of Japanese and U.S. legal systems that "explain away Japan by attributing every finding to 'Japanese uniqueness' [rather than] treat Japan as a point on a universal continuum" (Miyazawa 1987, p. 239). The case for engaging in the search for such universal continua is made by Black (1976, 1997).

Much current research, however, continues to be guided by one or a combination of the four general theories that initially defined the field. Bentham's utilitarian philosophy underlies rational choice theories of the behavior of law. Studies of deterrence at both individual and organizational levels of analysis continue to pursue this line of theorizing (see Vaughn 1998 for a summary and critique of organizational analysis). Alternatively, the sociological theories of Marx, Durkheim, and Weber articulate properties of social organization that shape and constrain the choices of persons and firms (for an overview, see Garland 1990). Work in the sociology of law thus not only illuminates the institution of law in unique ways but contributes more fundamentally to basic knowledge about human social organization.

REFERENCES

Albonetti, Celesta A. 1987 "Prosecutorial Discretion: The Effects of Uncertainty." *Law and Society Review* 21:291–313.

Black, Donald 1976 *The Behavior of Law.* New York: Academic Press.

—— 1997 *The Social Structure of Right and Wrong.* Revised edition. San Diego: Academic Press.

Blumberg, Abraham S. 1967 "The Practice of Law as a Confidence Game: Organization Cooptation of a Profession." *Law and Society Review* 1:15–39.

Burstein, Paul 1985 *Discrimination, Jobs and Politics: The Struggle for Equal Employment Opportunity in the U.S. Since the New Deal.* Chicago: University of Chicago Press.

Chambliss, William J. 1964 "A Sociological Analysis of the Law of Vagrancy." *Social Problems* 12:67–77.

Dobbin, Frank R., Lauren Edelman, John W. Myer, W. Richard Scott, and Ann Swindler 1988 "The Expansion of Due Process in Organizations." In Lynne G. Zucker, ed., *Institutional Patterns and Organizations: Culture and Environment.* Cambridge, Mass.: Ballinger.

Edelman, Lauren B., Steven E. Abraham, and Howard S. Erlanger 1992 "Professional Construction of Law: The Inflated Threat of Wrongful Discharge." *Law and Society Review* 26:47–83.

Emerson, Robert M. 1969 *Judging Delinquents: Context and Process in Juvenile Court.* Chicago: Aldine.

Feeley, Malcolm M. 1979 *The Process Is the Punishment: Handling Cases in a Lower Court.* New York: Russell Sage Foundation.

—— 1997 "Legal Complexity and the Transformation of the Criminal Process: The Origins of Plea Bargaining." *Israel Law Review* 31:183–222.

Freeman, Alan D. 1978 "Legitimizing Racial Discrimination through Antidiscrimination Law: A Critical Review of Supreme Court Doctrine." *Minnesota Law Review* 62:1049–1119.

Galanter, Marc 1974 "Why the 'Haves' Come Out Ahead." *Law and Society Review* 9:95–160.

Garland, David 1990 *Punishment and Modern Society: A Study in Social Theory.* Chicago: University of Chicago Press.

Grattet, Ryken, Valerie Jenness, and Theodore R. Curry 1998 "The Homogenization and Differentiation of Hate Crime Law in the United States, 1978 to 1995: Innovation and Diffusion in the Criminalization of Bigotry." *American Sociological Review* 63:286–307.

Hagan, John 1980 "The Legislation of Crime and Delinquency: A Review of Theory, Method, and Research." *Law and Society Review* 14:603–628.

Hall, Jerome 1952 *Theft, Law and Society,* 2nd ed. Indianapolis: Bobbs-Merrill.

Heimer, Carol A. 1995 "Explaining Variation in the Impact of Law: Organizations, Institutions, and Professions." *Studies in Law, Politics and Society* 15:29–59.

Holmes, Malcom D., Howard C. Daudistel, and William A. Taggart 1992 "Plea Bargaining Policy and State District Court Caseloads: An Interrupted Time Series Analysis." *Law and Society Review* 26:139–159.

Horney, Julie, and Cassia Spohn 1991 "Rape Law Reform and Instrumental Change in Six Urban Jurisdictions." *Law and Society Review* 25:117–154.

Humphries, Drew, and David Greenberg 1981 "The Dialectics of Crime Control." In David Greenberg, ed., *Crime and Capitalism* Palo Alto, Calif.: Mayfield.

Hunt, Alan 1978 *The Sociological Movement in Law.* Philadelphia: Temple University Press.

Kelman, Mark 1987 *A Guide to Critical Legal Studies.* Cambridge, Mass.: Harvard University Press.

Klare, Karl E. 1978 "Judicial Deradicalization of the Wagner Act and the Origins of Modern Legal Consciousness, 1937–1941." *Minnesota Law Review* 62:265–339.

Lewis, Anthony 1964 *Gideon's Trumpet.* New York: Random House.

Miyazawa, Setsuo 1987 "Taking Kawashima Seriously: A Review of Japanese Research on Japanese Legal Consciousness and Disputing Behavior." *Law and Society Review* 21:219–241.

Mnookin, Robert H., and Lewis Kornhauser 1979 "Bargaining in the Shadow of the Law: The Case of Divorce." *Yale Law Journal* 88:950–997.

Myers, Martha, and Susette M. Talarico 1987 *The Social Contexts of Criminal Sentencing.* New York: Springer-Verlag.

Ofshe, Richard J., and Richard A. Leo 1997 "The Social Psychology of Police Interrogation: The Theory and Classification of True and False Confessions." *Studies in Law, Politics and Society* 16:189–251.

Rosenberg, Gerald N. 1991 *The Hollow Hope: Can Courts Bring about Social Change?* Chicago: University of Chicago Press.

Shapiro, Susan 1990 "Collaring the Crime, Not the Criminal: Reconsidering the Concept of White Collar Crime." *American Sociological Review* 55:346–365.

Soule, Sarah A., and Yvonne Zylan 1997 "Runaway Train?: The Diffusion of State-Level Reform in ADC/AFDC Eligibility Requirements, 1950–1967." *American Journal of Sociology* 103:733–762.

Sudnow, David 1965 "Normal Crimes: Sociological Features of the Penal Code in a Public Defender's Office." *Social Problems* 12:255–276.

Trubek, David 1984 "Where the Action Is: Critical Legal Studies and Empiricism." *Stanford Law Review* 36:575–622.

Vaughn, Dianne 1998 "Rational Choice, Situated Action, and the Social Control of Organizations." *Law and Society Review* 32:23–61.

Walker, Samuel, Cassia Spohn, and Miriam DeLorme 1996 *The Color of Justice: Race, Ethnicity and Crime in America.* Belmont, Calif.: Wadsworth.

Wallace, Michael, Beth A. Rubin, and Brian T. Smith 1988 "American Labor Law: Its Impact on Working-class Militancy, 1901–1980." *Social Science History* 12:1–29.

Watson, Alan 1985 *The Evolution of Law.* Baltimore: Johns Hopkins University Press.

JAMES M. INVERARITY

SOCIOLOGY OF RELIGION

An important intellectual shift has taken place in the social scientific study of religion as many of its longest held theoretical positions, passed down from the founders of the field, have been overturned. These changes have been so dramatic and far-reaching that Warner (1993, p. 1044) identified them "as a paradigm shift in progress," an assessment that since that time "has been spectacularly fulfilled" (Greeley 1996, p. 1).

Typically, the emergence of a new paradigm rests on both an empirical basis and a theoretical basis. Over the past thirty years, there has been an explosion of research on religious topics and a substantial number of new facts have accumulated. The bulk of these discoveries have turned out to be inconsistent with the old paradigm. In response to the growing incompatibility between fact and traditional theory, new theories have been constructed to interpret the empirical literature.

There are five major points of dispute between the old and new paradigms. In this article, each one is described, followed by a brief summary of the pertinent evidence. Finally, additional recent trends in the field are noted.

RELIGION IS HARMFUL

For nearly three centuries, social scientists condemned religion as harmful to the individual because it impedes rational thought and harmful to society because it sanctifies tyrants (Stark 1999b). The premise that religion is irrational and psychologically harmful has taken many forms, all of them notable for the open contempt and antagonism they express toward faith. Thus, as Freud explained on one page of his psychoanalytic exposé of faith, *The Future of an Illusion* (1961 [1927], p. 88), religion is an "illusion," a "sweet—or bitter-sweet—poison," a "neurosis," an "intoxicant," and "childishness to be overcome." More recently, Carroll (1987, p. 491) claimed that praying the Rosary is "a disguised gratification of repressed anal-erotic desires," a substitute for playing "with one's feces." In a similar fashion, Ostow (1990, p. 113) asserted that evangelical Protestantism is a matter of regression "to the state of mind of the child who resists differentiation from its mother. The messiah and the group itself represent the returning mother."

In rejecting assertions that religion is rooted in irrationality, proponents of the new paradigm cite a growing literature that finds religion to be a reliable source of better mental and even physical health (Ellison 1991, 1993; Idler and Kasl 1997; Levin 1996; Pargament and Park 1995). Two literature reviews published in 1987, pointed to the positive health effects of religious involvement regardless of the age, sex, race, ethnicity, or nationality of the population being studied (Jarvis and Northcutt 1987; Levin and Schiller 1987). In a more recent review, Levin (1996, p. 850) found that that relationship still holds and suggests that these results point to a "protective epidemiologic effect of religiosity."

In the field of gerontology, of research on religion and aging has grown so rapidly that a new journal (*Journal of Religious Gerontology*) has emerged and older journals have devoted special issues or sections to discussions of the topic. Krause (1997, p. S291) summarized the literature: "[A]n impressive body of research indicates that elderly people who are involved in religion tend to enjoy better physical and mental health than older adults who are not as religious."

Not only is religion associated with better mental and physical health, all the current theorizing about religion accepts the rational choice principle as its first axiom (Gill 1998; Greeley 1995; Iannaccone 1990, 1995a, 1995b; Miller 1995; Sherkat 1997; Stark 1996a, 1996b, 1999a; Stark and Bainbridge 1980 [1987], 1996; Stark and Finke 2000; Stark and Iannaccone 1993, 1994). Most of these scholars do not employ the "thin" version of rational choice currently used in economics (Iannaccone 1995b) but the "thick" version (Ferejohn 1991), similar to what Weber ([1922] 1993, p. 1) had in mind when he wrote that

> *religiously or magically motivated behavior is relatively rational behavior . . . It follows rules of experience. . . . Thus, religious and magical behavior or thinking must not be set apart from the range of everyday purposive conduct . . .*

What about the harmful *social* effects of religion as it sustains the powerful and dispenses false consciousness to the exploited and debased? Engels (Marx and Engels 64 195, p. 316) claimed that early Christianity "first appeared as a religion of slaves and emancipated slaves, of poor people deprived of all rights, of peoples subjugated and dispersed by Rome." Does it not follow that *religion appeals most strongly to the lower classes*?

While the old paradigm identified religion as the opiate of the people, the new paradigm notes that religion also often is the "amphetamines" of the people in that religion animated many medieval peasant and artisan rebellions (Cohn 1961), generated repeated uprisings among the native peoples of Africa and North America against European encroachment (Wilson 1975), and recently served as a major center of mobilization against tyranny in eastern Europe (Echikson 1990). The notion that religion primarily serves to compensate the deprived and dispossessed has become untenable. The consensus among scholars rejects as "imaginary history" Engels's notion that the early Christian movement was rooted in proletarian suffering. The facts force the conclusion that Christianity's greatest early appeal was to the privileged classes (Stark 1996a). In similar fashion, since the early 1940s many researchers have attempted to connect religiousness to social class, but their findings have been weak and inconsistent (Stark and Finke 2000). Consequently, the need for new theorizing on the role of religion in the political affairs of nations has been recognized (Gill 1998).

RELIGION IS DOOMED IN MODERN TIMES

As the social sciences emerged in the wake of the Enlightenment, the leading figures eagerly proclaimed the demise of religion. Toqueville wrote in his famous early nineteenth-century study, *Democracy in America* ([1840] 1956, vol. II, p. 319):

> *The philosophers of the eighteenth century explained in a very simple manner the gradual decay of religious faith. Religious zeal, said they, must necessarily fail the more generally liberty is established and knowledge diffused.*

This came to be known as the *secularization thesis*: In response to modernization, "religious institutions, actions, and consciousness, [will] lose their social significance" (Wilson 1982, p. 149). Toqueville was virtually alone in rejecting the secularization thesis; perhaps no other social scientific prediction enjoyed such nearly universal acceptance for so long. Thus, the anthropologist Wallace (1966, p. 265) wrote in an undergraduate textbook:

> *The evolutionary future of religion is extinction. Belief in supernatural beings and supernatural forces that affect nature without obeying nature's laws will erode and become only an interesting historical memory . . . Belief in supernatural powers is doomed to die out, all over the world, as the result of the increasing adequacy and diffusion of scientific knowledge.*

In the late 1990s, the secularization thesis has been buried under a mountain of contrary facts (Bossy 1985; Duffy 1992; Greeley 1989, 1995, 1996; Murray 1972; Stark 1999c). The primary empirical basis for claims of ongoing secularization has been the very low rates of religious participation in contemporary European nations, where weekly rates of church attendance often are below 5 percent. However, the overwhelming weight of historical research shows that these low rates do not represent a decline. Church attendance always was extremely low in those nations, and it is not clear that they ever were effectively Christianized (Greeley 1995; Stark 1999c). Furthermore, in those nations the overwhelming majority express firm belief in the supernatural, pray, and describe themselves as religious. It is perverse to describe a nation as highly secularized (as those committed to the old paradigm still do) when two-thirds or more of its residents say they are "religious persons" and fewer than 5 percent say they are atheists. The interesting question thus does not concern secularization but is, "[W]hy are these societies of believing non-belongers?" as Davie (1994) has expressed it. What is it about the churches in those nations that prevents them from mobilizing participation?

Looking to the world as a whole, there is no consistent relationship between religious participation and modernization. Indeed, the very few significant, long-term declines in religious participation that have been seen in the world are greatly outnumbered by remarkable increases (Stark and Finke 2000). What needs to be explained, therefore, is not religious decline but *variation*. Finally, the spread of science cannot cause secularization, because science and religion are unrelated. Scientists are as religious as anyone else, and the more scientific their fields, the more religious are American academics (Stark et al. 1996).

ONE LAST SPASM

The twin propositions that religious behavior is rooted in irrationality and that religion must soon yield to secularization have been dealt a blow by the finding that the more liberal (or secularized) a religious body becomes, the more rapidly it loses members, while denominations that sustain more vigorous and traditional theologies have prospered (Finke and Stark 1992; Iannaccone 1994; Kelley 1972; Stark and Finke 2000). How can it be that the "fundamentalists" grow while the liberals lose out? Proponents of the old paradigm have invoked the notion that this is but one final, dying spasm of piety. They claim that the expansion of evangelical Protestant churches in the United States (and presumably in Latin America, where they are experiencing explosive growth) is a frantic "flight from modernity," that people who feel threatened by the erosion of traditional morality are flocking to religious havens (Berger 1967; Hunter 1987, 1983). Berger (1967, p. 11) described American evangelical Protestant churches as follows: "They are like besieged fortresses, and their mood tends toward a militancy that only superficially covers an underlying sense of panic." Nearly thirty years later Thurow (1996, p. 232) explained, "Those who lose out economically or who cannot stand the economic uncertainty of not knowing what it takes to succeed in the new era ahead retreat into religious fundamentalism."

A fatal problem with this explanation is that, as was noted above, the relationship between social class and religiousness is weak and inconsistent. Conservative churches actually include a fair share of highly educated, successful, and sophisticated people who display no apparent fears of modernity (Smith 1998, 2000; Stark and Finke 2000; Woodberry and Smith 1998).

The new paradigm has no difficulty explaining the growth of evangelical churches because it does not confuse price with value. As Iannaccone (1994, 1992) has demonstrated, "strict" churches—those which require more from their members—are a better value because they offer far more in the way of rewards, both worldly and otherworldly. In this sense, to opt for a more traditional religious affiliation is to make the more rational choice, in that it yields a greater ratio of rewards over costs.

IDEALISTIC HUMBUG

Generations of social scientists have embraced the notion that religion is a dependent variable and that whatever appears to be a religious effect is ultimately merely a mask for something more basic, something "material."

Although social scientists in most other areas of study have long acknowledged the truism that if people define something as real, it can have real consequences, this concession usually has been denied in the area of religion. Instead, there has been a general willingness to agree with Marx that any attempt to explain "reality" by reference to an unreality such as religion is "idealistic humbug." Rather, one must explain religion by reference to "realities" such as "the mode of production." That is, one "does not explain practice from the idea but explains the formation of ideas from material practice" (Marx [1845] 1998, p. 61). As Marx's collaborator Engels explained, "All religion . . . is nothing but the fantastic reflection in men's minds of those external forces which control their daily life . . . the economic conditions . . . the means of production" (Marx and Engels 1964, pp. 147–148).

These views did not originate with Marx; they have been nearly universal among social scientists for close to three centuries (Stark 1999b). Even Weber, having attributed the rise of capitalism to the "Protestant ethic," traced the source of that ethic to material conditions (including the rise of the bourgeoisie, population growth, and colonialism), thus limiting Calvinist doctrines to being at most a *proximate* rather than a *fundamental* cause of capitalism. Even so, Weber has been bitterly criticized for affording religion *any* causal role. Emile Durkheim and his functionalist heirs dismissed religious belief as an insignificant epiphenomenon, regarding ritual as the only active religious ingredient and as being only a proxy for a more basic factor, social solidarity (Stark and Bainbridge 1997).

The new paradigm is committed to the proposition that people often act from religious motives and that in many cases no more fundamental or material cause can be found. Four historical examples reveal the conflict between paradigms on this central issue.

Crusading for Land and Loot. For centuries, historians believed that the Crusades to the Holy Land were motivated by faith, that tens of thousands of European nobles and knights marched to the Holy Land to rescue it from Muslim "desecration." However, by the end of the nineteenth century social scientists had penetrated those appearances to discover that the crusaders really went in pursuit of land and loot. Having summarized the many economic problems facing Europe in the eleventh century, including the population pressures and land shortages that were said to beset the knightly class, Mayer (1972, pp. 22–25) stressed the "lust for booty" and the "hunger for loot" that motivated the crusaders: "Obviously the crusade acted as a kind of safety valve for a knightly class which was constantly growing in numbers." He went on to emphasize the need to recognize "the social and economic situation of a class which looked upon the crusade as a way of solving its material problems."

Although there is extensive evidence that the crusaders truly believed they were going for purely religious reasons, this material can be ignored because there exists a definitive refutation of the materialist position. In 1063, thirty-two years before Urban II called for the First Crusade to the Holy Land, Pope Alexander II, backed by the evangelical efforts of the monks of Cluny, attempted to organize a Crusade to reclaim Moorish Spain.

Here, very close at hand, lay great wealth and an abundance of fertile land, and the Pope had declared that all who fought for the Cross in Spain were entitled not only to absolution for their sins but to all the wealth and "lands they conquered from the infidel" (Runciman 1951, vol. 1, p. 91). However, hardly anyone responded, and little or nothing was achieved. The materialist interpretation of the Crusades fails when faced with the fact that crusaders were not lured to nearby Spain in pursuit of rich and relatively easy pickings, while soon afterward tens of thousands set off for the dry wastes of faraway Palestine and did so again and again. Why did they do that rather than go to Spain? Because Spain was not the Holy Land. Jesus had not walked the streets of Toledo or been crucified in Seville.

Heresy and Class Struggle. Beginning in the eleventh century and lasting though the sixteenth, Europe was swept by mass heretical movements—Waldensians, Cathars (called Albigensians in southern France), Hussites, and many others—culminating in the Reformation. Tens of thousands died on behalf of their religious beliefs, but maybe not.

Many historians possessed of an excessive sociological imagination have claimed that these great heretical movements were not primarily about doctrines and morals, if indeed religious factors were of any significance at all. Instead, they argue, the religious aspect of these movements masked their real basis, which was of course class struggle. Engels (Marx and Engels 1964, pp. 97–123) identified some of these movements, including the Albigensians, as urban heresies in that they represented the class interests of the town bourgeoisie against those of the feudal elites of church and state. But most of the heretical movements were, according to Engels, based on the proletariat, which demanded restoration of the equality and communalism of early Christianity (Engels and many other Marxists have claimed that the early Christians briefly achieved true communism). Engels granted that these class struggles were characterized by religious and mystical rhetoric but dismissed this as false consciousness. Following Engels, many Marxist historians have "exposed" the materialism behind the claims of religious dissent. Thus, in 1936 the Italian historian Antonino de Stefano claimed, "At bottom, the economic argument must have constituted, more than any

dogmatic or religious discussions, the principle motive of the preaching of heresy" (quoted in Russell 1965, p. 231). Even many historians not committed to orthodox Marxism have detected materialism behind medieval dissent. For example, the non-Marxist historian Cohn (1961, p. xiii) reduced medieval heresies to "the desire of the poor to improve the material conditions of their lives," which "became transfused with phantasies of a new Paradise."

It is not necessary for proponents of the new paradigm to deny that class conflicts existed in medieval times or to suppose that people participating in heresy never paid any heed to their material interests to reaffirm that religion lay at the heart of these conflicts. If their primary concerns had been worldly, surely most heretics would have recanted when that was the only way out. It was, after all, only their religious notions they had to give up, not their material longings. However, large numbers of them chose death instead. Moreover, these movements drew participants from all levels of the class system. The Albigensians, for example, enlisted not only the bourgeoisie but, in contradiction to Engels, most of the nobility as well as the clergy of southern France and indeed the "masses" (Costen 1997; Lambert 1992; Mundy 1985). Finally, the claim that the majority of the participants in any given heresy consisted of peasants and the poor is lacking in force, even in the instances in which it might be true. Almost everyone in medieval Europe was poor and a peasant. Gauged against this standard, it seems likely that the "proletarian masses" were quite underrepresented in most of these movements (Lambert 1992).

Medieval Jewish Messianic Movements. For Jews the messiah has yet to come, but again and again over the centuries, groups of Jews have hailed his arrival. An early episode resulted, of course, in Christianity, but it would not be an exaggeration to say that hundreds of other messianic movements have occurred in Jewish communities over the past two millennia, and such movements were especially common in the European diaspora during medieval times (Cohen 1967; Lenowitz 1998; Sharot 1982).

In a sophisticated analysis of these religious movements, Sharot (1982, p. 18) noted the huge literature that stresses that messianic movements are

*responses to the disruption of social and
cultural patterns . . . [produced by] a disaster
such as an epidemic, famine, war, or massacre.
Following a disaster, persons feel vulnerable,
confused, full of anxiety, and they turn to
millennial beliefs in order to account for
otherwise meaningless events. They interpret
the disaster as a prelude to the millennium;
thus their deepest despair gives way to the
greatest hope.*

Although some messianic Jewish movements did
erupt after a disaster, as he worked his way through
all the better-known cases, Sharot (1982, pp. 65–
66) was forced to agree with Cohen's (1967) earlier
study that many movements seemed to come out
of nowhere in the sense that they arose during
periods of relative quiet and therefore that "disaster was not a necessary condition of a messianic
outburst."

Sharot made this concession very reluctantly,
and often seems to forget it. Nevertheless, his
scrupulous accounts of specific incidents frequently
show that a movement was the direct result of
religious rather than secular influences. In many
cases, an episode began with an individual or small
group poring over the *Kabbalah* (a collection of
Jewish mystical writings) out of purely personal
motives and then "discovering" that the millennium was at hand. Thereafter, they shared this
knowledge with others, who in turn assisted in
arousing a mass following. In other instances,
someone became convinced that he was the messiah and was able to convince his family and friends
(Stark 1999d).

One can of course argue that Jews in medieval
Europe were always victims and hence always ripe
for millenarian solutions. However, constants cannot explain variations, and in as many cases as not,
nothing special was going on to cause a movement
to arise then rather than at some other time except for direct religious influences in the form of
people advocating a new religious message or
circumstance.

Of course, people often do turn to religion in
times of trouble and crisis, but the new paradigm
rejects the claim that crises are a necessary condition for religious innovations and recognizes that
religious phenomena can be caused by other religious phenomena.

The Mystical 1960s. A huge literature attributes the "explosive growth" of new religious
movements in the United States in the late 1960s
and early 1970s to profound social causes. Particular attention has been given to uncovering the
secular causes of the special appeal of Eastern
faiths for Americans in that period. Cox (1983, p.
42) blamed "the most deteriorated, decadent phase
of consumer capitalism," charging that converts to
Eastern faiths had "been maddened by consumer
culture" (p. 40). Serious journals published equally
hysterical explanations. As Robbins summarized
(1988, p. 60), each of these analyses identified one
or more "acute and distinctively modern dislocation which is said to be producing some mode of
alienation, anomie or deprivation to which Americans are responding." With a fine grasp of the
essentials, Barker (1986, p. 338) commented that
"those who have read some of the sociological
literature could well be at a loss to understand why
all young adults are not members [of new religious
movements], so all-encompassing are some of the
explanations."

In fact, there was no growth, explosive or
otherwise, of new religious movements in this era
(Melton 1988; Finke and Stark 1992); the rate of
new movement formation was constant from 1950
through 1990. As for the brief increase in the
proportion of Eastern faiths among new American
movements, capitalism had nothing to do with it.
Rather, in 1965 the elimination of exclusionary
rules against Asian immigration made it possible
for the first time for authentic Eastern and Indian
religious leaders to seek American followers directly. Consequently, there was an increase in the
number of Eastern religious organizations, but
the number of actual converts was minuscule.
Even so, these movements were the result of *religious* efforts, of face-to-face recruitment activities motivated by the religious convictions of
missionizing gurus.

THE EVILS OF PLURALISM

More than three centuries ago, early scholars of
comparative religion assumed that by publicizing
the beliefs of the world's many faiths, they could
advance the cause of atheism, that by virtue of
their competing claims, each religion would refute
the others (Preus 1987). This view has led to the

claim that faith is a very fragile thing that cannot survive challenge; hence, *pluralism*—the existence of several competing religious bodies in a society—is said to be incompatible with strong religiosity. Durkheim ([1897] 1951, p. 159) asserted that when multiple religious groups compete, religion becomes open to question, dispute, and doubt and thus "the less it dominates lives." Eventually these views were formulated into elegant sociology by Berger (1967, 1979), who repeatedly argued that pluralism inevitably destroys the plausibility of all religions and only where one faith prevails can there exist a "scared canopy" that is able to inspire universal confidence and assent.

These notions are mistaken, having been taken over uncritically from the justifications given by European state churches for their monopolies. It is indicative of the undue respect given European social science that American sociologists accepted this view, since religious competition is an obvious basis for the extraordinary levels of religious participation in the United States, in contrast to the religious apathy prevalent in societies with a monopoly church. Indeed, the positive role of competition is obvious in American history. In 1776, when most American colonies were dominated by a state-supported church, about one person in five belonged to any church. After the Revolution, the onset of vigorous religious competition eventually resulted in about two-thirds of Americans belonging to a church (Finke and Stark 1992)

To fully appreciate the power of pluralism, it was necessary to cease treating religion as primarily a psychological phenomenon and take a more sociological view, an approach that also has been characteristic of the new paradigm. The concept of a *religious economy* (Stark 1985) made it possible to adopt an overall perspective on the religious activities in a society and examine the interplay among religious groups. This analysis quickly revealed that the main impact of religious competition on individuals is not confusion or the corrosion of faiths but to present the individual with vigorously offered choices. As Adam Smith pointed out more than two centuries ago, monopoly religions are as subject to laziness and inefficiency as are monopoly business firms. Thus, it is axiomatic in the new paradigm that religious competition strengthens religion because as firms vie for supporters, they tend to specialize their ap-

peals, with the overall result that a higher proportion of the population will be enrolled. As of 1999 there had been more than twenty-five published studies based on many different societies and different eras, offering overwhelming support for this view (Finke and Stark 1998; Stark and Finke 2000).

A FOCUS ON RELIGION

Despite emphasizing that religion does have effects, the new paradigm is not limited to that perspective. Rather, in addition to a sociology of religious effects, the new paradigm has promulgated a sociology of religion per se.

For a long time sociologists interested in religion attempted to justify their topic by demonstrating its importance to those who specialized in one of the more of the "secular" areas of the field. Thus, some sociologists devoted studies to demonstrating religious effects on political behavior such as voting and opinions on current issues. Others sought to convince demographers that religion was crucial to fertility studies. This trend has been enshrined in textbooks on the sociology of religion, all of which have consisted almost entirely of chapters on "religion and family," "religion and economics," "religion and prejudice," and so on.

However, having become part of a relatively large and well-established specialty, sociologists in this area have become sufficiently confident to made religion the real center of study rather than trying to draw legitimacy from its connections to other topics. Consequently, there has been renewed attention to what religion is as well as what it does (Boyer 1994; Greeley 1995; Guthrie 1996; Stark 1999a). There also is much new work on religious and mystical experiences (Hood 1997; Howell 1997; Neitz and Spickard 1990; Stark 1999d). Other scholars have focused not on the causes or consequences of prayer but on its nature and practice (Poloma and Gallup 1991; Swatos 1987). Also, increasing attention is being paid to images of God (Barrett 1998; Greeley 1995; Stark forthcoming).

In addition, there is an impressive new literature on religious socialization (Ellison and Sherkat 1993a, 1993b; Granqvist 1998; Kirkpatrick and Shaver 1990; Smith 1998), on denominational switching (Musick and Wilson 1995; Perrin et al.

1997; Sherkat and Wilson 1995), and on conversion (Hall 1998; Rambo 1993; Stark and Finke 2000). Amid all this activity, the case study literature is blooming as never before (Davidman 1991; Goldman 1999; Heelas 1996; Lang and Ragvald 1993; Lawson 1995, 1996, 1998; Neitz 1987; Poloma 1989; Washington 1995).

REFERENCES

Barker, Eileen 1986 "Religious Movements: Cult and Anti-Cult Since Jonestown." *Annual Review of Sociology* 12:329–346.

Barrett, Justin L. 1998 "Cognitive Constraints on Hindu Concepts of the Divine." *Journal for the Scientific Study of Religion* 37:608–619.

Berger, Peter 1967 *The Sacred Canopy*. New York: Doubleday.

—— 1979 *The Heretical Imperative: Contemporary Possibilities of Religious Affiliation*. New York: Doubleday.

Bossy, John 1985 *Christianity in the West: 1400–1700*. New York: Oxford University Press.

Boyer, Pascal 1994 *The Naturalness of Religious Ideas: A Cognitive Theory of Religion*. Berkeley: University of California Press.

Carroll, Michael P. 1987 "Praying the Rosary: The Anal-Erotic Origins of a Popular Catholic Devotion." *Journal for the Scientific Study of Religion* 26:486–498.

Cohen, Gershon D. 1967. "Messianic Postures of Ashkenazim and Sephardim (Pior to Sabbatai Zevi)." In Max Kreutzberger, ed., *Studies of the Leo Baeck Institute*. New York:

Cohn, Norman 1961 *The Pursuit of the Millennium*. New York: Harper and Row.

Costen, Michael 1997 *The Cathars and the Albigensian Crusade*. Manchester, UK: Manchester: University Press.

Cox, Harvey 1983 "Interview." In Steven J. Gelberg, ed., *Hare Krishna, Hare Krishna*. New York: Grove Press.

Davidman, Lynn 1991 *Tradition in a Rootless World: Women Turn to Orthodox Judaism*. Berkeley: University of California Press.

Davie, Grace. 1994. *Religion in Britain Since 1945: Believing without Belonging*. Oxford:Blackwell.

Duffy, Eamon. 1992. *Stripping of the Altars*. New Haven, Conn.: Yale University Press.

Durkheim, Emile (1897) 1951 *Suicide*. Glencoe, Ill.: Free Press.

Echikson, William 1990 *Lighting the Night: Revolution in Eastern Europe*. New York: Morrow.

Ellison, Christopher G. 1991 "Religious Involvement and Subjective Well-Being." *Journal of Health and Social Behavior* 32:80–99.

—— 1993. "Religion, the Life Stress Paradigm, and the Study of Depression." In Jeffrey S. Levin, ed., *Religious Factors in Aging and Health: Theoretical Foundations and Methodological Frontiers*. Newbury Park, Calif.: Sage

Ferejohn, John A. 1991 "Rationality and Interpretation: Parliamentary Elections in Early Stuart England." In Kristen Renwick Monroe, ed., *The Economic Approach to Politics: A Critical Reassessment of the Theory of Rational Action*. New York: HarperCollins.

—— 1992 *The Churching of America, 1776–1990: Winners and Losers in our Religious Economy*. New Brunswick, N. J.: Rutgers University Press.

Finke, Roger, and Rodney Stark 1998 "Religious Choice and Competition." *American Sociological Review*. 63:761–766.

Freud, Sigmund (1927) 1961 *The Future of an Illusion*. Garden City, N.Y.: Doubleday.

Gill, Anthony J. 1998 *Rendering Unto Caesar: The Roman Catholic Church and the State in Latin America*. Chicago: University of Chicago Press.

Goldman, Marion 1999 *Passionate Journies: Why Successful Women Joined a Cult*.

Granqvist, Pehr 1998 "Religiousness and Perceived Childhood Attachment: On the Question of Compensation or Correspondence." *Journal for the Scientific Study of Religion*. 37:350–367.

Greeley, Andrew M. 1989 *Religious Change in America*. Cambridge, Mass.: Harvard University Press.

—— 1995 *Religion as Poetry*. New Brunswick, N.J.: Transaction.

—— 1996 "The New American Paradigm: A Modest Critique." Paper read at the German Sociological Association annual meetings, Cologne.

Guthrie, Stewart Elliott 1996 "Religion: What Is It?" *Journal for the Scientific Study of Religion*. 35:412–419.

Heelas, Paul 1996 *The New Age Movement*. Oxford: Blackwell.

Hood, Ralph W., Jr. 1997 "The Empirical Study of Mysticism." In Bernard Spilka and Daniel N. McIntosh, eds., *The Psychology of Religion: Theoretical Approaches*. Boulder, Colo. Westview Press.

Howell, Julia Day 1997 "ASC Induction Techniques, Spiritual Experiences, and Commitment to New Religious Movements." *Sociology of Religion*. 58:141–164.

Hunter, James Davison 1983 *American Evangelicalism: Conservative Religion and the Quandary of Modernity*. New Brunswick, N.J.: Rutgers University Press.

—— 1987 *Evangelicalism: The Coming Generation*. Chicago: University of Chicago Press.

Iannaccone, Laurence R. 1990 "Religious Practice: A Human Capital Approach." *Journal for the Scientific Study of Religion*. 29:297–314.

—— 1992 "Sacrifice and Stigma: Reducing Free-Rising in Cults, Communes, and other Collectives." *Journal of Political Economy*. 100(2):271–292.

—— 1994 "Why Strict Churches Are Strong." *American Journal of Sociology*. 99:1180–1211.

—— 1995a "Risk, Rationality, and Religious Portfolios." *Economic Inquiry*. 33:285–295.

—— 1995b "Voodoo Economics? Reviewing the Rational Choice Approach to Religion." *Journal for the Scientific Study of Religion*. 34:76–89.

Idler, Ellen L. and Stanislav V. Kasl 1997b "Religion among Disabled and Nondisabled Persons: II. Attendance at Religious Services as a Predictor of the Course of Disability. *Journal of Gerontology* 52B(6):S306–316.

Jarvis, G. K. and H. C. Northcutt 1987 "Religion Differences in Morbidity and Mortality." *Social Sciences and Medicine* 25:813–824.

Kelley, Dean M. 1972 *Why Conservative Churches Are Growing*. New York: Harper and Row.

Kirkpatrick, Lee A., and Philip R. Shaver 1990 "Attachment Theory and Religion: Childhood Attachments, Religious Beliefs, and Conversion." *Journal for the Scientific Study of Religion*. 29:315–334.

Krause, Neal 1997 "Religion, Aging, and Health: Current Status and Future Prospects." *Journal of Gerontology* 52B(6):S291–293.

Lambert, Malcolm 1992 *Medieval Heresy*. Oxford, UK: Basil Blackwell.

Lang, Graeme, and Lars Ragvald 1993 *The Rise of a Refugee God: Hong Kong's Wong Tai Sin*. Hong Kong: Oxford University Press.

Lawson, Ronald 1995 "Sect-State Relations: Accounting for the Differing Trajectories of Seventh-Day Adventists and Jehovah's Witnesses."

—— 1996 "Church and State at Home and Abroad: The Evolution of Seventh-Day Adventist Relations with Governments." *Journal of the American Academy of Religion* 64:279–311.

—— 1998 "From American Church to Immigrant Church: The Changing Face of Seventh-Day Adventism in Metropolitan New York." *Sociology of Religion* 59:329–351.

Lenowitz, Harris 1998 *The Jewish Messiahs: From Galilee to Crown Heights*. New York: Oxford University Press.

Levin, Jeffrey S. 1996 "How Religion Influences Morbidity and Health." *Social Science and Medicine* 43(5):849–864.

——, and P. L. Schiller 1987 "Is There a Religious Factor in Health?" *Journal of Religion Health* 26:9–36.

Marx, Karl, with Frederich Engels (1845) 1998 *The German Ideology*. Amherst. N.Y. Prometheus.

——, and Friedrich Engels 1964 *On Religion*. New York: Schocken.

Mayer, Hans Eberhard 1972 *The Crusades*. London: Oxford University Press.

Miller, Alan 1995 "A Rational Choice Model of Religious Behavior in Japan." *Journal for the Scientific Study of Religion* 34:234–244.

Mundy, John Hine 1985 *The Repression of Catharism and Toulouse*. Toronto: Pontifical Institute of Mediaeval Studies.

Murray, Alexander 1972 "Piety and Impiety in Thirteenth-Century Italy." *Studies in Church History*. 8:83–106.

Musick, Marc, and John Wilson 1995 "Religious Switching for Marriage Reasons." *Sociology of Religion* 56:257–270.

Neitz, Mary Jo 1987 *Charisma and Community: A Study of Religious Commitment within the Charismatic Renewal*. New Brunswick, N.J.: Transaction.

——, and James V. Spickard 1990 "Steps toward a Sociology of Religious Experience: The Theories of Mihal Csikszentmihayi and Alfred Schutz." *Sociological Analysis* 51:15–33.

Ostow, Mortimer 1990 "The Fundamentalist Phenomenon: A Psychological Perspective." In Norman J. Coher, ed., *The Fundamentalist Phenomenon: A View from Within, a Response from Without*. Grand Rapids, Mich.: Eerdmans.

Pargament, K. I. and C. L. Park 1995 "Merely a Defense?: The Variety of Religious Ends and Means." *Journal of Social Issues*, 51(2):13–32.

Perrin, Robin D., Paul Kennedy, and Donald Miller 1997 "Examining the Sources of Conservative Church Growth: Where Are the New Evangelical Movements Getting their Numbers?" *Journal for the Scientific Study of Religion* 36:71–80.

Poloma, Margaret M. 1989 *The Assemblies of God at the Crossroads*. Knoxville: University of Tennessee Press.

——, and George H. Gallup, Jr. 1991 *Varieties of Prayer: A Survey Report*. Philadelphia: Trinity Press International.

Preus, J. Samuel 1987 *Explaining Religion: Criticism and Theory from Bodin to Freud*. New Haven, Conn.: Yale University Press.

Rambo, Lewish R. 1993 *Understanding Religious Conversion*. New Haven, Conn.: Yale University Press.

Robbins, Thomas 1988 *Cults, Converts and Charisma: The Sociology of Religious Movements*. Beverly Hills, Calif.: Sage.

Runciman, Steven 1951 *A History of the Crusades* (3 vols.). Cambridge, UK: Cambridge University Press.

Russell, Jeffrey Burton 1965 *Dissent and Reform in the Early Middle Ages*. Berkeley: University of California Press.

Sharot, Stephen 1982 *Messianism, Mysticism, and Magic: A Sociological Analysis of Jewish Religious Movements*. Chapel Hill: University of North Carolina Press.

Sherkat, Darren E. 1997 "Embedding Religious Choices: Preferences and Social Constraints into Rational Choice Theories of Religious Behavior." In Lawrence A. Young, ed., *Rational Choice Theory and Religion: Summary and Assessment*. New York: Routledge.

Smith, Christian. 2000. *Christian America? What Evangelicals Really Want*. Berkeley: University of California Press.

——, with Michael Emerson, Sally Gallagher, Paul Kennedy, and David Sikkink 1998 *American Evangelism: Embattled and Thriving*. Chicago: University of Chicago Press.

Stark, Rodney 1985 "From Church-Sect to Religious Economies" In Phillip E. Hammond, ed., *The Sacred in a Post-Secular Age*. Berkeley: University of California Press.

—— 1996a *The Rise of Christianity: A Sociologist Reconsiders History*. Princeton, N.J. Princeton University Press.

—— 1996b "Why Religious Movements Succeed or Fail: A Revised General Model." *Journal of Contemporary Religion* 11:133–146.

—— 1999a "The Micro Foundations of Religion: A Revised Theory." *Sociological Theory* 17:

—— 1999b "Atheism, Faith, and the Social Scientific Study of Religion." *Journal of Contemporary Religion:* 14:41–62.

—— 1999c "Secularization, R.I.P." *Sociology of Religion* 60:

—— 1999d "A Theory of Revelations," *Journal for the Scientific Study of Religion* 37:

—— Forthcoming. *Gods: Their Social and Historical Power.*

——, and William Sims Bainbridge 1980 "Towards a Theory of Religion: Religious Commitment," *Journal for the Scientific Study of Religion,* 19:114–128.

—— (1987) 1996 *A Theory of Religion*, Republished ed. New Brunswick, N.J.: Rutgers University Press.

—— 1997 *Religion, Deviance, and Social Control*. New York: Routledge.

——, and Roger Finke 2000 *The Human Side of Religion: A Social Science Paradigm*. Berkeley: University of California Press.

——, and Laurence R. Iannaccone 1993 "Rational Choice Propositions about Religious Movements." In David G. Bromley and Jeffrey K. Hadden, ed., *Religion and the Social Order, (vol. 3–A:): Handbook on Cults and Sects in America*. Greenwich, Conn.: JAI Press.

——, 1994 "A Supply-Side Reinterpretation of the "Secularization" of Europe." *Journal for the Scientific Study of Religion*. 33:230–252.

——, Laurence R. Iannaccone, and Roger Finke 1996 "Religion, Science and Rationality." *American Economic Review* (papers and proceedings):433–437.

Swatos, William H., Jr. 1987 "The Power of Prayer: Observations and Possibilities." In W. H. Swatos, ed., *Religious Sociology: Interfaces and Boundaries*. New York: Greenwood Press.

Thurow, Lester 1996 *The Future of Capitalism*. New York: Morrow.

Tocqueville, Alexis de. (1840) 1956 *Democracy in America* (2 vols). New York: Vintage.

Wallace, Anthony F. C. 1966 *Religion: An Anthropological View*. New York: Random House.

Warner, R. Stephen 1993 "Work in Progress towards a New Paradigm for the Sociological Study of Religion in the United States." *American Journal of Sociology* 98:1044–1093.

Washington, Peter 1995 *Madame Blavatsky's Baboon*. New York: Schoecken.

Weber, Max (1922) 1993 *The Sociology of Religion*. Boston: Beacon.

Wilson, Bryan 1975 *Magic and the Millennium*. Frogmore, UK: Paladin.

—— 1982 *Religion in Sociological Perspective*. Oxford: UK: Oxford University Press.

Woodberry, Robert D., and Christian S. Smith 1998 "Fundamentalism et al.: Conservative Protestants in America." *Annual Review of Sociology*. 22:25–56.

RODNEY STARK

SOCIOMETRY

See Social Networks; Social Psychology.

SOUTHEAST ASIA STUDIES

Southeast Asia consists of the ten countries that lie between the Indian subcontinent and China. On the mainland of Southeast Asia are Myanmar (Burma), Thailand, Laos, Cambodia, and Vietnam. Insular Southeast Asia includes Indonesia, the Philippines, Brunei, Malaysia, and Singapore. While most of Malaysia (Peninsular Malaysia) is on the mainland, that country usually is considered part of insular Southeast Asia because the Malay population (the majority ethnic population) shares a common language and religion with much of the Indonesian population. The city-state of Singapore (on an island connected by a mile-long causeway to Peninsular Malaysia) was historically part of Malaysia, but because of its unique ethnic composition (three-quarters of the population is of Chinese origin), it is more similar to East Asia than to Southeast Asia.

While there are some common geographic and cultural features, diversity is the hallmark of the region. Incredible indigenous cultural variation has been overlaid by centuries of contact, trade, migration, and cultural exchange from within the region, from other parts of Asia, and for the past five hundred years from Europe (for general overviews of the region, see Osborne 1985; Wertheim 1968). The common characteristic of mainland Southeast Asia is Buddhism, although there are very significant variations across and within countries: Islam is the majority religion in Indonesia, Brunei, and Malaysia, while Christianity is the major religion in the Philippines. The lowlands of both mainland and insular Southeast Asia tend to be densely settled, and wet (irrigated) rice agriculture is the predominant feature of the countryside. Rural areas are knitted together with small- and medium-sized market towns. The major metropolitan areas of the region (Jakarta, Bangkok, Singapore, Manila, Rangoon, Kuala Lumpur, Ho Chi Minh City) are typically port cities or are located along major rivers. Many of these towns and cities have significant Chinese minorities (often intermarried with the local population) that play an important role in commerce. Every country has remote highland and mountainous regions that often are populated by ethnic minorities.

In terms of land area, population size, and cultural and linguistic diversity, Southeast Asia is comparable to Europe (excluding the former Soviet Union). By the year 2000, the population of Southeast Asia will exceed 500 million, about 8 percent of the world's total. Indonesia is the fifth most populous country in the world, while the oil-rich sultanate of Brunei (on the island of Borneo) is one of the smallest. The other large countries of the region—Thailand, Vietnam, and the Philippines—are more populous than all European countries except for the former Soviet Union and Germany. The sea (South China Sea and Indian and Pacific Oceans) surrounds much of the region, especially the immense Indonesian and Filipino archipelagoes. While the sea can be a barrier, the ocean and the rivers of the region are avenues that have fostered local and long-distance trade throughout history. Moreover, the ease of movement throughout the region seems to have shaped cultures that easily absorbed new ideas and immigrants and have been tolerant of diversity.

HISTORY

The contemporary political divisions of the region are largely a product of European imperialism, especially of the nineteenth century. Before European intervention, there were great regional civilizations, both agrarian states and maritime empires that waxed and waned over the millennium. The remains of the temple complexes of Angkor (Cambodia) and Pagan (Burma) rival the architectural achievements of any premodern world civilization. Early Western observers of the city of Melaka (a fifteenth-century maritime empire centered on the west coast of the Malayan peninsula) described it as more magnificent than any contemporary European city. These early polities were founded on intensive rice cultivation with complex irrigation systems, the dominance of regional and long-distance trade, or both. The region also has been deeply influenced by contacts with the great civilizations of India and China. The cultural influences from outside have invariably been transformed into distinctive local forms in different Southeast Asian contexts. Because relatively few written records have survived the tropical environment of Southeast Asia, historical research relies heavily on archeological investigations, epigraphs, and records from other world regions, especially Chinese sources.

European influence began in the sixteenth century with the appearance of Portuguese and Spanish naval forces, followed by the arrival of the

Dutch in the seventeenth century and then by that of the British and French. In the early centuries of contact, European powers were able to dominate the seas and thus limit the expansion of Southeast Asian polities, but they rarely penetrated very far inland from their coastal trading cities. All Southeast Asia was transformed, however, in the nineteenth century as the Industrial Revolution in the West stimulated demand for mineral and agricultural products around the globe. New economic organizations of plantations, mines, and markets led to large-scale migration of people and capital to frontier areas and to the cities of Southeast Asia. There was an accompanying flurry of imperialist wars to grab land, people, and potential resources. In a series of expansions, the British conquered the area of present-day Myanmar (Burma) and Malaysia, the Dutch completed their conquest of the East Indies (now Indonesia), and the French took the areas that formed their Indochina empire (present-day Vietnam, Cambodia, and Laos). At the turn of the twentieth century, the United States defeated nationalist forces to take control of the Philippines just as the Spanish Empire was crumbling. Siam (Thailand) was the only indigenous Southeast Asian state to escape the grip of colonialism.

The political history of the region has not been stable. As Western countries moved toward more democratic social and political institutions over the first decades of the twentieth century, the colonists (British, Dutch, American, and French) constructed authoritarian dependencies in the tropics that were based on export economies and racial ideologies. Although there were stirrings of nationalist sentiment in the first half of the twentieth century, it was only after World War II that the nationalist forces were strong enough and the international environment favorable enough to bring political independence to the region. The critical turning point was the Japanese conquest and occupation of Southeast Asia from 1942 to 1945, which permanently shattered the myth of European superiority. The colonial powers returned after World War II, but they encountered popular nationalist movements that demanded the end of colonialism.

Independence was negotiated peacefully by the Americans in the Philippines and the British in Burma and Malaya, but nationalist forces had to wage wars of independence against the Dutch in Indonesia (1945–1950) and the French in Vietnam (1945–1954). The interplay of nationalist struggles, class conflicts, and East-West cold war rivalry had a marked influence on political developments in the region. In almost every country there were radical and communist movements that held the allegiance of significant sectors of the population. In several cases, communist parties were part of the nationalist movement but left (or were driven out of) the political arena as domestic and international tensions escalated. Vietnam was unique in that the nationalist movement was led by Communists. After the French were defeated in 1954 and agreed to grant independence to Vietnam, the United States intervened to set up a non-Communist Vietnamese state in the southern region of the country. After another twenty years of war and a million casualties, Vietnam was finally united as an independent state in 1975. Since 1975, however, political tension between the socialist states of Vietnam, Cambodia, and Laos and the other countries in the region has been the dominant feature of international relations there.

Domestic political developments within individual countries in the region have been no less dramatic. Governments have oscillated between authoritarian and democratic forms, with no linear trend. Behind the headlines of military coups, regional wars for autonomy, and "managed" elections have been complex political struggles among various contending groups defined by class, region, ethnicity, and kinship. These struggles have ranged from civil war to fairly open elections. Large-scale violence is not the norm, but massacres in Indonesia, Cambodia, and East Timor have been among the worst of such episodes in modern times. Popular civil protests against ruling elites in the Philippines and Burma had significant domestic and international reverberations. Neither academic scholarship nor political reporting has offered generalizations about or convincing interpretations of the postwar political change in Southeast Asia.

Many of the countries in Southeast Asia have experienced remarkable socioeconomic modernization in the postindependence era. This is most evident for the ASEAN (Association of Southeast Asian Nations) countries of Thailand, Malaysia, Singapore, Indonesia, the Philippines, and Brunei. All indicators of socioeconomic development (gross national product, educational levels, occupational structure, infant mortality) suggest that Southeast Asia has successfully narrowed the gap with the first world, while other regions of the third world have fallen farther behind. The reasons for the success of some countries and the economic stagnation in other countries are a matter of dispute. The East Asian model of state-sponsored export industrialization is widely discussed in policy and academic circles, but the parallels between East Asian and Southeast Asian economic development strategies are still a matter of considerable uncertainty. Few scholarly studies have examined the causes and consequences of the economic modernization of Southeast Asia.

THE STATUS OF WOMEN

Several theoretical concepts and empirical generalizations have arisen from studies of Southeast Asian societies that have relevance far beyond the region. Empirically, the most common cultural characteristic across the region is the relatively high status of women in Southeast Asian societies, especially compared with East Asia and South Asia. While women still face many social and cultural obstacles in Southeast Asia, the situation appears much different from that in the patriarchal societies of other Asian societies and the traditional female domesticity of many Western societies. While there are a few matrilineal societies in the region, Southeast Asian kinship systems are typically bilateral, with equal importance attached to the husband's and wife's families. The patrilocal custom of an obligatory residence of a newly married couple with or near the groom's family is largely absent in Southeast Asia. The residence of young couples after marriage seems to be largely a matter of choice or is dependent on relative economic opportunities. There is no strong sex preference for children in Southeast Asia, with both girl and boy children seen as desirable.

The relatively positive status of women was evident in earlier times. Reid (1988, pp. 146–172) reports that early European observers were struck by the active role of women in economic and political affairs in Southeast Asia. Traditional folklore also suggests that women play an active role in courtship and that female sexual expectations were as important as men's. Perhaps most unusual was the custom (reported in the fifteenth and sixteenth centuries) of inserting spurs or balls in male

genitals to enhance the sexual pleasure of women (Reid 1988, pp. 148–151).

At present, women seem to be well represented in schools, universities, and employment in all modern sectors of the economy in almost every country in Southeast Asia. There is only a modest scholarly literature on the higher status of women in Southeast Asia (Van Esterik 1982), and few efforts have been made to explain the links between the traditional roles of women as productive workers in the rural rice economy and their relative ease of entry into the modern sector. Demographic research has revealed very rapid declines in fertility in several Southeast Asian countries, particularly Singapore, Thailand, Malaysia, and Indonesia. If the current pace of decline continues, replacement-level fertility (two children per woman) should be reached in the near future (Hirschman and Guest 1990).

AGRICULTURAL INVOLUTION

Scholarship on Southeast Asia often has reached beyond the boundaries of the region to influence debates over social science concepts, theory, and models. Perhaps most influential have been the books and articles on Indonesia by the anthropologist Geertz. His evocative concepts of the "theatre state," "thick description," and "agricultural involution" have stimulated debate and research in several social science disciplines, including sociology. His model of agricultural involution (Geertz 1968) has been one of the most provocative developments in scholarship on Indonesia over the last generation.

A strikingly bold thesis, agricultural involution is an attempt to explain how Java became one of the most densely settled populations in the world within a traditional agricultural economy. To address this question, Geertz presents an ecological interpretation of the evolution (involution) of Javanese social structure in the face of rapid population growth and Dutch colonialism within the constraints (and possibilities) of a wet rice economy. The colonial system prevented industrialization and the development of an indigenous entrepreneurial class. The traditional rice economy, however, could absorb a larger population because additional labor inputs in the maintenance of irrigation facilities, water control, weeding, and harvesting yielded marginal increments in rice production. Over the decades, this refinement of traditional production technology (involution) led to an increasing rigidification of traditional Javanese culture, thus discouraging innovation and any efforts at social change and reinforcing the structural limits of the colonial system. Even after independence, when structural limits were lifted, the legacy of the past, as reflected in Javanese culture, remained.

Geertz's thesis remains highly controversial, and many of its components have been confronted with negative evidence (for a review of the debate, see White 1983; and Geertz 1984). For example, Geertz deemphasized social class divisions with his interpretation of "shared poverty" as the traditional social strategy. Most research has shown significant inequality of landholding and other socioeconomic dimensions in Javanese villages, although it is not clear if inequality is permanently perpetuated between families across generations. Even accepting many of the criticisms, agricultural involution is a seminal sociological model that should generate empirical research on the historical development of Asian societies.

THE MORAL ECONOMY

A classic question in social science involves the causes of revolution or rebellion. Neither Marxian theory, which emphasizes exploitation, nor relative deprivation theory seems to be a satisfactory model to explain the occurrence of revolutions or rebellions. The most sophisticated sociological theory of peasant rebellion is based on historical materials from Burma and Vietnam by the political scientist J Scott (1976) in *The Moral Economy of the Peasant: Subsistence and Rebellion in Southeast Asia*. Scott argues that peasants rebel only when their normative expectations of a minimum subsistence level are not met. These conditions are more likely to occur when capitalist market relations and colonial states erode traditional societies and the reciprocal obligations of peasants and their patrons.

Scott's thesis has been criticized and hotly debated (Popkin 1979; Keyes 1983). One criticism is that Scott believes that peasants prefer traditional societies and are not responsive to economic opportunity. Scott acknowledges that peasants can be quite innovative and individualistic as long as their minimum subsistence is not at risk.

This debate, however, does not really address the central theoretical contribution of Scott's thesis about the specification of the causes of peasant rebellion.

In a more recent study based on fieldwork in a rural Malaysian village, Scott (1985) examines how class antagonisms are displayed in everyday life. Given that rebellion is a very rare event in most societies, Scott calls attention to political, social, and linguistic behaviors that reveal the depth of descensus and potential social conflict but do not risk violent reaction from the state and powerful elites. In these two books and related publications, Scott has provided original interpretations of peasant political behavior in Southeast Asia and set a research agenda for scholars of other world regions and, more generally, the development of social theory.

CONCLUSION

Scholarship on Southeast Asia, whether in sociology or in other disciplines, has tended to focus on individual countries rather than on the region. Different languages (colonial and indigenous) as well as variations in religious traditions and political and economic systems have reinforced the image of a heterogenous collection of countries that is labeled a region largely by default. There is tremendous political, economic, and sociocultural diversity in the region; many of these differences, however, are a product of the colonial era and its legacy. The similarity of family systems and the status of women throughout Southeast Asia suggest some common historical and cultural roots for the region. There may well be other social and cultural parallels across Southeast Asia that will be revealed as more comparative research is undertaken (Wolters 1982).

Many indicators of development in Southeast Asia, including very low levels of mortality and almost universal secondary schooling, are approaching the prevailing standards of developed countries. Assuming that current socioeconomic trends continue, several countries in the region probably will follow Japan, Korea, and Taiwan along the path of development in the early decades of the twenty-first century. The study of these processes of modernization and the accompanying changes in politics, family structure, ethnic relations, and other social spheres should make Southeast Asia an extraordinarily interesting sociological laboratory.

Evolutionary—and sometimes revolutionary—social change continued throughout much of Southeast Asia in the 1990s. After the collapse of the Soviet Union, the socialist countries in the region, including Vietnam, Cambodia, and Laos, moved rapidly toward more market-driven economies. Several political regimes that appeared to be stable for long periods have been transformed. The "people power" popular protests that ended the Marcos regime in the Philippines in the 1980s was echoed by the peaceful transition of power from a military regime in Thailand in the early 1990s and by the ending of the Suharto regime in Indonesia in 1998.

For much of the 1990s, most of Southeast Asia experienced rapid economic growth and the major question was the emerging role of the new middle class (McVey 1992; Girling 1996). This trend was halted in late 1997 by the "Asian economic crisis" that hit the region and affected Thailand, Malaysia, and Indonesia in particular. Both the causes of this crisis and its consequences are currently the subject of much debate. The change of regime in Indonesia and political protests in Malaysia may be the most visible long-term impact may be more profound.

Scholarship inevitably lags behind current events. Several important publications, including the second volume of Reid's (1990, 1995) *Southeast Asia in the Age of Commerce 1450–1680* and a much expanded version of Wolters's classic *History, Culture, and Region in Southeast Asian Perspectives 1999*, offer a new understanding of the history of the premodern era. Although the definition of Southeast Asia as a region sometimes has been considered arbitrary, historical studies show common cultural, political, and social forms in many places throughout the region.

One of the defining features of the region has been the relatively easy absorption of peoples, ideas, and cultural practices from elsewhere. In the twentieth century, assimilation into Southeast Asian societies became more difficult with the creation of political and social barriers. These issues are illuminated with considerable insight in Chirot and Reid's (1997) edited collection that compares the experience of the Chinese in Southeast Asia with that of the Jews in central Europe.

Research on Southeast Asia over the last decade also has been influenced by Anderson's (1991) *Imagined Communities*, a book originally published in the 1980s. Although Anderson is a specialist on Southeast Asia, his book on the development of nationalism provides comparisons from across the world.

REFERENCES

Anderson, Benedict 1991 *Imagined Communities: Reflections on the Origin and Spread of Nationalism*, rev. ed. London: Verso.

Chirot, Daniel, and Anthony Reid, eds. 1997 *Essential Outsiders: Chinese and Jews in the Modern Transformation of Southeast Asia and Central Europe*. Seattle: University of Washington Press.

Geertz, Clifford 1968 *Agricultural Involution: The Processes of Ecological Change in Indonesia*. Berkeley: University of California Press.

—— 1984 "Culture and Social Change." *Man* 19:511–532.

Girling, John 1996 *Interpreting Development: Capitalism, Democracy, and the Middle Class in Thailand*. Ithaca, N.Y.: Southeast Asia Program, Cornell University.

Hirschman, Charles, and Philip Guest 1990 "The Emerging Demographic Transitions of Southeast Asia." *Population and Development Review* 16:121–152.

Keyes, Charles F., ed. 1983 "Peasant Strategies in Asian Societies: Moral or Rational Economic Approaches—A Symposium." *Journal of Asian Studies* 42:753–868.

McVey, Ruth, ed. 1992 *Southeast Asian Capitalists*. Ithaca, N.Y.: Southeast Asia Program, Cornell University.

Osborne, Milton 1985 *Southeast Asia: An Illustrated Introductory History*. Sydney: Allen and Unwin.

Popkin, Samuel L. 1979 *The Rational Peasant*. Berkeley: University of California Press.

Reid, Anthony 1988 *Southeast Asia in the Age of Commerce, 1450–1680*, vol. 1: *The Lands below the Winds*. New Haven, Conn.: Yale University Press.

——1990 *Southeast Asia in the Age of Commerce 1450–1680: The Lands below the Winds*. New Haven, Conn.: Yale University Press.

——1995 *Southeast Asia in the Age of Commerce 1450–1680: Expansion and Crisis*. New Haven, Conn.: Yale University Press.

Scott, James C. 1976 *The Moral Economy of the Peasant: Subsistence and Rebellion in Southeast Asia*. New Haven, Conn.: Yale University Press.

——1985 *Weapons of the Weak: Everyday Forms of Peasant Resistance*. New Haven, Conn.: Yale University Press.

Van Esterik, Penny 1982 *Women of Southeast Asia*. Dekalb: Center for Southeast Asian Studies, Northern Illinois University.

Wertheim, W. F. 1968 "Southeast Asia." In David Sills, ed., *International Encyclopedia of the Social Sciences*. New York: Macmillan and Free Press.

White, Benjamin 1983 "Agricultural Involution and Its Critics: Twenty Years After." *Bulletin of Concerned Asian Scholars* 15:18–41.

Wolters, O. W. 1982 *History, Culture, and Region in Southeast Asian Perspectives*. Singapore: Institute of Southeast Asian Studies.

——1999 *History, Culture, and Region in Southeast Asian Perspectives*, rev. ed. Ithaca, N.Y.: Southeast Asia Program, Cornell University.

CHARLES HIRSCHMAN

SOVIET AND POST-SOVIET SOCIOLOGY

In prerevolutionary Russia, sociology occupied a marginal position. The state universities offered no instruction in the field, but there was a solid intellectual tradition of historical and theoretical sociology (Maxim Kovalevsky, Nikolai Mikhailovsky, Evgeny de Roberty), the sociology of law (Leon Petrajizky, Pitirim Sorokin), and the sociology of social problems (living conditions of industrial workers and peasants, public health, crime and prostitution in the cities). Beginning in the 1860s, the provincial intelligentsia initiated a kind of social movement, *Zemskaja statistika* (Statistics for Local Administration). Since official governmental statistics were unreliable, local statisticians made systematic surveys of households, daily life and public health conditions, and the reading preferences of the population (N. A. Rubakin). A modern system of sampling was elaborated by the statistician A. A. Chuprov for those surveys; K. M. Takhtarev introduced the concept of statistical sociological methods in social research.

In 1916, the Russian Sociological Society was founded, along with the "Sociological Institute," where M. M. Kovalevsky, K. M. Takhtarev, N. I. Kareev, and P. A. Sorokin gave lectures. Western sociological classics by Auguste Comte, Herbert Spencer, Emile Durkheim, Gabriel Tarde, Gustave Le Bon, Georg Simmel, Lester Ward, and others were available in Russian translations. Most important European sociological papers were immediately translated in the series *New Ideas in Sociology*. There was also a well-developed ethnography and a literary genre of sociological journalism.

The Bolshevik Revolution provided strong stimulus to sociological reflection and empirical social research. In the Soviet government decree "About the Socialist Academy of the Social Sciences," drafted in May 1918, Lenin (1962, p. 372) stressed the need "to organize a series of social researches" and called it "one of the most urgent tasks of the day." However, the Bolsheviks tolerated research only from Marxist and procommunist positions. In the early postrevolutionary years, censorship was relatively weak or inefficient. For example, Sorokin not only established the first sociological laboratory in Pertograd University but also succeeded in publishing (illegally) his two-volume *System of Sociology* (Sorokin 1920), for which he was awarded a doctorate in April 1922. He also conducted important empirical investigations on mass starvation in the districts of Samara and Saratov and examined its influence on various aspects of social life and human behavior.

However, this liberalism or negligence on the part of the authorities was short-lived. In autumn 1922, a group of leading Russian intellectuals, including Sorokin and other prominent social philosophers, was expelled from the county, ending non-Marxist sociology in Soviet Russia.

The tightening ideological control proved detrimental to socialist and Marxist social research as well. Nevertheless, the 1920s was a fruitful period both in empirical research and in theoretical-methodological work. The most important theoretical contributions were in the field of economic sociology (A. V. Chajanov, N. D. Kondratjev). There were also interesting studies on the social organization of labor, the budgeting of time in work and leisure activities (S. G. Strumilin), population dynamics, rural and urban ways of life (A. I. Todorsky, V. E. Kabo), marriage and sexual behavior, social psychology (V. M. Bekhterev), social medicine, and other topics. All this research was finished by the early 1930s.

The Stalinist totalitarian system was incompatible with any kind of social criticism, problem-oriented thinking, or empirical research. Most creative original thinkers were liquidated, and their books were prohibited. Sociology was declared "bourgeois pseudo-science." Official social statistics were kept secret or falsified. Empirical research that relied on questionnaires, participant observation, and similar methods was forbidden. All social theory was reduced to the official dogmatic version of historical materialism, which had very little in common with genuine Marxist dialectics. Practically no firsthand information about Western sociology was available.

The revival of sociology in the Soviet Union began during the Khrushchev's era in the late 1950s. It was initiated by a group of young philosophers and economists with a liberal political orientation. This intellectual initiative received support from reformist and technocratically oriented people in the party and state leadership. The first organizational step in this direction was the establishment in 1958 of the Soviet Sociological Association (SSA). The primary aim of this move was to facilitate participation in international sociological congresses by Soviet ideological bureaucrats in administrative academic positions. Gradually, thanks to personal efforts of Gennady Ossipov, among others, the SSA became a sort of organizational center for the emerging discipline.

To avoid conflicts with the dominant ideology, it was unanimously agreed that the only acceptable "scientific" general sociological theory was Marxist historical materialism but that it should be supplemented by "concrete social research" and eventually some middle-range theories. In 1960 Ossipov organized in the Institute of Philosophy of the USSR Academy of Sciences in Moscow a small unit for research on the new forms of work and daily life. This unit later was transformed into the Department of Concrete Social Research. At about the same time, Vladimir Iadov organized, within the philosophical faculty of Leningrad State University, the Laboratory of Concrete Social Research, which was dedicated to the study of job orientation and workers' personalities. At the Novosibirsk Institute of Industrial Economics and Organization, Vladimir Shubkin developed a unit for studies of youth issues, including high school children's professional orientations and social mobility, and Tatiana Zaslavskaia initiated the fields of economic and rural sociology. Sociology research units appeared under various names at the universities of Sverdlovsk and Tartu (Estonia). In 1968, the independent Institute of Concrete So-

cial Research of the USSR Academy of Sciences was established in Moscow, headed by the eminent economist and vice-president of the USSR Academy of Sciences A. M. Rumiantsev.

According to Shlapentokh (1987), 1965–1972 were the golden years of Soviet sociology. Important original research was done on workers' attitudes toward their jobs and on the interrelationship of work and personality (Iadov et al. 1970), professional orientations of youth, rural sociology and population migrations (Zaslavskaia 1970 Zaslavskaia and Ryvkina 1980; Arutiunian 1971), public opinion and mass media (Grushin 1967; Shlapentokh 1970), industrial sociology (Shkaratan 1978), marriage and the family (Kharchev 1964), personality (Kon 1967), leisure (Gordon and Klopov 1972), political institutions (F. M. Burlatsky, A. A. Galkin), and other topics. At the same time, research on the history of sociology had begun, and a dialogue with Western theoretical ideas instead of a blunt ideological denunciation of everything "non-Marxist" was initiated (Andreeva 1965; Kon Zamoshkin 1966). In theoretical terms, structural functionalism, symbolic interactionism, and C. Wright Mills's "new sociology were of particular interest to Soviet sociologists. The American Sociological Association aided these developments by arranging to send professional books and journals to the Soviet Union. In the 1960s, a few Western sociological books and textbooks, beginning with *Modern Sociological Theory in Continuity and Change* edited by H. Becker and A. Boskoff, were translated and published in Russian.

The social and intellectual situation of Soviet sociology was very uncertain. It was completely dependent on the official ideology and the goodwill of party authorities. Even a hint of social criticism was deemed dangerous, and such work could be published only if it was formulated in the ESOPs language. The Institute of Concrete Social Research was under constant attack. Especially devastating and venomous was an attack on Levada's *Lectures on Sociology* (1969); soon after the attack, Levada was dismissed from Moscow University and deprived of a professorial title. In 1972, the liberal head of the Institute, A. M. Rumiantsev, was replaced by the reactionary Mikhail Rutkevich, who had initiated an ideological campaign against "Western influences." As a result of his policies, the most prominent and qualified scholars were forced to leave the institute.

Until 1986, Soviet sociology was in bad shape, but the process of its institutionalization continued. It was a period of extensive growth of sociological units. Many new laboratories and departments of applied social research in the universities and sociological and social psychological laboratories in the big industrial plants had been established. Industrial sociologists (the most numerous and active group in the SSA) studied motivation to work, trends in the workforce, the efficiency of different forms of labor organization, in-group relations between workers and employers, and systems of management. The managers, who pretended to be "progressive," elaborated and reported to the party authorities "the plans of social developments" based on sociological studies (later, some of these industrial sociologists were able to consult the new post-soviet businessmen).

In 1972, the Institute of Concrete Social Research was renamed the Institute for Sociological Research. In 1974, the first professional journal, *Sotsiologicheskie Issledovania (Sociological Research)*, was inaugurated (the first editor in chief was Anatoly Kharchev). SSA membership grew continuously. In the late 1980s, the SSA had about 8,500 individual and 300 collective members and twenty-one regional branches. The technical and statistical level of sociological research in the 1970s and 1980s improved considerably. Some new sociological subdisciplines emerged. At its apogee, before the collapse of the Soviet Union, the SSA had thirty-eight specialized sections, including twelve research committees, directly connected with the respective International Sociological Association (ISA) committees. The geography of sociological research centers has also expanded.

The general intellectual and theoretical level of Soviet sociology was, with few exceptions, inadequate. Relatively free theoretical reflection was limited to the marginal fields of social psychology, anthropology, and history. Most sociological research was done on the micro level and involved separate industrial plants, without any attempt at broad theoretical generalization. Publications of a more general character were mostly apologies for the so-called real socialism. Sociological theories were divided between historical materialism and dogmatic ideological scholasticism, "the theory of scientific communism." Attempts to narrow the gap between sociological statements and social realities were ruthlessly punished by the authorities. The Leningrad sociological school, perhaps the best in the country, was decimated by the local party leadership in the mid-1980s. Zaslavskaia was in serious trouble when her report, which was highly critical of the prospects for economic reforms without parallel political changes, was published in the West. The public image of sociology had changed dramatically: In the 1960s, the new discipline was associated in the public's mind with social criticism and progressive economic reforms, and in the late 1970s, industrial sociologists sometimes were represented in the mass media as sly manipulators helping plant managers play down workers' discontent.

Perestroika and glasnost drastically changed the place of sociology in Soviet society. Mikhail Gorbachev and his team claimed that they needed an objective social science for information and advice, and the majority of Soviet sociologists were, from the beginning, strong supporters of reforms. In 1986, Zaslavskaia was elected president of the SSA. In 1987, a special resolution of the Communist Party Central Committee acknowledged that sociology was an important scientific discipline. In 1988, the Institute of Sociological Research was transformed into the Institute of Sociology, and V. Iadov was appointed its director. Sociologists (for example, Galina Starovoitova) took an active part in political life not only as advisers to the government but as deputies of central and local soviets and, after 1991, the post-Soviet parliaments of independent states. There were no longer official restrictions on the topics suitable for sociological research, and the publication of results became much easier. Some newspapers introduced regular sociological columns.

However, the relationship between sociology and political power is always problematic. On the one hand, neither Gorbachev nor Boris Yeltsin really needed or followed sociological advice. Very often, they did the opposite of what they have been advised to do. For example, Gorbachev's catastrophic antialcohol campaign, which was the first irreparable blow to the state budget and created the first wave of organized crime, was initiated despite strong and unanimous objections from social scientists. While making his fatal decisions about the Chechen war, Yeltsin completely ignored professional opinions. These experiences made sociologists more critical of the regime.

On the other hand, sociologists have been neither intellectually nor morally ready for new social responsibilities. The lack of a sociological imagination and their predominantly functionalist or empiricist mentality made them more comfortable with post hoc explanations of events than with responsible and reliable predictions. Social scientists are always more sure about what should not be done than about what to do, and Soviet sociology had never had a unified professional body.

By 1991 but especially after 1993, there was a deep political and intellectual schism in the former Soviet sociology. The majority of its founders remained faithful to liberal, democratic, and pro-Western ideas. However, liberal politicians, they often did not know how to apply those general principles to particular Russian, Ukrainian, or other situations. On the contrary, the former "scientific communists," who declared themselves sociologists or politologists after 1991 and who hold now many if not most university chairs, proclaim their fidelity to Marxism-Leninism, often with a strong flavor of Russian nationalism, traditionalism, and religious orthodoxy. The gap between these two wings is irreconcilable, and that gap has many organizational, ideological, and educational implications.

In the 1990s, there were essential changes in the institutional structure of sociological communities in all the post-Soviet states as well as in areas of research. To replace the SSA, several national, republican sociological associations have been formed. Sometimes there are more than one sociological association in the same country. Alongside the national Sociological Association of Russia (Russian Sociological Society), which is a collective member of the ISA, Ossipov organized an alternative Association of Sociologists and Demographers; he also initiated the split in the Institute of Sociology (IS) of RAS and created in the framework of RAS a new Institute of Social and Political Problems (ISPP), that became one of the main intellectual centers of communist and nationalist opposition to reforms. The coexistence of the two centers is by no means peaceful.

The main research projects of the IS include the theory and history of the discipline, quantitative and qualitative methodology, social stratification, sociocultural processes in Russia in the context of global social and economic changes, changes in personality, social identities and new forms of solidarities, economic and political elites, environmental studies, family and gender, social organizations, and social conflicts. The IS has an affiliation in St. Petersburg (director Serguei Golod). The IS is also combining research with teaching undergraduates and postgraduate students. The European University in St. Petersburg (rector Boris Firsov), has departments of history, political sciences, and sociology.

Fundamental sociological research is also being done in other academic institutions and universities, such as those in Novosibirsk (rural and regional sociology), Samara (sociology of labor), and Niznii Novgorod (stratification and regional studies). Research on interethnic relationships and conflicts is concentrated in the Institute of Ethnology and Anthropology of the RAS; population and gender studies are conducted in the Institute for Social-Economic Studies of Population, and so on. Many sociological groups and centers are moving from one academic institute to another or becoming fully independent, especially if they can make money by doing applied research.

Public opinion and market surveys centers became independent enterprises, some of which were united in the Russian Guild of Pollsters and Marketing Researchers. The All-Russian Public Opinion Research Center (directed by Yuri Levada) is a leading national center for public opinion polls; among many others, the Independent Public Opinion Research Service Vox Populi (VP), founded by Boris Grushin, and *Obshechesvennoe mnenie* (the Foundation of Public Opinion polls) are the most visible. Many sociologists are working as political image makers, speechwriters, economic consultants, and so on.

Sociology is now an institutionalized discipline in Baltic states, Armenia, Georgia, Kazakhstan, Uzbekistan, Belarus, and Ukraine. Especially visible progress in research and teaching sociology has occurred in Estonia and Ukraine. In the Soviet Union, Estonia was one of the few places where Western traditions of sociology were known and maintained. Since 1991, the main focus of sociological research in Estonia has been the empirical description and theoretical interpretation of the rapid social changes taking place in all spheres of society. The main traditional branches of Estonian sociology were social structure and stratification

(M. Titma, E. Saar); family and living conditions (Narusk 1995); the environment (M. Heidmets, Y. Kruusvall); urban sociology (M. Pavelson, K. Paadam), the mass media; youth; and education (P. Kenkmann). New situations have stimulated theoretical analyses of transitional processes (Lauristin and Vihalemm 1997) and explorations of new areas of research, such as the integration of the Russophone minority in Estonian society, poverty and social deprivation, political sociology, and public opinion research. In the second half of the 1990s, the dominant theoretical paradigm of social research in Estonia shifted from traditional structural functionalism to social constructivism. The main centers of sociological research in Estonia are the University of Tartu, the Pedagogical University of Tallinn, and the Institute for International and Social Studies in Tallinn.

In 1991, the Institute of Sociology of the Academy of Sciences of Ukraine and the first independent research center, the Kiev International Institute of Sociology, were founded. Together with the universities of Kiev, Kharkiv, Lviv, and Odessa, these Institutes have become centers of the development of sociological science in Ukraine. The basic topics of studies are social transformations and change (E. Golorakha, V. Khmelko, O. Kutsenko, E. Yakuba), economic and political sociology (I. Bekestina, N. Panina), ethnosociology, (N. Chernysh, M. Shulga, and B. Yertukh) sociology of mass consciousness (N. Kostenko, V. Ossorskiy, I. Popora), social psychology, relationships between social structures and personality under conditions of radical social change, the sociology of the Chernobyl catastrophe, and gender studies. In 1992, the Sociological Association of Ukraine was reorganized as an independent national association. Since 1993, the preparation of sociologists, using the programs and textbooks of Western universities, began at the oldest university in eastern Europe, Kiev-Mohyla Academy (founded in 1632). The academic journal *Sociology: Theory, Methods, Marketing* began to be issued in Ukrainian (1998) and Russian (1999).

The main problem confronting Russian sociology is the shortage of money and professional personnel. Until 1989 in the Soviet Union, there was practically no undergraduate sociological education; only a few courses in applied (mainly industrial) sociology were offered. Now sociological departments and schools have established in Moscow, Saint Petersburg, Novosibirsk, Ekaterinburg, and some other state universities, and there are about two hundred departments of sociology and political science in other colleges. The Russian Ministry of Higher Education issued the "State Standard" in sociology, which prescribed teaching the discipline as a multitheoretical one, not merely Marxist-oriented. Up-to-date methods of teaching sociology are provided by new educational centers: the Moscow School of Social and Economic Sciences, the European University in Saint Petersburg, the Faculty of Sociology of the Academic Institute of Sociology, and the High School of Economics in Moscow. According to the official statistics, in 1998 more than 6,600 university students studied sociology as their main subject. The discipline is taught also in many high schools and lyceums. With the financial support of different foundations (George Soros is the leading donor), sociological classics, world-recognized modern authors (P. Bourdieu, Z. Bauman, A. Giddens, Y. Habermas, and many others) and teaching materials (handbooks and readers) have been published. New professional journals, including *The Russian Public Opinion Monitor* (edited by T. Zaslavskaia and Y. Levada), *Sociological Journal* (edited by G. Batygin), *Sociology–4M: Methodology, Methods, Mathematical Models* (edited by V. Iadov); *The World of Russia* (edited by O. Shkaratan), have been published. In Russia, the Baltic states, and Ukraine, there are summer schools and advanced courses in theory and subdisciplines of sociology for young teachers and postgraduates where internationally renown scholars lecture. The exchange of graduate students in sociology between post-Soviet, U.S., and west European universities is growing rapidly. Prominent Western sociologists are invited regularly to give lectures and seminars at Russian and other independent state universities and vice versa.

Post-Soviet sociology is now ideologically and organizationally open and interested in international contacts and exchanges on all levels. There are many joint research projects with American, Canadian, German, French, Finnish, Japanese, and other scholars. Most of these projects are related to current political attitudes and value orientations, ethnic relations and regional studies, stratification, personality studies, social minorities, organizational culture, and modernization. The annual international symposia "Where Is Russia going?" are organized by the Independent Moscow School of Economics and Political Sciences (T. Shanin and T. Zaslavskaja).

High-level studies are being conducted on the problems of the economic and political elites (Kryshtanovskaja 1997), environmental sociology (Yanitsky 1993), gender and life stories (Semenova and Foteeva 1996), political sociology (Zdravomyslova 1998), and the sociology of culture (Ionin 1996). Some of these projects are the result of academic international cooperation, while others are financed by charity funds the State foundation for humanities (John D. and Catherine T. MacArthur Foundation, Open Society Institute, Ford Foundation, and others), and voluntary associations.

The prospects for the development of post-Soviet sociology depend on the fate of economic and democratic transformations. The gigantic social experiment unfolding in the post-Soviet region needs creative support from the social sciences. It is a powerful stimulus for sociological imagination and theory construction. Today sociologists in these countries are overburdened by the need to search for immediate practical solutions to urgent political and economic issues and have no time for quiet theoretical reflection. The most important sociological contributions to reforms are still the public opinion polls and information about current social processes. The next step seems to be the emergence of a sociology of social problems interpreted not only in the specific national contexts but in the context of the global problems of civilization as well. This, may lead to the revival of historical and comparative macrosociology and produce new theoretical insights. All this will be feasible, however, only as the result of intensive international and interdisciplinary intellectual cooperation.

REFERENCES

Andreeva, G. M. 1965 *Sovremennaia Bourzhuaznaia Empiricheskaia Sotsiologia*. Moscow: Mysl'.

Arutiunian, I. V. 1971 *Structura Sel'skogo Naselenia SSSR*. Moscow: Mysl'.

Batygin, G. S., and I. F. Deviatko 1994 "Russian Sociology: Its Origins and Current Trends." In R. P. Mohan and A. S. Wilke, eds., *International Handbook of Contemporary Developments in Sociology*. Westport, Conn.: Greenwood.

Gordon, L. A., and E. V. Klopov 1972 *Chelovek Posle Raboty*. Moscow: Nauka.

Grushin, B. A. 1967 *Mnenia o Mire i Mir Mnenij*. Moscow: Politizdat.

Iadov, V. A., V. Rozhin, and A. Zdravomyslov, 1970 *Man and His Work*. White Plains, N.Y.: International Arts and Sciences Press.

———, eds. 1998 *Sotsiologia v Rossii*. Moscow: Institut Sotsiologii Press.

Ionin, L. 1996 *Russishe Metamorphosen: Aufsetze zu Politik: Alltag und Kultur*. Berlin: Berliner Debatte.

Kohn, M., K. Slomczynski, K. Janicka, V. Khmelko, B. Mach, V. Paniotto, W. Zaborowski, R. Guttierez, and C. Heyman 1997 "Social Structure and Personality under Conditions of Radical Social Change: A Comparative Analysis of Poland and Ukraine." *American Sociological Review* 62:614–638.

Kon, I. S. 1967 *Sotsiologia Lichnosti*. Moscow: Politizdat.

Kryshtanovskaia, O. V. 1997 "The Emerging Russian Elite: Old & New; The Aftermath of 'Real Existing Socialism'" in Jacquez Heshz Johannes, ed., Eastern Europe." vol. 1. London: Macmillan.

Lauristin, M, and P. Vihalemm, eds. 1997 *Return to the Western World: Cultural and Political Perspectives on the Estonian Post-Communist Transition*. Tartu, Estonia: Tartu University Press.

Lenin, V. I. 1962 *O Sotsialisticheskoi Akademii Obshchestvennykh Nauk*. Vol. 36 of *Polnoe Sobranie Sochinenij*. Moscow: Politizdat.

Levada, I. A. 1969 *Lektsii po Sotsiologii*, Vols. 1 and 2. Moscow: IKSI AN SSSSR.

Lewada, Y. 1992 *Die Sovietmenshen* 1989–1991: Sociogram eines Zehrfall. Berlin: Argon Verlag

Narusk, A., ed. 1995 *Every-Day Life and Radical Social Change in Estonia*. Tallin, Estonia: Institute of International and Social Studies.

Moskvichev, P. N. 1997 *Sotsiologia i Vlast: Dokumenty 1953–1968*. Moscow: Academia Press.

Semenova, V., and E. Foteeva E. 1996 *Sudby Ludei. Rossia XX vek. Biografii Semei Kak Objekt Sotsiologicheskogo Issledovania*. Moscow: Institut Sotsiologii RAN.

Shlapentokh, V. 1987 *The Politics of Sociology in the Soviet Union*. Boulder and London: Westview.

Sorokin, P. A. 1920 *Sistema Sotsiologii*. Petrograd

Yanitsky, O. 1993 *Russian Environmentalism*. Moscow: Mezhdunarodnye Otnoshenia.

Zamoshkin, Iu. A. 1966 *Krizis Burzhuaznogo Individual izma i Lichnost'*. Moskva: Mysl'.

Zaslavskaia, T. (ed.) 1970 *Migratsia Sel'skogo Nasleniia*. Voskva: Mysl'.

——, and R. Ryvkina (eds.) 1980 *Metodologia Metodika Sistemnogo Izucheniia Derevni.* Novosibirsk Nauka.

—— 1990 *The Second Socialist Revolution and Alternative Soviet Strategy.* London: I.B. Tauris.

Zdravomyslov, A. G., ed. 1986 *Developments in Marxist Sociological Theory.* New York and London: Sage.

—— 1998. "Becoming of Political Sociology in Russia: The First Steps." In P. Sztompka, ed., *Building Open Society in East-Central Europe.* London: JSE Allen.

IGOR S. KON
VLADIMIR A. IADOV

SPORT

People in all cultures have always engaged in playful physical activities and used human movement as part of their everyday routines and collective rituals (Huizinga 1955). The first examples of organized games in societies worldwide probably emerged in the form of various combinations of physical activities and religious rituals (Guttmann 1978). Those games were connected closely with the social structures, social relations, and belief systems in their societies. Although they often recreated and reaffirmed existing systems of power relations and dominant ideologies, they sometimes served as sites for resistant or oppositional behaviors (Guttmann 1994; Sage 1998). Variations in the forms and dynamics of physical activities and games indicate that they are cultural practices that serve different social purposes and take on different meanings from time to time and place to place. Research on these variations has provided valuable insights into social processes, structures, and ideologies (Gruneau 1999; Sage 1998).

The physical activities that most sociologists identify as "modern sports" emerged in connection with a combination of rationalization, industrialization, democratization, and urbanization processes in the eighteenth and nineteenth centuries. As various forms of physical activities and play were constructed as institutionalized, competitive, rule-governed challenges and games, they became associated with a range of processes and structures in societies. To varying degrees in different settings, "organized sports" were implicated in processes of social development and the structure of family life, socialization and education, identity formation and government policy, commodification and the economy, and globalization and the media. Today, sports constitute a significant part of the social, cultural, political, and economic fabric of most societies.

As cultural practices, organized sports constitute an increasingly important part of people's lives and collective life in groups, organizations, communities, and societies. In addition to capturing individual and collective attention, they are implicated in power relations and ideological formation associated with social class, gender, race and ethnicity, sexuality, and physical ability. Because sports are social constructions, they may develop around particular ideas about the body and human nature, how people should relate to one another, expression and competence, human abilities and potential, manhood and womanhood, and what is important and unimportant in life. These ideas usually support and reproduce the dominant ideology in a society, but this is not always the case. Ideology is complex; therefore, the relationship between sports and ideological formation and transformation is sometimes inconsistent or even contradictory. Furthermore, sports come in many forms, and those forms can have many different associated social meanings.

Although sports continue to exist for the enjoyment of the participants, commercialized forms are planned, promoted, and presented for the entertainment of vast numbers of spectators. Sport events such as the Olympic Games, soccer's World Cup (men's and women's), the Tour de France, the tennis championships at Wimbledon, American football's Super Bowl, and championship boxing bouts capture the interest of billions of people when they are televised by satellite in over 200 countries around the world. These and other formally organized sports events are national and global industries. They are implicated in processes of state formation and capitalist expansion and are organized and presented as consumer activities for both participants and spectators. Although sport programs, events, and organizations may be subsidized directly or indirectly by local or national governments, support increasingly comes from corporations eager to associate their products and images with cultural activities and events that are a primary source of pleasure for people all over the world. Corporate executives have come to realize, as did Gramsci (1971) when he discussed hegemony and consensus-generating processes, that sponsoring people's pleasures can be crucial in creating a consensus to support corporate expansion. At the same time, most sport organizations have sought corporate support.

People of all ages connect with sports through the media. Newspapers in many cities devote entire sections of their daily editions to sports, especially in North America, where the space devoted to sports frequently surpasses that given to the economy, politics, or any other single topic of interest (Lever and Wheeler 1993). Major magazines and dozens of specialty magazines cater to a wide range of interests among participants and fans. Radio coverage of sporting events and sports talk shows capture the attention of millions of listeners every day in some countries. Television coverage of sports, together with commentary about sports, is the most prevalent category of video programming in many countries. First the transistor radio and more recently satellites and Internet technology have enabled millions of people around the world to share their interest in sports. As Internet technology expands, these media-facilitated connections that revolve around sports will take new forms with unpredictable social implications.

Worldwide, many people recognize high-profile teams and athletes, and this recognition fuels everything from product consumption to tourism. Sports images are a pervasive part of life in many cultures, and the attention given to certain athletes today has turned them into celebrities, if not cultural heroes. In cultures in which there have been assumed connections between participation in sports and character formation, there has been a tendency to expect highly visible and popular athletes to become role models of dominant values and lifestyles, especially for impressionable young people. This has created a paradoxical situation in which athletes often are held to a higher degree of moral accountability than are other celebrities while at the same time being permitted or led to assume permission to act in ways that go beyond traditional normative boundaries.

People around the world increasingly talk about sports. Relationships often revolve around sports, especially among men but also among a growing number of women. Some people identify with teams and athletes so closely that what happens in sports influences their moods and overall sense of well-being. In fact, people's identities as athletes and fans may be more important to them than their identities related to education, religion, work, and family.

Overall, sports and sports images have become a pervasive part of people's everyday lives, especially among those who live in countries where resources are relatively plentiful and the media are widespread. For this reason, sports are logical topics for the attention of sociologists and others concerned with social life.

USING SOCIOLOGY TO STUDY SPORTS

Although play and games received attention from various European and North American behavioral and social scientists between the 1880s and the middle of the 20th century, sports received scarce attention in that period (Loy and Kenyon 1969). Of course, there were notable exceptions. Thorstein Veblen wrote about college sports in the United States in 1899 in *Theory of the Leisure Class*. Max Weber mentioned English Puritan opposition to sports in the 1904 and 1905 volumes of *The Protestant Ethic and the Spirit of Capitalism*, and William Graham Sumner discussed "popular sports" in his 1906 *Folkways*. Willard Waller devoted attention to the "integrative functions" of sports in U.S. high schools in *The Sociology of Teaching* in 1932.

The first analyst to refer to a "sociology of sport" was Theodor Adorno's student Heinz Risse, who published *Sociologie des Sports* in 1921. Sports received little or no further analytic attention from social scientists until after World War II. Then, in the mid-1950s, there was a slow but steady accumulation of analyses of sports done by scholars in Europe and North America (Loy and Kenyon 1969; Dunning 1971).

The origins of the sociology of sport can be traced to both sociology and physical education (Ingham and Donnelly 1997; Sage 1997). The field initially was institutionalized in academic terms through the formation of the International Committee for Sport Sociology (ICSS) and the publication of the *International Review for Sport Sociology* (IRSS) in the mid-1960s. The ICSS was a subcommittee of the International Council of Sport Science and Physical Education and the International Sociological Association, and it sponsored the publication of the IRSS. Other publications in the 1960s and 1970s provided examples of the research and conceptual issues discussed by scholars who claimed an affiliation with the sociology of sport (Kenyon 1969; Krotee 1979; Lüschen 1970). In addition to meeting at the annual conferences of the ICSS beginning in the mid-1960s, many scholars in the sociology of sport also met at the annual conferences of the North American Society for the Sociology of Sport (NASSS). This organization was founded in 1978. It has sponsored conferences every year since then, and its membership has been as high as 326 in 1998. In 1984, the *Sociology of Sport Journal* was published under the sponsorship of the NASSS.

Although the sociology of sport involves scholars from many countries and has its foundations in traditional academic disciplines, its early growth was fueled partly by the radical and reform-oriented work of social activists trained in a variety of social sciences. That work attracted the attention of a number of young scholars in both sociology and physical education. For example, in U.S. universities, many courses devoted to the analysis of sport in society in the 1970s highlighted sport as a social institution, but many also used sports as a focal point for critical analyses of U.S. society as a whole. Objections to the war in Vietnam inspired analyses of autocratic and militaristic forms of social organization in sports and other spheres of social life. Critiques of capitalism were tied to research on the role of competition in social life and the rise of highly competitive youth and interscholastic sports. Concern with high rates of aggression and violence in society was tied to an analysis of contact sports that emphasize the physical domination of opponents. Analyses of racial and civil rights issues were tied to discussions of racism in sports and to issues that precipitated the boycott of the 1968 Mexico City Olympic Games by some black American athletes (Edwards 1969). Analyses of gender relations were inspired by the widespread failure of U.S. high schools and universities to comply with Title IX legislation that, among other things, mandated gender equity in all sport programs sponsored by schools that received federal funds.

Today, those who are dedicated to studying sports as social and cultural phenomena constitute a small but active, diverse, and steadily expanding collection of scholars from sociology, physical education and kinesiology, sport studies, and cultural studies departments. This has made the field unique because many of these scholars have realized that to maintain the field they must engage each other despite differences in the research questions they ask and the theoretical perspectives and methodologies they use.

Mainstream sociology has been slow at the institutional level to acknowledge the growing social and cultural significance of sports and sports participation. The tendency among sociologists to give priority to studies of work over studies of play, sports, or leisure accounts for much of this disciplinary inertia. Furthermore, sports have been seen by many sociologists as nonserious, nonproductive dimensions of society and culture that do not merit scholarly attention. Consequently, the sociology of sport has continued to exist on the fringes of sociology, and studying sports generally does not forward to a scholar's career in sociology departments. For example, in 1998–1999, only 149 (1.3 percent) of the 11,247 members of the American Sociological Association (ASA) declared "Leisure/Sport/Recreation" as one of their three major areas of interest, and over half those scholars focused primarily on leisure rather than sports. Only thirty-seven ASA members identified "Leisure/Sports Recreation" as their primary research and/or teaching topic (0.3 percent of ASA members), and only two Canadian and two U.S. sociology departments offer a graduate program in the sociology of sport, according to the 1998 Guide to Graduate Departments of Sociology. At the 1998 annual ASA meeting, there were approximately 3,800 presenters and copresenters, and only 20 dealt with sport-related topics in their presentations; only 2 of the 525 sessions were devoted to the sociology of sport. Patterns are similar in Canada, Great Britain, and Australia (Rowe et al. 1997).

In physical education and kinesiology, the primary focus of most scholars has been on motor learning, exercise physiology, biomechanics, and physical performance rather than the social dimensions of sports (see Sage 1997). Social and cultural issues have not been given a high priority in the discipline except when research has had practical implications for those who teach physical education, coach athletes, or administer sport programs. As the legitimacy and role of physical education departments have been questioned in many universities, the scholars in those departments have been slow to embrace the frequently critical analyses of sports done by those who use sociological theories and perspectives. Therefore, studying sports as social phenomena has not earned many scholars high status among their peers in physical education and kinesiology departments. However, the majority of sociology of sport scholars with doctorates have earned their degrees and now have options in departments of physical education or kinesiology and departments of sport studies and human movement studies.

There have been noteworthy indications of change. For example, there are a number of journals devoted to social analyses of sports (*Sociology of Sport Journal, International Review for the Sociology of Sport, Journal of Sport & Social Issues, Culture, Sport, Society*). Many mainstream journals in sociology and physical education now accept and publish research that uses sociological perspectives to study sports. National and regional professional associations in sociology and physical education in many countries sponsor regular sessions in the sociology of sport at their annual conferences. Annual conferences also are held by a number of national and regional sociology of sport associations around the world, including those in Japan, Korea, and Brazil as well as the countries of North America and Europe. The International Sociology of Sport Association (ISSA, formerly the ICSS) holds annual conferences and meets regularly with the International Sociological Association. Attendance at many of these conferences has been consistent, and the quality of the programs has been impressive. The existence of such organizational endorsement and support, along with continued growth in the pervasiveness and visibility of sports in society, suggests that the discipline will continue to grow.

Among other indications of growth, articles in the *Sociology of Sport Journal* are cited regularly in social science literature. Scholars in the field are recognized as "public intellectuals" by journalists and reporters associated with the mass media. Quotes and references to sociology of sport research appear increasingly in the popular print and electronic media. Amazon.com, the world's major Internet bookseller, listed over 260 books in its "Sociology of Sport" reference category in March 1999. Most important, major publishers such as McGraw-Hill estimate that every year nearly 30,000 university students take courses in the "sport in society" category.

Complicating the issue of future growth is the fact that scholars in this field regularly disagree about how to "do" the sociology of sport. Some prefer to see themselves as scientific experts who do research on questions of organization and efficiency, while others prefer to see themselves as facilitators or even agents of cultural transformation whose research gives a voice to and empowers people who lack resources or have been pushed to the margins of society. This and other disagreements raise important questions about the production and use of scientific knowledge, and many scholars in the sociology of sport are debating those questions. As in sociology as a whole, the sociology of sport is now a site for theoretical and paradigmatic debates that some scholars fear will fragment the field and subvert the maintenance of an institutionalized professional community (Ingham and Donnelly 1997). Of course, this is a challenge faced in many disciplines and their associated professional organizations.

CONCEPTUAL AND THEORETICAL ISSUES

Through the mid-1980s, most research in the sociology of sport was based on two assumptions. First, sport was assumed to be a social institution similar to other major social institutions (Lüschen and Sage 1981). Second, sports were assumed to be institutionalized competitive activities that involve physical exertion and the use of physical skills by individuals motivated by a combination of personal enjoyment and external rewards (Coakley 1990). These conceptual assumptions identified the focus of the sociology of sport and placed theory and research on sports within the traditional parameters of sociological theory and research.

Theory and research based on these assumptions were informative. However, many scholars in the field came to realize that when analytic attention is focused on institutionalized and competitive activities, there is a tendency to overlook the lives of people who have neither the resources to formally organize their physical activities nor the desire to make them competitive. Scholars became sensitive to the possibility that this tendency can reinforce the ideologies and forms of social organization that have disadvantaged certain categories and collections of people in contemporary societies (Coakley 1998). This encouraged some scholars to ask critical questions about sports as contested activities in societies. Consequently, their research has come to focus more on the connections between sports and systems of power and privilege and the changes needed to involve more people in the determination of what sports can and should be in society.

These scholars used an alternative approach to defining sports that revolved around two questions: What gets to count as a sport in a group or society? and Whose sports count the most? These questions forced them to focus more directly on the social and cultural contexts in which ideas are formed about physical activities and the social processes that privilege some forms of physical activities. Those who have used this approach also note numerous cultural differences in how people identify sports and include them in their lives. In cultures that emphasize cooperative relationships, the idea that people should compete for rewards may be defined as disruptive, if not immoral, and for people in cultures that emphasize competition, physical activities and games that have no winners may seem pointless. These cultural differences are important because there is no universal agreement about the meaning, purpose, and organization of sports. Similarly, there is no general agreement about who will participate in sports, the circumstances in which participation will occur, or who will sponsor sports or the reasons for sponsorship. It is now assumed widely by scholars who study sports that these factors have varied over time from group to group and society to society and that sociological research should focus on the struggle over whose ideas about sports become dominant at any particular time in particular groups or societies. This in turn has highlighted issues of culture and power relations in theory and research in the sociology of sport.

Before the mid-1980s, most research and conceptual discussions in the sociology of sport were inspired or informed by structural functionalist theories and conflict theories (Lüschen and Sage 1981; Coakley 1990), and in parts of western Europe, figurational sociology was used by some scholars who studied sports (see Dunning 1992). Those with structural functionalist perspectives often focused on questions about sports and issues of socialization and character development, social integration, achievement motivation, and struc-

tural adaptations to change in society. The connections between sports and other major social institutions and between sports and the satisfaction of social system needs were the major topics of concern.

Those who used conflict theories viewed sports as an expression of class conflict and market forces and a structure linked to societal and state institutions. Their work was inspired by various interpretations of Marxist theory and research focused generally on connections between capitalist forms of production and consumption and social behaviors in sports and on the ways in which sports promote an ideological consciousness that is consistent with the needs and interests of capital. Specifically, they studied the role of sports in processes of alienation, capitalist expansion, nationalism and militarism, and racism and sexism (Brohm 1978; Hoch 1972).

Figurational, or "process," sociology was and continues to be inspired by the work of Elias (Elias 1978; Elias and Dunning 1986; Jarvie and Maguire 1994). Figurational sociologists have focused on issues of interdependence and interaction in social life and have identified historical linkages between the structure of interpersonal conduct and the overall structure of society. Unlike other theoretical approaches, figurational sociology traditionally has given a high priority to the study of sport. Figurational analyses have emphasized sports as a sphere of social life in which the dichotomies between seriousness and pleasure, work and leisure, economic and noneconomic phenomena, and mind and body can be shown to be false and misleading. Before the mid-1980s, research done by figurational sociologists focused primarily on the historical development of modern sport and the interrelated historical processes of state formation, functional democratization, and expanding networks of international interdependencies. Their best known early work focused on linkages between the emergence of modern sports and the dynamics of civilizing processes, especially those associated with the control of violence in society (Elias and Dunning 1986).

Since the mid-1980s, the sociology of sport has been characterized by theoretical and methodological diversity. Fewer scholars use general theories of social life such as structural functionalism and conflict theories. The theories more often used are various forms of critical theories, including feminist theories and hegemony theory; also used are interpretive sociology (especially symbolic interactionism), cultural studies perspectives, and various forms of poststructuralism (Rail 1998). Figurational sociology still is widely used, especially by scholars outside North America. A few scholars have done research informed by the reflexive sociology of Pierre Bourdieu (Laberge and Sankoff 1988; Wacquant 1995a, 1995b) and the structuration theory of Anthony Giddens (Gruneau 1999).

Methodological approaches also vary. Quantitative data and statistical analyses remain popular, although various qualitative methods and interpretive analyses have become increasingly popular, if not the dominant research approaches in the field (Donnelly 2000). Ethnography and in-depth interviewing, along with textual and discourse analysis, have emerged as common methodologies among many scholars studying sports and sport participation (Coakley and Donnelly 1999). Quantitative methods have been used most often to study issues and questions related to sport participation patterns, the attitudinal and behavioral correlates of participation, and the distribution of sports-related resources in society. Both quantitative and interpretive methods have been used to study questions and issues related to socialization, identity, sexuality, subcultures, the body, pain and injury, disability, deviance, violence, emotions, the media, gender relations, homophobia, race and ethnic relations, new and alternative sports forms, and ideological formation and transformation (Coakley and Dunning 2000).

FINAL NOTE

Sociologists study sports because they are prominent and socially significant cultural practices in contemporary societies. The sociology of sport contains an active, diverse, and slowly expanding collection of scholars united by professional organizations and academic journals. Continued growth of the field depends on whether these scholars continue to do research that makes meaningful contributions to the way people live their lives and recognized and visible contributions to knowledge in sociology as a whole.

REFERENCES

Brohm, Jean-Marie 1978 *Sport–A Prison of Measured Time*, trans. I. Frasier. London: Ink Links.

Coakley, J. 1990 *Sport in Society: Issues and Controversies*, (4th ed.). St. Louis: Mosby.

——, 1998 *Sport in Society: Issues and Controversies*, 6th ed. New York: McGraw-Hill.

——, and P. Donnelly, eds. 1999 *Inside Sports*. London: Routledge

—— eds. 2000 *Handbook of Sport and Society*. London: Sage.

Donnelly, P. 2000 "Interpretive Approaches to the Sociology of Sport." In J. Coakley and E. Dunning. eds., *Handbook of Sport and Society*. London: Sage.

Dunning, E., ed. 1971 *The Sociology of Sport*. London: Cass.

—— 1992 "Figurational Sociology and the Sociology of Sport: Some Concluding Remarks." In E. Dunning, and C. Rojek, eds., *Sport and Leisure in the Civilizing Process*. Toronto: University of Toronto Press.

Edwards, H. 1969 *The Revolt of the Black Athlete*. New York: Free Press.

Elias, N. 1978 *The Civilizing Process*, vol. 1: *The History of Manners*. Oxford, UK: Blackwell.

——, and E. Dunning, eds. 1986 *Quest for Excitement: Sport and Leisure in the Civilizing Process*. Oxford, UK: Blackwell.

Gramsci, A. 1971 *Selections from the Prison Notebooks*, trans. and ed. Q. Hoare and G. Smith. New York: International Publishers.

Gruneau. R. 1999 *Class, Sports, and Social Development*. Champaign, Ill. Human Kinetics.

Guttmann, A. 1978 *From Ritual to Record: The Nature of Modern Sports*. New York: Columbia University Press.

—— 1994 *Games and Empires: Modern Sports and Cultural Imperialism*. New York: Columbia University Press.

Hoch, P. 1972 *Rip Off the Big Game: The Exploitation of Sports by the Power Elite*. Garden City, N.Y.: Anchor.

Huizinga, J. 1955 *Homo Ludens: A Study of the Play Element in Culture*. Boston: Beacon Press.

Ingham, A. G., and P. Donnelly 1997 "A Sociology of North American Sociology of Sport: Disunity in Unity, 1965–1996." *Sociology of Sport Journal* 14(4):362–418.

Jarvie, G., and J. Maguire 1994 *Sport and Leisure in Social Thought*. London: Routledge.

Kenyon, G. S., ed. 1969 *Aspects of Contemporary Sport Sociology*. Chicago: Athletic Institute.

Krotee, M., ed. 1979 *The Dimensions of Sport Sociology*. West Point, N.Y.: Leisure Press.

Laberge, S., and D. Sankoff 1988 "Physical Activities, Body Habitus and Lifestyles." In J. Harvey and H. Cantelon eds., *Not Just a Game: Essays in Canadian Sport Sociology*. Ottawa: University of Ottawa Press.

Lever, J., and S. Wheeler 1993 "Mass Media and the Experience of Sport." *Communication Research* 20(1):299–313.

Loy, J. W., G. S. and Kenyon, eds. 1969 *Sport, Culture, and Society*. London: Collier-Macmillan.

Lüschen. G. ed. 1970 *The Cross-Cultural Analysis of Sport and Games*. Champaign, Ill. Stipes.

——, and G. H. Sage 1981 "Sport in Sociological Perspective." In G. Lüschen and G. H. Sage, eds., *Handbook of Social Science of Sport*. Champaign, Ill. Stipes.

Rail, G., ed. 1998 *Sport and Postmodern Times*. Albany: State University of New York Press.

Rowe, D., J. McKay, and G. Lawrence 1997 "Out of the Shadows: The Critical Sociology of Sport in Australia, 1986–1996." *Sociology of Sport Journal* 14(4):340–361.

Sage, G. H. 1997 "Physical Education, Sociology, and Sociology of Sport: Points of Intersection." *Sociology of Sport Journal* 14(4):317–339.

—— 1998. *Power and Ideology in American Sport*. Champaign, Ill. Human Kinetics.

Wacquant, L. J. D. 1995a "The Pugilistic Point of View: How Boxers Feel about Their Trade." *Theory and Society* 24:489–535.

—— 1995b "Pugs at Work: Bodily Capital and Bodily Labour among Professional Boxers." *Body & Society* 1(1):65–93.

JAY COAKLEY
JANET LEVER

STANDARDIZATION

Standardization is a technique used in comparing indicators from two or more populations. The goal of the standardization procedure is to control for compositional differences between these groups that may influence the indicator that is being examined. This method allows a researcher to determine the extent to which differences in the rates of events between populations are due to differences in population characteristics. Often sociologists ask questions, that require comparisons between groups of people: Which city has a higher crime rate? Which country has lower mortality? Which ethnic group is more likely to coreside with elderly family members? In making these comparisons, one usually calculates a summary measure: crimes per capita, crude death rate, or the proportion of elders living with family members. However, any two groups of people are likely to differ along several dimensions, such as age, educational level, race, and income. These dimensions, or factors, also may be related to the event being explored. As a result, the summary measure to some extent reflects the compositional differences in the groups being studied.

Standardization historically has been a central aspect of demographic methods (Bogue 1969; Hinde 1998; Murdock and Ellis 1991; Shryock and Siegel 1980), but its importance extends beyond that use to a way of thinking about summary or aggregate measures. While offering the advantage of conciseness, aggregate measures mask underlying compositional differences, and the use of standardization represents an acknowledgment that population characteristics influence the rate at which events occur in a population. Summary indicators are very useful; they provide a single number for comparison rather than a whole series of numbers, and they are easily calculated. However, comparisons among population groups or among subgroups in a population should account for the differing compositional makeup of those groups. Demographers have been led to standardization for several reasons. First, there is a natural desire to make comparisons between groups along demographic indicators: crude death rates, crude birthrates, marriage rates, and employment, among others. Standardization allows these comparisons to reflect differences in the underlying processes, rather than being confounded by the effects of composition. Standardization procedures can accommodate the effects of a single factor or many factors, leaving the technique bounded only by the available data. Standardization also allows the estimation of indicators for groups for which data are incomplete or of poor quality.

Many demographic measures are affected by the composition of the population, particularly the age distribution. Age composition is especially critical in considering crude death rates, since mortality rates have a very distinctive age-specific pattern: high at very young and very old ages.

Populations with a large proportion of persons in those age groups experience a large number of deaths, regardless of age-specific rates of mortality. Two populations with identical sets of age-specific rates of mortality but different age distributions will have different crude death rates. The removal of the "interference" of age distribution from the summary measure—the crude death rate—is the goal of the standardization procedure. In the rest of this article, the standardization procedure will be explained using mortality rates, and then several other examples of standardization will be presented.

The first step in a comparison is to calculate a crude rate or proportion. Crude rates or proportions are calculated by the formula

$$CR = \frac{E}{P} \qquad (1)$$

where E refers to the number of events of interest in the population during the time period and P refers to the population during that period. If the population is measured at the middle of the year and the events occur throughout the year, this proportion can be interpreted as a rate. In cases where this proportion is small, for instance, mortality rates, the crude rate commonly is multiplied by 1,000 and reported as the number of events per 1,000 people.

Crude rates or proportions are used to represent a variety of characteristics of a population. These rates have an advantage over a comparison of absolute numbers, since they account for differences in size between two populations. Obviously, in a comparison of the annual number of homicides in Chicago versus that in Seattle, one must account for the fact that the population of Chicago is 2.8 million people compared to about one-half million in Seattle. Similarly, comparing the number of deaths in the United States (over 2 million) to those in Sweden (about 90,000) in 1994 would be unreasonable without knowing that the population of the United States is three times that of Sweden.

Despite the advantage of crude rates over absolute numbers, crude rates are influenced by the composition of the populations being compared. If the event of interest varies by some factor and the two populations have varying levels of that

factor, the crude rates will partly reflect this compositional variation rather than only a difference in the rate at which the event is occurring. If the populations being compared are standardized with respect to the factor, any remaining difference between the crude rates can be attributed to a true difference in rates of occurrence. If the difference in the crude rate disappears, one can conclude that the compositional variation rather than a difference in the underlying rates of occurrence led to a difference in the crude of events.

To understand the rationale of standardization, it is necessary to recognize that in essence, the crude rate is a weighted average of a set of factor-specific rates, where the weights are the distribution of the factor in the population. Thinking in this manner, one can rewrite the crude rate as

$$CR = \sum \frac{e_a}{p_a} \frac{p_a}{P} \qquad (2)$$

where p_a is the population in group a and e_a is the number of events occurring in group a. The sum of all e_a equals the total number of events, E, and the sum of all p_a equals the total population, P. Note that this equation has two components. The first, e_a/p_a, represents the group-specific rate of events or the group-specific proportion, which sometimes is expressed as m_a. The second component of the rate calculation, p_a/P, represents the proportion of the population in each of the a groups. These are the two series of elements needed to apply the direct standardization technique. Using this notation, the crude rate can be rewritten as

$$CR = \sum m_a \cdot \frac{p_a}{P} \qquad (3)$$

When the formula for the crude rate is written in this manner, it is easy to see how the composition of the population, that is, its distribution among the a groups, affects the crude rate. If the group-specific rate m_a is high when the proportion of the population in that group, p_a/P, is large, more events will be observed in the total population than will be observed if p_a/P is small. Similarly, if m_a is small when p_a/P is small, few events will occur.

A comparison of the crude death rates in Sweden and the United States provides an example of the use of standardization. Sweden has one of the world's highest life expectancies at birth, approximately 76 years for men and 81.4 years for women in 1994. The crude death rate of Sweden, however, was about 10.4 deaths per 1,000 in that year. In contrast, life expectancy at birth in the United States was 72.2 years for mens and 78.8 years for women in 1993, and the crude death rate was about 8.6 deaths per 1,000 in that year (United Nations 1997). It seems natural to expect that the country with the longest life expectancy would also have the lowest crude death rate, so what accounts for this discrepancy? To understand the reason for this difference in the crude rates, it is necessary to observe the differing age distributions of the two populations. In the United States about 13 percent of the population is over age of 65; while in Sweden over 17 percent of people are over that age. Since death rates are highest in this age range, the larger proportion of the Swedish population in old age creates more deaths, even with lower age-specific death rates. Standardization demonstrates the extent to which these differences in age distribution account for the difference in the crude death rate.

As was mentioned above, this method of standardization—direct standardization—requires a standard population distribution and a set of factor-specific rates for the populations being studied. Direct standardization uses this standard population to calculate new standardized crude rates for the populations of interest. In this case, the population distribution of the standard population replaces the observed population distribution. Since each population's crude rate will be calculated with the same distribution, the effect of the compositional differences will be eliminated and each population will have the same composition. To apply direct standardization, the formula

$$DSR = \sum \frac{e^j_a}{p^j_a} \cdot \frac{p^s_a}{P^s} \qquad (4)$$

is used, where e^j_a represents the number of events occurring in group a in population j, p^j_a represents the population size of group a in population j, p^s_a represents the number of people in group a in the standard population s, and P^s represents the standard population. Comparing equations (2) and (4) shows the similarities. The second term in equation (2), the compositional distribution of the population of interest, p_a/P, has been replaced with the compositional distribution of the standard population, p^s_a/P^s. The first term in the crude rate calculation remains the factor-specific rate in the population of interest, population j.

Returning to the example of the United States and Sweden, using the age distribution of the United States as the standard distribution and computing a standardized crude death rate for Sweden by applying the age-specific death rates of Sweden yields a standardized crude death rate of 7.6 deaths per 1,000 for Sweden. Instead of being higher than the crude death rate in the United States, Sweden's crude death rate falls below that of the United States. At least part of the difference in the crude rates therefore is due to Sweden's older population rather than to a difference in age-specific death rates. In general, populations with a relatively old age distribution tend to have higher crude death rates than do populations with similar age-specific mortality patterns, since death rates are higher at older ages.

The data demands for direct standardization, while not overwhelming, can be difficult to meet if there is limited information on factor-specific rates in one of the populations of interest. For example, in many studies of mortality in less developed countries or in a historical perspective, information on age-specific death rates may be missing or unreliable. In these cases, an alternative method referred to as indirect standardization can be used. Indirect standardization requires knowledge only of the composition of the population and the total number of events of interest. Direct standardization involves the application of population-specific sets of rates to a standard population; conversely, indirect standardization involves the application of a standard set of rates to individual population distributions. In indirect standardization, a set of standard rates is applied to the population and the expected number of events is compared to the actual number. This standardizing ratio is estimated by the formula

$$SR = \frac{E^j}{\sum m^s_a \, p^j_a} \qquad (5)$$

where E^j is the actual number of events in the population j, m^s_a is the factor-specific rate in the standard population s, and p^j_a is the number of people in population j who are in group a. The denominator of the ratio calculates the number of events that would be expected in population j if the factor-specific rates of the standard population were applied to the population. When the event of interest is death, this ratio often is referred to as the standardized mortality ratio. To obtain the new indirectly standardized crude rate, this standardizing ratio is multiplied by the crude rate for the standard population:

$$ISR = SR \cdot CR^s \qquad (6)$$

where CR^s is the crude rate in the standard population. These indirectly standardized crude rates then can be compared to each other. Obviously, when the standardizing ratio is greater than 1.0, the ISR will be larger than the crude rate for the standard population, and when the standardizing ratio is less than 1.0, the ISR will be smaller than the standard population's crude rate.

Indirect standardization does not control for composition as well as the direct standardization method does but should yield similar results in terms of direction and magnitude. Returning to the example of Sweden and the United States, the actual number of recorded deaths in Sweden would be greater than the observed number if U.S. age-specific death rates were applied to the Swedish population's age distribution. The resulting standardized mortality ratio would be 0.912, and when that was multiplied by the crude rate for the United States, the ISR for Sweden would be 7.8, very similar to the result obtained through direct standardization.

When indirect standardization is employed, there is no choice to be made about the standard population; this method is used when only one population distribution is available. The choice of the standard population for direct standardization should be considered carefully, but within reasonable bounds the choice of standard should not alter the conclusions radically. Researchers generally are interested in the direction and approximate size of differences between the groups, and these values are preserved with the choice of any of a number of reasonable standard populations. There are three general choices for the standard: use one of the populations being studied, use an average of the populations, or use a population outside those being studied. Each of these choices has advantages and disadvantages. Theoretically,

the choice of standard should be made to minimize the effects of that choice on the results.

Using one of the populations being studied eliminates the need to standardize that population and often makes the explication of comparisons easier. For instance, in comparing crime rates across several cities, choosing one city as the basis for comparison may be appropriate. When comparisons are made of a population over time, it is standard procedure to choose a distribution that is representative of the middle of the time period. For instance, in a study of mortality change between 1950 and 1990 in the United States, it would be appropriate to use the 1970 census for the standard age distribution. A drawback to using one of the study populations as the standard, however, can be that the population chosen has an unusual distribution of factors. This unusual distribution may skew the summary measures in a way that is inconsistent or difficult to interpret. Also, choosing one of the populations as a standard can carry implications that this distribution is the "ideal" or "correct" distribution and may place interpretational burdens on the results.

Using an average of the populations eliminates the problem of setting one population as the ideal and ameliorates the problem of unusual distributions. A comparison of racial differences in mortality in the United States, for example, might use the age distribution of the total U.S. population, an unweighted average of the distribution of each racial group, as the standard. This choice eliminates the assumption that any one population has a preferred distribution and allows for meaningful comparisons among groups. The use of an aggregate population as the standard is encountered frequently in comparisons of subgroups within a national population.

A third choice is to pick a population completely exogenous to the study as a standard. This choice most often involves an artificial population that is representative of a standard pattern of factor distributions. Several sources of standard populations exist. In the case of age, Coale and Demeny's (1983) set of regional model life tables contains sets of age distributions typical of a variety of mortality levels and patterns. The use of an external standard eliminates any value judgments associated with the choice of standard. An external standard also can be chosen to minimize or eliminate extreme distributions of factors. The external standard also provides a way of comparing very diverse populations. Again, the choice of standard should match the populations being studied as closely as possible to minimize the effect of that choice on the results.

An exogenous standard also might be employed as a way to simulate the effects of a variety of changes in population composition on the crude rate. This use of the standardization technique highlights the underlying logic of the procedure by using the method to investigate the extent to which compositional chances influence aggregate comparisons. Here the technique is used as a methodological device to explore the effects of changes. For instance, a researcher might be interested in the effects on average wages of changing occupational structures among men and women. A testable hypothesis could be that as women approach men in terms of occupational distribution, the gender gap in wages will disappear. If a variety of simulated occupational structures are applied to a set of gender- and occupation-specific wage rates, the effect of occupational structure on the wage gap can be examined.

Since standardization developed in the field of demography, most applications involve the study of demographic phenomena. The example of the United States and Sweden involved comparisons of mortality rates. However, standardization is used widely in other areas as well. For example, the U.S. Census Bureau routinely reports the distribution of the American population aged 15 and older among marital states, and historical comparisons of this distribution are used to examine changes in marital behavior over time. However, the age composition of the population can greatly influence the distribution among marital states, particularly when the proportion of the population in the age range of 15 to 25 years is very large. In 1960, 65.6 percent of women aged 15 and older were married compared to 60.4 percent of similarly aged women in 1975 (United States Bureau of the Census 1976). At first glance, these comparisons seem to signal a retreat from marriage: A smaller proportion of women was married in 1975 than in 1960. However, when the age distribution of the population is standardized to the 1960 population, the proportion married in 1975 in-

creases to 63.5. While this is still a decline compared to 1960, the magnitude of the change is much less. The difference in the proportion married is due largely to a difference between 1960 and 1975 in the proportion of women just over the age of 15, the baby boomers, who were young teenage women who had not yet married.

Standardization can be used to control for characteristics other than age. Suppose, for instance, one is comparing the health status of two different groups: elderly white Americans and elderly African-Americans. If we compare the proportion of each group in poor health, we find that 34 percent of elderly whites and 50 percent of elderly African-Americans report their health as fair or poor. However, we know that health status varies by education and that the educational distributions of these two groups differ. Among elderly whites, about 12 percent have fewer than eight years of school, compared to 39 percent of elderly African-Americans. Clearly, since lower levels of education are associated with poorer health and elderly African-Americans have lower levels of educational attainment, some of the difference in observed health status between the groups can be expected to result from the different educational compositions.

It is desirable to compare these two groups without the influence of education. Using the educational distribution of the elderly white population as a standard and applying the observed education-specific rates of poor health among elderly African-Americans, one obtains an overall proportion of 42 percent in poor health, compared to the unstandardized proportion of 50 percent. Thus, if the African-American older population had an educational distribution similar to that of the more highly educated white elderly population, the expected health status of older African-Americans would improve.

Lichter and Eggebeen (1994) used standardization techniques to examine the effects of parental employment on rates of child poverty. In their work these researchers use direct standardization techniques in two different ways. In the first, they simulate the effects of a variety of assumptions about parental employment patterns on children's poverty rates. This is an illustration of using an "exogenous" or artificial population distribution as a standard population. By changing the employment distribution of the parents of children in poverty, they determine that only modest declines in child poverty would result from increasing those levels of employment. Their second application of standardization compares the poverty rates of black children obtained by using the employment distribution of white parents as the standard to the rates directly observed. In this case, they have chosen one of the study populations as the standard and are interested in the extent to which differences in child poverty between blacks and whites are determined by factors other than parental employment distributions. They find in fact that parental employment differences among female-headed families account for a substantial portion of the observed differences in child poverty.

Standardization can control for more than one factor at a time and can be applied to more than two groups. Himes et al. (1996) standardize for age, sex, and marital status in an examination of the living arrangements of minority elderly in the United States. Living arrangements are known to be different for men and women, for married and unmarried, and for younger and older elderly. These factors—age, sex, and marital status—also are known to vary across racial and ethnic subgroups. Therefore, the observed differences in living arrangements are likely to be due in part to these underlying characteristics rather than being a reflection of differences in attitudes or beliefs. Standardization allows a comparison among groups without the influence of these compositional differences. In this research, the compositional distribution of the entire United States with respect to age, sex, and marital status was chosen as the standard. In this analysis, the standardization procedure had the greatest effect on comparisons of the African-American population and much smaller effects on the white, non-Hispanic, Hispanic, Asian, and Native American populations.

Standardization is widely used in a variety of sociological inquiries. While it originated in demographic analyses, it can be applied to a variety of questions in which a researcher wants to determine the extent to which compositional differences in population groups account for observed differences in summary measures. Standardization is also useful as a simulation technique, allowing researchers to explore the effects of a variety of compositional changes on a summary indicator. Researchers should bear in mind, however, that the results of standardization are merely artificially constructed indicators; they do not represent a real population or circumstance.

REFERENCES

Bogue, Donald J. 1969 *Principles of Demography*. New York: Wiley.

Coale, Ansely J., and Paul Demeny 1983 *Regional Model Life Tables and Stable Populations, 2nd ed.* New York: Academic Press.

Himes, Christine L., Dennis P. Hogan, and David J. Eggebeen 1996 "Living Arrangements of Minority Elders." *Journal of Gerontology: Social Sciences* 51B:S42–S48.

Hinde, Andrew 1998 *Demographic Methods*. New York: Oxford University Press.

Lichter, Daniel T., and David J. Eggebeen 1994 "The Effect of Parental Employment on Child Poverty." *Journal of Marriage and the Family* 56:633–645.

Murdock, Steve H., and David R. Ellis 1991 *Applied Demography: An Introduction to Basic Concepts, Methods, and Data*. Boulder, Colo.: Westview Press.

Shryock, Henry S., and Jacob S. Siegel 1980. *The Methods and Materials of Demography*, 4th printing (rev.). Washington, D.C.: U.S. Government Printing Office.

United Nations 1997 *Demographic Yearbook 1995*. New York: United Nations.

United States Bureau of the Census 1976 *Social Indicators 1976*. Washington, D.C.: U.S. Government Printing Office.

CHRISTINE L. HIMES

STATE, THE

The term "state" denotes the complex of organizations, personnel, regulations, and practices through which political power is exercised in a territory. In simple societies organized as bands of families, as tribes, or as chiefdoms, political power is not separated from power relationships rooted in kinship structures or religion. Those societies also lack organizations and specialized personnel (beyond the chief) for exercising political authority and therefore have no real states. The state emerged only with the development of more complex societies, either cities or tribal confederations, which formed the bases for city-states, monarchies, and empires. Monarchies and empires in turn have given way to liberal states, modernizing dictatorships, and one-party states as the most widespread current forms of states.

The "state" is a rather abstract term. Over time and space, the concrete organizational forms, the kinds of personnel, the specific laws and regulations, and the practices of states have varied greatly with the historical development of societies and across different cultures and regions. The modern nation-state is a very particular kind of state that developed in Europe in the eighteenth and nineteenth centuries and currently is spreading across the world (Poggi 1990). However, like other forms of the state, this organizational form is likely to have its day and then fade; already various kinds of supranational and international bodies have begun to take over some of the political power formerly monopolized by nation-states.

The basis of the state is political power. This article examines the roots of that power and then explores the various forms taken by states from their beginnings to the present day.

POLITICAL POWER

All forms of power involve the ability of powerholders to coerce others into giving up their property, their free choice of action, and even their lives. Political power, as opposed to economic power (based on money or other forms of wealth), religious power (based on relationships to transcendent forces), family power (based on sex, seniority, and kin relationships), and pure coercion (based on brute force), is rooted in the recognition of the rightful authority of the ruler (Weber 1968). That authority stems from the demands within a society for specialists with the ability to mediate and coordinate.

Any group of human beings in regular interaction among themselves is prone to conflict over possessions, decisions regarding group actions (to hunt or not, to camp here or there, to fight or flee from a threat), and individual actions that give offense (insults, injury, infidelity). In small groups, such conflicts usually can be settled through the arbitration of respected family members or elders, but in larger groups or groups in which much interaction occurs among nonkin, those conflicts produce demands for justice that require a more broadly recognized form of mediation. Individuals who are particularly skilled at mediating such conflicts, who gain a reputation for wisdom and justice, can acquire the role of a specialist in settling conflicts. In addition, every group of human beings faces external threats from wild animals, the weather, and other human groups. Individuals who are particularly skilled at coordinating actions within a group for the purposes of attack, hunting, and defense can gain a reputation that translates into a calling as a specialist in coordinating group actions to meet threats.

The functions of mediation to produce internal justice and of coordination to deal with external threats are distinct; indeed Native American tribes sometimes had a "peace chief" and a "war chief" who specialized in those functions. Modern societies have legal-judicial systems and executive-military systems that show a similar division of functions. However, these functions tended to merge because in both cases it was necessary to have mechanisms to compel compliance with the arbitration decisions of the mediator or the action directives of the coordinator. Once a society develops regular means to compel compliance with those decisions and directives (generally armed warriors closely attached to or under the direct supervision of the mediator or coordinator), that society is on its way to developing a state. Political power is thus the authority given to a recognized leader (whether judge or general) to compel compliance with his or her decisions.

Political power, however, is a two-edged sword. On the one hand, the power of the leader must be sufficient to ensure that arbitration is enforced and that the coordination of military, hunting, or building activities is effective. The larger a society is, the more complex its economy is, the stronger its enemies are, and the more threatening and varied its environment is, the greater are the tasks facing the state. Thus, for a society to avoid turmoil and defend itself, it must grow in organizational size, complexity, and power along with the society of which it is a part. On the other hand, as the leaders acquire control of larger and richer organizations and larger and more powerful coercive forces, there is a danger that that organizational and coercive force will be used to enrich and serve the desires of the ruler, not to meet the demands for justice and protection of the population (Mann 1986).

The history of the state is thus a history of balancing acts and often of overreaching. State rulers frequently use their organization and authority to expand their power and wealth. Some rulers invest heavily in conquest, acquiring power over new regions and peoples by brute force and then setting up organizations and laws to acquire and enforce political authority. Other rulers have sought to distinguish themselves primarily as lawgivers or (e.g., King Solomon) paragons of justice. Still others have simply taken their power as given and abused it. Sometimes they gain mightily from such abuse, but at other times—under very particular conditions—they may become the object of elite revolts or popular revolutions.

For sociologists, the key to understanding the state is knowledge about the shifting relationships between state rulers, their organizations and resources, and their societies. Much of the history of the development of state forms comes from the competition between rulers seeking to extend their control of political organizations and coercive force and elite and popular groups seeking to limit or channel political authority into socially acceptable goals and actions.

CITY-STATES, EMPIRES, AND FEUDALISM

Although cities and states initially may have developed independently, with both gradually moving forward between 8000 and 3000 B.C., by the third millennium B.C., the conjunction between urbanization and state making was firmly established in the Middle East. Elsewhere—in sub-Saharan Africa and southeast Asia (especially Java and Cambodia)—states and even empires developed without true cities; those states operated through dense clusters of villages that often centered on great temple complexes. By contrast, in the Middle East and the New World, large cities grew up around the temple complexes that served as the headquarters and ceremonial centers of the new states. Several of those city-states had great success in

expansion and became the nucleus of larger empires, such as Sumer, Akkad, Assyria, and the empire of the Aztecs.

City-states continued to emerge throughout history, especially in periods of early settlement of new lands (such as the Greek city-states that spread throughout the Mediterranean in the second millennium B.C.) or after the breakup of large empires (as occurred in Italy and along the Rhine in Germany after the collapse of Charlemagne's empire in the ninth century A.D.). The legacy of these city-states is that they experimented with a wide array of state forms. At various times, the Greek and Roman city-states of the eighth through fourth centuries B.C.—including Athens, Sparta, Thebes, Corinth, and Rome—were ruled by a single monarch, pairs of kings (or consuls), oligarchies of the wealthy or well-born aristocrats, and popular assemblies. The modern forms of democracy and monarchy can be traced back to the Greek and Roman city-states of that period. However, city-states generally did not survive in any area for more than a few centuries before being swallowed up by large territorial empires.

Those large territorial empires became the dominant form of the state in much of the world for the next 5,000 years, from roughly 3000 B.C. to A.D. 1900 (Eisenstadt 1963). In the Middle East, the major empires included of Sumer, Akkad, Egypt, Assyria, Babylonia, and Persia and the Hellenistic empires founded by the generals of Alexander the Great. These empires were followed by the Roman Empire, the Byzantine Empire, and the Islamic empires founded by the followers of Mohammed. These empires were followed by the vast empires of the Mongols and the Turks, the last of which was the Ottoman Empire, which ruled large portions of north Africa, the Middle East, and southeastern Europe and lasted until 1923. In Europe, after the fall of the Roman Empire there followed the empires of Charlemagne and his sons. That empire left as a legacy the Holy Roman Empire, which eventually evolved into the Austro-Hungarian Empire, which survived until 1918. After roughly A.D. 1500, much of eastern Europe and central Asia was under the control of the Russian Empire, which lasted until 1917. In China and India, large empires emerged in the third and fourth centuries B.C. In China, the Qin and Han dynasties initiated a pattern of imperial rule that lasted until the birth of the Chinese Republic in 1911; in India, the Maurya and Gupta dynasties briefly unified the subcontinent and were followed by the Mughal Empire, which lasted until India came under British domination in the eighteenth century.

In Africa, there also were large Empires, including the Aksum Empire in Ethiopia which was (founded around 300 B.C. and whose successor empires and dynasties lasted until 1974), the Ghana Empire and Mali Empire in west Africa, Great Zimbabwe and Mutapa in southern Africa, and the Zulu Empire, which ruled over much of southeastern Africa until it was defeated by the British in the late nineteenth century. In the Americas, three major indigenous empires developed: the Maya and the Aztecs in what is today Mexico and the Incas centered in modern-day Peru. After defeating the Aztecs and Incas in the sixteenth century, Spain established an empire in the Americas extending from Chile to California that it ruled for nearly 300 years.

The vast majority of these empires were conquest empires in which strong imperial centers acquired territory, troops, and resources to build ever-larger empires and thus conquer ever more territory. However, many imperial rulers also were famous lawgivers renowned for establishing justice and order in their empires; they included Hammurabi of Babylonia, Justinian of Rome, and Suleyman the Magnificent of the Ottoman Empire. Their lawcodes were established not to give "rights" to subjects but to produce order by making a clear list of crimes and the penalties that would be imposed.

Though powerful, these empires were not immune to decay and disintegration. Even the longest-lived empires, such as those of Egypt and China, had periods of civil war and broke up into multiple states. Population growth that created pressure on the capacity of the land to yield taxes, military defeat by powerful neighbors, and conflicts among elite factions could all produce disorganization and decay of the imperial state administration. In times of decay, a locally based form of rule known as feudalism often arose.

Feudalism in the strict sense is a pattern of allegiance by oath taking in which a lord gives control of land (a "fief") to a vassal in return for a promise of service. This pattern may have one dominant lord controlling many vassals, or there may be many lords and many vassals, with some vassals dispensing fiefs and thus becoming lords themselves. In this sense, feudalism is not a state, for no centralized administration has full control of the territory. However, if a single lord manages to emerge as dominant over all the other lords and vassals in a territory and is able to expand his own household and personal administration to exert his will throughout the territory, one can then speak of a state, which usually is described as a kingdom or monarchy. Kingdoms were known throughout the world and generally appear in periods in which large empires have broken down or before they are established. In most of the world, empires continued to reestablish themselves, often building on the strongest kingdom in a region. However, in western and central Europe, no empire ever reestablished lasting control over the area that had been controlled by the Romans. Instead, the period of feudalism in Europe (roughly A.D. 600 through 1300) was followed by many centuries in which a number of competing kingdoms controlled major portions of the European continent.

ABSOLUTISM AND BUREAUCRATIC-AUTHORITARIAN STATES

The early empires and kingdoms all had rudimentary administrations and relatively undifferentiated elites. That is, the officers of the state were mainly family members of the ruler or personal favorites appointed at the ruler's pleasure; many were also high-ranking officials in the church. They gained much of their income from the control of personal properties or privileges granted by the ruler. The mingling of state and church was based on a strong connection between religious and state power; there was usually an official state religion that supported the state and was in turn supported by the ruler.

By around the sixteenth century A.D., however, most of the kingdoms and empires of Europe and Asia had begun to develop into more impersonal and bureaucratic states. State offices were fixed in a "table of ranks," and officers were expected to undergo rigorous academic training to qualify for their positions. The number of state offices multiplied greatly, and while favorites still were chosen for key positions, an increasing number were chosen and promoted for their merit and services. States also began to diversify their sources of income. Most early empires relied on various forms of tribute collection or taxes paid "in kind," such as set amounts of grain, cloth, or labor services. In contrast, by the sixteenth century, most states had begun to specify and collect taxes in cash, with which they paid regular salaries to state officials. In those states, subjects still had few rights and no participation in politics; rulers remained absolute in authority. However, those states became "bureaucratic-authoritarian" in the sense that authority increasingly was exercised through uniform rules enforced by bureaucratic officials rather than through local and customary practices enforced by fairly autonomous local notables.

Dependence on cash meant that many states also placed a greater emphasis on trade and on taxes on commerce as an alternative to taxes on land. For some states (e.g., the Netherlands and Great Britain), taxes on trade and industry soon exceeded revenues from traditional land taxes (Tilly 1990). In the period 1500–1900, the promotion of trade and commerce led to a vast expansion of long-distance trade, both ocean-borne and land-based, across the globe. European kingdoms, stymied in creating empires in Europe, created them overseas. Seeking natural resources and new markets, European states (and later Japan) invested in colonies and overseas companies and administrations to control them in the Americas, Africa, India, southeastern Asia, Korea, and along the Chinese coast.

While this period remained one of kingdoms and empires, bureaucratic-authoritarian states faced two extensive periods of challenge. From the late sixteenth to the mid-seventeenth century and again from the late eighteenth to the mid-nineteenth century, all of Eurasia experienced several trends that reshaped states. First, in those two periods the population grew dramatically, doubling or more, while in other periods the population declined or was stable. These periods of population growth were also periods of rising prices as a result of more extensive commerce and a rising demand for basic goods. Pay to laborers and available land for peasants, however, declined as the population grew faster than did the agricultural economy. Population growth also led to factional conflicts among elite groups competing for control of state offices and to greater demands on state administrations. However, states were run-

ning into financial trouble, for population growth was reducing the surplus available for taxation and the rapid growth of commerce was shifting more resources into areas where traditional tax collection was weak, leaving more resources in the hands of merchants, local landowners, and urban and regional elites. Toward the end of those two periods—roughly 1580–1660 and 1770–1860—conflicts between state rulers and elites over the rulers' prerogatives and resources triggered worldwide waves of revolutions and rebellions in kingdoms and empires; these included the English, American, and French revolutions, the anti-Habsburg revolts, and the revolutions of 1848 in Europe; the collapse of the Ming Empire and the Taiping rebellion in China; and the janissary, Balkan, and Egyptian revolts in the Ottoman Empire (Goldstone 1991).

REVOLUTIONS, NATIONALISM, AND NATION-STATES

Those revolutions and rebellions all involved popular uprisings and elite rebellions against the ruler and loyal elements of the state but had different outcomes in different areas. In most societies, the elites were deeply frightened by popular uprisings and sought to reestablish state power more firmly by tightening the reins of state power and enforcing allegiance to the state-sponsored religion. This was the case in Catholic Spain, Italy, and Austria under the Counter-Reformation; in Confucian China under the Qing dynasty; and in the Islamic Ottoman Empire. However, in England 1689, America in 1776, and France in 1789, the elites were more concerned that excessive state power would damage their positions and fuel future revolutions. Reviving ideas and institutions from the days of democratic Greece and republican Rome, they attempted to place limits on state power and reserve specific rights to elites and even to ordinary workers and peasants. Those limits and rights were codified in a variety of documents, including "declarations of rights", and especially in constitutions that became the basis for state power. Those constitutions marked a distinctively modern turn in the history of state. Previously, state authority had always rested on coercion and demands for the dispensation of order and been supported by religious belief and tradition, but from the age of constitutions, the legitimacy of state authority rested on whether the ruler abided by the limits in the constitution and recognized the rights of the elites and popular groups that had established that constitution.

Constitutions meant that a new relationship was forged between the state and the population of the territory it ruled. Under empires, the state established order and most people were simply economic producers, not political actors. By contrast, under constitutions, the people, or at least those involved in creating and establishing constitutional rule, were the ultimate controllers and beneficiaries of state power. This new relationship led to new demands by various groups.

One demand was for greater and more regular political participation by groups that had been excluded: religious and ethnic minority groups, women, and the poor. Though frequently resisted by elites and state rulers, in many areas those groups gained elite allies and acquired rights to regular political participation, most notably through voting (Reuschemeyer et al. 1992). States where voting rights are widespread and the state's power over its subjects has significant limits are commonly described as democratic or "liberal" states. By the late nineteenth century, most of the states in Europe west of Russia and in North and South America were liberal states.

Another demand came from professionals, merchants, and sometimes military officers who lived under empires and wanted to take control of their positions and territories under something like the relationship that prevailed in constitutional regimes, where the state was identified as an instrument of the people rather than the reverse. Those elites argued that every ethnic group should be entitled to its "own" state and its own rulers. The resulting ideology was known as "nationalism" (Calhoun 1998), and it spread widely throughout the world. Nationalism fueled the revolutions of 1830 in Poland and Greece; those of 1848 in Hungary, Germany, Italy, and Romania; the effort to expel the Austro-Hungarians and unify Italy under Italian rule in the 1860s; and the Serb liberation movement that helped start World War I. Nationalist sentiments also fueled revolts in Ireland throughout the nineteenth and twentieth centuries; the Chinese Republican Revolution of 1911; the anticolonial revolutions in India, Algeria, Indonesia, and Vietnam after World War II; and a host of other anticolonial revolts in Africa and Asia.

Nationalism fostered the ideal that states should be "national" states, reflecting the identity and promoting the aspirations of their inhabitants as a united community rooted in shared traditions and culture (Anderson 1991). In fact, to comply with this ideal, many traditions had to be invented and national languages had to be created. Even today, it often is ambiguous whether a given nation-state reflects a nation (Is there is British nation or only English, Welsh, and Scottish nations plus portions of Scot-settled Ireland sharing the state of Great Britain?). However, the ideal of the nation-state spread widely, even to older states, so that it became expected that modern nation-states would have a national language, a national flag and anthem, national systems of schooling and communications (newspapers, radio, and television), national systems of transportation (highways, railways, and airlines), and a national army.

Nonetheless, since almost all existing states included members of more than one ethnic, linguistic, or cultural group within their boundaries, most nation-states inevitably failed to satisfy to a greater or lesser degree the aspirations of subnational groups, which in turn often developed their own nationalist ambitions. A large number of the violent conflicts in the world in recent years are the result of nationalist movements within nation-states, such as the Chechens in Russia, the Basques in Spain, the Kurds in Turkey, the Uighurs in China, and the Albanian Kosovars in Yugoslavia.

While nationalism seemed poised to bring more liberal, constitutional states into being, things did not develop that way. The defeat of many early nationalist movements led nationalist leaders to conclude that above all else, a people needed a strong state to protect them from control by others, whether multinational empires or other nations. As a result, many nationalist movements gave rise to authoritarian, populist dictatorships. Those dictatorships often promulgated constitutions and claimed to draw their legitimacy—in the modern fashion—from their service to and identification with the people of the territories they ruled, but in fact they operated in as absolute a manner as any older imperial state, only now they were backed by the latest industrial and military technology. Thus, while nationalism was destroying the old traditional empires and replacing them with modern states, those modern states were following divergent paths into democracy and dictatorship.

DEMOCRACIES AND DICTATORSHIPS

The history of the state in the twentieth century has largely been one of a struggle between democracies and dictatorships. In the liberal states over the course of the twentieth century, the range of citizen rights has been expanding, the participation in politics of ordinary citizens (through rallies, financial contributions, petitions, and voting) has grown, and the obligations of the state to support its citizens (the modern "welfare state") have been extended. A major result of these patterns is that women, the working class, and the poor are far more closely integrated into political life in liberal states as voters and direct recipients of state actions than ever before (O'Conner et. al, 1999). To accommodate and channel this political participation, most liberal states have a number of political parties that organize and control the competition for political power. At the end of the twentieth century, as a result of growing state obligations, the personnel and budget of modern liberal states has swollen to the point where state expenditures make up one-quarter to one-half of the entire national product of their societies.

However, the model of the liberal state did not triumph in every place where empires collapsed. In many regions, spurred by nationalist sentiment and the failure of liberal states to provide economic and military security under the chaotic conditions that followed military defeat or economic crises, modern dictatorships emerged. Some of those dictatorships, such as those of Adolph Hitler and his Nazi Party in Germany and Benito Mussolini and his Fascist Party in Italy, did not outlast their founders. However, in Russia and China, Communist parties took on a dominant life of their own, and those countries became one-party states in which everything of economic, military, and political importance was controlled by the party-state. In other countries, notably in Africa (e.g., Nigeria), Latin America, and eastern Asia (e.g., Korea and Indonesia), military personnel seized power and held on for periods ranging from years to generations. For most of the twentieth century, such modern one-party and military dictatorships, all professing nationalist ideals and even staging (controlled) popular elections, controlled the vast majority of the states and peoples of the world.

In the last two decades of the twentieth century, however, the majority of those one-party states and military dictatorships collapsed (Walder 1995; Goldstone et al. 1991). Their extensive control of the economy stifled innovation and encouraged corruption, leading their revenues to fall well below those of the leading liberal states. Within dictatorial states, even the elites looked on the far greater material wealth and personal freedom of their counterparts in liberal states with envy. Efforts at reform in one-party and military states thus quickly turned into movements to establish liberal regimes. As a result, for the first time in history, it appears that humankind will enter a new millennium with a majority of its nations and populations living under liberal constitutional states (Huntington 1991).

BEYOND THE NATION-STATE

While the twentieth century has closed with the national, liberal state seemingly triumphant, there is no assurance that this form of state will endure. Constitutional states often have been overthrown by dictatorships, both military and populist, when they encounter severe military or economic setbacks. The Great Depression led a host of democracies to collapse into dictatorships, and struggles with economic development led many Latin American and African states into communist takeovers and military coups in the 1960s and 1970s. In most of the world outside Europe and North America, liberal states are not firmly established and may be vulnerable if another major economic trauma sweeps the globe. Thus, the past threats to the continuance of liberal states may reemerge.

In addition, new threats to the primacy of the nation-state have arisen in the form of supranational organizations with genuine sovereignty and military power. The most notable of these organizations are NATO (a military alliance with a unified command embracing the forces of most European nations and the United States) and the European Union (a supranational body ruled by representatives from most European nations with taxing and legislative authority over certain aspects of its member states). A variety of cooperative multinational organizations established by treaty, such as the United Nations, the International Monetary Fund, the International Court of Justice, and various environmental commissions and human rights organizations, also have impinged on state sovereignty. The future may see still greater transfers of state power to such supranational bodies as the problems of establishing human rights, safeguarding the global environment, and maintaining stable and sound financial institutions may grow beyond the capacity of any single state or ad hoc arrangement of states to resolve.

REFERENCES

Anderson, Benedict 1991 *Imagined Communities*. London: Verso.

Calhoun, Craig 1998 *Nationalism*. Minneapolis: University of Minnesota Press.

Eisenstadt, S. N. 1963 *The Political Systems of Empires*. London: Macmillan.

Goldstone, Jack A. 1991 *Revolution and Rebellion in the Early Modern World*. Berkeley: University of California Press.

——, Ted Robert Gurr, and Farrokh Moshiri 1991 *Revolutions of the Late Twentieth Century*. Boulder, Colo.: Westview.

Huntington, Samuel P. 1991 *The Third Wave: Democratization in the Late Twentieth Century*. Norman: Oklahoma University Press.

Mann, Michael 1986 *The Sources of Social Power*. Cambridge, U.K: Cambridge University Press.

O'Conner, Julia S, Ann Shola Orloff, and Sheila Shaver 1999 *States, Markets, Families: Gender, Liberalism, and Social Policy in Australia, Canada, Great Britain, and the United States*. Cambridge: Cambridge University Press.

Poggi, Gianfranco 1990 *The State: Its Nature, Development, and Prospects*. Stanford, Calif.: Stanford University Press.

Rueschemeyer, Dietrich, Evelyn Huber Stephens, and John D. Stephens 1992 *Capitalist Development and Democracy*. Chicago: University of Chicago Press.

Tilly, Charles 1990 *Coercion, Capital, and European States, AD 990–1990*. Oxford, UK: Basil Blackwell.

Walder, Andrew 1995 *The Waning of the Communist State*. Berkeley and Los Angeles: University of California Press.

Weber, Max 1968 *Economy and Society*, edited by Guenther Roth and Claus Wittich. New York: Bedminster.

JACK A. GOLDSTONE

STATISTICAL GRAPHICS

Statistical graphs present data and the results of statistical analysis, assist in the analysis of data, and occasionally are used to facilitate statistical computation. Presentation graphs include the familiar bar graph, pie chart, line graph, scatterplot, and statistical map. Data analysis employs these graphical forms as well as others. Computational graphs ("nomographs") sometimes display data but usually show theoretical quantities such as power curves for determining sample size. Computational graphs are convenient when statistical tables would be unwieldy, but computer programs are even more convenient, and so nomographs are used with decreasing frequency. This article emphasizes the role of graphs in data analysis, although many of the considerations raised here also apply to graphical presentation.

Although it generally is recognized that the pictorial representation of information is a par-

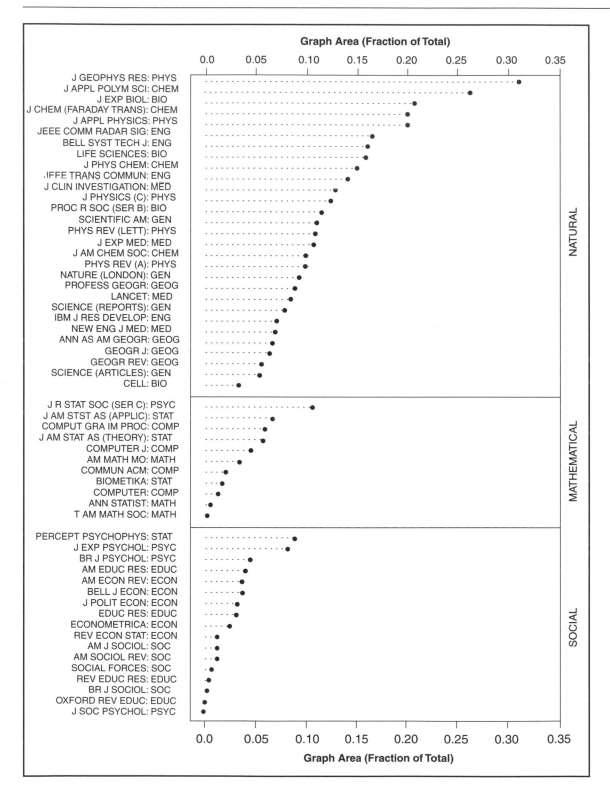

Figure 1. Dot graph showing the fractional area devoted to graphs in fifty-seven journals in the natural, mathematical, and social sciences. Four sociology journals appear near the bottom of the graph. To construct the graph, fifty articles were sampled from each journal in 1980 and 1981.

SOURCE: Reprinted from Cleveland (1984) with the permission of the American Statistical Association.

ticularly effective mode of communication, statistical graphs seldom appear in sociological publications. Figure 1, from Cleveland (1984), shows the relative space devoted to graphs in leading scientific publications, including four sociology journals. Sociology, of course, is not a wholly quantitative discipline. Nevertheless, even a cursory examination of publications in the field reveals that sociologists much more frequently report numerical information in tabular than in graphical form. Informal observation also suggests that sociologists usually analyze numerical data without the assistance of statistical graphs, a situation that may be changing.

HISTORY

Broadly construed, graphic communication dates to the cave paintings of human prehistory and to the earliest forms of writing, which were pictorial or semipictorial. The first diagrams to communicate quantitative information—about location and distance—were maps: Egyptian cartographers employed coordinate systems in maps prepared 5,000 years ago, and cartography remains a relatively well developed area of graphical representation. Musical notation, which charts pitch as a function of time, also has an ancient origin and illustrates the spatial display of essentially nonspatial information. Rectilinear coordinate graphs are so familiar that it is easy to lose sight of the radical abstraction required to represent diverse quantities, such as pitch, as distances along an axis.

In the seventeenth century, the French mathematician and philosopher René Descartes established the relationship between algebraic equations and curves in a rectilinear coordinate space. The graphical representation of functions is not logically necessary for the display of empirical data as points in space, and there are isolated examples before Descartes of statistical graphs that employ abstract coordinate systems. Nevertheless, Descartes's analytic geometry no doubt provided the impetus for the development of statistical graphics, and the most common forms of statistical graphs evolved slowly over the subsequent three and a half centuries.

Among many individuals' contributions to this evolution, the work of William Playfair at the turn of the nineteenth century is of particular importance. First, Playfair either invented or popularized several common graphical forms, including the line graph, the bar graph, the pie chart, and the circle chart (in which areas of circles represent quantities). Second, Playfair employed statistical graphs to display social and economic data. Figure 2a, from Playfair's 1786 *Commercial and Political Atlas*, is a time series line graph of imports to and exports from England in the period 1771–1782. In the original graph, the space between the two curves is colored green when the balance of trade favors England (i.e., when the curve for exports is above that for imports) and red when the balance favors England's trading partners. Of the forty-two graphs in Playfair's atlas, all but one depict time series. The sole exception is a bar graph of imports to and exports from Scotland (Figure 2b), the data for which were available only for the year 1780–1781, precluding the construction of time series plots. Playfair's 1801 *Statistical Breviary* included a wider variety of graphical forms.

The first half of the nineteenth century was a period of innovation in and dissemination of statistical graphics, particularly in England and France. The ogive (cumulative frequency curve), the histogram, the contour map, and graphs employing logarithmic and polar coordinates all appeared before 1850. Later in the century, the British scientist Sir Francis Galton exploited an analogy to contour maps in his determination of the bivariate–normal correlation surface, illustrating the role of graphs in discovery.

The nineteenth-century enthusiasm for graphic representation of data produced many memorable and high-quality statistical graphs, such as those of Playfair, Florence Nightingale, E. J. Marey, and Charles Joseph Minard (several of which are reproduced in Tufte 1983). The same enthusiasm produced early abuses, however, including the graph from M. G. Mulhall's 1892 *Dictionary of Statistics* shown in Figure 3: The heights of the triangles indicate the accumulated wealth of each country, but their areas are wildly disproportionate to the quantities represented, conveying a misleading

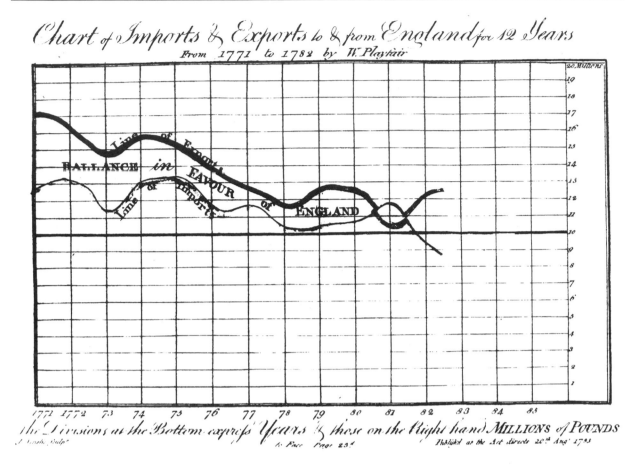

Figure 2a

impression of the data. Furthermore, the horizontal arrangement of the countries bears no relationship to the purpose of the graph and apparently was done for artistic effect: It would be more natural to order the countries by wealth. Many modern graphs have similar problems, a situation that has motivated a substantial literature of graphic criticism (such as the works by Schmidt, Tufte, and Wainer discussed below).

The evolution of statistical graphics paralleled the general growth of statistical science well into the twentieth century. This relationship changed radically in the 1930s as statisticians such as R. A. Fisher emphasized the development of procedures for statistical inference. Fisher's influential *Statistical Methods for Research Workers*, first published in 1925, includes a brief chapter on "diagrams"; this chapter incorporates line graphs, scatterplots, and a histogram with a superimposed normal-density curve. The remainder of the book, however, contains many numerical tables but just five additional figures, none of which presents empirical information. Fisher's 1935 *The Design of Experiments* includes just three graphs, all of which are theoretical.

The rebirth of interest in statistical graphics may be traced to John W. Tukey's work on exploratory data analysis, beginning in the 1960s and culminating in the publication of his text on this subject in 1977. Tukey's coworkers and students, most importantly the group at Bell Laboratories and its successors associated with William S. Cleveland, continue to contribute to the modern development of statistical graphics (see, in particular, Chambers et al. 1983; Cleveland 1993, 1994). Further information on the history of statistical graphics can be found in Funkhouser (1937), Tufte (1983), and Beninger and Robyn (1978), the last of which contains a useful chronology and bibliography.

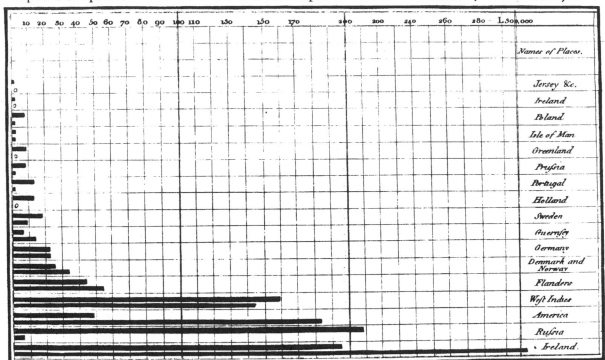

Figure 2b. Two graphs from Playfair's 1786 Commercial and Political Atlas*: (a) A time series line graph showing imports to and exports from England, 1771–1782. (b) A bar graph showing imports to and exports from Scotland for the year 1780–1781. The originals are in color.*

SOURCE: Photographs courtesy of the William Clements Library, University of Michigan, Richard W. Ryan, curator of books.

GRAPHIC STANDARDS

After several abortive efforts, the International Statistical Congresses held in Europe in the nineteenth century abandoned the attempt to formulate graphical standards. Since that time, many authors have proposed standards and principles for the construction of statistical graphs, but consensus on these matters remains elusive. Schmidt (1983, p. 17), for example, suggests that grid lines should always appear on rectilinear line graphs, while Tufte (1983, p. 112) maintains that grids "should usually be muted or completely suppressed," an instance of his more general principle that good graphs maximize the "dataink ratio" (the amount of ink devoted to the display of data as a proportion of all the ink used to draw the graph) and eliminate "chartjunk" (extraneous graphical elements).

Disagreements such as this are due partly to the lack of systematic data on graphical perception (a situation that is improving), partly to differences in style and taste, and partly to the absence of adequate general theories of graph construction and perception (although there have been attempts, such as Bertin 1973). Also, good graphical display depends on the purposes for which a graph is drawn and on particular characteristics of the data, factors that are difficult to specify in advance and in a general manner.

Huff (1954, chap. 5), for example, argues that scales displaying ratio quantities should always start at zero to avoid exaggerating the magnitude

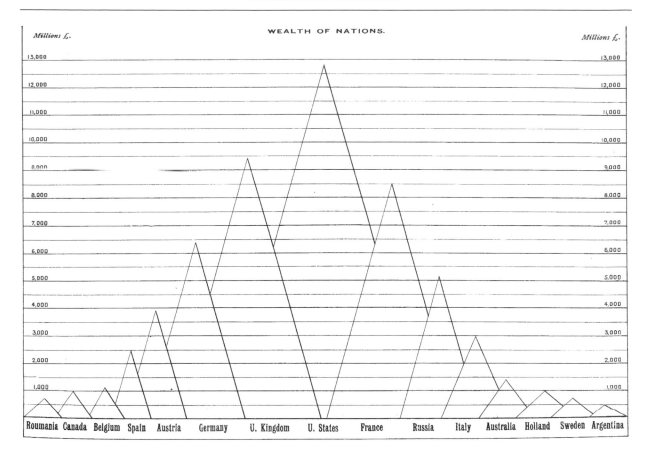

Figure 3. A modified bar graph from Mulhall's 1892 Dictionary of Statistics, *substituting triangles with unequal bases for equal-width rectangular bars. The height of each triangle represents accumulated national wealth in 1888. The original is in color.*

SOURCE: Photograph by University of Michigan Photographic Services.

of differences between data values. This principle, however, often disguises patterns in data that are revealed clearly by graphical magnification. Consider Figure 4, a and b, which shows the relative value of the Canadian and U.S. dollars in the eight weeks surrounding the June 23, 1990, deadline for the ratification of the ill-fated "Meech Lake" amendment to the Canadian constitution. This period was widely interpreted, both domestically and abroad, as one of constitutional crisis and uncertainty for Canada. Because in the short term the Canadian dollar traditionally trades in a narrow range against the U.S. dollar, Figure 4a is essentially uninformative, while Figure 4b reveals that the Canadian dollar fell slightly as the Meech deadline approached and rose afterward.

Despite some areas of disagreement, commentators on the design of statistical graphs, such as Tufte (1983, 1990, 1997), Schmidt, and Wainer, offer a great deal of uncontroversially sound advice. In a tongue-in-cheek essay (reprinted in Wainer 1997: chap. 1), Wainer enumerates twelve rules to help the reader "display data badly." Several of these rules are illustrated in Figure 5a, which appeared in the *Miami Herald* in 1984: "Rule 7, Emphasize the trivial (ignore the important)"; "Rule 11, More is murkier: (a) more decimal places and (b) more dimensions"; and "Rule 12, If it has been done well in the past, think of a new way to do it." The graph in Figure 5a is meant to show the presumably negative relationship between the success of the twenty-six major league baseball teams in the 1984 season and the average salaries paid to the players on those teams. The lengths of the bars represent average players' salaries, while the teams' records of wins and losses are hidden in parenthe-

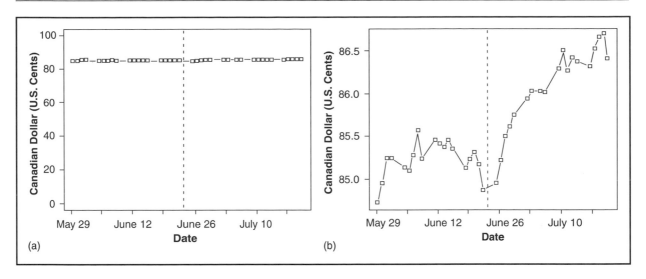

Figure 4. The relative value of the Canadian and U.S. dollar in an eight-week period in 1990 surrounding the failure of the Meech Lake amendment to the Canadian constitution. (a) Beginning the vertical axis at zero. Note that the upper end point of one is arbitrary, since the Canadian dollar can (at least in theory) trade above par with the U.S. dollar. (b) Scaling the vertical axis to accommodate the range of the data. The vertical line in each graph is drawn at the June 23 deadline for ratifying the Meech Lake accord.

SOURCE: Daily foreign exchange quotations in the *New York Times*.

ses within the bars, making it essentially impossible to tell whether the two variables are related—ostensibly the point of the graph. The bars are drawn in three-dimensional perspective, apparently for artistic effect, but the result is that the quantities represented are slightly distorted: For example, the average salary of the New York Yankees, $458,544, appears to be about $410,000. A standard representation of these data appears in the scatterplot in Figure 5b, revealing a slight *positive* relationship between salary and success.

RESEARCH ON GRAPHIC PERCEPTION

The earliest psychophysical research on perception of graphs, conducted in the 1920s, focused on the relative merits of pie charts and bar charts for displaying percentage data and was inconclusive. More recently, statisticians and psychologists have undertaken systematic experimentation on graphical perception. Spence and Lewandowsky (1990) review the literature in this area up to 1990.

Cleveland and McGill (1984), for example, conducted a series of experiments to ascertain the relative accuracy of ten elementary perceptual tasks that extract quantitative information from graphs, as represented schematically in Figure 6. Ranked in order of decreasing average accuracy, these tasks involve judgment of position along a common scale; position along nonaligned scales; length, direction, or angle; area; volume or curvature; and shading or color saturation. Similarly, Spence (reported in Spence and Lewandowsky 1990) has shown in an experiment that categorical information differentiating points on a scatterplot is encoded most effectively by colors and least effectively by confusable letters (e.g., E, F, H); other coding devices, such as different shapes (circles, squares, triangles), degrees of fill, and discriminable letters (H, Q, X), were intermediate in effectiveness.

Cleveland (1993) demonstrates that slope judgments are most accurate for angles close to forty-five degrees and least accurate for angles near zero or ninety degrees. Cleveland therefore suggests that the aspect ratio of graphs (the relative lengths of the axes) be set so that average slopes are close to forty-five degrees, a procedure he terms "banking to forty-five degrees." This process is illus-

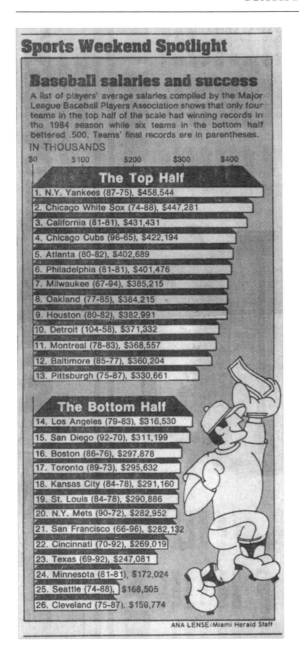

Figure 5a

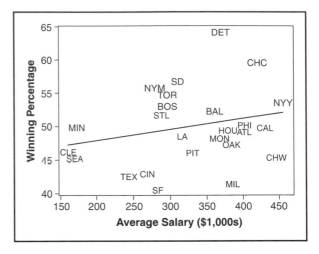

Figure 5b. Major League Baseball salaries and team success in the 1984 season. (a) As depicted in the Miami Herald. *The lengths of the bars (slightly distorted) represent the average salaries paid to players from each team; the teams' won–lost records appear in parentheses within the bars. The apparent point of the graph is that there is a negative relationship between salaries and success. (b) The same data in standard scatterplot. The line on the plot, derived from a logistic regression of wins on average salaries, indicates a weak positive relationship between salaries and success.*

trated in Figure 7. Both graphs in this figure plot the same data, but the periodic pattern of the data is nearly impossible to discern in Figure 7a because the average slope of the curve is too steep.

Cleveland and his colleagues have designed new graphical forms that apply these and similar findings by encoding important information through the employment of accurately judged graphic elements. One such form is the dot graph, an exam-

ple of which appears in Figure 1. Similarly, Cleveland and McGill (1984) suggest the replacement of quantitative statistical maps that use shading or hue (e.g., Figure 8a) with maps that employ framed rectangles (Figure 8b), which exploit the more accurate judgment of position along nonaligned scales. Despite the inferiority of Figure 8a for judging differences in murder rates among the states, however, this map more clearly reveals regional variations in rates, illustrating the principle that the purpose for which a graph is drawn should influence its design.

The effectiveness of statistical graphs is rooted in the remarkable ability of people to apprehend, process, and remember pictorial information. The human visual system, however, is subject to distortion and illusion, processes that can affect the perception of graphs. Good graphical design can minimize and counteract the limitations of human vision. In Figure 9, for example, it appears that the difference between the hypothetical import and export series is changing when this difference

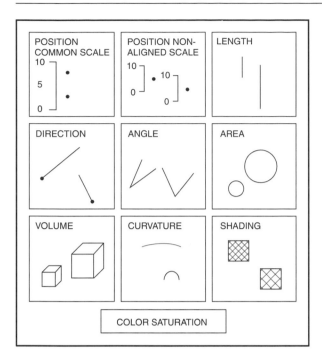

Figure 6. Ten elementary perceptual tasks for decoding quantitative information from statistical graphs.

SOURCE: Reprinted from Cleveland and McGill (1984) with the permission of the American Statistical Association.

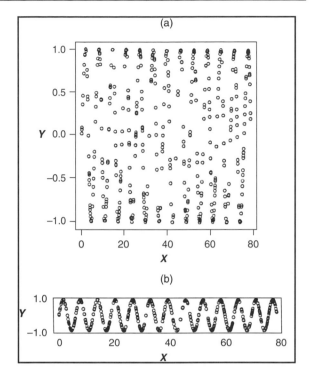

Figure 7. Two scatterplots of the same data. Five hundred X-values were randomly generated in the interval [0,25π], and Y=sin X. The periodic pattern of the data is clear in (b), where the aspect ratio of the plot is adjusted so that the average slope of the curve is not too steep, but not in panel (a).

actually is constant (cf., Playfair's time series graph in Figure 2a). The source of the illusion is the tendency to attend to the least distance between the two curves rather than to the vertical distance. Thus, an alternative is to graph the difference between the two curves—the balance of trade—directly (cf. Figure 12, b and c, below), exploiting the relatively accurate judgment of position along a common scale, or to show vertical lines between the import and export curves, employing the somewhat less accurate judgment of position along nonaligned scales.

GRAPHS IN DATA ANALYSIS

Statistical graphs should play a central role in the analysis of data, a common prescription that is most often honored in the breach. Graphs, unlike numerical summaries of data, facilitate the perception of general patterns and often reveal unusual, anomalous, or unexpected features of the data—characteristics that might compromise a numerical summary.

The four simple data sets in Figure 10, from Anscombe (1973) and dubbed "Anscombe's quartet" by Tufte (1983), illustrate this point well. All four data sets yield the same linear least-squares outputs when regression lines are fitted to the data, including the regression intercept and slope, coefficient standard errors, the standard error of the regression (i.e., the standard deviation of the residuals), and the correlation, but—significantly—not residuals. Although the data are contrived, the four graphs tell very different imaginary stories: The least-squares regression line accurately summarizes the tendency of y to increase with x in Figure 10a. In contrast, the data in Figure 10b clearly indicate a curvilinear relationship between y and x, a relationship the linear regression does not capture. In Figure 10c, one point is out of line with the rest and distorts the regression. Perhaps the outlying point represents an error in recording the data or a y-value that is influenced by factors other than x. In Figure 10d, the ability to fit a line

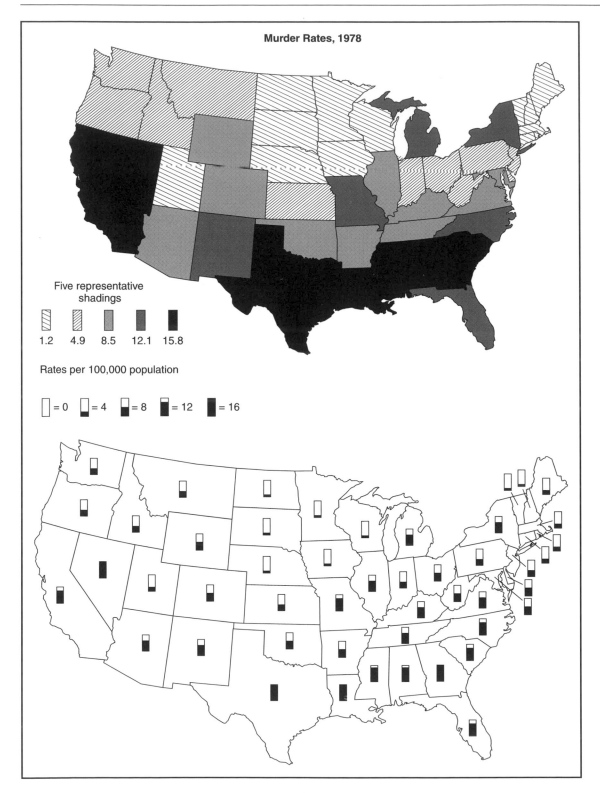

Figure 8. Statistical maps of state murder rates in 1978 employing (a) shading and (b) framed rectangles.

SOURCE: Reprinted from Cleveland and McGill (1984) with the permission of the American Statistical Association.

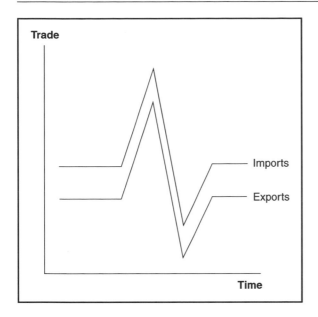

Figure 9. Despite appearances, the vertical separation between the curves for imports and exports is constant. The "data" are contrived.

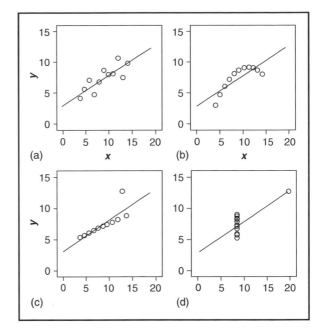

Figure 10. The four data sets have the same linear least-squares regression, including the regression coefficients, their standard errors, the correlation between the variables, and the standard error of the regression.

SOURCE: Redrawn from Anscombe (1973) with the permission of the American Statistical Association.

and the line's specific location depend on the presence of a single point.

Diverse graphical forms are adapted to different purposes in data analysis. Many important applications appear in the figures below, roughly in order of increasing complexity, including graphs for displaying univariate distributions, bivariate relationships, diagnostic quantities in regression analysis, and multivariate data.

Particularly useful for graphically screening data are methods for displaying the distributions of quantitative variables. Several univariate displays of the distribution of infant mortality rates for 201 countries are shown in Figure 11, using data compiled by the United Nations.

Figure 11a is a traditional histogram of the infant mortality data, a frequency bar graph formed by dissecting the range of infant mortality into class intervals or "bins" and then counting the number of observations in each bin; the vertical axis of the histogram is scaled in percent. Figure 11b shows an alternative histogram that differs from Figure 11a only in the origin of the bin system (the bars are shifted five units to the left). These graphs demonstrate that the impression conveyed by a histogram depends partly on the

arbitrary location of the bins. Figure 11c is a stem-and-leaf display, a type of histogram (from Tukey) that records the data values directly in the bars of the graph, thus permitting the recovery of the original data. Here, for example, the values given as 1:2 represent infant mortality rates of 12 per 1,000.

Figure 11d is a kernel density estimate, or smoothed histogram, a display that corrects both the roughness of the traditional histogram and its dependence on the arbitrary choice of bin location. For any value x of infant mortality, the height of the kernel estimate is

$$\hat{f}(x) = \frac{1}{nh} \sum_{i=1}^{n} K\left(\frac{x - x_i}{h}\right) \qquad (1)$$

where n is the number of observations (here, 201); the observations themselves are $\chi_1, \chi_2, \ldots, \chi_n$, h is the "window" half-width for the kernel estimate, analogous to bin width for a histogram; and K is

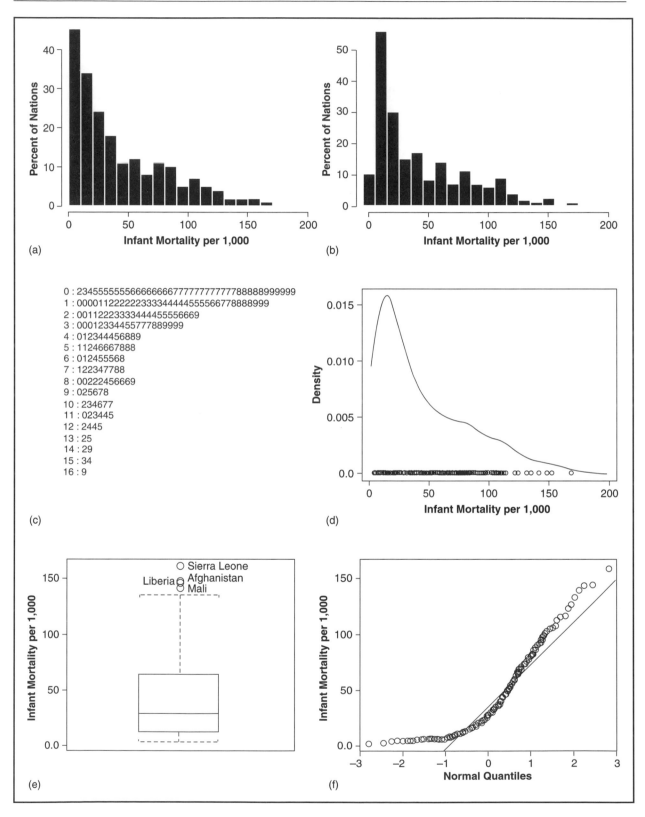

Figure 11. Six univariate displays of the distribution of infant mortality rates in 201 nations. The histograms (a) and (b) both have bins of width ten, but the bars of (b) are five units to the left of those of (a). A stem-and-leaf display is shown in (c), a kernel density estimate in (d), a boxplot in (e), and a normal quantile comparision plot in (f).

SOURCE: United Nations, http://www.un.org/Depts/unsd/social/main.htm.

some probability–density function, such as the unit-normal density, ensuring that the total area under the kernel estimate is one. A univariate scatterplot — another form of distributional display giving the location of each observation — is shown at the bottom of Figure 11d.

Figure 11e, a "boxplot" of the infant mortality data (a graphic form also from Tukey), summarizes a variety of important distributional information. The box is drawn between the first and third quartiles and therefore encloses the central half of the data. A line within the box marks the position of the median. The whiskers extend either to the most extreme data value (as on the bottom) or to the most extreme nonoutlying data value (as on the top). Four outlying data values are represented individually. The compactness of the boxplot suggests its use as a component of more complex displays; boxplots may be drawn in the margins of a scatterplot to show the distribution of each variable, for example.

Figure 11f shows a normal quantile comparison plot for the infant mortality data. As the name implies, this graph compares the ordered data with corresponding quantiles of the unit-normal distribution. By convention, the ith largest infant mortality rate, denoted $\chi_{(i)}$, has $P_i = (i - 1/2)/n$ proportion of the data below it. The corresponding normal quantile is z_i, located so that $Pr(Z \leq z_i) = P_i$, where Z follows the unit-normal distribution. If X is normally distributed with mean μ and standard deviation σ, then within the bounds of sampling error, $x_{(i)} \cong \mu + \sigma z_i$. Departure from a linear pattern therefore indicates nonnormality. The line shown in Figure 11f passes through the quartiles of X and Z. The positive skew of the infant mortality rates is reflected in the tendency of the plotted points to lie above the fitted line in both tails of the distribution.

While the skewness of the infant mortality data is apparent in all the displays, the possibly multimodal grouping of the data is clearest in the kernel density estimate. The normal quantile comparison plot, in contrast, retains the greatest resolution in the tails of the distribution, where data are sparse; these are the regions that often are problematic for numerical summaries of data such as means and regression surfaces.

Many useful graphs display relationships between variables, including several forms that ap-

peared earlier in this article: bar graphs (Figure 2b), dot graphs (Figure 1), and line graphs such as time series plots (Figures 2a and 4). Parallel boxplots are often informative in comparing the distribution of a quantitative variable across several categories. Scatterplots (as in Figure 10) are invaluable for examining the relationship between two quantitative variables. Other data-analytic graphs adapt these forms.

In graphing quantitative data, it is sometimes advantageous to transform variables. Logarithms, the most common form of transformation, often clarify data that extend over two or more orders of magnitude (i.e., a factor of 100 or more) and are natural for problems in which ratios of data values, rather than their differences, are of central interest.

Consider Figure 12, which shows the size of the Canadian and U.S. populations for census years between 1790 and 1990 in the United States and between 1851 and 1991 in Canada. The data are graphed on the original scale in Figure 12a and on the log scale in Figure 12b. Because the Canadian population is much smaller than that of the United States, it is difficult to discern the Canadian data in Figure 12a. Moreover, Figure 12b shows more clearly departures from a constant rate of population growth, represented by linear increase on the log scale, and permits a direct comparison of the growth rates in the two countries. These rates were quite similar, with the U.S. population roughly ten times as large as the Canadian population throughout the past century and a half. Figure 10c, however, which graphs the difference between the two curves in Figure 10b (i.e., the log population ratio), reveals that the United States was growing more rapidly than Canada was before 1900 and more slowly afterward.

Graphs also can assist in statistical modeling. Least-squares regression analysis, for example, which fits the model

$$Y_i = \beta_0 + \beta_1 x_{1i} + \beta_2 x_{2i} + \cdots + \beta_k x_{ki} + \varepsilon_i \qquad (2)$$

makes strong assumptions about the structure of the data, including assumptions of linearity, equal error variance, normality of errors, and independence. Here Y_i is the dependent variable score for the ith of n observations; $\chi_{1i}, \chi_{2i}, \ldots, \chi_{ki}$, are independent variables; ε_i, is an unobserved error that is assumed to be normally distributed with zero ex-

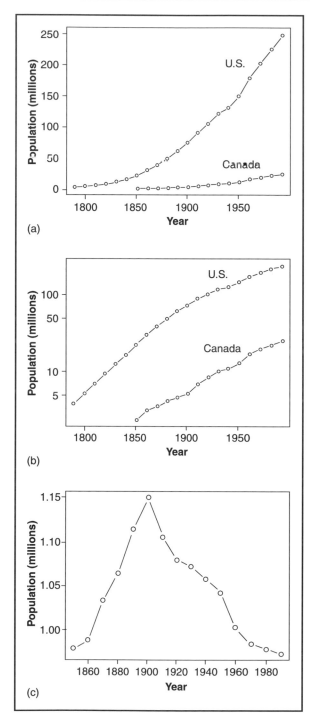

(a)

(b)

(c)

Figure 12. Canadian and U.S. population figures are plotted directly in (a) and on a log scale in (b). The difference between the two log series is shown in (c).

SOURCE: *Canada Yearbook 1994* and *Statistical Abstract of the United States: 1994.*

pectation and constant variance σ^2, independent of the x's and the other errors; and the ß's are regression parameters, which are to be estimated along with the error variance from the data.

Graphs of quantities derived from the fitted regression model often prove crucial in determining the adequacy of the model. Figure 13, for example, plots a measure of leverage in the regression (the "hat values" h_i) against a measure of discrepancy (the "studentized residuals" t_i). Leverage represents the degree to which individual observations can affect the fitted regression, while discrepancy represents the degree to which each observation departs from the pattern suggested by the rest of the data. Actual influence on the estimated regression coefficients is a product of leverage and discrepancy and is displayed on the graph by Cook's $D_i i$, represented by the areas of the plotted circles. The data for this graph are drawn from Duncan's (1961) regression of the rated prestige of forty-five occupations on the educational and income levels of the occupations. The plot suggests that two of the data points (the occupations "minister" and "conductor") may unduly affect the fitted regression.

Figure 14 is a scatterplot of residuals against fitted Y-values,

$$\hat{Y}_i = b_0 + b_1 x_{1i} + b_2 x_{2i} + \mathrm{K} + b_k x_{ki} \qquad (3)$$

where the b's are sample estimates of the corresponding ß's. If the error variance is constant as assumed, the variation of the residuals should not change systematically with the fitted values. The data for Figure 14 are drawn from work by Ornstein (1976) relating the number of interlocking directorate and executive positions maintained by 248 dominant Canadian corporations to characteristics of the firms. The plot reveals that the variation of the residuals appears to increase with the level of the fitted values, casting doubt on the assumption of constant error variance.

Figure 15 shows a partial residual (also called a component plus residual) plot for the relationship between occupational prestige and income, a diagnostic useful for detecting nonlinearity in regression. The plot is for a regression of the rated prestige of 102 Canadian occupations on the gender composition, income level, and educational level of the occupations (see Fox and Suschnigg

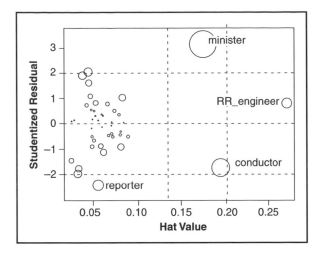

Figure 13. Influence plot for Duncan's regression of the rated prestige of forty-five occupations on their income and educational levels. The hat values measure the leverage of the observations in the regression, while the studentized residuals measure their discrepancy. The plotted circles have area proportional to Cook's D, a summary measure of influence on the regression coefficients. Horizontal lines are drawn at plus and minus 2; in well-behaved data, only about 5 percent of studentized residuals should be outside these lines. Vertical lines are drawn at two and three times the average hat value; hat values greater than two or three times the average are noteworthy. Observations that have relatively large residuals or leverages are identified on the plot.

1989). The partial residuals are formed as $e_{1i} = b_1 \chi_{1i} + e_i$, where b_1 is the fitted income coefficient in the linear regression, χ_{1i} is the average income of incumbents of occupation i, and e_i is the regression residual. The nonlinear pattern of the data, which is apparent in the graph, suggests modification of the regression model. Similar displays are available for generalized linear models such as logistic regression. Further information on the role of graphics in regression diagnostics can be found in Atkinson (1985), Fox (1991, 1997), and Cook and Weisberg (1994).

Scatterplots are sometimes difficult to interpret because of visual noise, uneven distribution of the data, or discreteness of the data values. Visually ambiguous plots often can be enhanced by smoothing the relationship between the variables, as in Figure 15. The curve drawn through this plot was determined by a procedure from

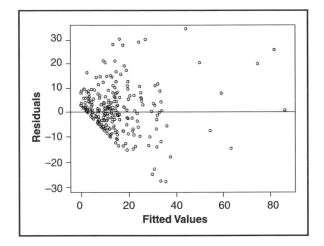

Figure 14. Plot of residuals by fitted values for Ornstein's regression on interlocks maintained by 248 dominant Canadian corporations on the characteristics of the firms. The manner in which the points line up diagonally at the lower left of the graph is due to the lower limit of zero for the dependent variable.

SOURCE: Personal communication from M. Ornstein.

Cleveland (1994) called *locally weighted scatterplot smoothing* ("lowess"). Lowess (also called "loess," for *local regression*) fits n robust regression lines to the data, with the ith such line emphasizing observations whose χ-values are closest to χ_i. The lowess fitted value for the ith observation, $\hat{y}_i$, comes from the ith such regression. Here x and y simply denote the horizontal and vertical variables in the plot. The curve plotted on Figure 15 connects the points $(\chi_i, \hat{y}_i)$. Lowess is one of many methods of nonparametric regression analysis, including methods for multiple regression, described, for example, in Hastie and Tibshirani (1990) and Fox (forthcoming a and b). Because there is no explicit equation for a nonparametric regression, the results are most naturally displayed graphically.

Scatterplots for discrete data may be enhanced by paradoxically adding a small amount of random noise to the data to separate the points in the plot. Cleveland (1994) calls this process "jittering." An example is shown in Figure 16a, which plots scores on a vocabulary test against years of education; the corresponding jittered plot (Figure 16b) reduces the overplotting of points, making the relationship much clearer and revealing other characteristics

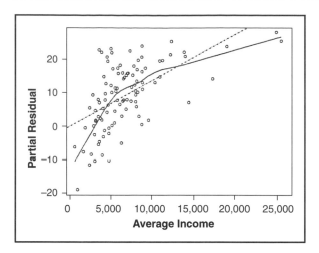

Figure 15. Partial residual (component+residual) plot for income in the regression of occupational prestige on the gender composition and income and education levels of 102 Canadian occupations in 1971. The broken line gives the linear least-squares fit, while the solid line shows the lowess (nonparametric regression) fit to the data.

SOURCE: Fox and Suschnigg (1989).

of the data, such as the concentration of points at twelve years of education.

Because graphs commonly are drawn on two-dimensional media such as paper and computer screens, the display of multivariate data is intrinsically more difficult than that of univariate or bivariate data. One solution to the problems posed by multivariate graphic representation is to record additional information on a two-dimensional plot. Symbols such as letters, shapes, degrees of fill, and color may be used to encode categorical information on a scatterplot, for example (see Figure 19, below). Similarly, there are many schemes for representing additional quantitative information, as shown in Figures 8 and 13.

A scatterplot matrix is the direct graphic analogue of a correlation matrix, displaying the bivariate relationship between each pair of a set of quantitative variables and thus providing a quick overview of the data. In contrast to a correlation matrix, however, a scatterplot matrix can reveal nonlinear relationships, outlying data, and so on. The scatterpiot matrix in Figure 17 is for rates of seven different categories of crime in the thirty largest U.S. cities (excluding Chicago) in 1996.

The regression curve shown in each scatterplot was determined by the lowess procedure described above.

A limitation of the scatterplot matrix is that it displays only the *marginal* relationships between the variables, while *conditional* (or *partial*) relationships are more often the focus of multivariate statistical analysis. This limitation sometimes can be overcome, however, by highlighting individual observations or groups of observations and following them across the several plots (see the discussion of "brushing" in Cleveland 1994). These methods are most effective when they are implemented as part of an interactive computer system for graphic data analysis.

One approach to displaying conditional relationships is to focus on the relationship between the dependent variable and each independent variable fixing the other independent variable (or variables) to particular, possibly overlapping ranges of values. A nonparametric regression smooth then can be fitted to each partial scatterplot. Cleveland (1993) calls this kind of display a "conditioning plot" or "coplot." The strategy breaks down, however, when there are more than two or three independent variables, or when the number of observations is small.

Many of the most useful graphical techniques for multivariate data rely on two-dimensional projections of the multivariate scatterplot of the data. A statistical model fitted to the data often determines these projections. An example of a display employing projection of higher-dimensional data is the partial residual plot shown in Figure 15. Another common application of this principle is the similarly named but distinct partial regression (or added-variable) plot. Here the dependent variable (Y) and one independent variable in the multiple regression model (say, x_1) are each regressed on the other independent variables in the model (i.e., $\chi_2, \ldots, \chi_k$), producing two sets of residuals (which may be denoted $y_{(1)}$ and $\chi_{(1)}$). A scatterplot of the residuals (that is, $y_{(1)}$ versus $\chi_{(1)}$) is frequently useful in revealing high-leverage and influential observations. Implementation on modern desktop computers, which can exploit color, shading, perspective, motion, and interactivity, permits the effective extension of projections to three dimensions (see Monette 1990; Cook and Weisberg 1994; Cook 1998).

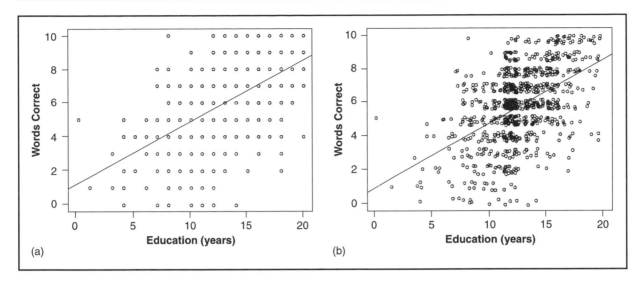

Figure 16. Randomly "jittering" a scatterplot to clarify discrete data. The original plot in (a) shows the relationship between score on a ten-item vocabulary test and years of education. The same data are graphed in (b) with a small random quantity added the each horizontal and vertical coordinate. Both graphs show the least-squares regression line.

SOURCE: 1989 General Social Survey, National Opinion Research Center.

When there are relatively few observations and each is of separate interest, it is possible to display multivariate data by constructing parallel geometric figures for the individual observations. Some feature of the figure encodes the value of each variable. One such display, called a "star plot," is shown in Figure 18 for the U.S. cities crime rate data. The cities are arranged in order of increasing general crime rate.

Other common and essentially similar schemes include "trees" (the branches of which represent the variables), faces (whose features encode the variables), and small bar graphs (in which each bar displays a variable). None of these graphs is particularly easy to read, but judicious ordering of observations and encoding of variables sometimes can suggest natural clusterings of the data or similarities between observations. Note in Figure 18, for example, that Oklahoma City and Jacksonville have roughly similar "patterns" of crime, even though the rates for Oklahoma City are generally higher. If similarities among the observations are of central interest, however, it may be better to address the issue directly by means of clustering or ordination (also called multidimensional scaling); see, e.g., Hartigan (1975), and Kruskal and Wish (1978).

THE PRESENT AND FUTURE OF STATISTICAL GRAPHICS

Computers have revolutionized the practice of statistical graphics much as they earlier revolutionized numerical statistics. Computers relieve the data analyst of the tedium of drawing graphs by hand and make possible displays—such as lowess scatterplot smoothing, kernel density estimation, and dynamic graphs—that previously were impractical or impossible. All the graphs in this article, with the exception of several from other sources, were prepared with widely available statistical software (most with *S-Plus*, the graphical and other capabilities of which are ably described by Venables and Ripley 1997). Virtually all general statistical computer packages provide facilities for drawing standard statistical graphs, and many provide specialized forms as well.

Dynamic and interactive statistical graphics, only a decade ago the province of high-performance graphics workstations and specialized software, are now available on inexpensive desktop computers. Figure 19 illustrates the application of Cook and Weisberg's (1999) state-of-the-art *Arc* package to Duncan's occupational prestige data.

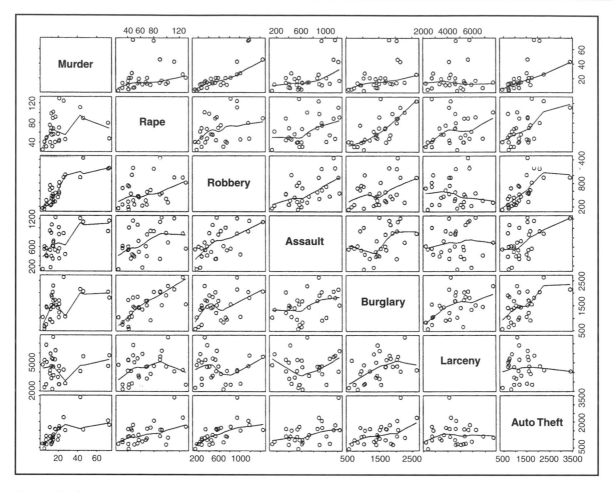

Figure 17. Scatterplot matrix for the rates of seven categories of crime in the thirty largest U.S. cities in 1996 (Chicago is omitted because of missing data). The rate labeled "Murder" represents both murder and manslaughter. The line shown in each panel is a lowess scatterplot smooth.

SOURCE: *Statistical Abstract of the United States: 1998.*

Arc, programmed in Tierney's (1990) *Lisp-Stat* statistical computing environment, is freely available software that runs on Windows computers, Macintoshes, and Unix workstations. Standard statistical packages such as *SAS* and *SPSS* are gradually acquiring these capabilities as well.

The other edge of the computing sword cuts in the direction of ugly, poorly constructed graphs that obfuscate rather than clarify data: Modern software facilitates the production of competent (if not beautiful) statistical graphs. Nevertheless, a data analyst armed with a "presentation graphics" package can, with little effort or thought and less taste, produce elaborate, difficult to read, and misleading graphs.

REFERENCES

Anscombe, Frank J. 1973 "Graphs in Statistical Analysis." *American Statistician* 27:17–22.

Atkinson, A. C. 1985 *Plots, Transformations, and Regression: An Introduction to Graphical Methods of Diagnostic Regression Analysis.* Oxford, UK: Clarendon Press.

Beninger, James R., and Dorothy L. Robyn 1978 "Quantitative Graphics in Statistics: A Brief History." *American Statistician* 32:1–11.

Bertin, Jacques 1973 *Semiologie graphique*, 2nd ed. Paris: Mouton.

Chambers, J. M., William S. Cleveland, Beat Kleiner, and Paul A. Tukey 1983 *Graphical Methods for Data Analysis.* Belmont Calif.: Wadsworth.

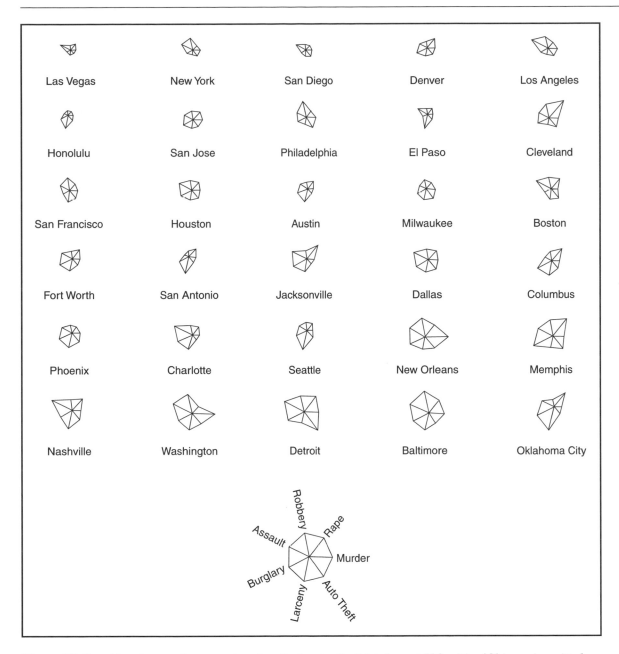

Figure 18. Star plot of rates of seven categories of crime in the thirty largest U.S. cities (Chicago is omitted because of missing data). The plot employs polar coordinates to represent each observation: Angles (the "points" of the star) encode variables, while distance from the origin (the center of the star) encodes the value of each variable. The crime rates were scaled (by range) before the graph was constructed. A key to the points of the star is shown at the bottom of the graph: "Murder" represents both murder and manslaughter.

SOURCE: *Statistical Abstract of the United States: 1998.*

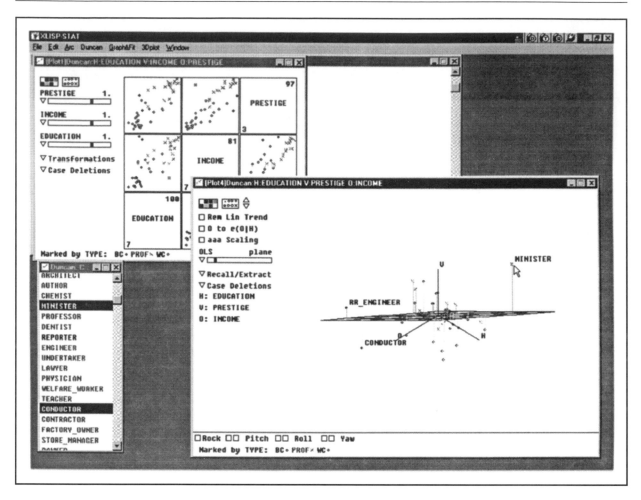

Figure 19. Modern statistical computer graphics: Cook and Weisberg's Arc. *The window in the foreground contains a rotating three-dimensional scatterplot of Duncan's occupational prestige data. The points in the plot are marked by type of occupation; a regression plane and residuals to the plane also are shown. Several occupations have been identified with a mouse. (The mouse cursor currently points at the occupation "minister.") To the left and bottom of the window, a variety of controls for manipulating the plot appear. The small window at the bottom left of the screen contains the names of the observations; note that this window is linked to the three-dimensional scatterplot. At the upper left, partly hidden, is a window containing a scatterplot matrix of the data, which also is linked to the other windows. Plot controls for this graph include power-transformation sidebars at the left of the window.*

Cleveland, William S. 1984 "Graphs in Scientific Publications." *American Statistician* 38:261–269.

—— 1993 *Visualizing Data*. Summit N.J.: Hobart Press.

—— 1994 *The Elements of Graphing Data*, rev. ed. Summit N.J.: Hobart Press.

——, and Robert McGill 1984 "Graphical Perception: Theory, Experimentation, and Application to the Development of Graphical Methods." *Journal of the American Statistical Association* 79:531–554.

Cook, R. Dennis 1998 *Regression Graphics: Ideas for Studying Regressions through Graphics*. New York: Wiley.

——, and Sanford Weisberg 1994 *An Introduction to Regression Graphics*. New York: Wiley.

—— 1999 *Applied Regression Including Computing and Graphics*. New York: Wiley.

Duncan, Otis Dudley 1961 "A Socioeconomic Index for All Occupations." In Albert J. Reiss, Jr., Otis Dudley Duncan, Paul K. Hatt, and Cecil C. North, eds., *Occupations and Social Status*. New York: Free Press.

Fox, John 1991 *Regression Diagnostics*. Newbury Park, Calif.: Sage.

——— 1997 *Applied Regression Analysis, Linear Models, and Related Methods*. Thousand Oaks, Calif.: Sage.

——— forthcoming (*a*) *Nonparametric Simple Regression: Scatterplot Smoothing*. Thousand Oaks, Calif.: Sage.

——— forthcoming (*b*) *Multiple and Generalized Nonparametric Regression*. Thousand Oaks, Calif.: Sage.

———, and Carole Suschnigg 1989 "A Note on Gender and the Prestige of Occupations." *Canadian Journal of Sociology* 14:353–360.

Funkhouser, H. Gray 1937 "Historical Development of the Graphical Representation of Statistical Data." *Osiris* 3:267–404.

Hartigan, John A. 1975 *Clustering Algorithms*. New York: Wiley.

Hastie, Trevor J., and Robert J. Tibshirani 1990 *Generalized Additive Models*. London: Chapman and Hall.

Huff, Darrell 1954 *How to Lie with Statistics*. New York: Norton.

Kruskal, Joseph B., and Myron Wish 1978 *Multidimensional Scaling*. Beverly Hills, Calif.: Sage.

Monette, Georges 1990 "Geometry of Multiple Regression and Interactive 3-D Graphics." In John Fox and J. Scott Long, eds., *Modern Methods of Data Analysis*. Newbury Park, Calif.: Sage.

Ornstein, Michael D. 1976 "The Boards and Executives of the Largest Canadian Corporations: Size, Composition, and Interlocks." *Canadian Journal of Sociology* 1:411–437.

Schmidt, Calvin F. 1983 *Graphics: Design Principles and Practices*. New York: Wiley.

Spence, Ian, and Stephan Lewandowsky 1990 "Graphical Perception." In John Fox and J. Scott Long, eds., *Modern Methods of Data Analysis*. Newbury Park, Calif.: Sage.

Tierney, Luke 1990. *Lisp-Stat: An Object-Oriented Environment for Statistical Computing and Dynamic Graphics*. New York: Wiley.

Tufte, Edward R. 1983 *The Visual Display of Quantitative Information*. Cheshire, Conn.: Graphics Press.

——— 1990 *Envisoning Information*. Cheshire, Conn.: Graphics Press.

——— 1997 *Visual Explanations: Images and Quantities, Evidence and Narrative*. Cheshire, Conn.: Graphics Press.

Tukey, John W. 1977 *Exploratory Data Analysis*. Reading, Mass.: Addison-Wesley.

Venables, W. N., and B. D. Ripley 1997 *Modern Applied Statistics with S-PLUS*, 2nd ed. New York: Springer-Verlag.

Wainer, Howard 1997. *Visual Revelations: Graphical Tales of Fate and Deception from Napoleon Bonaparte to Ross Perot*. New York: Springer-Verlag.

JOHN FOX

STATISTICAL INFERENCE

Making an inference involves drawing a general conclusion from specific observations. People do this every day. Upon arising in the morning, one observes that the sun is shining and that the day will be nice. The news reports the arrest of a military veteran for child abuse, and a listener infers that military veterans have special adjustment problems. Statistical inference is a way of formalizing the process of drawing general conclusions from limited information. It is a way of stating the degree of confidence one has in making an inference by using probability theory. Statistically based research allows people to move beyond speculation.

Suppose a sociologist interviews two husbands. Josh, whose wife is employed, does 50 percent of the household chores; Frank, whose wife does not work for pay, does 10 percent. Should the sociologist infer that husbands do more housework when their wives are employed? No. This difference could happen by chance with only two cases. However, what if 500 randomly selected husbands with employed wives average 50 percent of the chores and randomly selected husbands with nonemployed wives average 10 percent? Since this difference is not likely to occur by chance, the sociologist infers that husbands do more housework when their wives are employed for pay.

Researchers perform statistical inferences in three different ways. Assume that 60 percent of the respondents to a survey say they will vote for Marie Chavez. The *traditional hypothesis testing* approach infers that Chavez will win the election if chance processes would account for the result (60 percent support in this survey) with less than some a priori specified statistical significance level. For example, if random chance could account for the result fewer than five times in a hundred, one would say the results are statistically significant. Statistical significance levels are called the *alpha* (e.g., α = .05 for the 5 percent level). If Chavez would get 60 percent support in a sample of the size selected less than 5 percent of the time by chance, one would infer that she will win. The researcher picked the 5 percent level of significance before doing the survey. (The test, including the α level, must be planned *before* one looks at the findings.) If one would get this result 6 percent of the time by chance, there is no inference. Note that not making the inference means just that: One does not infer that Chavez's opponent will win.

A second strategy involves stating the *likelihood of the result occurring by chance* without an a priori level of significance. This strategy reports the result (60 percent of the sample supported Chavez) and the probability of getting that result by chance, say, .042. This gives readers the freedom to make their inferences using whatever level of significance they wish. Sam Jones, using the .01 level (α = .01) in the traditional approach would see that the results do not meet his criterion. He would not conclude that Chavez will win. Mara Jabar, using the .05 level, would conclude that Chavez would win.

The third strategy places a *confidence interval around a result*. For example, a researcher may be 95 percent confident that Chavez will get between 55 percent and 65 percent of the votes. Since the entire interval—55 percent to 65 percent—is enough for a victory, that is, is greater than 50 percent one infers that Chavez will win.

Each approach has an element of risk attached to the inference. That risk is the probability of getting the result by chance alone. Sociologists tend to pick low probabilities (e.g., .05, .01, and even .001), because they do not want to conclude that something is true when it is at all likely to have occurred by chance.

TRADITIONAL TESTS OF SIGNIFICANCE

Traditional tests of significance involve six steps. Three examples are used here to illustrate these steps: (1) A candidate will win an election, (2) mothers with at least one daughter will have different views on abortion than will mothers with only sons, and (3) the greater a person's internal political efficacy is, the more likely that person is to vote.

Step 1: State a hypotheses (H_1) in terms of statistical parameters (characteristics such as means, correlations, proportions) of the population:

H1: P(vote for the candidate) $<$ .50. [Read: The mean for mothers with daughters is not equal to the mean for mothers with sons.]

H2: μ mothers with daughters $\neq$ μ mothers with sons. [Read: The means for mothers with daughters is not equal to the mean for mothers with sons.]

H3: ρ $<$ 0.0. [Read: The population correlation ρ (rho) between internal political efficacy and voting is greater than zero.]

H2 says that the means are different but does not specify the direction of the difference. This is a two-tail hypothesis, meaning that it can be significant in either direction. In contrast, *H1* and *H2* signify the direction of the difference and are called one-tail hypotheses.

These three hypotheses are not directly testable because each involves a range of values. *Step 2* states a null hypothesis, which the researcher usually wishes to reject, that has a specific value.

H1$_0$: P(vote for the candidate) = .50.

H2$_0$: μ mothers with daughters = μ mothers with sons.

H3$_0$: ρ = 0.

An important difference between one-tail and two-tail tests may have crossed the reader;s mind. Consider *H1$_0$*. If 40 percent of the sample supported the candidate, one fails to reject *H1$_0$* because the result was in the direction opposite of that of the one-tail hypothesis. In contrast, whether mothers with daughters have a higher or lower mean attitude toward abortion than do mothers with sons, one proceeds to test *H2$_0$* because a difference in either direction could be significant.

Step 3 states the a priori level of significance. Sociologists usually use the .05 level. With large samples, they sometimes use the .01 or .001 level. This paper uses the .05 level (α = .05). If the result would occur in fewer than 5 percent (corresponding to the .05 level) of the samples if the null hypothesis were true in the population, the null hypothesis is rejected in favor of the main hypothesis.

Suppose the sample correlation between internal political efficacy and voting is .56 and this would occur in fewer than 5 percent of the samples this size if the population correlation were 0 (as specified in $H3_0$). One rejects the null hypothesis, $H3_0$, and accepts the main hypothesis, $H3$, that the variables are correlated in the population. What if the sample correlation were .13 and a correlation this large would occur in 25 percent of the samples from a population in which the true correlation were 0? Because 25 percent exceeds the a priori significance level of 5 percent, the null hypothesis is not rejected. One cannot infer that the variables are correlated in the population. Simultaneously, the results do not prove that the population correlation is .00, simply that it could be that value.

Step 4 selects a test statistic and its critical value. Common test statistics include z, t, F, and χ^2 (chi-square). The *critical value* is the value the test statistic must exceed to be significant at the level specified in step 3. For example, using a one-tail hypothesis, a z must exceed 1.645 to be significant at the .05 level. Using a two-tail hypothesis, a z, must exceed 1.96 to be significant at the .05 level. For t, F, and χ^2, determining the critical value is more complicated because one needs to know the degrees of freedom. A formal understanding of degrees of freedom is beyond the scope of this article, but an example will give the reader an intuitive idea. If the mean of five cases is 4 and four of the cases have values of 1, 4, 5, and 2, the last case must have a value of 8 (it is the only value for the fifth case that will give a mean of 4, since $1 + 4 + 5 + 2 + x = 20$, only if $x = 8$ and $20/5 = 4$). Thus, there are $n - 1$ degrees of freedom. Most test statistics have different distributions for each number of degrees of freedom.

Figure 1 illustrates the z distribution. Under the z distribution, an absolute value of greater than 1.96 will occur by chance only 5 percent of the time. By chance a $z > 1.96$ occurs 2.5 percent of the time and a $z < -1.96$ occurs 2.5 percent of the time. Thus, 1.96 is the critical z-score for a two-tail .05 level test. The critical z-score for a one-tail test at the .05 level is 1.645 or -1.645, depending on the direction specified in the main hypothesis.

Step 5 computes the test statistic. An example appears below.

Step 6 decides whether to reject or fail to reject the null hypothesis. If the computed test statistic exceeds the critical value, one rejects the null hypothesis and makes the inference to accept the main hypothesis. If the computed test statistic does not exceed the critical value, one fails to reject the null hypothesis and make no inference.

Example of Six Steps Applied to *H1*. A random sample of 200 voters shows 60 percent of them supporting the candidate. Having stated the main hypothesis (step 1) and the null hypothesis (step 2), step 3 selects an a priori significance level at $\alpha = .05$, since this is the conventional level. Step 4 selects the test statistic and its critical level. To test a single percentage, a z test is used (standard textbooks on social statistics discuss how to select the appropriate tests statistics; see Agresti and Finlay 1996; Loether and McTavish 1993; Raymondo 1999; Vaughan 1997). Since the hypothesis is one-tail, the critical value is 1.645 (see Figure 1).

The fifth step computes the formula for the test statistic:

$$z = \frac{p_s - p}{\sqrt{\dfrac{pq}{n}}}$$

where p_s is the proportion in the sample

p is the proportion in the population under H_0

q is $1 - p$

n is the number of people in the sample.

Thus,

$$z = \frac{.6 - .5}{\sqrt{(.5 \times .5)/200}}$$

$$z = 2.828$$

The sixth step makes the decision to reject the null hypothesis, since the difference is in the predicted direction and $2.828 > 1.645$. The statistical inference is that the candidate will win the election.

REPORTING THE PROBABILITY LEVEL

Many sociological researchers do not use the traditional null hypothesis model. Instead, they report the probability of the result. This way, a reader knows the probability (say, .042 or .058) rather than the significant versus not significant status. Reporting the probability level removes the "magic

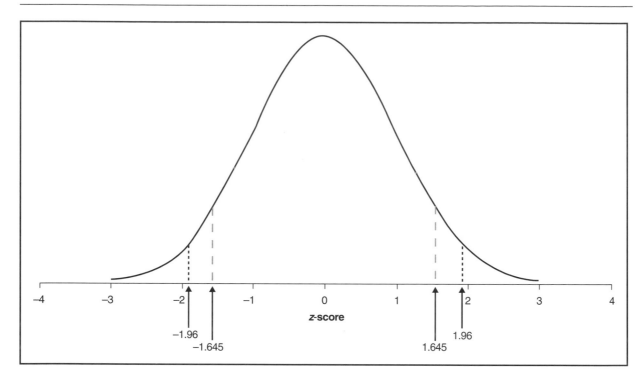

Figure 1. Normal deviate (z) distribution.

of the level of significance." A result that is significant at the .058 level is not categorically different from one that is significant at the .042 level. Where the traditional null hypothesis approach says that the first of these results is not significant and the second is, reporting the probability tells the reader that there is only a small difference in the degree of confidence attached to the two results. Critics of this strategy argue that the reader may adjust the significance level post hoc; that is, the reader may raise or lower the level of significance after seeing the results. It also is argued that it is the researcher, not the reader, who is the person testing the hypotheses; therefore, the researcher is responsible for selecting an a priori level of significance.

The strategy of reporting the probability is illustrated for *H1*. Using the tabled values or functions in standard statistical packages, the one-tail probability of a $z = 2.828$ is .002. The researcher reports that the candidate had 60 percent of the vote in the sample and that the probability of getting that much support by chance is .002. This provides more information than does simply saying that it is significant at the .05 level. Results that could happen only twice in 1,000 times by chance

(.002) are more compelling than are results that could happen five times in 100 (.05).

Since journal editors want to keep papers short and studies often include many tests of significance, reporting probabilities is far more efficient than going through the six-step process outlined above. The researcher must go through these steps, but the paper merely reports the probability for each test and places an asterisk along those which are significant at the .05 level. Some researchers place a single asterisk for results significant at the .05 level, two asterisks for results significant at the .01 level, and three asterisks for results significant at the .001 level.

CONFIDENCE INTERVALS

Rather than reporting the significance of a result, this approach puts a confidence interval around the result. This provides additional information in terms of the width of the confidence interval.

Using a confidence interval, a person constructs a range of values such that he or she is 95 percent confident (some use a 99 percent confidence interval) that the range contains the population parameter. The confidence interval uses a two-tail approach on the assumption that the population value can be either above or below the sample value.

For the election example, *H1*, the confidence interval is

$$p_s \pm z_{a/2} \sqrt{\frac{pq}{n}}$$

where $z_{a/2}$ is the two-tail critical value for the alpha level

p_s is the proportion in the sample

p is the proportion in the population under H_0

q is $1 - p$

n is the number of people in the sample

$$= .6 \pm 1.96 \sqrt{\frac{.5 \times .5}{200}}$$

$$= .6 \pm 1.96 \times .03535$$

$$= .6 \pm .0693$$

| upper limit | .669 |
| lower limit | .531 |

The researcher is 95 percent confident that the interval, .531 to .669, contains the true population proportion. The focus is on the confidence level (.95) for a result rather than the low likelihood of the null hypothesis (.05) used in the traditional null hypothesis testing approach.

The confidence interval has more information value than do the first two approaches. Since the value specified in the null hypothesis (H_0: P = .50) is not in the confidence interval, the result is statistically significant at the .05 level. Note that a 95 percent confidence level corresponds to a .05 level of significance and that a 99 percent confidence interval corresponds to a .01 level of significance. Whenever the value specified by the null hypothesis is not in the confidence interval, the result is statistically significant. More important, the confidence interval provides an estimate of the range of possible values for the population. With 200 cases and 60 percent support, there is confidence that the candidate will win, although it may be a close election with the lower limit indicating 53.1 per-

cent of the vote or a landslide with the upper limit indicating 66.9 percent of the vote. If the sample were four times as large, $n = 800$, the confidence interval would be half as wide (.565–.635) and would give a better fix on the outcome.

COMPUTATION OF TESTS AND CONFIDENCE INTERVALS

Table 1 presents formulas for some common tests of significance and their corresponding confidence intervals where appropriate. These are only a sample of the tests that are commonly used, but they cover means, differences of means, proportions, differences of proportions, contingency tables, and correlations. Not included are a variety of multivariate tests for analysis of variance, regression, path analysis, and structural equation models. The formulas shown in Table 1 are elaborated in most standard statistics textbooks (Agresti and Finlay 1996; Blalock 1979; Bohrnstedt and Knoke 1998: Loether and McTavish 1993; Raymondo 1999; Vaughan 1997).

LOGIC OF STATISTICAL INFERENCE

A formal treatment of the logic of statistical inference is beyond the scope of this article; the following is a simplified description. Suppose one wants to know whether a telephone survey can be thought of as a random sample. From current census information, suppose the mean, μ, income of the community is $31,800 and the standard deviation, σ, is $12,000. A graph of the complete census enumeration appears in Panel A of Figure 2. The fact that there are a few very wealthy people skews the distribution.

A telephone survey included interviews with 1,000 households. If it is random, its sample mean and standard deviation should be close to the population parameters, μ and σ, respectively. Assume that the sample has a mean of $33,200 and a standard deviation of $10,500. To distinguish these sample statistics from the population parameters, call them *M* and *s*. The sample distribution appears in Panel B by Figure 2. Note that it is similar to the population distribution but is not as smooth.

One cannot decide whether the sample could be random by looking at Panels A and B. The distributions are different, but this difference might

Common Tests of Significance Formulas

What is Being Tested?	H_1	H_0	Test Statistic	Large-Scale Confidence Interval
Single mean against value specified as χ in H_o	1-tail: $\mu > \chi$ 2-tail: $\mu \neq \chi$	$\mu = \chi$	t with $n-1$ degrees of freedom $t = \dfrac{M - \chi}{s/\sqrt{n}}$	$M \pm t_{\alpha/2}\sigma/\sqrt{n}$
Single proportion against value specified as χ in H_o	1-tail: $P > \chi$ 2-tail: $P \neq \chi$	$P = \chi$	$z = \dfrac{P_{s-\chi}}{\sqrt{\Gamma Q/N}}$	$P_s \pm z_{\alpha/2}\sqrt{\dfrac{PQ}{n}}$
Difference between two means	1-tail: $\mu_1 > \mu_2$ 2-tail: $\mu_1 \neq \mu_2$	$\mu_1 = \mu_2$	t with $n_1 + n_1$ degrees of freedom: $t = \dfrac{M_1 - M_2}{\sqrt{s^2\left(\frac{1}{n_1} + \frac{1}{n_2}\right)}}$, where $s^2 =$ $\dfrac{(n_1-1)s_1^2 + (n_2-1)s_2^2}{n_1 + n_2 - 2}$	$M_1 - M_2 \pm t_{\alpha/2}\sigma_{M_1-M_2}$ where $\sigma_{M_1-M_2}$ is defined as the denominator of the t- test in the cell to the immediate left
Difference between two proportions	1-tail: $P_1 > P_2$ 2-tail: $P_1 \neq P_2$	$P_1 = P_2$	$z = \dfrac{Ps_1 - Ps_2}{\sqrt{PQ}\sqrt{\frac{n_1+n_2}{n_1 n_2}}}$	$Ps_1 - Ps_2 \pm z_{\alpha/2}\sigma_{Ps_1-Ps_2}$ where $\sigma_{Ps_1-Ps_2}$ is defined as the numerator of the z- test in the cell to the immediate left
Significance of contingency table	The level on one variable depends on the level on the second variable	No dependency between the variables	$\chi^2 = \dfrac{\Sigma(F_o - F_e)^2}{F_e}$	Not applicable
Single correlation	1-tail $\rho > 0$ 2-tail $\rho \neq 0$	$\rho = 0$	F with 1 and $n-2$ degrees of freedom: $F = \dfrac{r^2(n-2)}{1-r^2}$	Complex, since it is not symmetrical

Table 1

have occurred by chance. Statistical inference is accomplished by introducing two theoretical distributions: the sampling distribution of the mean and the z-distribution of the normal deviate. A theoretical distribution is different from the population and sample distributions in that a theoretical distribution is mathematically derived; it is not observed directly.

Sampling Distribution of the Mean. Suppose that instead of taking a single random sample of 1,000 people, one took two such samples and determined the mean of each one. With 1,000 cases, it is likely that the two samples would have means that were close together but not the same. For instance, the mean of the second sample might be $30,200. These means, $33,200 and $30,200, are pretty close to each other. For a sample to have a mean of, say $11,000, it would have to include a

greatly disproportionate share of poor families; this is not likely by chance with a random sample with $n = 1,000$. For a sample to have a mean of, say, $115,000, it would have to have a greatly disproportionate share of rich families. In contrast, with a sample of just two individuals, one would not be surprised if the first person had an income of $11,000 and the second had an income of $115,000.

The larger the samples are, the more stable the mean is from one sample to the next. With only 20 people in the first and second samples, the means may vary a lot, but with 100,000 people in both samples, the means should be almost identical. Mathematically, it is possible to derive a distribution of the means of all possible samples of a given n even though only a single sample is observed. It can be shown that the mean of the

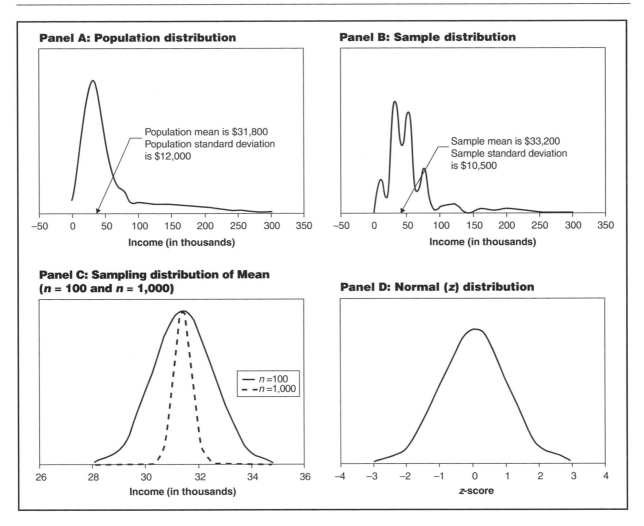

Figure 2. Four distributions used in statistical inference: (A) population distribution; (B) sample distribution; sampling distribution for n=100 and n=1,000; and (D) normal deviate (z) distributions

sampling distribution of means is the population mean and that the standard deviation of the sampling distribution of the means is the population standard deviation divided by the square root of the sample size. The standard deviation of the mean is called the *standard error of the mean:*

$$\text{Standard error of the mean (SEM)} = \sigma_M = \frac{\sigma}{\sqrt{n}}$$

This is an important derivation in statistical theory. Panel C shows the sampling distribution of the mean when the sample size is $n = 1,000$. It also shows the sampling distribution of the mean for $n = 100$. A remarkable property of the sampling distribution of the mean is that with a large sample

size, it will be normally distributed even though the population and sample distributions are skewed.

One gets a general idea of how the sample did by seeing where the sample mean falls along the sampling distribution of the mean. Using Panel C for $n = 1,000$, the sample $M = \$33,200$ is a long way from the population mean. Very few samples with $n = 1,000$ would have means this far way from the population mean. Thus, one infers that the sample mean probably is based on a nonrandom sample.

Using the distribution in Panel C for the smaller sample size, $n = 100$, the sample $M = \$33,200$ is not so unusual. With 100 cases, one should not be surprised to get a sample mean this far from the population mean.

Being able to compare the sample mean to the population mean by using the sampling distribution is remarkable, but statistical theory allows more precision. One can transform the values in the sampling distribution of the mean to a distribution of a test statistic. The appropriate test statistic is the distribution of the normal deviate, or z-distribution. It can be shown that

$$z = \frac{M - \mu}{\sigma/\sqrt{n}}$$

If the z-value were computed for the mean of all possible samples taken at random from the population, it would be distributed as shown in Panel D of Figure 2. It will be normal, have a mean of zero, and have a variance of 1.

Where is $M = \$33,200$ under the distribution of the normal deviate using the sample size of $n = 1,000$? Its z-score using the above formula is

$$z = \frac{33,200 - 31,800}{12,000/\sqrt{1,000}}$$
$$= 3.689$$

Using tabled values for the normal deviate, the probability of a random sample of 1,000 cases from a population with a mean of $31,800 having a sample mean of $33,200 is less than .001. Thus, it is extremely unlikely that the sample is purely random.

With the same sample mean but with a sample of only 100 people,

$$z = \frac{33,200 - 31,800}{12,000/\sqrt{100}}$$
$$= 1.167$$

Using tabled values for a two-tail test, the probability of getting the sample mean this far from the population mean with a sample of 100 people is .250. One should not infer that the sample is nonrandom, since these results could happen 25 percent of the time by chance.

The four distributions can be described for any sample statistic one wants to test (means, differences of means, proportions, differences of proportions, correlations, etc). While many of the calculations will be more complex, their logic is identical.

MULTIPLE TESTS OF SIGNIFICANCE

The logic of statistical inference applies to testing a single hypothesis. Since most studies include multiple tests, interpreting results can become extremely complex. If a researcher conducts 100 tests, 5 of them should yield results that are statistically significant at the .05 level by chance. Therefore, a study that includes many tests may find some "interesting" results that appear statistically significant but that really are an artifact of the number of tests conducted.

Sociologists pay less attention to "adjusting the error rate" than do those in most other scientific fields. A conservative approach is to divide the Type I error by the number of tests conducted. This is known as the Dunn multiple comparison test, based on the Bonferroni inequality. For example, instead of doing nine tests at the .05 level, each test is done at the $.05/9 = .006$ level. To be viewed as statistically significant at the .05 level, each specific test must be significant at the .006 level.

There are many specialized multiple comparison procedures, depending on whether the tests are planned before the study starts or after the results are known. Brown and Melamed (1990) describe these procedures.

POWER AND TYPE I AND TYPE II ERRORS

To this point, only one type of probability has been considered. Sociologists use statistical inference to minimize the chance of accepting a main hypothesis that is false in the population. They reject the null hypothesis only if the chances of it's being true in the population are very small, say, $\alpha = .05$. Still, by minimizing the chances of this error, sociologists increase the chance of failing to reject the null hypothesis when it should be rejected. Table 2 illustrates these two types of error.

Type I, or α, error is the probability of rejecting H_0 falsely, that is, the error of deciding that H_1 is right when H_0 is true in the population. If one were testing whether a new program reduced drug abuse among pregnant women, the H_1 would be that the program did this and the H_0 would be that the program was no better than the existing one. Type I error should be minimized because it would be wrong to change programs when the new program was no better than the existing one. Type I

Type I (α) and Type II (β) Errors

Decision Made by the Researcher	True Situation in the Population	
	H_0, the null hypothesis, is true	H_1, the main hypothesis, is true
H_0, the null hypothesis is true	$1 - \alpha$	β
H_r, the main hypothesis is true	α	$1 - \beta$

Table 2

error has been described as "the chances of discovering things that aren't so" (Cohen 1990, p. 1304). The focus on Type I error reflects a conservative view among scientists. Type I error guards against doing something new (as specified by H_1) when it is not going to be helpful.

Type II, or ß, error is the probability of failing to reject H_0 when H_1 is true in the population. If one failed to reject the null hypothesis that the new program was no better (H_0) when it was truly better (H_1), one would put newborn children at needless risk. Type II error is the chance of missing something new (as specified by H_1) when it really would be helpful.

Power is $1 - \beta$. Power measures the likelihood of rejecting the null hypothesis when the alternative hypothesis is true. Thus, if there is a real effect in the population, a study that has a power of .80 can reject the null hypothesis with a likelihood of .80. The power of a statistical test is measured by how likely it is to do what one usually wants to do: demonstrate support for the main hypothesis when the main hypothesis is true. Using the example of a treatment for drug abuse among pregnant women, the power of a test is the ability to demonstrate that the program is effective if this is really true.

Power can be increased. First, get a larger sample. The larger the sample, the more power to find results that exist in the population. Second, increase the α level. Rather than using the .01 level of significance, a researcher can pick the .05 or even the .10. The larger α is, the more powerful the test is in its ability to reject the null hypothesis when the alternative is true.

There are problems with both approaches. Increasing sample size makes the study more costly. If there are risks to the subjects who participate,

adding cases exposes additional people to that risk. An example of this would be a study that exposed subjects to a new drug treatment program that might create more problems than it solved. A larger sample will expose more people to these risks.

Since Type I and Type II errors are inversely related, raising α reduces ß thus increasing the power of the test. However, sociologists are hesitant to raise α since doing so increases the chance of deciding something is important when it is not important. With a small sample, using a small α level such as .001 means there is a great risk of ß error. Many small-scale studies have a Type II error of over .50. This is common in research areas that rely on small samples. For example, a review of one volume of the *Journal of Abnormal Psychology* (this journal includes many small-sample studies) found that those studies average Type II error of .56 (Cohen 1990). This means the psychologist had inadequate power to reject the null hypothesis when H_1 was true. When H_1 was true, the chance of rejecting H_0 (i.e., power) was worse than that resulting from flipping a coin.

Some areas that rely on small samples because of the cost of gathering data or to minimize the potential risk to subjects require researchers to plan their sample sizes to balance α, power, sample size, and the minimum size of effect that is theoretically important. For example, if a correlation of .1 is substantively significant, a power of .80 is important, and an $\alpha = .01$ is desired, a very large sample is required. If a correlation is substantively and theoretically important only if it is over .5, a much smaller sample is adequate. Procedures for doing a power analysis are available in Cohen (1988); see also Murphy and Myous (1998).

Power analysis is less important for many sociological studies that have large samples. With a large sample, it is possible to use a conservative α error rate and still have sufficient power to reject the null hypothesis when H_1 is true. Therefore, sociologists pay less attention to ß error and power than do researchers in fields such as medicine and psychology. When a sociologist has a sample of 10,000 cases, the power is over .90 that he or she will detect a very small effect as statistically significant. When tests are extremely powerful to detect small effects, researchers must focus on the substantive significance of the effects. A correlation of

.07 may be significant at the .05 level with 10,000 cases, but that correlation is substantively trivial.

STATISTICAL AND SUBSTANTIVE SIGNIFICANCE

Some researchers and many readers confuse statistical significance with substantive significance. Statistical inference does not ensure substantive significance, that is, ensure that the result is important. A correlation of .1 shows a weak relationship between two variables whether it is statistically significant or not. With a sample of 100 cases, this correlation will not be statistically significant; with a sample of 10,000 cases, it will be statistically significant. The smaller sample shows a weak relationship that might be a zero relationship in the population. The larger sample shows a weak relationship that is all but certainly a weak relationship in the population, although it is not zero. In this case, the statistical significance allows one to be confident that the relationship in the population is substantively weak.

Whenever a person reads that a result is statistically significant, he or she is confident that there is some relationship. The next step is to decide whether it is substantively significant or substantively weak. Power analysis is one way to make this decision. One can illustrate this process by testing the significance of a correlation. A population correlation of .1 is considered weak, a population correlation of .3 is considered moderate, and a population correlation of .5 or more is considered strong. In other words, if a correlation is statistically significant but .1 or lower, one has to recognize that this is a weak relationship—it is statistically significant but substantively weak. It is just as important to explain to the readers that the relationship is substantively weak as it is to report that it is statistically significant. By contrast, if a sample correlation is .5 and is statistically significant, one can say the relationship is both statistically and substantively significant.

Figure 3 shows power curves for testing the significance of a correlation. These curves illustrate the need to be sensitive to both statistical significance and substantive significance. The curve on the extreme left shows the power of a test to show that a sample correlation, r, is statistically significant when the population correlation, ρ (rho), is .5. With a sample size of around 100, the power

of a test to show statistical significance approaches 1.0, or 100 percent. This means that any correlation that is this strong in the population can be shown to be statistically significant with a small sample.

What happens when the correlation in the population is weak? Suppose the true correlation in the population is .2. A sample with 500 cases almost certainly will produce a sample correlation that is statistically significant, since the power is approaching 1.0. Many sociological studies have 500 or more cases and produce results showing that substantively weak relationships, $\rho = .2$, are statistically significant. Figure 3 shows that even if the population correlation is just .1, a sample of 1,000 cases has the power to show a sample result that is statistically significant. Thus, any time a sample is 1,000 or larger, one has to be especially careful to avoid confusing statistical and substantive significance.

The guidelines for distinguishing between statistical and substantive significance are direct but often are ignored by researchers:

1. If a result is not statistically significant, regardless of its size in the sample, one should be reluctant to generalize it to the population.

2. If a result is statistically significant in the sample, this means that one can generalize it to the population but does not indicate whether it is a weak or a strong relationship.

3. If a result is statistically significant and strong in the sample, one can both generalize it to the population and assert that it is substantively significant.

4. If a result is statistically significant and weak in the sample, one can both generalize it to the population and assert that it is substantively weak in the population.

This reasoning applies to any test of significance. If a researcher found that girls have an average score of 100.2 on verbal skills and boys have an average score of 99.8, with girls and boys having a standard deviation of 10, one would think this as a very weak relationship. If one constructed a histogram for both girls and boys, one would find them almost identical. This difference is not substantively significant. However, if there was a sufficiently

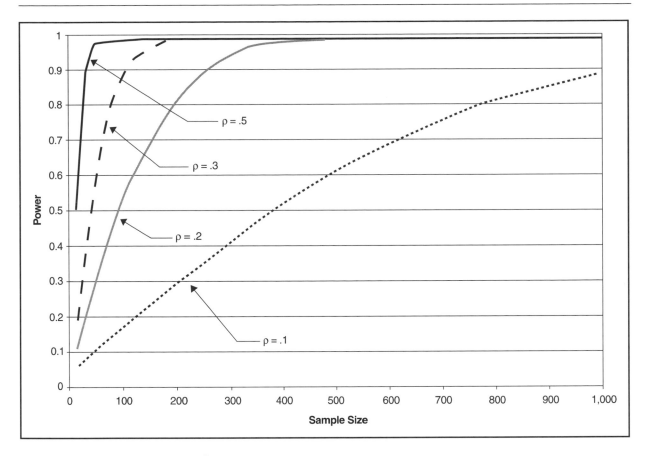

Figure 3. Power of test of r, α = .05

large sample of girls and boys, say, $n = 10,000$, it could be shown that the difference is statistically significant. The statistical significance means that there is some difference, that the means for girls and boys are not identical. It is necessary to use judgment, however, to determine that the difference is substantively trivial. An abuse of statistical inference that can be committed by sociologists who do large-scale research is to confuse statistical and substantive significance.

NONRANDOM SAMPLES AND STATISTICAL INFERENCE

Very few researchers use true random samples. Sometimes researchers use convenience sampling. An example is a social psychologist who has every student in a class participate in an experiment. The students in this class are not a random sample of the general population or even of students in a university. Should statistical inference be used here?

Other researchers may use the entire population. If one wants to know if male faculty members are paid more than female faculty members at a particular university, one may check the payroll for every faculty member. There is no sample—one has the entire population. What is the role of statistical inference in this instance?

Many researchers would use a test of significance in both cases, although the formal logic of statistical inference is violated. They are taking a "what if" approach. If the results they find could have occurred by a random process, they are less confident in their results than they would be if the results were statistically significant. Economists and demographers often report statistical inference results when they have the entire population. For example, if one examines the unemployment rates of blacks and whites over a ten-year period, one may find that the black rate is about twice the white rate. If one does a test of significance, it is unclear what the population is to which one wants to generalize. A ten-year period is not a random selection of all years. The rationale for doing statistical inference with population data and nonprobability samples is to see if the results could have been attributed to a chance process.

A related problem is that most surveys use complex sample designs rather than strictly random designs. A stratified sample or a clustered sample may be used to increase efficiency or reduce the cost of a survey. For example, a study might take a random sample of 20 high schools from a state and then interview 100 students from each of those schools. This survey will have 2,000 students but will not be a random sample because the 100 students from each school will be more similar to each other than to 100 randomly selected students. For instance, the 100 students from a school in a ghetto may mostly have minority status and mostly be from families that have a low income in a population with a high proportion of single-parent families. By contrast, 100 students from a school in an affluent suburb may be disproportionately white and middle class.

The standard statistical inference procedures discussed here that are used in most introductory statistics texts and in computer programs such as SAS and SPSS assume random sampling. When a different sampling design is used, such as a cluster design, a stratified sample, or a longitudinal design, the test of significance will be biased. In most cases, the test of significance will underestimate the standard errors and thus overestimate the test statistic (z, t, F). The extent to which this occurs is known as the "design effect." The most typical design effect is greater than 1.0, meaning that the computed test statistic is larger than it should be. Specialized programs allow researchers to estimate design effects and incorporate them in the computation of the test statistics. The most widely used of these procedures are WesVar, which is available from SPSS, and SUDAAN, a stand-alone program. Neither program has been widely used by sociologists, but their use should increase in the future.

REFERENCES

Agresti, Alan, and Barbara Finlay 1996 *Statistical Methods for the Social Sciences*. Englewood Cliffs, N.J.: Prentice-Hall.

Blalock, Hubert M., Jr. 1979 *Social Statistics*. New York: McGraw-Hill.

Bohrnstedt, George W., and David Knoke 1988 *Statistics for Social Data Analysis*, 2nd ed. Itasca, Ill.: F.E. Peakcock.

Brown, Steven R., and Lawrence E. Melamed 1990 *Experimental Design and Analysis*. Newbury Park, Calif.: Sage.

Cohen, Jacob 1988 *Statistical Power Analysis for the Behavioral Sciences*, 2nd ed. Hillsdale, N.J.: Erlbaum.

—— 1990 "Things I Have Learned (So Far)." *American Psychologist* 45:1304–1312.

Loether, Herman J., and Donald G. McTavish 1993 *Descriptive and Inferential Statistics*. New York: Allyn and Bacon.

Murphy, Kelvin R., and Brentt Myous, eds. 1998 *Statistical Power Analysis: A Simple and Graphic Model for Traditional and Modern Hypothesis Tests*. Hillsdale, N.J.: Erlbaum.

Raymondo, James 1999 *Statistical Analysis in the Social Sciences*. New York: McGraw-Hill.

Vaughan, Eva D. 1997 *Statistics: Tools for Understanding Data in Behavioral Sciences*. Englewood Cliffs, N.J.: Prentice-Hall.

ALAN C. ACOCK

STATISTICAL METHODS

In the 1960s, the introduction, acceptance, and application of multivariate statistical methods transformed quantitative sociological research. Regression methods from biometrics and economics; factor analysis from psychology; stochastic modeling from engineering, biometrics, and statistics; and methods for contingency table analysis from sociology and statistics were developed and combined to provide a rich variety of statistical methods. Along with the introduction of these techniques came the institutionalization of quantitative methods. In 1961, the American Sociological Association (ASA) approved the Section on Methodology as a result of efforts organized by Robert McGinnis and Albert Reiss. The ASA's yearbook, *Sociological Methodology*, first appeared in 1969 under the editorship of Edgar F. Borgatta and George W. Bohrnstedt. Those editors went on to establish the quarterly journal *Sociological Methods and Research* in 1972. During this period, the National Institute of Mental Health began funding training programs that included rigorous training in quantitative methods.

This article traces the development of statistical methods in sociology since 1960. Regression, factor analysis, stochastic modeling, and contingency table analysis are discussed as the core methods that were available or were introduced by the early 1960s. The development of additional methods through the enhancement and combination of these methods is then considered. The discussion emphasizes statistical methods for causal modeling; consequently, methods for data reduction (e.g., cluster analysis, smallest space analysis), formal modeling, and network analysis are not considered.

THE BROADER CONTEXT

By the end of the 1950s, the central ideas of mathematical statistics that emerged from the work of R. A. Fisher and Karl Pearson were firmly established. Works such as Fisher's *Statistical Methods for Research Workers* (1925), Kendall's *Advanced Theory of Statistics* (1943, 1946), Cramér's *Mathematical Methods of Statistics* (1946), Wilks's *Mathematical Statistics* (1944), Lehman's *Testing Statistical Hypotheses* (1959), Scheffé's *The Analysis of Variance* (1959), and Doob's *Stochastic Processes* (1953) systematized the key results of mathematical statistics and provided the foundation for developments in applied statistics for decades to come. By the start of the 1960s, multivariate methods were applied routinely in psychology, economics, and the biological sciences. Applied treatments were available in works such as Snedecor's *Statistical Methods* (1937), Wold's *Demand Analysis* (Wold and Juréen, 1953), Anderson's *An Introduction to Multivariate Statistical Analysis* (1958), Simon's *Models of Man* (1957), Thurstone's *Multiple-Factor Analysis* (1947), and Finney's *Probit Analysis* (1952).

These methods are computationally intensive, and their routine application depended on developments in computing. BMD (Biomedical Computing Programs) was perhaps the first widely available statistical package, appearing in 1961 (Dixon et al. 1981). SPSS (Statistical Package for the Social Sciences) appeared in 1970 as a result of efforts by a group of political scientists at Stanford to develop a general statistical package specifically for social scientists (Nie et al. 1975). In addition to these general-purpose programs, many specialized programs appeared that were essential for the methods discussed below. At the same time, continuing advances in computer hardware increased the availability of computing by orders of magnitude, facilitating the adoption of new statistical methods.

DEVELOPMENTS IN SOCIOLOGY

It is within the context of developments in mathematical statistics, sophisticated applications in other fields, and rapid advances in computing that major changes occurred in quantitative sociological research. Four major methods serve as the cornerstones for later developments: regression, factor analysis, stochastic processes, and contingency table analysis.

Regression Analysis and Structural Equation Models. Regression analysis is used to estimate the effects of a set of independent variables on one or more dependent variables. It is arguably the most commonly applied statistical method in the social sciences. Before 1960, this method was relatively unknown to sociologists. It was not treated in standard texts and was rarely seen in the leading sociological journals. The key notions of multiple regression were introduced to sociologists in Blalock's *Social Statistics* (1960). The generalization of regression to systems of equations and the accompanying notion of causal analysis began with Blalock's *Causal Inferences in Nonexperimental Research* (1964) and Duncan's "Path Analysis: Sociological Examples" (1966). Blalock's work was heavily influenced by the economist Simon's work on correlation and causality (Simon 1957) and the economist Wold's work on simultaneous equation systems (Wold and Juréen 1953). Duncan's work added the influence of the geneticist Wright's work in path analysis (Wright 1934). The acceptance of these methods by sociologists required a substantive application that demonstrated how regression could contribute to the understanding of fundamental sociological questions. In this case, the question was the determination of occupational standing and the specific work was the substantively and methodologically influential *The American Occupational Structure* by Blau and Duncan (1967), a work unsurpassed in its integration of method and substance. Numerous applications of regression and path analysis soon followed. The diversity of influences, problems, and approaches that resulted from Blalock and Duncan's work is shown in Blalock's reader *Causal Models in the Social Sciences* (1971), which became the handbook of quantitative methods in the 1970s.

Regression models have been extended in many ways. Bielby and Hauser (1977) have reviewed developments involving systems of equations. Regression methods for time series analysis and forecasting (often called Box-Jenkins models) were given their classic treatment in Box and Jenkins's *Time Series Analysis* (1970). Regression diagnostics have provided tools for exploring characteristics of the data set that is to be analyzed. Methods for identifying outlying and influential observations have been developed (Belsley et al. 1980), along with major advances in classic problems such as heteroscedasticity (White 1980) and specification (Hausman 1978). All these extensions have been finding their way into sociological practice.

Factor Analysis. Factor analysis, a technique developed by psychometricians, was the second major influence on quantitative sociological methods. Factor analysis is based on the idea that the covariation among a larger set of *observed* variables can be reduced to the covariation among a smaller set of *unobserved* or latent variables. By 1960, this method was well known and applications appeared in most major sociology journals. Statistical and computational advances in applying maximum-likelihood estimation to the factor model (Jöreskog 1969) were essential for the development of the covariance structure model discussed below.

Stochastic Processes. Stochastic models were the third influence on the development of quantitative sociological methods. Stochastic processes model the change in a variable over time in cases where a chance process governs the change. Examples of stochastic processes include change in occupational status over a career (Blumen et al. 1955), friendship patterns, preference for job locations (Coleman 1964), and the distribution of racial disturbances (Spilerman 1971). While the mathematical and statistical details for many stochastic models had been worked out by 1960, they were relatively unknown to sociologists until the

publication of Coleman's *Introduction to Mathematical Sociology* (1964) and Bartholomew's *Stochastic Models for Social Processes* (1967). These books presented an array of models that were customized for specific social phenomena. While these models had great potential, applications were rare because of the great mathematical sophistication of the models and the lack of general-purpose software for estimating the models. Nonetheless, the influence of these methods on the development of other techniques was great. For example, Markov chain models for social mobility had an important influence on the development of loglinear models.

Contingency Table Analysis and Loglinear Models. Methods for categorical data were the fourth influence on quantitative methods. The analysis of contingency tables has a long tradition in sociology. Lazarsfeld's work on elaboration analysis and panel analysis had a major influence on the way research was done at the start of the 1960s (Lazarsfeld and Rosenberg 1955). While these methods provided useful tools for analyzing categorical data and especially survey data, they were nonstatistical in the sense that issues of estimation and hypothesis testing generally were ignored. Important statistical advances for measures of association in two-way tables were made in a series of papers by Goodman and Kruskal that appeared during the 1950s and 1960s (Goodman and Kruskal 1979). In the 1960s, nonstatistical methods for analyzing contingency tables were replaced by the loglinear model. This model made the statistical analysis of multiway tables possible. Early developments are found in papers by Birch (1963) and Goodman (1964). The development of the general model was completed largely through the efforts of Frederick Mosteller, Stephen E. Fienberg, Yvonne M. M. Bishop, Shelby Haberman, and Leo A. Goodman, which were summarized in Bishop et al.'s *Discrete Multivariate Analysis* (1975). Applications in sociology appeared shortly after Goodman's (1972) didactic presentation and the introduction of ECTA (Fay and Goodman 1974), a program for loglinear analysis. Since that time, the model has been extended to specific types of variables (e.g., ordinal), more complex structures (e.g., association models), and particular substantive problems (e.g., networks) (see Agresti [1990] for a treatment of recent developments). As with regression models, many early applications appeared in the area of stratification research. Indeed, many developments in loglinear analysis were motivated by substantive problems encountered in sociology and related fields.

ADDITIONAL METHODS

From these roots in regression, factor analysis, stochastic processes, and contingency table analysis, a wide variety of methods emerged that are now applied frequently by sociologists. Notions from these four areas were combined and extended to produce new methods. The remainder of this article considers the major methods that resulted.

Covariance Structure Models. The covariance structure model is a combination of the factor and regression models. While the factor model allowed imperfect multiple indicators to be used to extract a more accurately measured latent variable, it did not allow the modeling of causal relations among the factors. The regression model, conversely, did not allow imperfect measurement and multiple indicators. The covariance structure model resulted from the merger of the structural or causal component of the regression model with the measurement component of the factor model. With this model, it is possible to specify that each latent variable has one or more imperfectly measured observed indicators and that a causal relationship exists among the latent variables. Applications of such a model became practical after the computational breakthroughs made by Jöreskog, who published LISREL (*li*near *s*tructural *rel*ations) in 1972 (Jöreskog and van Thillo 1972). The importance of this program is reflected by the use of the phrase "LISREL models" to refer to this area.

Initially, the model was based on analyzing the covariances among observed variables, and this gave rise to the name "covariance structure analysis." Extensions of the model since 1973 have made use of additional types of information as the model has been enhanced to deal with multiple groups, noninterval observed variables, and estimation with less restrictive assumptions. These extensions have led to alternative names for these methods, such as "mean and covariance structure models" and, more recently, "structural equation modeling" (see Bollen [1989] and Browne and

Arminger [1995] for a discussion of these and other extensions).

Event History Analysis. Many sociological problems deal with the occurrence of an event. For example, does a divorce occur? When is one job given up for another? In such problems, the outcome to be explained is the time when the event occurred. While it is possible to analyze such data with regression, that method is flawed in two basic respects. First, event data often are censored. That is, for some members of the sample the event being predicted may not have occurred, and consequently a specific time for the event is missing. Even assuming that the censored time is a large number to reflect the fact that the event has not occurred, this will misrepresent cases in which the event occurred shortly after the end of the study. If one assigns a number equal to the time when the data collection ends or excludes those for whom the event has not occurred, the time of the event will be underestimated. Standard regression cannot deal adequately with censoring problems. Second, the regression model generally assumes that the errors in predicting the outcome are normally distributed, which is generally unrealistic for event data. Statistical methods for dealing with these problems began to appear in the 1950s and were introduced to sociologists in substantive papers examining social mobility (Spilerman 1972; Sorensen 1975; Tuma 1976). Applications of these methods were encouraged by the publication in 1976 of Tuma's program RATE for event history analysis (Tuma and Crockford 1976). Since that time, event history analysis has become a major form of analysis and an area in which sociologists have made substantial contributions (see Allison [1995] and Petersen [1995] for reviews of these methods).

Categorical and Limited Dependent Variables. If the dependent variable is binary, nominal, ordinal, count, or censored, the usual assumptions of the regression model are violated and estimates are biased. Some of these cases can be handled by the methods discussed above. Event history analysis deals with certain types of censored variables; loglinear analysis deals with binary, nominal, count, and ordinal variables when the independent variables are all nominal. Many other cases exist that require additional methods. These methods are called quantal response models or models for categorical, limited, or qualitative dependent variables. Since the types of dependent variables analyzed by these methods occur frequently in the social sciences, they have received a great deal of attention by econometricians and sociologists (see Maddala [1983] and Long [1997] for reviews of these models and Cameron and Trivedi [1998] on count models).

Perhaps the simplest of these methods is logit analysis, in which the dependent variable is binary or nominal with a combination of interval and nominal independent variables. Logit analysis was introduced to sociologists by Theil (1970). Probit analysis is a related technique that is based on slightly different assumptions. McKelvey and Zavoina (1975) extend the logit and probit models to ordinal outcomes. A particularly important type of limited dependent variable occurs when the sample is selected nonrandomly. For example, in panel studies, cases that do not respond to each wave may be dropped from the analysis. If those who do not respond to each wave differ nonrandomly from those who do respond (e.g., those who are lost because of moving may differ from those who do not move), the resulting sample is not representative. To use an example from a review article by Berk (1983), in cases of domestic violence, police may write a report only if the violence exceeds some minimum level, and the resulting sample is biased to exclude cases with lower levels of violence. Regression estimates based on this sample will be biased. Heckman's (1979) influential paper stimulated the development of sample selection models, which were introduced to sociologists by Berk (1983). These and many other models for limited dependent variables are extremely well suited to sociological problems. With the increasing availability of software for these models, their use is becoming more common than even that of the standard regression model.

Latent Structure Analysis. The objective of latent structure analysis is the same as that of factor analysis: to explain covariation among a larger number of observed variables in terms of a smaller number of latent variables. The difference is that factor analysis applies to interval-level observed and latent variables, whereas latent structure analysis applies to observed data that are noninterval. As part of the American soldier study, Paul F. Lazarsfeld, Sam Stouffer, Louis Guttman, and others developed techniques for "factor ana-

lyzing" nominal data. While many methods were developed, latent structure analysis has emerged as the most popular. Lazarsfeld coined the term "latent structure analysis" to refer to techniques for extracting latent variables from observed variables obtained from survey research. The specific techniques depend on the characteristics of the observed and latent variables. If both are continuous, the method is called factor analysis, as was discussed above. If both are discrete, the method is called latent class analysis. If the factors are continuous but the observed data are discrete, the method is termed latent trait analysis. If the factors are discrete but the data are continuous, the method is termed latent profile analysis. The classic presentation of these methods is presented in Lazarsfeld and Henry's *Latent Structure Analysis* (1968). Although these developments were important and their methodological concerns were clearly sociological, these ideas had few applications during the next twenty years. While the programs ECTA, RATE, and LISREL stimulated applications of the loglinear, event history, and covariance structure models, respectively, the lack of software for latent structure analysis inhibited its use. This changed with Goodman's (1974) algorithms for estimation and Clogg's (1977) program MLLSA for estimating the models. Substantive applications began appearing in the 1980s, and the entire area of latent structure analysis has become a major focus of statistical work.

Multilevel and Panel Models. In most of the models discussed here, observations are assumed to be independent. This assumption can be violated for many reasons. For example, in panel data, the same individual is measured at multiple time points, and in studies of schools, all the children in each classroom may be included in the sample. Observations in a single classroom or for the same person over time tend to be more similar than are independent observations. The problems caused by the lack of independence are addressed by a variety of related methods that gained rapid acceptance beginning in the 1980s, when practical issue of estimation were solved. When the focus is on clustering with social groups (such as schools), the methods are known variously as hierarchical models, random coefficient models, and multilevel methods. When the focus is on clustering with panel data, the methods are referred to as models for cross-section and time series data, or simply panel analysis. The terms "fixed and random effects models" and "covariance component models" also are used. (See Hsiao [1995] for a review of panel models for continuous outcomes and Hamerle and Ronning [1995] for panel models for categorical outcomes. Bryk and Raudenbush [1992] review hierarchical linear models.)

Computer-Intensive Methods. The availability of cheap computing has led to the rapid development and application of computer-intensive methods that will change the way data are analyzed over the next decade. Methods of resampling, such as the bootstrap and the jackknife, allow practical solutions to previously intractable problems of statistical inference (Efron and Tibshirani 1993). This is done by recomputing a test statistic perhaps 1,000 times, using artificially constructed data sets. Computational algorithms for Bayesian analysis replace difficult or impossible algebraic derivations with computer-intensive simulation methods, such as the Markov chain algorithm, the Gibbs sampler, and the Metropolis algorithm (Gelman et al. 1995). Related developments have occurred in the treatment of missing data, with applications of the EM algorithm and Markov chain Monte Carlo techniques (Schafer 1997).

Other Developments. The methods discussed above represent the major developments in statistical methods in sociology since the 1960s. With the rapid development of mathematical statistics and advances in computing, new methods have continued to appear. Major advances have been made in the treatment of missing data (Little and Rubin 1987). Developments in statistical graphics (Cleveland 1985) are reflected in the increasing number of graphics appearing in sociological journals. Methods that require less restrictive distributional assumptions and are less sensitive to errors in the data being analyzed are now computationally feasible. Robust methods have been developed that are insensitive to small departures from the underlying assumptions (Rousseeuw and Leroy 1987). Resampling methods (e.g., bootstrap methods) allow estimation of standard errors and confidence intervals when the underlying distributional assumptions (e.g., normality) are unrealistic or the formulas for computing standard errors are intractable by letting the observed data assume the role of the underlying population (Stine 1990). Recent work by Muthén (forthcom-

ing) and others combines the structural component of the regression model, latent variables from factor and latent structure models, hierarchical modeling, and characteristics of limited variables into a single model. The development of Mplus (Muthén and Muthén 1998) makes routine application of this general model feasible.

CONCLUSIONS

The introduction of structural equation models in the 1960s changed the way sociologists viewed data and viewed the social world. Statistical developments in areas such as econometrics, biometrics, and psychometrics were imported directly into sociology. At the same time, other methods were developed by sociologists to deal with substantive problems of concern to sociology. A necessary condition for these changes was the steady decline in the cost of computing, the development of efficient numerical algorithms, and the availability of specialized software. Without developments in computing, these methods would be of little use to substantive researchers. As the power of desktop computers grows and the ease and flexibility of statistical packages increase, the application of sophisticated statistical methods has become more accessible to the average researcher than the card sorter was for constructing contingency tables in the 1950s and 1960s. As computing power continues to develop, new and promising methods are appearing with each issue of the journals in this area.

Acceptance of these methods has not been universal or without costs. Critiques of the application of quantitative methods have been written by both sympathetic (Lieberson 1985; Duncan 1984) and unsympathetic (Coser 1975) sociologists as well as statisticians (Freedman 1987) and econometricians (Leamer 1983). While these critiques have made practitioners rethink their approaches, the developments in quantitative methods that took shape in the 1960s will continue to influence sociological practice for decades to come.

REFERENCES

Agresti, Alan 1990 *Categorical Data Analysis*. New York: Wiley.

Allison, Paul D. 1995 *Survival Analysis Using the SAS® System: A Practical Guide*. Cary, NC: SAS Institute.

Anderson, T. W. 1958 *An Introduction to Multivariate Statistical Analysis*. New York: Wiley.

Bartholomew, D. J. 1967 *Stochastic Models for Social Processes*. New York: Wiley.

Belsley, David A., Edwin Kuh, and Roy E. Welsch 1980 *Regression Diagnostics: Identifying Influential Data and Sources of Collinearity*. New York: Wiley.

Berk, R. A. 1983 "An Introduction to Sample Selection Bias in Sociological Data." *American Sociological Review* 48:386–398.

Bielby, William T., and Robert M. Hauser 1977 "Structural Equation Models." *Annual Review of Sociology*. 3:137–161.

Birch, M. W. 1963. "Maximum Likelihood in Three-Way Contingency Tables." *Journal of the Royal Statistical Society Series B* 27:220–233.

Bishop, Y. M. M., S. E. Fienberg, and P. W. Holland 1975 *Discrete Multivariate Analysis: Theory and Practice*. Cambridge, Mass.: MIT Press.

Blalock, Hubert M., Jr. 1960 *Social Statistics*. New York: McGraw-Hill.

—— 1964. *Causal Inferences in Nonexperimental Research*. Chapel Hill: University of North Carolina Press.

——, 1971 *Causal Models in the Social Sciences*. Chicago: Aldine.

Blau, Peter M., and Otis Dudley Duncan 1967 *The American Occupational Structure*. New York: Wiley.

Blumen, I., M. Kogan, and P. J. McCarthy 1955 *Industrial Mobility of Labor as a Probability Process*. Cornell Studies of Industrial and Labor Relations, vol. 6. Ithaca, N.Y. Cornell University Press.

Bollen, Kenneth A. 1989 *Structural Equations with Latent Variables*. New York: Wiley.

Borgatta, Edgar F., and George W. Bohrnstedt, eds. 1969 *Sociological Methodology*. San Francisco: Jossey-Bass.

——, eds. 1972 *Sociological Methods and Research*. Beverly Hills, Calif.: Sage.

Box, George E. P., and Gwilym M. Jenkins 1970 *Time Series Analysis*. San Francisco: Holden-Day.

Browne, Michael W., and Gerhard Arminger 1995 "Specification and Estimation of Mean- and Covariance-Structure Models." In Gerhard Arminger, Clifford C. Clogg, and Michael E. Sobel, eds., *Handbook of Statistical Modeling for the Social and Behavioral Sciences*. New York: Plenum.

Bryk, Anthony S., and Stephen W. Raudenbush 1992 *Hierarchical Linear Models: Applications and Data Analysis Methods*. Newbury Park, Calif.: Sage.

Cameron, A. Colin, and Pravin K. Trivedi 1998 *Regression Analysis of Count Data*. New York: Cambridge University Press.

Cleveland, William S. 1985 *The Elements of Graphing Data*. Monterey, Calif.: Wadsworth.

Clogg, Clifford C. 1977 *MLLSA: Maximum Likelihood Latent Structure Analysis*. State College: Pennsylvania State University.

Coleman, James S. 1964 *Introduction to Mathematical Sociology*. Glencoe, Ill.: Free Press.

Coser, Lewis F. 1975 "Presidential Address: Two Methods in Search of Substance." *American Sociological Review* 40:691–700.

Cramér, Harald 1946 *Mathematical Methods of Statistics*. Princeton, N.J.: Princeton University Press.

Dixon, W. J. chief ed. 1981 *BMD Statistical Software*. Berkeley: University of California Press.

Doob, J. L. 1953. *Stochastic Processes*. New York: Wiley.

Duncan, Otis Dudley 1966 "Path Analysis: Sociological Examples." *American Journal of Sociology* 72:1–16.

—— 1984 *Notes on Social Measurement: Historical and Critical*. New York: Russell Sage Foundation.

Efron, Bradley, and Robert J. Tibshirani 1993 *An Introduction to the Bootstrap*. New York: Chapman and Hall.

Fay, Robert, and Leo A. Goodman 1974 *ECTA: Everyman's Contingency Table Analysis*.

Finney, D. J. 1952 *Probit Analysis, 2nd ed.* Cambridge, UK: Cambridge University Press.

Fisher, R. A. 1925 *Statistical Methods for Research Workers*. Edinburgh: Oliver and Boyd.

Freedman, David A. 1987 "As Others See Us: A Case Study in Path Analysis." *Journal of Educational Statistics* 12:101–128.

Gelman, Andrew, John B. Carlin, Hal S. Stern, and Donald B. Rubin 1995 *Bayesian Data Analysis*. New York: Chapman and Hall.

Goodman, Leo A. 1964 "Simple Methods of Analyzing Three-Factor Interaction in Contingency Tables." *Journal of the American Statistical Association* 58:319–352.

—— 1972. "A Modified Multiple Regression Approach to the Analysis of Dichotomous Variables." *American Sociological Review* 37:28–46.

—— 1974 "The Analysis of Systems of Qualitative Variables When Some of the Variables Are Unobservable. Part I: A Modified Latent Structure Approach." *American Journal of Sociology* 79:1179–1259.

——, and William H. Kruskal 1979 *Measures of Association for Cross Classification*. New York: Springer-Verlag.

Hamerle, Alfred, and Gerd Ronning 1995 "Panel Analysis for Qualitative Variables." In Gerhard Arminger, Clifford C. Clogg, and Michael E. Sobel, eds., *Handbook of Statistical Modeling for the Social and Behavioral Sciences*. New York: Plenum.

Hausman, J. A. 1978 "'Specification Tests in Econometrics." *Econometrica* 46:1251–1272.

Heckman, James J. 1979 "Sample Selection Bias as a Specification Error." *Econometrica* 47:153–161.

Hsiao, Cheng 1995 "Panel Analysis for Metric Data." In Gerhard Arminger, Clifford C. Clogg, and Michael E. Sobel, eds., *Handbook of Statistical Modeling for the Social and Behavioral Sciences*. New York: Plenum.

Jöreskog, Karl G. 1969 "A General Approach to Confirmatory Maximum Likelihood Factor Analysis." *Psychometrika* 34:183–202.

———, and Marielle van Thillo 1972 *LISREL: A General Computer Program for Estimating a Linear Structural Equation System Involving Multiple Indicators of Unmeasured Variables*. Princeton, N.J.: Educational Testing Service.

Kendall, Maurice G. 1943 *Advanced Theory of Statistics*, vol. 1. London: Griffin.

——— 1946. *Advanced Theory of Statistics*, vol. 2. London: Griffin.

Lazarsfeld, Paul F., and Neil W. Henry 1968 *Latent Structure Analysis*. New York: Houghton Mifflin.

———, and Morris Rosenberg, eds. 1955 *The Language of Social Research*. New York: Free Press.

Leamer, Edward E. 1983 "Let's Take the Con Out of Econometrics." *American Economic Review* 73:31–43.

Lehmann, E. L. 1959 *Testing Statistical Hypotheses*. New York: Wiley.

Lieberson, Stanley 1985 *Making It Count: The Improvement of Social Research and Theory*. Berkeley: University of California.

Little, Roderick J. A., and Donald B. Rubin 1987 *Statistical Analysis with Missing Data*. New York: Wiley.

Long, J. Scott 1997 *Regression Models for Categorical and Limited Dependent Variables*. Newbury Park, Calif.: Sage.

Maddala, G. S. 1983 *Limited-Dependent and Qualitative Variables in Econometrics*. Cambridge, UK: Cambridge University Press.

McKelvey, Richard D., and William Zavoina 1975 "A Statistical Model for the Analysis of Ordinal Level Dependent Variables." *Journal of Mathematical Sociology* 4:103–120.

Muthén, Bengt O. 1998 "Second-Generation Structural Equation Modeling with a Combination of Categorical and Continuous Latent Variables: New Opportunities for Latent Class/Latent Growth Modeling." In A. Sayer and L. Collins, eds., *New Methods for the Analysis of Change*. Washington D.C.: APA.

Muthén, Linda K., and Bengt O. Muthén 1998 *Mplus: The Comprehensive Modeling Program for Applied Researchers*. Los Angeles: Muthén & Muthén.

Nie, Norman H., C. Hadlai Hull, Jean G. Jenkins, Karin Steinbrenner, and Dale H. Bent 1975 *Statistical Package for the Social Sciences, 2nd ed.* New York: McGraw-Hill.

Petersen, Trond 1995 "Analysis of Event Histories." In Gerhard Arminger, Clifford C. Clogg, and Michael E. Sobel, eds., *Handbook of Statistical Modeling for the Social and Behavioral Sciences*. New York: Plenum.

Rousseeuw, Peter J., and Annick M. Leroy 1987 *Robust Regression and Outlier Detection*. New York: Wiley.

Schafer, J. L. 1997 *Analysis of Incomplete Multivariate Data*. New York: Chapman and Hall.

Scheffé, H. 1959 *The Analysis of Variance*. New York: Wiley.

Simon, Herbert 1957 *Models of Man*. New York: Wiley.

Snedecor, George W. 1937 *Statistical Methods*. Ames: Iowa State University Press.

Sorensen, Aage 1975 "The Structure of Intragenerational Mobility." *American Sociological Review* 40:456–471.

Spilerman, Seymour 1971 "The Causes of Racial Disturbances: Tests of an Explanation." *American Sociological Review* 36:427–442.

——— 1972 "The Analysis of Mobility Processes by the Introduction of Independent Variables Into a Markov Chain." *American Sociological Review* 37:277–294.

Stine, Robert 1990 "An Introduction to Bootstrap Methods." In John Fox and J. Scott Long, eds., *Modern Methods of Data Analysis*. Newbury Park, Calif.: Sage.

Theil, H. 1970 "On the Estimation of Relationships Involving Qualitative Variables." *American Journal of Sociology* 76:103–154.

Thurstone, L. L. 1947 *Multiple-Factor Analysis*. Chicago: University of Chicago Press.

Tuma, Nancy B. 1976 "Rewards, Resources, and the Rate of Mobility." *American Sociological Review* 41:338–360.

———, and D. Crockford 1976 *Invoking RATE*. Center for the Study of Welfare Policy. Menlo Park, Calif.: Stanford Research Institute.

White, Halbert 1980 "A Heteroskedasticity-Consistent Covariance Matrix and a Direct Test for Heteroskedasticity." *Econometrica* 48:817–838.

Wilks, S. S. 1944 *Mathematical Statistics*. Princeton, N.J.: Princeton University Press

Wold, Herman, and Lars Juréen 1953 *Demand Analysis.* New York: Wiley.

Wright, Sewall 1934 "The Method of Path Coefficients." *Annals of Mathematical Statistics* 5:161–215.

J. SCOTT LONG

STATUS ATTAINMENT

Status attainment is the process by which individuals attain positions in the system of social stratification in a society. If one thinks of social stratification as referring to the rewards society offers and the resources individuals use to obtain those rewards, education, occupation, and income are the key factors. The amount and kind of education people attain determine the kinds of jobs they get. The kind of work people do is the main determinant of their income. Moreover, the education, occupation, and income of parents largely determine the kinds of advantages or disadvantages they create for their children. Sociologists usually think of education, occupation, and income as the main aspects of socioeconomic status, and the study of status attainment is therefore the study of how these attributes of people are related both within and across generations.

ESTABLISHMENT OF THE FIELD

As a distinctive area of research, status-attainment research had its origins in the work of Otis Dudley Duncan in the 1960s. Duncan (1961) reconceptualized the study of intergenerational occupational mobility—which is concerned with the degree and pattern of association between the kinds of work done by parents and offspring (in practice, fathers and sons)—as the study of the factors that determine who gets what sort of job, with the father's occupation being only one of several determining factors. Other researchers extended Duncan's findings to take account of the factors that determine how much schooling people get and how much money they make.

Duncan's conceptual reformulation was accompanied by two important technical innovations. The first was the creation of a socioeconomic status scale for occupations. Unlike education and income, occupation has no intrinsic metric: No natural ordering of occupations exists in terms of relative status. For many kinds of research, however, especially the study of status attainment, it is desirable to arrange occupations into some sort of status hierarchy, that is, a hierarchy of the relative socioeconomic advantage enjoyed by people in different occupations. Duncan created such an ordering of occupations for the categories of the 1950 U.S. Census classification by taking the weighted average of the education and income of typical incumbents, with the weights chosen to maximize the association between the resulting socioeconomic status scale and the relative prestige of occupations as measured by popular evaluations. He was able to do this because prestige and socioeconomic status are very highly correlated: Occupations that have high socioeconomic status (that is, that require a great deal of education and pay well) also tend to have high prestige, and jobs that require little education and pay poorly tend to have low prestige.

Second, Duncan introduced path analysis into sociology. Path analysis is a way of statistically representing the relative strength of different relationships between variables, both direct and indirect. For example, it is known that educated people tend to earn more than do uneducated people, but it is not clear whether this is the case simply because they have jobs of higher status or whether, among those who have jobs of similar status, the better educated earn more than do the less well educated. Path analysis provides a way of answering this question: Even among people doing the same sort of work, the better educated tend to earn more.

SUBSTANTIVE ISSUES

Four central issues have dominated research on status attainment. The first issue is the extent of "social reproduction," the tendency for class and socioeconomic status position to be perpetuated, or "reproduced," from generation to generation. A value assumption underlies this question. "Open" societies, that is, societies with low rates of social reproduction or, to put it differently, high rates of intergenerational social mobility, are regarded as desirable since they are assumed to have relatively high equality of opportunity and to emphasize "achievement" rather than "ascription" as the basis for socioeconomic success.

The second issue is the factors other than the status of parents that affect education, occupation, and income. Of course, some factors may be correlated with the status of parents and also may have an independent effect. For example, there is a modest negative correlation between socioeconomic status and fertility—high-status people tend to have fewer children—and there is also a tendency for people from large families not to go as far in school as people from small families do. Thus, part of the reason the children of high-status people go further in school is that such people have smaller families. However, it is also true that at any given level of parental status (e.g., for families where both parents are college-educated professionals), people from smaller families go further in school. Therefore, the number of siblings has an *independent* effect on educational attainment apart from its correlation with parental status. Sorting out such effects is facilitated by the application of path analysis.

The third issue is the extent to which there are sex and racial (or ethnic) differences in patterns of status attainment. With respect to gender, the questions are: Do men and women from similar social origins go equally far in school? Do equally qualified men and women get jobs of equal status? Are women paid as well as men doing similar work? The same set of questions is asked with respect to differences between racial and ethnic groups.

The fourth issue is whether the process of status attainment operates the same way in different countries or in the same country in different historical periods. What follows is a summary of what is known about each of these four issues with respect to educational attainment, occupational attainment, and income attainment.

EDUCATION

Reproduction. In regard to the extent of educational reproduction, the evidence in the United States in the late twentieth century is clear: America is an "open" society. Educational attainment (how far people go in school) is only weakly dependent on parental status. Only about 20 percent of the variability in years of school completed can be attributed to the level of education attained by one's father or mother. When several different family background characteristics are taken into account, the connection is not much stronger; at most, about one-third of the variability in educational attainment can be attributed to the status of the family one comes from. The rest is due to factors unrelated to social origins.

Other Factors. Apart from the social status of parents, the main factors that affect educational attainment are intelligence, the number of siblings (as was noted above, all else being equal, people from large families get less schooling), family stability (those from nonintact families, people whose parents have divorced or died—one or both— go less far in school), the influence of "significant others" (family members, friends, and teachers), and academic performance (the better people do in school, the longer they continue to go to school).

The question naturally arises as to why and how origin status and these other factors affect educational attainment. In a country such as the United States, where education up to the college level is free, parental wealth has relatively little effect on whether people stay in school. This claim is supported by the observation that the effect of social origins on educational attainment declines with each successive educational transition. That is, social origins have a stronger influence on whether people graduate from high school than on whether high school graduates go on to college and an even weaker influence on the graduation chances of those who begin college. If parental wealth is not important, what is?

There are two underlying factors: "Human capital" (sometimes called "cultural capital") is the most important, but "social capital" is involved as well. Human capital refers to the knowledge, skills, and motivations of individuals. The basic argument here is that growing up in a high-status family enhances one's human capital and that those with high human capital do better in school and therefore gain more education, which of course further enhances their human capital. The idea is that children who grow up in well-educated families or professional families learn the kinds of skills and acquire the kinds of motivations that enable them to do well in school. There are many books in such houses, and there are often computers. Schoolwork is familiar to these children because it is the same sort of thing they find at home.

Social capital refers to the social connections people have with others. Here the idea is that people are strongly influenced by the company they keep. Young people whose friends drop out of high school are more likely to drop out of high school themselves than are others whose friends have a social background and academic performance level that encourage educational attainment. Similarly, those whose friends go to college are more likely to go themselves than are others whose friends go to work after high school, and those whose teachers encourage them to continue their education are more likely to do so than are others whose records are just as good. Since people with high-status origins tend to live in neighborhoods with others of similar origins, they tend to have greater social capital than do those with low-status origins.

Sex and Racial Differences. In the United States, there is little difference in the average amount of education attained by men and women, but more men than women tend to be very well educated or very poorly educated; that is, more men than women graduate from college, but more men than women drop out of high school. However, the effect of social origins and other factors on educational attainment is very similar for men and women. Race and ethnicity are a different story. Blacks are substantially less well educated than are whites and those of other races. In part, this is the case because the parents of blacks are poorly educated. However, blacks are also less able to convert whatever advantage they do have into a corresponding advantage for their children. In particular, blacks do not go as far in school as would be predicted from their parents' status. The sharp difference between blacks and other groups is a continuing legacy of slavery. While there are differences in the educational attainment levels of other ethnic groups, those differences are largely the result of differences among those groups in the average status of parents.

In nations such as South Africa, where until 1994 racial distinctions were embedded in law and social institutions (as in the American South before 1964), racial differences in educational attainment are much larger than they are in the United States. Whereas in the United States in 1990 whites averaged 13.1 years of schooling and blacks averaged 12.3 years, a difference of 0.8 year in South Africa in 1991 whites averaged 10.0 years of schooling and blacks averaged 4.5 years, a difference of 5.5 years, with the other racial groups falling be-

tween these values This was a direct consequence of government policies that created separate and unequal school systems for South Africa's four "official" racial groups.

Cross-Cultural and Cross-Temporal Variations. Differences between countries in the educational attainment process are due both to general factors such as the level of industrialization and to specific differences in the way education is organized. In general, in places were the level of educational inequality in the parents' generation is high, educational attainment is more dependent on social origins than it is in countries where the level of educational inequality in the parents' generation is low. This is a consequence of the effect of human capital acquired at home. In a country such as the United States, where janitors have about ten years of school and high school teachers have about sixteen, the son of a janitor will be able to compete in school much more effectively with the son of a high school teacher than is the case in a society such as India where high school teachers also have about sixteen years of schooling but janitors have no schooling at all and are illiterate. Second, in highly industrialized countries schooling is less dependent on social origins than it is in less industrialized countries, in part because schooling tends to be free in industrialized countries. Third, in countries where the state provides not only free education but financial subsidies to students, as has been done in eastern Europe and in some western European countries, education tends to be less dependent on social origins than it is in countries without such subsidies.

There is a worldwide trend for educational attainment to become less "ascriptive" over time. That is, in almost all countries-educational attainment has become less and less dependent on social origins throughout most of the twentieth century. The reason for this is straightforward. As was mentioned above, the effect of social origins on the probability that people will move from one level of education to the next declines with each higher level of education. Therefore, since the average *level* of educational attainment has been steadily increasing in most countries, it follows that more and more people are in educational categories where social origins matter relatively little.

An important distinction in educational systems is that between divided and unitary systems.

In the United States, there is, with only modest exceptions, a single path to educational attainment: primary school, to secondary school, to college or university, to graduate or professional school. Students achieve a certain level of education and then leave school to take up other pursuits. Thus, years of schooling is a very good indicator of educational attainment. In Europe and elsewhere, schooling tends to be divided into parallel tracks. In particular, a distinction is made between academic and vocational tracks, beginning in secondary school. Thus, in Europe, educational attainment must be measured not only by the amount of schooling but by the type of schooling a student has. In general, academic credentials have more value in the labor market than do vocational credentials in that they lead to jobs with higher status and higher income.

Among nations at a similar level of economic development, there often are substantial variations in the dependence of education on social origins. For example, in the 1970–the latest period for which there are systematic comparative data–55 percent of French male university graduates were the sons of managers or professionals, while in Great Britain this was true of only 35 percent. In general, at every selection point, social origins mattered more in France than they in Great Britain. In this sense, one can say that the British educational system was (and probably still is) substantially more egalitarian than the French system.

Finally, particular historical events can have a major impact on educational attainment. For example, the 1966–1977 Cultural Revolution in China caused massive disruptions in almost all aspects of social life. Secondary schools were closed from 1966 to 1968; universities were closed until 1972 and, when they reopened, accepted students on the basis of political status rather than academic merit until 1977. The results were twofold. First, the educational advantage of high-status origins—particularly growing up in a professional family—were very reduced substantially for those who would have entered secondary school or university during that period. Second, the quality of education declined because even when the schools remained open, they were devoted largely to political indoctrination rather than conventional studies. The evidence indicates that those educated during the Cultural Revolution read less well than do those with the same amount of schooling who were educated before or after the Cultural Revolution.

OCCUPATIONAL STATUS

Reproduction. Like educational status, occupational status is only weakly related to social origins. However, it is somewhat harder to pin this down than is true for education since, unlike education, which is completed by most people early in life, occupational status may vary over the life course, as people change jobs. The convention in most research on occupational attainment therefore is to restrict the analysis to men (since women not only change jobs but move in and out of the labor force for marriage or childbearing) and to compare the occupations held by men at the time they are interviewed with the occupations of their fathers when the interviewed men were teenagers, usually age 14. The relationship between fathers' and sons' occupational statuses turns out to be even weaker than the relationship between parents' and offspring's educational attainment. Thus, with respect to occupational statuses as well as educational attainment, America is an open society.

Other Factors. In the analysis of occupational attainment, an important issue has been to assess the relative importance of social origins (measured by the father's occupational status) and education as determinants of men's occupational status. The ratio of these two effects has been taken as an indicator of the degree of societal openness. In the United States and most industrial societies, education is by far the most important determinant of occupational status, while the direct effect of a father's occupational status is very limited. In the past, many people directly inherited their occupational position from their parents (for example, the sons of farmers were likely to take over their fathers' farms, the sons of shopkeepers to take over their fathers' shops, and so on), but in modern societies such as the United States, where people tend to work in large organizations, most jobs cannot be inherited directly. Instead, occupational status inheritance, insofar as it occurs at all, results mainly from the children of high-status people going further in school and those going further in school attaining better jobs. However, since, as was shown above, education is largely independent of social origins, the results is that education serves mainly as a vehicle of social mobility rather than a mechanism of social reproduction or status inheritance.

Sex and Racial Differences. The most striking difference between men and women is that most men work most of the time once they complete their schooling, whereas the work lives of many women are interrupted for childbearing and child rearing. However, the labor-force participation rates or women and men are converging in the United States as more women remain in the labor force even when their children are very young. In general, men and women work at jobs of equal status, although the specific jobs held by men and women are very different. Most managers, skilled and unskilled manual workers, and farm workers are men; most clerical and service workers are women; and professional, sales, and semiskilled manual jobs tend to be performed by both men and women. The sex segregation of the labor force has important implications for income differences between men and women, as is discussed below.

Blacks tend to work at lower-status occupations than do whites and others. In part this is due to their lower levels of educational attainment, but in part it is due to the fact that black are not able to obtain jobs as good as those which can be obtained by equally well-educated members of other groups. Again, as in the case of education, differences in occupational status among nonblack ethnic groups are largely attributable to differences in educational attainment.

Cross-Cultural and Cross-Temporal Variations. In highly industrialized societies and in relatively egalitarian societies, there is little direct transmission of occupational status from one generation to the next; in those societies, occupational transmission is largely indirect, occurring through education. In less industrialized and less egalitarian societies, the importance of the father's occupation as a determinant of occupational status increases and the importance of education decreases, although education always remains more important than the father's occupation even in the least-developed societies.

Although the association between father's and son's occupational statuses has been declining over time and is weaker in industrialized societies, the *pattern* of intergenerational occupational mobility appears to be largely invariant, with only minor variations across societies caused by specific historical circumstances, at least in industrialized societies and probably in nonindustrialized societies as well. That is, the relative chances that, say, the son of a professional and the son of a laborer will become professionals, rather than skilled workers, appear to be essentially similar in all societies.

Despite the commonality in intergenerational mobility patterns, there are substantial national variations in the strength of the linkage between schooling and career beginnings. In general, there is a tighter connection between education and the status of one's first job in countries, such as Germany and Switzerland, where there are separate vocational and academic tracks and assignment to one or the other is made early and where vocational secondary education provides occupation-specific skills than there is in countries, such as Great Britain, Japan, and the United States, where neither condition holds. Japan is, however, a special case. Japanese secondary schools and universities are highly stratified on the basis of prestige. Schools have close connections with large business firms and are able to place their students there. Students from the best schools go to the best firms, where they are trained by being rotated through a series of jobs. Thus, there is very tight schooling–first job connection in Japan, but of a kind not well captured by the association between the amount of schooling and the prestige of the first job.

There are also national differences in the sensitivity of career opportunities to the expansion or contraction of the economy, depending on institutional differences, particularly in welfare state policies and labor market structures. In the United States, for example, rates of job mobility show great sensitivity to structural change and to the labor market resources of individual workers, whereas in the Netherlands, jobs are largely insulated from structural forces.

Finally, careers can be strongly affected by specific historical events. The collapse of communism in eastern Europe in 1989 forced many political officials and administrators into early retirement. However, since the political transformation was accompanied by an economic collapse, with the economies of many former communist countries shrinking by about one-third in the early 1990s, unemployment increased and many women and older workers left the labor force. At the same time, there were substantial new opportunities, particularly in the newly emerging private sector of the economy. Thus, there was a substantial increase in occupational mobility, at least in the short run.

As with education, the extent of reproduction of occupational status has been systematically decreasing over time in almost all societies. The reasons for this are not clear. There may be a worldwide shift toward an emphasis on achievement as opposed to ascription, although the likelihood that a shift in value orientations could have such a large and systematic effect does not seem great. More likely, the systematic increase in the average level of education in almost all countries is responsible, since it is known that the association between fathers' and sons' occupational statuses decreases for those who have obtained higher levels of education.

INCOME

Reproduction. Little is known about the extent of income reproduction because it is very difficult to measure income in the parents' generation. Most data used in intergenerational analyses are obtained by asking people to report on their parent's characteristics. While people tend to know how much schooling their parents had and what sort of work their fathers were doing when the respondents were teenagers, few people have a very good idea of what their parents' income were. However, one major study has obtained such information: a study of the graduating class of 1957 from Wisconsin high schools conducted by Sewell and Hauser (1975). This cohort of graduates has been followed up in a number of surveys over the years, so that information has become available about its members' occupations and incomes at various stages after completing school. In addition, with careful arrangements to guard confidentiality, the researchers were able to obtain information from the Wisconsin Department of Taxation and the Social Security Administration regarding the incomes of the parents at the time the students were in high school. These data suggest that the intergenerational transmission of income is even weaker than is true for education or occupation. Other ways of indirectly estimating this relationship yield similar results.

One possible reason for this is that income (measured in real dollars, that is, adjusted for inflation) is highly variable over the life cycle and, for some workers—particularly those who are self-employed or whose jobs are dependent on the weather—even from year to year. Moreover, age differences in earnings vary systematically for different occupational groups. The earnings of professionals tend to increase steadily over the course of their careers, while at the other extreme, the earnings of unskilled laborers do not change at all. Thus, when they first start working, unskilled laborers earn as much as or more than do professionals just beginning their careers, but by the time they near retirement, professionals earn several times as much as laborers of the same age earn. Incomes are also highly variable from place to palace, reflecting differences in the cost of living, and even within cities, different firms pay different wages or salaries for the same job. All these factors make individual variations in income rather unpredictable.

Other Factors. Unlike parental education and occupational status, which affect educational attainment but have little direct effect on occupational attainment or income, parental income directly affects the income of offspring even when education and occupational attainment are taken into account. In fact, parental income is nearly as important as occupational status in determining income and is more important than education. Apparently, there is a propensity to earn money, and this propensity is transmitted from generation to generation. Whether this reflects differences in values that transmitted from parents to their children—with some people choosing jobs on the basis of how well they pay and others choosing jobs on the basis of their intrinsic interest, how secure they are, and so on—or in another factor is not known.

Other factors that affect income even when parental education and the respondent's own education and occupational status are taken into account include ability, the quality of the college attended, and the kind of work people do. Doctors earn more than professors do even though the jobs are of similar status, and garbage collectors earn more than ditch diggers earn. There is an extensive, although inconclusive, literature on differences in earnings across industrial sectors, and there is some evidence that earnings are higher in more strongly unionized occupations and industries.

Sex and Racial Differences. Gender is the big story here. In the United States, among full-time year-round workers, women earn about 60 percent of what men earn, and this ratio has remained essentially unchanged since the 1950s. Of the 40 percent gender difference, about 20 percent can be accounted for by the greater work experience of men, differences in the kinds of education received, and similar factors. The other 20 percent is due in part to the fact that the jobs performed mainly by women tend to pay less than do the jobs performed mainly by men even though many of these jobs are similar with respect to the skill required, the effort involved, and the responsibility entailed, and in part to the fact that women tend to earn less than do men in the same occupations. This state of affairs is possible because of the extreme gender segregation of the labor force. Most jobs tend to be performed either mostly by men or mostly by women, with relatively few jobs open to both sexes.

One consequence of this is that, at least in the United States, poverty is concentrated in female-headed households, especially where there are young children present. Not only do women in such situations find it difficult to work because of their child care responsibilities, even when they do work, their earnings tend to be low. Thus, the total income of such households is often below the poverty line.

In the United States, racial differences in income are somewhat smaller than gender differences and have been declining steadily for the last half century, as has occupational segregation by race. There is little evidence that the racial composition of jobs affects their pay levels. Instead, racial differences in income are attributable both to the fact that many blacks tend to be less educated and to work at lower-status jobs than most whites and others and to the fact that blacks get a lower return on their education and occupational status than do whites and others. Interestingly, there appears to be an across-the-board difference between the earnings of black and other males at any given level of education, occupational status, and so forth. However, the racial difference in the earnings of women is somewhat more complicated. At low levels of education and occupational status, black women earn much less than do other women, but at high levels of education and occupational status, there is little or no difference in earnings among women of all races.

Cross-Cultural and Cross-Temporal Variations. While international comparisons of the determinants of personal or family income are scarce, probably because of the difficulty in measuring income in a comparable way across countries, differences in the *distribution* of income across nations and over time are well established. Income inequality is related to the level of economic development in a curvilinear way: It is low for the least developed nations, where most people are peasants; high for nations at medium levels of development, which often display large regional differences as a result of uneven economic development; and low for the most developed nations, where a combination of tax and welfare policies tends to ensure that most of the population enjoys at least a moderately adequate standard of living and constrains opportunities to become extremely rich. Because of restrictions on the accumulation of private property in communist regimes, income inequality tends to be smaller than it is in capitalist nations at a corresponding level of economic development. Finally, rampant inflation, such as that which occurred in eastern Europe after the collapse of communism, may cause dramatic reversals of fortune, impoverishing those on fixed incomes, such as government employees and pensioners, and enriching sellers of goods and services whose prices keep pace with inflation.

REFERENCES

Allmendinger, Jutta 1989 "Educational Systems and Labor Market Outcomes." *European Sociological Review* 5:231–250.

Blau, Peter, and Otis Dudley Duncan 1957 *The American Occupational Structure*. New York: Wiley.

Deng, Zhong, and Donald J. Treiman 1997 "The Impact of the Cultural Revolution on Trends in Educational Attainment in the People's Republic of China." *American Journal of Sociology* 103:391–428.

DiPrete, Thomas A., Paul M. de Graaf, Ruud Laijkx, Michael Tåhlin, and Hans-Peter Blossfeld 1997 "Collectivist versus Individualist Mobility Regimes? Structural Change and Job Mobility in Four Countries." *American Journal of Sociology* 103:318–358.

Duncan, Otis Dudley 1961 "A Socioeconomic Index for All Occupations," In Albert J. Reiss, Jr., ed., *Occupations and Social Structure*. New York: Free Press.

Erikson, Robert, and John H. Goldthorpe 1992 *The Constant Flux: A Study of Class Mobility in Industrial Societies.* Oxford, UK: Clarendon.

Featherman, David L., and Robert M. Hauser, 1978 *Opportunity and Change.* New York: Academic Press.

Ganzeboom, Harry B. G., Ruud Luijkx, and Donald J. Treiman 1989 "Intergenerational Class Mobility in Comparative Perspective." *Research in Social Stratification and Mobility* 8:3–84.

——, and Donald J. Treiman 1993 "Preliminary Results on Educational Expansion and Educational Achievement in Comparative Perspective." In Henk A. Becker and Piet L. J. Hermkens, eds., *Solidarity of Generations: Demographic, Economic and Social Change, and Its Consequences.* Amsterdam, thesis.

——, ——, and Wout C. Ultee 1990 "Comparative Intergenerational Stratification Research: Three Generations and Beyond." *Annual Review of Sociology* 17:277–302.

Hout, Michael 1988 "More Universalism, Less Structural Mobility: The American Occupational Structure in the 1980s." *American Journal of Sociology* 93:1358–1400.

Mare, Robert D. 1980 "Social Background and School Continuation Decisions." *Journal of the American Statistical Association* 75:295–305.

Müller, Walter, and Wolfgang Karle 1993 "Social Selection in Educational Systems in Europe." *European Sociological Review* 9:1–24.

Roos, Patricia A. 1985 *Gender and Work: A Comparative Analysis of Industrial Societies.* Albany: State University of New York Press.

Rosenbaum, James E., and Takehiko Kariya 1991 "Do School Achievements Affect the Early Jobs of High School Graduates in the United States and Japan?" *Sociology of Education* 64:78–95.

Sewell, William H., and Robert M. Hauser 1975 *Education, Occupation, and Earnings: Achievement in the Early Career.* New York: Academic Press.

Shavit, Yossi, and Hans-Peter Blossfeld, eds., 1993 *Persistent Inequality: Changing Educational Attainment in Thirteen Countries.* Boulder, Colo.: Westview.

——, and Walter Müller, eds., 1998 *From School to Work: A Comparative Study of Educational Qualifications and Occupational Destinations.* Oxford, UK: Clarendon.

Treiman, Donald J. 1998. "Results from the Survey of 'Social Stratification in Eastern Europe after 1989': What We Have Learned and What We Need to Find Out." In *Transformation Processes in Eastern Europe, 1997,* proceedings of an NWO workshop, Amsterdam, March. The Hague: NWO.

——, and Kam-Bor Yip 1989 "Educational and Occupational Attainment in 21 Countries." In Melvin L. Kohn, ed., *Cross-National Research in Sociology.* Newbury Park, Calif.: Sage.

——, Matthew McKeever, and Eva Fodor 1996 "Racial Differences in Occupational Status and Income in South Africa, 1980 and 1991." *Demography* 33:111–132.

DONALD J. TREIMAN

STATUS INCONGRUENCE

The phenomenon sociologists call "status incongruence" has equivalents in many languages. Expressions such as *"nouveau riche," "déclassé," "roturier"* and *"parvenu"* show that people in many societies perceive the incongruence between various statuses. The popular dictum "the heart on the left, the pocket on the right" expresses this incongruence between positions and feelings.

As a sociological concept, status incongruence is relatively recent. It was devised some time after the adoption of the notion of "status," following the discovery of Max Weber's writings on this subject by American sociologists in the late 1930s. In the 1950s, some twelve articles were published on "status inconsistency," most of them in the *American Sociological Review.* Those articles had a cumulative effect. At a certain point in the 1960s, it was felt that the debate on this topic had become saturated. In the absence of more empirical evidence, the theoretical discussion on status incongruence stagnated, but in the meantime the concept had been diffused in textbooks and compendiums.

After a period of neglect, the concept of status inconsistency has been reinvigorated over the last two decades as sociologists on both sides of the Atlantic have acknowledged a "decline of social classes." However despite the fact that the idea of social class has been dethroned, social inequalities persist.

The concept of status incongruence is a companion of the theory of cross-pressure. The first article focusing directly on status incongruence appeared in the same year (1944) as *The People's Choice* by Lazarsfeld, Berelson, and McPhee. The two notions nevertheless remain distinct in the sociological literature because they respond to different analytic needs.

The incidence of status incongruence increases in times of social upheaval, such as the period of the Weimar Republic, the economic depression in the United States in the early 1930s, and that in Russia after the implosion of the Soviet regime. In the two decades before the French Revolution of 1789, the incidence of status incongruence was particularly high.

In emphasing the revolutionary potential of downward mobility, which he called the "proletarization of middle classes," Marx paid little attention to upward mobility and the effects of status incongruence. That neglect has been considered by some scholars to be one of his more glaring errors (Lopreato and Hazelrigg, 1972 p. 445). In contemporary sociological literature, the notion of status incongruence is related to role theory, rational theory, the theory of relative deprivation, and the theory of social movements.

This article considers only advanced Western societies, partly because the empirical evidence on status incongruence is available primarily for those countries and partly because social mobility and its impact on status incongruence are a less widespread phenomenon in developing countries.

STATUS INCONSISTENCY AS A CORRECTION OF WEAK CORRELATIONS

For a long time in sociological research, correlation between levels of social stratifications and other variables were rarely as significant as expected in light of the hypotheses and theoretical frameworks that had been adopted. Even when the rudimentary dichotomy of manual and nonmanual was abandoned and more categories were taken into consideration, the empirical results did not provide satisfactory explanations. Even when class as a rigid and restricted concept was largely replaced by the dimension of occupational status, the research strategy was not improved. Certainly, the emphasis on status groups is one of Weber and Pareto's chief corrections of Marx's theory (Lopreato and Hazelrigg 1972, p. 83). Nevertheless, an essential approach was missing until the 1950s, that of status inconsistency, which marked an advance in sociological thinking. It has been demonstrated that the consistency or inconsistency of a person's status based on various criteria is a better predictor of social behavior than is the level of status based on a single criterion.

FROM SOCIAL CLASS TO STATUS INCONSISTENCY

Status incongruence is generated by gaps in income, occupation, education, and ethnic origin and other inconsistencies between a person's social position in one domain and that person's relatively lower status in another dimension. Status incongruence can be found in census results by cross-tabulating indicators such as education, income, professional hierarchical position, qualification, and racial origin. There is a logical relationship between the spread of status incongruencies and the weakening of social class consciousness.

Status inconsistency has become an essential aspect of social stratification in contemporary postindustrial society. It has been exacerbated by the growth of the middle classes and the decline of the peasantry and the industrial working class. Vertical mobility is the main source of status discrepancy. Most studies of social mobility have focused on upward mobility, particularly during the postwar period of economic development, but in more recent times, downward mobility has become equally important. Today, social mobility consists mostly in what Lipset and Zetterberg (1956, p. 563) called "the interchange of ranks." For every upward move, there must be a downward move. What was then only a hypothesis has been confirmed empirically: "[S]ome proportion of the children of the middle class fall in socio-economic status; some do not have the abilities to complete higher education or to get along in a bureaucratic hierarchy, and fall by the wayside. Whatever the reason that some persons of middle class origin move downward, they leave room for others of lower-class background to rise" (p. 570). Today, millions of Europeans and Americans born into the middle classes are in such incongruent situations. The downward move can be intragenerational or intergenerational.

Another source of status incongruence is liberation from primary social groups, particularly religious communities and families. More and more, through schooling, individual achievement negates the constraints of family background. For this reason, status inconsistency is a fertile ground for individualistic tendencies.

The concept of status inconsistency raises the concept of status crystallization, which was proposed by Lenski (1954) as a nonvertical dimension of social status. Strong or weak status crystallization refers to the degree of incongruence or coherence of a person's ranking according to various criteria. A strong status crystallization implies that a person is rated consistently on all important criteria, whether the rating is high or low. Today, a large part of the population in Western societies finds itself in a situation of weak status crystallization. Solid social class can exist only if the majority of the population experiences strong status crystallization.

One of the most visible varieties of status incongruence occurs among schoolteachers, who are more numerous today than were workers in the heavy industry plants four decades ago. For many teachers there is a serious gap between the level of their education and their role in society and income level. The left-wing orientation of most teachers in European countries can be explained in terms of status incongruence, rather than class. Even some college professors experience this incongruence.

If one compares status incongruence today and in the past, two important categories have become prominent over the last two decades: the "intellectual proletarian" and the "ethnic achiever" (as opposed to the "skidder").

The spread of education in most advanced societies has highlighted the need of postindustrial economies for highly educated people. Today, two-thirds of people aged 18 are still in school. At the end of their college years, most of them do not find a job that corresponds to their expectations in terms of intellectual and economic rewards. It is in this category of the population—young educated people "with diplomas in their pockets"—that the rate of unemployment is the highest in most west European countries. This overabundance of graduates results from the incapacity of a highly technological society to absorb them in "interesting" occupations, with the existing jobs being protected by unions. This imbalance between the level of education, the quality of the job, and the amount of income generates status incongruences for "overeducated" young people. An advanced postindustrial society in search of productivity replaces people with machines, producing a new kind of educated proletariat that was born into the middle class. In western Europe in the last decade (except in Germany), one of every four or five young people under age 25 was unemployed, and others were pushed down into "degraded" jobs. Those who accept jobs beneath their abilities, "degraded jobs," represent one of the most frequent varieties of status incongruence, a "reserve army" of alienated people.

The ethnic achiever is a new variety in western Europe and an old one in the United States. Status inconsistency can be found among ethnic and racial minorities in Great Britain, France, Germany, Belgium, the Netherlands, Switzerland, and Austria. Immigrants of European origin in Europe are integrated and assimilated in a single generation, with the best example being the eight million French citizens of Italian, Spanish, Portuguese, Polish, or Armenian origins. The children of these European immigrants are not normally in a position of status inconsistency. When language is combined with ethnicity and religion, as with immigrants from the southern rim of the Mediterranean, the integration process takes two generations and the younger generation often experiences status incongruence. When skin color skin is considered, the difficulties of integration are compounded. Many immigrants from southern Asia and Africa feel excluded from the host society. Nevertheless, a substantial minority are economically well integrated, and many climb the income ladder. They are ethnic achievers, more than completely assimilated immigrants. They are deeply rooted in status incongruences.

In Europe, these two varieties of status incongruence contrast with a social category of status crystallization at the bottom of society. According to a recent survey by the Organization for Economic Cooperation and Development (OECD), almost one-fourth of the adult population in Western advanced societies is functionally semi-illiterate and coexists with a high proportion of functionally overeducated younger adults. Strong status crystallization arises from the fact that these semi-illiterates are also those who receive the lowest salaries and perform the most menial work, and the large majority of them are of non-European origin. The status crystallization that occurs in

Europe has a similar and more deeply ingrained counterpart in the United States.

MINORITY STATUS AND STATUS INCONGRUENCE

In many studies of electoral behavior (which are preferred because of the availability of statistics), particularly those conducted by means of survey research, the issue of social context has been neglected. Only the characteristics of individuals are taken into consideration, while the parameters of the social milieu are ignored. With some notable exceptions, too many sociologists have forgotten that the behavior of people is conditioned by their social context. This mistake has been denounced by the German sociologist Scheuch (1969) as the "individualistic fallacy," a complement to the "ecological fallacy." The direct consequence of "individualistic research" is the dismissal of the notion of a "minority" in spite of the fact that its importance has been demonstrated repeatedly. Examples are found in the contrasting behaviors of the same "unidimensional category," whether they are a frustrated minority or a dominant majority. Examples include Irish Catholics who vote for the leftist party in Britain versus "good" Catholics who vote conservative in France or Catholics in Germany who vote for the Christian democratic party and industrial workers who live in densely populated working-class areas versus the same kind of workers who live in middle-class districts. These notions of "minority context" and "majoritarian context" are directly related to the issue of status incongruence, because in many places minorities live in a more or less hostile environment. In such cases, three concepts are involved: status incongruence, minority complex, and cross-pressure.

Contradictory propositions have been suggested concerning the political effects of upward and downward mobility in terms of status incongruence. According to some scholars, upward mobility favors a conservative orientation, and downward mobility a liberal-leftist tendency. Others scholars have arrived at the opposite conclusion. This confusing situation can be explained by the neglect of the social context by those who extrapolate at the national level the results obtained at the local level. Most studies of status incongruence have been conducted in individual cities (including Lenski's 1954 and 1966 studies). It is misleading to generalize from a series of local monographs that do not represent a truly national sample: "Consistency theory seeks to show that predictable effects result from the combination or interaction of statuses, and that these effects differ from the effects of several independent variables" (Rossides 1976, p. 87). However, in practice it is difficult to weigh the importance of each variable in the social context. In one case, it may be a question of race; in another, income; and in still another, professional position. Extrapolated at national level, these variables conceal important variations across local social contexts.

STATUS INCONGRUENCE AND INDIVIDUALISM

Most frequently, status inconsistency refers to individuals, not to collectivities. Incongruence of status is a characteristic of a relationship between individuals. When an individual cannot raise the lower factors of the incongruence, he or she tends to avoid people who react to them (Malewski 1963, p. 306). He or she makes an individual move. If an individual can raise the lower factor, "he has a natural tendency to think of himself in terms of that status or rank which is highest, and to expect others to do the same, [but] others, who come in contact with him, have a vested interest in doing just the opposite, that is, in treating him in terms of the lowest status or rank" (Lenski 1966, p. 87). Even in this case, the relationship is between individuals. Vertical mobility separates ascending individuals from nonmobile peers who remain in their status of origin. A high rate of individual upward mobility breaks the unity of the social class by effectively promoting certain people and generating in the minds of others expectations of moving out of the class and into a better one. As Dahrendorf has noted, a high rate of upward mobility favors individualism to the detriment of class consciousness.

However, high rates of downward mobility may have the opposite effect, favoring, as Marx emphasized, the spread of class consciousness. In that case, the tendency is not to leave the group but to identify oneself with others in the same situation of incongruence of status. In some social contexts that aggregate individuals, such as large factories, mines, railways, working-class suburbs, and ghettos in large cities, the phenomenon of individual status incongruence blooms into a collective social consciousness and a "minority complex."

CONFIGURATIONS OF STATUS INCONGRUENCES

The amount of status inconsistencies depends on the configuration of three dimensions that may be dichotomized for analytic purposes.

1. Culturally homogeneous societies versus heterogeneous societies. In recent decades, immigration in Western countries has differed from that of former times. In most cases, immigrants coming from Western Europe to the United States and Canada require only two generations for complete assimilation into the dominant culture. More recent immigrants in Western countries came from the southern rim of the Mediterranean and Africa. Not only are their distinctive characteristics are not only religious and linguistic, they also differ in skin color. Their integration requests more than two generations, and many of them manifest a preference for multiculturalism, that is, for a recognition and institutionalization of ethnic diversity. Such diversity is currently a source of status inconsistencies but may have different effects in the future.

2. Segmented versus fluid societies. Heterogeneous countries may be segmented or fluid. Segmented societies are divided into religious or linguistic communities, as in Belgium and Northern Ireland, or into "pillars," as in the Netherlands until the middle of 1980s (Lijphart 1977). In these societies, there is little room for ethnic status inconsistency. By contrast, in fluid societies, the crossing of vertical and transversal cleavages is relatively common and generates incongruences.

3. High versus low vertical mobility. Another dichotomy is related to the amount of vertical social mobility on the economic scale, which may be relatively high or relatively low. The fact that high vertical mobility, either upward or downward, increases the frequency of incongruence of statuses is well established.

These three factors have a cumulative effect on the proportion of people who experience incongruence of status.

STATUS INCONGRUENCE AT THE ELITE LEVEL

What is missing in Pareto's "circulation of elites" is the concept of status incongruence. This is surprising in the writings of someone who emphasized the importance of upward and downward social mobility. If the concept of status incongruence was applied to the highest levels of society, elite studies would be enhanced. The psychological portrait of some of the world's most famous painters could be better understood in the light of status inconsistency. The biographies of masters such as Michelangelo, Bellini, Bosch, Goya, van Gogh, and Toulouse Lautrec could be enriched by an interpretation in terms of status incongruence. Many novelists, including Dostoievsky, Tolstoy, Stendhal, Balzac, de Lampedusa, Proust, and Dumas, have analyzed the psychological aspects of status inconsistency even if they have not used that sociological term. One of the main themes of *The Red and the Black* and *The Leopard* is status inconsistency. The most common case is that of the rich man's daughter who becomes enamored of a young man of lower status. No sociologist has explored the hundreds of cases of status incongruence described by famous writers, starting with Shakespeare's Romeo and Juliet.

The concept of status incongruence should be applied even to saints. The best analyses of the personality of the evangelist Paul have been written by theologians and religious historians, who have used the notion of status inconsistency implicitly. The subtitle of Dieter Hilbrand's *Saul-Paul: A Double Life* is significant. Baslez insists on the status incongruence of Saint Paul: Born as a Roman citizen but at the periphery, in Syria; he was a stranger in Ephesus; a polyglot Jew, an apostate, and the son of a Pharisiee, he was rejected as a missionary in many communities. Paul accumulated many incongruencies. Moses, as the nephew of the pharaoh, and Muhammad, as the poor husband of a rich wife, are examples of status inconsistencies.

The use of the concept of status incongruence is appropriate for a better understanding of political leaders from Spartacus to Robespierre and from Trotsky to Castro. There are numerous examples of the status incongruence of athletes, clergymen, businessmen, politicians: poets, and movie stars, but this notion has been insufficiently used to explain the metamorphosis of labor leaders. The concept could even be applied to sociologists for a better understanding of the theories and motivations of scholars such as Pareto, Michels, Veblen, Sorokin, Mills, and Lazarsfeld.

THE RELEVANCE OF STATUS INCONGRUENCE TODAY

The incidence of status incongruence in advanced societies today is many times higher than it was in earlier generations. This upsurge is a result of increasing upward and downward economic mobility, the increasing ethnic heterogeneity of Western societies (as a consequence of massive non-European immigration), and a better perception of inequalities and the spread of "multiculturalism" as opposed to the doctrine of the melting pot, particularly among the so-called second generation, which is composed of the sons and daughters of immigrants.

Four decades ago, status incongruence was usually a question of an imbalance between education, income, occupation, religion, and gender. Today it originates primarly in ethnic and racial intermingling. Religious differences have become less prominent.

In most Western societies on both sides at the Atlantic, a homogeneous majority no longer exists. Any conceivable majority is necessarily composed of multiple minorities of all kinds. An advanced society is a multidimensional society that includes many parallel hierarchies. The political game consists precisely in building coalitions of minorities to crystallize a temporary and unstable political-electoral majority. In almost all these countries, the leftist party has become the party of amalgamated minorities, of those who experience frustrations generated by status incongruences and the psychological complex of belonging to a minority. In the United States, the electorate of the Democratic Party is much more ethnically heterogeneous than is its adversary. It is a conglomerate of minorities. In France, the leftist coalition has officially adopted the label "plural majority." Without the concept of status incongruence, it would be difficult to explain its electoral success.

Projections of demographic trends suggest that Western societies are becoming increasingly diversified along a noneconomic axis and that the amount of status incongruence nourished by ethnic and racial characteristics will increase.

A mountain of statistics has been collected showing that objective inequality and social consciousness explain only a relatively small part of the variance in studies of social stratification. What must be added is an interpretation in terms of status congruence–incongruence.

REFERENCES

Barber, Bernard 1957 *Social Stratification.* New York: Harcourt Brace.

Bendix, Reinhard, and Seymour M. Lipset, eds. 1966 *Class, Status, and Power.* Free Press.

Bourdieu, Pierre 1978 "Classement, Déclassement, Reclassement." *Actes de la Recherche in Sciences Sociales* 24:2–22.

Clark, T. N., and S. M. Lipset 1991 "Are Social Classes Dying?" *International Sociology* 6(4):397–410.

Dogan, Mattei 1995 "Erosion of Class Voting and of the Religious Vote in Western Europe." *International Social Science Journal* 146:525–538.

——— 1999 "Marginality." *In Encyclopedia of Creativity,* vol. I. London: Academic Press.

Esping-Andersen, Costa 1992 "Post-Industrial Class Structures: An Analytical Framework," working paper, Madrid: Juan March Institute.

Goldthorpe, John H. 1996 "Class Analysis and the Reorientation of Class Theory." *British Journal of Sociology* 47(3):481–505.

Feagin, Joe 1997 "The Future of U.S. Society in the Era of Racism, Group Segregation and Demographic Revolution." *The Heritage and Future of Sociology in the North American Region.* International Sociological Association.

Lenski Gerhard E. 1954 "Status Crystallization: A Non-Vertical Dimension of Social Status." *American Sociological Review* 19:405–413.

——— 1966 *Power and Privilege.* New York: McGraw-Hill.

Lijphart, Arend 1977 *Democracy in Plural Societies.* New Haven, Conn.: Yale Universtity Press.

Lipset, S. M., and R. Bendix 1959 *Social Mobility in Industrial Society.* University of California Press.

——— and H. Zetterberg 1956 "A Theory of Social Mobility." In Reinhard Bendix and Seymour M. Lipset, eds., *Class, Status, and Power.* New York: Free Press.

Lopreato, Joseph, and Lawrence Hazelrigg 1972 *Class, Conflict, and Mobility*. San Francisco: Chandler.

Malewski, Andrej 1963 "The Degree of Status Incongruence and its Effects." In Reinhard Bendix and Seymour M. Lipset, eds., *Class, Status, and Power*. New York: Free Press.

Paugam, S. 1994 *La Disqualification Sociale: Essai sur la Nouvelle Pauvreté*. Paris: Presses Universitaires de France.

Rossides, Daniel 1976 *The American Class System*. Boston: Houghton-Mifflin.

Scheuch, Erwin 1969 "Social Context and Individual Behavior." in M. Dogan and S. Rokkan, eds., *Quantitative Ecological Analysis in the Social Sciences*. Cambridge, Mass.: M. I. T. Press.

Thelat, Claude 1982 *Tel Père, Tel Fils: Position Sociale et Origine Familiale*. Paris: Dunod.

Turner, Frederick 1992 *Social Mobility and Political Attitudes*. New Brunswick: Transaction Publishers.

Wilenski, Harold L., and Hugh Edwards 1959 "The Skidders: Ideological Adjustments of Downwardly Mobile Workers." *American Sociological Review* 24:215–231.

MATTEI DOGAN

STEREOTYPES

See Attitudes; Discrimination; Prejudice.

STRESS

NOTE: *Although the following article has not been revised for this edition of the Encyclopedia, the substantive coverage is currently appropriate. The editors have provided a list of recent works at the end of the article to facilitate research and exploration of the topic.*

The theoretical interest in social epidemiology, the study of effects of social conditions on the diffusion of distress and diseases in the population, can be traced to Durkheim's study of suicide in 1897 (1951). Since then, theory and research have elaborated on the associations among the various forms of social integration and psychiatric disorder. Among the classic works are Faris and Dunham's study of the ecology of mental disorders in urban areas (1939), Hollingshead and Redlick's research on social class and mental illness in New Haven (1958), the midtown Manhattan studies (Srole et al. 1962; Langner and Michael

1962; Srole 1975), the Sterling County studies by the Leightons and their colleagues (A. H. Leighton 1959; C. C. Hughes et al. 1960; D. Leighton et al. 1963) and the British studies by Brown and his associates (Brown and Harris, 1978). Each study illuminates the linkage between social conditions and distress and advances theories, hypotheses and empirical evidence in the specification of the relationships.

A parallel theoretical development has also taken place, over the past thirty-five years, in the formulation of the life stress paradigm in social psychiatry. The birth of this paradigm can be dated to the work of Hans Selye (1956) whose study of the undifferentiated response (physiological and psychological) that is generated by diverse external stimuli (stressors) linked sociological constructs to the internal individualistic responses made by individuals to their environment. This stress-distress model provided impetus for a convergence between the earlier sociological concerns with consequences of social integration and the physiological modeling of internal responses to the external environment.

The stress research enterprise gained further momentum when Holmes and Rahe, and subsequently other researchers, developed measures of life experiences that require social adjustments, known as inventories of life events (Holmes and Rahe 1967; Dohrenwend and Dohrenwend 1974, 1981; Myers and Pepper 1972). The life events schedules provide a convenient instrument that can be applied to a wide range of populations and administered with ease. The instrument has shown a high degree of validity and reliability relative to many measures of distress across populations and time lags.

In general, the research shows that life stressors, as measured by the life events schedules, exert a significant but moderate influence on mental and physical well-being. In a simple zero-order correlation, the relationship between life stressors and well-being (e.g., depressive symptoms) ranges between .25 and .40 (Rabkin and Struening 1976). This figure is somewhat less for physical health (House 1981; Wallston et al. 1987; Ensel 1986). The magnitude of this relationship seems to hold up when other factors are taken into account (e.g., general socioeconomic status measures; age; gender; psychological resources such as self-esteem, personal competence, and locus of control; physical health; and prior mental state).

MODIFICATIONS AND EXTENSIONS–THE MEDIATION PROCESSES

Modifications of the stressors-distress paradigm have taken several directions. In one direction, the conceptualization of stress as undifferentiated response has been modified so that the nature of stressors entails further specification. For example, in the analysis of life events, desirability, controllability, and importance are identified as dimensions exerting differential effects on distress (Thoits 1981; Tausig 1986). Research has shown that when only self-perceived undesirable life events are considered, the effect of the stressor instrument on distress increases marginally but significantly. It has also been shown that when items pertaining to psychological states (sleeping and eating problems) or illnesses are deleted, the magnitude of its effect is only marginally reduced (Ensel and Tausig 1982; Tausig 1982, 1986).

Conceptualization and operationalization of stressors have also been extended to include role strains (Pearlin and Schooler 1978) and daily hassles (Lazarus and Folkman 1984). Generally speaking, these stressors have demonstrated consistent but moderate effects on mental health, with zero-order correlations with various measures of mental health ranging from .15 to .35.

Another direction focuses attention on factors mediating or buffering the stressors-distress relationship. Researchers have identified three major components involved in the stress process: stressors, mediating factors, and outcome variables. Pearlin et al. (1981) viewed these constructs as multifaceted. Mediators consist of both external coping resources (i.e., social support) and internal coping resources (i.e., mastery and self-esteem). Outcome factors consist of psychological and physical symptomatology.

Social support, for example, has been considered a major candidate variable, and the cumulative evidence is that it exerts both direct and indirect effects on mental health (Cobb 1976; Cassel 1974, 1976; Nuckolls, Cassel, and Kaplan 1972; Dean and Lin 1977; Lin et al 1979; Turner 1981; Barrera and Ainlay 1983; Aneshensel and Huba 1984; Sarason and Sarason 1985; Kessler and McLeod 1985; Lin, Dean, and Ensel 1986; Berkman 1985; Cohen and Wills 1985; House, Umberson, and Landis 1988). Coping has also received substantial research attention and been found to be an effective mediator (Pearlin et al, 1981; Wheaton 1983, 1989; Lazarus and Folkman 1984). This type of research has served as the prototype for the sociopsychological study of stress in the 1980s (Pearlin, 1989). Emphasis has been placed on the mechanisms by which social resources, provided or called upon in the presence of a stressor, operate to alter the effect of the stressor (House, Umberson, and Landis 1988; Kessler, Price, and Wortman 1985; Thoits 1985).

DEVELOPMENT OF INTEGRATIVE AND TIME-LAGGED MODELS

While conceptual analysis and research attention have been given to life stress, resources (social support and coping), and psychological stress for their potential effects on health and mental health, only recently have specific proposals emerged in integrating these elements into a coherent theoretical framework. Dohrenwend and Dohrenwend (1981) summarized various formulations of life stress processes involving stressors (life events) and the psychological and social contexts in which they occurred. These formulations were synthesized into six hypotheses, each of which was shown to provide viable conceptual linkages between stressors (life events) and health outcomes and to have received some empirical support. The hypotheses in these models share two common features: (1) The ultimate dependent variable is adverse health or adverse health change rather than mental health problems or disorders, and (2) each hypothesis delineates and explains the possible empirical association between life events and health. Some of the hypotheses affirm the primary role of life events as causing health problems, while others incorporate mediating factors to explain health problems. The Dohrenwends (1974) proposed that these hypotheses should be examined together for their relative merits. Golden and Dohrenwend (1981) outlined the analytic requirements for testing these causal hypotheses.

Further elaboration of these hypotheses formed the basis of an integrative life stress paradigm in which stressors and resources in three environments—social, psychological, and physiological—

are considered as the factors impinging on well-being (Lin and Ensel 1989). This model specifies the enhancing (resources) and detrimental (stressing) forces in each environment. These stressors and resources in the three environments interact in affecting one's physical and mental health. Empirical evidence suggests that social resources tend to mediate the stress process involving mental health, whereas psychological resources are more prominent in mediating the process involving physical health.

Another integrative attempt incorporates multidisciplinary and multilevel variables in the study of life stress. For example, Lazarus and Folkman (1984) and Trumbull and Appley (1986) have conceptualized cognitive mechanisms involved in the stress process. Lazarus and Folkman proposed a model in which three levels of analysis (social, psychological, and physiological) are conducted to understand the antecedent, mediating, and immediate as well as long-term effects on distress. Trumbull and Appley (1986) proposed the simultaneous assessment of the physiological system, psychological system, and social system functioning. These functionings have both intrasystem and intersystem reciprocal relationships and exert joint effects on distress. In the later paradigms, emphasis has been placed on personality factors and coping skills. Additionally, the importance of linking social, psychological, and physical factors in the study of the stress process has been noted. Causal antecedents of both depressive and physical symptomatology are viewed as coming from social, psychological, and physiological sources and are hypothesized to be mediated by a variety of coping factors and perceived social support.

Pearlin and Aneshensel have proposed a synthesized paradigm (Pearlin 1989; Pearlin and Aneshensel 1986) in which health behaviors and illness behaviors have been incorporated into the basic stress process and in which equal attention has been given to the potential mediating and moderating roles of social and psychological resources. Thus, in addition to mediating the effect of stressors on illness outcomes, coping and social support are viewed as having the potential to mediate health and illness behaviors. An important element of this synthesizing paradigm is the recognition that physical illness creates life problems that are reflected in an increase in undesirable life events—that is, in addition to stressors affecting physical illnesses, physical illness also has the potential to bring about the occurrence of stressors. In such a synthesized paradigm, stressors embedded in social structure (e.g., role strains and problems) interact with illness behavior and illnesses. These interactions are mediated by coping and social support.

Finally, growing attention has been given to the need for studying the stress process over time (Wheaton 1989). Not only have there been concerns with causal interpretations of cross-sectional data, but more importantly, a call for longer lags in the panel design to capture the stress process in the life course more realistically (Thoits 1982). Some of the earlier panel studies, such as the midtown Manhattan study (Srole and Fischer 1978), the Kansas City study (Pearlin et al. 1981), the New Haven study (Myers, Lindenthal, and Pepper 1975), and the Cleveland GAO study (Haug and Folmar 1986) have all made significant contributions to understanding the stress process in urban communities. More current efforts, incorporating prevailing models and variables, would substantially add to the knowledge about stress in the life course. Current panel studies, such as those mounted by Aneshensel in Southern California; House and his associates on a national sample; Berkman in New Haven; Murrell in Kentucky; and Lin, Dean, and Ensel in upstate New York have the potential to expand research programs into investigations of the life-course process of stress.

(SEE ALSO: *Mental Illness and Mental Disorders; Personality Theories*)

REFERENCES

Aneshensel, Carol S. 1992 "Social Stress: Theory and Research." *Annual Review of Sociology* 18:15–38.

Aneshensel, C. S., and G.J. Huba 1984 "An Integrative Causal Model of the Antecedents and Consequences of Depression over One Year." In James R. Greenley, ed., *Research in Community and Mental Health.* Greenwich, Conn.: JAI Press.

Avison, William R. and Ian H Gotlib (eds.) 1994 *Stress and Mental Health: Contemporary Issues and Prospects for the Future.* New York: Plenum Press.

Barrera, M., and S. L. Ainlay 1983 "The Structure of Social Support: A Conceptual and Empirical Analysis." *Journal of Community Psychology* 11:133–143.

Berkman 1985 "The Relationship of Social Networks and Social Support to Morbidity and Mortality." In S. Cohen and S. L. Syme, eds., *Social Support and Health.* New York: Academic Press.

Brown, G. W., and T. Harris 1978 *Social Origins of Depression: A study of Psychiatric Disorder in Women.* New York: The Free Press.

Cassel, J. 1974 "An Epidemiological Perspective of Psychosocial Factors in Disease Etiology." *American Journal of Public Health* 64:1040–1043.

—— 1976 "The Contribution of the Social Environment to Host Resistance." *American Journal of Epidemiology* 104:107–123.

Cobb, S. 1976 "Social Support as a Moderator of Life Stress." *Psychosomatic Medicine* 38:300–314.

Cohen, S., and T. A. Wills 1985 "Stress, Social Support, and the Buffering Hypothesis." *Psychological Bulletin* 98(2):310–357

Coyne, James C. and Geraldine Downey 1991 "Social Factors and Psychopathology: Stress, Social Support, and Coping Processes." *Annual Review of Psychology* 42:401–425.

Dean, Alfred, and Nan Lin 1977 "The Stress Buffering Role of Social Support." *Journal of Nervous and Mental Disease* 165(2):403–13.

Dohrenwend, B. S., and B. P. Dohrenwend 1974 *Stressful Life Events: Their Nature and Effect.* New York: Wiley.

—— 1981 "Life Stress and Illness: Formulation of the Issues." In B. S. Dohrenwend and B. P. Dohrenwend, eds., *Stressful Life Events: Their Nature and Effects.* New York: Prodist.

Durkheim, Emile 1951 *Suicide.* Glencoe, Ill.: The Free Press.

Ensel, Walter M. 1986 "Measuring Depression: The CES-D scale." In Nan Lin, Alfred Dean, and Walter M. Ensel, eds., *Social Support, Life Events, and Depression.* Orlando, Fla.: Academic Press.

——, and Mark Tausig 1982 "The Social Context of Undesirable Life Events." Presented October 11–12 at the National Conference on Social Stress, DurHam, N.H.

—— and Nan Lin 1991 "The Life Stress Paradigm and Psychological Distress." *Journal of Health and Social Behavior* 32:321–341.

Faris, Robert E. K., and H. Warren Dunham 1939 *Mental Disorders in Urban Areas.* Chicago: University of Chicago Press.

Fernandez, Maria E., Elizabeth J. Mutran, and Donald C. Reitzes 1998 "Moderating the Effects of Stress on Depressive Symptoms." *Research on Aging* 20:163–182.

George, Linda K. 1993 "Sociological Perspectives on Life Transitions." *Annual Review of Sociology* 19:353–373.

Golden, R. R., and B. S. Dohrenwend 1981 "Teating Hypotheses about the Life Stress Process: A Path Analytic Method for Testing Causal Hypotheses." In B. S. Dohrenwend and B. P. Dohrenwend, eds., *Stressful Life Events: Their Nature and Effects.* NY: Prodist.

Gotlib, Ian H. and Blair Wheaton, eds. 1997 *Stress and Adversity over the Life Course: Trajectories and Turning Points.* Cambridge: Cambridge University Press

Haug, M. R., and S. J. Folmar 1986 "Longevity, Gender, and Life Quality." *Journal of Health and Social Behavior* 27:332–346.

Hollingshead, August, and Fredrick Redlick 1958 *Social Class and Mental Illness.* New York: Wiley.

Holmes, T., and R. Rahe 1967 "The Social Readjustment Rating Scale." *Journal of Psychosomatic Research* 11:213–218.

House, James S. 1981 *Work Stress and Social Support.* Reading, Mass.: Addison-Wesley.

——, Karl R. Landis, and Debra Umberson 1988 "Social Relationships and Health." *Science* 241 (July 29):540–545.

—— 1988 "Structures and Processes of Social Support." *Annual Review of Sociology* 14:293–318.

Hughes, C. C., M. A. Tremblay, et al. 1960 *People of Cove and Woodlot,* vol. 2 of the Sterling County Study. New York: Basic Books.

Kessler, R. C., and J. McLeod 1985 "Sex Differences in Vulnerability to Undesirable Life Events." *American Sociological Review* 49 (5):620–631.

Kessler, R. C., R. H. Price, and C. B. Wortman 1985 "Social Factors in Psychopathology: Stress, Social Support, and Coping Processes." *Annual Review of Psychology* 36:531–572.

Langner, T. S., and S. T. Michael 1962 *Life Stress and Mental Health.* New York: The Free Press.

Lazarus, Richard S. 1991 "Psychological Stress in the Workplace." *Journal of Social Behavior and Personality* 7:1–13.

——, and S. Folkman 1984 *Stress, Appraisal, and Coping.* New York: Springer.

Leighton, A. H. 1959 *My Name Is Legion.* New York: Basic Books.

Leighton, D. C., et al. 1963 *The Character of Danger.* New York: Basic Books.

Lin, Nan, Alfred Dean, and Walter M. Ensel 1986 *Social Support, Life Events, and Depression.* Orlando, Fla.: Academic Press.

Lin, Nan, and Walter M. Ensel 1989 "Life Stress and Health: Stressors and Resources." *American Sociological Review* 54:382–399.

Lin, Nan, Ronald Simeone, Walter M. Ensel, and Wen Kuo 1979 "Social Support, Stressful Life Events, and Illness: A Model and an Empirical Test." *Journal of Health and Social Behavior* 20 (1):108–119.

Myers, J. K., and M.P. Pepper 1972 "Life Events and Mental Status: A Longitudinal Study." *Journal of Health and Social Behavior* 13:398–406.

Myers, J. K., J. J. Lindenthal, and M. P. Pepper 1975 "Life Events, Social Integration, and Psychiatric Symptomatology." *Journal of Health and Social Behavior* 16:421–429.

Nuckolls, C. G., J. Cassel, and B. H. Kaplan 1972 "Psychosocial Assets, Life Crises, and the Prognosis of Pregnancy." *American Journal of Epidemiology* 95:431–441.

Pearlin, L. I. 1989 "The Sociological Study of Stress." *Journal of Health and Social Behavior* 30:241–256.

——, and C. Aneshensel 1986 "Coping and Social Supports: Their Function and Applications." In L. Aiken and D. Mechanic, eds., *Applications of Social Science in Clinical Medicine and Health*. New Brunswick, N.J.: Rutgers University Press.

——, M. A. Lieberman, E.G. Menaghan, and J. T. Mullan 1981 "The Stress Process." *Journal of Health and Social Behavior* 22:337–356.

——, and C. Schooler 1978 "The Structure of Coping." *Journal of Health and Social Behavior* 19 (1):2–21.

Rabkin, J. G., and E. L. Struening 1976 "Life Events, Stress, and Illness." *Science* 194:1013–1020.

Sarason, I. G., and B. R. Sarason 1985 *Social Support: Theory, Research, and Application*. The Hague: Martinus-Nijhoff.

Scheck, Christine L., Angelo J. Kinicki, and Jeannette A. Davy 1995 "A Longitudinal Study of a Multivariate Model of the Stress Process Using Structural Equations Modeling." *Human Relations* 48:1481–1510.

Seyle, Hans 1956 *The Stress of Life*. New York: Mc-Graw-Hill.

Srole, L. 1975. "Measurements and Classification in Sociopsychiatric Epidemiology: Midtown Manhattan Study I (1954) and Midtown Manhattan Restudy II (1974)." *Journal of Health and Social Behavior* 16: 347–364.

——, T. S. Langner, S. T. Michael, et al. 1962 *The Midtown Manhattan Study*. New York: McGraw-Hill.

Tausig, Mark 1982 "Measuring Life Events." *Journal of Health and Social Behavior* 23 (March):52–64.

—— 1986 "Measuring Life Events." In Nan Lin, Alfred Dean, and Walter M. Ensel, eds., *Social Support, Life Events, and Depression*. Orlando, Fla.: Academic Press.

Thoits, Peggy A. 1981 "Undesirable Life Events and Psychophysiological Distress: A Problem of Operational Confounding." *American Sociological Review* 46 (1):97–109.

—— 1982 "Conceptual, Methodological, and Theoretical Problems in Studying Social Support as a Buffer Against Life Stress." *Journal of Health and Social Behavior* 24:145–159.

—— 1985 "Social Support Processes and Psychological Well-being: Theoretical Possibilities." In I. G. Sarason and B. R. Sarason, eds., *Social Support: Theory, Research, and Application*. The Hague: Martinus-Nijhoff.

—— 1995 "Stress, Coping, and Social Support Processes: Where Are We? What Next?" *Journal of Health and Social Behavior*, extra issue: 53–79.

Tijhuis, M. A. R., H. D. Flap, M. Foets, and P. P. Groenewegen 1995, "Social Support and Stressful Events in Two Dimensions: Life Events and Illness as an Event." *Social Science and Medicine* 40:1513–1526.

Trumbull, R., and M. H. Appley 1986 "A Conceptual Model for the Examination of Stress Dynamics." In M. H. Appley and R. Trumbull, eds., *Dynamics of Stress: Physiological, Psychological, and Social Perspectives*. New York: Plenum.

Turner, R. J. 1981 "Social Support as a Contingency in Psychological Well-being." *Journal of Health and Social Behavior* 22:357–367.

Uhlenhuth, E. H., et al. 1982 "Symptom Checklist Syndromes in the General Population: Correlations with Psychotherapeutic Drug Use." *Archives of General Psychiatry* 40:1167–1173.

Unger, Jennifer B., C. Anderson Johnson, and Gary Marks 1997 "Functional Decline in the Elderly: Evidence for Direct and Stress-Buffering Protective Effects of Social Interactions and Physical Activity." *Annals of Behavioral Medicine* 19:152–160.

Wallston, B. S., et al. 1987 "Social Support and Physical Health." *Health Psychology* 2 (4):367–391.

Wheaton, B. 1983 "Stress, Personal Coping Resources, and Psychiatric Symptoms: An Investigation of Interactive Models." *Journal of Health and Social Behavior* 24:208–229.

—— 1989 "Life Transitions, Role Histories, and Mental Health." *American Sociological Review* 2:209–223.

NAN LIN

STRIKES

See Labor Movements and Unions; Industrial Sociology.

STRUCTURAL EQUATIONS

See Causal Inference Models; Correlation and Regression Analysis; Multiple Indicator Models.

STRUCTURAL LAG

The concept of structural lag originally was suggested by the observation that in the late twentieth century there was a discrepancy between the growing number of older healthy people and the meaningful roles available to them. This simple empirical observation is only one instance of a more general phenomenon: a mismatch between the numbers and kinds of people of a given age and existing patterns in the social structures into which people must fit. This mismatch occurs because changes in people's lives and changes in social structures typically are not synchronic. When social structures fail to adapt to new cohorts with characteristics different from those of previous cohorts, there is a situation of structural lag (Riley et al. 1994).

PREMISES ABOUT AGE AND SOCIETY

How and why structural lags emerge and how they are dealt with can be better understood by considering the underlying principles of age as both an individual and a social phenomenon and its relationship to social change.

1. Age not only is a characteristic of people but is built into social structures in the form of criteria for entering or leaving social roles, expectations about behavior in those roles, and resources and rewards for role performance. Formal and informal rules govern the age at which children enter and stay in school, age patterns in the family such as the appropriate age at first marriage, and age of entry into and retirement from the work force. Age norms influence behavior and orientations in these roles, and conformity is but-tressed by material rewards and social approval.

2. Both the process of aging from birth to death and social structures related to age are subject to change. The aging process is not the same for all cohorts, since members of each cohort (those born in the same period) grow up and grow older under unique social, political, and environmental circumstances. For example, cohorts of people born around the beginning of the twentieth century differ from those born a half century later in level of education, exposure to illness, size of the family, job skills, the likelihood of being married and divorced, and attitudes and worldviews. Cohorts born at the end of the twentieth century will differ from their predecessors in still other ways. For example, the birth weight of newborns in the 1980s and 1990s was greater than that of babies born in earlier times, and this undoubtedly will influence the way that members of those cohorts develop. Further, as the more recent cohorts grow up, it is likely that they will to benefit from new medical advances. Age patterns in social structures have changed as well. To cite two examples, schools have raised the school-leaving age, and government and corporate policies have encouraged a decline in the typical age of retirement.

3. Changes in patterns of aging and in social structures affect each other; they are interdependent. As an example, by altering long-standing employment practices, restructuring, downsizing, and mergers of large firms in the United States have led to a shift in the work lives of employees. Thus, compared to previous cohorts of workers, fewer workers now can look forward to lifetime employment in one firm; many have to make multiple career changes, and some have to make do with temporary and part-time employment at some time in their working lives. In turn, new patterns of careers over the life course are likely to have an impact on societal institutions. Firms are likely to reduce their commitment to training workers, with educational institutions as-

suming greater responsibility for training and retraining.

While changing aging processes and social structures affect each other, the two processes of change are distinct, with each following its own dynamics. The aging process, while varying across cohorts, has a distinct rhythm, as people are born and then proceed through childhood, adolescence, adulthood, and old age. Social structures do not have a similar rhythm. The economy has ups and downs; political shifts follow their own paths; and cataclysmic events such as wars, depressions, famines, and epidemics affect all social institutions. Consequently, in any period there is likely to be a poor fit between lives and structures: an imbalance between what people of given ages have to offer, what they need and expect in their lives, and their motivations versus what social structures can accommodate or demand.

4. Lags can occur in either direction. Sometimes people's lives lag behind changes in social structures. For example, many older people may be reluctant to learn and use new technologies, or adolescents may not be motivated to take the science courses that will prepare them for technological changes. At the end of the twentieth century, however, a key form of imbalance is the lag of social structures behind changes in people's lives. As the examples discussed below indicate, structural lag is pervasive, affecting people of all ages and many social institutions.

STRUCTURAL LAG AT THE MILLENNIUM

A focus on the fit or misfit between people and structures in three major age strata shows how these principles play themselves out and how structural lags have emerged.

The Old. The increase in the number and proportion of older people in the twentieth century is a dramatic example of a change in people's lives that has posed numerous problems for societal institutions. By the end of the century people 65 years old and over represented 13 percent of the U.S. population compared to about 4 percent at the beginning of the century. More than 70 percent of Americans now live to age 65, almost three times the proportion at the beginning of the century. These changes are in large part the result of public and private health care measures that reduced infant mortality decades ago, increasing the proportion of individuals who could survive to the later years. Reductions in infant and child mortality were followed by reductions in death rates among older people, partly as a result of public health and scientific and medical innovations and partly because of healthy practices in diet and exercise undertaken by individuals. Indeed, old people at the end of the twentieth century are a relatively healthy lot. Most report that they have no disabilities; even among those over age 85, about 40 percent report being able to function in daily life (Rowe and Kahn 1998). Thus, not only are more people growing old, they are aging well.

Social institutions have been slow to accommodate to the needs of this new kind of older population, a lag that represents not only lost opportunities for the old but a loss of the productive capabilities of older people to society. Consider the organization of work and retirement. Although 65 is the age of eligibility for full Social Security benefits, most people in recent years have been retiring before that age. This pattern of early retirement was facilitated by Social Security regulations, devised in an earlier period, that exact little or no cost for retiring before age 65. On their part, many employing organizations, driven by changing personnel requirements, offer financial incentives for early retirement. Also, in the process of restructuring their firms or merging with others, employers let many long-term employees go, many of whom retired early rather than face the uncertainties of the job market. If they are assured of financial security in retirement, some workers welcome the opportunity to retire early, perhaps because of their health or because of the onerous or stultifying nature of their jobs. Nevertheless, surveys find that a sizable proportion of older workers prefer not to sever their ties to the labor force completely (Burkhauser and Quinn 1994). However, few firms permit workers to continue at their old jobs under the more flexible working conditions many workers prefer. Available part-time or temporary jobs typically have few, if any, of the benefits of workers' former employment, and the pay is generally low. The result is that many older workers withdraw from the labor force completely—often unwillingly. Employing organizations thus lose the benefits that experienced workers can bring to their firms.

Paid employment is not the only way older workers can make productive contributions to society. A sizable minority of older people do volunteer work that has social value—in religious, charitable, and civic organizations, for example. Structural lag and resistance to new ideas and values consistent with a changed society may explain why more older persons do not volunteer. Volunteer organizations often do not have recruiting mechanisms to draw on the large pool of potential older volunteers. With respect to societal values, volunteer work is not accorded the same respect as paid employment (Kahn 1994).

Societal institutions are lagging behind the needs of an unfortunate sector of the older population: those in poor health who need support. Especially among the oldest old, there is a need for long-term care either in the home or in a nursing facility, but affordable arrangements for such care are inadequate. As a result some older people are not getting the care they need, and the burden for caring for them falls on their elderly spouses or their middle-aged offspring or other relatives. In such ways, structural lag in care institutions affects both the old and the middle-aged. Unless there are relevant structural changes in these care institutions and/or government programs to shore them up, there will be problems for the baby boom cohorts when they reach their later years. They will have fewer kin available to provide the needed support, since the baby boom cohorts were followed by relatively small cohorts.

Children. Children's lives also have changed dramatically; today they have vastly different growing up experiences than did earlier cohorts. As a consequence, children now differ from their predecessors in attitudes, capabilities, motivations, behaviors, and the choices they make. These dispositions will affect their paths of future development: their school careers, job choices and opportunities, and marriage and family decisions.

One development that has altered the lives of children has been the increase in single-parent families. On average, these families are poorer than two-parent families, and there are long-term consequences for children raised under condi-

tions of poverty. Experiencing poverty as infants and young children (zero to 5 years of age) affects people's subsequent educational achievement and employability (Duncan, et al. 1998). The increase in single-parent families thus does not bode well for the future of their young offspring, many of whom will not be prepared to fill the roles available in a technologically advanced and constantly changing society.

There has also been a marked increase in families where both the father and the mother work outside the home. Unless they have high incomes, dual-earner families, share with single-parent families the problem of finding adequate child care arrangements. A small proportion of mothers cope with both work and taking care of children, and a similarly small percentage of fathers care for children while mothers work away from the home. In some cases, grandparents or other relatives care for children outside the children's home. The well off can afford paid babysitters, and about one-quarter of preschoolers of working mothers are in some form of organized day care. Many of these facilities, however, have been judged unsafe or unsanitary and do not offer a warm and intellectually stimulating environment.

While the long-term outcome of these new socialization environments for infants and children cannot be known yet, social structures outside the family clearly are not filling the gaps created by changed family arrangements. Most important, there has been no institutionalization of satisfactory nonparental child care arrangements; social structures outside the family are lagging behind changes in children's lives and changes in the family.

There is also a gap between the lives of school-age children and social structures. Consider institutions of public education. Among the many undertakings of public schools at the end of the twentieth century, there are two major tasks: educating students raised in changed family environments and preparing those students for a changed society in which people increasingly will need the ability to adapt to continual changes and more jobs will require high levels of conceptual thinking.

By and large, experimental programs and various changes in schools notwithstanding, schools are falling behind in meeting these challenges. For example, many teachers have inadequate knowledge of subject matter; curricula often lag behind new knowledge and are too often shaped by the nature of national or statewide tests; frequently there is administrative inertia and resistance to change; and students often are not challenged sufficiently in terms of, for example, the amount and nature of homework. These patterns militate against the goal of inculcating the kinds of thinking and other skills that will be needed in the next decades, when today's students will enter the labor force and take on adult responsibilities.

Adults. Structural lags affecting the old and the young have an impact on people in their middle years. It is those people years who must undertake the care of the young and the old when there are no alternatives, but it is precisely when people are in their prime years that they have heightened job and career responsibilities. Social structures are lagging in providing arrangements— such as flexible hours or flexible workplace settings and respite care from social agencies—that would ease the multiple burdens of those with career and family care responsibilities.

It is not only work organizations and social agencies that are not helping workers undertake their multiple responsibilities: Family structures are not adapting to the new realities either. It is women who typically bear the brunt of multiple burdens of work and family care. While most married women with children work outside the home, they still have the main responsibility for tasks in the home. More husbands—when they are present—are "helping" with household work than was the case in earlier times, but the norm of equal sharing has not been institutionalized. There is a gap between the changed lives of women and the way most families are structured.

Class, Gender, and Race Differences. There are differences within the several age strata (layers of people who differ in age and confront structures differentially appropriate for particular ages) in the degree of fit between changed people and changed institutions. The match or mismatch between people of given ages and institutions often depends on the gender, ethnicity, race, or class of the people involved.

Thus, the impact of structural lag is uneven. In some instances it is the most disadvantaged segments of the different age strata that are most likely to feel the brunt of the lag.

CLOSING THE GAP: PRESSURES FOR CHANGE

The gap between structures and the lives of the individuals in those structures creates tensions, inefficiencies, and other problems that are potent stimuli for change in both people and structures. Whatever the constraints, social structures tend to respond to these forces.

Social Structural Responses. Social structural responses to an increase in cohort size—a key source of pressure on structures—are illustrative. Beginning in midcentury, the pressure on social institutions came from the unexpectedly large number of people in the baby boom cohorts, whose large size created a lag in structures at every life stage. As Waring (1976) shows, social institutions coped with these large cohorts in myriad ways. When the baby boom cohorts were newborns, hospitals reduced the typical length of stay of new mothers and their babies to accommodate the flood of new births. When the baby boomers entered school, new schools were built and younger teachers were hired to compensate for the teacher shortage. In their college years, educational requirements were extended, with the result that entry into the labor force was delayed, helping to prevent a labor glut. These changes generally came piecemeal, but many of them, such as shorter maternal hospital stays, have turned out to be long-lasting.

As the number of old people has increased and as the baby boomers approach old age, there are signs that social institutions are making further changes. Indeed, as the changes made in many different institutional settings accumulate, new social meanings of age may arise. Age barriers to entry into a broad range of social roles are being relaxed and even breakingdown. For individuals this means increased opportunities to intersperse periods of education, work, family time, and leisure over the life course, unlike the more rigid pattern of education in youth, work in adulthood, and retirement and leisure in old age that has been the typical shape of the life course (Riley et al. 1999). Within institutions, as more roles become available to people of all ages, cross-age interactions are likely to increase. Also, the pool of human capital available to varied social institutions will no longer be limited by rigid age norms.

Mechanisms of Change. Changes, whether piecemeal or encompassing, do not come about automatically. A number of processes operate singly or in combination to bring about change.

Actions of policymakers. Some individuals and agencies are in a good position to make and implement policy—government officials and company executives, for example—because they have an overview of their organizations and can propose or institute policies that will reduce the gap between people and structures.

One of the portents of more flexible age criteria has been the opening up of colleges and universities to older students. Educational administrators have played an important role in this development. They saw an opportunity to expand the pool of prospective students and felt a responsibility to offer access to their schools to older people. They have devised special degree programs for older people along with a wide range of nondegree classes. On a less formal level, other organizational leaders have developed elder hostel programs that give older people a chance to combine education and recreation, programs that have expanded beyond college settings and beyond the United States.

Undoubtedly, these policy initiatives were influenced by the actions of older people who were seeking avenues for enriching their lives or for filling in gaps in their education. Indeed, people inside social structures often act as agents of change, sometimes engaging in purposeful action with others and sometimes acting independently, as in the case of cohort norm formation, another mechanism of change.

Cohort norm formation. As formulated by Riley (1978), cohort norm formation is a process that occurs when the members of a cohort, reacting independently but in like fashion to changes in society, create new patterns of behavior and attitudes. These changes often spread to the succeeding cohorts, contributing to the establishment of new norms.

The centurylong increase in women's labor force participation is a prime example of this process. Since the early decades of the twentieth century, in successive cohorts, increasing proportions of women have worked outside the home. They were, of course, responding to broad social forces that eased household burdens, facilitated control of family size, and introduced workplace technologies that women could manage efficiently. However, it was individual women who made the decision to enter and remain in the labor force after marriage. As they did so, norms for women's labor force participation changed. Early in the century the typical married woman did not hold a job outside the home and was not expected to, but as increasing numbers of women sought employment, it became acceptable for them to work for pay. At the end of the twentieth century, not only are high proportions of single and married women in the labor force, it is expected that women will have paying jobs regardless of their marital status. This norm was embodied in welfare legislation in the 1990s: Poor women were given time limits for welfare payments to support them and their dependent children. After that deadline, they were expected to be self-supporting.

Among older people at terminal stages of the life course, another set of norms has been forming (Riley 1990). Older people have been pressing for new norms that will help them avoid a prolonged, painful process of dying, provide palliative care, and give them more control of the way they die. New norms for the dying process and arrangements to implement them are being put in place. Hospice care that eschews heroic measures for those near death has been more widely accepted, more people are writing living wills detailing measures to be taken near the end, and hospitals have been forming medical ethics committees to deal with these issues. The "right to die" movement has gained power and, with it, some of the structural changes it supports. However, this movement has taken on a new cast as it has focused more on improving caretaking arrangements than on the psychosocial needs of patients (see "Death and Dying" in this encyclopedia).

What started out as individual but uncoordinated responses of numerous older people and others concerned about unacceptable practices in the American way of dying—an example of cohort norm formation—have taken on the shape of a social movement, a more organized effort to change customary practices.

Social movements. Social movements have played a role in effecting many age-related changes. These movements take several forms. They may involve organized groups exerting pressure for change or may entail collective actions that arise more spontaneously. Whether organized or not, they bring issues of concern to public attention. Sometimes their actions lead to conflicts with groups that have different interests and agendas.

Organized social movements encompassing large segments particular age strata have emerged relatively infrequently. Most noteworthy was the Townsend movement in the 1930s, which organized older people to work for a publicly supported pension program for the elderly in the United States. At its height it had organized groups in almost every state. It played a role in the eventual enactment of Social Security legislation.

Although broad-based movements involving age-related issues are difficult to organize, more limited movements for structural change crop up. In the recent past there has been the "right to die" movement with its shifting emphases, as noted above, and organizations focusing on the problems of older women. At the other end of the age spectrum there is a children's rights movement concerned particularly about neglected children. By bringing problems to public attention and by lobbying policymakers directly, these social movements are able to stimulate at least piecemeal changes.

At times, social movements can trigger conflict among age strata. In the 1980s, for example, some pressure groups attempted to pit younger people against the old with dire predictions of intergenerational conflict in the future. Those groups argued that the elderly receive undue advantages from U.S. government programs and that younger adults are unfairly burdened with supporting those programs. Such age conflicts have not emerged, however, and challenges from younger adults that might provide the impetus for changes in government policies seem unlikely. The cross-age support for Social Security suggests why this is so. Younger adults want to maintain the Social Security program to safeguard their own future as well as to protect their parents' present status. Apart from affection for their parents, self-interest is involved. Without publicly supported pensions, those under age 65 would have to bear an increased financial burden to support their elderly parents. Moreover, many adults under age 65 benefit indirectly from gifts and ultimately

from inheritances made possible by the financial security afforded to the old by Social Security pensions. In short, the inevitability of growing old and the intergenerational bonds and exchanges within the family are powerful deterrents to conflicts between the young and the old (Foner 1974).

Obstacles to Change. Changing age-related components of social structures does not necessarily proceed smoothly. Long-held values, institutional rigidities, and the possible costs involved create impediments to effective change.

Proposals to make lifelong education a reality—not only educational opportunities for the old but also time off for retraining and sabbaticals for educational enrichment among those of working age—may seem simple to implement. However, many employers perceive that giving time off for sabbaticals is costly and often see no payoff from retraining mature workers when newly trained and cheaper young workers are available.

More equal sharing of household and child care responsibilities by young and middle-aged married adults can be thwarted by entrenched values about the appropriate roles of men and women.

Giving sick and dying patients increased autonomy in regard to their care does not comport with common practices such as rigid scheduling and beliefs of physicians and authorities in medical institutions that patients do not have the professional expertise needed to deal with their illness.

Unintended Consequences. Such obstacles notwithstanding, change does occur, but sometimes it has unforeseen results. For example, the spread of hospices that provide relief and palliative care for near-death patients has been a welcome alternative for people who do not want heroic—and often painful and expensive—measures. However, as the number of hospices and their patients has increased in the United States, federal regulatory agencies have found themselves hard put to monitor them and fraud has increased (New York Times 1998).

New norms about extending the work life will give healthy and eager older workers productive roles while at the same time addressing certain problems of the financial viability of the Social Security system. However, these new norms could undermine the right to retirement, discrediting those who are unable to work or those who need a rest after long years of toil. Further, an increase in the number of older workers in the labor market looking for good part-time jobs could lead to competition with young and female workers also looking for such jobs. One result could be depressed wages in this sector of the labor market.

Viewed in their particulars, changes in social structures do not always neatly adjust social institutions to the changed lives of people. The change may be only partial, some changes may work out well for some people but not for others, and new problems may emerge, calling for additional changes. Viewed in the long run, however, structural lag turns out to be a frequently unrecognized but powerful force for change.

STRUCTURAL LAG AND THEORIES OF CHANGE

The concept of structural lag as a force for change has a ring of familiarity. Many analysts have put forth theories about discrepancies among the several parts of the society that press for change.

Perhaps the idea seemingly most similar to structural lag is Ogburn's (1932) concept of "cultural lag." Ogburn conceived of culture as complex, consisting of interdependent parts. There is the material culture with its technology, raw materials, manufactured products, and the like, and the nonmaterial culture that includes folkways, mores, social institutions, beliefs, laws, and governments. Ogburn thought that changes in the nonmaterial culture generally were dependent on changes in the material culture and often lagged behind changes in the material culture, hence the notion of cultural lag.

While Ogburn's concept of culture includes many of the same components of social structure posited in the theory of structural lag, his approach to social change differs from the analysis of structural lag in a number of ways. Ogburn's emphasis is on the relationship among elements in the culture. The theory of structural lag introduces the lack of fit between *people* and structures. Moreover, not only are changes in the lives of people not synchronized with changes in social structures, people act as agents of change in trying to align structures with their changing lives. A related difference is that Ogburn views the motive power of change as residing in the material culture. By

contrast, the analysts of structural lag consider changing lives and changing social structures as interdependent, with no claim for the priority of one over the other.

Others also have proposed that inconsistencies in social structures create pressures for social change. For example, Marx and Engels (1848) discussed contradictions within capitalism, and Merton (1938, 1957) analyzed the disjunction between culturally defined goals and socially differential access to the opportunity structure for achieving those goals, but these theories differ from the analysis of structural lag in a number of ways.

For Marx, change has its source in a fundamental contradiction of capitalism between private ownership of the means of production and the social nature of the production process, a contradiction that results in the exploitation of wage laborers employed by and dependent on capitalist employers. As workers struggle to improve their working conditions, their actions lead to fundamental change in the social relations of production. However, Marx's analysis of capitalist contradictions focuses on the crucial role of the productive sphere, whereas the analysis of structural lag does not give preeminence to any particular institution. Structural lag can and does occur in all societal structures, and pressures for change can emanate from all of them. Nor is social conflict the major mechanism of social change posited in the theory of structural lag, where, as was noted above, other mechanisms of change are generally more important.

In Merton's theory, the disjunction between goals and means leads to several modes of deviant adaptation, of which one, "rebellion", clearly augurs social change. In rebellion, one segment of the population rejects both goals and means as socially defined and seeks to replace them with a "greatly modified social structure" (Merton 1957, p. 155). Thus, this theory suggests a mechanism for changing the existing cultural and social structure. It is not concerned with the continuous entry into society of new cohorts whose changing lives confront social structures with the need for change, a central focus of the theory of structural lag.

In summary, the theory of structural lag, while rooted in the special qualities of age and aging as social phenomena—seemingly a narrow focus—is a broad theory that links age and aging to both social structures and social change. In its structural aspects, it views age as a key element with which social structures must cope. From a dynamic perspective, it sees social forces bringing about change in people's lives, with those changing lives in turn causing pressure for changes in social structures. Structural lag thus is both a consequence of social change and an impetus for further change.

REFERENCES

Burkhauser, Richard V., and Joseph F. Quinn 1994 "Changing Policy Signals." In Matilda White Riley, Robert L. Kahn, and Anne Foner, eds., *Age and Structural Lag: Society's Failure to Provide Meaningful Opportunities in Work, Family, and Leisure.* New York: Wiley.

Duncan, Greg, J. W. Jean Yeung, Jeanne Brooks-Gunn, and Judith R. Smith 1998 "How Much Does Childhood Poverty Affect the Life Chances of Children?" *American Sociological Review* 63:406–423.

Foner, Anne 1974 "Age Stratification and Age Conflicts in Political Life." *American Sociological Review* 39:187–196.

Kahn, Robert L. 1994 "Opportunities, Aspirations, and Goodness of Fit," In Matilda White Riley, Robert L. Kahn, and Anne Foner, eds., *Age and Structural Lag: Society's Failure to Provide Meaningful Opportunities in Work, Family, and Leisure.* New York: Wiley.

Marx, Karl, and Frederich Engels. (1848) 1978 "Manifesto of the Communist Party." In R. Tucker, ed., *The Marx-Engels Reader,* 2nd ed. New York: Norton.

Merton, Robert K. 1938 "Social Structure and Anomie." *American Sociological Review* 3:672–682.

—— 1957 "Social Structure and Anomie," In *Social Theory and Social Structure.* Glencoe, Ill.: Free Press.

New York Times, May 10, 1998. "Hospice Boom Is Giving Rise to New Fraud" by Douglas Frantz, pp. 1, 8.

Ogburn, William F. 1932 *Social Change.* New York: Viking.

Riley, John, Jr. 1990 "Death and Dying." In E. Borgatta and M. Borgatta, eds., *The Encyclopedia of Sociology.* New York: Macmillan.

Riley, Matilda White 1978 "Aging, Social Change, and the Power of Ideas." *Daedalus* 107:39–52.

——, Anne Foner, and John W. Riley, Jr. 1999 "The Aging and Society Paradigm: From Generation to Generation." In Vern L. Bengtson and K. Warner Schaie, eds., *Handbook of Theories of Aging.* New York: Springer.

——, Robert L. Kahn, and Anne Foner, eds. 1994. *Age and Structural Lag: Society's Failure to Provide Meaning-ful Opportunities in Work, Family, and Leisure.* New York: Wiley.

Rowe, John W. and Robert L. Kahn 1998 *Successful Aging.* New York: Pantheon.

Waring, Joan 1976 "Social Replenishment and Social Change: The Problem of Disordered Cohort Flow." In Anne Foner, ed., *Age in Society.* Beverly Hills, Calif.: Sage.

ANNE FONER

STUDENT MOVEMENTS

Student movements generally are thought of college student movements. These young adult movements have a long history in widely differing societies. Some have been characterized as direct student redress of situational grievances, such as the seventeenth-century sacking of the English Jesuit College of La Fleche to protest a rigid, strained regimen and the student protests led by African-American and Hispanic students on over a hundred campuses in the 1980s and 1990s to protest cutbacks in governmental aid and scholarships for lower-income students. Other student protest movements have been related to larger social movements. Examples are evident over time and space, including the nineteenth-century Russian revolutionary student movement, the American civil rights and antiwar student movements of the 1930s and 1960s, the 1970s Greek student Polytechnic protest that precipitated the downfall of that country's military dictatorship, and the ill-fated Chinese Tianenmen Square democratic movement in the late 1980s.

Student movements have the potential to generate major social change in the context of underlying economic, demographic, and other social forces. This makes student movement a strategic factor in assessing the nature of some consequential social change developments in society. The recent history of the United States exemplifies this idea. The far-reaching Civil Rights Act of 1964, the public shift from support of to opposition to the Vietnam War, and the pressure to diversify college student bodies and curricula racially and ethnically all involved student protest–induced changes that have affected the lives of people throughout American society and influenced student movements in other societies, as movements in other societies have influenced American students.

Other examples of consequential student protest movements extend back a millennium or more. What is different about contemporary student movements is the combination of their frequency and their consequences for social change in society. This is a reflection of the central role of formal education in economic and social stability and development in both advanced technological and developing societies.

The massive growth of higher education, with the concomitant potential for student movements, is evident from the change in the proportion of young adults in their late teens and early twenties attending college. Before World War II, even in the advanced industrial nations of Japan, the United States, and Canada, as well as in Great Britain and western Europe, less than 10 percent of the young adult age cohort attended college. The figure was less than 1 percent in emerging, often formerly colonial, developing nations. In contrast, by the late twentieth century, close to half of young adults were in college in advanced technological societies, and the fastest growing student body in developing countries had become collegiate. Overall, instead of a few hundred or a few thousand students, major state universities in the United States now generally have between 20,000 and 40,000 or more students, with long-established private universities typically having over 10,000. Similarly, large national universities such as those in Beijing, Tehran, Madrid, Mexico City, and Moscow have student bodies larger than those of the largest U.S. state universities.

The growth of public education generally, and collegiate education in particular, has placed young adult students in a strategic position in respect to the potential of protest movements to induce social change. Prototypical examples at the end of the twentieth century range from the student protests that keyed the unexpected election of the former professional wrestler Jesse Ventura to the governorship of Minnesota and the overthrow of the authoritarian Suharto regime after over thirty years in Indonesia, the fourth most populous nation in the world.

The precipitating causes of these student protest activities were very different. In the case of Minnesota, the economy was strong and played no discernible role. Key factors were the intense national political conflict between Republicans and Democrats over President Clinton's sexual scandal, charges of obstruction of justice, and partisan controversy over a presidential impeachment. This induced many students and other young people to change allegiance from the established national parties to a reform party candidate. In Indonesia, the Asian economic crisis of 1998 played a key role in the protest activity of students demanding a more democratic government and more equitable economic opportunities.

In terms of real or potential effects on the direction of society, it is not only that college students represent a high proportion of influential future economic, political, and social leaders. The growth of colleges since the middle of the twentieth century is also an international reflection of the general public's and democratic and authoritarian regimes' recognition of the importance of the educational training of students. This training represents a key element in the future of various societies in the modern cybernetic economic era.

There has been extensive research on what motivates consequential proportions of students to engage in protest movements. There is irony in the fact that students represent a relatively privileged and prospectively influential group in society. These characteristics generally are associated with support for the established social order, yet students are often in the activist forefront of protest movements aimed at changing that order.

This seeming contradiction has been addressed in intergenerational conflict terms since the time of Socrates and Plato. In sociology, Mannheim (1952) addressed specific attention to this phenomenon as part of his concern with the sociology of knowledge. Building on Mannheim's analyses, Feuer (1969) holds that the need for the emerging young to replace older adults in societies generates inherent intergenerational conflict that crystallizes in increasingly influential collegiate settings.

In this context, it is held that students act out their traditional intergenerational conflicts in a setting that is particularly conducive to challenging the older generation. Colleges, and to a lesser extent primary and secondary schools, remove students from familial and kinship settings. While faculty members present an adult schooling influence, in the increasingly large school settings, students are placed in a peer-related situation removed from both direct familial influences and the later pressures of occupational positions.

This relatively separated, peer-influenced life pattern is evident in the precipitating protest actions of many student movements. Most sociological research has dealt with student participation in major protest movements involving civil rights, environmental protection, war, and other momentous public issues. However, a review of the student movement literature demonstrates that often the early motivation for student protest against university administrators and more general societal authorities has been related to specific student-experienced grievances over American-based situational concerns such as poor dormitory food in the 1950s and concerns among Italian and Chinese students in the 1960s and 1980s that growing numbers of college graduates were unemployed or were receiving lower pay than were undegreed manual laborers (Altbach and Peterson 1971; Lipset 1971).

Immediate student self-interest also can be seen in respect to student participation in larger social movements. This has been evident in respect to direct student concerns about conscription and being forced into combat situations. The 1860s Harvard University economic and social elite student anticonscription protests during the Civil War helped precipitate congressional modification of who was subject to the draft. Those with several hundred dollars were allowed to commute their draft status to the next young man called up who could not afford to commute being drafted. This was a central factor in the poor nonstudent Irish Catholic, conscription riots of 1863 in New York City that left several hundred dead.

Similar immediate self-interest was a part of the American Student Union antiwar movement before World War II in the 1930s as well as the anti–Vietnam War movement led by the Students for a Democratic Society (SDS) in the 1960s. These student protests partially reflected general public disagreement about war support, but the most common precipitating thread was immediate student interest. A particularly clear case of student self-interest was the high involvement of African-American students in the civil rights movements of the 1960s, working for more openings and support for African-Americans, who had long been excluded from equal higher educational opportunity.

However, immediate self-interest does not explain the active involvement of most participants in student movements to support disadvantaged minority and low-income groups. This is seen in protest actions such as extensive involvement in the Student Non-Violent Coordinating Committee and other American civil rights organizations in the 1960s and the 1989 student effort to establish democracy in China. In this respect, students tend to activate parental ideals and values that are perceived to be falling short in their implementation (Davies 1969). What has become evident in the extensive empirical research on student movement participants since the 1960s is that the conflict of generations thesis advanced by Mannheim, Feuer, and others is less a conflict of generations than an active attempt among the student generation to realize the values to which they have been socialized by the parental generation.

Rather than challenging the values of the parental generation, student activists generally support those values and work to see them actualized (DeMartini 1985). A case in point is the background characteristics of students who were active in the politically liberal SDS, which was strongly against the Vietnam War, and that of those in the politically conservative Young Americans for Freedom (YAF), which was strongly supportive of that war. As Lipset (1971) reports, SDS students were mostly from high-status Protestant homes where secular, liberal values prevailed. In contrast, but in intergenerational concurrence, YAF student activists generally were drawn from strongly religiously observant and conservative homes in lower middle-class and working-class settings. Another example of this intergenerational confluence is Bell's (1968) documentation that the largest proportion of white student activists in the Congress of Racial Equality (CORE) were Jewish and were actively expressing their home-based familial values in support of minority rights.

Student movement concerns with actualizing ideals have been a dynamic aspect of those movements. The national student Free Speech Movement in 1964 was precipitated by University of

California at Berkeley students who protested a specific ban on allowing a CORE civil-rights-information table on the campus in an open mall area. While a relatively small number of students were actively involved with the CORE table, a large majority of students, first at Berkeley and then nationally, supported the First Amendment right of open expression, leading to the larger Free Speech Movement (Altbach and Peterson 1971).

Protest movements generally are time-delimited. Given the relatively short age dimensions of student status, student movements tend to have even shorter time spans. Even with time and leadership delimitations, student movements are sufficiently common and consequential that more systematic research is needed on not only who the student protestors are but also where they go after a student activist movement ends. Research is beginning to ascertain the extent to which former student protest activists' ideas and behaviors continue to reflect their protest values.

It is clear that most student activists enter into business and professional, high-socioeconomic-status positions. What is not as clear is the extent to which they continue to adhere to the values and related issues that motivated them to engage in student movements. Research in this area of student movements is suggestive of long-term consequences.

An analysis over time of 1960s student protest activists and nonactivists indicates that protest values continue to influence social, economic, and political behavior. Well over a decade after their civil rights and anti–Vietnam War activity, former activists continued to be more change-oriented than average, and given the nature of their protests, they were more liberal on issues of civil rights and civil liberties. Their orientation was to support more than did nonactivists government action to address a wide range of social problems and support specific policies such as abortion rights and affirmative action for minorities' and women's educational and employment opportunities (Sherkat and Blocker 1997). Further research may demonstrate additional social change consequences on society long after specific student movements have ended.

(SEE ALSO: *Protest Movements; Social Movements*)

REFERENCES

Altbach, Philip G., and Patti Peterson 1971 "Before Berkeley: Historical Perspectives on American Student Activism." *Annals of the American Academy of Political and Social Science* 395:1–14.

Bell, Inge Powell 1968 *CORE and the Strategy of Non-Violence*. New York: Random House.

Davies, James C. 1969 "The J-Curve of Rising Expectations and Declining Satisfactions as a Cause of Some Great Revolutions and Contained Rebellions." In H. Graham and T. Gurr, eds., *Violence in America*. New York: Bantam.

DeMartini, Joseph R. 1985 "Change Agents and Generational Relationships: A Reevaluation of Mannheim's Problem of Generations." *Social Forces* 64:1–16.

Feuer, Lewis S. 1969 *The Conflict of Generations: The Character and Significance of Student Movements*. New York: Basic Books.

Lipset, Seymour M. 1971 *Rebellion in the University*. Boston: Little, Brown.

Mannheim, Karl 1952 *Essays on the Sociology of Knowledge*. New York: Oxford University Press.

Sherkat, Darren E., and T. Jean Blocker 1997 "Explaining the Political and Personal Consequences of Protest." *Social Forces* 75:1049–1076.

LEONARD GORDON

SUBURBANIZATION

Suburbanization is one aspect of the more general process of the expansion and spatial reorganization of metropolitan settlements. Settled areas that are beyond the historical boundaries of what have been considered cities but still are clearly functionally linked to the cities or may not be considered suburban. What is suburban is a matter of social definition. For example, when small cities are enveloped by the expansion of larger cities, at what point should they be considered suburbs, if they should be called suburbs at all? As some cities extend their boundaries outward, will the newly settled areas not be considered suburban if they are within the new boundaries?

Many researchers in the United States have chosen to adopt conventions established by the U.S. Bureau of the Census. The term "suburban" refers to the portion of a metropolitan area that is not in the central city. This definition depends on what is defined as metropolitan and central city, and those definitions change over the years. Such changes are not simply technical adjustments; they respond (among other criteria) to assumptions about what cities and suburbs are. For example, as many U.S. "suburbs" have become employment centers in the last two decades, altering traditional patterns of commuting to work, Census Bureau scientists have adjusted the definition of "central city" to include some of those peripheral areas.

For many purposes, it may be preferable to avoid these categories altogether. "Suburban" may be intended to reflect distance from the city center, recency of development, residential density, or commuting patterns—all of which can be measured directly. The main substantive rationale for accepting definitions tied to the juridical boundaries of cities is to emphasize the differences between cities and suburbs (and among suburbs) that are related to municipal governance. An important class of issues revolves around disparities in public resources: In what parts of the metropolis are taxes higher, where are better schools available, where is police protection greater? What are the effects of these differences on the opportunities available to people who live in different parts of the metropolis? Another dimension concerns local politics: How do localities establish land use and budget policies, and what are the effects of those policies on growth?

Because many suburban residents have worked in central cities while paying taxes in the suburbs, John Kasarda has described the city–suburb relationship in terms of "exploitation." Political scientists in particular have studied this issue in terms of arguments for the reform of structures of metropolitan governance. The normative implications of their arguments have explicit ideological underpinnings. Some, such as Dennis Judd, emphasize the value of equality of life chances and interpret differences between cities and suburbs as disparities; others (public choice theorists such as Elinor Ostrom) emphasize freedom of choice and interpret differences as opportunities for the exercise of choice.

Sociologists on the whole have been less willing to be proponents of metropolitan solutions and have shown more interest in the causes than in the consequences of suburbanization. Nevertheless, there are differences in theoretical perspective that closely parallel those in political science,

and they hinge in part on the importance of political boundaries and the political process. The main lines of explanation reflect two broader currents in sociological theory: Structural functionalism is found in the guise of human ecology and neoclassical economics, and variants of Marxian and Weberian theory have been described as the "new" urban theory.

Ecologists and many urban economists conceptualize suburbanization as a process of decentralization, as is reflected in Burgess's (1967) concentric-zone model of the metropolis. Burgess accepted the postulate of central place theory that the point of highest interaction and most valued land is naturally at the core of the central business district. The central point is most accessible to all other locations in the metropolis, a feature that is especially valuable for commercial firms. At the fringes of the business district, where land is held for future commercial development, low-income and immigrant households can compete successfully for space, though only at high residential densities. Peripheral areas, by contrast, are most valued by more affluent households, particularly those with children and a preference for more spacious surroundings.

The key to this approach is its acceptance of a competitive land market as the principal mechanism through which locational decisions are reached. More specific hypotheses are drawn from theories about people's preferences and willingness (and ability) to pay for particular locations or structural changes (e.g., elevators, transportation technology, and the need for space of manufacturers) that affect the value of a central location. Many researchers have focused on gradients linking distance from the center to various compositional characteristics of neighborhoods: population density (Treadway 1969), household composition (Guest 1972), and socioeconomic status (Choldin and Hanson 1982). Comparatively little research has been conducted on the preferences of residents or the factors that lead them to select one location or another.

Other sociologists have argued that growth patterns result from conscious policies and specific institutional interventions in the land and housing markets. Representative of this view is the study done by Checkoway (1980), who emphasizes the role of federal housing programs and institutional support for large-scale residential builders in the suburbanization process of the 1950s. The move to suburbs, he argues, was contingent on the alternatives offered to consumers. The redlining of inner-city neighborhoods by the Federal Housing Administration, its preference for large new subdivisions, and its explicit discrimination against minority home buyers are among the major forces structuring these alternatives.

There have been few studies of the housing market from an institutional perspective, although the restructuring of real estate financing and the emergence of new linkages between large-scale developers and finance capital have begun to attract attention. More consideration has been given to the explicitly political aspects of land development (Logan and Molotch 1987). Following Hunter (1953), who believed that growth questions are the "big issue" in local politics, later studies found that the most powerful voices in local politics are the proponents of growth and urban redevelopment and, in this sense, that a city is a growth machine.

In applying this model to suburbs, most observers portray suburban municipalities as "exclusionary." Suburban municipalities have long used zoning to influence the location and composition of land development. Since environmentalism emerged as a formidable political movement in the early 1970s, it has become commonplace to hear about localities that exercise their power to preserve open space and historic sites by imposing restraints or even moratoriums on new development. The "no-growth movement" is a direct extension of earlier exclusionary zoning policies.

SOCIOECONOMIC DIFFERENCES BETWEEN CITIES AND SUBURBS

These two theoretical perspectives can be illustrated through their application to research on socioeconomic differences between cities and suburbs. It is well known that central cities in most metropolitan regions have a less affluent residential population than do the surrounding suburbs. There is much debate, however, whether this class segregation between cities and their suburbs represents a natural sorting out of social classes through the private market or whether its causes are political and institutional. Similar debate surrounds the phenomenon of differentiation *within* suburbia,

where there is great variation in economic function, class and racial composition, and other characteristics of suburbs.

Research from an ecological perspective has stressed a comparison between the older, larger, denser cities of the North and the more recently growing cities of the South and West. The principal consistent findings have been that (1) the pattern of low central city relative to suburban social status is more pronounced in older metropolitan regions but that (2) controlling for metropolitan age, there appears to be a universal generalization of this pattern over time (Guest and Nelson 1978). These sociologists propose that suburbs have natural advantages over central cities. For example, their housing stock is newer, their land is less expensive, and they are more accessible to freeways and airports. The socioeconomic differences between cities and suburbs reflect those advantages.

Others argue that disparities are generated primarily by political structures that allocate zoning control and responsibility for public services to local governments and require those governments to finance services from local sources such as taxes on real property. They propose that the typical fragmentation of metropolitan government creates the incentive and opportunity for suburbs to pursue exclusionary growth policies (Danielson 1976).

Seeking to test these theories, Logan and Schneider (1982) found greater disparities in metropolitan areas where central cities were less able to grow through annexation (thus where suburban municipal governments were more autonomous) and where localities were more reliant on local property taxes (hence had greater incentive to pursue exclusionary policies). They also found a significant racial dimension: Greater disparities were evident in both 1960 and 1970 in metropolitan areas in the North with a larger proportion of black residents. (This did not hold for the South and West, however.) This disparity is due both to the concentration of lower-income blacks in central cities and to a greater propensity of higher-status whites to live in suburbs in those metropolitan areas. This finding is reinforced by Frey (see Frey and Speare 1988; Shihadeh and Ousey 1996), who reported that the central-city proportion of black residents is a significant predictor of white flight, independent of other causes.

If suburbs follow exclusionary growth policies, it seems counterintuitive that suburbs experienced much more rapid growth than did cities in the postwar decades. The findings on city–suburb disparities, of course, indicate that exclusion has selective effects. Nevertheless, it is surprising that in a study of northern California cities, Baldassare and Protash (1982), found that communities with more restrictive planning controls actually had higher rates of population growth in the 1970s. Similarly, Logan and Zhou (1989) found that suburban growth controls had little, if any, impact on development patterns (population growth, socioeconomic status, and racial composition). In their view, the exclusionary policies of suburbs may be more apparent than real. The more visible actions, such as growth moratoriums, often are intended to blunt criticisms by residents concerned with problems arising from rapid development. Unfortunately, few studies have looked in depth at the political process within suburbs; there is as little direct evidence on the role of local politics as there is on the operation of the land market. Most research from both the ecological and the political-institutional perspectives has inferred the *processes* for controlling growth from evidence about the *outcomes*.

SUBURBANIZATION OF EMPLOYMENT

A central problem for early studies of suburban communities was to identify the patterns of functional specialization among them. It was recognized that older industrial satellites coexisted with dormitory towns in the fringe areas around central cities. Both were suburban in the sense that they were integrated into a metropolitan economy dominated by the central city. Their own economic role and the nature of the populations they housed were quite distinct, however. The greatest population gains in the 1950s occurred in residential suburbs, communities that were wealthier, younger, newer, and less densely settled than the towns on the fringes of the region that had higher concentrations of employment. Schnore (see Schnore and Winsborough 1972) distinguished "suburbs" from "satellites" to acknowledge these different origins.

The metaphors of suburbs and satellites reflected the reality of early postwar suburbanization, a period when established towns and small cities were surrounded by successive waves of new subdivisions. Those metaphors are no longer appropriate. Since the late 1950s, the bulk of new manufacturing and trade employment in the metropolis has been located in small and middle-sized cities in the suburban ring (Berry and Kasarda 1977, chap. 13). Downtown department stores compete with new suburban shopping malls. The highly developed expressway network around central cities frees manufacturing plants to take advantage of the lower land prices and taxes and the superior access to the skilled workforce offered by the suburbs. For the period 1963–1977, in the largest twenty-five metropolitan areas, total manufacturing employment in central cities declined by about 700,000 (19 percent), while their suburbs gained 1.1 million jobs (36 percent). At the same time, total central-city retail and wholesale employment was stagnant (dropping by 100,000). Trade employment in the suburbs increased 1.8 million (or 110 percent) in that period. Thus, total employment growth in the suburbs outpaced the growth of population (Logan and Golden 1986). This is the heart of the phenomenon popularized by Garreau (1991) as the creation of "Edge City."

How has suburbanization of employment affected suburban communities? According to microeconomic and ecological models, locational choices by employers reflect the balance of costs and benefits of competing sites. New employment maintains old patterns because the cost–benefit equation is typically stable, including important considerations such as location relative to workforce, suppliers, markets, and the local infrastructure. In the terms commonly used by urban sociologists, this means that communities find their "ecological niche." Stahura's (1982) finding of marked persistence in manufacturing and trade employment in suburbs from 1960 to 1972 supports this expectation. Once it has "crystallized," the functional specialization of communities changes only under conditions of major shifts in the needs of firms.

In this view, to the extent that changes occur, they follow a natural life cycle (Hoover and Vernon 1962). Residential suburbs in the inner ring, near the central city, tend over time to undergo two related transformations: to higher population density and a conversion to nonresidential development and to a lower socioeconomic status. Thus, inner suburbs that gain employment are—like older satellites—less affluent than residential suburbs.

By contrast, those who emphasize the politics of land development suggest very different conclusions. A growing number of suburbs perceive business and industry as a significant local resource. Once shunned by the higher-status suburbs, they now contribute to property values and the local tax base. Prestigious communities such as Greenwich, Connecticut, and Palo Alto, California, house industrial parks and corporate headquarters. The "good climate for business" they offer includes public financing of new investments, extensive infrastructure (roads, utilities, parking, police and fire protection), and moderate taxes (Logan and Molotch 1987).

Competition among suburbs introduces a new factor that has the potential to reshape suburban regions. Schneider (1989) reports that location of manufacturing firms is affected by the strength of the local tax base, suggesting that wealthy suburbs are advantaged in this competition. Logan and Golden (1986) find that newly developing suburban employment centers have higher socioeconomic status, as well as stronger fiscal resources, than other suburbs; this is a reversal of the pattern of the 1950s.

MINORITY SUBURBANIZATION

The suburbanization process also increasingly involves minorities and immigrants, and the incorporation of those groups into suburban areas has become an important topic for research on racial and ethnic relations. As Massey and Denton (1987) document, the rate of growth of nonwhites and Hispanics in metropolitan areas is far outstripping the rate of growth of non-Hispanic whites. Much of this growth is occurring in suburbs. During the 1970s, for example, the number of blacks in the non-central-city parts of metropolitan areas increased 70 percent compared with just 16 percent in central cities, and the number of other nonwhites in those locations shot up 150 percent compared with approximately 70 percent in central cities. One reason for the rapidly increasing racial and ethnic diversity of suburbs may be that some new immigrant groups are bypassing central cities and settling directly in suburbs. Equally important is the increasing suburbanization of older racial and ethnic minorities, such as blacks (Frey and Speare 1988).

This phenomenon has encouraged researchers to study suburbanization as a mirror on the social mobility of minorities. Consistent with classical ecological theory, suburbanization often has been portrayed broadly as a step toward assimilation into the mainstream society and a sign of the erosion of social boundaries. For European immigrant groups after the turn of the century, residential decentralization appears to have been part of the general process of assimilation (Guest 1980).

Past studies have found that suburbanization of Hispanics and Asians in a metropolitan area is strongly associated with each group's average income level (Massey and Denton 1987, pp. 819–820; see also Frey and Speare 1988, pp. 311–315). Further, again for Hispanics and Asians, Massey and Denton (1987) demonstrate that suburban residence typically is associated with lower levels of segregation and, accordingly, higher probabilities of contact with the Anglo majority. However, these and other authors report very different results for blacks. Black suburbanization is unrelated to the average income level of blacks in the metropolitan area and does not result in higher intergroup contact for blacks. The suburbanization process for blacks appears largely to be one of continued ghettoization (Farley 1970), as is indicated by high and in some regions increasing levels of segregation and by the concentration of suburban blacks in communities with a high incidence of social problems (e.g., high crime rates), high taxes, and underfunded social services (Logan and Schneider 1984; Reardon 1997).

These findings regarding black suburbanization have been interpreted in terms of processes that impede the free mobility of racial minorities: steering by realtors, unequal access to mortgage credit, exclusionary zoning, and neighbor hostility (Foley 1973). Home ownership indeed may be one of the gatekeepers for suburban living. Stearns and Logan (1986) report that blacks were less likely to live in suburban areas where higher proportions of the housing stock were owner-occupied.

Further evidence is offered by Alba et al (1999), who based their conclusions on an analysis of individual-level data from the 1980 and 1990 censuses. They find that suburban residence is more likely among homeowners and persons of higher socioeconomic status. There are strong effects of family status (marriage and the presence of children in the household), but for many immigrant groups, measures of cultural assimilation (English language use, nativity, and period of immigration) have declining relevance for suburban location. Assimilation traditionally has been a major part of the suburbanization process for most groups, especially those arising out of immigration, but large pockets of relatively new immigrants have now appeared in the suburban ring.

Parallel results are found for the racial and ethnic sorting process within a suburban region (the New York–New Jersey suburban region, as reported by Logan and Alba 1993; Alba and Logan 1993). Two sorts of analyses were conducted. First, members of different racial and ethnic groups were compared on the average characteristics of the suburbs in which they resided. Second, regression models were estimated for members of each major racial or ethnic group to predict several of these indicators of place advantages or community resources.

There are important differences between whites, blacks, Hispanics, and Asians in regard to the kinds of suburbs in which they live. As some researchers have suspected, suburban Asians have achieved access to relatively advantaged communities that are similar in most respects to those of suburban non-Hispanic whites. Hispanics in the New York region have not. Suburban Hispanic by and large live in communities that are about the same as black suburbs: communities with low average income levels and low rates of home ownership and, perhaps more important, high crime rates (Alba et al. 1994).

Is the disadvantage of blacks and Hispanics attributable to individual qualities of group members, or do these groups face collective disadvantages? Analysis of individual characteristics that may predict the quality of the suburb in which one resides shows that the same location process does not apply equally to all minorities. The pattern for whites, who are relatively advantaged in terms of access to community resources, lends clear support to assimilation theory. Human capital and indicators of cultural assimilation are strongly associated with access to higher-status suburbs. The same can be said of Asians (who are relatively advantaged overall), with the exception that cultural assimilation variables seem not to be important for Asians.

The results for blacks call attention to processes of racial stratification. Even controlling for many other individual characteristics, blacks live in suburbs with lower ownership and income levels than do non-Hispanic whites. Further, most human capital and assimilation variables have a smaller payoff for blacks than they do for whites. The findings for Hispanics are supportive of the assimilation model in several respects. Hispanics gain more strongly than whites do from most human capital characteristics; therefore, at higher levels of socioeconomic achievement and cultural assimilation, Hispanics come progressively closer to matching the community resources of whites. It should be noted, however, that Hispanics begin from a lower starting point and that black Hispanics face a double disadvantage that is inconsistent with an assimilation perspective.

LOOKING TO THE FUTURE

Suburbanization continues to be a key aspect of metropolitan growth and is perhaps of growing importance in the global era (Muller 1997). The political boundaries between cities and suburbs accentuate interest in substantive issues of metropolitan inequality. They also create special opportunities for theories of urbanization to go beyond economic models and incorporate an understanding of the political process. Research on suburbanization has been most successful in describing patterns of decentralization and spatial differentiation. The movements of people and employment and the segregation among suburbs by social class, race, ethnicity, and family composition have been well documented. However, these patterns are broadly consistent with a variety of interpretations, ranging from those which assume a competitive land market (human ecology) to those which stress the institutional and political structuring of that market.

The principal gaps in knowledge concern the processes that are central to these alternative interpretations. Few sociologists have directly studied the housing market from the perspective of either demand (how do people learn about the alternatives, and how do they select among them?) or supply (how does the real estate sector operate, how is racial and ethnic segmentation of the market achieved, how is the complex of construction industries, developers, and financial institutions tied to the rest of the economy?). Rarely have sociologists investigated government decisions (at any level) that impinge on development from the point of view either of their effects or of the political process that led to them. Of course, these observations are not specific to research on suburbanization. It is important to bear in mind that neither the theoretical issues nor the research strategies in this field distinguish suburbanization from other aspects of the urban process.

(SEE ALSO: *Cities; Community; Urbanization*)

REFERENCES

Alba, Richard and John R. Logan 1993 "Minority Proximity to Whites in Suburbs: An Individual-Level Analysis of Segregation" *American Journal of Sociology* 98:1388–1427.

——, ——, and Paul Bellair 1994 "Living with Crime: The Implications of Racial and Ethnic Differences in Suburban Location" *Social Forces* 73:395–434.

——, ——, Brian Stults, Gilbert Marzan, and Wenquan Zhang 1999 "Immigrant Groups and Suburbs: A Reexamination of Suburbanization and Spatial Assimilation." *American Sociological Review* 64:446–460.

Baldassare, Mark, and William Protash 1982 "Growth Controls, Population Growth, and Community Satisfaction." *American Sociological Review* 47:339–346.

Berry, Brian, and John Kasarda 1977 *Contemporary Urban Ecology*. New York: Macmillan.

Burgess, Ernest W. 1967 "The Growth of the City." In R. E. Park, E. W. Burgess, and R. D. McKenzie, eds., *The City*. Chicago: University of Chicago Press.

Checkoway, Barry l980 "Large Builders, Federal Housing Programmes, and Postwar Suburbanization." *International Journal of Urban and Regional Research* 4:21–44.

Choldin, Harvey M., and Claudine Hanson 1982 "Status Shifts within the City." *American Sociological Review* 47:129–41.

Danielson, Michael 1976 *The Politics of Exclusion*. New York: Columbia University Press.

Farley, Reynolds 1970 "The Changing Distribution of Negroes within Metropolitan Areas: The Emergence of Black Suburbs." *American Journal of Sociology* 75:512–529.

Foley, Donald 1973 "Institutional and Contextual Factors Affecting the Housing Choices of Minority Residents." In Amos Hawley and Vincent Rock, eds., *Segregation in Residential Areas*. Washington, D.C.: National Academy of Sciences.

Frey, William, and Alden Speare 1988 *Regional and Metropolitan Growth and Decline in the United States*. New York: Russell Sage Foundation.

Garreau, Joel 1991 *Edge City: Life on the New Frontier*. New York: Doubleday.

Guest, Avery M. 1972 "Patterns of Family Location." *Demography* 9:159–171.

—— 1980 "The Suburbanization of Ethnic Groups." *Sociology and Social Research* 64:497–513.

——, and G. Nelson 1978 "Central City/Suburban Status Differences: Fifty Years of Change." *Sociological Quarterly* 19:723.

Hoover, Edgar, and Raymond Vernon 1962 *Anatomy of a Metropolis*. Garden City, N.Y.: Doubleday.

Hunter, Floyd 1953 *Community Power Structure*. Chapel Hill: University of North Carolina Press.

Liska, Allen, John R. Logan, and Paul Bellair 1998 "Race and Violent Crime in the Suburbs." *American Sociological Review* 63:27–38.

Logan, John R. and Richard Alba 1993 "Locational Returns to Human Capital: Minority Access to Suburban Community Resources." *Demography* 30:243–268.

——, and Reid Golden 1986 "Suburbs and Satellites: Two Decades of Change." *American Sociological Review* 51:430–437.

——, and Harvey L. Molotch 1987 *Urban Fortunes: The Political Economy of Place*. Berkeley: University of California Press.

——, and Mark Schneider 1982 "Governmental Organization and City-Suburb Income Inequality, 1960–1970." *Urban Affairs Quarterly* 17:303–318.

—— 1984 "Racial Segregation and Racial Change in American Suburbs: 1970–1980." *American Journal of Sociology* 89:874–888.

——, and Min Zhou 1989 "Do Growth Controls Control Growth?" *American Sociological Review* 54:461–471.

Massey, Douglas, and Nancy Denton 1987 "Trends in the Residential Segregation of Blacks, Hispanics, and Asians: 1970–1980." *American Sociological Review* 52:802–825.

Muller, Peter O. 1997 "The Suburban Transformation of the Globalizing American City." *Annals of the American Academy of Political and Social Science* 551:44–58.

Reardon, Kenneth M. 1997 "State and Local Revitalization Efforts in East St. Louis, Illinois." *Annals of the American Academy of Political and Social Science* 551:235–247.

Schneider, Mark 1989 *The Competitive City: The Political Economy of Suburbia.* Pittsburgh: University of Pittsburgh Press.

Schnore, Leo, and Hall Winsborough 1972 "Functional Classification and the Residential Location of Social Classes." In Brian Berry, ed., *City Classification Handbook: Methods and Application.* New York: Wiley.

Shihadeh, Edward S., and Graham C. Ousey 1996 "Metropolitan Expansion and Black Social Dislocation: The Link between Suburbanization and Center-City Crime." *Social Forces* 75:649–666.

Stahura, John 1982 "Determinants of Suburban Job Change in Retailing, Wholesaling, Service, and Manufacturing Industries: 1960–1972." *Sociological Focus* 15:347–357.

Stearns, Linda, and John Logan 1986 "The Racial Structuring of the Housing Market and Segregation in Suburban Areas." *Social Forces* 65:28–42.

Treadway, Roy C. 1969 "Social Components of Metropolitan Population Densities." *Demography* 6:55–74.

Warner, Kee, and Harvey Molotch 1995 "Power to Build: How Development Persists Despite Local Limits." *Urban Affairs Review* 30:378–406.

JOHN R. LOGAN

SUICIDE

To many people, suicide—intentional self-murder—is an asocial act of a private individual, yet sociology grew out of Durkheim's argument ([1897] 1951) that suicide rates are social facts and reflect variation in social regulation and social interaction. The concept of suicide derives from the Latin *sui* ("of oneself") and *cide* ("a killing"). Shneidman (1985) defines "suicide" as follows: "currently in the Western world a conscious act of self-induced annihilation best understood as a multidimensional malaise in a needful individual who defines an issue for which suicide is perceived as the best solution." Several conceptual implications follow from this definition.

Although suicidal types vary, there are common traits that most suicides share to some extent. (Shneidman 1985). Suicides tend to

- Seek a solution to their life problems by dying
- Want to cease consciousness
- Try to reduce intolerable psychological pain
- Have frustrated psychological needs
- Feel helpless and hopeless
- Be ambivalent about dying
- Be perceptually constricted and rigid thinkers
- Manifest escape, egression, or fugue behaviors
- Communicate their intent to commit suicide or die
- Have lifelong self-destructive coping responses (sometimes called "suicidal careers")

Completed suicides must be differentiated from nonfatal suicide attempts, suicide ideation, and suicide talk or gestures. Sometimes one speaks of self-injury, self-mutilation, accident proneness, failure to take needed medications, and the like—where suicide intent cannot be demonstrated—as "parasuicide." The most common self-destructive behaviors are indirect, such as alcoholism, obesity, risky sports, and gambling. There are also mass suicides (as in Jonestown, Guyana, in 1978 and in Masada in A.D. 72–73) and murder suicides. Individual and social growth probably require some degree of partial self-destruction.

Although most suicides have much in common, suicide is not a single type of behavior. Suicidology will not be an exact science until it specifies its dependent variable. The predictors or causes of suicide vary immensely with the specific type of suicidal outcome. Suicidologists tend to recognize three to six basic types of suicide, each with two or three of its own subtypes (Maris et al. 1992, chap. 4). For example, Durkheim ([1897] 1951) thought all suicides were basically anomic, egoistic, altruistic, or fatalistic. Freud (1917 [1953]) and Menninger (1938) argued that psychoanalytically, all suicides were based on hate or revenge (a "wish to kill"); on depression, melancholia, or hopelessness (a "wish to die"); or on guilt or shame (a "wish to be killed"). Baechler (1979) added "oblative" (i.e., sacrifice or transfiguration) and "ludic" (i.e., engaging in ordeals or risks and games) suicidal types.

EPIDEMIOLOGY, RATES, AND PREDICTORS

Suicide is a relatively rare event, averaging 1 to 3 in 10,000 in the general population per year. In 1996 (the most recent year for which U. S. vital statistics are available), there were 31,130 suicides, accounting for about 1.5 percent of all deaths. This amounts to an overall suicide rate of 11.6 per 100,000. Suicide is now the ninth leading cause of death, ranking just ahead of cirrhosis and other liver disease deaths and just behind human immunodeficiency virus (HIV) deaths. Suicide also has been moving up the list of the leading causes of death in this century (Table 1).

Suicide rates in the United States vary considerably by sex, age, and race (Table 2). The highest rates are consistently observed among white males, who constitute roughly 73 percent of all suicides. White females account for about 17 percent of all suicides. American blacks, especially females, rarely commit suicide (except for some young urban males). Some scholars have argued that black suicides tend to be disguised as homicides or accidents. In general, male suicides outnumber female suicides three or four to one. Generally, suicide rates gradually increase with age and then drop off at the very oldest ages. Female suicide rates tend to peak earlier than do those of males. Note in Table 3 that from about 1967 to 1977, there was a significant increase in the suicide rate of 15- to 24-year-olds and that suicide rates among the elderly seem to be climbing again.

Typically, marrying and having children protect one against suicide. Usually suicide rates are highest for widows, followed by the divorced and the never-married or single. Studies of suicide rates by social class have been equivocal. Within each broad census occupational category, there are job types with high and low suicide rates. For example, psychiatrists have high suicide rates, but pediatricians and surgeons have low rates. Operatives usually have low rates, but police officers typically have high rates.

The predominant method of suicide for both males and females in 1992 was firearms (Table 4).

Ten Leading Causes of Death in the United States, 1996 (total of 2,314,690 deaths)

Rank	Cause of Death	Rate per 100,000	No. of Deaths (all causes)
1	Disease of the heart	276.4	733,361
2	Malignant neoplasms	203.4	539,533
3	Cerebrovascular disease	60.3	159,942
4	Chronic obstructive pulmonary disease	40	106,027
5	Accidents	35.8	94,943
6	Pnuemonia and influenza	31.6	83,727
7	Diabetes mellitus	23.3	61,767
8	HIV infection	11.7	31,130
9	Suicide	11.6	30,903
10	Chronic liver disease and cirrhosis	9.4	25,047

Table 1

SOURCE: Data from U.S. National Center for Health Statistics, 1998.

The second most common method among males is hanging, and among females it is a drug or medicine overdose. Females use a somewhat greater variety of methods than males do. Suicide rates tend to be higher on Mondays and in the springtime (Gabennesch 1988).

Prediction of suicide is a complicated process (Maris et al. 1992). As is the case with other rare events, suicide prediction generates many false positives, such as identifying someone as a suicide when that person in fact is not a suicide. Correctly identifying true suicides is referred to as "sensitivity," and correctly identifying true nonsuicides is called "specificity." In a study using common predictors (Table 5) Porkorny (1983) correctly predicted fifteen of sixty-seven suicides among 4,800 psychiatric patients but also got 279 false positives.

Table 5 lists fifteen major predictors of suicide. Single predictor variables seldom correctly identify suicides. Most suicides have "comorbidity" (i.e., several key predictors are involved), and specific predictors vary with the type of suicide and other factors. Depressive disorders and alcoholism are two of the major predictors of suicide. Robins (1981) found that about 45 percent of all

Rates of Completed Suicide per 100,000 Population by Race and Gender, 1996

Race and Gender Group	No. of Suicides	Percent of Suicides	Rate per 100,000
White males	22,547	73	20.9
White females	5,309	17.1	4.8
Black males	(1,389)	(4.5)	(11.4)
Black females	(204)	(0.8)	(2.0)
Nonwhite males*	2,451	8.0	11.3
Nonwhite females*	596	1.9	2.5
Totals	30,903	100.0	11.6

Table 2

NOTE: *Includes American Indian, Chinese, Hawaiian, Japanese, Filipino, Other Asian or Pacific Islander, and Other.

SOURCE: Data from Centers for Disease Control, 1998.

completed suicides involved either depressed or alcoholic persons. Roughly 15 percent of all those with depressive illness and 18 percent of all alcoholics eventually commit suicide. Repeated depressive illness that leads to hopelessness is especially suicidogenic.

Nonfatal suicide attempts, talk about suicide or dying, and explicit plans or preparations for dying or suicide all increase suicide risk. However, for the paradigmatic suicide (older white males), 85 to 90 percent of these individuals make only one fatal suicide attempt and seldom explicitly communicate their suicidal intent or show up at hospitals and clinics. Social isolation (e.g., having no close friends, living alone, being unemployed, being unmarried) and lack of social support are more common among suicides than among controls. Suicide tends to run in families, and this suggests both modeling and genetic influences. Important biological and sociobiological predictors of suicide have been emerging, especially low levels of central spinal fluid serotonin in the form of 5-HIAA (Maris 1997).

HISTORY, COMPARATIVE STUDIES, AND SOCIAL SUICIDOLOGISTS

The incidence and study of suicide have a long history and were fundamental to the development of sociology. The earliest known visual reference to suicide is Ajax falling on his sword (circa 540 B.C.). Of course, it is known that Socrates (about 399 B.C.) drank hemlock. In the Judeo-Christian scriptures there were eleven men (and no women) who died by suicide, most notably Samson, Judas, and Saul. Common biblical motives for suicide were revenge, shame, and defeat in battle. Famous suicides in art history include paintings of Lucretia stabbing herself (after a rape), Dido, and work by Edvard Munch and Andy Warhol.

Suicide varies with culture and ethnicity. Most cultures have at least some suicides. However, suicide is rare or absent among the Tiv of Nigeria, Andaman islanders, and Australian aborigines and relatively infrequent among rural American blacks and Irish Roman Catholics. The highest suicide rates are found in Hungary, Germany, Austria, Scandinavia, and Japan (Table 6). The lowest rates are found in several South American, Pacific Island, and predominantly Roman Catholic countries, including Antigua, Jamaica, New Guinea, the Phillipines, Mexico, Italy, and Ireland.

The sociological study of suicide started with Durkheim ([1897] 1951) and has continued to the present day primarily in the research and publications of the following sociologists: Short, (1954), J.P. Gibbs (1964), J.T. Gibbs (1988), Douglas (1967), Maris (1969, 1981), Phillips (1974), Phillips et al. (1991), Stack (1982), Wasserman (1989), and Pescosolido and Georgianna (1989). It is impossible in an encyclopedia article to do justice to the full account of the sociological study of suicide. For a more complete review, the reader is referred to Maris (1989).

Durkheim ([1897] 1951) claimed that the suicide rate varied inverely with social integration and that suicide types were primarily ego-anomic. However, Durkheim did not operationally define "social integration." Gibbs and Martin (1964) created the concept of "status integration" to correct this deficiency. They hypothesized that the less frequently occupied status sets would lead to lower status integration and higher suicide rates. Putting it differently, they expected status integration and suicide rates to be negatively associated. In a large series of tests from 1964 to 1988, Gibbs confirmed his primary hypothesis only for occupational statuses, which Durkheim also had said were of central importance.

Rates of Completed Suicide per 100,000 Population by Year and Age in the United States

	YEAR				
Age*	1957	1967	1977	1987	1992
5–14	0.2	0.3	0.5	0.7	0.9
15–24	4.0	7.0	13.6	12.9	12.9
25–34	8.6	12.4	17.7	15.4	14.6
35–44	12.8	16.6	16.8	15.0	15.1
45–54	18.0	19.5	18.9	15.9	14.7
55–64	22.4	22.4	19.4	16.6	14.9
65–74	25.0	19.8	20.1	19.4	16.6
75–84	26.8	21.0	21.5	25.8	23.1
>85	26.3	22.7	17.3	22.1	21.9
Total	9.8	10.8	13.3	12.7	12.0

Table 3

NOTE: Suicide not reported for individuals under 5 years of age.
SOURCE: Data from Centers for Disease Control, 1995.

Short (Henry and Short 1954) expanded Durkheim's concept of external and constraining social facts to include interaction with social psychological factors of "internal constraint" (such as strict superego restraint) and frustration-aggression theory. Short reasoned that suicide rates would be highest when external restraint was low and internal restraint was high and that homicide rates would be highest when internal restraint was low and external restraint was high.

A vastly different sociological perspective on suicide originated with the work of enthnomethodologist Douglas. Douglas, in the tradition of Max Weber's subjective meanings, argued that Durkheim's reliance on official statistics (such as death certificates) as the data base for studying suicide was fundamentally mistaken (Douglas 1967). Instead, it is necessary to observe the accounts or situated meanings of individuals who are known to be suicidal, not rely on a third-party official such as a coroner or medical examiner who is not a suicide and may use ad hoc criteria to classify a death as a suicide. There are probably as many official statistics as there are officials.

Maris (1981) extended Durkheim's empirical survey of suicidal behaviors, but not just by measuring macrosocial and demographic or structural variables. Instead, Maris focused on actual interviews ("psychological autopsies") of the intimate survivors of suicides (usually their spouses) and compared those cases with control or comparison groups of natural deaths and nonfatal suicide attempts. Maris claimed that suicides had long "suicidal careers" involving complex mixes of biological, social, and psychological factors.

Phillips (1974) differed with Durkheim's contention that suicides are not suggestible or contagious. In a pioneering paper in the *American Sociological Review*, he demonstrated that front-page newspaper coverage of celebrity suicides was associated with a statistically significant rise in the national suicide rate seven to ten days after a publicized suicide. The rise in the suicide rate was greater the longer the front-page coverage, greater in the region where the news account ran, and higher if the stimulus suicide and the person supposedly copying the suicide were similar. In a long series of similar studies, Phillips et al. (1991) expanded and documented the suggestion effect for other types of behavior and other groups. For example, the contagion effect appears to be especially powerful among teenagers. Nevertheless, contagion accounts only for a 1 to 6 percent increase over the normal expected suicide rates in a population.

Percent of Completed Suicides in 1987 and 1992 by Method and Gender

METHOD	Male % 1987	Male % 1992	Female % 1987	Female % 1992
Firearms (E955.0–955.4)	64.0	65	39.8	39
Drugs/medications (E950.0–950.5)	5.2	–	25.0	–
Hanging (E953.0)	13.5	16	9.4	14
Carbon monoxide (E952.0–952.1)	9.6	–	12.6	–
Jumping from a high place (E957)	1.8	–	3.0	–
Drowning (E954)	1.1	–	2.8	–
Suffocation by plastic bag (E953.1)	0.4	–	1.8	–
Cutting/piercing instruments (E965)	1.3	1	1.4	1
Poisons (E950.6–950.9)	0.6	–	1.0	–
Other*	2.5	18	3.2	45
Totals	100.0	100.0	100.0	99.0

Table 4

NOTE: *Includes gases in domestic use (E951), other specified and unspecified gases and vapors (E952.8–952.9), explosives (E955.5), unspecified firearms and explosives (E955.9), and other specified or unspecified means of hanging, strangulation, or suffocation (E953.8–953.9).

SOURCE: Data from National Center for Health Statistics, 1995.

Common Single Predictors of Suicide

1. Depressive illness, mental disorder
2. Alcoholism, drug abuse
3. Suicide ideation, talk, preparation, religion
4. Prior suicide attempts
5. Lethal methods
6. Isolation, living alone, loss of support
7. Hopelessness, cognitive rigidity
8. Older white males
9. Modeling, suicide in the family, genetics
10. Work problems, economics, occupation
11. Marital problems, family pathology
12. Stress, life events
13. Anger, aggression, irritability, 5-HIAA
14. Physical illness
15. Repetition and comorbidity of factors 1–14, suicidal careers

Table 5

SOURCE: Maris et al. 1992, chap. 1.

Phillips's ideas about contagion dominated the sociological study of suicide in the 1980s. Works by Stack (1982), Wasserman (1989), Kessler and Strip (1984), and others have produced equivocal support for the role of suggestion in suicide (Diekstra et al. 1989). Wasserman (1989) feels that the business cycle and unemployment rates must be controlled for. Some have claimed that imitative effects are statistical artifacts. Most problematic is the fact that the theory of imitation in suicide is underdeveloped.

The most recent sociologist to study suicide is the medical sociologist Pescosolido. She has claimed, contrary to Douglas, that the official statistics on suicide are acceptably reliable and, as Gibbs said earlier, are the best basis available for a science of suicide. Her latest paper (Pescosolido and Georgianna 1989) examined Durkheim's claim that religious involvement protects against suicide. Pescosolido and Georgianna find that Roman Catholicism and evangelical Protestantism protect one against sui-cide (institutional Protestantism does not) and that Judaism has a small and inconsistent protective effect. Those authors conclude that with disintegrating network ties, individuals who lack both integrative and regulative supports commit suicide more often.

ISSUES AND FUTURE DIRECTIONS

Much of current sociological research on suicide appears myopic and sterile compared to the early work of Durkheim, Douglas, and Garfinkel. Not only is the scope of current research limited, there is very little theory and few book-length publications. Almost no research mongraphs on the sociology of suicide were written in the 1980s. Highly focused scientific journal articles on imitation have predominated, but none of these papers have been able to establish whether suicides ever were exposed to the original media stimulus. Since suicide does not concern only social relations, the study of suicide needs more interdisciplinary syntheses. The dependent variable (suicide) must include comparisons with other types of death and

Suicide Rates per 100,000 Population in 62 Countries, 1980–1986

COUNTRY	RATE
1. Hungary	45.3
2. Federal Republic of Germany	43.1
3. Sri Lanka	29.0
4. Austria	28.3
5. Denmark	27.8
6. Finland	26.6
7. Belgium	23.8
8. Switzerland	22.8
9. France	22.7
10. Suriname	21.6
11. Japan	21.2
12. German Democratic Republic	19.0
13. Czechoslovakia	18.9
14. Sweden	18.5
15. Cuba	17.7
16. Bulgaria	16.3
17. Yugoslavia	16.1
18. Norway	14.1
19. Luxemborg	13.9
20. Iceland	13.3
21. Poland	13.0
22. Canada	12.9
23. Singapore	12.7
24. United States	12.3
25. Hong Kong	12.2
26. Australia	11.6
27. Scotland	11.6
28. Netherlands	11.0
29. El Salvador	10.8
30. New Zealand	10.3
31. Puerto Rico	9.8
32. Uruguay	9.6
33. Northern Ireland	9.3
34. Portugal	9.2
35. England and Wales	8.9

Suicide Rates per 100,000 Population in 62 Countries, 1980–1986

COUNTRY	RATE
36. Trinidad and Tobago	8.6
37. Guadeloupe	7.9
38. Ireland	7.8
39. Italy	7.6
40. Thailand	6.6
41. Argentina	6.3
42. Chile	6.2
43. Spain	4.9
44. Venezuela	4.8
45. Costa Rica	4.5
46. Ecuador	4.3
47. Greece	4.1
48. Martinique	3.7
49. Colombia	2.9
50. Mauritius	2.8
51. Dominican Republic	2.4
52. Mexico	1.6
53. Panama	1.4
54. Peru	1.4
55. Philippines	0.5
56. Guatemala	0.5
57. Malta	0.3
58. Nicaragua	0.2
59. Papua New Guinea	0.2
60. Jamaica	0.1
61. Egypt	0.1
62. Antigua and Barbuda	—

Table 6

SOURCE: World Health Organization data bank, latest year of reporting as of July 1, 1988.

violence as well as more nonsocial predictor variables (Holinger 1987).

A second issue concerns methods for studying suicide (Lann et al. 1989). There has never been a truly national sample survey of suicidal behaviors in the United States. Also, most suicide research is retrospective and based on questionable vital statistics. More prospective or longitudinal research design are needed, with adequate sample sizes and comparison or control groups. Models of suicidal careers should be analyzed with specific and appropriate statistical techniques such as logistic regression, log-linear procedures, and event or hazard analysis. Federal funds to do major research on suicide are in short supply, and this is probably the major obstacle to the contemporary scientific study of suicide.

Most studies of suicide are cross-sectional and static. Future research should include more social developmental designs (Blumenthal and Kupfer 1990). There is still very little solid knowledge about the social dynamics or "suicidal careers" of eventual suicides (Maris 1990). For example, it is well known that successful suicides tend to be socially isolated at the time of death, but how they came to be that way is less well understood. Even after almost a hundred years of research the relationship of suicide to social class, occupation, and socioeconomic status is not clear.

A major issue in the study of suicide is rational suicide, active euthanasia, the right to die, and appropriate death. With a rapidly aging and more secular population and the spread of the acquired immune defiency (AIDS) virus, the American public is demanding more information about and legal rights to voluntary assisted death (see the case of Nico Speijer in the Netherlands in Diekstra et al. 1989). The right to die and assisted suicide have been the focus of a few recent legal cases (Humphry and Wickett 1986; Battin and Maris 1983). Rosewell Gilbert, an elderly man who was sentenced to life imprisonment in Florida for the mercy killing of his sick wife, was pardoned by the governor of Florida (1990). However, in 1990, the U.S. Supreme Court (*Cruzon v. the State of Missouri*) ruled that hospitals have the right to force-feed even brain-dead patients. The Hemlock Society has been founded by Derek Humphry to assist those who wish to end their own lives, make living wills, or pass living will legislation in their states

(however, see the *New York Times*, February 8, 1990, p. A18). Of course, the state must assure that the right to die does not become the obligation to die (e.g., for the aged). These issues are further complicated by strong religious and moral beliefs.

Should society help some people to die, and if so, who and in what circumstances? All people have to die, after all, so why not make dying free from pain, as quick as is desired, and not mutilating or lonely? One cannot help thinking of what has happened to assisted death at the other end of the life span, when help has not been available, in the case of abortion. Women often mutilate themselves and torture their fetuses by default. The same thing usually happens to suicides when they shoot themsleves in the head in a drunken stupor in a lonely bedroom or hotel room. Obviously, many abortions and most suicides are not "good deaths."

Euthanasia is not a unitary thing. It can be active or passive, voluntary or involuntary, and direct or indirect. A person can be against one type of euthanasia but in favor of another. "Active euthanasia" is an act that kills, while "passive euthanasia" is the omission of an act, which results in death. For example, passive or indirect euthanasia could consist of "no-coding" terminal cancer or heart patients instead of resuscitating them or not doing cardiopulmonary resuscitation after a medical crisis.

"Voluntary euthanasia" is death in which the patient makes the decision (perhaps by drafting a living will), as opposed to "involuntary euthanasia," in which someone other than the patient (e.g., if the patient is in a coma) decides (the patient's family, a physician, or a nurse).

"Direct euthanasia" occurs when death is the primary intended outcome, in contrast to "indirect euthanasia," in which death is a by-product, for example, of administering narcotics to manage pain but secondarily causes respiratory failure.

All the types of euthanasia have asssociated problems. For example, active euthanasia constitutes murder in most states. It also violates a physician's Hippocratic oath (first do no harm) and religious rules (does all life belong to God?) and has practical ambiguities (when is a patient truly hopeless?).

Passive euthanasia is often slow, painful, and expensive. For example, the comatose patient Karen Anne Quinlan lived for ten years (she survived even after the respirator was turned off) and seemed to grimace and gasp for breath. Her parents and their insurance company spent thousands of dollars on what proved to be a hopeless case. The U.S. Supreme Court ruled in *Cruzan* (1990) that hospitals cannot be forced to discontinue feeding comatose patients.

In a case in which the author served as an expert, Elizabeth Bouvia, a quadriplegic cerebral palsy patient in California, sued to avoid being force-fed as a noncomatose patient. Her intention was to starve herself to death in the hospital. The California Supreme Court upheld Bouvia's right to refuse treatment, but others called the court's decision "legal suicide."

A celebrated spokesperson for euthanasia in the form of assisted suicide has been Derek Humphry, especially in his best-selling book *Final Exit* (1996). Rational assisted suicide (Humphry assisted in his first wife's death and in the death of his father-in-law), even for the terminally ill within six months of death, has proved highly controversial, particularly to Catholics and the religious right. Basically, Humphry has written a "how-to" book on the practicalities of suicide for the terminaly ill.

His preferred rational suicide technique is to ingest four or five beta-blocker tablets and 40 to 60 100-mg tablets of a barbituate (perhaps in pudding or Jell-O), taken with Dramamine (to settle the stomach), vodka (or one's favorite whiskey), and a plastic bag over the head loosely fixed by a rubber band around the neck. Humphry recommends against guns (too messy), cyanide (too painful), hanging (too graphic), jumping (one could land on another person), and other mutilating, violent, painful, or uncertain methods.

One of the big questions about *Final Exit* is its potential abuses, for example, by young people with treatable, reversible depression. Having the lethal methods for suicide described in such vivid, explicit details worries many people that suicide will become too easy and thus often will be inappropriate. Yet Humphry shows that it is hard to get help with self-deliverance without fear of penalties. He argues that laws need to be changed to permit and specify procedures for physician-assisted suicide for the terminally ill under highly controlled conditions.

A few states have undertaken such reforms to permit legal assisted death. For example, Initiative 119 in the fall of 1991 in Washington and Proposition 161 in the fall of 1992 in California would have provided "aid in dying" for a person if (1) two physicians certified that the person was within six months of (natural) death (i.e., terminally ill), (2) the person was conscious and competent, and (3) the person signed a voluntarily written request to die witnessed by two impartial, unrelated adults. Both referenda failed by votes of about 45 percent in favor and 55 percent against.

Humphry waged a similar legal battle in Oregon, first as president of the Hemlock Society and later as president of the Euthanasia Research and Guidance Organization (ERGO) and the Oregon Right to Die organization. On November 4, 1994, Oregon became the first state to permit a doctor to prescribe lethal drugs expressly and explicitly to assist in a suicide (see Ballot Measure 16). The National Right to Life Committee effectly blocked the enactment of this law until-1997, when the measure passed overwhelmingly again. On March 25, 1998, an Oregon woman in her mid-eighties stricken with cancer became the first known person to die in the United States under a doctor-assisted suicide law (most, if not all, of Dr. Jack Kervorkian's assisted suicides have probably been illegal).

Physician-assisted suicide has been practiced for some time in the Netherlands. On February 10, 1993, the Dutch Parliment voted 91 to 45 to allow euthanasia. To be eligible for euthanasia or assisted-suicide in the Netherlands, one must (1) act voluntarily, (2) be mentally competent, (3) have a hopeless disease without prospect for improvement, (4) have a lasting longing (or persistent wish) for death, (5) have assisting doctor consult at least one colleague, and (6) have written report drawn up afterward.

The Dutch law opened the door for similar legislation in the United States, although the U.S. Supreme court seems to have closed that door shut in Washington and New York. Box 1 discusses reviews of Dr. Herbert Hendin's *Seduced by Death*, which opposes physician-assisted death the United States and the Netherlands. While the idea of legal assisted suicide will remain highly controversial and devisive, it is quite likely that bills similar to Oregon's Measure 16 will pass in other states in the next decade. A key issue will be safeguards against abuses (for example, Hendin argues that physicians in the Netherlands have decided on their own in some cases to euthanize patients).

THE DUTCH CASE

The following are excerpts from reviews of Dr. Herbert Hendin's Seduced by Death, Doctors, Patients, and the Dutch Cure *(Norton 1997). See* Suicide and Life-Threatening Behavior 28:2, 1998.

On June 26, 1997, the United States Supreme Court handed down a unanimous decision on physician-assisted suicide. All nine justices concurred that both New York and Washington's state bans on the practice should stand.

The picture [Hendin paints in the Netherlands] is a frightening one of excessive reliance on the judgment of physicians, a consensual legal system that places support of the physician above individual patient rights in order to protect the euthanasia policy, the gradual extension of practice to include administration of euthanasia without consent in a substantial number of cases, and psychologically naive abuses of power in the doctor-patient relationship.

*[For example:] Many patients come into therapy with sometimes conscious but often more unconscious fantasies that cast the therapist in the role of executioner . . . It may also play into the therapist's illusion that if he cannot cure the patient, no one else can either." (*Seduced by Death*, p. 57)*

Samuel Klagsburn, M.D., says of Hendin's argument: "He is wrong . . . suffering needs to be addressed as aggressively as possible in order to stop unnecessary suffering."

Hendin claims that in the Netherlands, "despite legal sanction, 60% of [physician-assisted suicide and death] cases are not reported, which makes regulation impossible."

Hendin goes on to argue that "a small but significant percentage of American doctors are now practicing assisted suicide, euthanasia, and the ending of patients' lives without their consent." But one also has to wonder: what about all those patients being forced to live and suffer without the patients' consent?

Dr. Hendin is, after all, the former Executive Director and current Medical Director of the American Foundation for Suicide Prevention. What would really be news is if Hendin came out in favor of physician-assisted death. Certainly, there are abuses of any policy. But is that enough of a reason to fail to assist fellow human beings in unremitting pain to die more easily? Death is one the most natural things there is and often is the only *relief.*

One of the most controversial advocates of physician-assisted suicide ("medicide") has been Dr. Kervorkian (Kevorkian 1991). Public awareness of assisted suicide and whether it is rational has foused largely on Kervorkian, the "suicide doctor." As of early 1999, Kervorkian had assisted in over 100 suicides.

Initially, with Janet Adkins, Kervorkian used a suicide machine, which he dubbed a "mercitron." This machine provided a motor-driven, timed release of three intravenous bottles; in succession, they were (1) thiopental or sodium pentathol (an anesthetic that produces rapid unconsciousness), (2) succinycholine (a muscle paralyzer like the curare used in Africa use in poison darts to hunt monkeys), and (3) postassium chloride to stop the heart. The metcitron was turned on by the would-be suicide. Because of malfunctions in the suicide machine, almost all of Kervorkian's suicides after Atkins were accomplished with a simple facial mask hooked up to a hose and a carbon monoxide cannister, with the carbon monoxide flow being initiated by the suicide. For most nonnarcotic users or addicts, 20 to 30 milligrams of intravenous injected morphine would cause death.

All of Kervorkian's first clients were women, and most were single, divorced, or widowed. Almost all were not terminally ill or at least probably would not have died within six months. The toxicology reports at autopsy (by Frederick Rieders; the author spoke with Dr. Dragovic, the Oakland County, Michigan, medical examiner to obtain these data) showed that only two of the eight assisted suicides had detectable levels of antidepressants in their blood at the time of death. It could be concluded that Kervorkian's assisted suicides were for the most part not being treated for depressive disorders.

Given Kervorkian's zealous pursuit of active euthanasia, one suspects that at least his early assisted suicides were not adequately screened or processed, for example, in accordance with the Dutch rules (above) or other safeguards. Strikingly, Hugh Gale is reputed to have asked Kervorkian to take off the carbon monoxide mask and terminate the dying process and perhaps was ignored by Kervorkian.

It is difficult to be objective about assisted suicide. Paradoxically, Kevorkian may end up setting euthanasia and doctor-assisted suicide back several years. Not only has he lost (1991) his Michigan medical license (he was a pathologist) and been charged with murder (after videotaping the dying of an assisted suicide for a television program), but Michigan and many other states (including South Carolina) have introduced bills to make previously legal assisted suicide a felony, with concurrent fines and imprisonment.

These new laws may have a chilling effect on both active and passive euthanasia, even in the case of legitimate pain control ("palliative care") previously offered to dying patients by physicians and nurses. For example, in Michigan it is now a felony to assist a suicide. People who want self-deliverance from their final pain and suffering will be more likely to mutilate themselves, die alone and disgraced, and feel generally abandoned in their time of greatest need.

Kervorkian needs to be separated from the issue of assisted suicide. However, the issue of physician-assisted suicide or death itself is not silly and transitory.

Everyone has to die eventually, and many people will suffer machine-prolonged debilitating illness and pain that diminishes the quality of their lives. Suicide and death and permanent annnihilation of consciousness (if there is no afterlife) are effective means of pain control. This refers primarily to physical pain, but psychological pain also can be excruciating. Pain cannot always be controlled short of death. Most narcotics risk respiratory death. Furthermore, narcotics often cause altered consciousness, nightmares, nausea, panic, long periods of disrupted consciousness and confusion, and addiction.

Pain control technology is progressing rapidly (e.g., spinal implant morphine pumps). There are hospices that encourage the use classic painkilling drinks such as Cicely Saunder's "Brompton's cocktail" (a mixed drink of gin, Thorazine, cocaine, heroin, and sugar). It is also possible to block nerves or utilize sophisticated polypharmacy to soften pain.

However, some pain is relatively intractable (e.g., that from bone cancer, lung disease with pneumonia, congestive heart failure in which patients choke to death on their own fluids, gastrointestinal obstructions, and amputation). A few physicians have made the ludricrous death-in-life proposal to give hopeless terminally ill patients general anesthesia to control their pain. People do always get well or feel better. Sometimes they just need to die, not be kept alive to suffer pointlessly. Anyone deserves to be helped to die in such instances.

REFERENCES

Baechler, Jean 1979 *Suicides*. New York: Basic Books.

Battin, Margaret P., and Ronald W. Maris, eds. 1983 *Suicide and Ethics*. New York: Human Sciences Press.

Blumenthal, Susan J., and David J. Kupfer, eds. 1990. *Suicide over the Life Cycle: Risk Factor Assessment, and Treatment of Suicidal Patients*. Washington, D.C.: American Psychiatric Press.

Diekstra, René F. W., Ronald W. Maris, Stephen Platt, Armin Schmidtke, and Gernot Sonneck, eds. 1989 *Suicide and Its Prevention: The Role of Attitude and Imitation*. Leiden: E.J. Brill.

Douglas, Jack D. 1967 *The Social Meanings of Suicide*. Princeton, N.J.: Princeton University Press.

Durkheim, Emile. (1897) 1951 *Suicide*. New York: Free Press.

Freud, Sigmund (1917) 1953 "Mourning and Melancholia." In *Standard Edition* of the Complete Works of Sigmund Freud. London: Hogarth Press.

Gabennesch, Howard 1988 "When Promises Fail: A Theory of Temporal Fluctuations in Suicide." *Social Forces* 67:129–145.

Gibbs, Jack P., and W. T. Martin 1964 *Status Integration and Suicide*. Eugene: University of Oregon Press.

Gibbs, Jewelle Taylor, ed. 1988 *Young, Black, and Male in America: An Endangered Species*. Dover, Mass.: Auburn House.

Henry, Andrew F., and James F. Short 1954 *Suicide and Homicide*. New York: Free Press.

Holinger, Paul C. 1987 *Violent Deaths in the United States: An Epidemiological Study of Suicide, Homicide, and Accidents*. New York: Guilford.

Humphry, Derek 1996 *Final Exit*. New York: Dell.

——, and Ann Wickett 1986 *The Right to Die: Understanding Euthanasia*. New York: Harper & Row.

Kessler, Ronald C., and H. Stripp 1984 "The Impact of Fictional Television Stories on U.S. Fatalities: A Replication." *American Journal of Sociology* 90:151–167.

Kervorkian, Jack 1991 *Prescription Medicine*. Buffalo, N.Y.: Prometens.

Lann, Irma S., Eve K. Mościcki, and Ronald W. Maris, eds. 1989 *Strategies for Studying Suicide and Suicidal Behavior*. New York: Guilford.

Maris, Ronald W. 1969 *Social Forces in Urban Suicide*. Chicago: Dorsey.

—— 1981. *Pathways to Suicide: A Survey of Self-Destructive Behaviors*. Baltimore: Johns Hopkins University Press.

—— 1989. "The Social Relations of Suicide." In Douglas Jacobs and Herbert N. Brown, eds., *Suicide, Understanding and Responding: Harvard Medical School Perspectives*, Madison, Conn.: International Universities Press.

—— 1990. The Developmental Perspective of Suicide." In Antoon Leenaars, ed., *Life Span Perspectives of Suicide*. New York: Plenum.

—— 1997 "Suicide." In Renato Pulbecco, ed., *Encyclopedia of Human Biology*.

——, Alan L. Berman, John T. Maltsberger, and Robert I. Yufit, eds. 1992 *Assessment and Prediction of Suicide*. New York: Guilford.

Menninger, Karl 1938 *Man against Himself*. New York: Harcourt, Brace.

Pescosolido, Bernice A., and Sharon Georgianna 1989 "Durkheim, Suicide, and Religion: Toward a Network Theory of Suicide." *American Sociological Review* 54:33–48.

Phillips, David P. 1974 "The Influence of Suggestion on Suicide." *American Sociological Review* 39:340–354.

Pokorny, Alex D. 1983 "Prediction of Suicide in Psychiatric Patients." *Archives of General Psychiatry* 40:249–257.

——, Katherine Lesyna, and David T. Paight 1991 "Suicide and the Media." In Ronald W. Maris, et al., eds., *Assessment and Prediction of Suicide*. New York: Guilford.

Robins, El: 1981 *The Final Months*. New York: Oxford University Press.

Shneidman, Edwin S. 1985 *Definition of Suicide*. New York: Wiley Interscience.

Stack, Stephen 1982 "Suicide: A Decade Review of the Sociological Literature." *Deviant Behavior* 4:41–66.

Wasserman, Ira M. 1989 "The Effects of War and Alcohol Consumption Patterns on Suicide: United States, 1910–1933." *Social Forces* 67:129–145.

RONALD W. MARIS

SUPERNATURALISM

See Religious Orientations.

SURVEY RESEARCH

Survey research is the method most frequently used by sociologists to study American society and other large societies. Surveys allow sociologists to move from a relatively small sample of individuals who are accessible as carriers of information about themselves and their society to the broad contours of a large population, such as its class structure and dominant values. Surveys conform to the major requirements of the scientific method by allowing a considerable (though by no means perfect) degree of objectivity in approach and allowing tests of the reliability and validity of the information obtained.

Like many other important inventions, a survey is composed of several more or less independent parts: sampling, questioning, and analysis of data. The successful combination of those elements early in the twentieth century gave birth to the method as it is known today. (Converse 1987 provides a history of the modern survey).

SAMPLING

The aspect of a survey that laypersons usually find the most mysterious is the assumption that a small sample of people (or other units, such as families or firms) can be used to generalize about the much larger population from which that sample is drawn. Thus, a sample of 1,500 adults might be drawn to represent the population of approximately 200 million Americans over age 18 in the year 2000. The sample itself is then used to estimate the extent to which numerical values calculated from it (for example, the percentage of the sample answering "married" to a question about marital status) are likely to deviate from the values that would have been obtained if the entire population over age 18 had been surveyed. That estimate, referred to as "sampling error" (because it is due to having questioned only a sample, not the full population), is even stranger from the standpoint of common sense, much like pulling oneself up by one's own bootstraps.

Although a sample of only 1,500 may be needed to obtain a fairly good estimate for the entire U.S. adult population, this does not mean that a much smaller sample is equally adequate for, say, a city of only 100,000 population. It is the absolute size of the sample that primarily determines the precision of an estimate, not the proportion of the population that is drawn for the sample—another counterintuitive feature of sampling. This has two important implications. First, a very small sample, for example, two or three hundred, is seldom useful for surveys, regardless of the size of the total population. Second, since it is often subparts of the sample, for example, blacks or whites, that are of primary interest in a survey report, it is the size of each subpart that is crucial, not the size of the overall sample. Thus, a much larger total sample may be required when the goal is to look separately at particular demographic or social subgroups.

All the estimates discussed in this article depend on the use of probability sampling, which implies that at crucial stages the respondents are selected by means of a random procedure. A nonprobability sampling approach, such as the proverbial person-in-the-street set of interviews, lacks scientific justification for generalizing to a larger population or estimating sampling error. Consumers of survey information need to be aware of the large differences in the quality of sampling that occur among organizations that claim to do surveys. It is not the case in this or other aspects of survey research that all published results merit equal confidence. Unfortunately, media presentations of findings from surveys seldom provide the information needed to evaluate the method used in gathering the data.

The theory of sampling is a part of mathematics, not sociology, but it is heavily relied on by sociologists and its implementation with real populations of people involves many nonmathematical problems that sociologists must try to solve. For example, it is one thing to select a sample of people according to the canons of mathematical theory and quite another to locate those people and persuade them to cooperate in a social survey. To the extent that intended respondents are missed, which is referred to as the problem of nonresponse, the scientific character of the survey is jeopardized. The degree of jeopardy (technically termed "bias") is a function of both the amount of nonresponse and the extent to which the nonrespondents differ from those who respond. If, for example, young black males are more likely to be missed in survey samples than are other groups in the population, as often happens, the results of the survey will not represent the entire population adequately. Serious survey investigators spend a great deal of time and money to reduce nonresponse to a minimum, and one measure of the scientific adequacy of a survey report is the information provided about nonresponse. In addition, an active area of research on the survey method consists of studies both of the effects of nonresponse and of possible ways to adjust for them. (for an introduction to sampling in social surveys, see Kalton 1983; for a more extensive classic treatment, see Kish 1965).

QUESTIONS AND QUESTIONNAIRES

Unlike sampling, the role of questions as a component of surveys often is regarded as merely a matter of common sense. Asking questions is a part of all human interaction, and it is widely assumed that no special skill or experience is needed to design a survey questionnaire. This is true in the sense that questioning in surveys is seldom very different from questioning in ordinary life but incorrect in the sense that many precautions are needed in developing a questionnaire for a general population and then interpreting the answers.

Questionnaires can range from brief attempts to obtain factual information (for example, the number of rooms in a sample of dwelling units) or simple attitudes (the leaning of the electorate toward a political candidate) to extensive explorations of the respondents' values and worldviews. Assuming that the questions have been framed with a serious purpose in mind—an assumption not always warranted because surveys are sometimes initiated with little purpose other than a desire to ask some "interesting questions"—there are two important principles to bear in mind: one about the development of the questions and the other about the interpretation of the answers.

The first principle is the importance of carrying out as much pilot work and pretesting of the questions as possible, because not even an experienced survey researcher can foresee all the difficulties and ambiguities a set of questions holds for the respondents, especially when it is administered to a heterogeneous population such as that of the United States. For example, a frequently used question about whether "the lot of the average person is getting worse" turned out on close examination to confuse the respondents about the meaning of "lot,"—with some taking it to refer to housing lots. Of course, it is still useful to draw on expert consultation where possible and to become familiar with discussions of questionnaire design in texts, especially the classic treatment by Payne (1951) and more recent expositions such as that by Sudman and Bradburn (1987).

Pilot work can be done in a number of ways, for example, by having a sample of respondents think aloud while answering, by listening carefully to the reactions of experienced interviewers who have administered the questionnaire in its pretest form, and, perhaps best of all, by having investigators do a number of practice interviews. The distinction between "pilot" and "pretest" questionnaires is that the former refer to the earlier stages of questionnaire development and may involve relatively unstructured interviewing, while the latter are closer to "dress rehearsals" before the final survey.

The main principle in interpreting answers is to be skeptical of simple distributions of results often expressed in percentage form for a particular question, for example, 65 percent "yes," 30 percent "no," 5 percent "don't know." For several reasons, such absolute percentages suggest a meaningfulness to response distributions that can be misleading. For one thing, almost any important issue is really a cluster of subissues, each of which can be asked about and may yield a different distribution of answers. Responses about the issue of "gun control" vary dramatically in the United States depending on the type of gun referred to, the amount and method of control, and so forth. No single percentage distribution or even two or three distributions can capture all this variation, nor are such problems confined to questions about

attitudes: Even a seemingly simple inquiry about the number of rooms in a home involves somewhat arbitrary definitions of what is and is not to be counted as a room, and more than one question may have to be asked to obtain the information the investigator is seeking. By the same token, care must be taken not to overgeneralize the results from a single question, since different conclusions might be drawn if a differently framed question were the focus. Indeed, many apparent disagreements between two or more surveys disappear once one realizes that somewhat different questions had been asked by each even though the general topic (e.g., gun control) may look the same.

Even when the substantive issue is kept constant, seemingly minor differences in the order and wording of questions can change percentage distributions noticeably. Thus, a classic experiment from the 1940s showed a large difference in the responses to a particular question depending on whether a certain behavior was said to be "forbidden" rather than "not allowed": To the question, "Do you think the United States should forbid public speeches against democracy?" 54 percent said yes, [Forbid], but to the question, "Do you think the United States should allow public speeches against democracy?" 75 percent said no (do not allow). This is a distinction in wording that would not make a practical difference in real life, since not allowing a speech would have the same consequence as forbidding it, yet the variation in wording has a substantial effect on answers. Experiments of this type, which are called "split-ballot experiments," frequently are carried out by dividing a national sample of respondents in half and asking different versions of the question to each half on a random basis. If the overall sample is large enough, more than two variations can be tested at the same time, and in some case more complex "factorial designs" are employed to allow a larger number of variations (see Rossi and Nock [1982] for examples of factorial surveys).

The proportion of people who answer "don't know" to a survey question also can vary substantially—by 25 percent or more—depending on the extent to which that answer is explicitly legitimized for respondents by mentioning it along with other alternatives ("yes," "no," "don't know") or omitted. In other instances, the location of a question in a series of questions has been shown to affect answers even though the wording of the question is not changed. For example, a widely used question about allowing legalized abortion in the case of a married woman who does not want more children produces different answers depending entirely on its position before or after a question about abortion in the case of a defective fetus. Thus, the context in which a question is asked can influence the answers people give. These and a large number of other experiments on the form, wording, and context of survey questions are reported by Schuman and Presser (1981) (see Turner and Martin [1984] for several treatments of survey questioning, as well as more recent volumes by Schwarz and Sudman [1996] and Sudman et al. [1996] with a cognitive psychological emphasis).

ANALYSIS

Although questioning samples of individuals may seem to capture the entire nature of a survey, a further component is vital to sociologists: the logical and statistical analysis of the resulting data. Responses to survey questions do not speak for themselves, and in most cases even the simple distribution of percentages to a single question calls for explicit or implicit comparison with another distribution, real or ideal. To report that 60 percent of a sample is satisfied with the actions of a particular leader may be grounds for either cheering or booing. It depends on the level of satisfaction typical for that leader at other times or for other individuals or groups in comparable leadership positions. Thus, reports of survey data should include these types of comparisons whenever possible. This is why for sociologists the collection of a set of answers is the beginning and not the end of a research analysis.

More generally, most answers take on clear meaning primarily when they are used in comparisons across time (for example, responses of a sample this year compared with responses of a sample from the same population five years ago), across social categories such as age and education, or across other types of classifications that are meaningful for the problem being studied. Moreover, since any such comparison may produce a difference that is due to chance factors because only a sample was drawn rather than to a true difference between time points or social categories, statistical testing is essential to create confidence that the difference would be found if the

entire population could be surveyed. In addition, individual questions sometimes are combined into a larger index to decrease idiosyncratic effects resulting from any single item, and the construction of this type of index requires other preliminary types of statistical analysis.

As an example of survey analysis, sociologists often find important age differences in answers to survey questions, but since age and education are negatively associated in most countries—that is, older people tend to have less education than do younger people—it is necessary to disentangle the two factors in order to judge whether age is a direct cause of responses or only a proxy for education. Moreover, age differences in responses to a question can represent changes resulting from the aging process (which in turn may reflect physiological, social, or other developmental factors) or reflect experiences and influences from a particular historical point in time ("cohort effects"). Steps must be taken to distinguish these explanations from one another. At the same time, a survey analyst must bear in mind and test the possibility that a particular pattern of answers is due to "chance" because of the existence of sampling error.

Thus, the analysis of survey data can be quite complex, well beyond, though not unrelated to, the kinds of tables seen in newspaper and magazine presentations of poll data. (The terms "poll" and "survey" are increasingly interchangeable, with the main difference being academic and governmental preference for "survey" and media preference for "poll.") However, such thorough analysis is important if genuine insights into the meaning of answers are to be gained and misinterpretations are to be avoided. (A comprehensive but relatively nontechnical presentation of the logic of survey analysis is provided by Rosenberg [1968]. Among the many introductory statistical texts, Agresti and Finlay [1997] leans in a survey analytic direction.)

MODE OF ADMINISTRATION

Although sampling, questioning, and analysis are the most fundamental components, decisions about the mode of administering a survey are also important. A basic distinction can be made between self-administered surveys and those in which interviewers are used. If it is to be based on probability sampling of some sort, self-administration, usually is carried out by mailing questionnaires to respondents who have been selected through a random procedure. For instance, a sample of sociologists might be chosen by taking every twentieth name from an alphabetical listing of all regular members of the American Sociological Association, though with the recognition that any such listing would be incomplete (e.g., not everyone with an advanced degree in sociology belongs to the association).

The major advantage of mail surveys is their relatively low cost, which is limited to payments to clerical employees, stamps, and perhaps financial incentive for the respondents. One disadvantage of mail surveys is that they traditionally have produced low response rates; many obtain only 25 percent or less of the target sample. However, Dillman (1978) argues that designing mail surveys in accordance with the principles of *exchange theory* can yield response rates at or close to those of other modes of administration. Whether this is true for a sample of the U.S. population remains in doubt for the reason given below, although Dillman has implemented some of his strategies in government census-type surveys. It is clear from numerous experiments that the use of two specific features—monetary incentives (not necessarily large) provided in advance and follow-up "reminders"—can almost always improve mail questionnaire response rates appreciably. However, another important disadvantage of mail surveys in the United States is the absence of an available centralized national listing of households for drawing a sample; because of this situation, it is difficult to say what response rate could be obtained from a nongovernmental national mail sample in this country.

Mail surveys generally are used when there is a prior list available, such as an organization's membership, and this practice may add the benefit of loyalty to the organization as a motive for respondent cooperation. Other disadvantages of mail surveys are lack of control over exactly who answers the questions (it may or may not be the target respondent, assuming there is a single target), the order in which the questionnaire is filled out, and the unavailability of an interviewer for respondents who cannot read well or do not understand the questions. One compensating factor is the greater privacy afforded respondents, which may lead to more candor, although evidence of this is still limited. Sometimes similar privacy is attempted an interview survey by giving a portion of the questionnaire to respondents to fill out themselves and even providing a separate sealed envelope to mail back to the survey headquarters, thus guaranteeing that the interviewer will not read the answers. This strategy was used by Laumann et al. (1994) in a major national survey of sexual behavior, but no comparison with data obtained in a more completely private setting was provided. Tourangeau and Smith (1996) provide a different type of evidence by showing that respondents who answer directly into a computer appear more candid than do respondents who give answers to interviewers. Recently, the Internet has been investigated as a vehicle for self-administered surveys, although there are formidable problems of sampling in such cases.

Because of these difficulties, most surveys aimed at the general population employ interviewers to locate respondents and administer a questionnaire. Traditionally, this has been done on a face-to-face (sometimes called "personal") basis, with interviewers going to households, usually after a letter of introduction has been mailed describing the survey. The sample ordinarily is drawn by using "area probability" methods: To take a simple example, large units such as counties may be drawn first on a random basis, then from the selected counties smaller units such as blocks are drawn, and finally addresses on those blocks are listed by interviewers and a randomly drawn subset of the listed addresses is designated for the actual sample, with introductory letters being sent before interviewing is attempted. In practice, more than two levels would be used, and other technical steps involving "stratification" and "clustering" would be included to improve the efficiency of the sampling and data collection.

A major advantage of face-to-face interviewing is the ability of the interviewer to find the target respondent and persuade her or him to take part in the interview. Face-to-face interviewing has other advantages: Graphic aids can be used as part of a questionnaire, interviewers can make observations of a respondent's ability to understand the questions and of other behavior or characteristics of a respondent, and unclear answers can be clarified. The major disadvantage of face-to-face interviewing is its cost, since much of the time of interviewers is spent locating respondents (many are not at home on a first or second visit). For every actual hour spent interviewing, five to ten hours may be needed for travel and related effort. Furthermore, face-to-face surveys require a great deal of total field time, and when results are needed quickly, this is difficult to accomplish and may add more expense. Another disadvantage is the need for an extensive supervisory staff spread around the country, and yet another is that survey administrators must rely on the competence and integrity of interviewers, who are almost always on their own and unsupervised during interviews. This makes standardization of the interviewing difficult.

Increasingly since the early 1970s, face-to-face interviewing has been replaced by telephone interviewing, usually from a centralized location. Telephone surveys are considerably less expensive than face-to-face surveys, though the exact ratio is hard to estimate because they also are normally shorter, usually under forty-five minutes in length; the expense of locating people for face-to-face interviews leads to hourlong or even lengthier interviews, since these usually are tolerated more readily by respondents who are interviewed in person. Telephone surveys can be completed more rapidly than can face-to-face surveys and have the additional advantage of allowing more direct supervision and monitoring of interviewers. The incorporation of the computer directly into interviewing—known as computer-assisted telephone interviewing (CATI)—facilitates questionnaire formatting and postinterview coding, and this increases flexibility and shortens total survey time. Still another advantage of telephone surveys is the relative ease of probability sampling: Essentially random combinations of digits, ten at a time, can be created by computer to sample any telephone number in the United States (three-digit area code plus seven-digit number). There are a variety of practical problems to be overcome (e.g., many of the resulting numbers are nonworking, account must be taken of multiple phones per household, and answering machines and other devices often make it difficult to reach real people), but techniques have been developed that make such samples available and inexpensive to a degree that was never true of the area sampling required for face-to-face interviewing. Perhaps the largest problem confronting survey research is the proliferation of telemarketing, which makes many potential respondents wary of phone calls and reluctant to devote time to a survey interview.

Because speaking on the telephone seems so different from speaking face to face, survey methodologists initially thought that the results from the two types of survey administration might be very different. A number of experimental comparisons, however, have failed to find important differences, and those which do occur may have more to do with different constraints on sampling (telephone surveys obviously miss the approximately 8 percent of the American households without telephones and produce somewhat higher levels of refusal by the intended respondents). Thus, the remaining reasons for continuing face-to-face surveys have to do with the need for longer interviews and special additions such as graphic demonstrations and response scales. (Groves [1989] discusses evidence on telephone versus face-to-face survey differences, and Groves et al. [1988] present detailed accounts of methodological issues involving telephone surveys.)

Face-to-face and telephone surveys share one important feature: the intermediate role of the interviewer between the questionnaire and the respondent. Although this has many advantages, as was noted above, there is always the possibility that some behavior or characteristic of the interviewer will affect responses. For example, as first shown by Hyman (1954) in an effort to study the interview process, a visible interviewer characteristic such as racial appearance can have dramatic effects on answers. This is probably the largest of all the effects discovered, no doubt because of the salience and tension that racial identification produces in America, but the possibility of other complications from the interview process—and from the respondent's assumption about the sponsorship or aim of the survey—must be borne in mind. This is especially true when surveys are attempted in societies in which the assumption of professional neutrality is less common than in the United States, and some recent failures by surveys to predict elections probably are due to bias of this type.

THE SEQUENCE OF A SURVEY

Surveys should begin with one or more research problems that determine both the content of the questionnaire and the design of the sample. The two types of decisions should go hand in hand, since each affects the other. A questionnaire that is intended to focus on the attitudes of different ethnic and racial groups makes sense only if the population sampled and the design of the sample will yield enough members of each group to provide sufficient data for adequate analysis. In addition, decisions must be made early with regard to the mode of administration of the survey—whether it will be conducted through self-administration or interviewing and, if the latter, whether in person, by telephone, or in another way—since these choices also influence what can be asked. Each decision has its trade-offs in terms of quality, cost, and other important features of the research.

After these planning decisions, the development of the questionnaire, the pretesting, and the final field period take place. The resulting data from closed, or fixed-choice, questions can be entered directly in numerical form (e.g., 1 = yes, 2 = no, 3 = don't know) into a computer file for analysis. If open-ended questions—questions that do not present fixed alternatives—are used and the respondents' answers have been recorded in detail, an intermediate step is needed to code the answers into categories. For example, a question that asks the respondents to name the most important problems facing the country today might yield categories for "foreign affairs," "inflation," "racial problems," and so forth, though the words used by the respondents ordinarily would be more concrete. Finally, the data are analyzed in the form of tables and statistical measures that can form the basis for a final report.

MODIFICATIONS AND EXTENSIONS OF THE SURVEY METHOD

This discussion has concerned primarily the single cross-sectional or one-shot survey, but more informative designs are increasingly possible. The most obvious step now that surveys of the national population have been carried out for more than half a century is to study change over time by repeating the same questions at useful intervals. The General Social Survey (GSS) has replicated many attitude and factual questions on an annual or biennial basis since 1972, and the National Election Study (NES) has done the same thing in the political area on a biennial basis since the 1950s. From these repeated surveys, sociologists

have learned about substantial changes in some attitudes, while in other areas there has been virtually no change (see Niemi et al. [1989] and Page and Shapiro [1992] for examples of both change and stability). An important variant on such longitudinal research is the panel study, in which the same respondents are interviewed at two or more points in time. This has certain advantages; for example, even where there is no change for the total sample in the distribution of responses, there may be counterbalancing shifts that can be best studied in this way.

Surveys are increasingly being carried out on a cross-national basis, allowing comparisons across societies, though usually with the additional obstacle of translation to be overcome. Even within the framework of a single survey in one country, comparisons across different types of samples can be illuminating, for example, in an important early study by Stouffer (1955) that administered the same questionnaire to the general public and to a special sample of "community leaders" in order to compare their attitudes toward civil liberties. Finally, it is important to recognize that although the survey method often is seen as entirely distinct from or even opposite to the experimental method, the two have been usefully wedded in a number of ways. Much of what is known about variations in survey responses caused by the form, wording, and context of the questions has been obtained by means of split-ballot experiments, while attempts to study the effects of policy changes sometimes have involved embedding surveys of attitudes and behaviors within larger experimental designs.

ETHICAL AND OTHER PROBLEMS

As with other social science approaches to the empirical study of human beings, surveys raise important ethical issues. The success of survey sampling requires persuading individuals to donate their time to being interviewed, usually without compensation, and to trust that their answers will be treated confidentially and used for purposes they would consider worthwhile. A related issue is the extent to which respondents should be told in advance and in detail about the content and aims of a questionnaire (the issue of "informed consent"), especially when this might discourage their willingness to answer questions or affect the kinds of answers they give (Singer 1993). The purely professional or scientific goal of completing the survey thus can conflict with the responsibility of survey investigators to the people who make surveys possible: the respondents. These are difficult issues, and there probably is no simple overall solution. There is a need in each instance to take seriously wider ethical norms as well as professional or scientific goals.

From within sociology, reliance on surveys has been criticized on several grounds. Sociologists committed to more qualitative approaches to studying social interaction often view surveys as sacrificing richness of description and depth of understanding to obtain data amenable to quantitative analysis. Sociologists concerned with larger social structures sometimes regard the survey approach as focusing too much on the individual level, neglecting the network of relations and institutions of societies. Finally, some see the dependence of surveys on self-reporting as a limitation because of the presumed difference between what people say in interviews and how they behave outside the interview situation (Schuman and Johnson 1976). Although there are partial answers to all these criticisms, each has some merit, and those doing survey research need to maintain a self-critical stance toward their own approach. However, the survey is the best-developed and most systematic method sociologists have to gather data. Equally useful methods appropriate to other goals have yet to be developed.

REFERENCES

Agresti, Alan, and Barbara Finlay 1997 *Statistical Methods for the Social Sciences.* Upper Saddle River, N.J.: Prentice Hall.

Converse, Jean M. 1987 *Survey Research in the United States: Roots and Emergence, 1890–1960.* Berkeley: University of California Press.

Dillman, Don A. 1978 *Mail and Telephone Surveys: The Total Design Method.* New York: Wiley.

Groves, Robert M. 1989 *Survey Errors and Survey Costs.* New York: Wiley.

—— Paul P. Biemer, Lars E. Lyberg, James T. Massey, William L. Nicholls II, and Joseph Waksberg 1988 *Telephone Survey Methodology.* New York: Wiley.

Hyman, Herbert H. 1954 *Interviewing in Social Research.* Chicago: University of Chicago Press.

Kalton, Graham 1983 *Introduction to Survey Sampling.* Beverly Hills, Calif.: Sage.

Kish, Leslie 1965 *Survey Sampling.* New York: Wiley.

Laumann, Edward O., Robert T. Michael, John H. Gagnon, and Stuart Michaels 1994 *The Social Organization of Sexuality: Sexual Practices in the United States.* Chicago: University of Chicago Press.

Niemi, Richard, John Mueller, and Tom W. Smith 1989 *Trends in Public Opinion: A Compendium of Survey Data.* Westport, Conn.: Greenwood Press.

Page, Benjamin I., and Robert Y. Shapiro 1992 *The Rational Public: Fifty Years of Trends in Americans' Policy Preferences.* Chicago: University of Chicago Press.

Payne, Stanley L. 1951. *The Art of Asking Questions.* Princeton, N.J.: Princeton University Press.

Rosenberg, Morris 1968. *The Logic of Survey Analysis.* New York: Basic Books.

Rossi, Peter H., and Steven L. Nock, eds. 1982 *Measuring Social Judgments: The Factorial Survey Approach.* Beverly Hills, Calif.: Sage.

Schuman, Howard, and Michael P. Johnson 1976 "Attitudes and Behavior." *Annual Review of Sociology,* vol. 2. Palo Alto, Calif.: Annual Reviews.

—— and Stanley Presser 1981 *Questions and Answers in Attitude Surveys: Experiments on Question Form, Wording, and Context.* New York: Academic Press.

Schwarz, Norbert, and Seymour Sudman, eds. 1996 *Answering Questions: Methodology for Determining Cognitive and Communicative Processes in Survey Research.* San Francisco: Jossey-Bass.

Singer, Eleanor 1993 "Informed Consent in Surveys: A Review of the Empirical Literature." *Journal of Official Statistics.* 9:361–375.

Stouffer, Samuel A. 1955 *Communism, Conformity, and Civil Liberties.* Garden City, N.Y.: Doubleday.

Sudman, Seymour, and Norman M. Bradburn 1987 *Asking Questions: A Practical Guide to Question Design.* San Francisco: Jossey-Bass.

——,——, and Norbert Schwarz 1996 *Thinking About Answers: The Application of Cognitive Processes to Survey Methodology.* San Francisco: Jossey-Bass.

Tourangeau, Roger, and Tom W. Smith 1996 "Asking Sensitive Questions: The Impact of Data Collection Mode, Question Format, and Question Content." *Public Opinion Quarterly* 60:275–304.

Turner, Charles, and Elizabeth Martin, eds. 1984 *Surveying Subjective Phenomena,* 2 vols. New York: Russell Sage Foundation.

HOWARD SCHUMAN

SYMBOLIC INTERACTION THEORY

The term "symbolic interactionism" was invented by Blumer (1937) to describe sociological and social psychological ideas he presented as emanating directly from Mead, especially but not exclusively in *Mind, Self, and Society* (1934). "Symbolic interaction theory" is a term that is related to those ideas, though not necessarily in the specific forms presented by Blumer or Mead.

FUNDAMENTAL IMAGERY

The fundamental character of symbolic interactionist ideas is suggested by the theoretical proposition that the self reflects society and organizes behavior and by related imagery that addresses the nature of society and the human being, the nature of human action and interaction, and the relationship between society and the person. That imagery begins with a vision of society as a web of communication: Society *is* interaction, the reciprocal influence of persons who, as they relate, take into account each other's characteristics and actions, and interaction is communication. Interaction is "symbolic," that is, conducted in terms of the meanings persons develop in the course of their interdependent conduct. The environment of human action and interaction is symbolically defined: It is the environment as it is interpreted that is the context, shaper, and object of action and interaction. Persons act with reference to one another in terms of symbols developed through interaction and act through the communication of those symbols. Society is a label aggregating and summarizing such interaction. Society does not "exist"; it is created and continuously re-created as persons interact. Social reality is a flow of events joining two or more persons. More than simply being implicated in the social process, society and the person derive from that process: They take on their meanings as those meanings emerge in and through social interaction.

Neither society nor the individual is ontologically prior to the other in this imagery; persons create society through their interaction, but it is society, a web of communication and interaction, that creates persons as social beings. Society and the individual presuppose each other; neither exists except in relation to the other. This conception of society implicitly incorporates a view of the human being as "minded" and that "mindedness" as potentially reflexive. That is, people can and sometimes do take themselves as the object of their own reflection, thus creating selves, and do this from the standpoint of the others with whom they interact. Selves are inherently social products, although they involve more than reflected appraisals of others in the immediate situation of interaction; in particular, selves involve persons as subjects responding to themselves as objects. Thinking takes place as an internal conversation that uses symbols that develop in the social process. Mind arises in both the evolutionary and individual senses in response to problems (interruptions in the flow of activities) and involves formulating and selecting from symbolically defined alternative courses of action to resolve those problems. Choice is an omnipresent reality in the human condition, and the content of choices is contained in the subjective experience of persons as that experience develops in and through the social process.

Following from this imagery is a view of human beings, both collectively and individually, as active and creative rather than simply responsive to environmental stimuli. Since the environment of human action and interaction is symbolic; because the symbols attaching to persons (including oneself), things, and ideas are the products of interaction and reflexivity and can be altered and manipulated in the course of that interaction; since thought can be used to anticipate the effectiveness of alternative courses of action in resolving problems; and because choice among alternatives is an integral feature of social conduct, one arrives at an image of social interaction as literally constructed, although not necessarily anew in each instance, in the course of interaction. One also arrives at an image that entails a degree of indeterminacy in human behavior in the sense that the course and outcome of social interaction cannot as a matter of principle (not uncertain knowledge) be completely predicted from conditions and factors existing before that interaction.

THE SYMBOLIC INTERACTIONIST FRAMEWORK

Labeling the ideas of symbolic interactionism a "theory" is misleading. If one distinguishes between a systematic set of interrelated propositions about how a segment of the world is organized and functions and assumptions about and conceptualizations of the parts of that segment, symbolic interactionism has more the character of the latter than the former. That is, it is more a theoretical framework than a theory per se. While features of the framework appear to militate against attempts to formulate systematic theory by using it as a base and various proponents deny that possibility, a few sociologists have employed the framework in efforts to elaborate specific theories (e.g., Heise 1979; Stryker 1980, forthcoming; Stryker and Serpe 1982; Rosenberg 1984; Thoits 1983; MacKinnon 1994; Burke 1991). It is not possible to review such specific theories nor characterize the research that derives from that framework here. (For extensive references to classic literature and research literature before 1985, see Stryker and Statham [1985]. For more recent research, see one of the texts written from a symbolic interactionist perspective, such as Hewitt [1997], or *Symbolic Interaction*, a journal sponsored by the Society for the Study of Symbolic Interaction and devoted to work emanating from the framework.)

In the work of some (e.g., Blumer 1969), symbolic interaction "theory" is intended to be a general sociological frame that is applicable to the intellectual problems of sociology as a discipline from the most micro to the most macro levels. In the work of others (e.g., Stryker 1980), it is a frame restricted in utility to issues of social psychology. The first position does not seem defensible, because any framework brings into special focus particular variables and leaves unattended—at least relatively—other variables and because the symbolic interaction framework highlights interaction, social actors related through interaction, and subjective variables "internal" to those actors. It thus neglects features of the sociological landscape relating to large-scale social systems—the state, the economy, the "world system," demographic variables, and so forth—and does not easily pose sociological questions involving interrelationships among those features of large-scale social systems. This neglect has led to criticism of the symbolic interactionist framework as lacking the social structural concepts needed for the analysis of power and consequently as an ideological apology for the status quo (see Meltzer et al. 1975; Stryker 1980; Reynolds 1990). Although many (e.g., Maines 1977) deny the validity of this criticism, pointing to work

by Hall (1972) and others, the criticism may be justified if the claim is that symbolic interactionism is a general sociological framework; it is not valid if the more restricted claim for its utility is made. However, there remains concern about the adequacy of the framework for problems of a distinctively *sociological* social psychology that centers on the reciprocal relationships of social units and social persons. There also is concern about whether the framework admits of and provides readily for the articulation of sociological and social psychology concepts. These concerns arise from the ways in which social structural concepts enter, or fail to enter, the symbolic interactionist frame (for presentations of an avowedly social structural version of the framework, see Stryker 1980, forthcoming). Whatever the intended coverage—from all of sociology to a limited social psychology—the framework traditionally has been conceived as knowing no cultural boundaries; that view, however, has been questioned (Hewitt 1990).

CENTRAL CONCEPTS

Implicated in the description of symbolic interactionist imagery provided above are many of the central concepts of the framework. The meaning of "meaning" is fundamental. By definition, social acts involve at least two persons taking each other into account in satisfying impulses or resolving problems. Since social acts occur over time, *gestures*—parts of an act that indicate that other parts are still to come—can appear. Vocal sounds, physical movements, bodily expressions, clothing, and so forth, can serve as gestures. When they do, they have meaning: Their meaning lies in the behavior that follows their appearance. Gestures that have the same meaning (implying the same future behavior) to those who make them and those who perceive them are *significant symbols*.

Things, ideas, and relationships among things and ideas can all be symbolized and enter the experience of human beings as objects; objects whose meanings are anchored in and emerge from social interaction constitute social reality. Although meanings are unlikely to be identical among participants, communication and social interaction presuppose significant symbols that allow meanings to be "sufficiently" shared. Because significant symbols anticipate future behavior, they entail plans of action: They organize behavior with reference to what they symbolize. In the context of the ongoing social process, meanings must be at least tentatively assigned to features of the interactive situations in which persons find themselves; without the assignment of meanings, behavior in those situations is likely to be disorganized or random. The situation must be symbolized, as must its constituent parts; it must be defined or interpreted, and the products of that symbolization process are *definitions of the situation*. Those definitions focus attention on what is pertinent (satisfying impulses or resolving problems) in an interactive setting and permit a preliminary organization of actions appropriate to the setting. Tentative definitions are tested and may be reformulated through ongoing experience.

From the point of view of the actors involved, the most important aspects of a situation requiring definition are who or what they are in the situation and who or what the others with whom they interact are. Defining the others in the situation typically is accomplished by locating them as members of a socially recognized category of actors, one (or more) of the kinds of persons it is possible to be in a society (e.g., male or female, young or old, employed or unemployed). Doing this provides cues to or predictors of their behavior and permits the organization of one's own behavior with reference to them. When others are recognized as instantiations of a social category, behaviors are expected of them and actions that are premised on those expectations can be organized and directed toward them. Through this process, the introduction of early definitions of the situation can produce, although not inevitably, behavior that validates the definitions. This is an insight that underlies the notion of altercasting (Weinstein and Deutschberger 1963) and appears in the development of expectation states theory (Berger et al. 1974). When such behavior becomes routinized and organized, it also can serve to reproduce the existing social structure.

While some interactionists disdain the term, expectations attached to social categories—again, the kinds of persons it is possible to be in a society—are *roles*. Situations frequently allow one to locate others in multiple categories and open the possibility that conflicting expectations will come into play; in this circumstance, no clear means of organizing responses may be available. Defining oneself in a situation also involves locating oneself in socially recognized categories; to respond reflexively to oneself by classifying, naming, and defining who and what one is is to have a *self*. The self, conceived in this manner, involves viewing oneself as an object. The meaning of self, like that of any object, derives from interaction: To have a self is to view oneself from the standpoint of those with whom one interacts. The self, like any significant symbol, provides a plan of action. By definition, that plan implicates the expected responses of others.

People learn, at least provisionally, what they can expect from others through *role taking*, a process of anticipating the responses of the others with whom one interacts. In effect, one puts oneself in the place of those people to see the world as they do, using prior experience with them, knowledge of the social categories in which they are located, and symbolic cues available in interaction. On such bases, tentative definitions of others' attitudes are formulated and then validated or reshaped in interaction. Role taking permits one to anticipate the consequences of one's own and others' plans of action, monitor the results of those plans as they are carried out behaviorally, and sustain or redirect one's behavior on the basis of the monitoring. Because roles often lack consistency and concreteness while actors must organize their behavior as if roles were unequivocal, interaction is also a matter of *role making*: creating and modifying roles by devising performances in response to roles imputed to others (Turner 1962).

Many social acts take place within organized systems of action; consequently, both role taking and role making can occur with reference to a *generalized other*, that is, a differentiated but interrelated set of others (Mead's example involves baseball players anticipating the responses of other members of their team and those of their opponents). Not all others' perspectives are equally relevant to an actor; the concept of *significant other* indicates that some persons will be given greater weight when perspectives differ or are incompatible. It is implied here that meanings are not likely to be universally shared or shared in detail; if they are not, accuracy in role taking and difficulty in role making also will vary. It also is implied that smooth and cooperative interpersonal relations do not necessarily follow from accurate role taking: Conflict may result from or be sharpened by such accuracy.

The symbolic interactionist ideas reviewed here have a history. Many issue directly from Mead. Mead's ideas are part of a tradition of philosophical thought with roots in the Scottish moral philosophers Adam Smith, David Hume, Adam Ferguson, and Francis Hutcheson and, more proximately, in the American pragmatists Charles Peirce, William James, and John Dewey. They also contain important admixtures of evolutionary and dialectic premises. Mead's thought overlaps considerably with that of a number of sociologists who also wrote in the first decades of the twentieth century, in particular Charles Horton Cooley and William Isaac Thomas. Cooley's axiom that society and the person are two sides of the same coin (the coin, he added, is communication) and that of Thomas asserting that if humans define situations as real, the situations are real in their consequences, capture much of the essence of symbolic interactionism. A host of sociologists connect that past with the present; among others, Burgess, Blumer, Waller, Sutherland, Hughes, Shibutani, Kuhn, Cottrell, Hill, Lemert, Lindesmith, Mills, Miyamoto, and Stone are linked to a more contemporary set of persons that includes Goffman, Lofland, Becker, Lopata, Strauss, Geer, Weinstein, Farberman, Couch, Denzin, Bart, Maines, Reynolds, Turner, Daniels, Scheff, Wiseman, Heise, Stryker, Burke, Heiss, Fine, Hochschild, Weigert, McCall, Snow, and Hewitt. (For reviews of the history and literature of symbolic interactionism, see Stryker and Statham 1985; Meltzer et al. 1975; Reynolds 1990; Lewis and Smith 1980.) The presence of these researchers in a common listing does not indicate their adherence to a common credo; there may be as much conceptual difference as similarity among them.

COMMONALITIES AND VARIATIONS

Thus, no single version of symbolic interaction theory satisfies all who find its core ideas appealing and useful in conducting research and analyses. There appear to be three fundamental premises of a symbolic interactionist perspective that are shared by those who acknowledge their intellectual roots in this tradition of sociological thought (Stryker 1988). The first holds that an adequate account of human social behavior must incorporate the perspective of participants in interaction and cannot rest entirely on the perspective of the observer. The second is that the self, that is, persons' reflexive responses to themselves, links the larger social organization or structure to the social interaction of those persons. The third asserts that processes of social interaction are prior to both self and social organization, both of which derive and emerge from social interaction.

Each of these premises leaves open issues of considerable importance with respect to the content, methods, and objectives of interactionist analyses on which symbolic interactionists can differ. Some sociologists for whom the three core premises serve as a starting point believe that social life is so fluid that it can be described only in process terms, that concepts purportedly describing social structures or social organization belie the reality of social life. Relatedly, some believe that actors' definitions, which theoretically are central and powerful as generators of lines of action, are reformulated continuously in immediate situations of interaction, making it impossible to use preexistent concepts to analyze social life (Blumer 1969). Others accept the "reality" of social structural phenomena, viewing the social structure as relatively stable patternings of social interaction that operate as significant constraints on actors' definitions. Social structure is thought to make for sufficient continuity in definitions to allow the use of concepts derived from past analyses of social interaction in the analysis of present and future interaction (Stryker 1980). The first premise hides, in the term "account," the important difference between those who seem to believe that given the constructed character of social behavior, only an "after the fact" understanding of past events is possible (Weigert 1981) and those who believe that sociology can build testable predictive explanations of social behavior (Kuhn 1964). Similarly, some argue that the perspective of a sociological observer of human social behavior is likely to distort accounts of that behavior and so must be abjured in seeking to capture the perspectives of those who live the behavior that is observed (Denzin 1970), and others argue directly or by implication that the requirement that accounts incorporate the perspective of the actors whose behavior is observed dictates only that actors' definitions be included in developed explanations, not that they constitute those explanations (Burke 1991). The first group tends to argue that the best, if not the only "legitimate," methods are naturalistic, primarily observational (Becker and Geer 1957); the second group tends to be catholic with respect to methods, refusing to rule out categorically any of the full range of possible social science methods and techniques (Heise 1979).

With respect to the second premise, interactionists differ in the degree to which they assign an independent "causal" role to the self as the link between social organization or structure and social behavior. For many, self can and does serve as an independent source of that behavior (McCall and Simmons 1978). For others, social organization or structure (as the residue of prior interaction) builds selves in its image, thus making the self essentially a conduit through which these structures shape behavior, not an independent source of that behavior (Goffman 1959). Similarly, there is variation among symbolic interactionists in the degree to which the self is seen as the source of creativity and novelty in social life, the degree to which creativity and novelty in social life are seen as probable as opposed to simply possible (occurring only under a specific and limited set of social circumstances), and the degree to which social life is constructed anew rather than "merely" reconstructed in the image of prior patterns (Turner 1962; Hewitt 1997; Stryker and Statham 1985).

The third premise is interpreted by some as denying that social organization and selves have sufficient constancy to permit generalized conceptualization or the development of useful a priori theory on the basis of any investigation that can carry over reasonably to any new investigation (Glaser and Strauss 1967). In the view of others, this premise does not deny that there is in social life a reasonable constancy that implies a sufficient constancy in both selves and social organization to permit the elaboration of useful theories employing general concepts that potentially are applicable to wide instances of social behaviors (Heise 1986). Some emphasize the behavioristic elements in their intellectual heritage from Mead, concentrating on how concerted lines of social action are constructed (Couch et al. 1986; McPhail and Wohlstein 1986), while others adopt a stance that attends primarily to the phenomenological worlds of the actors (or interactors) they study (Denzin 1984).

Clearly, these possibilities for important variations in symbolic interactionist thought are not independent of one another: Those who subscribe to a view emphasizing the fluidity of social life and the moment-to-moment situated character of definitions also are likely to emphasize the degree to which social order continuously emerges from fluid process, the self organizes social behavior in an unconstrained fashion, and creativity and novelty characterize human behavior. They also tend to insist that the point of view of the observer contaminates reasonable accounts of social interaction, that there is little utility in an analysis of conceptualizations and theory emanating from earlier analyses, and that understanding, not explanation, is the point of sociological efforts.

The set of views presented in the preceding paragraph identifies symbolic interactionism for many of its most passionate adherents and perhaps for a majority of its critics. Those approaching their work from symbolic interactionism so defined tended to present what they did in both conceptual and methodological opposition to available alternatives in sociology. For example, Blumer (1969) devoted much of his career to championing direct and participant observation aimed at accessing the interpretations of those whose ongoing interaction sociologists sought to understand as opposed to both statistical and structural analyses, whose categories, data, and mathematical manipulations seemed to him devoid of actors' meanings. Critics of symbolic interactionism attacked it and its adherents for being nonscientific and asociological. To circumscribe symbolic interactionism in the manner of these adherents and critics belies the diversity in views on key issues represented in the work of those who use the framework.

CONTEMPORARY VITALITY

Interest in the symbolic interactionist framework within sociology has fluctuated. That interest was great from 1920 to 1950, reflecting in part the dominance of the University of Chicago in producing sociologists as well as the institutional structure of sociology. Through the 1950s and into the 1970s, interest waned, first as the structural functionalism of Parsons and Merton gained ascendance intellectually and Harvard and Columbia became institutionally dominant and later as Marxist and structuralist emphases on macro social processes swept the field. Symbolic interactionism, when not decried as reactionary or asociological, became the loyal opposition (Mullins 1973). Indeed, Mullins predicted that it would disappear as a viable socio-logical framework.

More recent events contradict that prediction: Symbolic interaction' has had a remarkable revitalization in the past three decades (Stryker 1987), and there has been a corresponding resurgence of interest in the framework. The revitalization and resurgent interest reflect various sources. One is an emerging realization among sociologists with a structural orientation that their theories could benefit from the sociologically sophisticated theory of the social actor and action that symbolic interactionism can provide and the related increasing interest in linking micro to macro social processes. A second lies in a series of changing emphases in the work of contemporary symbolic interactionists. Although much recent work in a symbolic interactionist framework reflects traditional conceptual, theoretical, and methodological themes, on the conceptual level, newer work tends to adopt a "multiple selves" perspective, drawing on William James (Stryker 1989; McCall and Simmons 1978) rather than viewing the self as singular or unitary. Theoretically, there is greater attention to emotion, to affective dimensions of social life (Hochschild 1979; Thoits 1989; MacKinnon 1994; Ervin and Stryker, forthcoming), correcting for a "cognitive bias" in the framework; there is also greater appreciation for structural facilitators of and constraints on interaction and on self processes. While not yet prominent in contemporary interactionism, the groundwork has been laid (e.g., in Stryker and Statham 1985) for the reintroduction of the concept of habit, which was central in the writings of John Dewey and other forerunners of interactionism, in recognition that social life is not invariablyreflexive and minded. Current symbolic interactionism is methodologically eclectic and tends to be more rigorous than it was in the past, whether the methods are ethnographic (Corsaro 1985) or involve structural equation modeling (Serpe 1987). Also contributing to the revitalization of symbolic interactionism is the attention to its ideas, often unacknowledged but sometimes recognized, paid by a psychological social psychology that is predominately cognitive in its orientation. For cognitive social psychology, concepts are mental or subjective structures formed through experience, and these structures affect recognizing, attending, storage, recall, and utilization of information impinging on the person; of prime significance among concepts functioning in these ways are self-concepts. The link thus forged between cognitive social psychology and symbolic interactionism is mutually advantageous. Symbolic interactionism benefits from the "legitimacy" implicit in the attention given to its ideas and from the expanded pool of researchers focusing on those ideas; cognitive social psychology can benefit from understanding that cognitions are rooted in social structures and processes.

(SEE ALSO: *Identity Theory; Role Theory; Self-Concept; Social Psychology*)

REFERENCES

Becker, Howard S., and Blanche Geer 1957 "Participant Observation and Interviewing: A Comparison."*Human Organization* 16:28–32.

Berger, Joseph, Thomas L. Connor, and M. Hamit Fisek, eds. 1974 *Expectation States Theory: A Theoretical Research Program*. Cambridge, Mass.: Winthrop.

Blumer, Herbert 1937 "Social Psychology." In Emerson P. Schmidt, ed., *Man and Society*. New York: Prentice-Hall.

—— 1969 *Symbolic Interactionism: Perspective and Method*. Englewood Cliffs, N.J.: Prentice-Hall.

Burke, Peter J. 1991. "Attitudes, Behavior, and the Self." In Judith A. Howard and Peter L. Callero, eds., *The Self-Society Dynamic*. New York: Cambridge University Press.

Corsaro, William A. 1985 *Friendship and Peer Culture in the Early Years*. Norwood, N.J.: Ablex.

Couch, Carl J., Stanley L. Saxon, and Michael A. Katovich 1986 *Studies in Symbolic Interaction: The Iowa School*, 2 vols. Greenwich, Conn.: JAI Press.

Denzin, Norman K. 1984 *On Understanding Emotion*. San Francisco: Josey Bass.

—— 1970 *The Research Act*. New York: McGraw-Hill.

Ervin, Laurie, and Sheldon Stryker forthcoming. "Self-Esteem and Identity." In Timothy J. Owens, Sheldon Stryker, and Norman Goodman, eds., *Extending Self-Esteem Theory and Research: Sociological and Psychological Currents*. New York: Cambridge University Press.

—— 1984 "Toward a Phenomenology of Domestic Family Violence." *American Journal of Sociology* 3:483–513.

Glaser, Barney G., and Anselm L. Strauss 1967 *The Discovery of Grounded Theory*. Chicago: Aldine.

Goffman, Erving 1959 *The Presentation of Self in Everyday Life*. Garden City, N.Y.: Doubleday.

Hall, Peter M. 1972 "A Symbolic Interactionist Analysis of Politics." *Sociological Inquiry* 42:35–75.

Heise, David R. 1979 *Understanding Events*. New York: Cambridge University Press.

—— 1986 "Modeling Symbolic Interaction." In Siegwart Lindenberg, James S. Coleman, and Stefan Nowak, eds., *Approaches to Social Theory*. New York: Russell Sage Foundation.

Hewitt, John P. 1990 *Dilemmas of the American Self*. Philadelphia: Temple University Press.

—— 1997. *Self and Society: A Symbolic Interactionist Social Psychology*, 7th ed. Boston: Allyn and Bacon.

Hochschild, Arlie R. 1979 "Emotion Work, Feeling Rules, and Social Structure." *American Journal of Sociology* 85:551–575.

Kuhn, Manfred H. 1964 "Major Trends in Symbolic Interaction Theory in the Past Twenty-Five Years." *Sociological Quarterly* 5:61–84.

Lewis, J. David, and Richard J. Smith 1980 *American Sociology and Pragmatism: Mead, Chicago Sociology, and Symbolic Interaction*. Chicago: University of Chicago Press.

McCall, George J., and J. L. Simmons 1978. *Identities and Interaction*, rev. ed. New York: Free Press.

McPhail, Clark, and Ronald T. Wohlstein 1986 "Collective Locomotion as Collective Behavior." *American Sociological Review* 51:447–464.

MacKinnon, Neil J. 1994. *Symbolic Interactionism as Affect Control*. Albany, NY: State University of New York Press.

Maines, David 1977 "Social Organization and Social Structure in Symbolic Interactionist Thought." *Annual Review of Sociology* 3:235–259.

Mead, George H. 1934 *Mind, Self, and Society*. Chicago: University of Chicago Press.

Meltzer, Bernard N., John W. Petras, and Larry T. Reynolds 1975 *Symbolic Interactionism: Genesis, Varieties, and Criticism*. London: Routledge and Kegan Paul.

Mullins, Nicholas 1973 *Theories and Theory Groups in Contemporary American Sociology*. New York: Harper and Row.

Reynolds, Larry T. 1990 *Interactionism: Exposition and Critique*, 2nd ed. Dix Hills, N.Y.: General Hall.

Rosenberg, Morris 1984 "A Symbolic Interactionist View of Psychosis." *Journal of Health and Social Behavior* 25:289–302.

Serpe, Richard T. 1987 "Stability and Change in Self: A Structural Symbolic Interactionist Explanation." *Social Psychology Quarterly* 50:44–55.

Stryker, Sheldon 1980 *Symbolic Interactionism: A Social Structural Version*. Menlo Park, Calif.: Benjamin/Cummings.

—— 1987 "The Vitalization of Symbolic Interactionism." *Social Psychology Quarterly* 50:83–94.

—— 1988 "Substance and Style: An Appraisal of the Sociological Legacy of Herbert Blumer." *Symbolic Interaction* 11:33–42.

—— 1989 "Further Developments in Identity Theory: Singularity versus Multiplicity of Self." In Joseph Berger, Morris Zelditch, Jr., and Bo Anderson, eds., *Sociological Theories in Progress: New Formulations*. Newbury Park, Calif.: Sage.

—— 1997 "In the Beginning There Is Society: Lessons from a Sociological Social Psychology." In Craig McGarty and S. Alexander Haslam, eds., *The Message of Social Psychology*. Cambridge, Mass.: Blackwell.

—— forthcoming "Identity Competition: Key to Differential Social Movement Participation?" In Sheldon Stryker, Timothy J. Owens, and Robert W. White, eds., *Self, Identity, and Social Movements*. Minneapolis: University of Minnesota Press.

——, and Richard T. Serpe 1982 "Commitment, Identity Salience, and Role Behavior." In William Ickes and Eric Knowles, eds., *Personality, Roles, and Social Behavior*. New York: Springer-Verlag.

——, and Anne Statham 1985 "Symbolic Interactionism and Role Theory." In Gardner Lindzey and Elliot Aronsen, eds., *The Handbook of Social Psychology*, 3rd ed. New York: Random House.

Tamas Rudas, Clifford C. Clogg, Bruce G. Lindsay 1994. "A New Index of Fit Based on Mixture Methods for the Analysis of Contingency Tables" *Journal of the Royal Statistical Society. Series B (Methodological)* 56:623–639.

Thoits, Peggy A. 1983 "Multiple Identities and Psychological Well-Being: A Reformulation and Test of the Social Isolation Hypothesis." *American Sociological Review* 48:174–187.

—— 1989 "The Sociology of Emotions." *Annual Review of Sociology* 15:317–342.

Turner, Ralph H. 1962 "Role-Taking: Process versus Conformity." In Arnold M. Rose, ed., *Human Behavior and Social Process*. Boston: Houghton-Mifflin.

Weigert, Andrew J. 1981 *Sociology of Everyday Life*. New York: Longman.

Weinstein, Eugene, and Paul Deutschberger 1963 "Some Dimensions of Altercasting." *Sociometry* 26:454–466.

Wong, Raymond Sin-Kwok Wong 1990 "Understanding Cross-National Variation in Occupational Mobility." *American Sociological Review*, Vol. 55:560–573.

——— 1992 "Vertical and Nonvertical Effects in Class Mobility: Cross-National Variations." *American Sociological Review* 57:396–410.

——— 1995 "Extensions in the Use of Log-Multiplicative Scaled Association Models in Multiway Contingency Tables." Sociological Methods and Research 23:507–538.

Xie, Yu 1992 "The Log-Multiplicative Layer Effect Model for Comparing Mobility Tables" *American Sociological Review* 57:380–395.

SHELDON STRYKES

SYSTEMS THEORY

NOTE: *Although the following article has not been revised for this edition of the Encyclopedia, the substantive coverage is currently appropriate. The editors have provided a list of recent works at the end of the article to facilitate research and exploration of the topic.*

Systems theory is much more (or perhaps much less) than a label for a set of constructs or research methods. The term *systems* is used in many different ways (Boguslaw 1965; 1981, pp. 29–46). Inevitably this creates considerable confusion. For some it is a "way" of looking at problems in science, technology, philosophy, and many other things; for others it is a specific mode of decision making. In the late twentieth-century Western world it has also become a means of referring to skills of various kinds and defining professional elites. Newspaper "want ads" reflect a widespread demand for persons with a variety of "system" skills, for experts in "systems engineering," "systems analysis," "management systems," "urban systems," "welfare systems," and "educational systems."

As a way of looking at things, the "systems approach" in the first place means examining objects or processes, not as isolated phenomena, but as interrelated components or parts of a complex. An automobile may be seen as a system; a car battery is a component of this system. The automobile, however, may also be seen as a component of a community or a national transportation system. Indeed, most systems can be viewed as subsystems of more encompassing systems.

Second, beyond the idea of interrelatedness, systems imply the idea of control. This always includes some more or less explicit set of values. In some systems, the values involved may be as simple as maintaining a given temperature range. The idea of control was implicit in Walter B. Cannon's original formulation of the concept of homeostasis. Cannon suggested (Cannon 1939, p. 22) that the methods used by animals to control their body temperatures within well-established ranges might be adapted for use in connection with other structures including social and industrial organizations. He referred to the body's ability to maintain its temperature equilibrium as *homeostasis.*

A third idea involved in the system way of looking at things is Ludwig von Bertalannfy's search for a "general systems theory" (von Bertalannfy 1968; Boguslaw 1982, pp. 8–13). This is essentially a call for what many would see as an interdisciplinary approach. Von Bertalannfy noted the tendency toward increased specialization in the modern world and saw entire disciplines—physics, biology, psychology, sociology, and so on—encapsulated in their private universes of discourse, with little communication between any of them. He failed to note, however, that new interdisciplinary disciplines often quickly tend to build their own insulated languages and conceptual cocoons.

A fourth idea in the systems approach to phenomena is in some ways the most pervasive of all. It focuses on the discrepancy between objectives set for a component and those required for the system. In organizations this is illustrated by the difference between goals of individual departments and those of an entire organization. For example, the sales department wants to maximize sales, but the organization finds it more profitable to limit production, for a variety of reasons. If an entire community is viewed as a system, a factory component of this system may decide that short-term profitability is more desirable as an objective than investment in pollution-control devices to protect the health of its workers and community residents. Countless examples of this sort can be found. They all seem to document the idea that system objectives are more important than those of its subsystems. This is a readily understandable notion with respect to exclusively physical systems. When human beings are involved on any level, things become much more complicated.

Physical components or subsystems are not expected to be innovative. Their existence is ideal when it proceeds in a "normal" routine. If they wear out they can be replaced relatively cheaply, and if they are damaged they can be either repaired or discarded. They have no sense of risk and can be required to work in highly dangerous environments twenty-four hours a day, seven days a week, if necessary. They do not join unions, never ask for increases in pay, and are completely obedient. They have no requirements for leisure time, cultural activities, or diversions of any kind. They are completely expendable if the system demands sacrifices. They thrive on authoritarian or totalitarian controls and cannot deal with the notion of democracy.

As a specific mode of decision making, it is this top-down authoritarianism that seems to characterize systems theory when it is predicated on a physical systems prototype. Computerization of functions previously performed by human beings ostensibly simplifies the process of converting this aspect of the theory into action. Computer hardware is presumably completely obedient to commands received from the top; software prepared by computer programers is presumably similarly responsive to system objectives. Almost imperceptibly, this has led to a condition in which systems increasingly become seen and treated as identical to the machine in large-scale "man-machine systems." (The language continues to reflect deeply embedded traditions of male chauvinism.)

These systems characteristically have a sizable computerized information-processing subsystem that keeps assuming increasing importance. For example the U.S. Internal Revenue Service (IRS) obviously has enormous quantities of information to process. Periodically, IRS officials feel the necessity to increase computer capacity. To accomplish this, the practice has been to obtain bids from computer manufacturers. One bid, accepted years ago at virtually the highest levels of government, proposed a revised system costing between 750 million and one billion dollars.

Examination of the proposal by the congressional Office of Technology Assessment uncovered a range of difficulties. Central to these was the fact that the computer subsystem had been treated as the total system (perhaps understandably since the contractor was a computer corporation). The existing body of IRS procedures, internal regulations, information requirements, and law (all part of the larger system) was accepted as an immutable given. No effort had been made to consider changes in the larger system that could conceivably eliminate a significant portion of the massive computer installation (Office of Technology Assessment 1972).

Almost two decades after attention had been called to these difficulties, system problems at the IRS continued to exist. A proposed Tax System Modernization was formulated to solve them. The General Accounting Office raised questions about whether this proposal, estimated to cost several billion dollars, was in fact "a new way of doing business" or simply intended to lower costs and increase efficiency of current operations. Moreover, the Accounting Office suggested that the lack of a master plan made it difficult to know how or whether the different component subsystems would fit together. Specifically, for example, it asked whether the proposal included a telecommunications subsystem and, if so, why such an item had not been included among the budgeted items (Rhile 1990).

To exclude the larger system from consideration and assume it is equivalent to a subsystem is to engage in a form of fragmentation that has long been criticized in related areas by perceptive sociologists (see Braverman 1974; Kraft 1977). Historically, fragmentation has led to *deskilling* of workers, that is, replacing craft tasks with large numbers of relatively simpler tasks requiring only semi-skilled or unskilled labor. This shields the larger system from scrutiny and facilitates centralization of control and power. It also facilitates computerization of work processes and even more control.

In the contemporary industrial and political worlds, power is justified largely on the basis of "efficiency." It is exercised largely through monopolization of information. Various forms of social organization and social structure can be used for the exercise of this power. Systems theory focuses not on alternative structures but, rather, on *objectives*, a subset of what sociologists think of as *values*. To hold power is to facilitate rapid implementation of the holder's values.

Fragmentation, in the final analysis, is an effort to divide the world of relevant systems into tightly enclosed cubbyholes of thought and practice controlled from the top. This compartmentalization is found in both government and private enterprises. The compartments are filled with those devoid of genuine power and reflect the limitation of decisions available to their occupants. Those at the summit of power pyramids are exempt from these constraints and, accordingly, enjoy considerably more "freedom" (Pelton, Sackmann, and Boguslaw 1990).

An increasingly significant form of fragmentation is found in connection with the operation of many large-scale technological systems. Sociologist Charles Perrow has, in a path-breaking study, examined an enormous variety of such systems. He has reviewed operations in nuclear power, petrochemical, aircraft, marine, and a variety of other systems including those involving dams, mines, space, weapons, and even deoxyribonucleic acid (DNA). He developed a rough scale of the potential for catastrophe, assessing the risk of loss of life and property against expected benefits. He concluded that people would be better off learning to live without some, or with greatly modified, complex technological systems (Perrow 1984). A central problem he found involved "externalities," the social costs of an activity *not* shown in its price, such as pollution, injuries, and anxieties. He notes that these social costs are often borne by those who do not even benefit from the activity or are unaware of the externalities.

This, of course, is another corollary to the fragmentation problem. To consider the technological system in isolation from the larger social system within which it is embedded is to invite enormous difficulties for the larger system while providing spurious profits for those controlling the subsystem.

Another interesting manifestation of the fragmentation problem arises in connection with two relatively new disciplines that address many problems formerly the exclusive province of sociology: operations research and management science. Each of these has its own professional organization and journal.

Operations research traces its ancestry to 1937 in Great Britain when a group of scientists, mathematicians, and engineers was organized to study some military problems. How do you use chaff as a radar countermeasure? What are the most effective bombing patterns? How can destroyers best be deployed if you want to protect a convoy?

The efforts to solve these and related problems gave rise to a body of knowledge initially referred to as Operations Analysis and subsequently referred to as Operations Research. A more or less official definition of the field tells us Operations Research is concerned with scientifically deciding how to best design and operate man-machine systems usually under conditions requiring the allocation of scarce resources. In practice, the work of operations research involved the construction of models of operational activities, initially in the military, subsequently in organizations of all kinds. *Management science*, a term perhaps more congenial to the American industrial and business ear, emerged officially as a discipline in 1953 with the establishment of the Institute of Management Sciences.

In both cases, the declared impetus of the discipline was to focus on the entire system, rather than on components. One text points out that subdivisions of organizations began to solve problems in ways that were not necessarily in the best interests of the overall organizations. Operations research tries to help management solve problems involving the interactions of objectives. It tries to find the "best" decisions for "as large a portion of the *total system* as possible" (Whitehouse and Wechsler 1976).

Another text, using the terms *management science* and *operations research*, interchangeably defines them (or it) as the "application of scientific procedures, techniques, and tools to operating, strategic, and policy problems in order to develop and help evaluate solutions" (Davis, McKeown, and Rakes 1986, p. 4).

The basic procedure used in operations research/management science work involves defining a problem, constructing a model, and, ultimately, finding a solution. An enormous variety of mathematical, statistical, and simulation models have been developed with more or less predictable consequences. "Many management science specialists were accused of being more interested in manipulating problems to fit techniques than . . . (working) to develop suitable solutions" (Davis, McKeown, and Rakes 1986, p. 5). The entire field often evokes the tale of the fabled inebriate who persisted in looking for his lost key under the lamppost, although he had lost it elsewhere, because "it is light here."

Under the sponsorship of the Systems Theory and Operations Research program of the National

Science Foundation, a Committee on the Next Decade in Operations Research (CONDOR) held a workshop in 1987. A report later appeared in the journal *Operations Research*. The journal subsequently asked operation researchers to comment on the report (Wagner et al. 1989). One of the commentators expressed what appears to be a growing sentiment in the field by pointing out the limitations of conventional modeling techniques for professional work. Criticizing the CONDOR report for appearing to accept the methodological status quo, he emphasized the character of models as "at best abstractions of selected aspects of reality" (Wagner et al. 1989). He quoted approvingly from another publication, "thus while exploiting their strengths, a prudent analyst recognizes realistically the limitations of quantitative methods" (Quade 1988).

This, however, is an unfortunate repetition of an inaccurate statement of the difficulty. It is not the limitations of quantitative methods that is in question but rather the recognition of the character of the situations to which they are applied. Sociologists distinguish between *established* situations, those whose parameters can be defined precisely and for which valid analytic means exist to describe meaningful relationship within them and *emergent* situations, whose parameters are known incompletely and for which satisfactory analytic techniques are not available within the time constraints of necessary action (Boguslaw [1965] 1981). In established situations mathematical or statistical models are quite satisfactory, along with other forms of rational analysis. In emergent situations, however, they can yield horrendous distortions. Fifty top U.S. corporation executives, when interviewed, recognized and acted upon this distinction more or less intuitively, although the situations presented to them were referred to as Type 1 and Type 2, respectively (Pelton, Sackmann, and Boguslaw 1990).

Individual persons, organizations, or enterprises may be viewed, on the one hand, as self-contained systems. On the other, they may be viewed as subsystems of larger social systems. Unfortunately, efforts are continually made to gloss over this dichotomy through a form of fragmentation, by treating a subsystem or collection of subsystems as equivalent to a larger system. It is this relationship between system and subsystem that constitutes the core of the dilemma continuing to confront systems theory.

Achieving a satisfactory resolution of the discrepancy between individual needs and objectives of the systems within which individuals find themselves embedded or by which they are affected remains an unsolved problem as the twentieth century draws to a close.

(SEE ALSO: *Decision-Making Theory and Research; Social Dynamics; Social Structure*)

REFERENCES

Bernik, Ivan 1994 "Double Disenchantment of Politics: A Systems Theory Approach to Post-Socialist Transformation." *Innovation* 7:345–356.

Bivins, Thomas H. 1992 "A Systems Model for Ethical Decision Making in Public Relations." *Public Relations Review* 18:365–383.

Boguslaw, Robert (1965) 1981 *The New Utopians: A Study of Systems Design and Social Change*. Englewood Cliffs, N.J.: Prentice-Hall.

—— 1982 *Systems Analysis and Social Planning: Human Problems of Post-Industrial Society*. New York: Irvington.

Braverman, Harry 1974 *Labor and Monopoly Capital: The Degradation of Work in the Twentieth Century*. New York: Monthly Review Press.

Cannon, Walter B. 1939 *The Wisdom of the Body*, rev. ed. New York: Norton.

Cohen-Rosenthal, Edward 1997 "Sociotechnical Systems and Unions: Nicety or Necessity." *Human Relations* 50:585–604.

Creedon, Pamela J. 1993 "Acknowledging the Infrasystem: A Critical Feminist Analysis of Systems Theory." *Public Relations Review* 19:157–166.

Davis, K. Roscoe, Patrick G. McKeown, and Terry R. Rakes 1986 *Management Science*. Boston, Mass.: Kent.

Garnsey, Elizabeth 1993 "Exploring a Critical Systems Perspective." *Innovation* 6:229–256.

Janeksela, Galan M. 1995 "General Systems Theory and Structural Analysis of Correctional Institution Social Systems." *International Review of Modern Sociology* 25:43–50.

Kraft, Philip 1977 *Programmers and Managers: The Routinization of Computer Programming in the United States*. New York: Springer-Verlag.

Office of Technology Assessment 1977 *A Preliminary Assessment of the IRS Tax Administration System*. Washington, D.C.: Office of Technology Assessment.

Pelton, Warren, Sonja Sackmann, and Robert Boguslaw 1990 *Tough Chokes: Decision-Making Styles of America's Top 50 CEO's*. Homewood, Ill.: Dow Jones-Irwin.

Perrow, Charles 1984 *Normal Accidents: Living with High-Risk Technologies*. New York: Basic Books.

Quade, E. S. 1988 "Quantitative Methods: Uses and Limitations" In H. J. Miser and E. S. Quade, eds., *Handbook of Systems Analysis: Overview of Uses, Procedures, Applications and Practice*, pp. 283–324. New York: North-Holland.

Rhile, Howard G. (March 22) 1990 "Progress in Meeting the Challenge of Modernizing IRS' Tax Processing System." Testimony before the Subcommittee on Oversight, Committee on Ways and Means, House of Representatives. Washington, D.C.: General Accounting Office.

Searight, H. Russell and William T. Merkel 1991 "Systems Theory and Its Discontents: Clinical and Ethical Issues." *American Journal of Family Therapy* 19:19–31.

Stichweh, Rudolf 1995 "Systems Theory and Rational Choice Theory; Systemtheorie und Rational Choice Theorie." *Zeitschrift fur Soziologie* 24:395–406.

Turner, Jonathan H. 1991 *The Structure of Sociological Theory*, 5th ed. Belmont, Calif.: Wadsworth.

von Bertalannfy, Ludwig 1968 *General Systems Theory: Foundations, Development, Applications*. New York: George Braziller.

Wagner, Harvey M., Michael H. Rothkopf, Clayton J. Thomas, and Hugh J Miser 1989 "The Next Decade in Operations Research: Comments on the CONDOR Report," *Operations Research* 37:664–672.

Warren, Keith, Cynthia Franklin, and Calvin L. Streeter 1998 "New Directions in Systems Theory: Chaos and Complexity." *Social-Work* 43 (4):357–372.

Whitehouse, Gary E., and Ben L. Wechsler 1976 *Applied Operations Research*. New York: Wiley.

ROBERT BOGUSLAW

T

TABULAR ANALYSIS

In its most general form, tabular analysis includes any analysis that uses tables, in other words, almost any form of quantitative analysis. In this article, however, it refers only to the analysis of categorical variables (both nominal and ordered) when that analysis relies on cross-classified tables in the form of frequencies, probabilities, or conditional probabilities (percentages). In general, the use of such cross-tabulated data is practical only with variables that have a limited number of categories. Therefore, this article deals with some of the *analytic* problems of *categorical data analysis*. Although it sometimes is difficult to separate analysis from methods of data presentation, the emphasis here is decidedly on analysis (see Davis and Jacobs 1968).

Tabular analysis can take many different forms, but two methods deserve special attention. The first is known as *subgroup analysis*. The underlying logic of this type of analysis was codified under the name "elaboration paradigm" by Lazarsfeld and his colleagues (Kendall and Lazarsfeld 1950; Lazarsfeld 1955; Hyman 1955; Rosenberg 1968; Lazarsfeld et al., 1972; Zeisel 1985). Because of the simplicity of the method and the ease with which it can facilitate communication with others, subgroup analysis has been the mainstay of research reports dealing with categorical data.

The second is based on the use of *log-linear* and related models and has become increasingly popular (Bishop et al. 1975; Goodman 1978; Haberman 1978, 1979; Fienberg 1980; Agresti 1984; 1990; Clogg and Shihadeh 1994). (For other related models, see McCullagh and Nelder 1983; Thiel 1991; Long 1997; Press and Wilson 1998). This method is flexible, can handle more complex data (with many variables), and is more readily amenable to statistical modeling and testing (Clogg et al. 1990). For this reason, the log-linear method is rapidly emerging as the standard method for analyzing multivariate categorical data. Its results, however, are not easily accessible because the resulting tabular data are expressed as multiplicative functions of the parameters (i.e., log-linear rather than linear), and the parameters of these models tend to obscure descriptive information that often is needed in making intelligent comparisons (Davis 1984; Kaufman and Schervish 1986; Alba 1988; Clogg et al. 1990).

These two methods share a set of analytic strategies and problems and are complementary in their strengths and weaknesses. To understand both the promises and the problems of tabular analysis, it is important to understand the logic of analysis and the problems that tabular analyses share with the simpler statistical analysis of linear systems. As a multivariate analysis tool, tabular analysis faces the same problems that other well-developed linear statistical models face in analyzing data that are collected under less than ideal experimental conditions. It therefore, is important to have a full understanding of this foundation, and the best way to do that is to examine the simplest linear system.

STATISTICAL CONTROLS, CAUSAL ORDERING, AND IMPROPER SPECIFICATIONS

Consider the simplest linear multivariate system:

$$Y = Xb_{yx \cdot z} + Zb_{yz \cdot x} + e \qquad (1)$$

where all the variables, including the error term, are assumed to be measured from their respective means. When this equation is used merely to describe the relationship between a dependent variable Y and two other variables X and Z, the issue of misspecification—in other words, whether the coefficients accurately reflect an intended relationship—does not arise because the coefficients are well-known partial regression coefficients. However, when the linear model depicted in equation (1) is considered as a representation of an underlying theory, these coefficients receive meaning under that theory. In that case, the issue of whether the coefficients really capture the intended relationship becomes important. Causal relationships are not the only important relationships, but it is informative to examine this equation with reference to such relationships since this is the implicitly implied type of system.

Many different conceptions of causality exist in the literature (Blalock 1964, 1985a, 1985b; Duncan 1966, 1975; Simon 1954, 1979; Heise 1975; Mostetler and Tukey 1977; Bunge 1979; Singer and Marini 1987). However, the one undisputed criterion of causality seems to be the existence of a relationship between manipulated changes in one variable (X) and attendant changes in another variable (Y) in an ideal experiment. That is, a causal connection exists between X and Y if changes in X and X *alone* produce changes in Y. This is a very restrictive criterion and may not be general enough to cover all important cases, but it is sufficient as a point of reference. This definition is consistent with the way in which effects are measured in controlled experiments. In general, even in an ideal experiment, it is often impossible to eliminate or control all the variations in other variables, but their effects are made random by design. A simple linear causal system describing a relationship produced in an ideal experiment thus takes the following familiar form:

$$Y = Xd_{yx} + e \qquad (2)$$

where e stands for all the effects of other variables that are randomized. The randomization makes the expected correlation between X and e zero. (Without loss of generality, it is assumed that all the variables [X, Y, and e] are measured as deviations from their respective means.) For the sake of simplicity, it is assumed for now that Y does not affect X. (For an examination of causal models dealing with reciprocal causation and with more complex systems in general, see Fisher 1966; Goldberger and Duncan 1973; Alwin and Hauser 1975; Duncan 1975; Blalock 1985a, 1985b.)

The coefficient d_{yx} measures the expected change in Y given a unit change in X. It does not matter whether changes in X affect other variables and whether some of those variables in turn affect Y. As long as all the changes in Y ultimately are produced by the manipulated initial changes in X and X alone, X receives total credit for them. Therefore, d_{yx} is a coefficient of *total causal effect* (referred to as an *effect coefficient* for short).

The customary symbol for a simple regression coefficient, b_{yx} is not used in equation (2) because b_{yx} is equivalent to d_{yx} only under these very special conditions. If one uses a simple regression equation in the form similar to equation (2) above and assumes that b_{yx} is equivalent to d_{yx}, the model is misspecified as long as the data do not meet all the assumptions made about the ideal experiment. Such errors in model specification yield biased estimates in general. Implications of some specification errors may be trivial, but they can be serious when one is analyzing nonexperimental data (see Kish 1959; Campbell and Stanley 1966; Leamer 1978; Cook and Campbell 1979; Lieberson 1985; Arminger and Bohrnstedt 1987).

Many underlying causal systems are compatible with the three-variable linear equation shown above. For the purpose at hand, it is enough to examine the simple causal systems shown in Figure 1. These causal systems imply critical assumptions about the error term and the causal ordering. If these assumptions are correct, there is a definite connection between the underlying causal parameters and the regression coefficients in equation (1). However, if some of these assumptions are wrong, equation (1) is a misrepresentation of

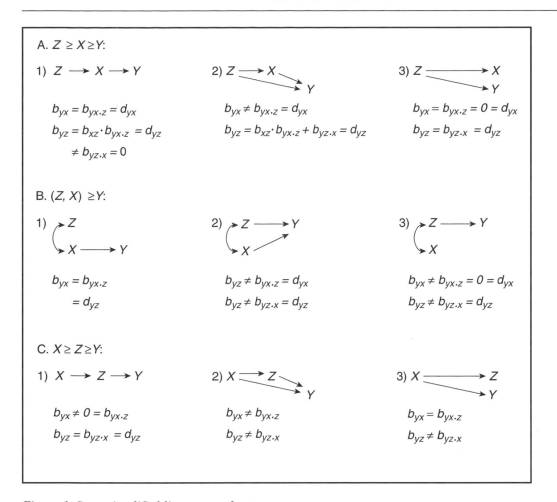

Figure 1. Some simplified linear causal systems

the assumed causal model (for a fuller description of other possible systems, see Duncan 1975).

The notation for causal hierarchy ($\geq$) means that the preceding variable may affect the variables after it, but variables after ($\geq$) may not affect the preceding variables. A connecting arrow between two variables indicates both the existence and the direction of effects; lack of a connecting arrow indicates no known effects. (For convenience, these diagrams do not show random errors, but their presence is assumed.)

For each causal system in Figure 1, the key relationships among simple regression coefficients, partial regression coefficients, and effect coefficients are listed below each causal diagram. Look at the simple causal chain (or a cascading system) shown in A1, for instance. The introduction of Z as a control variable has no effect on the observed relationship between X and Y. Note also that the simple regression coefficient is equivalent to the effect coefficient ($b_{yx} = b_{yx \cdot z} = d_{yx}$); similarly, the simple b_{yz} is equivalent to d_{yx}, but the partial $b_{yz \cdot x}$ becomes zero. (If one were to control Y, the X–Z relationship would not change, but such control is superfluous given the assumptions about the causal ordering.) In fact, one could argue that these two conditions, given the assumptions about the causal hierarchy, uniquely define a simple causal chain. If the control variable Z enters the X–Y causal system only through X (or the effects of a set of variables are mediated completely through [an]other variable[s] in the system), there is no need to introduce Z (or a set of such variables) as a control to correctly specify the X–Y relationship.

In A2, the two partials ($b_{yx \cdot z}$ and $b_{yz \cdot x}$) are different from the respective bivariate coefficients (b_{yx}

and b_{yz}). The key point is that the partial $b_{yx \cdot z}$ is equivalent to d_{yx}, while the partial between Z and Y ($b_{yz \cdot x}$) simply reflects the portion of the causal effect from Z to Y that is not mediated by X.

In A3, there is no direct connection between X and Y once the effect of Z is controlled: The observed bivariate relation between X and Y is spurious or, more accurately, the observed association between X and Y is explained by the existence of a common cause. In this case, the introduction of Z, controlling its effects on both X and Y, is critical in ascertaining the true causal parameter of the system (d_{yx}), which happens to be zero.

All the causal systems shown in B share similar patterns with A; the pattern of the relationship between the bivariate coefficients and the partials remains the same. For this reason, the X–Y relationship in particular is examined in the same way by introducing Z as a control variable regardless of the specification of causal hierarchy between X and Z. Note in particular that introducing Z as a control variable in B1 and B3 is a misspecification of the model, but such misspecifications (including an irrelevant variable in the equation) do not lead to biased estimation (for a related discussion, see Arminger and Bohrnstedt 1987).

The systems shown in C do not require additional comments. Except for the changes in the order of the two variables X and Z, they are exact replicas of the systems in A. The resulting statistics show the same patterns observed in A. Nevertheless, the attendant interpretation of the results is radically different. For instance, when the partial $b_{yx \cdot z}$ disappears, one does not consider that there is no causal relationship between X and Y; instead, one's conviction about the causal relationship is reinforced by the fact that an intervening causal agent is found.

In summary, the assumptions about the causal ordering play a critical role in the interpretation of the coefficients of the linear model shown in equation (1). The assumptions about the order must come from outside knowledge.

There is one more type to note. All the systems examined so far are linear and additive. The partial coefficients reflect the expected change in the dependent variable given a unit change in a given independent variable while the other independent variables are kept constant. If two or more independent variables interact, such simplicity does not exist. A simple example of such a system is given below:

$$Y = X_1 \cdot b_1 + X_2 \cdot b_2 + (X_1 \cdot X_2) \cdot b_3 + e \qquad (3)$$

which is the same as equation (1) except for the simplification of labels for the variables and coefficients and the addition of a multiplicative term ($X_1 \cdot X_2$).

The partial for X_1 in such a system, for example, no longer properly represents the expected change in Y for a unit change in X_1, even if the assumptions about the causal order are correct. A partial differentiation of the equation with respect to X_1 for instance, gives $b_1 + X_2 \cdot b_3$, which implies that the rate of change introduced by a change in X_1 is also dependent on the values of the other causal variable (X_2) and the associated coefficient (b_3). One therefore cannot interpret the individual coefficients as measuring something independently of others. This point is important for a fuller understanding of the log-linear models introduced below, because a bivariate relationship is represented by interaction terms. The notion of control often invoked with *ceteris paribus* (other things being unchanged) also becomes ambiguous.

The logic of causal analysis for the additive systems can be extended easily to a system with more variables. If the assumptions about the causal order, the form of the relationship, and the random errors are correct, one can identify the causal parameters, such as d_{yx}, and decompose the linear connection between any set of variables into spurious (noncausal) and genuine (causal) components, d_{yx}, and the latter (d_{yx}) into indirect (mediated) and direct (residual) components.

To identify d_{yx}, one must control all the potentially relevant variables that precede X in causal ordering but not the variables that might intervene between X and Y. Under this assumption, then, the partial b_{yx} ($z \cdots$), where the variables in parentheses represent all such "antecedent" variables, is equivalent to dyx. In identifying this component, one must not control the variables that X may affect; these variables may work as mediating causal agents and transmit part of the effect of X to Y.

The partial of a linear system in which both antecedent variables (Zs) and intervening variables (Ws) are included ($b_{yx} \cdot [x \cdots w \cdots]$) will represent the residual causal connection between X and Y that is not mediated by any of the variables included in the model. As more Ws are included, this residual component may change. However, the linear representation of a causal system without these additional intervening variables is not misspecified. By contrast, if the introduction of additional Zs will change the X–Y partial, an omission of such variables from the equation indicates a misspecification of the causal system because some of the spurious components will be confounded with the genuine causal components.

For nonexperimental data, the problems of misspecification and misinterpretation are serious. Many factors may confound the relationships under consideration (Campbell and Stanley 1966; Cook and Campbell 1979; Lieberson 1985; Arminger and Bohrnstedt 1987; Singer and Marini 1987). There is no guarantee that a set of variables one is considering constitutes a closed system, but the situation is not totally hopeless. The important point is that one should not ignore these issues and assume away potentially serious problems. Selection biases, contagion effects, limited variations in the data, threshold effects, and so on, can be modeled if they are faced seriously (Rubin 1977; Leamer 1978; Hausman 1978; Heckman 1979; Berk 1983, 1986; Heckman and Robb 1986; Arminger and Bohrnstedt 1987; Long 1988; Bollen 1989; Xie 1989). Furthermore, this does not mean that one has to control (introduce) every conceivable variable. Once a few key variables are controlled, additional variables usually do not affect the remaining variables too much. (This observation is a corollary to the well-known fact that social scientists often have great difficulty finding any variable that can substantially improve R^2 in regression analysis.)

FREQUENCY TABLES, CONDITIONAL PROBABILITIES, AND ODDS RATIOS

To fix the ideas and make the following discussions concrete, it is useful to introduce basic notations and define two indicators of association for a bivariate table. Consider the simplest contingency table, one given by the cross-classification of two dichotomous variables. Let f_{ij} denote the observed frequencies; then the observed frequency distribution will have the following form:

Observed Frequencies

		Variable X		
		1	2	Total
Variable Y	1	f_{11}	f_{12}	$f_{1\cdot}$
	2	f_{21}	f_{22}	$f_{2\cdot}$
	total	$f_{\cdot 1}$	$f_{\cdot 2}$	N

Note the form of marginal frequencies. Now let p_{ij} denote the corresponding observed probabilities: $p_{ij} = f_{ij}/N$. Let the uppercase letters, F_{ij} and P_{ij}, denote the corresponding expected frequencies and probabilities under same model or hypothesis.

If X and Y are statistically independent,

$$\frac{p_{ij}}{p_{\cdot j}} = \frac{p_{i\cdot}p_{\cdot j}}{p_{\cdot j}} = p_{i\cdot}$$

That is, the conditional probability of Y_i given X_j is the same as the marginal probability of Y_i. Thus, a convenient descriptive indicator of statistical independence is that $b_{yx} = p_{11}/p_{\cdot 1} - p_{12}/p_{\cdot 2} = 0$. The percentage difference is simply 100 times b_{yx}. The symbol b_{yx} is quite appropriate in this case, for it is equivalent to the regression coefficient. The fact that $b_{yx} \neq 0$ implies a lack of statistical independence between X and Y.

Another equally good measure is the odds ratio or cross-product ratio:

$$\text{Odds ratio } (t) = \frac{F_{11}/F_{12}}{F_{21}/F_{22}}$$

$$= \frac{F_{11}/F_{21}}{F_{12}/F_{22}}$$

$$= \frac{F_{11}/F_{22}}{F_{12}/F_{21}}$$

The first line shows that the odds ratio is a ratio of ratios. The second line shows that it is immaterial whether one starts with odds (ratio) in one direction or the opposite direction. The final line indicates that the odds ratio is equivalent to the cross-product ratio. In general, if all the odds ratios in a table for two variables are 1, the two variables are statistically independent; the converse is also true. The fact that t equals 1 implies that X is independent of Y. Therefore, both the odds ratio (t) and the percent age difference (b_{yx}) can serve equally well as descriptive indicators of association between variables.

Given that observed frequencies are unstable because of sampling variability, it is useful to test the null hypothesis that $t = b_{yx} = 0$ in the population. Such a hypothesis is evaluated by using either the conventional chi-square statistic or the -2*(likelihood ratio):

$$\chi^2 = \sum\sum (f_{ij} - F_{ij})^2 / F_{ij}$$
$$L^2 = -2\sum\sum (f_{ij} \log(F_{ij}/f_{ij}))$$
$$= 2\sum\sum (f_{ij} \log(f_{ij}/F_{ij}))$$

These values are evaluated against the theoretical distribution with the appropriate degrees of freedom. These two tests are equivalent for large samples. (For a related discussion, see Williams 1976; Tamas et al. 1994)

ELABORATION AND SUBGROUP ANALYSIS

The logic of linear systems that was presented earlier was introduced to social scientists through the elaboration paradigm and through an informal demonstration of certain patterns of relationship among variables (Kendall and Lazarsfeld 1950; Lazarsfeld 1955). Statistical control is achieved by examining relationships within each subgroup that is formed by the relevant categories of the control variable. The typical strategy is to start the analysis with an examination of the association between two variables of interest, say, X and Y. If there is an association of some sort between X and Y, the following two questions become relevant: (1) Is the observed relationship spurious or genuine? (2) If some part of the relationship is genuine, which variables mediate the relationship between the two? (The question of sampling variability is handled rather informally, relying on the magnitude of the percentage differences as a simple guide. Moreover, two variables that seemingly are unrelated at the bivariate level may show a stronger association after suppressor variables are controlled. Therefore, in some situations, applying such a test may be premature and uncalled for.)

To answer these questions adequately, one must have a fairly good knowledge of the variables under consideration and the implications of different causal systems. It is clear from the earlier examination of the linear causal systems that to answer the first question, one must examine the X–Y relationship while controlling for the factors that are antecedent to X (assuming that $X \geq Y$). To answer the second question, one also must control factors that X may affect and that in turn may affect Y. Controlling for many variables is possible in theory but is impractical for two quite different reasons: (1) One runs out of cases very quickly as the number of subgroups increases, and (b) as the number of subgroups increases, so does the number of partial tables to examine and evaluate. Nevertheless, it is quite possible that one might find a strategically critical variable that might help explain the observed relationship either by proving that the observed relationship is spurious or by confirming a causal connection between the two variables.

To make the discussion more concrete, consider the hypothetical bivariate percentage table between involvement in car accidents (Y) and the gender of the driver (X). The percentage difference (10% = 30% − 20%) indicates that men are more likely to be involved in car accidents while driving than are women. Because there are only two categories in Y, this percentage difference (b_{yx}) captures all the relationship in the table. Given the large sample size and the magnitude of the percentage difference, it is safe to assume that this is not an artifact of sampling variability.

Suppose a third variable (Z = amount of driving) is suspected to be related to both gender (X) and involvement in accidents (Y). It therefore is prudent to examine whether the X–Y relationship remains the same after the amount of driving is controlled or eliminated. Whether this conjecture is reasonable can be checked before one examines the three-variable subgroup analysis: There has to be some relationship between X and Z and between X and Y. Table 1b shows the bivariate relationship between gender (X) and driving (Z). Note that there is a very strong association: $b_{yx} = .333$ (33.3%) difference between the genders.

The conditional tables may show one of the following four patterns: (1) The observed relationship between X and Y disappears within each subgroup: $b_{yx \cdot z} = 0$, (2) the relationship remains the same: $b_{yx \cdot z} = b_{yx}$, (3) the relationships change in magnitude but remain the same across the groups:

Hypothetical Bivariate Tables

	Men	Women
a) Car Accidents (Y) by Gender (X)		
Had at least one accident while driving	30%	20%
Never had an accident while driving	<u>70%</u>	<u>80%</u>
Total	100%	100%
(Number of cases)	(3,000)	(3,000)
b) Amount of Driving (Z) by Gender (X)		
More than 10,000 miles	67.7%	33.3%
Less than 10,000 miles	<u>33.3%</u>	<u>67.7%</u>
Total	100%	100%
(Number of cases)	(3,000)	(3,000)

Table 1

SOURCE: Adapted from Ziesel (1985), p. 146.

$b_{yx\cdot z(1)} = b_{yx\cdot z(2)} \neq b_{yx}$, (4) the X–Y relationship in one group is different from the relationship in the other group: $b_{yx\cdot z(1)} \neq b_{yx\cdot z(2)}$. These examples are shown in Table 2. Compare these patterns with the corresponding causal systems shown in Figure 1.

Whether Z should be considered as antecedent or intervening depends on the theory one is entertaining. One's first interpretation might be that the original relationship has sexist implications in that it may mean that men are either more aggressive or less careful. Against such a hypothesis, the amount of driving is an extraneous variable. By contrast, one may entertain a social role theory stating that in this society men's roles require more driving and that more driving leads to more accidents. Then Z can be considered an intervening variable.

Pattern (1) will help undermine the psychological or biological hypothesis, and pattern (2) will enhance that hypothesis. Pattern (1) also will lend weight to the social role hypothesis. These patterns are the simplest to deal with but rarely are encountered in real life (see Lazarsfeld 1955; Rosenberg 1968; Zeisel 1985 for interesting examples). If one were lucky enough to come across such a pattern, the results would be considered important findings. Note that there are three causal systems in Figure 1 that share the same statistical pattern (the relationship between partials and original coefficients) with each of these two. Of course, the choice must be dictated by the theory and assumptions about the causal ordering that one is willing to entertain.

Patterns (3) and (4) are more likely outcomes in real life. In (3), the magnitude of the X–Y relationship within each subgroup is reduced. (Sometimes the X–Y relationship may turn out to be even stronger.) This pattern is compatible with three causal systems—A2, B2, and C2—in Figure 1. Assume that one takes the causal order indicated in C; that is, one takes the gender role theory to account for the observed relationship. Part of the original relationship (.04 out of .10) is mediated by the amount of driving, but a greater part (.06) remains unexplained. If one believes that all the difference in the accident rate has nothing to do with psychological or biological differences between the genders, one has several other potential role-related connections to consider: Men may drive more during the rush hours than women do, men may drive during worse weather conditions than women do, and so on. One could introduce these variables as additional controls. By contrast, if one believes in the validity of the psychological explanation, one could collect data on the aggressiveness of each individual and introduce aggressiveness as a control variable.

Table 2d illustrates a pattern in which the effects of the two explanatory variables interact: X's effect on Y varies across the categories of Z, and Z's effect on Y varies across the categories of X. A corresponding example in linear systems was given by equation (3). One must consider both variables at the same time because the effect of one variable depends on the other.

In general, empirical data may exhibit patterns that are mixtures of 2c and 2d. In cross-tabulations of variables with more than two categories, it is often not easy, purely on the basis of eyeballing, to discern the underlying pattern. At this point, there is a need for more refined and systematic tools. Moreover, in some instances, an application of a log-linear model may indicate patterns that are different from what a linear model (such as using percentage tables) might indicate.

Before ending this section, it should be mentioned that some examples in the literature use the

Percent Ever Had Accident (Y) by Gender (X) by Amount of Driving (Z)

a) Original X–Y Relationship Disappears

(Compatible with causal systems A3, B3, and C1)

Gender (X)	Amount of Driving (Z)		
	> 10,000 miles	< 10,000 miles	
Men	40% (2,000)	10% (1,000)	$b_{yx \cdot z} = 0$
Women	40% (2,000)	10% (1,000)	$b_{yz \cdot x} = .30$

b) Original X–Y Relationship Unchanged

(Compatible with causal systems AI, B1, and C3)

Gender (X)	> 10,000 miles	< 10,000 miles	
Men	30% (2,000)	30% (1,000)	$b_{yx \cdot z} = .10$
Women	20% (1,000)	20% (2,000)	$b_{yz \cdot x} = 0$

c) Original X–Y Relationship Diminishes

(Compatible with causal systems A2, B2, and C2)

Gender (X)	> 10,000 miles	< 10,000 miles	
Men	34% (2,000)	24% (1,000)	$b_{yx \cdot z} = .06$
Women	28% (1,000)	18% (2,000)	$b_{yz \cdot x} = .10$

d) X–Y Relationship Varies

Gender (X)	> 10,000 miles	< 10,000 miles	
Men	40% (2,000)	20% (1,000)	$b_{yx \cdot z\,(1)} = .20$
Women	20% (1,000)	20% (2,000)	$b_{yx \cdot z\,(2)} = 0$
			$b_{yz \cdot x\,(1)} = .20$
			$b_{yz \cdot x\,(2)} = 0$

Table 2

NOTE: Number of cases for the percentage base are in parentheses. Throughout these tables, $b_{xz} = .40$ and $b_{yx} = .10$ remain constant. Compare percents across the categories of that variable.

subgroup analysis as a full-fledged multivariate analysis tool. For instance, Davis (1984) shows how the logic of elaboration can be combined with the standardization technique to derive, among other things, the following decomposition of the relationship between the father's and the son's occupational statuses, where Zs represent the father's education and the mother's education and W represents the son's education.

a. Total observed relationship:
   b_{yx} = .256

b. Spurious connection resulting from environmental variables (Zs) (a–c)   .052

c. Total causal effect: $b_{yx \cdot z \cdots}$ = .204

c1. Unmediated causal effect:
   $b_{yx \cdot z \cdots w}$ = .138

c2. Effect mediated by education
   $(b_{yx \cdot z \cdots} - b_{yx \cdot z \cdots w})$ = .066

The power of subgroup analysis comes mainly from the close analogy between the percentage differences and the coefficients of the linear system illustrated in Figure 1, but its uses need not be confined to the analysis of causal systems. There are various applications of this logic to survey data (Hyman 1955; Rosenberg 1968; Zeisel 1985). These accounts remain one of the best sources for learning the method as well as the art of pursuing research ideas through the use of percentage tables.

ODDS RATIOS AND LOG-LINEAR MODELS

A more formal approach to categorical data analysis is provided by the log-linear model and related models (Bishop et al. 1975; Goodman 1978; Haberman 1978, 1979; Fienberg 1980; Agresti 1984; Clogg and Shihadeh 1994; Long 1997). Some of these models are not even log-linear (Clogg 1982a, 1982b, Goodman 1984, 1990; Wong 1995; Xie 1992). Only the log-linear models are examined here.

By means of an ingenious device, the log-linear model describes the relationships among categorical variables in a linear form. The trick is to treat the logarithms of the cell frequencies as the (titular) dependent variable and treat design vectors as independent variables. The design vectors represent relevant features of the contingency table and hypotheses about them.

Once again consider a concrete example; the simplest bivariate table, in which each variable has only two categories. Such a table contains four frequencies. Logarithms of these frequencies (log-frequencies for short) can be expressed as an exact function of the following linear equation:

$$Y = b_0 + X_1 \cdot b_1 + X_2 \cdot b_2 + (X_1 \cdot X_2) b_3 \qquad (4)$$

In this equation, Y stands for the log-frequencies ($\log(F_{ij})$). X_1 is a design vector for the first (row) variable, and X_2 is a design vector for the second (column) variable. The last vector ($X_1 - X_2$) is a design vector for interaction between X_1 and X_2, and it is produced literally by multiplying the respective components of X_1 and X_2. It is important to note that the model is linear only in its parameters and that there is an interaction term. As is the case with linear models that contain interaction terms, one must be careful in interpreting the coefficients for the variables involved in the interaction term.

This type of model in which the observed frequencies are reproduced exactly also is known as a saturated model. (The model is saturated because all the available degrees of freedom are used up. For instance, there are only four data points, but this model requires that many parameters.) Of course, if one can reproduce the exact log-frequencies, one also can reproduce the actual frequencies by taking the exponential of $Y - F_{ij} =$

$\exp(Y_{ij})$. Note also the similarities between equations (3) and (4); both contain a multiplicative term as a variable. (For more general models, a maximum likelihood estimation requires an iterative solution, but that is a technical detail for which readers should consult standard texts (such as Nelder and Wedderburn 1972; Plackett 1974; Goodman 1978, 1984; Haberman 1978, 1979; Fleiss 1981; Agresti 1984). Many computer packages routinely provide solutions to these types of equations. Therefore, what is important is the logic underlying such analysis, not the actual calculation needed.)

It is no exaggeration to say that in more advanced uses of the model, what distinguishes a good and creative analysis from a mundane analysis is how well one can translate one's substantive research ideas into appropriate design vectors. Thus, it is worthwhile to examine these design vectors more carefully. Constructing a design matrix (the collection of vectors mentioned above) for a saturated model is easy, because one is not pursuing any specific hypothesis or special pattern that might exist in the relationship. Categories of each variable have to be represented, and there are many equivalent ways of doing that. This section will examine only the two most often used ones: effect coding and dummy coding. These design matrices for a 2 × 2 table are shown in Table 3.

The first column (X_0) in each coding represents a design vector for the constant term (b_0); X_1 is for the row categories, and X_2 is for the column categories. The last column (X_3) is the product of the preceding two, needed to represent interaction between X_1, and X_2. Note the pattern of these design vectors. In the effect coding, except for the constant vector, each vector or column sums to zero. Moreover, the interaction vector sums to zero for each column and row of the original bivariate table. This pattern assures that each effect is measured as a deviation from its respective mean.

In dummy coding, the category effect is expressed as a deviation from one reference category, in this case, the category that is represented by zero. Whatever codings are used to represent the categories of each variable, the interaction design vector is produced by multiplying the design vector for the column variable by the design

Design Vectors Used in Log-Linear Model for 2×2 Table

a) Design Matrices for Saturated Model

	Effect Coding				Dummy Coding			
Frequency	X_0	X_1	X_2	X_3	X_0	X_1	X_2	X_3
Y_{11}	1	1	1	1	1	1	1	1
Y_{12}	1	1	−1	−1	1	1	0	0
Y_{21}	1	−1	1	−1	1	0	1	0
Y_{22}	1	−1	−1	1	1	0	U	0

b) Representation of Log-Frequencies in Terms of Parameter

$b_0+b_1+b_2+b_3$	$b_0+b_1-b_2-b_3$	$b_0+b_1+b_2+b_3$	b_0+b_1
$b_0-b_1+b_2-b_3$	$b_0-b_1-b_2+b_3$	b_0+b_2	b_0

c) Representation of Frequencies in Terms of Multiplicative Parameters, where $t_i = \exp(b_i)$

$t_0{}^*t_1{}^*t_2{}^*t_3$	$t_0{}^*t_1/(t_2{}^*t_3)$	$t_0{}^*t_1{}^*t_2{}^*t_3$	$t_0{}^*t_1$
$t_0{}^*t_2/(t_1{}^*t_3)$	$t_0{}^*t_3(t_1{}^*t_2)$	$t_0{}^*t_2$	t_0

d) Parameters for Interaction in Log-Linear Model

b_3	$-b_3$	b_3	0
$-b_3$	b_3	0	0

Log (odds ratio)

4^*b_3	b_3

e) Multiplicative Parameter for Interaction ($t_3 = \exp(b_3)$)

t_3	$1/t_3$	t_3	1
$1/t_3$	t_3	1	1

Odds ratio

$t_3{}^*t_3{}^*t_3{}^*t_3 = t_3{}^4$	t_3

Table 3

vector for the row variable. Normally, one needs as many design vectors for a given variable as there are categories, minus one: $(R\text{-}1)$ for the row variable and $(C\text{-}1)$ for the column variable. In that case, there will be $(C\text{-}1)(R\text{-}1)$ interaction design vectors for the saturated model. These interaction vectors are created by cross-multiplying the vectors in one set with those of the other set. There is only one vector for each of the three independent variables in equation (4) because both variables are dichotomous.

The names for these codings come from the fact that the first coding is customarily used as a convenient way of expressing factor effects in an analysis of variance (ANOVA), while the second coding often is used in regression with dummy variables. As a result of coding differences in the representation of each variable, the constant term in each coding has a different meaning: In effect, coding it measures the unweighted grand mean, while in dummy coding, it measures the value of the category with all zeros (in this particular case, Y_{22}). (For other coding schemes, see Haberman 1979; Agresti 1984; Long 1984.) Some parameter estimates are invariant under different types of coding, and some are not (Long 1984); therefore, it is important to understand fully the implications of a particular design matrix for a proper interpretation of the analysis results.

Panel (b) of Table 3 expresses each cell as a product of the design matrix and corresponding parameters. Since the particular vectors used contain 1, -1, or 0, the vectors do not seem to appear in these cell representations. However, when design vectors contain other numbers (as will be shown below), they will be reflected in the cell representation. Panel (c) is obtained by exponentiation of the respective cell entries in (b), the individual t-parameter also being the corresponding exponential of the log-linear parameter in panel (b).

Panel (d) isolates parameters associated with the interaction design vector. Panel (e) contains corresponding antilogs or multiplicative coefficients. These parameters play a critical role in representing the degree and nature of association between the row variables and the column variables. If all the odds ratios are 1, one variable is statistically independent from the other; in other words, information about the association between variables is totally contained in the pattern of odds ratios. Panels (d) and (e) show that the odds ratio in turn is completely specified by the parameter(s) of the interaction vector(s). In forming the odds ratio, all the other parameters cancel out (in logarithms, multiplication becomes addition and division becomes subtraction).

In short, this is an indirect way to describe a pattern of association in a bivariate table. Unfortunately, doing this requires a titular dependent variable and multiplicative terms as independent variables. Also, in effect coding, the log-odds ratio is given by 4 x b_3, but in dummy coding, it is given by b_3. This is a clear indication that one cannot assume that there is only one way of describing the parameters of a log-linear model. These facts make the interpretation of these parameters tricky, but the process is worth it for two reasons.

First, the advantage of this method for analyzing a 2 X 2 table is trivial, but the model can be generalized and then applied to more complex contingency tables. Because of the ANOVA-like structure, it is easy to deal with higher-level interaction effects. Second, the parameters of the log-linear models (obtained through the likelihood procedure) have very nice sampling properties for large samples. Therefore, better tools for statistical testing and estimating are available. Without this second advantage, the fact that the approach allows the construction of ANOVA-like models may not be of much value, for the log-linear models only indirectly and by analogy reflect the relationship between variables.

Consider the bivariate tables in Table 4. In all these tables, the frequencies are such that they add up to 100 in each column. Thus, one can take these frequencies as percentages as well. The first table shows a 20 percent difference and an odds ratio of 2.25. The second table shows only half the percentage difference of the first but the same odds ratio. The last table shows the same percentage difference as the second one, but its odd ratio is greater at 6.68. These descriptive measures indicate that there is some association between the two variables in each table.

Whether this observed association is statistically significant can be tested by applying a model in which the coefficient for the interaction design vector is constrained to be zero. (Here one is utilizing the properties of the log-linear model that were asserted earlier.) Constraining the interaction parameter to zero is the same as deleting the interaction design vector from the model. This type of a design matrix imposes the model of statistical independence (*independence* model for short) on the data. If such a log-linear model does not fit the data (on the basis of some predetermined criteria), the observed association is accepted as significant. For large samples, both the conventional chi-square test and the likelihood ratio (L^2) test can be used for this purpose. The results of these tests are included in each table, and they indicate that all three associations are statistically significant at the conventional α level of .05.

Thus, to describe fully the underlying pattern of the association in Table 4, one needs to introduce the interaction parameter, which in these cases is the same as it is using the saturated model. The right-hand tables show the multiplicative parameters (t-parameters) for the interaction term. (Here only the results of applying effect coding are included.) First, examine the patterns of these parameters. In each of the three tables, the t-parameters indicate that the main diagonal cells have higher rates than do the off-diagonal cells. This tendency is slightly higher in the last table than it is in the first two. This interpretation follows from the fact that to reproduce the observed frequency in each cell, the respective t-

Odds Ratios (*t*) and Percentage Differences

FREQUENCIES				MULTIPLICATIVE PARAMETERS			
a)		X_1	X_2	*Effect Coding*		*Dummy Coding*	
	Y_1	60	40	1.225	.816	2.25	1
	Y_2	40	60	.816	1.225	1	1
		100	100				
b_{yx}= .20		t = 2.25					
L^2= 8.05		p = .005					
b)		X_1	X_2				
	Y_1	20	10	1.225	.816	2.25	1
	Y_2	80	90	.816	1.225	1	1
		100	100				
b_{yx} = .10		t = 2.25					
L^2 = 3.99		p = .046					
c)		X_1	X_2				
	Y_1	12	2	1.608	.622	6.68	1
	Y_2	88	98	.622	1.608	1	1
		100	100				
b_{yx} = .10		t = 6.68					
L^2 = 8.46		p = .004					

Table 4

parameter must be multiplied to whatever value may be implied by other parameters in the model. In the first and second tables, the frequencies in the main diagonal are about 22 percent higher (1.22 times) than they would be without the inter-action effect. The frequencies in the off-diagonal cells are about 18 percent lower than they otherwise would be. If one were to examine only the statistics generated by log-linear models, however, it would be easy to overlook the fact that the percentage of the first cell in the last table is only 12 percent (see Kaufman and Schervish 1986 for a more extended discussion). This is one of the reasons why it is advisable to examine the percentage tables even if one is using the log-linear model almost exclusively.

There are other reasons, too. By the linear standard (percentage difference), the first table shows a greater degree of association than does the second or the third. By the standard of a log-linear model or odds ratio, the last table shows the

greatest degree of association. In most cases, where the percentages remain within the range of 20 to 80 percent, these two standards are roughly comparable, and the linear and log-linear models may produce similar results (see Goodman 1981). More important, in examining three-way interactions, if two subtables have the patterns shown in Table 4a and 4b, log-linear models will indicate no three-way interaction, while linear models will indicate it. There are models in which a particular standard is justified explicitly by the phenomenon under consideration, but one should not adopt a standard merely because a particular statistical model does so. It is important to understand the differences in the implicit standards that are used in different methods.

SOME MODELS OF ASSOCIATION

The flexibility of log-linear models is not obvious until one deals with several variables. However, even in a bivariate table, if there is an underlying order in the categories of variables involved and the pattern of association, the model allows some flexibility for exploring this pattern. Consider the hypothetical table shown in Table 5a. The marginal totals are such that each column may be read as percentages. There is a definite pattern in the direction of the relationship, although the tendency is fairly weak. If one were to apply a test of independence, such a null hypothesis would not be rejected. (L^2 = 6.56 with four degrees of freedom has a probability of .161.) Against an unspecified alternative hypothesis, the null hypothesis cannot be rejected at the conventional level of α.

Knowing that almost every society values these two variables in the same order, one may expect that the underlying pattern of association reflects the advantages of the upper class over the lower class in obtaining valued objects. Both the pattern of percentage differences and the odds ratios seem to indicate such an ordering in the pattern: The advantage the upper class has over the lower class is greater than the one it has over the middle class. Furthermore, the upperclass does better in relation to educational levels that are farther apart (the odds ratio involving the corner cells is 2.87).

A conjecture or hypothesis like this can be translated into a design vector. Assign any consecutive numbers to the categories of each variable, but to be consistent with the effect coding, express them as deviations from the mean. One such scaling is to use $(R+1)/2-i$ for the row variable and $(C+1)/2-j$ for the column variable. (The mean and category values can be reversed, but this scheme assigns a higher value to a higher class and a higher educational level to be consistent with everyday language.) Recalling once again that only the interaction terms are relevant for the description of association, one needs to create such an interaction term by multiplying these two vectors component by component. An example is shown in Table 6.

The log-linear model, then, will include design vectors for the constant term, two vectors for the row and two vectors for the column, and one vector for the "linear-by-linear" interaction. This type of model is known as a *uniform association* model (for a fuller discussion of this and related models, see McCullagh 1978; Haberman 1979; Clog 1982a, 1982b; Anderson 1984; Goodman 1984, 1985, 1987, 1990, 1991 Clogg and Shihadeh 1994). The results of applying such a model to

Table 5a are presented in Table 5b and 5c. First, this model fits the data extremely well. Moreover, the reduction of the L^2 statistic (6.557 − .008 = 6.549) with one degree of freedom is statistically significant. Therefore, the null hypothesis cannot be accepted against this specific alternative hypothesis (see Agresti 1984 for a fuller discussion of hypothesis testing of this type). Note the pattern of the expected frequencies and the interaction parameters. Both indicate that the odds ratio for every consecutive four cells is uniform. Moreover, the other odds ratios are exact functions of this basic odds ratio and the distances involved. For instance, the odds ratio for the four corner cells is $2.87 = 1.303^{2*2}$, with each exponent indicating the number of steps between respective categories in each variable. A degree of parsimony has been achieved in describing the pattern of association and some statistical power has been gained in proposing a more definite alternative hypothesis than the general one that stipulates any lack of statistical independence (and hence uses up four degrees of freedom).

The introduction of different design matrices allows one to explore different patterns very easily. Just two are examined here. Consider the hypothetical tables shown in Table 7. In the first table, the odds ratios remain the same across the columns but vary across the rows, perhaps indicating that the order inherent in the row categories is not uniform, while that in the column category is. Differently stated, the *distance* between two consecutive row categories varies, while it remains constant for the column categories. Such an association pattern is known as the *row-effects association* model not because the column variable does not have any effect but because an equal-interval scale works well for it. In this case, one needs two design vectors to accommodate the unequal distances in the row categories. In general, the most one needs is the number of categories in the row minus one. As is shown in Table 6, these design vectors are obtained by cross-multiplying the linear distance vector of the column and the two vectors that already have been used to represent the row categories. (It works just as well to use the dummy coding.) The *column-effects* model is obtained if one reverses the role of these variables.

Table 7b is an example of the simplest possible *homogeneous row–column effects* model. The odds

A Hypothetical Table: Level of Educational Attainment (Y) by Social Class (X)

a) Observed Table

		Social Class		
Level of Education	High	Middle	Low	
College	17	12	8	
High school	41	38	34	
Less than high school	42	50	58	
Total	100	100	100	

b) Expected Frequencies under the Assumption of Independence

12.33	12.33	12.33	$L^2 = 6.56$
37.67	37.67	37.67	$df_1 = 4$
50.00	50.00	50.00	$p = .161$

c) Expected Frequencies under the Assumption of Uniform Association

16.90	11.90	8.20	$L^2 = .0082$
41.30	38.00	33.80	$df_2 = 3$
41.80	50.10	58.10	$p = .161$

d) Log-Linear and Multiplicative Parameters

.264	0	−.264	1.303	1	.768
0	0	0	1	1	1
−.264	0	.264	.768	1	1.303

$L_1^2 - L_2^2 = 6.48$; $\qquad df_1 - df_2 = 1$; $\qquad p = .0109$

Table 5

ratios change across the row and across the column, but the corresponding pair of categories in the row and in the column share the same odds ratio. In this particular example, there is a greater distance between the first two categories than there is between the second two. In general, a homogeneous row–column effects model can accommodate different intervals in each variable as long as the corresponding intervals are homogeneous across the variables. The design matrix for such a pattern is easily obtained by adding the row-effects model vectors and the column-effects model vectors. This is also how two variables are constrained to have equal coefficients in any linear model. Such a design matrix for a 3×3 table is also contained in Table 6. The examples shown in that table should be sufficient to indicate strategies for generalizing to a larger table.

There are many other possibilities in formulating specific hypotheses. These relatively simple models are introduced not only for their intrinsic value but also as a reminder that one can incorporate a variety of specialized hypotheses into the log-linear model (for other possibilities, see Goodman 1984; Clogg 1982a, 1982b; Agresti 1983, 1984). Before ending this section, it should be noted that when design vectors such as the ones for the homogeneous row–column effects model are used, the connection between the parameters for linear models indicated in this article and the usual ANOVA notation used in the literature is not

Design Matrices for Row-Column Association Models for 3 × 3 Table

T	A		B		C	D	E	F		G		H		I			J			
							C*D	A*~D		B*~D		F+G		(F~G)†			A*~B			
1	1	0	1	0	1	1	1	1	0	1	0	2	0	1	0	0	1	0	0	0
1	1	0	0	1	1	0	0	0	0	0	1	0	1	0	0	1	0	0	1	0
1	1	0	−1	−1	1	−1	−1	−1	0	−1	−1	−2	−1	−1	0	−1	−1	0	−1	0
1	0	1	1	0	0	1	0	0	1	0	0	0	1	0	1	0	0	1	0	0
1	0	1	0	1	0	0	0	0	0	0	0	0	0	0	0	0	0	0	0	1
1	0	1	−1	−1	0	−1	0	0	−1	0	0	0	−1	0	−1	0	0	−1	0	−1
1	−1	−1	1	0	−1	1	−1	−1	−1	−1	0	−2	−1	−1	−1	0	−1	−1	0	0
1	−1	−1	0	1	−1	0	0	0	0	0	−1	0	−1	0	0	−1	0	0	−1	−1
1	−1	−1	−1	−1	−1	−1	1	1	1	1	1	2	2	1	1	1	1	1	1	1

T: design vector for the constant term.
A: effect coding for row variable.
B: effect coding for column variable.
C: linear contrasts for row variable—$(R + 1)/2 - i$; any consecutive numbering will do; for variables with three categories, this is the same as the first code for the row variable.
D: linear contrasts for column variable—$(C + 1)/2 - j$.
E: design for the linear-by-linear interaction or uniform association, obtained by multiplying the linear contrast vector for the row and for the column.
F: design vectors for the row effects model, obtained by multiplying the design vectors for the row categories and the linear contrast vector for the column.
G: design vectors for column effects model, obtained by multiplying the design vectors for the column variable and the linear contrast for the row variable.
H: homogeneous row-column effects model, obtained by adding each vector in the matrix for the row and the corresponding vector in the matrix for the column.
 I: row and column effects model—concatenation of F and G minus the redundant linear-by-linear interaction vector.
J: interaction vectors for saturated model, obtained by multiplying each vector in A with each vector in B.

Design matrix for each type of model is obtained by concatenating relevant vectors from above, and the degrees of freedom by number of cells in the table minus the number of columns in the design matrix.

	Vectors	df
Independence model	T~A~B	4
Uniform association model	T~A~B~E	3
Row-effects model	T~A~B~F	2
Column-effects model	T~A~B~G	2
Homogeneous row–column effects model	T~A~B~H	2
Row and column effects model	T~A~B~I	1
Saturated model	T~A~B~J	0

Note: ~ (Horizontal concatenation); * (Multiplication); *~ (Horizontal direct product); † (Excluding redundant vector).

Table 6

obvious. Those parameters pertaining to each cell, denoted by t_{ij}, are equivalent to the product of the relevant part of the design matrix and the corresponding coefficients.

SOME EXTENSIONS

There are several ways in which one can extend the basic features of the log-linear models examined so far. Among these, the following three seem important: (1) utilizing the ANOVA-like structure

Hypothetical Tables Illustrating Some Association Models

a) Row-Effects Association Model

	Frequency				Odds Ratio	
		X				
	400	400	50		4	4
Y	200	800	400		2	2
	100	800	800			

	Log Parameters				Multiplicative Parameter	
	1.155	0	−1.555		3.175	1	.315
	−.231	0	.231		.794	1	1.260
	−.924	0	.924		.397	1	2.520

b) Homogeneous Row–Column Effects Model

	Frequency				Odds Ratio	
		X				
	400	100	100		4	2
Y	100	100	200		2	1
	100	200	400			

	Log Parameters				Multiplicative Parameters	
	.924	−.231	−.693		2.520	.794	.500
	−.231	0	.231		.794	1	1.260
	−.693	.231	.462		.500	1.260	1.587

Table 7

of the log-linear model and the well-developed sampling theory to explore interaction patterns of multivariate categorical data, (2) manipulating the design matrices to examine more specific hypotheses and models, and (3) combining the strategic features of subgroup analysis and the flexibility and power of the log-linear models to produce more readily accessible analysis results. These three extensions are discussed below.

General Extension of Log-Linear Models. The most straightforward and widely used application of the log-linear model is to explore the interaction pattern of multivariate data by exploiting the ANOVA-like structure of the model. Given several variables to examine, especially when each variable contains more than two categories, it is almost impossible to examine the data structure in detail.

The ANOVA-like structure allows one to develop a convenient strategy to explore the existence of multiway relationships among the variables.

This strategy requires that one start with a design matrix for each variable (containing k-1 vectors, where k is the number of categories in the variable). It does not matter whether one uses dummy coding or effect coding. To examine all the possible interrelationships in the data, one needs design matrices corresponding to each two-way interaction to m-way interaction where m is the number of variables. To construct a design matrix for a two-way interaction between variable A and variable B, simply cross-multiply the design vectors for A with those for B. (This method is illustrated in Table 6.) This general approach to design matrices is extended to m-way. For example, a three-way interaction is handled by cross-multiplying each two-way vector with the basic design vectors for a third variable, and so on.

If one includes in the model all the vectors covering up to m-way interactions, the resulting model is saturated, and each frequency in the multiway table is completely described. In general, one wants to explore and, if possible, find a parsimonious way to describe the data structure. One general strategy, perhaps overused, is to examine systematically the hierarchical pattern inherent in the design constraints and serially examine a nested set of models. To illustrate, consider that there are three variables and that the basic design vectors for each variable are represented by A, B, and C, respectively. Let T stand for the constant vector. Then an example of a nested set of models is illustrated below. The commas indicate concatenation, and two or more letters together indicate cross-multiplication of the basic design vectors for each variable.

$$H_1: \quad T$$
$$H_2: \quad T, A, B, C$$
$$H_{3a}: \quad T, A, B, C, AB$$
$$H_{3b}: \quad T, A, B, C, AB, AC$$
$$H_{3c}: \quad T, A, B, C, AB, AC, BC$$
$$H_4: \quad T, A, B, C, AB, AC, BC, ABC$$

(H_1)	Equiprobability
(H_2)	Total independence
(H_{3a})	One two-way interaction
(H_{3b})	Two two-way interactions
(H_{3c})	No three-way interaction
(H_4)	Saturated model

Each hypothesis is tested, using the appropriate degrees of freedom, which is given by the number of the cells in the frequency table minus the number of vectors contained in the design matrix and the χ^2 or L^2 statistics associated with each model. The sequence from the hypotheses in set (3) is arbitrary; one may choose any nested set or directly examine 3c. One usually would accept the simplest hypothesis that is compatible with the data.

If variables contain many categories, even the simplest two-way interactions will use up many

degrees of freedom. This type of generic testing does not incorporate into the design matrix any special relationships that may exist between variables. Models of this type are routinely available in standard computer packages and therefore are quite accessible. For that reason, they are overused. Moreover, the sequential nature of the testing violates some of the assumptions of classical hypothesis testing. Nevertheless, in the hands of an experienced researcher, they become a flexible tool for exploring the multivariate data structure.

The Uses of Constrained Models. The flexibility and power of log-linear models are fully realized only when one incorporates a specific hypothesis about the data into the design matrices. There are virtually endless varieties one can consider. Some of the simple but strategic models of association were introduced in the preceding section.

Incorporating such models into a multivariate analysis is not difficult if one views the task in the context of design matrices. For instance, suppose one suspects that a certain pattern of relationship exists between X and Y (for instance, the social class of origin and destination in intergenerational mobility). Furthermore, one may have an additional hypothesis that these relationships vary systematically across different political systems (or across societies with different levels of economic development). If one can translate these ideas into appropriate design matrices, using such a model will provide a much more powerful test than the generic statistical models described in the previous section can provide. Many social mobility studies incorporate such design matrices as a way of incorporating a special pattern of social mobility in the overall design (for some examples, see Duncan 1979; Hout 1984; Yamaguchi 1987 and for new developments, see DiPrete 1990; Stier and Grusky 1990; Wong 1990, 1992, 1995; Xie 1992).

In general, there are two problems in using such design matrices. The first, which depends in part on the researcher's creative ability, is the problem of translating theoretically relevant models into appropriate design matrices. The second is finding a way to obtain a good statistical solution for the model, but this is no longer much of a problem because of the wide availability of computer programs that allow the incorporation of design matrices (see Breen 1984 for a discussion of preparing design matrices for a computer program that handles generalized linear systems).

One of the general problems has been that researchers often do not make the underlying design matrices explicit and as a result sometimes misinterpret the results. A solution for this problem is to think explicitly in terms of the design matrices, not in analogy to a generic (presumed) ANOVA model.

Use of Percentage Tables in Log-Linear Modeling. Multivariate analysis is in general complex. Categorical analysis is especially so, because one conceptual variable has to be treated as if it were (k- 1) variables, with k being the number of categories in the variable. Therefore, even with a limited number of variables, if each variable contains more than two categories, examining the multivariate pattern becomes extremely difficult. Therefore, the tendency is to rely on the general hypothesis testing discussed earlier.

It is useful to borrow two of the strategies of subgroup analysis: focusing on a bivariate relationship and using percentage distributions. After an acceptable log-linear model is identified, one therefore may display the relationship between two key variables while the effects of other variables are controlled or purged (Clogg 1978; Clogg and Eliason 1988a; Clogg et al. 1990; Kaufman and Schervish 1986). Furthermore, a percentage distribution for the bivariate distribution may be compared with the corresponding percentage distributions when different sets of variables are controlled in this manner. Fortunately, the log-linear modeling can provide a very attractive way in which the confounding effects of many variables can be purged from the relationship that is under special scrutiny (Clogg 1978; Kaufman and Schervish 1986; Clogg and Eliason 1988a; Clogg et al. 1990). Clogg et al. (1990) show a general framework under which almost all the known variations in adjustments can be considered a special case. Furthermore, they also describe statistical testing procedures for variety of statistics associated with such adjustments.

Tables 8 and 9 contain examples of traditional subgroup analysis, log-linear analysis, and the uses of standardization or purging methods. The upper panel of Table 8 contains a bivariate table showing (1) the race of the defendant (X) and (2) the

Death Penalty Verdict (Y) by Defendant's Race (X) and Victim's Race (Z)

Victim's Race	Defendant's Race	Death Penalty		
		Yes	No	Percentage Yes
Total	White	53	430	11.0
	Black	15	176	7.9
White	White	53	414	11.3
	Black	11	37	22.9
Black	White	0[†]	16	0.0
	Black	4	139	2.8

Table 8

SOURCE: Radelet and Pierce (1991), p. 25, and Agresti (1996), p. 54.

NOTE: (1) For log-linear analysis, 0.5 is added to zero cell. (2) In the original data, there are two cases that involve both white and black victims. (3) The data do not consistently identify Spanish ancestry. Most defendants and victims with Spanish ancestry are coded as white. For detailed information, see Radelet and Pierce (1991).

verdict—death penalty versus other penalties (Y), while the lower panel contains the result of traditional three-variables subgroup analysis, in which the original relationship between X and Y is reanalyzed within the categories of the third variable, the race of the victims (Z). (These data are based on individuals who were convicted of multiple homicides in Florida. See Radelet and Peierce 1991; Agresti 1996.)

The original bivariate relationship seems to indicate that whites are more likely to receive the death penalty than are blacks. However, when the race of the victims is controlled, the partial relationship between X and Y is reversed: Within each category of victim, blacks are more likely to receive the death penalty than are whites. The underlying reasons for this reversal are two related facts: (1) There is a strong association between the race of the defendant (X) and the race of the victims (Z): white defendants are more likely to kill whites than blacks, while black defendants are more likely to kill blacks than whites, and (2) there is a strong relationship between the race of the victims and the death penalty: those who killed white victims are more likely to receive the death penalty than are those who killed blacks. Once these relation-

Design Matrix, Expected Frequencies, and Standardized Percentages under the Model without Three-Way Interaction

a) Design Matrix and Coefficients for the Model without Three-Way Interaction

T	Z	X	Y	XZ	YZ	XY	Parameter	Coefficient	z-value
1	1	1	1	1	1	1	Constant (T)	2.959	21.0
1	1	1	−1	1	−1	−1	Z	1.039	6.9
1	1	−1	1	−1	1	−1	X	−0.135	−1.3
1	1	−1	−1	−1	−1	1	Y	−1.382	−11.1
1	−1	1	1	−1	−1	1	XZ	1.137	14.7
1	−1	1	−1	−1	1	−1	YZ	0.558	3.9
1	−1	−1	1	1	−1	−1	XY	−0.201	−2.2
1	−1	−1	−1	1	1	1	$L^2 = 0.284$	df =1	Prob. = 0.594

b) Expected Frequencies under the Model without Three-Way Interaction

		Death Penalty		
Victim's Race	Defendant's Race	Yes	No	Percentage Yes
Total	White	53.5	430.0	11.1
	Black	15.0	176.0	7.9
White	White	53.3	413.7	11.4
	Black	10.7	37.3	22.3
Black	White	0.2	16.3	1.2
	Black	4.3	138.7	3.0

c) Direct Standardization

Total	White	35.87	447.62	7.4
	Black	28.16	162.84	14.7
White	White	33.58	260.67	11.4
	Black	25.91	90.33	22.3
Black	White	2.29	186.95	1.2
	Black	2.25	72.51	3.0

d) Purging XZ (= purging XZ and XYZ)

Total	White	17.7	183.2	8.8
	Black	34.9	160.9	17.8
White	White	17.0	132.3	11.4
	Black	33.5	116.6	22.3
Black	White	0.7	50.9	1.4
	Black	1.4	44.4	3.1

e) Purging XZ and YZ (= purging XZ, YZ, and XYZ)

Total	White	11.0	260.9	4.0
	Black	21.5	228.7	8.6
White	White	9.8	231.9	4.0
	Black	19.1	203.2	8.6
Black	White	1.2	29.0	4.0
	Black	2.4	25.4	8.6

Table 9

ships are taken into consideration, blacks receive a higher rate of the death penalty than do whites.

The log-linear analysis can supplement such a traditional subgroup analysis in several convenient ways. Panel (a) of Table 9 shows design matrix, coefficients, and standardized values under the model without three-way interaction. These statistics show several things that are not obvious in the conventional subgroup analysis: (1) The three-way interaction is not statistically significant, (2) all three bivariate relationships are statistically significant, and (3) in some sense, the association between X and Z is the strongest and that between X and Y is the weakest among the three bivariate relationships.

Panel (b) shows expected frequencies and relevant percentages under the model (where the three-way interaction is assumed to be zero). The pattern revealed in each subtable is very similar to that under the traditional subgroup analysis shown in Table 8. (This is as it should be, given no three-way interaction effect.) Within each category of victim's race, black defendants are more likely to receive the death penalty than are white defendants. The standardization or purging, then, allows one to summarize this underlying relationship between X and Y under the hypothetical condition that the effect of the third variable is controlled or purged. There are many different ways of controlling the effects of the third variable: (1) direct standardization, panel (c), (2) when the effects of XZ relationship are purged (in addition to the purging of the three-way interaction) panel (d), (3) when, in addition to the previous purging, the effects of the YZ relationship are also purged, panel (e). Although the percentage differences seem to vary, the underlying log-linear effect remains constant: Blacks are twice more likely to receive the death penalty than are whites when both kill a victim of the same race (see Clogg 1978; Clogg and Eliason 1988b; Clogg et al. 1990).

(SEE ALSO: *Analysis of Variance and Covariance; Causal Inference Models; Measures of Association; Nonparametric Statistics; Statistical Methods*)

REFERENCES

Agresti, Alan 1983 "A Survey of Strategies for Modeling Cross-Classifications Having Ordinal Variables." *Journal of the American Statistical Association* 78:184–198.

—— 1984 *Analysis of Ordinal Categorical Data.* New York: Wiley.

—— 1990 *Categorical Data Analysis.* New York: Wiley.

—— 1996 *An Introduction to Categorical Data Analysis.* New York: Wiley.

Alba, Richard D. 1988 "Interpreting the Parameters of Log-Linear Models." In J. Scott Long, ed., *Common Problems/Proper Solutions.* Beverly Hills, Calif.: Sage.

Alwin, Dwane F., and Robert M. Hauser 1975 "The Decomposition of Effects in Path Analysis." *American Sociological Review* 40:37–47.

Anderson, J. A. 1984 "Regression and Ordered Categorical Variables." *Journal of the Royal Statistical Society* B46:1–30.

Arminger, G., and G. W. Bohrnstedt 1987 "Making It Count Even More: A Review and Critique of Stanley Lieberson's *Making It Count: The Improvement of Social Theory and Research.*" *Sociological Methodology* 17:347–362.

Berk, R. A. 1983 "An Introduction to Sample Selection Bias in Sociological Data." *American Sociological Review* 48:386–398.

—— 1986 "Review of *Making It Count: The Improvement of Social Research and Theory.*" *American Journal of Sociology* 92:462–465.

Bishop, Yvonne M. M., Stephen E. Fienberg, and Paul W. Holland 1975 *Discrete Multivariate Analysis: Theory and Practice.* Cambridge, Mass.: MIT Press.

Blalock, Hubert M., Jr. 1964 *Causal Inferences in Nonexperimental Research.* Chapel Hill: University of North Carolina Press.

——, ed. 1985a *Causal Models in the Social Sciences*, 2nd ed. New York: Aldine.

——, ed. 1985b *Causal Models in Panel and Experimental Designs.* New York: Aldine.

Bollen, K. A. 1989 *Structural Equations with Latent Variables.* New York: Wiley.

Breen, Richard 1984 "Fitting Non-Hierarchical and Association Models Using GLIM." *Sociological Methods and Research* 13:77–107.

Bunge, Mario 1979 *Causality and Modern Science*, 3rd rev. ed. New York: Dover.

Campbell, D. T., and J. C. Stanley 1966 *Experimental and Quasi-Experimental Designs for Research.* Boston: Houghton Mifflin.

Clogg, Clifford C. 1978 "Adjustment of Rates Using Multiplicative Models." *Demography* 15:523–539.

—— 1982a "Using Association Models in Sociological Research: Some Examples." *American Journal of Sociology* 88:114–134.

—— 1982b "Some Models for the Analysis of Association in Multiway Cross-Classifications Having Ordered Categories." *Journal of the American Statistical Association* 77:803–815.

——, and Scott R. Eliason 1988a "A Flexible Procedure for Adjusting Rates and Proportions, Including Statistical Methods for Group Comparisons." *American Sociological Review* 53:267–283.

—— 1988b "Some Common Problems in Log-Linear Analysis." In J. Scott Long, ed., *Common Problems/ Proper Solutions*. Beverly Hills, Calif.: Sage.

——, and Edward S. Shihadeh 1994 *Statistical Models for Ordinal Variables*. Thousand Oaks, Calif.: Sage.

——, James W. Shockey, and Scott R. Eliason 1990 "A General Statistical Framework for Adjustment of Rates." *Sociological Methods and Research* 19:156–195.

Cook, Thomas D., and Donald T. Campbell 1979 *Quasi-Experimentation: Design and Analysis Issues for Field Settings*. Chicago: Rand McNally.

Davis, James A. 1984 "Extending Rosenberg's Technique for Standardizing Percentage Tables." *Social Forces* 62:679–708.

——, and Ann M. Jacobs 1968 "Tabular Presentations." In David L. Sills, ed., *The International Encyclopedia of the Social Sciences*, vol.15. New York: Macmillan and Free Press.

Duncan, Otis Dudley 1966 "Path Analysis: Sociological Examples." *American Journal of Sociology* 72:1–16.

—— 1975 *Introduction to Structural Equation Models*. New York: Academic Press.

—— 1979 "How Destination Depends on Origin in the Occupational Mobility Table." *American Journal of Sociology* 84:793–803.

Fienberg, Stephen E. 1980 *The Analysis of Cross-Classified Data*, 2nd ed. Cambridge, Mass.: MIT Press.

Fisher, F. M. 1966 *The Identification Problem in Econometrics*. New York: McGraw-Hill.

Fleiss, J. L. 1981 *Statistical Methods for Rates and Proportions,* 2nd ed. New York: Wiley Interscience.

Goldberger, Arthur S., and Otis Dudley Duncan (eds.) 1973 *Structural Equation Models in the Social Sciences*. New York and London: Seminar Press.

Goodman, Leo A. 1978 *Analyzing Qualitative/Categorical Data: Log-Linear Analysis and Latent Structure Analysis*. Cambridge, Mass.: Abt.

—— 1981 "Three Elementary Views of Loglinear Models for the Analysis of Cross-Classifications Having Ordered Categories." In Karl F. Schuessler, ed., *Sociological Methodology*. San Francisco: Jossey-Bass.

—— 1984 *The Analysis of Cross-Classified Categorical Data Having Ordered Categories*. Cambridge, Mass.: Harvard University Press.

—— 1985 "The Analysis of Cross-Classified Data Having Ordered and/or Unordered Categories: Association Models, Correlation Models, and Asymmetry Models for Contingency Tables with or without Missing Entries." *Annals of Statistics* 13:10–69.

—— 1987 "The Analysis of a Set of Multidimensional Contingency Tables Using Log-Linear Models, Latent Class Models, and Correlation Models: The Solomon Data Revisited." In A. E. Gelfand, ed., *Contributions to the Theory and Applications of Statistics: A Volume in Honor of Herbert Solomon*. New York: Academic Press.

—— 1990 "Total-Score Models and Rasch-Type Models for the Analysis of a Multidimensional Contingency Table, or a Set of Multidimensional Contingency Tables, with Specified and/or Unspecified Order for Response Categories." In Karl F. Schuessler, ed., *Sociological Methodology*. San Francisco: Jossey-Bass.

Haberman, Shelby J. 1978 *Analysis of Qualitative Data*, vol. 1: *Introductory Topics*. New York: Academic Press.

—— 1979 *Analysis of Qualitative Data*, vol. 2: *New Developments*. New York: Academic Press.

Hausman, J. A. 1978 "Specification Tests in Econometrics." *Econometrica* 46:1251–1272.

Heckman, J. J. 1979 "Sample Selection Bias as a Specification Error." *Econometrica* 47 153–161.

——, and R. Robb 1986 "Alternative Methods for Solving the Problem of Selection Bias in Evaluating the Impact of Treatments on Outcomes." In H. Wainer, ed., *Drawing Inferences from Self-Selected Samples.* New York: Springer-Verlag.

Heise, David R. 1975 *Causal Analysis*. New York: Wiley.

Hout, Michael 1984 "Status, Autonomy, Training in Occupational Mobility." *American Journal of Sociology* 89:1379–1409.

Hyman, Herbert 1955 *Survey Design and Analysis: Principles, Cases and Procedures*. Glencoe, Ill.: Free Press.

Kaufman, Robert L., and Paul G. Schervish 1986 "Using Adjusted Crosstabulations to Interpret Log-Linear Relationships." *American Sociological Review* 51:717–733.

Kendall, Patricia L., and Paul Lazarsfeld 1950 "Problems of Survey Analysis." In Robert K. Merton and Paul F. Lazarsfeld, eds., *Continuities in Social Research: Studies in the Scope and Method of the American Soldier*. Glencoe, Ill.: Free Press.

Kish, Leslie 1959 "Some Statistical Problems in Research Design." *American Sociological Review* 24:328–338.

Lazarsfeld, Paul F. 1955 "Interpretation of Statistical Relations as a Research Operation." In Paul F. Lazarsfeld and Morris Rosenberg, eds., *The Language of Social Research*. Glencoe, Ill.: Free Press.

———, Ann K. Pasanella, and Morris Rosenberg, eds. 1972 *Continuities in the Language of Social Research*. New York: Free Press.

Leamer, E. E. 1978 *Specification Searches: Ad Hoc Inference with Nonexperimental Data*. New York: Wiley Interscience.

Lieberson, Stanley 1985 *Making It Count: The Improvement of Social Research and Theory*. Berkeley and Los Angeles: University of California Press.

Long, J. Scott 1984 "Estimable Functions in Loglinear Models." *Sociological Methods and Research* 12:399–432.

———, ed. 1988 *Common Problems/Proper Solutions: Avoiding Error in Quantitative Research*. Beverly Hills, Calif.: Sage.

Mare, Robert D., and Christopher Winship 1988 "Endogenous Switching Regression Models for the Causes and Effects of Discrete Variables." In J. Scott Long, ed., *Common Problems/Proper Solutions*. Beverly Hills, Calif: Sage.

McCullagh, P. 1978 "A Class of Parametric Models for the Analysis of Square Contingency Tables with Ordered Categories." *Biometrika* 65:413–418.

———, and J. Nelder 1983 *Generalized Linear Models*. London: Chapman and Hall.

Mosteller, F. 1968 "Association and Estimation in Contingency Tables." *Journal of the American Statistical Association* 63:1–28.

———, and John W. Tukey 1977 *Data Analysis and Regression*. Reading, Mass.: Addison-Wesley.

Nelder, J. A., and R. W. M. Wedderburn 1972 "Generalized Linear Models." *Journal of the Royal Statistical Society* A135:370–384.

Plackett, R. L. 1974 *The Analysis of Categorical Data*. London: Griffin.

Press, S. L., and S. Wilson 1978 "Choosing between Logistic Regression and Discriminant Analysis." *Journal of the American Statistical Association* 73:699–705.

Radelet, Michael I., and Glenn L. Pierce 1991 "Choosing Those Who Will Die: Race and the Death Penalty in Florida." *Florida Law Review* 43:1–34.

Rosenberg, Morris 1968 *The Logic of Survey Analysis*. New York: Basic Books.

Rubin, D. B. 1977 "Assignment to Treatment Group on the Basis of a Covariance." *Journal of Educational Statistics* 2:1–26.

Simon, Herbert A. 1954 "Spurious Correlation: A Causal Interpretation." *Journal of the American Statistical Association* 49:467–479.

——— 1979 "The Meaning of Causal Ordering." In Robert K. Merton, James S. Coleman, and Peter H. Rossi, eds., *Qualitative and Quantitative Social Research: Papers in Honor of Paul F. Lazarsfeld*. New York: Free Press.

Singer, Burton, and Margaret Mooney Marini 1987 "Advancing Social Research: An Essay Based on Stanley Lieberson's *Making It Count*." In Clifford C. Clogg, ed., *Sociological Methodology*. Washington, D.C.: American Sociological Association.

Thiel, Henri 1971 *Principles of Econometrics* New York: Wiley.

Williams, D. A. 1976 "Improved Likelihood Ratio Tests for Complete Contingency Tables." *Biometrika* 63:33–37.

Xie, Yu 1989 "An Alternative Purging Method: Controlling the Composition-Dependent Interaction in an Analysis of Rates." *Demography* 26:711–716.

Yamaguchi, Kazuo 1987 "Models for Comparing Mobility Tables: Toward Parsimony and Substance." *American Sociological Review* 52:482–494.

Zeisel, Hans 1985 *Say It with Figures*, 6th ed. New York: Harper & Row.

JAE-ON KIM
MYOUNG-JIN LEE

TECHNOLOGICAL RISKS AND SOCIETY

See Society and Technological Risks.

TERRITORIAL BELONGING

DEFINITION

Belonging is defined as the state of being part of something. Territorial belonging implies being part of a territory. The definition of a territory, although it is conditioned by the morphology of space, is essentially a social operation that is connected with the factors that induce the perception of boundaries. These are complex factors that researchers in the "psychology of form" (*Gestaltpsychologie*) have attempted to specify (Reusch 1956, pp. 340–361). Campbell has identified seven of these factors. Those analytically most relevant to social systems are similarity and shared destiny or "common fate" (Campbell 1958), to which the ecological, economic, and sociological traditions (Hawley 1950, p. 258) add interdependence, which is related to Campbell's (1958) notion of internal diffusion.

Territorial belonging is therefore a form of social belonging (for a detailed treatment, see Pollini 1987) that is displayed by a spatially defined collectivity. Spatial definition more or less precisely and more or less sharply delimits (where the concept of a boundary refers to a line or zone) a territory to which a name is given. Belonging to a spatially defined collectivity thus may be related to the name given to a territory, so that it becomes simply territorial without ceasing to be social as well. To emphasize its twofold nature, it also may be called "socioterritorial belonging" (Pollini 1992, pp. 55–58).

THE MULTIPLICITY OF TERRITORIAL BELONGINGS

Like any form of social belonging, territorial belonging may relate to objective or subjective elements and may be defined by the self or by others (Merton 1963). Like social belonging, it may be largely exclusive or admit to multiplicity and may be ascribed or acquired (Simmel 1908).

Workers in human ecology, human geography, sociology, and land economics have long attempted to provide a definition of the most suitable territorial units for social purposes. They have oscillated between emphasizing the principle of similarity (the morphology of the territory, the physical and cultural features of the individuals who inhabit it, the predominant type of economic activity, etc.) and emphasizing the principle of interdependence (on the basis of gravitational flows for work and services, areas of relatively intense exchange, etc.) (see Galtung 1968). The implementation of the political function of governing human communities, moreover, has led to the fixing of territorial boundaries that express (and produce) a common fate (Hawley 1950, p. 258).

Reciprocal relations are among the main criteria used to define territorial units (similarity, interdependence, and common fate, taking the proximity of elements for granted). As studies of "nation building" have shown (see Deutsch [1953] 1966), similarity tends to create relations of interdependence and interdependence generates perceptions of similarity (Simmel 1890, p. 40; Shils 1975, p. 17); in the same manner, a common fate induces perceptions of similarity and interdependence and similarity and interdependence heighten the perception of a common fate.

The most enduring and significant spatial units are those with multi-confirmed boundaries (Campbell 1958), that is, those for which the criteria of similarity, functional interdependence, and common fate are congruent. The European nation-states of the nineteenth and twentieth centuries exemplify the successful achievement of this congruence (Eisenstadt 1973, pp. 231–235).

In traditional nomadic and agricultural societies, similarity, interdependence, and common fate are properties that relate substantially to a single socioterritorial unit that includes everyday life almost in its entirety, except when extraordinary occasions (great feasts and celebrations, great markets, wars, etc.) demonstrate the importance of a broader socioterritorial unit that is ethnic and/or tribal in nature or sometimes is of state dimension (kingdoms and empires, churches and great religious organizations). This is the social order that is called the "segmentary society of mechanical solidarity" by Durkheim (1893), *Gemeinschaft* by Toennies (1887), and the "independent community" by Hawley (1950, pp. 223 ff) and is exemplified by numerous contemporary societies (Dyson Hudson 1966).

As a significant division of territorial labor develops—induced by the reduced spatial friction brought about by advances in transport and communications that allow more frequent exchanges over longer distances (the "mobiletic revolution" of Russet 1967) and by technical progress, which requires the greater accumulation of capital and is not uniformly distributed across the territory (industrial revolution)—the areas of interdependence expand and are structured into several levels (Hawley 1950, pp. 236–257). This has evident effects on areas of common fate. Increased interdependence facilitates temporary or permanent movements across the territory and thus alters similarities and differences as well as the criteria for their definition and perception (Sola Pool 1965).

In short, mainly as a result of these phenomena, a socioterritorial structure grows more complex. Important socioterritorial units proliferate, intersect, and are organized into larger (Parsons 1961, pp. 123 ff) and relatively fluid systems, while the congruence among the three main principals of sociospatial structuring diminishes. These changes have been interpreted as the decay of *Gemeinschaft* (Toennies 1887) and of the territorial state (Herz 1957), as stages in an ongoing evolution into cosmopolitanism, and as the onset of a single overarching socioterritorial unit: the world in its entirety. Parsons (1951) introduced in his theoretical pattern of variables for the definition of roles the dichotomy between particularism and universalism. Although of general analytic significance, this dichotomy also has been used to characterize the process of modernization (Parsons 1971), which, with reference to territorial belonging, includes the localism–cosmopolitanism dichotomy. The term "globalization," which now has general currency although it dates from the early 1970s (Kaufman 1974), has been employed more recently to define this trend.

The increased complexity of socioterritorial belonging is obviously correlated to the complexity of the social structuring of the territory. All individuals are involved in relational networks that may be micro-local (habitation), local, regional, national, continental, and global, and they shift easily and rapidly from one level to another by virtue of the ease of communications and transportation or simply pass subjectively from one role to another (Webber 1963, 1964).

Owing to the ease of communications and transport, every individual may encounter and assimilate elements of other cultures. Cultural diversity has dwindled before the advance of modern culture as it is interpreted by Western society.

Intellectual elements ("scientific" criteria for the reliability of knowledge) and most emotional (aspirations and values) and evaluative ones (ethics and hierarchies of values) are widely shared by humankind (Inglehart 1997). Consequently, similarities and differences are difficult to define in territorial terms, and when they are thus definable, they are increasingly so only as symbols (languages, flags, cultural artifacts, physical resemblances, etc.), since knowledge-evoking and evaluative elements have been reduced to being options that are private, individual, and socially irrelevant (ethical and gnoseological relativism, individualism) (Thomas and Znaniecki 1918–1920; Halman, et al. 1987).

The state itself, which is called on to define the conditions of the collective control of the collective destiny, although it is still characterized by distinct territorial boundaries, is undergoing profound change as a result of the erosion of its sovereignty and power by the rise of supranational political organizations (e.g., the United Nations) and, in centralized states, infrastate political organizations (Galtung 1967), as well as by the growth of multinational economic enterprises and other noneconomic associations over which it can exert little or no control.

Consequently, if the continuing determination of the territorial boundaries of political and/or administrative units (Herz 1968) allows belongings to be related to them, those belongings grow increasingly less socially significant in regards to not only interdependencies and similarities but also common destiny. This occurs because social relevance is divided among several units organized into a system of relationships that need not be hierarchical and may indeed compete with each other.

TERRITORIAL BELONGING SUBJECTIVELY DEFINED BY REFERENCE TO THE SELF (THE SENTIMENT OF TERRITORIAL BELONGING)

The localism–cosmopolitanism of territorial belonging: A single-or multidimensional concept?

The growing complexity of territorial belonging,

along with the hypothesis that it is the manifestation of an ongoing process whose final outcome is cosmopolitanism (or the erasure of any nonglobal, nonecumenical sense of belonging), has prompted sociologists to study the phenomenon empirically by focusing on the subjective definition of belonging provided by individuals with reference to themselves. Taking the process of growing systemization at the "energetic" level for granted, attention has been focused on how the phenomenon is subjectively reflected in the subjective definition individuals give to their territorial belongings. The aim of these studies has been to single out the factors that induce a person to feel that she or he belongs primarily to one unit rather than to another and, more generally, why she or he expresses a primarily cosmopolitan sense of belonging rather than one anchored in a particular geographic unit. Other studies have explored attachment to units of a particular size (home and neighborhood, local community, region, nation, continent, etc.).

The data gathered in both types of studies have included highly modernized contexts. On the home and neighborhood, see Fried and Gleicher (1961), Galster and Hesser (1981), and Fried (1982). On the local community, see Kasarda and Janowitz (1974), Rojek et al. (1975), Taylor and Townsend (1976), Wasserman (1982), Fried (1982), Goudy (1990), and Beggs et al. (1996). On regional units, see Piveteau (1969) and Gubert (1997). On belongings and national pride, apart from studies of nationalism and ethnicity, see the European Values Study in Ashford and Timms (1992, pp. 89–91) and the World Values Study in Ingleheart (1997, pp.303–305). On territorial belongings on the localism–cosmopolitanism contiuum, see Treinen (1965), Gubert and Struffi (1987), Gubert (1992a), and Strassoldo and Tessarin (1992). These data confirm the complexity of the phenomenon of territorial belonging when it is defined subjectively (a sentiment of belonging). Subjectively felt belongings are multiple, and each has its own role to play; that is, they become socially important in accordance with the particular context, which may change rapidly. For example, the sense of national belonging is exalted during international sports events, but local and regional senses of belonging emerge during sports events within a country. This multiplicity of territorial belongings therefore rules out their mutual exclusiveness; this emerges clearly when subjects are asked to declare the absolute level of attachment they feel to different territorial units (Gubert 1998).

It is probable that partly diversified belongings underlie this multiplicity. This diversity was not grasped in early empirical studies of the sentiment of belonging, which relied largely on relative measures of the strength of attachment to socioterritorial units arranged along a continuum, with the neighborhood and community at one extreme and cosmopolitanism at the other (Terhune 1965; Gubert 1972, p. 181). Relative measures also were used in later large-scale surveys such as the European Values Study and the World Values Study. It is difficult to imagine that a Pole's identification with his or her nation is the same as his or her attachment to his or her place of residence. One may feel strongly Polish while also having close bonds with one's local community, and this cannot be explained by a single-dimensional conception of localism–cosmopolitanism, which instead suggests a social experience in which the nation as a sociospatial unit has weaker emotional connotations.

Further evidence that feelings of belonging to diverse socioterritorial units differ is provided by analyses of the attitudes of subjects who declare that they do not feel attached to any particular territorial unit. These individuals may be called cosmopolitans, but their cosmopolitanism is not only the extreme position on the localism–cosmopolitanism continuum; it is also symptomatic of difficulties of social integration, or anomie (Bertelli 1992). The distribution of the strength of socioterritorial belonging therefore measures not only the territorial size of the main social collectivities of reference but also the intensity of social integration, which in the case of declared nonbelonging to any territorial unit is markedly diminished, perhaps more in some cases than in others; therefore, cosmopolitanism is internally differentiated or heterogeneous. Parsons's assumption that there is social belonging (and therefore loyalty and attachment) if there is social conformity—if, that is, the subject conforms with the institutional obligations of solidarity (Parsons 1951)—receives empirical support in that a lack of social integration is connected with a lack of belonging to any socioterritorial unit.

Localism–cosmopolitanism as a single-dimensional continuum. Taken for granted (or given) the multiplicity of socioterritorial belongings and their partly diverse nature a further finding of empirical surveys concerns the relative importance of each of these belongings with respect to the others. It is assumed here that, to some extent, they express the localism–cosmopolitanism dimension and therefore can be plotted along a continuum.

When asked about the matter, even interviewees in highly modernized contexts tend to assign more importance to local belongings than to national and supranational ones. Overall, the two units that predominate are the commune and the nation or state. The importance of the other subnational and supracommunal units (province, region) depends on the structure of the public powers (the federal or nonfederal structure of the state) (Gubert 1995) or on whether an ethnic and/or national minority constitutes the majority in a subnational unit (Gubert 1975, p. 305). By contrast, the emergence of subcommunal units (neighborhoods, districts) depends on the settlement pattern of a commune: When it is articulated into several settlements (districts), importance is more frequently ascribed to subcommunal units, while the neighborhood acquires more importance when it constitutes a "natural area" within the communal settlement and has weak links with the rest of the urban territory.

If, rather than proposing a predetermined set of spatial units largely defined in political-administrative terms, individuals who declare their attachment to a particular territory are asked to freely describe it, to give it a name or define its boundaries, the area of belonging is generally more circumscribed. Indeed, it is sometimes restricted to the domestic ambit and its immediate surroundings, with little consideration of supralocal spatial units (Gubert 1992b, pp. 266–277). One therefore may conclude that the immediate bond with a territory is mainly local or microlocal and that only the mention of larger socioterritorial units prompts individuals to consider supralocal territorial attachments.

Between negation of the hypothesis of an evolution toward cosmopolitanism and the reasons for the persistence of localism in a modern society. Multiple regression analysis shows that the social conditions that orient people to cosmopolitan or supralocal belongings (e.g., higher educational level, greater geographic mobility, residence in a metropolis) attenuate local attachments, although they do not entirely eliminate them (Gubert 1992d, pp. 506–523). These conditions seeming to affect the intensity of territorial attachment, attenuating it all levels rather than eliminating its primacy at the local level. Residential mobility seems to multiply local attachments rather than creating a single cosmopolitan attachment (Rubinstein and Parmalee 1992, 1996; Gubert 1992b, pp. 326–330; Feldman 1996).

This phenomenon can be explained to some extent by the reasons adduced to account for the most important territorial attachments. These reasons mainly concern day-to-day living (Kasarda and Janowitz's [1974] duration of residence) and the places of infancy and the family (Taylor and Townsend 1976); much less important are the physical characteristics of places (except for places which are morphologically very distinct, such as mountains and coastlines, partially confirming Fried's [1982] argument) or utility and opportunity.

Therefore, the strongest territorial attachment is connected with strongly affective social relations or with affectively important individual experiences, such as those of a child who progressively establishes a relationship with his or her immediate surroundings.

It is evident that the geographic mobility for mainly utilitarian reasons (work, access to services, use of free time) typically induced by life in modern society does not affect this type of attachment greatly. For the same reason, little influence is exerted by educational level: Although it may extend relational ambits, it does so mainly for utilitarian reasons or ones tied to a person's professional role (Webber 1964). This has evident consequences for the territorial area of matrimonial choice and the areas which contain a person's best friends or relatives; these areas have increased in size, but they are nevertheless of modest proportions. Also, as was found for residential mobility, the consequence of this extension is more to increase the number of places of particular attachment than to induce an attachment to broader spatial units. In other words, the elasticity of relational ambits to the reduced costs of overcoming distance is much greater for secondary instrumental relationships than it is for primary relationships, especially family ones, which are firmly anchored in residence (Parsons 1951, p. 180 ff; 1960, p. 250 ff).

Regression analysis not of the size of the area of main attachment but of the (absolute) intensity of the feeling of belonging to it reveals, as was already mentioned, that the social conditions most typical of modernity (residence in large cities, geographic mobility, residential mobility, higher levels of education, secularization, ethical relativism, individualism, etc.) tend to attenuate the intensity of local attachment but do not erase it. Another explanation for the continuing primacy of local attachments over cosmopolitan ones is therefore that modernity tends to reduce the intensity of territorial belongings, but not to such a varied extent across territorial units that it alters the hierarchy of subjective importance assigned to them by most individuals. This sheds light on why the indicators of localism and cosmopolitanism with regard to the territorial extension of main attachments are determined by a factor independent of the one that groups together the indicators of the intensity of attachment (in any case, the correlation between the indicators is weak).

In addition to intensity, the features that connote greater "modernity" of ecological social and cultural positions in individuals exert a certain amount of influence on the social importance of the sentiment of territorial belonging (Gubert 1992d). Perception of the boundaries that mark the zone of principal attachment are less sharp: The inside–outside boundary, unless it is marked by obvious physical barriers against communica-

tion and vision, is not connected with the perception of distinct sociocultural differences and tends to assume the features of a zone rather than those of a line. The identifying features of the collectivity on the other side of the boundary, except in the case of physical barriers against communication or vision, display not abrupt discontinuities but gradual variations. Stereotypes and the ingroup–outgroup opposition are not as marked as those which arise when racial or ethnic differences are involved.

Moreover, the multiplicity of territorial belongings and their dependence on the particular and contingent nature of the context prevent the onset of radical in-group–out-group conflicts. Factor analysis has shown that the intensity of territorial attachment and in-group–out-group opposition (which is measurable, for example, by acceptance or rejection of immigrants in the area of principal belonging) are independent factors. Feeling stronger attachment to a particular territory therefore is weakly correlated with greater hostility toward or less acceptance of outsiders. The explanation of variance in these attitudes has more to do with the sphere of interests than with that of territorial belongings.

Equally independent (or weakly correlated) are factors relative to the social significance of the sentiment of territorial belonging and indicators of the territorial extension of the most important units.

Expectations of a positive relation between modernity and cosmopolitanism are not borne out by the data, although cross-sectional analysis is not conclusive on this matter. Certainly contradicted are claims that cosmopolitan attachments predominate in contemporary societies. What the advance of modernity seems to have done is breed a plurality of territorial belongings and reduce their intensity and social significance.

Distribution models of territorial attachments. Having ascertained that territorial attachment is felt mainly at the local level (the primary community of everyday life), one may inquire about the distribution pattern of the intensity of territorial attachment, extending the analysis to ambits that do not occupy the highest position in the hierarchy of spatial units.

Once again, the most detailed surveys have been carried out in Italy, a country where the dialectic among localism, nationalism, and cosmopolitanism is particularly lively. If one considers the first three positions in a decreasing scale of attachment from subcommunal units to the whole world, it is possible to identify the most common and significant rank orderings (Gubert 1992b, pp. 279–281). By far the most prevalent is a model one may call "lococentric:" Territorial units diminish in importance as they grow larger. In three-dimensional space, where a two-dimensional geographic plane constitutes the horizontal axes and the relative intensity of territorial attachment is the vertical axis, they assume a cone shape whose apex is the smallest spatial unit.

Two other patterns emerge: the opposite model (upside-down cone), where the importance of a territorial unit decreases as one moves from broader to narrower spatial units, and, more commonly, a volcano-shaped model, a variant of the cone where the greatest importance is attributed to intermediate units, the next greatest importance to smaller units, and the least importance to larger ones.

Despite the prevalence of the lococentric model, a model that might develop instead of the "cosmopolitan" one (upside-down cone) as a consequence of the continuing advance of modernity is the volcano model, which places greater emphasis on supralocal sociospatial units compared with smaller communal or subcommunal ones, but without the units assuming greater importance as they become more inclusive and extensive. This is a type of territoriality that reflects adaptation to the extension of relational spaces beyond the settlement of residence that assumes a form other than cosmopolitanism.

CONCLUSIONS

Sociological research into territorial belonging as it is subjectively defined by self-reference contradicts the claim that the extension of relational spaces and the increased frequency of relations across larger distances (continental and global) have led to the superseding of local or at least noncosmopolitan attachments. Attachment to local ambits still largely predominates. If anything, one discerns adaptations of a different kind, such as the increased complexity of the subjectively felt territorial bond and its closer dependence on changing contexts, the diminished intensity and social significance of various kinds of attachment, and a shift of primary attachment from the local level to one midway between localness and ecumene (the inhabited world). Rejection of any particular territorial attachment that might represent the outcome of cosmopolitan development is at least partly due to a lack of social integration.

Predictions that the demise of Toennies's *Gemeischaft* and Durkheim's segmentary society would indicate the end of the overriding importance of attachment to particular places is not supported by empirical inquiry. Toennies's *Gemeinschaft* has disappeared from modern society, but territorially restricted areas still have social relations of a communitarian nature, that is, relation in which community action in Weber's sense (Weber [1922] 1972, p. 21) predominates.

However, this may not explain the facts unless one refers to Pareto's assertion (1916, vol. II, sections 112–120, 1023–1041; Treinen 1965) that the sentiment of territorial belonging is a "residue" that can be included among those of the "persistence of aggregates." A sentiment springs from the psychological association between emotionally significant experiences and the context in which they happen. For example, emotionally positive experiences tied to childhood and the family and relationships involving sexuality are positively associated with the places in which they have occurred. This gives rise to deep emotional bonds with those places, bonds that lie beyond reasoning or rationalization. In Pareto's account, the attachment to places thus depends not on the communitarian or societal nature of the collectivity settled in the place of residence but instead on the fact that the most emotionally significant experiences in a person's life necessarily occur in a territorially limited context, if only because of the limits imposed by the perceptive horizon. This also explains why the dispersion of these emotionally significant experiences tends more to multiply the places of attachment than to create broad and inclusive attachments.

The technical progress of the means of communications and the means of transportation that facilitate the expansion of relational ambits, the individualization and secularization of culture, and the proliferation of the utilitarian businesslike relationships of *Gesellschaft* have had little or no effect on the processes that, according to Pareto's theory, cause the birth and persistence of attachment to place. As the negation of a particular bond with a particular place, cosmopolitanism unless it is not an ideological position that is deliberately assumed and declared to the interviewer, therefore may be a symptom of social marginalization caused by a lack of emotionally significant positive experiences. It is thus only rarely caused by the extreme territorial dispersion of those experiences and much more frequently caused by other personal and family events.

There are a number of reservations about the premises of the phenomenon known as globalization. Although relational ambits certainly extend over broader areas or, more precisely, relations have increased in intensity in even the largest of those areas, there is little evidence that the relative intensity of relations has increased. One cannot rule out the possibility that a diminution in the "friction of space" has intensified relations with all the territorial levels into which social life is structured, and it is likely that the intensification at medium and low levels is even greater for certain types of relation than it is at higher and broader ones. The increase in international trade, for example, does not mean that the system is becoming increasingly globalized; the increase may be greater at the national and regional levels, and so in relative terms, regional and national systems have become more self-contained (Deutsch 1960; Deutsch and Eckstein 1960–1961). The unproven assumption that the increase in the absolute density of relations has been accompanied by an increase in their relative density is credited to the existence of globalization processes that may not exist or may exist only for particular types of relations. Moreover, it is evident that in subjective perception (and not only in this area), the importance of the various levels depends much more on their relative density than on their absolute density.

If more detailed empirical research confirms the validity of these remarks, the persisting primacy of local, or at least noncosmopolitan, belongings may be explained not only by Paretian hypotheses but also by the predominance at the relational level of local, regional, and national systems compared with continental and global ones.

Belonging as being part of is a phenomenon of central importance in sociological analysis. Territorial belonging is only one way to manifest social belonging. It may be associated with (ethnic and national belonging) or in competition with (membership in universal religions or international interest groups) other forms of social belonging. It also is a complex phenomenon, but it nevertheless seems to be characterized by features more durable than those of other social or group belongings. It resembles ethnic and national belongings but may be less exposed to change if the Paretian hypothesis is correct. It is a phenomenon that probably is grounded in enduring features of human experience, in what once might have been called human nature. Even the dissolution of Toennies's *Gemeinschaft* into a nonorganic assembly of communitarian relations or the reduction of these relations to simple human relations confined to interindividual space has not severed the bond felt by individuals with the places where they had their most emotionally significant and gratifying personal experiences. Theories of modernity should take account of this fact, and the historicist paradigms that hypothesize a progressive evolution toward cosmopolitanism should be revised. Empirical research must continue, enrich itself with longitudinal surveys, and increase the number of cases observed. Feeling part of a territory and feeling tied to places are still important phenomena in numerous areas of social life.

REFERENCES

Ashford S., and N. Timms 1992 *What Europe Thinks: A Study of Western European Values*. Brookfield, Mass.: Dartmouth.

Beggs, J. J., J. S. Hurlbert, and V. Haines 1996 "Community Attachment in a Rural Setting: A refinement and

Empirical Test of the Systemic Model." *Rural Sociology* 61(3):407–426

Bertelli, B. 1992 "Assenza e Debolezza del Legame con il Territorio: Anomia, Devianza Sociale o Forme Diverse di Appartenenza?" In R. Gubert, ed., *L'Appartenenza Territoriale tra Ecologia e Cultura*. Trent, Italy: Reverdito.

Campbell, D. T. 1958 "Common Fate, Similarity and Other Indices of the Status of Aggregates of Persons as Social Entities." *Behavioral Science* 3:14–25

Deutsch, K. W. 1960 "The Propensity to International Transactions." *Political Studies* 8(8):147–155.

—— and A. Eckstein 1960–1961 "National Industrialization and the Declining Share of the International Economic Sector 1890–1959. *World Politics* 13.

—— 1966 *Nationalism and Social Communication*. Cambridge, Mass.: MIT Press.

Durkheim, E. 1893 *La Division du Travail Social*. Paris: F. Alcan.

Dyson Hudson, N. 1966 *Karimojong Politics*. Oxford, UK: Clarendon.

Eisenstadt S. N. 1973 *Tradition, Change and Modernity*. New York: Wiley.

Feldman, R. M. 1996 "Constancy and Change in Attachments to Types of Settlements." *Environment and Behavior* 28(4):419–445.

Fried, M. 1982 "Residential Attachment: Sources of Residential and Community Satisfaction." *Journal of Social Issues* 38(3):107–119.

——, and P. Gleicher 1961 "Some Sources of Residential Satisfaction in an Urban Slum." *Journal of the American Institute of Planners* 27:305–315.

Galster G. C., and G. W. Hesser 1981 "Residential Satisfaction: Compositional and Contextual Correlates." *Environment and Behavior* 13(6):735–758.

Galtung, J. 1967 "On the Future of the International System." *Journal of Peace Research* 4.

—— 1968 "A Structural Theory of Integration." *Journal of Peace Research* 5(4).

Goudy W. J. 1990 "Community Attachment in a Rural Region." *Rural Sociology* 55(2):178–198

Gubert, R. 1972 La Situazione Confinaria. Treiste, Italy: Lint.

—— 1975 "Entitività delle Etnie e Conflittualità Interetnica." *Studi di Sociologia*. 13n.(3–4):302–322.

——, and L. Struffi, (eds.) 1987 *Strutture Sociali del Territorio Montano*. Milan, Italy: Angeli.

—— 1992a L'appartenenza Territoriale tra Ecologia e Cultura. Trent, Italy: Reverdito. English translation 1999: The Territorial Belonging between Ecology and Culture. Trent: University of Trent Press.

—— 1992b "I Caratteri Generali degli Intervistati e del Loro Legame Socio-Territoriale. In R. Gubert, ed., L'Appartenenza Territoriale tra Ecologia e Cultura. Trent, Italy: Reverdito.

—— 1992c Gli Orientamenti Socio-Politici degli Italian." In R. Gubert ed., Persistenze e Mutamenti dei Valori degli Italiani nel Contesto Europeo. Trent, Italy: Reverdito.

—— 1992d "Le Dimensioni dell'Appartenza Territoriale: Verso un Modello Causale." In R. Gubert, ed., L'Appartenenza Territoriale tra Ecologia e Cultura. Trent, Italy: Reverdito.

—— 1995 "Analysis of Regional Differences in the Values of Europeans." In R. de Moor, ed., *Values in Western Societies*. Tilburg, The Netherlands: Tilburg University Press.

—— (ed.) 1997 *Specificità Culturale di Una Regione Alpina nel Contesto Europeo*. Milan, Italy: Angeli.

—— 1998 "Appartenenza e Mobilità Socio-Territoriali. Primi Risultati di un'Indagine su Operatori Turistici nel Nord.Est Italiano." In A. Gasparini, ed., *Nation, Ethnicity, Minority and Border: Contribution to an International Sociology*. Gorizia, Italy: ISIG.

Halman, L., F. Heunk, R. de Moor and H. Zaunders, (eds.) 1987 *Traditie, Secularisatie en Individualisering*. Tilburg: The Netherlands: University of Tilburg Press.

Hawley, A. 1950 *Human Ecology*. New York: Ronald Press.

Herz, J. H. 1957 "Rise and Demise of the Territorial State." *World Politics* 9(4).

—— 1968 "The Territorial State Revisited: Reflexions on the Future of the National State. *Polity, The Journal of Northeastern Political Science Association* 1(1):12–34.

Inglehart, R. 1997 *Modernization and Postmodernization: Cultural, Economic, and Political Change in 43 Societies*. Princeton, N.J.: Princeton University Press.

Kasarda, J., and M. Janowitz 1974 "Community Attachment in Mass Society." *American Sociological Review* 39:328–339.

Kaufman, G. 1974 *Il Sistema Globale*. Udine, Italy: Del Bianco.

Merton R. K. 1963 *Social Theory and Social Structure.* Glencoe, Ill.: Free Press.

Parsons, T. 1951 *The Social System.* Glencoe, Ill.: Free Press.

—— 1960 *Structure and Process in Modern Societies.* Glencoe, Ill.: Free Press.

—— 1961 "Order and Community in the International System." In J. N. Rosenau, ed., *International Politics and Foreign Policy.* New York and London: Free Press and Collier Macmillan.

—— 1971 *The System of Modern Societies.* Englewood Cliffs, N.J.: Prentice-Hall.

Piveteau, J. L. 1969 "Le Sentiment d'Appartenance Régionale en Suisse." *Revue de Geographie Alpine,* 57(3):361–386.

Pollini, G. 1987 *Appartenenza e Identità.* Milan, Italy: Angeli.

—— 1992 "L'Appartenenza Socio-Territoriale." In R. Gubert, ed., *L'Appartenenza Territoriale tra Ecologia e Cultura.* Trent, Italy: Reverdito.

Reusch, J. 1956 "Analysis of Various Types of Boundaries." In R. R. Grinker, ed., *Toward a Unified Theory of Human Behavior.* New York: Basic Books.

Rojeck D. G., F. Clemente and G. F. Summers 1975 "Community Satisfaction: A Study of Contentment with Local Services" *Rural Sociology* 40:177–192.

Rubinstein, R., P. A. Parmelee 1992 "Attachment to Place and the Representation of the Life Course by the Elderly." In I. Altman and S. Low, eds., *Place Attachment* New York: Plenum, pp. 139–164.

Russet, B. M. 1967 "The Ecology of Future International Politics." *International Studies Quarterly* 11.

Shils, E. 1975 *Center and Periphery: Essays in Macrosociology.* Chicago: University of Chicago Press.

Simmel, G. 1890 *Ueber Soziale Differenzierung, Soziologische und Psychologische Untersuchungen.* Leipzig, Germany: Dunker & Humblot.

—— 1908 *Soziologie. Untersuchungen ueber die Formen der Vergesellschaftung.* Leipzig, Germany: Dunker & Humblot.

Sola Pool I. 1965 "Effects of Cross-National Contact on National and International Images." In H. C. Kelman, ed., *International Behavior: A Social-Psychological Analysis.* New York: Holt, Rinehart and Winston.

Strassoldo, R., and N. Tessarin 1992 *Le Radici del Localismo: Indagine Sociologica sull'Appartenenza Territoriale in Friuli.* Trent, Italy: Reverdito.

Taylor, C. C. and A. R. Townsend 1976 "The Social 'Sense of Place' as Evidenced in North-East England." *Urban Studies* 13(2):133–146.

Terhune, K. W. 1965 "Nationalistic Aspiration, Loyalty and Internationalism." *Journal of Peace Research* 3.

Thomas, W. I. and F. Znaniecki 1918–1920 *The Polish Peasant in Europe and America.* Boston: Badger.

Toennies, F. 1887 *Gemeinschaft und Gesellschaft.* Leipzig, Germany: O. R. Reisland.

Treinen, H. 1965 "Symbolische Ortsbezogenhcit: Eine Soziologische Untersuchung zum Heimatproblem." *Koelner Zeitschrift fuer Soziologie und Sozialpsychologie.* 17(1–2):73–97, 254–297.

Wasserman, I. M. 1982 "Size of Place in Relation to Community Attachment and Satisfaction with Community Services." *Social Indicators Research* 11:421–436.

Webber, M. M. 1963 "Order in Diversity: Community without Propinquity." In L. Wingo, ed., *Cities and Space.* Baltimore: Johns Hopkins University Press.

—— 1964 *Culture, Territoriality, and the Elastic Mile. Regional Science Association Papers* 13:59–69

Weber, M. (1922) 1972 *Wirtschaft und Gesellschaft.* Tuebingen, Germany: J.C.B. Mohr (Paul Siebeck).

RENZO GUBERT

TERRORISM

Terrorism became an issue of worldwide concern in the last third of the twentieth century. Terrorist tactics were not new; they had been used for centuries before being defined as terrorism. The word "terror" entered the political lexicon during the French Revolution's "reign of terror." In the late nineteenth century, at the beginning of the twentieth, and again in the 1920s and 1950s—all periods between major wars on the European continents—terrorism became a technique of revolutionary struggle. Stalin's regime in the 1930s and 1940s was called a reign of terror, but from the late 1940s to the 1960s the word was associated primarily with the armed struggles for independence waged in Palestine and Algeria, from which later generations of terrorists took their inspiration and instruction. After World War II, "terror" emerged as a component of nuclear strategy; the fear of mutual destruction that would deter nuclear war between the United States and the Soviet Union was referred to as a balance of terror.

In the 1970s, "terrorism" became a fad word, promiscuously applied to a wide spectrum of conditions and actions. Bombs in public places were one form of terrorism, but some people asserted that oppression, poverty, hunger, racism, gang violence, spousal or child abuse, environmental destruction, and even medical malpractice were also forms of terrorism. Some governments labeled as terrorism all violent acts committed by their opponents, while antigovernment extremities claimed to be, and often were, the victims of government terror.

In an effort to get a firm hold on a slippery subject, those studying the phenomenon of terrorism were obliged to define it more precisely. Terrorism could be described simply as the use or threat of violence to create an atmosphere of fear and alarm and thus bring about a political result. But making this definition operative in political debate, rules of war, or criminal codes was anything but easy. Is all politically motivated violence terrorism? How does terrorism differ from ordinary crime? Should terrorism be considered a crime at all, or should it be seen as simply another form of armed conflict that is no less legitimate than any other form of war? Is the term properly reserved for those trying to overthrow governments, or can governments also be terrorists?

Definition was crucial because it ultimately determined the way in which terrorism has been studied. A major problem was that terrorism almost always has a pejorative connotation and thus falls in the same category of words as "tyranny" and "genocide," unlike such relatively neutral terms such as "war" and "revolution." One can aspire to objective and dispassionate research, but one cannot be neutral about terrorism any more than one can be neutral about torture. Thus, defining terrorism became an effort not only to delineate a subject area but also to maintain its illegitimacy. Even the most clinical inquiry was laden with values and therefore political issues. The very study of terrorism implied to some a political decision.

Terrorism can be defined objectively by the quality of the act, not by the identity of the perpetrators or the nature of their cause. All terrorist acts are crimes, and many also would be war crimes or "grave breaches" of the rules of war if one accepted the terrorists' assertion that they wage war. All terrorist acts involve violence or the threat of violence, sometimes coupled with explicit demands. The violence is directed against noncombatants. The purposes are political. The actions often are carried out in a way that will achieve maximum publicity, and the perpetrators are usually members of an organized group.

Terrorist organizations are by necessity clandestine, but unlike other criminals, terrorists often but not always claim credit for their acts. Finally—the hallmark of terrorism—the acts are intended to produce psychological effects. This introduces a distinction between the actual victims of terrorist violence and the target audience. The connection between the victim and the target of terrorism can be remote. The identity of the victims may be secondary or even irrelevant to the terrorist cause. "Pure terrorism" is entirely indiscriminate violence.

Terrorism differs from ordinary crime in its political purpose and its primary objective. However, not all politically motivated violence is terrorism, nor is terrorism synonymous with guerilla war or any other kind of war.

Terrorist techniques can be used by governments or those fighting against governments: however, scholars generally use the term "terror" when discussing fear-producing tactics employed by governments and "terrorism" when referring to tactics used by those fighting against governments. The distinction is primarily semantic. Both groups may use threats, assassinations, or abductions, but government terror also may include arbitrary imprisonment, concentration camps, torture, mind-affecting techniques, and the use of drugs for political purposes. Antigovernment terrorists generally lack the infrastructure for such tactics. Government terror produces more victims than terrorism does. Terrorists tend to seek more publicity than do governments.

Although a prerequisite to empirical research, the attempt to define terrorism inevitably lent greater coherence to disparate acts of violence than did any analysis offered by the terrorists themselves, few of whom thought of assassinations, bombings, kidnappings, and airline hijackings as elements of a unified tactical repertoire, let alone the basis of a strategy. Ironically, in an effort to understand a phenomenon, researchers ran the risk of attributing to terrorists a level of strategic thinking they may not have possessed.

The term "international terrorism" refers to terrorist attacks on foreign targets or the crossing of national frontiers to carry out terrorist attacks. It was the dramatic rise in international terrorism—especially in the form of attacks on diplomats and commercial aviation in the late 1960s—that caused mounting alarm on the part of governments not directly involved in those local conflicts.

Although terrorist tactics were centuries old, contemporary terrorism, especially in its international form, emerged in the late 1960s from a unique confluence of political circumstances and technological developments. The political circumstances included the failure of the rural guerrilla movements in Latin America, which persuaded the guerrilla movements to take their armed struggles into the cities, where, through the use of dramatic actions such as kidnappings, they could be assured of attracting national and international attention. Their actions also provoked terrorist responses by governments that resorted to using "disappearances" of suspected guerrillas and their supporters, torture, and other tactics of terror.

In the Middle East, the failure of the Arab armies in the Six-Day War in 1967 caused the Palestinians to abandon dependence on Arab military power to achieve their aims and rely more heavily on the tactics of terrorism with the approval of some Arab governments. Israel retaliated with both military attacks and assassinations of suspected terrorist leaders.

The third political root of contemporary terrorism grew from widespread antigovernment demonstrations in universities in western Europe, Japan, and the United States that were provoked in large measure but not exclusively by the war in Vietnam. By no stretch of the imagination could these antigovernment protests be called acts of terrorism, but the mass marches spawned extremist fringes that were inspired by third world guerrilla movements to carry on an armed struggle even after the student movements subsided.

Technological advances were equally important. Developments in communications—radio, television, communication satellites—made possible almost instantaneous access to global audiences, which was critical for a mode of violence aimed at publicity. Modern air travel provided terrorists with worldwide mobility and a choice of targets. Modern society's dependence on technology created new vulnerabilities. Global weapons production guaranteed a supply of guns and explosives.

Once the tactics of terrorism were displayed worldwide, they provided inspiration and instruction for other groups, and terrorism became a self-perpetuating phenomenon.

The 1980s saw a new form of international terrorism: state-sponsored terrorism. Some governments began to use terrorist tactics or employ those tactics as a mode of surrogate warfare. Unlike government-directed terror, which is primarily domestic, state-sponsored terrorism is directed against foreign governments or domestic foes abroad. International diplomacy, economic sanctions, and in some cases, military actions brought about a reduction in this type of terrorism in the 1990s.

Despite great differences in political perspectives and outlook toward armed conflict, the international community gradually came to accept at least a partial definition of terrorism and prohibited certain tactics and attacks on certain targets. This approach reflected that of the academic community, focusing on the terrorist act and rejecting judgment based on the political objective or cause behind an act. Thus, by 1985, the United Nations General Assembly unanimously condemned international terrorism, including but not limited to acts covered by previous treaties against airline hijacking, sabotage of aircraft, attacks at civil airports, attacks against maritime navigation and off-shore platforms, attacks in any form against internationally protected persons (i.e., diplomats), and the taking of hostages.

By 1998, there were ten multilateral counter-terrorism agreements that covered roughly half of all incidents of international terrorism but omitted primarily bombings of targets other than airlines or diplomatic facilities. One difficulty in delineating this type of terrorist act was distinguishing between terrorist bombings and aerial bombardment, which is considered a legitimate form of war. The rules of war prohibit indiscriminate bombing, thus providing at least a theoretical distinction between war and terrorism, although even with modern precision-guided munitions, collateral civilian casualties from aerial bombing in populated areas may fastly exceed casualties caused by the deliberate, indiscriminate bombs of terrorists.

In 1998, an International Convention for the Suppression of Terrorist Bombings attempted to address this lacuna. Unable to draw a clear distinction between terrorist bombings and other types of bombings, the treaty stated that the "activities of armed forces during an armed conflict . . . and the activities undertaken by military forces by a state in the exercise of their official duties, inasmuch as they are governed by other rules of international law, are not governed by this Convention."

Terrorism is a subject matter, not a discipline. It has been approached by scholars from various academic perspectives with political scientists in the lead. Psychologists and psychiatrists have examined individual and group behavior, while jurists have formulated international legal approaches. Sociologists have not played a major role in research focusing specifically on terrorism but have addressed it in the broader context of deviance or social control.

Much research on terrorism has focused more narrowly on the topic. In part, this reflects the desire of researchers to avoid the murky, politically loaded area of underlying causes, where any discussion might be seen as condemnation or rationalization of terrorist violence. Nonetheless, there have been excellent case studies of individual groups and their tactics.

Defining terrorism in terms of the act has enabled researchers to maintain a theoretically objective approach and conduct at least some primitive quantitative analysis. Event-based analysis has enabled them to discern broad patterns and trends and chart the growth of terrorism and its diffusion around the globe. They have been able to demonstrate statistically that as terrorism has increased in volume, it has also become bloodier. Researchers were able to illustrate a clear trend toward incidents of large-scale indiscriminate violence in the 1980s and infer that terrorists tend to be more imitative than innovative in their tactics. Event-based analysis also has permitted researchers to distinguish the operational profiles of specific terrorist groups, and these profiles have been useful in identifying changes in a group's *modus operandi*.

At the same time, event-based analysis has led the analysts into some methodological traps. An exclusive focus on terrorist actions, for example, resulted in terrorists being viewed first as if they were all part of a single entity and second as if they were almost extraterrestrial. While there are connections and alliances among some terrorist groups, the only thing the terrorists of the world have in common is a propensity for violence and certain tactics. Moreover, each group is rooted in its own social, political, and cultural soil, and cross-national comparisons are difficult. This has led to the question of whether there is such a thing as a terrorist-prone society.

It is, however, dangerous to attribute the actions of a few to perceived political defects or cultural flaws of a society as a whole, and researchers' attempts to discern deeper causes or conditions that lead to high levels of terrorism in certain societies have produced meager results. Terrorism is not demonstrably a response to poverty or political oppression. The liberal democracies of western Europe have suffered high levels of terrorist violence, while totalitarian states are virtually free of terrorism. Overall, countries with perceived terrorist problems tend to be comparatively advanced politically and economically. They are more highly urbanized and have higher per capita incomes, larger middle classes, more university students, and higher rates of literacy. One may ask whether political and economic advancement simply brings a more modern form of political violence.

One obstacle to linking high levels of terrorism with environmental factors is the problem of measuring terrorism. For the most part, this has been done by counting terrorist incidents, but international terrorism was narrowly and, more important, artificially defined to include only incidents that cause international concern, a distinction that has meant very little to the terrorists. Counting *all* terrorist incidents, both local and international, is better but still inadequate. Terrorist tactics, narrowly defined, represent most of what some groups, particularly those in western Europe, do but for other groups, terrorism represents only one facet of a broader armed conflict. In civil war situations, such as that in Lebanon in the 1970s, separating incidents of terrorism from the background of violence and bloodshed was futile and meaningless. And what about the extensive unquantified political and communal violence in the rural backlands of numerous third world countries? Broad statements about terrorist-prone or violence-prone societies simply cannot be made by measuring only a thin terrorist crust of that violence, if at all. The problem, however, is not merely one of counting. Although terrorists arise from the peculiarities of local situations, they may become isolated in a tiny universe of beliefs and discourse that is alien to the surrounding society. German terrorists were German, but were they Germany? In the final analysis, one is forced to dismiss the notion of a terrorist-prone society.

If terrorism cannot be explained by environmental factors, one must look into the mind of the individual terrorist for an explanation. Are there individuals who are prone to becoming terrorists—a preterrorist personality? Encouraged by superficial similarities in the demographic profiles of terrorists—many of them have been urban middle and upper class (not economically deprived) males in their early twenties with university or at least secondary school educations—researchers searched for commmon psychological features.

Behavioral analysts painted an unappealing portrait: The composite terrorist appeared to be a person who was narcissistic, emotionally flat, easily disillusioned, incapable of enjoyment, rigid, and a true believer who was action-oriented and risk seeking. Psychiatrists could label terrorists as neurotic and possibly sociopathic, but they found that most of them were not clinically insane. Some behavioral analysts looked for deeper connections between terrorists' attitude toward parents and their attitudes toward authority. A few went further in claiming a physiological explanation for terrorism based on inner ear disorders, but these assertions were not given wide credence in the scientific community. The growing number of terrorists apprehended and imprisoned in the 1980s permitted more thorough studies, but while these studies occasionally unearthed tantalizing similarities, they also showed terrorists to be a diverse lot.

Much research on terrorism has been government-sponsored and therefore oriented toward the practical goal of understanding terrorism in order to defeat it. While social scientists looked for environmental or behavioral explanations for terrorism, other researchers attempted to identify terrorist vulnerabilities and successful countermeasures. They achieved a measure of success in several areas. Studies of the human dynamics of hostage situations led to the development of psychological tactics that increased the hostages' chances of survival and a better understanding (and therefore more effective treatment) of those who had been held hostage. In some cases, specific psychological vulnerabilities were identified and exploited. With somewhat less success, researchers also examined the effects of broader policies, such as not making concessions to terrorists holding hostages and using military retaliation. The conclusion in this area were less clear-cut.

Another area of research concerned the effects of terrorism on society. Here, researchers viewed terrorism as consisting of not only the sum of terrorist actions but also the fear and alarm produced by those actions. Public opinion polls, along with measurable decisions such as not flying and avoiding certain countries, provided the measure of effect.

Some critics who are skeptical of the entire field of terrorism analysis assert that the state and its accomplice scholars have "invented" terrorism as a political issue to further state agendas through manipulation of fear, the setting of public discourse, preemptive constructions of "good" and "evil," and the creation of deliberate distractions from more serious issues. "Terrorism," a pejorative term that is useful in condemning foes, has generated a lot of fear mongering, and the issue of terrorism has been harnessed to serve other agendas, but one would have to set aside the reality of terrorist campaigns to see terrorism solely as an invention of the hegemonic state. While such deconstructions reveal the ideological prejudices of their authors, they nonetheless have value in reminding other analysts to be aware of the lenses through which they view terrorism.

Over the years, research on terrorism has become more sophisticated, but in the end, terrorism confronts people with fundamental philosophical questions: Do ends justify means? How far does one go on behalf of a cause? What is the value of an individual human life? What obligations do governments have toward their own citizens if, for example, they are held hostage? Should governments or corporations ever bargain for human life? What limits can be imposed on individual liberties to ensure public safety? Is the use of military force, as a matter of choice, ever appropriate? Can assassination ever be justified? These are not matters of research. They are issues that have been dictated through the ages.

(SEE ALSO: *International Law; Revolutions; Social Control; Violent Crime; War*)

REFERENCES

Barnaby, Frank 1996 *Instruments of Terror*. London: Satin.

Hoffman, Bruce 1998 *Inside Terrorism*. London: Gollancz.

Kushner, Harvey W. (ed.) 1998 *The Future of Terrorism: Violence in the New Millennium*. Thousand Oaks, Calif.: Sage.

Laquer, Walter 1977 *Terrorism*. Boston: Little Brown.

Lesser, Ian O. et al. 1999 *Countering the New Terrorism*. Santa Monica: Rand Corporation.

Oliverio, Annamarie 1998 *The State of Terror*. Albany: State University of New York Press.

O'Sullivan, Noel (ed.) 1986 *Terrorism, Ideology and Revolution*. Boulder, Colo: Westview.

Schmid, Alex P., and Albert J. Jongman 1988 *Political Terrorism*. Amsterdam: North Holland.

Simon, Jeffrey D. 1994 *The Terrorist Trap: America's Experience with Terrorism*. Bloomington: Indiana University Press.

Stern, Jessica 1999 *The Ultimate Terrorists*. Cambridge, Mass.: Harvard University Press.

Thackrah, John Richard 1987 *Terrorism and Political Violence*. London: Routledge & Kegan Paul.

Wilkinson, Paul, and Alasdair M. Stewart (eds.) 1987 *Contemporary Research on Terrorism*. Aberdeen, Scotland: Aberdeen University Press.

BRIAN MICHAEL JENKINS

THEOCRACY

See Religion, Politics, and War; Religious Organizations.

TIME SERIES ANALYSIS

Longitudinal data are used commonly in sociology, and over the years sociologists have imported a wide variety of statistical procedures from other disciplines to analyze such data. Examples include survival analysis (Cox and Oakes 1984), dynamic modeling (Harvey 1990), and techniques for pooled cross-sectional and time series data (Hsiao 1986). Typically, these procedures are used to represent the causal mechanisms by which one or more outcomes are produced; a stochastic model is provided that is presumed to extract the essential means by which changes in some variables bring about changes in others (Berk 1988).

The techniques called *time series analysis* have somewhat different intellectual roots. Rather than try to represent explicit causal mechanisms, the goal in classical time series analysis is "simply" to describe some longitudinal stochastic processes in summary form. That description may be used to inform existing theory or inductively extract new theoretical notions, but classical time series analysis does not begin with a fully articulated causal model.

However, more recent developments in time series analysis and in the analysis of longitudinal data more generally have produced a growing convergence in which the descriptive power of time series analysis has been incorporated into causal modeling and the capacity to represent certain kinds of causal mechanisms has been introduced into time series analysis (see, for example, Harvey 1990). It may be fair to say that differences between time series analysis and the causal modeling of longitudinal data are now matters of degree.

CLASSICAL TIME SERIES ANALYSIS

Classical time series analysis was developed to describe variability over time for a single unit of observation (Box and Jenkins 1976, chaps. 3 and 4). The single unit could be a person, a household, a city, a business, a market, or another entity. A popular example in sociology is the crime rate over time in a particular jurisdiction (e.g., Loftin and McDowall 1982; Chamlin 1988; Kessler and Duncan 1996). Other examples include longitudinal data on public opinion, unemployment rates, and infant mortality.

Formal Foundations. The mathematical foundations of classical time series analysis are found in difference equations. An equation "relating the values of a function y and one or more of its differences Δy, $\Delta^2 y$ . . . for each x-value of some set of numbers S (for which each of these functions is defined) is called a difference equation over the set S" ($\Delta y = y_t - y_{t-1}$, $\Delta^2 = \Delta(y_t - y_{t-1}) = y_t - 2y_{t-1} - y_{t-2}$, and so on) (Goldberg 1958, p. 50). The x-values specify the numbers for which the relationship holds (i.e., the domain). That is, the relationships may be true for only some values of x. In practice, the x-values are taken to be a set of successive integers that in effect indicate *when* a measure is taken. Then, requiring that all difference operations Δ be taken with an interval equal to 1 (Goldberg 1958, p. 52), one gets the following kinds of results (with t replacing x): $\Delta^2 y_t + k y_t = 2k + 7$, which can be rewritten $y_t - 2y_{t-1} + (1-k)y_{t-2} = 2k + 7$.

Difference equations are deterministic. In practice, the social world is taken to be stochastic. Therefore, to use difference equations in time series analysis, a disturbance term is added, much as is done in conventional regression models.

ARIMA Models. Getting from stochastic difference equations to time series analysis requires that an observed time series be conceptualized as a product of an underlying substantive process. In particular, an observed time series is conceptualized as a "realization" of an underlying process that is assumed to be reasonably well described by an unknown stochastic difference equation (Chatfield 1996, pp. 27–28). In other words, the realization is treated as if it were a simple random sample from the distribution of all possible realizations the underlying process might produce. This is a weighty *substantive* assumption that cannot be made casually or as a matter of convenience. For example, if the time series is the number of lynchings by year in a southern state between 1880 and 1930, how much sense does it make to talk about observed data as a representative realization of an underlying historical process that could have produced a very large number of such realizations? Many time series are alternatively conceptualized as a population; what one sees is all there is (e.g., Freedman and Lane 1983). Then the relevance of time series analysis becomes unclear, although many of the descriptive tools can be salvaged.

If one can live with the underlying world assumed, the statistical tools time series analysis provides can be used to make inferences about which stochastic difference equation is most consistent with the data and what the values of the coefficients are likely to be. This is, of course, not much different from what is done in conventional regression analysis.

For the tools to work properly, however, one must at least assume "weak stationarity." Drawing from Gottman's didactic discussion (1981, pp. 60–66), imagine that a very large number of realizations were actually observed and then displayed in a large two-way table with one time period in each column and one realization in each row. Weak stationarity requires that if one computed the mean for each time period (i.e., for each column), those means would be effectively the same (and identical asymptotically). Similarly, if one computed the variance for each time period (i.e., by column), those variances would be effectively the same (and identical asymptotically). That is, the process is characterized in part by a finite mean and variance that do not change over time.

Weak stationarity also requires that the covariance of the process between periods be independent of time as well. That is, for any given lag in time (e.g., one period, two periods, or three periods), if one computed all possible covariances between columns in the table, those covariances would be effectively the same (and identical asymptotically). For example, at a lag of 2, one would compute covariances between column 1 and column 3, column 2 and column 4, column 3 and column 5, and so on. Those covariances would all be effectively the same. In summary, weak stationarity requires that the variance-covariance matrix across realizations be invariant with respect to the displacement of time. Strong stationarity implies that the joint distribution (more generally) is invariant with respect to the displacement of time. When each time period's observations are normally distributed, weak and strong stationarity are the same. In either case, history is effectively assumed to repeat itself.

Many statistical models that are consistent with weak stationarity have been used to analyze time series data. Probably the most widely applied (and the model on which this article will focus) is associated with the work of Box and Jenkins (1976). Their most basic ARIMA (autoregressive-integrated moving-average) model has three parts: (1) an autoregressive component, (2) a moving average component, and (3) a differencing component.

Consider first the autoregressive component and y_t as the variable of interest. An autoregressive component of order p can be written as $y_t - \Phi_1 y_{t-1} - \cdots - \Phi_p y_{t-p}$.

Alternatively, the autoregressive component of order p (AR[p]) can be written in the form $\Phi(B) y_t$, where B is the backward shift operator—that is, $(B)y_t = y_{t-1}$, $(B^2)y_t = y_{t-2}$ and so on—and $\phi(B) =$ $1 - \phi_1 B - \cdots - \phi_p B^p$. For example, an autoregressive model of order 2 is $y_t - \phi_1 y_{t-1} - \phi_2 y_{t-2}$.

A moving-average component of order q, in contrast, can be written as $\varepsilon_t - \theta_1 \varepsilon_{t-1} - \cdots - \theta_q \varepsilon_{t-q}$. The variable ε_t is taken to be "white noise," sometimes called the "innovations process," which is much like the disturbance term in regression models. It is assumed that ε_t is not correlated with itself and has a mean (expected value) of zero and a constant variance. It sometimes is assumed to be Gaussian as well.

The moving-average component of order q (MA[q]) also can be written in the form $\Theta(B)\varepsilon_t$, where B is a backward shift operator and $\Theta(B) = 1 - \Theta_1 B - \cdots - \Theta_q B^q$. For example, a moving-average model of order 2 is $\varepsilon_t - \Theta_1 \varepsilon_{t-1} - \Theta_2 \varepsilon_{t-2}$.

Finally, the differencing component can be written as $\Delta^d y_t$, where the d is the number differences taken (or the degree of differencing). Differencing (see "Formal Foundations," above) is a method to remove nonstationarity in a time series mean so that weak stationarity is achieved. It is common to see ARIMA models written in general form as $\Theta(B)\Delta^d y_t = \Theta(B)\varepsilon_t$.

A seasonal set of components also can be included. The set is structured in exactly the same way but uses a seasonal time reference. That is, instead of time intervals of one time period, seasonal models use time intervals such as quarters. The seasonal component usually is included multiplicatively (Box and Jenkins 1976, chap. 9; Granger and Newbold 1986, pp. 101–114; Chatfield 1996 pp. 60–61), but a discussion here is precluded by space limitations.

For many sets of longitudinal data, nonstationarity is not merely a nuisance to be removed but a finding to be highlighted. The fact that time series analysis requires stationarity does not mean that nonstationary processes are sociologically uninteresting, and it will be shown shortly that time series procedures can be combined with techniques such multiple regression when nonstationarity is an important part of the story.

ARIMA Models in Practice. In practice, one rarely knows which ARIMA model is appropriate for the data. That is, one does not know what orders the autoregressive and moving-average components should be or what degree of differencing is required to achieve stationarity. The values of the coefficients for these models typically are unknown as well. At least three diagnostic procedures are commonly used: time series plots, the autocorrelation function, and the partial autocorrelation function.

A time series plot is simply a graph of the variable to be analyzed arrayed over time. It is always important to study time series plots carefully to get an initial sense of the data: time trends, cyclical patterns, dramatic irregularities, and outliers.

The autocorrelation function and the partial autocorrelation function of the time series are used to help specify which ARIMA model should be applied to the data (Chatfield 1996, chap. 4). The rules of thumb typically employed will be summarized after a brief illustration.

Figure 1 shows a time series plot of the simulated unemployment rate for a small city. The vertical axis is the unemployment rate, and the horizontal axis is time in quarters. There appear to be rather dramatic cycles in the data, but on closer inspection, they do not fit neatly into any simple story. For example, the cycles are not two or four periods in length (which would correspond to six-month or twelve-month cycles).

Figure 2 shows a plot of the autocorrelation function (ACF) of the simulated data with horizontal bands for the 95 percent confidence interval. Basically, the autocorrelation function produces a series of serial Pearson correlations for the given time series at different lags: 0, 1, 2, 3, and so on (Box and Jenkins 1976, pp. 23–36). If the series is stationary with respect to the mean, the autocorrelations should decline rapidly. If they do not, one may difference the series one or more times until the autocorrelations do decline rapidly.

For some kinds of mean nonstationarity, differencing will not solve the problem (e.g., if the nonstationarity has an exponential form). It is also important to note that mean nonstationarity may be seen in the data as differences in level for different parts of the time series, differences in slope for different parts of the data, or even some other pattern.

In Figure 2, the autocorrelation for lag 0 is 1.0, as it should be (correlating something with itself). Thus, there are three spikes outside of the 95 percent confidence interval at lags 1, 2, and 3. Clearly, the correlations decline gradually but rather rapidly so that one may reasonably conclude that the series is already mean stationary. The gradual decline also usually is taken as a sign autoregressive processes are operating, perhaps in combination with moving-average processes and perhaps not. There also seems to be a cyclical pattern, that is consistent with the patterns in Figure 1 and usually is taken as a sign that the autoregressive process has an order of more than 1.

Figure 3 shows the partial autocorrelation function. The partial autocorrelation is similar to the usual partial correlation, except that what is being held constant is values of the times series at lags shorter than the lag of interest. For example, the partial autocorrelation at a lag of 4 holds constant the time series values at lags of 1, 2, and 3.

From Figure 3, it is clear that there are large spikes at lags of 1 and 2. This usually is taken to mean that the p for the autoregressive component is equal to 2. That is, an AR[2] component is necessary. In addition, the abrupt decline (rather than a rapid but gradual decline) after a lag of 2 (in this case) usually is interpreted as a sign that there is no moving-average component.

The parameters for an AR[2] model were estimated using maximum likelihood procedures. The first AR parameter estimate was 0.33, and the second was estimate -0.35. Both had t-values well in excess of conventional levels. These results are consistent with the cyclical patterns seen in Figure 1; a positive value for the first AR parameter and a negative value for the second produced the apparent cyclical patterns.

How well does the model fit? Figures 4 and 5 show, respectively, the autocorrelation function and the partial autocorrelation function for the residuals of the original time series (much like

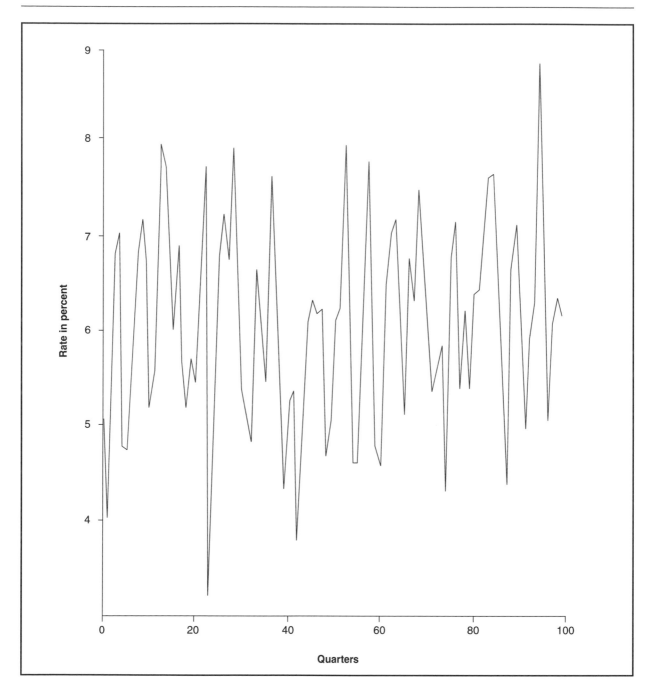

Figure 1. Unemployment Rate by Quarter

residuals in conventional regression analysis). There are no spikes outside the 95 percent confidence interval, indicating that the residuals are probably white noise. That is, the temporal dependence in the data has been removed. One therefore can conclude that the data are consistent with an underlying autoregressive process of order 2, with coefficients of 0.33 and -0.35. The relevance of this information will be addressed shortly.

To summarize, the diagnostics have suggested that this ARIMA model need not include any differences or a moving-average component but should include an autoregressive component of

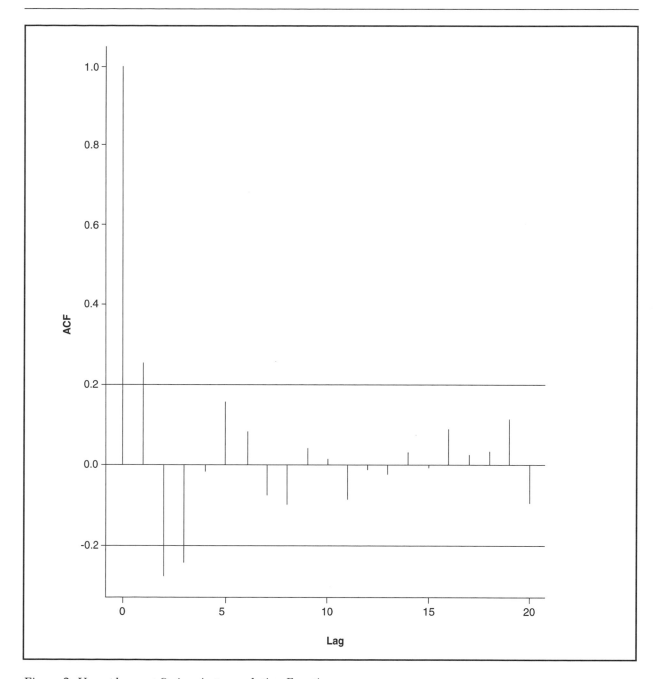

Figure 2. Unemployment Series: Autocorrelation Function

order 2. More generally, the following diagnostic rules of thumb usually are employed, often in the order shown.

1. If the autocorrelation function does not decline rather rapidly, difference the series one or more times (perhaps up to three) until it does.

2. If either before or after differencing the autocorrelation function declines very abruptly, a moving-average component probably is needed. The lag of the last large spike outside the confidence interval provides a good guess for the value of q. If the autocorrelation function declines rap-

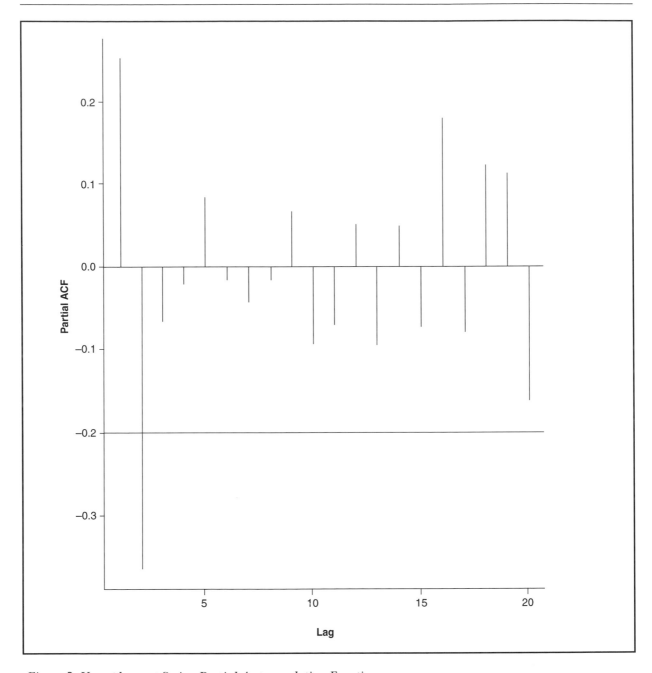

Figure 3. Unemployment Series: Partial Autocorrelation Function

idly but gradually, an autoregressive component probably is needed.

3. If the partial autocorrelation function declines very abruptly, an autoregressive component probably is needed. The lag of the last large spike outside the confidence interval provides a good guess for the value of p. If the partial autocorrelation function declines rapidly but gradually, a moving-average component probably is needed.

4. Estimate the model's coefficients and compute the residuals of the model. Use the rules above to examine the residuals. If there are no systematic patterns in the residuals, conclude that the model

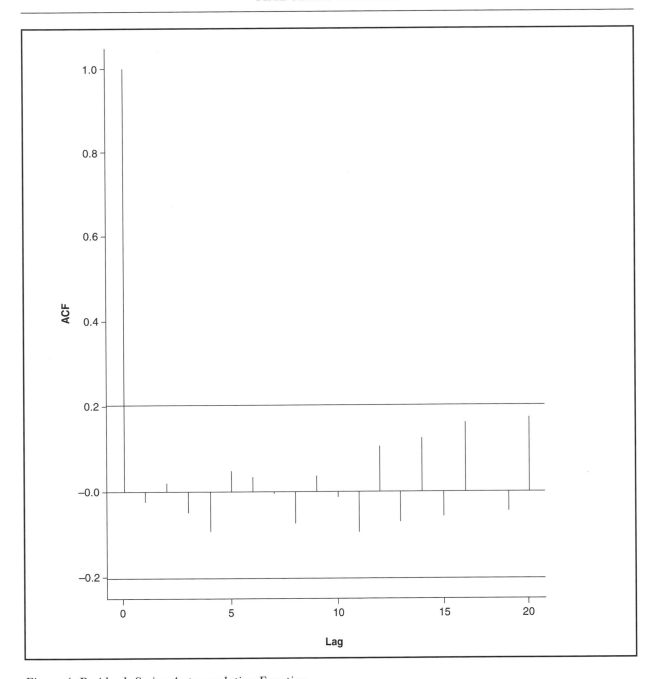

Figure 4. Residuals Series: Autocorrelation Function

is consistent with the data. If there are systematic patterns in the residuals, respecify the model and try again. Repeat until the residuals are consistent with a white noise process (i.e., no temporal dependence).

Several additional diagnostic procedures are available, but because of space limitations, they cannot be discussed here. For an elementary discussion, see Gottman (1981), and for a more advanced discussion, see Granger and Newbold (1986).

It should be clear that the diagnostic process is heavily dependent on a number of judgment calls about which researchers could well disagree. Fortunately, such disagreements rarely matter. First, the disagreements may revolve around differences

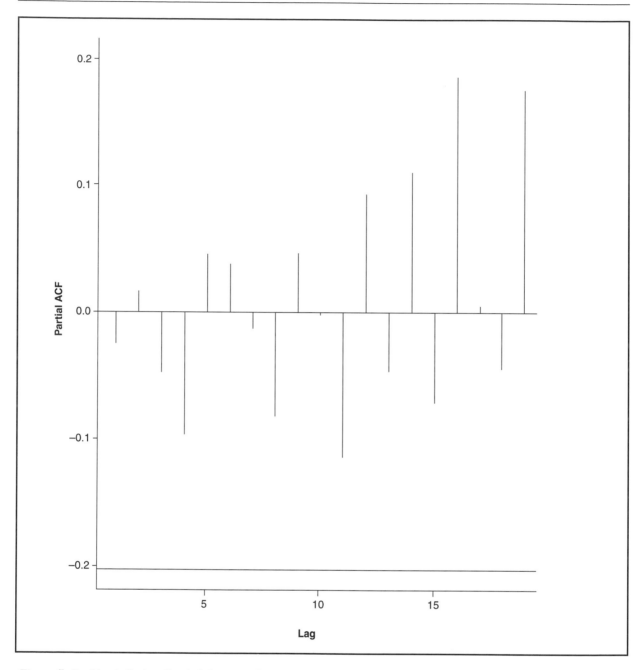

Figure 5. Residuals Series: Partial Autocorrelation Functions

between models without any substantive import. There may be, for instance, no substantive consequences from reporting an MA[2] compared with an MA[3]. Second, ARIMA models often are used primarily to remove "nuisance" patterns in time series data (discussed below), in which case the particular model used is unimportant; it is the result that matters. Finally and more technically, if certain assumptions are met, it is often possible to represent a low-order moving-average model as a high-order autoregressive model and a low-order autoregressive model as a high-order moving-average model. Then model specification depends solely on the criteria of parsimony. That is, models with a smaller number of parameters are preferred to models with a larger number of parameters. However, this is an aesthetic yardstick that may have nothing to with the substantive story of interest.

USES OF ARIMA MODELS IN SOCIOLOGY

It should be clear that ARIMA models are not especially rich from a substantive point of view. They are essentially univariate descriptive devices that do not lend themselves readily to sociological problems. However, ARIMA models rarely are used merely as descriptive devices (see, however, Gottman 1981). In other social science disciplines, especially economics, ARIMA models often are used for forecasting (Granger and Newbold 1986). Klepinger and Weiss (1985) provide a rare sociological example.

More relevant for sociology is the fact that ARIMA models sometimes are used to remove "nuisance" temporal dependence that may be obstructing the proper study of "important" temporal dependence. In the simplest case, ARIMA models can be appended to regression models to adjust for serially correlated residuals (Judge et al. 1985, chap. 8). In other words, the regression model captures the nonstationary substantive story of interest, and the time series model is used to "mop up." Probably more interesting is the extension of ARIMA models to include one or more binary explanatory variables or one or more additional time series. Nonstationarity is now built into the time series model rather than differenced away.

Intervention Analysis. When the goal is to explore how a time series changes after the occurrence of a discrete event, the research design is called an interrupted time series (Cook and Campbell 1979). The relevant statistical procedures are called "intervention analysis" (Box and Tiao 1975). Basically, one adds a discrete "transfer function" to the ARIMA model to capture how the discrete event (or events) affects the time series. Transfer functions take the general form shown in equation (1):

$$(1 - \delta_1 B - \cdots - \delta_i B^r)y_t = (\omega_0 - \omega_1 B - \cdots - \omega_s B^s)x_{t-b}.$$

If both sides of equation (1) are divided by the left-hand side polynomial, the ratio of the two polynomials in B on the right-hand side is called a transfer function. In the form shown in equation (1), r is the order of the polynomial for the "dependent variable" (y_t), s is the order of the polyno-

mial for the discrete "independent variable" (x_t), and b is the lag between when the independent "switches" from 0 to 1 and when its impact is observed. For example, if r equals 1, s equals 0, and b equals 0, the transfer function becomes $\omega_0 / 1 - \delta_1$. Transfer functions can represent a large number of effects, depending on the orders of the two polynomials and on whether the discrete event is coded as an impulse or a step. (In the impulse form, the independent variable is coded over time as $0,0, \ldots 0,1,0,0, \ldots ,0$. In the step form, the independent variable is coded over time as $0,0, \ldots 1,1 \ldots 1$. The zeros represent the absence of the intervention, while the ones represent the presence of the intervention. That is, there is a switch from 0 to 1 when the intervention is turned on and a switch from 1 to 0 when the intervention is turned off.) A selection of effects represented by transfer functions is shown in Figure 6.

In practice, one may proceed by using the time series data before the intervention to determine the model specification for the ARIMA component, much as was discussed above. The specification for the transfer function in the discrete case is more ad hoc. Theory certainly helps, but one approach is to regress the time series on the binary intervention variable at a moderate number of lags (e.g., simultaneously for lags of 0 periods to 10 periods). The regression coefficients associated with each of the lagged values of the intervention will roughly trace out the shape of the time path of the response. From this, a very small number of plausible transfer functions can be selected for testing.

In a sociological example, Loftin et al. (1983) estimated the impact of Michigan's Felony Firearm Statute on violent crime. The law imposed a two-year mandatory add-on sentence for defendants convicted of possession of a firearm during the commission of a felony. Several different crime time series (e.g., the number of homicides per month) were explored under the hypothesis that the crime rates for offenses involving guns would drop after the law was implemented. ARIMA models were employed, coupled with a variety of transfer functions. Overall, the intervention apparently had no impact.

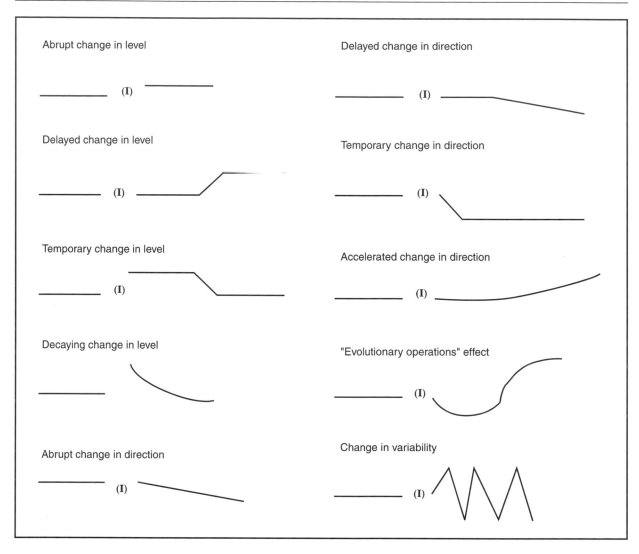

Figure 6. A Sampler of Intervention Effects. I = Intervention

Multiple Time Series. ARIMA models also may be extended to more than one time series (Chatfield 1996, Chap. 10) Just as the goal for the univariate case was to find a model that transformed the single time series into white noise, the goal for the multivariate case is to find a model that will transform a *vector* of time series into a white noise vector. In effect, each series is regressed simultaneously not only on lagged functions of itself and the disturbance term but on functions of all other time series and their disturbance terms. In practice, this sometimes reduces to building transfer function models that include a single response time series and several input time series, much as in multiple regression. For exam-

ple, Berk et al. (1980) explored how water consumption varied over time with the marginal price of water, weather, and a number of water conservation programs.

The mathematical generalization from the univariate case is rather straightforward. The generalization of model specification techniques and estimation procedures is not. Moreover, multivariate time series models have not made significant inroads into sociological work and therefore are beyond the scope of this chapter. Interested readers should consult Chatfield (1996) for an introduction or Granger and Newbold's (1986) for a more advanced treatment.

CONCLUSIONS

Time series analysis is an active enterprise in economics, statistics, and operations research. Examples of technical developments and applications can be found routinely in a large number of journals (e.g., *Journal of the American Statistical Association, Journal of Business and Economic Statistics, Journal of Forecasting*). However, time series analysis has not been especially visible in sociology. Part of the explanation is the relative scarcity of true time series for sociological variables collected over a sufficiently long period. Another part is that time series analysis is unabashedly inductive, often making little use of substantive theory; time series analysis may look to some a lot like "mindless empiricism." However, in many sociological fields, true time series data are becoming increasingly available. Under the banner of "data analysis" and "exploratory research," induction is becoming more legitimate. Time series analysis may well have a future in sociology.

(SEE ALSO: *Longitudinal Research; Statistical Methods*)

REFERENCES

Berk R. A. 1988 "Causal Inference for Sociological Data." In N. Smelser, ed., *The Handbook of Sociology*. Newbury Park, Calif.: Sage.

———, T. F. Cooley, C. J. LaCivita, S. Parker, K. Sredl, and M. Brewer 1980 "Reducing Consumption in Periods of Acute Scarcity: The Case of Water." *Social Science Research* 9:99–120.

Box, G. E. P., and G. M. Jenkins 1976 *Time Series Analysis: Forecasting and Control*. San Francisco: Holden-Day.

———, and G. C. Tiao 1975 "Intervention Analysis with Applications to Economic and Environmental Problems." *Journal of the American Statistical Association* 70:70–79.

Chamlin, Mitchel B. 1988 "Crime and Arrests: An Autoregressive Integrated Moving Average (ARIMA) Approach." *Journal of Quantitative Criminology* 4(3):247–258.

Chatfield, C. 1996 *The Analysis of Time Series: An Introduction*, 5th ed. New York: Chapman and Hall.

Cook, T. D., and D. T. Campbell 1979 *Quasiexperimentation*. Chicago: Rand McNally.

Cox, D. R., and D. Oakes 1984 *Analysis of Survival Data*: London: Chapman and Hall.

Freedman, D. A., and David Lane 1983 "Significance Testing in a Nonstochastic Setting." In P. J. Bickel, K. A. Doksum, and J. L. Hodges, Jr., eds., *A Festschrift for Erich L. Lehman*. Belmont, Calif.: Wadsworth International Group.

Goldberg, Samuel 1958 *Introduction to Difference Equations*. New York: Wiley.

Gottman, J. M. 1981 *Time-Series Analysis*. Cambridge, UK: Cambridge University Press.

Granger, C. W. J., and P. Newbold 1986 *Forecasting Economic Time Series*. Orlando, Fla.: Academic Press.

Harvey, A. C. 1990 *The Econometric Analysis of Time Series*, 2nd ed. London: Harvester Wheatshear.

Hsiao, Cheng 1986 *Analysis of Panel Data*. Cambridge, UK: Cambridge University Press.

Judge, D. G., W. E. Griffiths, R. C. Hill, H. Lutkepohl, and T.-C. Lee 1985 *The Theory and Practice of Econometrics*. New York: Wiley.

Kessler, D. A., and S. Duncan 1966 "The Impact of Community Policing in Four Houston Neighborhoods." *Evaluation Review* 6(20):627–669.

Klepinger, J. D. H., and J. G. Weis 1985 "Projecting Crime Rates: An Age, Period, and Cohort Model Using ARIMA Techniques." *Journal of Quantitative Criminology* 1:387–416.

Loftin, C., M. Heumann, and D. McDowall 1983 "Mandatory Sentencing and Firearms Violence: Evaluating an Alternative to Gun Control." *Law and Society Review* 17(2):287–318.

———, and D. McDowall 1982 "The Police, Crime, and Economic Theory." *American Sociological Review* 47:393–401.

RICHARD A. BERK

TIME USE RESEARCH

Time provides the organizational key to action at the level of individuals, groups, and institutions. It also defines a normative framework that regulates interpersonal relationships and allows synchronized operations in different parts of society. In the concept of time, structural as well as symbolic facets assume significance. In fact, as it is conceived in sociological theory, time is a means of social coordination as well as a dimension that assigns value to action schemes in a system assuring social order (Pronovost 1989; Sue 1994).

The empirical study of the temporal organization of human action reveals the functional characteristics of social roles and the societal division of social tasks. For instance, indicators of inequality and social exclusion can be derived and compared by referring to estimates of the amount of time involved in gender-related activities such as market work and housework. The time use of populations or subpopulations is studied mostly by means of diary procedures that assess individual "time budgets:" the sequence, timing, and duration of activities performed by individuals over a specified period. It is misleading to think that the aim of time budget research is time as either a physical or a subjectively perceived entity. As stressed by the major postwar promotor of this area of study, the Hungarian sociologist Szalai, the object of studying time is to discover the use people make of their time, or "the arrangement and the fit of people's activities in a temporal frame of reference, the temporal order and structure of everyday life" (1984, p. 20).

From this point of view, time is a special kind of resource. As with material goods and more symbolic commodities such as money, people have a "fund" of time at their disposition and make decisions on how to use, "spend," or "invest" it. However, time is a far more democratic resource in that every person deals with the same basic "stock" of it, such as the twenty hours in a day and the seven days in a week. This means that a shared reference of differential time allocation patterns can facilitate coherent comparisons and meaningful interpretations. It is this particular aspect that has made time use an important topic in quantitative social research. Both academic scholars and national statistical offices have shown a growing interest in time-budget data because those data permit policy-oriented microanalyses of changing lifestyles at the individual or household level as well as macroanalyses of social and economic inequalities in the context of cross-national comparative studies.

In contrast to the physical notion that attributes equivalent temporal resources to all people and therefore facilitates systematic accounts, from a subjective point of view, the length of a day is not always the same. Some people seem to have more time than others. This phenomenon reveals the sociopsychological dimension of time in which concepts such as stress and alienation are relevant. In a world where the quality of life depends largely on what one gets out of the time at one's disposal, coping with time and compressing multiple activities into the same time slot have become important skills. Furthermore, it is a universal observation that boring periods during a day, week, or year can seem long, whereas other, quantitatively equivalent but exciting periods of time are perceived as a passing moment. However, in studying social time, time-budget research adopts an activity-oriented approach and focuses only indirectly on subjective experiences. In substance, this means that observable patterns of behavior are selected as primary evidence and, in methodological terms, standard time units are chosen for measurement purposes.

THE TIME USE RESEARCH TRADITION

Although social time is not intrinsically quantitative, the use of standard time units for the purposes of analyzing the structure of everyday life seems legitimate, since the transfer of human work from agriculture to artificially controlled industrial environments and the subsequent changes in civilization have largely transformed natural time (tied to seasonal conditions and biological needs) into conventional, rational time (Elias 1988). As a corollary to this process, social life has become dominated by timekeeping. This chronometric function is characterized by a universally accepted "time" language that coordinates rhythms of action in the public and private spheres (Zerubavel 1982). Therefore, time budgets, which are concerned with different kinds of schedules for structuring the flow of events, are a key to the systematic investigation of the complex interdependencies and trade-offs of modern life.

The historical origins of the study of social time lie in both sociological theory and empirical research. With regard to theory, the early French school of sociology was interested in this phenomenon from the point of view of the historical and anthropological dimensions of social change (Pronovost 1989). Around the turn of the century, Hubert, Mauss, Durkheim, and Halbwachs conceived of social time as an intrinsically qualitative phenomenon that was relevant for the characterization of the sacred-profane symbolic dichotomy in the evolution of the collective consciousness or the formation of a collective memory. Their focus was a macro one, and their main interest was to explain long-term cultural change.

In contrast, Mead in the early 1930s chose an individualistic, micro-oriented approach that offered a philosophical rationale for studying time in the present. The present was conceived of as the context for the emergence and assimilation of various social time systems in interplay with the definition of different notions of "the self." Thus, the French and American approaches represent polar opposites, with one conceiving time within the matrix of historical societal relationships, and the other from the perspective of mutable configurations of symbolic interactions in small groups. The somewhat later work of Sorokin reflects both approaches. He presents the functionalist idea that the plurality of individual time schemes requires extensive synchronization to achieve social cohesion and that time expresses the sociocultural "pulsation" of a society.

In the 1960s, Gurvitch gave new impetus to the study of time after a considerable period of neglect. He was the first to conceive of time as an important source of contradictions and potential conflict. In particular, he stressed the hierarchically diversified aspects of the phenomenon (e.g., social time, time in organizations, time in special social groups) and raised the issues of power and legitimacy. More recently, Merton introduced the concept of "socially expected durations" that highlight the normative aspects of the embeddedness of time in social structures. In contrast, Elias stressed the role of time as a symbolic means of social regulation but also of increasingly unpredictable individual self-expression.

The historical origins of empirical investigations of social time are even older, going back to the middle of the nineteenth century. Three lines of research are significant: the research conducted by Friedrich Engels on the English working class, where the temporal organization of daily life was the issue; the studies undertaken by Frédéric LePlay, in which the economic "family-budgets" of workers in several European countries were assessed (similar to what "time budgets" do today); and the experimental work on time and motion performed by Frederick Taylor, based on carefully collected chronometric data. Taylor's aim was to introduce

strategies of scientific time management in industry. In regard to the adoption of time-budget methodologies, there were Bevans's pioneering studies (1913) of how workers spent their spare time and early Soviet inquiries by Strumilin into time use as the basis for rational social programming. Lundberg and Komarovsky's research into the organization of time within the realm of community research was conducted along the lines of American cultural anthropology.

Of more enduring interest, however, were two studies published in the 1930s. Jahoda et al.'s *Marienthal: The Sociography of an Unemployed Community* (1933) was a substantial contribution to the study of time use. It explores changes in the meaning of time for German working-class families when work, as a dominant regulating and legitimizing criterion for time use, has disappeared. Male workers tended to become severely disoriented and alienated after losing their work-based prestige, whereas their wives were successful in mastering that situation because they had much more positive attitudes based on more complex sources of social recognition. This research also shows how important it is to be aware that similar circumstances can assume diverse meanings for different groups.

The other study, whose importance lies in its methodological ideas, is Sorokin and Berger's *Time-Budgets and Human Behavior* (1939). Here the aim was to explore meaningful criteria for decision making conducive to different time structures. Information on motivations and the kinds of experiences associated with certain practices and future projects was collected to acquire a deeper understanding of how people deal with their time. Even more important, this research raised the crucial epistemological question of how to divide essentially continuous strings of behavior into activity segments that, beyond commonsense classifications, can be grouped into homogeneous and mutually exclusive categories (Kurtz 1984). The difficulty was that some activities that from an external viewpoint seemed identical could assume unequal functions in the eyes of those concerned, or conversely, that substantially different activities could assume similar functions. This means that any classification of activities presupposes an interpretive act. With this fundamental problem in mind, these authors were forced to approach earlier and purely descriptive assessments of time allocation with skepticism and spell out the methodological issues in their research.

After World War II, research took different directions in accordance with divergent political ideologies. The assessment of living conditions, which involved obtaining background data for economic planning and monitoring centrally initiated social change, continued to be of pivotal importance in research in eastern Europe's communist countries. Prudensky's time-budget studies in the Soviet Union in the 1960s not only followed the direction of Strumilin's work but also reflected these ideological concerns. The need to broaden data gathering to obtain effective guidance for public policy at the national level led Hungary's statistical office to begin the first microcensus research in this field.

In capitalist societies, time use research was concerned principally with mass media and leisure culture. Pioneering time use studies of audiences were undertaken by the BBC as well as NHK, the Japanese radio and television system, using large-scale survey techniques. From 1960 onward, NHK conducted regular five-year follow-up rounds of research to obtain time series statistics that showed long-term longitudinal development. This was a useful strategy because it produced an interesting account of how, in terms of time use, traditional ways of life are supplanted by innovative, primarily television-centered styles.

This was the situation in 1963, when the idea of conducting a Multinational Comparative Time Budget Research Project emerged. This was an ambitious sociological initiative in light of the organizational and data-processing difficulties of those years. Launched by a group of scholars directed by Szalai, sponsored by UNESCO's International Social Science Council, and coordinated by the Vienna Centre, this project attempted to obtain an interculturally valid body of knowledge that would shed light on regularities or variations in the functioning of human societies with regard to time use. This information was to be derived from a database of twelve different countries by using methodological instruments that assured a high level of analytic precision (Szalai 1977). In organizing the initiative, the basic concern was to avoid the emergence of a single central vantage point regarding the collection, elaboration, and interpretation of information. Therefore, research sites had considerable autonomy in studying the uniform data sets collected by means of strictly standardized survey instruments from probability samples of urban populations in the twelve countries under investigation.

From a positivist point of view, the focus on chronometric evidence and on an array of "hard" time use indicators enhanced the scientific character of the study and facilitated the collaboration of teams from such culturally and sociopolitically different environments as the United States and the Soviet Union. Of course, collaboration entailed the acceptance of common working hypotheses such as the expected influence of the major independent variables of industrialization and urbanization on the modalities of the division of market work and nonmarket work in households. By contrast, time for leisure was thought to be correlated with superior levels of modernization and democratization. These hypotheses clearly reflected the research traditions of the day, and so to connect the ideologically distant worlds of the 1960s, it was necessary to choose highly conventionalized and neutral time indicators as empirical evidence.

The Twelve Country Project, characterized by a strong belief in the "scientific *and* social import of cross-national comparative research" (Szalai 1977), did not go without criticism. Some thought that it was most important for cross-national research to contribute findings on general theoretical problems (Przeworski and Teune 1970). However the promoters were convinced that the discovery of the empirical peculiarities of cultural settings was at least as important as the verification of a priori hypotheses on common characteristics and trends. That the pragmatic point of view prevailed meant that the problem of a lack of reliable, relevant, and usable data had to be overcome.

In retrospect, it seems that this project did not contribute much to general theory, but it did produce an elaborate methodology whose essential lines are applied to basic and official survey research in many countries today. In fact, as Szalai hoped, the homogenization of time-budget methods now permits the drawing of "maps" of collective daily activity schemes at different levels of definition that have proved to be useful diagnostic elements for many policymakers and grassroots organizations. When economic indicators are insufficient, statistical information regarding the use of time can open up new policy perspectives and guide substantial change, especially when gaps in the quality of life manifest themselves and corrective action is needed to improve the conditions of disadvantaged social groups.

METHODOLOGICAL ASPECTS OF TIME-BUDGET RESEARCH

Since the work of Szalai, the methodology of time use research has been further refined. Under the auspices of the International Association of Time Use Research, in particular under the guidance of Harvey (1984, 1993), who has repeatedly codified the best practices, statistical bodies have reached a consensus on the format of official survey research.

The task of discovering the temporal order and structure of everyday life by means of time-budget methods involves fax more complex activities than gathering simple answers to questions of who does what, when, where, and with whom. In the design of a time-budget study, methodological issues such as the scope and scale of the research, the population from which the sample is to be drawn, the format of the data-gathering instruments, the classification and coding of activities, the choice of basic indicators, and the validity and reliability of the data must be resolved.

Defining the scope of a study also means fixing its scale. In fact, a time use survey may deal with a special group of persons, such as working women or teenagers, or with comprehensive national populations, perhaps excluding preschoolers. Or it may focus on a daily activity such as housework and child care or leisure. Alternatively, it may attribute equal weight to all everyday pursuits. Finally, the study may be aimed at discovering how the time of a special kind of day is spent, may take into account the rhythm of the week by distinguishing workdays from Sundays, or may be interested in longer periods such as the year with its seasonal differences and, in the extreme case, the life cycle (which of course would have to be studied on the basis of long-term recollections). Theo-

retically grounded sociological research is, for economic reasons, more likely to have circumscribed objectives, whereas national statistical offices have all-encompassing multipurpose datasets available. However, in both cases, the predominant tendency is to focus on the twenty-four hours of one or more single days in the life of the respondent. When these days are distributed over the week, month, or year, the average profiles of the period can be synthetically reconstructed. Such profiles most often refer to uninterrupted sequences of nonoverlapping main or "primary" activities. When there is interest in "secondary" activities or, more precisely, in contemporaneous activity episodes, the respondent usually is asked to designate the elements that represent the principal flow, which typically covers the 1,440-minute arc of the day. In fact, leaving secondary activity out of focus furnishes an unduly simplified picture of what is going on, since it ignores efficiency strategies that enable people who are short of time to deal simultaneously with multiple jobs. This frequently criticized weakness is compensated for by the heuristically valid fact that strict 24-hour accounts produce agile descriptive models. With such models, whatever time is saved on one kind of activity is strictly accredited, using zero-sum logic, to one or more other activities. Therefore "time set free" and the equivalent "time gained" concept furnish concise indicators of social change. Tracing the balance of the two magnitudes gives a dynamic slant to the analysis of time use and sheds light on the spectrum of strategic options.

Depending on the scope of the study, populations and samples are variously defined. From this point of view, the most significant difference between time use studies regards the choice of the sampling unit, which may be the individual or the household. In earlier studies, individual time use was of primary concern, and so estimates were obtained by classifying persons by their sociodemographic characteristics. More recent research, however, has looked more into how different types of families, as molecular units, manage time allocation with regard to income generation as well as work in the sphere of home and child care. Statistical offices now use very large probability samples of households to be able to generate cross-tabulated data on specific territorial areas and particular social groups. In Italy, for instance, the last national time use survey, conducted by Istat in 1988 and 1989, consisted of more than 38,000 persons belonging to almost 14,000 households. A survey conducted in Germany in 1991 and 1992 by the Statistisches Bundesamt included 7,200 households. One of the most difficult problems in time-budget research is the sample units' frequent refusal to respond once they see how much time is involved. In fact, nonresponse rates tend to be high and in some official surveys amount to almost 30 percent. This problem is easier to handle in smaller-scale studies, which often use quota sampling.

Data gathering in time use research begins with an interview (Scheuch 1972) to record the characteristics of the respondent and his or her family, contractual work arrangements, normal labor supply, and housing or other assets and to inquire into irregularities in the day designated for collecting the time-budget information. The time budget itself is registered in a protocol, a diary, or modular display where the beginning and the end of each activity can be indicated together with other information. The resulting datasets show for each day and respondent (1) the number of different activities performed and the frequency of each activity in separate episodes (for instance, the series of daily meals or the periods passed in front of the television set) and (2) the timing, duration, and sequence of activities or activity episodes. Most often, the interviewees register activities by using their own words. A grid of minimal time intervals is given (the "fixed interval" solution), where the task is to fill each interval with an activity, or the interviewee is asked to specify the exact time points of his or her schedule (the "open interval" solution). To obtain the essential elements of the interviewee's context, there is usually room to indicate contemporaneous activities (for instance, reading while using public transport or listening to music while doing homework); participation in activities with family members, neighbors, friends, and colleagues; and where the activity takes place. The least expensive method of data collection is the condensed telephone interview, which explores time use on the previous day. For field studies, there are other procedures, such as single face-to-face interviews and two personal interviews. In the first case, the person is asked to recall what he or she did the preceding day. This

procedure is complicated when a lot of detail is required. The second procedure involves two personal interviews. During the first, background information is collected and the time use diary is left behind, to be filled in the next day. During the second interview, on the day after the respondent's observation of his or her time use, the interviewer checks and refines the registrations. In Scandinavian countries, people were asked to return diaries by mail. This saves a second visit, but it is advisable only when intelligent and conscientious collaboration can be assumed.

The greatest methodological challenge in time use research is the choice of the scheme of classification of activities in terms of which the structure of everyday life is represented. Sorokin started to tackle this problem, but convincing theoretical or empirical criteria for constructing typological keys have not been found, and using conventional categories of ordinary language is not entirely satisfactory. Normative and/or contractual work arrangements suggest a fairly unambiguous specification of "market work," but there are some activities in the home that, according to circumstances, can be classified as either housework or leisure. This difficulty could be overcome if the respondent did the coding himself or herself, but usually the log of daily routines is described in the respondent's own words and codification is done by someone else, following criteria that exclude personal and/or subjective meanings. An even more fundamental issue is whether current classifications can be assumed to be meaningful in cross-cultural terms. Time use studies distinguish the minimal basic activity groupings of personal needs, formal work or education, household work, and leisure. The hidden dimension that is postulated by such groupings is obviously a reflection of the Western opposition between necessity and freedom of choice. It places market work immediately after biological needs and before domestic work, which is placed near leisure. This implicitly individualistic and work-oriented, contractual rationale probably is not well suited to representing the more solidarity-oriented temporal orders of everyday life in traditional societies (Bourdieu 1963).

Another difficulty concerns the level of specificity at which a common array of activities is reported at the collective level. The daily pursuits of persons who lead a busy life can be meaningfully recorded in great detail, whereas those of persons tied to the home usually have much less texture. One way to approach this difficulty is to construct hierarchical coding frameworks in which the first column in a multiple-digit code divides the day in terms of major classes of activities. Additional columns focus on increasingly more complex but exhaustive time accounts. The time use project coordinated by Szalai identified in its time-budget protocols ninety-six activity categories. For some purposes, these were reduced to thirty-seven and, for others, to the following ten main groups: work, housework, child care, shopping, personal needs, education, organizational activity, entertainment, active leisure, and passive leisure. Today the coding schemes for official statistical surveys often include many more basic activity categories because they have to accommodate the heterogeneity of lifestyles across gender groupings, generations, occupational categories, and rural versus urban residential environments.

Once time-budget data have been collected and coded, decisions about data processing and indicator construction can be made. According to the complexity of statistical data elaborations, there are three different levels of analysis (Stone 1972, pp. 96–97). First, activity arrays in terms of frequencies or durations, possibly taking company or locations into account, are cross-tabulated with the sociodemographic characteristics of the actors. Second, single activities and their positioning during the course of the day are studied. Finally, stochastic activity sequences are analyzed, focusing on the structure and rhythm of chronological daily routines. Since the 1960s, the following set of indicators generally have been used in computations: (1) the generic average duration of an activity, where the numerator refers to the total sample, disregarding whether there was involvement in the activity, (2) the rate of participation, or the percentage of interviewees who were involved in an activity, and (3) the specific average duration of an activity, where the denominator includes only those who have engaged in it.

Another issue in these surveys is the validity and reliability of data sets. Questions of validity can be raised by difficulties in recall and incorrect identification of activities among respondents or by possible alterations of spontaneous behavior after observation and the consequent distortions in reports or by research instruments that inadequately reflect the specificities of the observed sociocultural context. Research directed at data quality (Juster 1985; Niemi 1993) has shown that results obtained by means of time budgets present at the aggregate level a high correlation with those obtained by means of other forms of observation, such as interviews, workplace or school statistics, and telephone surveys. Moreover, the hypothesis that the desirability or social prestige of certain activities or lifestyles could influence time use reports has not been confirmed. In general, it seems that the twenty-four-hour frame of reference helps reduce such effects and brings informal and often undeclared work commitments to light. Certainly, activities that are assumed to be of secondary importance, such as conversations and listening to the radio, are under represented in current summary tables that restrict the attention to "primary" time allocations. However, this cannot be considered an invalidating shortcoming. Nevertheless, to assure validity, time budgets presuppose the concept of rational time. If a population does not live by the clock, any calculation of time budgets is meaningless.

CONTRIBUTIONS OF TIME USE RESEARCH

Time use research has gained momentum because of interest on the part of international agencies in comparing the functioning of societies in their national settings, the need to connect demographic change and social development, the need to focus on gender-related or generational variables to understand the changing role of the family, the awareness that economic variables reflect wealth and well-being only in very partial ways and that household and care activities must be brought into focus, and the need to construct articulated databases for decision making about social policy.

Since the late 1980s, nationally representative time use data sets have been available for several countries, but the evidence is not easy to compare because activity classifications do not always coincide. Therefore, with the hope that many European Union countries will participate in the very

Daily Time Use, in Hours and Minutes, for Primary Activities in the United States, France and Hungary, by Gender and Employment Status (1965–1966)

	United States (44 cities)	France (6 cities)	Hungary (Gyorz)
Employed men			
Personal needs	10:14	10:55	9:56
Work or study	7:36	7:29	8:47
Household work	1:17	1:33	1:48
Leisure	4:06	3:34	3:05
Non-work related travel	0:47	0:29	0:24
Total	*24:00*	*24:00*	*24:00*
Employed women			
Personal needs	10:20	10:53	9:30
Work or study	5:39	6:05	7:14
Household work	3:43	3:57	4:44
Leisure	3:33	2:40	2:03
Non-work related travel	0:45	0:25	0:29
Total	*24:00*	*24:00*	*24:00*
Unemployed women			
Personal needs	10:24	11:13	10:38
Work or study	0:35	0:09	0:52
Household work	7:12	8:13	9:19
Leisure	4:53	3:49	2:35
Non-work related travel	0:56	0:36	0:36
Total	*24:00*	*24:00*	*24:00*

Table 1

SOURCE: Adapted from A. Szalai, ed., *The Use of Time*, Statistical Appendix Table IV.4., 1972, p. 681.

expensive data-gathering process, Eurostat is preparing a standardized survey. Up to the present, only Japan has truly comparable five-year time series data to indicate trends and changes in lifestyle since 1970 (NHK 1991). In terms of Monday-to-Friday behavior, for instance, sleeping time and housework have decreased while market work has not. Over the years, leisure on all weekdays, especially hobbies, private lessons, and sports activities have grown steadily. Television viewing time reached a peak in 1975 (probably because of the advent of color television) but returned in 1990 to the 1970 level. The illustrations confirm the rule that trend-setting evidence of new life styles is found not so much in the main activity categories but in apparently marginal activities.

To demonstrate the interest of time-budget data in a comparative assessment of the different logics of time structurization, it is best to choose an example from the uniform data set gathered in the Twelve Country Study.

In Table 1, the patterns of daily urban time allocation ascertained in 1965–1966 for the United States, France, and Hungary are presented in the most synthetic form. The data refer to an average weekday and compare time use for personal needs (mostly sleep and meals), market work or study, household work, leisure, and non-work-related travel among adults aged 18–65, subdivided by gender and employment status.

When one compares the starkly different research contexts of those days (market economy, welfare state, state-controlled system), a set of clear-cut differences in time use emerge from these different ways of life; at one extreme the United States and at the other Hungary, with France in between. The average duration of market work was much shorter in American cities than in Hungarian ones; this was due mainly to the fact that employed women were more likely to hold part-time jobs in the United States, while in Hungary they held full-time jobs. Across the three countries, household work and leisure show systematic secular trends. Employed American men enjoyed one hour more of leisure and contributed half an hour less to housework than did their

Hungarian counterparts. For employed American women, housework lasted one hour less, and leisure lasted one and a half hours more than was the case for employed Hungarian women. Finally, household work among unemployed American women required two hours less time and leisure benefits lasted two hours longer than was the case for the corresponding group in Hungary. The uneven availability of household appliances and unequal access to leisure amenities (in particular, television) were the causes of these differences in lifestyles. In addition, the table reveals well-known inequalities in gender and employment status. If one combines the time invested in market work and housework, it appears, though less significantly in the west than in the east, that women in the labor force contributed a considerably larger share of work and enjoyed much less leisure than did employed men.

Table 2 shows that gender differences are clearly implicated in the discrepancies in the number of hours of economic activity and housework per week between men and women, indicating that there are analogous patterns of inequality in developing countries such as Bangladesh, India, and Nepal. In these countries, women are more likely to spend their time in subsistence activities, whereas men tend to have a monopoly of paid jobs. In addition, women's time investment in housework is six times that of men in Bangladesh and three times that of men in the other two countries. However, the gap in overall work hours, though disadvantaging women, is less evident. In fact, in Bangladesh they contribute 54 percent of the total micro-productive time input, in India 55 percent, and in Nepal 58 percent.

Data from the French national survey (Insee 1989) on the effect of cumulative social roles among women are much more analytic. In France, for mothers with husbands under 45 years of age and at least one child younger than 25 years old, increasing from one child to three and more children means, if they are unemployed, an increase of one hour and fifteen minutes of house work and, if they are employed, an increase of fifty-two minutes. Where does this extra time come from? In the case of especially pressured employed mothers, the time investment in human capital in the form of caring for additional children implies a

reduction of one hour and thirteen minutes in the duration of market work, including a seven-minute reduction in free time and fourteen minutes less of sleep. Especially for women with more than one child, this negatively affects their competitive position in the professional world. Data such as these should be of interest to policymakers.

This example also shows that considerable caution is required in interpreting time use data. In general, estimates of differential time allocations for men and women in certain activities do not reflect only gender differences. Demographic variables, especially family composition, the structure of the labor force, and the availability of household help, intervene in causal links between gender and time use. Particular attention must be paid to these influences in longitudinal analyses such as that of Gershuny and Robinson (1988), which analyzed U.S. and British time-budget data over three decades. Statistically controlling for female labor force participation, male unemployment, and declining family sizes, those authors concluded that in the 1980s, women did substantially less housework while men did a little more than in the 1960s. In another study that analyzed data from repeated surveys in eight Western countries, a general reduction in time dedicated to all kinds of work was found, along with a convergence of time use models among males and females and a growing international similarity in the patterns of the division of time between work and leisure (Gershuny 1992).

In recent decades, considerable progress has been made in representing the multidimensionality of time use phenomena because official data, instead of regarding samples of randomly chosen individuals, have been collected from all members of households. This has made it possible to observe how husbands' time management affects their wives and vice versa and to determine what it means for families if both husband and wife are employed and if children come into the family nucleus.

In Table 3, pertinent data on couples from the national time use survey conducted in Germany in 1990–1991 are presented. It shows time use models for types of families defined by employment status and the presence of children. Assuming the operation of compensatory mechanisms, it also

Time Use in Three Southern Asian Countries (1982–1992)

Countries:	Social Groups:	Hours per week of economic activity			Hours per week of housework	Total work hours per week
		Paid	Subsistence	Total		
Bangladesh	Ages 5+					
	Women	14	8	22	31	53
	Men	38	3	41	5	46
India	Ages 18+					
	Women	28	7	35	34	69
	Men	43	4	47	10	57
Nepal	Ages 15+					
	Women	18	17	35	42	77
	Men	29	12	41	15	56

Table 2

SOURCE: United Nations, *The World's Women 1995: Trends and Statistics*, Chart 5.3, 1995, New York.

takes the weekly rhythm of time use into account by distinguishing workdays (Monday to Friday) from weekends (Saturday and Sunday).

One model regards more traditional couples in which only husbands are employed and wives do most of the housework. Husbands increase their market work when there are children, but regardless of the presence of children, they defend their daily leisure and contribute to housework mostly on weekends. The other model concerns couples in which both partners are employed. In this case, it is not surprising that the wives' market work is considerably shorter than the husbands', but what is important is that in the presence of children, both partners increase their market work by more than one hour each. The housework of mothers increases on all days, whereas fathers limit increases in their domestic chores to the weekends.

From a micro perspective, what the German example shows are the implications of decisions made within the family. Here the family is seen as the institutional arena where partners search for a suitable compromise in their interlocking role definitions. From a macro perspective, the implications of gendered time use arrangements for the changing division of labor and the growing interaction between the market sector and the household sector are important. Sociologists and economists have often criticized the fact that mostly female domestic and caring activities, mostly male "do-it-yourself" repair initiatives, and voluntary

and other socially useful work done by both men and women go unrecorded in labor statistics and national accounts. These are "productive activities" insofar as they can be delegated to persons other than those who benefit from them.

Table 4 shows a selection of the results of a United Nations Development Programme analysis of a posteriori standardized time budget data from the most recent national surveys conducted in fourteen different countries (Goldschmidt-Clermont and Pagnossin-Aligisakis 1995). This analysis distinguishes between market oriented System of National Accounts (SNA) activities considered in the UN System of National Accounts and non-SNA activities, and introduces the necessary controls for the demographic structures of the populations.

Despite the nonhomogeneous social structures and value systems of France, Germany, Great Britain, and the United States, everywhere statistically unrecorded (non-SNA) activities absorb about as much labor time as do recorded (SNA) activities. Furthermore, total economic time allocations (SNA plus non-SNA) tend to be equal among men and women. Although this demonstates social equality in general terms, it can be seen that very strong gendered divisions of tasks prevail in all cases. In fact, in these four countries, women contribute only one-third of total market-oriented productive time, whereas they contribute two-thirds of total non-market-oriented productive time.

The availability of comparable time budget data is a prerequisite for official statistics that aim

Workday and Week-End Time Use of Husbands and Wives in German Households defined by the Employment Status of the Couple and the Presence of Children in the Family (1990–1991).

Activity categories	Husbands				Wives			
	Only husband employed		Both employed		Only husband employed		Both employed	
	Monday-Friday	Saturday-Sunday	Monday-Friday	Saturday-Sunday	Monday-Friday	Saturday-Sunday	Monday-Friday	Saturday-Sunday
Without children								
Personal needs	9:43	12:02	10:01	12:02	11:40	12:44	10:39	12:16
Market work and study	8:23	1:51	7:11	1:37	0:13	–	4:26	0:37
Household work	2:02	3:05	2:30	3:05	6:58	4:53	4:51	4:46
Free time	3:36	6:46	4:01	6:58	4:57	6:14	3:52	6:13
Other activities	0:16	0:16	0:17	0:18	0:12	0:09	0:12	0:08
Total:	24:00	24:00	24:00	24:00	24:00	24:00	24:00	24:00
With children								
Personal needs	9:25	11:43	9:22	11:39	10:24	11:31	9:46	11:42
Market work and study	8:44	1:16	8:49	1:23	0:24	–	5:36	0:45
Household work	2:16	3:59	2:23	3:49	8:55	6:18	5:23	5:45
Free time	3:22	6:37	3:15	6:47	3:57	5:51	3:06	5:42
Other activities	0:13	0:25	0:11	0:22	0:20	0:20	0:09	0:06
Total:	24:00	24:00	24:00	24:00	24:00	24:00	24:00	24:00

Table 3

SOURCE: Adapted from Statistisches Bundesamt, *Die Zeitverwendung der Bevoelkerung*, Tabellenband I, 1995, Wiesbaden.

to include the production value of nonmonetarized activities, through "satellite accounts," in their quantitative frameworks. The most recent national time use surveys have been conducted with these applications in mind.

THE RELEVANCE OF TIME-BUDGET DATA SETS FOR SOCIAL POLICY

Sociologists have often been skeptical about the utility of time-budget research. Time budgets are thought to provide data that are "broad but shallow" (Converse 1972, p. 46) and offer no more than static, tendentially commonsense descriptions of only the manifest aspects of everyday life. From a theoretical point of view, it is argued that there is a lack of explanatory hypotheses and relevant concepts that could bring norms, experiences, attitudes, and values to the fore. On the methodological side, the main criticism is that classification schemes of activities are imprecise, are unevenly general or detailed, and have barely changed since the 1920s (Pronovost 1989, pp. 78–80). Implicit in these observations is the dilemma Szalai faced earlier: whether priority should be assigned to the

testing of hypotheses or to multipurpose database construction. With the latter option comes the question of how to reconcile, in designing the studies, cross-national and longitudinal comparability and adherence to sociocultural settings and historically changing conditions.

Time-budget research is applied research that has increasingly been aimed at the design and evaluation of social policy. Its relevance in this context derives from the fact that in modern affluent societies, citizens often value scarce time more than material or monetary resources; thus, time use rationalization and efficient time management in the personal, family, and public sphere have become matters of general concern. Contingencies curtailing time use evidently are distributed unequally in the social world. For instance, health checks in public institutions often involve waiting times that private medical care does not, and not owning a means of transportation makes long commuting times unavoidable. Hence, social policies and their provisions try to make circumstances or opportunities more equal for everyone. Part-time employment, flexible worktimes, and compressed workweeks have been introduced mostly for pressured working mothers with small chil-

Distribution of Economic Time in Four Countries Between SNA and Non-SNA Activities, by Gender. Indices Showing Unequal Participation of Men and Women in Each Group of Activities

	Men (M)	Women (F)	Men and Women (M+F)	Inequality Index I=F/(M+F)
France (1985–1986)				
SNA activities	4:00	2:10	6:10	35%
Non SNA activities	2:28	4:59	7:27	67%
Total	6:50	7:09	13:37	52%
Germany (1991–1992)				
SNA activities	4:28	2:12	6:40	33%
Non SNA activities	2:53	5:08	8:01	64%
Total	7:21	7:20	14:41	50%
Great Britain (1985)				
SNA activities	4:39	2:34	7:13	36%
Non SNA activities	2:12	4:19	6:41	65%
Total	6:51	6:53	13:54	50%
United States (1985)				
SNA activities	4:31	2:47	7:18	38%
Non-SNA activities	2:37	4:46	7:23	65%
Total	7:08	7:33	14:41	51%

Table 4

SOURCE: Adapted from L. Goldschmidt-Clermont and E. Pagnossinn-Aligisakis, *Measures of Unrecorded Economic Activities in Fourteen Countries,* Occasional Papers no. 20, 1995, New York: UNDP.

dren. Shop-opening hours and office schedules have been changed to permit effective coordination and a better reconciliation of tasks. The effectiveness these measures can be monitored with the help of time-budget procedures.

The complexity of time-budget data sets has often been insufficiently exploited. Initially this was due to limitations in handling enormous data sets, but increased technological resources and new multivariate statistical techniques have opened new frontiers. Almost exclusive attention has been given to average durations and frequencies of primary activities, but the study of configurations emerging from an association of these activities with other contemporaneous activities promises a better understanding of modern time regimes. Until now, not much research has been done on routinized rhythms or the strategic sequencing of activities. Also, the collaborative or conflicting interface of the various schedules of family members, the reconstruction of networks of participative personal contacts (a topic of great significance in regard to lonely children, the ill, and the elderly), and the relationship of the use of urban spaces to time use (a problem studied by human geographers) are all interesting areas for future research because of the greater availability of important data sets.

Activity classifications will have to undergo critical study to better reflect changes in the activity patterns of everyday life. Statistical offices are presently reconceptualizing their taxonomies. Paid work might be broken down into its constituent parts and examined analytically, but other activities need redefinition. For example, some kinds of domestic work have been absorbed by the market; care activities now regard the elderly more than children; dealing with service bureaucracies has become a time-consuming task; there is a new spectrum of voluntary forms of participation at the social, political, and cultural levels; and leisure behavior has changed in relationship with new media.

However, the problem is not just a technical one regarding exclusively descriptive coding schemes. Time use data assume importance only when they provide a valid epistemological key for the interpretation of social change. As has already been pointed out, earlier lines of research identified two central components of time use: market work and leisure. Today, time use studies based on data from household samples may help identify other valid criteria of time use to better understand how families cope with growing structural unemployment and increasing social insecurity.

REFERENCES

Bevans, George Esdras 1913 *How Workingmen Spend Their Spare Time*. New York: Columbia University Press.

Bourdieu, Pierre 1963 "La Société Traditionelle: Attitude à l'Égard du Temps et Conduite Économique." *Sociologie du Travaille*, 5:24–44.

Converse, Philip E. 1968 "Time Budgets" In David L. Sills, ed., *The International Encyclopedia of Social Sciences*, vol. 16. New York: Macmillan–Free Press.

Elias, Norbert 1988 *Time*. New York: Basil Blackwell.

Gershuny, Jonathan 1992 "La répartition du temps dans les sociétés post-industrielles." *Futuribles*, Mai-Juin, 215–226.

——, and John P. Robinson 1988 "Historical Changes in the Household Division of Labor." *Demography* 25(4):537–552.

Goldschmidt-Clemont, Luisella, and Elisabetta Pagnossin-Aligisakis 1995 *Measures of Unrecorded Economic Activities in Fourteen Countries*, Occasional papers no. 20. New York: UNDP.

Harvey, Andrew S., Alexander Szalai, David Elliott, Philip J. Stone, and Susan M. Clark 1984 *Time Budget Research: An ISSC Workbook in Comparative Analysis*. Frankfurt: Campus.

—— 1993 "Guidelines for Time Use Data Collection." *Social Indicator Research* 30:197–228.

INSEE 1989 "Les Emplois du Temps des Français." *Economie et Statistique* 223.

Jahoda, Marie, Paul Lazarsfeld, and Hans Zeisel 1971 *Marienthal: The Sociography of an Unemployed Community*. Chicago: Aldine (German orig., 1933).

Juster, F. Thomas 1985 "The Validity and Quality of Time Use Estimates Obtained from Recall Diaries." In F. T. Juster and F. P. Stafford, eds., *Time, Goods, and Well-Being*. Ann Arbor: Institute of Social Research, University of Michigan.

Kurtz M.-F. D. 1984 "Les Budget-Temps: Réflexion Épistémologique," *L'année Sociologique* 34:9–27.

NHK 1991 *Japanese Time Use in 1990*. Japanese Broadcasting Corporation, Public Opinion Research Division.

Niemi, Iris 1993 "Systematic Error in Behavioural Measurement: Comparing Results from Interview and Time Budget Studies." *Social Indicators Research* 30:229–244.

Przeworski, Adam, and Henri Teune 1970 *The Logic of Comparative Inquiry*. New York–London: Wiley Interscience.

Pronovost, Gilles 1989 "The Sociology of Time." *Current Sociology* 37(3):1–129.

Scheuch, Erwin K. 1992 "The Time-Budget Interview." In Alexander Szalai, ed., *The Use of Time*. The Hague-Paris: Mouton.

Sorokin, P. A., and C. Q. Berger 1939 *Time-Budgets and Human Behavior*. Cambridge, Mass.: Harvard University Press.

Statistisches Bundesamt 1995 *Die Zeitverwendung der Bevoelkerung*, Tabellenband I. Wiesbaden.

Stone Philip J. 1972 "The Analysis of Time-Budget Data." In Alexander Szalai, ed., *The Use of Time*. The Hague–Paris: Mouton.

Sue, Roger 1994 *Temps et Ordre Social*. Paris: Presses Universitaires de France.

Szalai, Alexander, ed. 1972 *The Use of Time: Daily Activities of Urban and Suburban Populations in Twelve Countries*. The Hague–Paris: Mouton.

—— 1977 "The Organization and Execution of Cross-National Survey Research Projects." In Alexander Szalai and Riccardo Petrella, eds., *Cross-National Comparative Survey Research*. Oxford, UK: Pergamon.

—— 1984 "The Concept of Time Budget Research." In Andrew S. Harvey et al., eds., *Time Budget Research*. Frankfurt: Campus.

United Nations 1995 *The World's Women 1995: Trends and Statistics*. No. E.95. XVII.2.

Zerubavel, Eviatar 1982 "The Standardization of Time. A Sociohistorical Perspective." *American Journal of Sociology* 88 (1):1–23.

ELKE KOCH-WESER AMMASSARI

TOURISM

Tourism is an economic phenomenon with important sociocultural implications that acquired a fundamental significance in the last decades of the twentieth century. It is one of the economic sectors with the highest rates of growth, together with transportation, communications, and the computer industry, with which it works in a synergitic way.

According to a classic definition, tourism can be identified in the complex of relations and manifestations that rise from the travel and stay of foreigners when the stay is temporary and is not motivated by a lucrative occupation (Hunziker and Krapf 1942). "Foreigners" are persons who do not reside habitually in the zone in which the tourist activity is carried out; depending on wether the zone of residence is in the same state, one can distinguish between internal tourism and international tourism.

Other elements have to be considered in distinguishing fully-fledged tourism from similar activities. First, two "fundamental actors" have to be dealt with. On one side, there are tourists (*active tourism*), who decide to undertake this activity because of several motivations. This is one of the primary topics in the sociopsychological analysis of tourism. On the other side, there is *passive* (or receptive) *tourism* constituted by the technical and socioeconomic structures that exist in the zones of reception with the aim of hosting tourists. In modern tourism, a third actor, consisting of agents of tourist intermediation (travel agencies, tour operators, carriers, etc.), has assumed greater importance by connecting the demand for and the supply of tourism. The tourism described here is essentially a mass phenomenon that exists alongside elite tourism, which was the first type to appear.

Merchant writers such as Marco Polo, traveler-explorers, and missionaries, often accompanied by anthropologists and ethnologists, were the forerunners of tourists, but only after the "Grand Tours" of the eighteenth and nineteenth centuries can one speak of the emergence of the tourist phenomenon. The grand tour was considered a fundamental stage in the formation of young aristocrats and later of the children of the emergent high bourgeoisie. It consisted of a visit to the more centers of the culture of the age, with a predilection for southern Europe, in particular Italy and its remnants of classic culture.

Toward the end of nineteenth century, with the inauguration of the first seaside resorts, tourism began to acquire mass characteristics, a phenomenon that was facilitated by the improvement of transportation systems, especially the extension of the railway network (Urry 1990).

The transformation of elite tourism into a phenomenon that involved wide strata of the population did not occur until after the end of World War II and, in the more economically developed countries, the possession of the automobile as an individual and family means of transportation and the expansion of transcontinental and transoceanic flights.

Tourism is therefore facilitated, in addition to the elevation of individual incomes and better tariff conditions, by technical, political, and social factors. It also involves a psychological evolution in society, especially in the richer countries, where it provides an escape from the stresses of city life and the daily routine. A stronger desire for social intercourse has grown along with a desire for physical activity to compensate for a sedentary lifestyle.

Certain forms of travel have a demonstrative scope, since "to tour," in particular elite tourism but also mass tourism, may be thought of as an expression of one's prestige and social position.

Urry (1990) introduced the concept of the "tourist gaze," stating that "part at least of that experience is to gaze upon or view a set of different scenes, of landscapes or townscapes which are outside of the ordinary" (1990, p. 1). As Urry describes it:

1. "tourism is a leisure activity which presupposes its opposite, namely regulated and organized work, . . .

2. tourist relationships arise from a movement of people to, and their stay in, various destinations. This necessarily involves some movement through the space, that is the journey, and a period of stay in a new place or places,

3. the journey and stay are to, and in, sites which are outside the normal places of residence and work. Periods of residence elsewhere are of a short-term and temporary nature, . . .

4. the places gazed upon are for purposes which are not directly connected with the paid work and normally they offer some distinctive contrasts with work (both paid or unpaid);

5. a substantial proportion of the population of modern societies engages in such tourist practices, new socialized forms of

provision are developed in order to cope with the mass character of the gaze of tourist (as opposed to the individual character of "travel")

6. places are chosen to be gazed upon because there is an anticipation, especially through daydreaming and fantasy, of intense pleasures, either on a different scale or involving different senses from those customarily encountered, . . .

7. the tourist gaze is directed to features of landscape and townscape which separate them off from everyday experience. Such aspects are viewed because they are taken to be in some sense out of the ordinary, . . .

8. the gaze is constructed through signs, and tourism involves the collection of signs, . . .

9. an array of tourist professionals develop who attempt to reproduce ever-new objects of the tourist gaze. . . (Urry 1990, pp. 2–3 passim).

THE DIMENSIONS OF THE PHENOMENON

The modern growth of tourism (Prosser 1994, p. 19) has been referred to ironically by Lodge (1992) as the "new global religion," and a work on this phenomenon is entitled *The Golden Hordes*" (Turner and Ash 1975). Prosser also supplies some data on a "phenomenon" that he describes by using the metaphor of the tsunami: By the mid-1990s, the tourism sector constituted 6 percent of world gross national product and 13 percent of the money spent for consumption and could be defined as the fastest-growing industry. According to the forecasts of the World Tourism Organization, in the year 2005, the tourist industry will involve 40 million persons.

Taking into account only persons who cross their state borders for tourism (perhaps equally important is the internal tourist movement), more recent data show, in approximately a decade, a near doubling of the phenomenon and also indicate that total revenues have increased to three times their original amount (Table 1).

The distribution of tourism in a wide range of countries has occurred in time span of only a few years. Tourism in the industrialized countries, while

Arrivals and Revenues in International Tourism

Year	Arrivals ($ millions)	Revenue ($ billions)
1986	339	142
1987	362	175
1988	395	203
1989	427	219
1990	458	266
1991	464	273
1992	503	311
1993	518	318
1994	547	348
1995	566	393
1996	592	423

Table 1

SOURCE: World Tourism Organization.

declining in relative terms, accounts for ever 50 percent of the total, but the share of the developing countries has grown and now accounts for almost a third of the total. The countries of central and eastern Europe still suffer from the backwardness of decades of relative inaccessibility, but after the fall of the Berlin wall, their proportion of the world tourism has grown (Table 2).

France is the leader in tourist presence, followed by the United States and two countries of Mediterranean Europe, Spain and Italy. In fifth place is China, a country only recently opened to international tourism that has a large potential that bas been limited by a deficiency of infrastructure and receptive structures.

The forecasts of an increase of tourism are plausible because some countries of the former communist bloc already play an important role. Other developing countries (e.g., Brazil and South Africa), apart from China, have potential and will be able to play a more important role in international tourism if they stabilize their political and/or economic situation.

There currently is a remarkable concentration of tourist destinations in which the top ten countries together account for over 50 percent of tourism and top twenty countries account for over two-thirds (Table 3).

These figures suggest that the market for tourism will grow and become more differentiated, that there will be more specialization and segmentation of that market, and that organized travel

Percentage Distribution of Tourist Presences

	1990 (%)	1996 (%)
Industrialized countries	61.5	55.8
Developing countries	28.3	31.0
Central and eastern Europe	10.2	13.2

Table 2

SOURCE: World Tourism Organization.

packages will become more personalized to cope with the desire for greater individual freedom through a modular design of the product (Schwaninger 1989).

THE NATURE OF TOURISM

Mass tourism is the main concern of this article inasmuch as the current growth of the tourism industry essentially has resulted from it. Mass tourism is a "fickle" market in which status-elevating motivations are important. "If people do not travel, they lose status: travel is the maker of status" (Urry 1990, p. 5). The concept of conspicuous consumption (Veblen [1899] 1970) is operative here because in choosing a vacation, one takes into account the attributions of status defined on the basis of the place one visits and the characteristics of the other visitors.

One therefore is dealing with a market that is very sensitive to fashion and changes in values. The relative loss of importance of seaside resorts, which were the preferred destinations at the beginning of mass tourism, can be cited in this regard:

In the post-war period it has been the sun, not the sea, that is presumed to produce health and sexual attractiveness. The ideal body has come to be viewed as one that is tanned. This viewpoint has been diffused downwards through the social classes with the result that many package holidays present this as almost the reason for going on holiday. . . . Seaside resorts have also become less distinctive because of the widespread de-industrialization of many towns and cities so that there is less need to escape from them to the contrasting seaside. As the everyday has changed, as towns and cities have become de-industrialized and many have themselves become objects for the tourist gaze, with wave machines and other features of the

beach, so seaside resorts are no longer extraordinary. (Urry 1990, pp. 37–38)

Tourism is therefore a fashion phenomenon that goes through all the typical phases of a product of that type, from discovery and emergence, to increasing popularity, saturation, attenuation of its appeal, and eventually decline. It is sensitive to the relationship between demand and supply, based the on perceptions, expectations, attitudes, and values of people, and therefore is subject to cultural filters:

The various contents and destinations of tourism, from the nineteenth Century to our days, seem to follow a standardized route . . . They are invented by individuals that live in conditions of originality and marginality in relationship to the 'world.' Subsequently they are consecrated by the notables: the monarchs and their families, followed by the artists and the celebrities . . . Finally they are diffused through the capillary imitation of the behavior of one social layer by the immediately inferior one. As soon as a place or a tourist fashion is known, there begins an emulation process that leads quickly to congestion; processes of distinction are then activated by groups that address to other places and invent other activities, reopening a new cycle. The succession of dissemination and invention cycles leads to the need for distinction to introduce more and more far and unusual goals. (Savelli 1998, pp. 92–93).

One can speak of the "pleasure periphery," as in the case of the increase of Antarctic tourism (Prosser 1994, p. 22). For this aspect, the model of Plog (1973) is relevant. Plog analyzes the personality of the tourist: Along a continuum, one can go from psycho-centered, expectant subjects preoccupied with the small daily problems and escaping to adventures, to subjects who are as allocentered, confident in themselves, curious, and adventurous. The places visited by these varied subjects are obviously very different. In the survey conducted by Plog among the inhabitants of New York, while the psychocentered subjects do not venture beyond Coney Island, the midcentered travel to Europe and the allocentered do not dare to face the Pacific or Africa.

In dealing with tourism from a socioeconomic point of view, the "positional goods" concept

International Arrivals by Country, 1996

Country	Thousands of tourists	Country	Thousands of tourists
France	61,500	Austria	16,641
United States	44,791	Germany	15,070
Spain	41,295	Hong Kong	11,700
Italy	35,500	Switzerland	11,097
China	26,055	Portugal	9,900
Great Britain	25,800	Greece	9,725
Mexico	21,732	Russian Federation	9,678
Hungary	20,670	Turkey	7,935
Poland	19,420	Malaysia	7,742
Canada	17,345	Total	430,801
Czech Republic	17,205	World total	591,864

Table 3

SOURCE: World Tourism Organization.

(Hirsh 1978) can be used. This term refers to social goods, services, jobs, positions, and other relations that are scarce or subject to congestion and/or crowding. The competition is zero-sum: When someone consumes these kinds of goods in excess, someone else is forced to consume less. The supply is limited because quality would lessen as a result of quantitative growth.

One also can trace a conflict of interest between the actors described in the first part of this article (tourists, agencies, and the tourism industry in the hosting countries) and environmentalists. Since natural and cultural resources may be irremediably spoiled, there is thus a conflict of interest between present and future generations (Mishan 1969).

Another peculiar characteristic of tourism is that "almost all the services provided to tourists have to be delivered at the time and place at which they are produced. As a consequence the quality of the social interaction between the provider of the service, such as the waiter, flight attendant or hotel receptionist, and the consumer, is part of the 'product' being purchased by the tourist. If aspects of that social interaction are unsatisfactory (the offhand waiter, the unsmiling flight attendant, or the rude receptionist), then what is purchased is in effect a different service product" (Urry 1990, p. 40). Production of services for the consumer, in fact, cannot be done entirely behind the scenes, far away from the tourist gaze. Moreover, tourists have high expectations about what they will receive, since the search for the extraordinary is an essential aspect of the choice to travel.

"Spatial fixity" is a crucial characteristic of tourist services (Bagguley 1987), and customers are more mobile and now consume tourist services on a global scale. This means that "part of what is consumed is in effect the place in which the service producer is located. If the particular place does not convey appropriate cultural meanings, the quality of the specific service may well be tarnished" (Urry 1990, p. 40).

Since the services offered are intrinsically labor-intensive, employers try to diminish the costs. However, this may undermine the extraordinary character of the tourist experience (Urry 1990, p. 41).

TOURISTS AND THEIR MOTIVATIONS

In an attempt to grasp the features that distinguish tourists from other kinds of travelers, Cohen (1974) singles out certain dimensions that are thought to be essential: duration of the travel, voluntariness, direction, distance, recurrence, and purpose. On the basis of these elements, a tourist may be defined as a traveler who moves voluntarily and for a limited period of time to obtain pleasure from the experience of novelty and change, following a relatively long and non-recurring route.

For the sake of clarity, distinctions are introduced in the form of a dichotomy. However, one can assume that in many cases there are different degrees of distance from "full-fledged tourism."

When the *duration* of the travel and stay is short (less than twenty-four hours in the definition of the UN Conference on International Travel and

Tourism), there are trips and excursions. There is also an upper limit, more difficult to determine, beyond which one can speak of permanent travelers (wanderers, nomads).

When the element of *voluntariness* is lacking, one is dealing with the exile (sometimes voluntary), the slave, the prisoner of war, or the political refugee. The pilgrim also can be considered a type of traveler who differs from the full-fledged tourist inasmuch as in many cases there is a lack of voluntariness. This is the case because social expectations can determine the decision to travel and the stay (e.g., pilgrimages to Mecca by Muslim believers).

In terms of *direction*, tourists return to their countries of origin, while immigrants make a one-way trip. There are also intermediate categories that are less easy to classify, such as "tourist immigrants" and "permanent tourists." These people leave home as tourists but decide to stay for a longer time span in a foreign country. Persons such as the "expatriates" (e.g., the many foreign artists who reside in cities such as Paris) are also difficult to define. They decide to live in a foreign country for indefinite periods without completely cutting their ties with the country of origin.

If the *distance* is short, one can speak of excursionists and hikers, while if the distance is much longer, one could have spoken in the past of explorers. Today, nearly all the possible destinations on the face of the earth seem to be within the reach of the tourist. If the distance implies crossing a national border, there is the already mentioned distinction between internal tourism and international tourism.

When travel and stay have a season or weekend regularity (*recurrence*), one is dealing with the habitué, who often is the owner of a summer house. This person is not properly a tourist, because the elements of novelty and change are lacking.

Finally, the *purpose* for the tourist does not have to be instrumental but can involve the seeking of pleasure. If the purpose is instrumental or has another specific nature different from the search for novelty and change, one is dealing with students, old country visitors, conventioneers, business travelers, tourist employees, and the like.

However, this criterion is not as precise as it might appear at a first glance. The noninstrumental character of the purpose and the search for novelty and change has to be considered from a social point of view. When an individual takes a vacation for reasons of prestige, this travel is socially defined as a pleasure trip even if that individual will not enjoy the experience. More likely, there will be the opposite case: The purpose is declared as instrumental, but other instrumental (and not) purposes are also relevant (Savelli 1998, p. 57).

Tourists' motivations also can be analyzed by distinguishing the *push* factors that lead to the desire to go on vacation from the *pull* factors that the various areas of attraction exercise on the tourist (Savelli 1986, p. 2269).

To show the "versatility" of the tourism phenomenon, a relationship can be seen between some of its forms and the fundamental needs listed by Maslow. Therapeutic tourism satisfies physiological needs, while the needs of security and belonging are satisfied by familiar and "identity" tourism. The need for social recognition is catered to by tourism *à raconter*, (The French expression *à raconter* refers to a tourist who leads you to extraordinary places where extraordinary things happen that one is very pleased to narrate to friends, thereby obtaining social status.) and people satisfy the need for self-esteem through sport and cultural tourism (Kovacshazy and people 1998, p. 58).

To describe the psychological and social situation experienced by the tourist, some authors propose an interesting analogy between the tourist and the pilgrim. Both move from a familiar place to a distant one and then come back. In faraway localities, they dedicate themselves—although in different ways—to the "worship" of sacred places. These can be described as "liminoid" situations in which daily obligations are suspended (Turner and Truner 1978): "There is license for permissive and playful 'non-serious' behavior and the encouragement of a relatively unconstrained 'communitas' or social togetherness" (Urry 1990, p. 10). The purpose of a vacation thus consists of overturning the daily routine: Middle-class tourists try to be a "peasant for a day," while tourists with a lower social rank try to be "king/queen for a day" (Gottlieb 1982).

In a survey carried out in Italy (Isnart 1997) by interviewing only persons who go on vacation habitually, only the expenses for food and daily living were judged "more necessary" than those for traveling. The expenses for car use and maintenance and those undertaken to dress were lower than those for the consumption of vacations.

There often exists a link among subjective motivations, perception of the visited localities, and the objective connotations of those localities. Some connotations are always valid (effectiveness and efficiency, a proper quality–price ratio, a satisfactory environmental quality, the hospitality and warmth of the residents). Other connotations assume a nearly cyclical course: They gain a special reputation for one or two seasons and then fade out.

However, five major categories of motivations more or less summarize what this article has described so far:

1. *Subjectivity*: the sense of curiosity, interest, discovery, opportunity, and "digression" of the vacation

2. *Security*: the sense of confidence that vacation places must transmit and the possibility of relaxing (nearly the opposite of the insecurity of large cities)

3. *Transgression*: the willingness to have a good time, to push the limits, to have "extraordinary" and "sensual" experiences

4. *Budget*: the search for something that does not divert too many resources from other needs and opportunities

5. *Status*: the idea that travel is first of all social gratification, something to show, a reached goal (Isnart 1997, p. 16)

Among these categories of motivations, subjectivity prevails, with status and transgression not far behind. Obviously, budget is much more a concern of the elderly (who also appreciate security) and young people (who do not care much about status). Some of these differences are related to socioeconomic class.

THE IMPACT OF TOURISM

The tourist's role is a total one: "He cannot hide his own externality from the local population and all his relations are imprinted and denoted, in the first place, by the tourist role. In the same way, he is recognized as such from other tourists, regardless, in some manner, of his social condition, nationality, origin and race" (Savelli 1998, pp. 129–130).

The tourist's presence therefore cannot pass unnoticed, and the increase of tourism can carry, besides the obvious economic advantages, some negative consequence in the countries that receive tourist flows. In this regard, there are pessimistic visions that are valid, especially for developing countries. These are the countries in which tourism can be expected to show steadily increasing rates of growth and in which there is more to earn from this development.

Tourist destinations are vulnerable, and one can even speak about economic colonialism, because investments and the largest part of demand are controlled by the developed countries. Exploitation can be not only economic but also social and environmental, inasmuch as community displacement, societal dislocation, and cultural transformation may occur (Ryan 1991): "Village farmland is appropriated, there is inter-generational stress as younger groups succumb to the 'demonstration effect' of tourist material wealth and behavior, intra-family stress as male-female role balance shifts, and community disharmony as religious ceremonies and artforms are commercialized" (Prosser 1994, p. 29).

Therefore, it is necessary to foster a sustainable tourism that tries "to sustain the quantity, quality, and productivity both of human and natural resources systems over time, while respecting and accommodating the dynamics of such systems" (Prosser 1994, pp. 31–32). This alternative form of tourism must "search for spontaneity, enhanced interpersonal relations, creativity, authenticity, solidarity, and social and ecological harmony" (Pearce 1989, p. 101).

The social relations between tourists and indigenous populations are complex and can lead to conflict as a result of several factors. Among the more important ones are the number of tourists who visit a place in relation to the size of the hosting population, the type of organization of the tourist industry, the effects of tourism on preexisting agricultural and industrial activities, economic and social differences between the visitors and the majority of the hosts, and the degree to which visitors demand particular standards of lodging and service, that is, the expressed desire to be locked in an "environmental bubble" for protection from the "disappointing" characteristics of the hosting society (Urry 1990, p. 90).

As a counterbalance of these potential dangers, one has to consider that the cost of a new workplace in the tourist sector has been estimated at £4,000, compared with £32,000 in the manufacturing industry and £300,000 in mechanical engineering (Lumley 1988, cited by Urry 1990, p. 114). These are older figures, and therefore are not necessarily still valid, but the ratios probably continued to be valid. The "tourist prescription" therefore can be recommended particularly for countries that do not have many financial resources.

For tourism to be sustainable and respectful of the natural and social environment, the attitudes and behaviors of the three main actors must change:

- The attitudes of *tourists* must change. Tourists tend to believe that other tourists are the problem. Thus, their attitudes remain elitist and short-term.

- The *destination areas* must assume a longer-term attitude. An equilibrium between optimization of the revenues and protection of the resources must be found. Populations must be involved in all phases of development: ideation and planning, construction and implementation, conduction and management, and monitoring and modification.

- The *tourist industry* must find an equilibrium between opposing requirements. There is an unavoidable push for environmental control from foreign investors and operators in order to obtain greater profits that can be detrimental to local populations and governments. At the same time, the tourist industry feels the need to appear to be ecologically responsible (Prosser 1994, p. 32).

It has been proposed that tourism should be considered only a preliminary stage in which resources are obtained, that can be used later for "true" development through investment in other sectors. That is reasonable, because diversification is a key factor in economic security and stability, especially if tourism can be defined as a fashion

industry. However, one may question whether the impact of other industrial initiatives is less harmful and more sustainable than that of tourism. This opinion results from a dated attitude characterized by an ideologically rooted prejudice that is disappearing: "In the last few years in Britain many Labour councils have enthusiastically embraced local tourist initiatives, having once dismissed tourism as providing only 'candy-floss jobs'" (Urry 1990, p. 115).

POSTMODERN TOURISM

While the countries that receive tourist flows need to find a balance between the advantages and disadvantages and search for a sustainable "receipt," the benefits for tourists seem to be without shortcomings. Krippendorf (1987) speaks about "travel" that represents recuperation and regeneration, compensation and social integration, escape, and communication, intellectual expansion, freedom and self-determination, self-realization, and happiness.

The fact that the tourist industry continues to grow indicates that it is able to give a satisfactory answer to tourists' expectations; otherwise there would be frustration, and the phenomenon would recede. One can ask why tourists continue to travel and their numbers continue to increase in spite of the "alarm bells" that call attention to the problem of overcrowding and the relative nonauthenticity of the tourist experience.

This article has dealt with the problem of overcrowding in its characterization of the tourist product as a "positional good." This pessimistic thesis has been criticized by Beckerman (1974), who raises two interesting issues. First, the concern about the effects of the mass tourism is basically a "middle-class" anxiety (like many other environmental concerns) because the really rich "are quite safe from the masses in the very expensive resorts, or on their private yachts or private islands or secluded estates" (Beckerman 1974, pp. 50–51). Second, most people who are affected by mass tourism benefit from it, including the "pioneers," who, when they return to a place, find services that were not available when the number of visitors was small.

One also can criticize the applicability of the scarcity concept to the tourist industry. The implicit scarcities in the tourist industry are complex, and strategies can be adopted that allow the enjoyment of the same object by a greater number of persons. Thus, one must distinguish between the "physical capacity" and "perceptive capacity" of a tourist place (Walter 1982).

One also has to consider that in addition to the "romantic" tourist gaze, which emphasizes solitude, privacy, and a personal, quasi-spiritual relation with the observed object, there is an alternative "collective" gaze with different characteristics. The collective gaze demands the participation of wide numbers of other people to create a particular atmosphere: "They indicate that this is *the* place to be and that one should not be elsewhere." (Urry 1990, p. 46). This is the case for major cities, whose uniqueness lies in their cosmopolitan character: "It is the presence of people from all over the world (tourists in other words) that gives capital cities their distinct excitement and glamour" (Urry 1990, pp. 46).

Some people prefer to move around in compact formations because otherwise they will not enjoy themselves, while others prefer to travel in solitude. Therefore, Hirsh's (1978) thesis on scarcity and positional competition should be applied mainly to tourism characterized by the romantic gaze. When the collective gaze is more important, the problem of crowding and congestion is less marked. Moreover, the scarcity thesis would be totally applicable only if one maintained that there are severe limits to the number of "objects" worthy of the admiration of the tourist. However, "if Glasgow can be remade as a tourist attraction, one might wonder whether there are in fact any limits to the tourist, or post-tourist, gaze" (Urry 1990, p. 156).

Another issue refers to the nonauthenticity of the tourist experience. Turner and Ash (1975) describe a tourist who is placed at the center of a rigorously circumscribed world (the "environmental bubble"). Travel agents, couriers, and hotel managers are described as surrogate parents who relieve the tourist of every responsibility, protect the tourist from harsh reality, and decide for the tourist which objects are worthy to be admired.

Various types of tourists exist, and they are pushed by various needs and motivations for which various means are available to realize the tourist experience. In an age that is being defined as postmodern, the posttourist also is being redefined.

The post-tourist knows that they are a tourist and that tourism is a game, or rather a whole series of games with multiple texts and no single authentic tourist experience. The post-tourist thus knows that they will have to queue time and time again, that there will be hassles over foreign exchange, that the glossy brochure is a piece of pop culture, that the apparently authentic local entertainment is as socially contrived as an ethnic bar, and that the supposedly quaint and traditional fishing village could not survive without the income from tourism. (Urry 1990, p. 100).

The post-tourist knows that "he is not a time-traveller when he goes somewhere historic, not an instant noble savage when he stays on a tropical beach, not an invisible observer when he visits a native compound. Resolutely 'realistic,' he cannot evade his condition of outsider" (Feifer 1985, p. 271). This means that many travelers appreciate the "not-authenticity" of the tourist experience and "find pleasure in the multiplicity of tourist games. They know that there is *no* authentic tourist experience, that there are merely a series of games or texts that can be played" (Urry 1990, p. 11).

REFERENCES

Beckerman, W. 1974 *In Defense of Economic Growth.* London: Jonathan Cape.

Bugguley, P. 1987 *Flexibility, Restructuring and Gender: Changing Employment in Britain's Hotels.* Lancaster: Lancaster Regionalism Group, Working Paper no. 24.

Cohen, E. 1974 "Who Is a Tourist? A Conceptual Clarification." *Sociological Review* 4:527–556.

Feifer, M. 1985, *Going Places.* London: Macmillan.

Gottlieb, A. 1982 "Americans' Vacations." *Annals of Tourism Research* 9:165–187.

Hirsh, F. 1978 *Social Limits to Growth.* London: Routledge & Kegan Paul.

Hunziker, W. and K. Krapf 1942 *Grundriss der allgemeine Fremdenverkehrslehre.* Zurig.

Istituto Nazionale Ricerche Turistiche (National Institute for Tourism Research) 1997 *1997 Dove vanno in vacanza gli italiani.* Milan: Unioncamere.

Kovacshazy, M. C. 1998 "Le tourisme des seniors en 2010." *Futuribles* 233:47–64.

Krippendorf, J. 1987 *The Holiday Makers.* London: Heinemann.

Lodge, D. 1992 *Paradise News.* London: Penguin.

Lumley, R. (ed.) 1988 *The Museum Time-Machine.* London: Routledge.

Mishan, E. 1969 *The Costs of Economic Growth.* Harmondsworth, UK: Penguin.

Pearce, D. 1989 *Tourist Development.* Harlow, UK: Longman.

Plog, S. V. 1973 "Why Destination Areas Rise and Fall in Popularity." *Cornell Hotel and Restaurant Administration Quarterly*, November, pp. 13–16.

Prosser, R. 1994 "Societal Change and the Growth in Alternative Tourism." In E. Carter and G. Lowman, eds., *Ecotourism: A Sustainable Option?* New York: Wiley.

Ryan, C. 1991 *Recreational Tourism.* London: Routledge.

Savelli, A. 1986 "Turismo." In F. Demarchi, A. Ellena, and B. Cattarinussi, eds., *Nuovo dizionario di sociologia.* Rome: Paoline.

—— (1998), *Sociologia del turismo.* Milan: Angeli.

Schwaninger, M. 1989 "Trends in Leisure and Tourism for 2000–2010." In S. F. Witt and L. Moutinho, eds., *Tourism Marketing and Management Handbook.* Hemel Hempstead, UK: Prentice-Hall.

Turner, L., and J. Ash 1975 *The Golden Hordes.* London: Constable.

Turner, V., and E. Turner 1978 *Image and Pilgrimage in Christian Culture.* New York: Columbia University Press.

Urry, J. 1990 *The Tourist Gaze: Leisure and Travel in Contemporary Society.* Thousand Oaks, Calif.: Sage.

Veblen, T. [1899] 1970 *The Theory of the Leisure Class.* London: Allen & Unwin.

Walter, J. 1982 "Social Limits to Tourism." *Leisure Studies* 1:295–304.

GIOVANNI DELLI ZOTTI

TRANSNATIONAL CORPORATIONS

A transnational corporation (TNC) is "any enterprise that undertakes foreign direct investment, owns or controls income-gathering assets in more than one country, produces goods or services outside its country of origin, or engages in international production" (Biersteker 1978, p. xii). Variously termed multinational corporations (MNCs) and multinational enterprises (MNEs), transnational corporations are formal business organizations that have spatially dispersed operations in at least two countries. One of the most "transnational" major TNCs is Nestlé, the Swiss food giant; 91 percent of its total assets, 98 percent of its sales, and 97 percent of its workforce are foreign-based (UNCTAD 1998, p. 36).

TNCS AND THE GLOBAL ECONOMY

Although TNCs existed before the twentieth century (colonial trading companies such as the East India Company, the Hudson's Bay Company, and the Virginia Company of London were precursors of the modern TNC), only since the 1960s have they become a major force on the world scene (World Bank 1987, p. 45). Table 1 corroborates this by listing the foreign direct investment (FDI) stock of corporations by country from the beginning of the century to 1997. In 1900, only European corporations were major transnational players, but by 1930, American TNCs had begun to make their presence felt. The year 1960 marks the beginning of a new era in corporate transnationalization. In each of the decades from 1960 to the present, world FDI stock has more than tripled, whereas it only doubled during the first half of the century.

The phenomenal increase in transnational corporate activity in the latter part of the twentieth century can be accounted for in large part by technological innovations in transportation, communication, and information processing that have permitted corporations to establish profitable worldwide operations while maintaining effective and timely organizational control. The actual difference in foreign direct investment up to and after 1960 is even greater than the figures in Table 1 indicate. FDI for 1960 and before includes foreign *portfolio* investment, which is undertaken mainly by individuals, as well as foreign *direct* investment, which almost always is made by TNCs. These two types of investment were not reported separately for most countries before 1970. Thus, total FDI stocks are inflated. For example, Wilkins (1974, pp. 53–54) reports that in 1929–1930, U.S. foreign portfolio and direct investments were almost equal. American direct investment abroad was only $7.5 billion; the remaining $7.2 billion recorded in Table 1 was foreign portfolio investment.

Table 1 reveals that TNCs from only eleven countries accounted for almost 85 percent of all FDI in 1997. American TNCs accounted for more than one-quarter of total foreign investment, and

FDI Outward Investment Stock by Country, 1900–1997 (billions of US$)

Country	1900*	1930*	1960*	1971	1980	1990	1997†
United States	0.5	14.7	31.8	82.8	220.2	435.2	907.5
United Kingdom	12.1	18.2	13.2	23.1	80.4	229.3	413.2
Germany	4.8	1.1	0.6	7.0	43.1	151.6	326.0
Japan	Negligible	Negligible	Negligible	4.3	19.6	201.4	284.6
France	5.2	3.5	2.2	9.2	23.6	110.1	226.8
Netherlands	1.1	2.3	1.7	3.5	42.1	109.0	213.2
Switzerland	Negligible	Negligible	Negligible	6.5	21.5	65.7	156.7
Canada	Negligible	1.3	3.0	5.7	22.8	84.8	137.7
Italy	Negligible	Negligible	Negligible	NA	7.3	56.1	125.1
Belgium and Luxembourg	Negligible	Negligible	Negligible	NA	6.0	40.6	96.4
Sweden	Negligible	0.5	0.5	3.3	5.6	49.5	74.8
Others	Negligible	Negligible	Negligible	13.5	32.4	171.2	579.4
Total‡	23.8	41.6	53.8	159.2	524.6	1,704.5	3,541.4

Table 1

SOURCE: Data for 1900–1971 adapted from Buckley (1985), p. 200. Data for 1980–1997 from UNCTAD (1998), pp. 379–384.

NOTE: *Includes foreign portfolio investment as well as foreign direct investment.

†Estimates.

‡World total, excluding former Comecon countries, except for 1997.

corporations based in the Triad (United States, European Union, and Japan) were responsible for nearly four-fifths of world FDI stock (UNCTAD 1998, pp. 379–384). Clearly, TNCs largely operate out of and invest in the developed countries of the global economy.

The magnitude of FDI flow in the world is revealed by the fact that worldwide sales of foreign affiliates in 1997 totaled $9.5 trillion, almost one and a half times more than world exports of goods and services of $6.4 trillion (UNCTAD 1998, p. 5). Global sales of affiliates are considerably more important than exports in delivering goods and services to markets worldwide, underlining the importance of TNCs in structuring international economic relations. In 1997, 53,607 TNCs controlled nearly 450,000 foreign affiliates throughout the world (UNCTAD 1998, p. 4).

Table 2 presents the top 30 TNCs ranked by foreign assets. Although fewer than one-quarter of these corporations are American in origin, most names are well known in the United States. It is the

nature of transnational enterprise to generate this degree of familiarity. Among the top 100 TNCs in terms of foreign assets, 41 originate in the European Union, 28 in the United States, and 18 in Japan (UNCTAD 1998, p. 317). Most FDI inflows and outflows take place within the Triad. In 1996, approximately one-quarter of all foreign sales was accounted for by these top 100 firms. Among the major industries in which these TNCs operate, electronics and electrical equipment account for the largest number (17), followed by chemicals and pharmaceuticals (16), automotive (14), petroleum and mining (14), and food and beverages (12). In 1996, these transnational giants employed nearly 6 million foreign workers (UNCTAD 1998, pp. 35–43).

REASONS FOR BECOMING TRANSNATIONAL

The move toward integrated transnational investment can be seen as a logical and rational decision by business enterprises to adapt to their environ-

World's Leading Transnational Corporations by Foreign Assets, 1996 (billions of US$)

Corporation	Country	Industry	Foreign Assets	Total Assets
General Electric	United States	Electronics	82.8	272.4
Shell, Royal Dutch	United Kingdom/Netherlands	Petroleum	82.1	124.1
Ford Motors	United States	Automotive	79.1	258.0
Exxon	United States	Petroleum	55.6	95.5
General Motors	United States	Automotive	55.4	222.1
IBM	United States	Computers	41.4	81.1
Toyota	Japan	Automotive	39.2	113.4
Volkswagen	Germany	Automotive	—*	60.8
Mitsubishi	Japan	Diversified	—	77.9
Mobil	United States	Petroleum	31.3	46.4
Nestlé	Switzerland	Food	30.9	34.0
Asea Brown Boveri	Switzerland/Sweden	Electrical equipment	—	30.9
Elf Aquitaine	France	Petroleum	29.3	47.5
Bayer	Germany	Chemicals	29.1	32.0
Hoechst	Germany	Chemicals	28.0	35.5
Nissan	Japan	Automotive	27.0	58.1
FIAT	Italy	Automotive	26.9	70.6
Unilever	Neth/U.K.	Food	26.4	31.0
Daimler-Benz	Germany	Automotive	—	65.7
Philips Electronics	Netherlands	Electronics	24.5	31.7
Roche	Switzerland	Pharmaceuticals	24.5	29.5
Siemens	Germany	Electronics	24.4	56.3
Alcatel Alsthom Cie	France	Electronics	23.5	48.4
Sony	Japan	Electronics	23.5	45.8
Total	France	Petroleum	—	30.3
Novartis	Switzerland	Pharmaceuticals/ chemicals	21.4	43.4
British Petroleum	United Kingdom	Petroleum	20.7	31.8
Philip Morris	United States	Food/tobacco	20.6	54.9
ENI Group	Italy	Petroleum	—	59.5
Renault	France	Automotive	19.0	42.2

Table 2

SOURCE: UNCTAD (1998), p. 36.

NOTE: *Data on foreign assets are suppressed to avoid disclosure or are not available. In case of nonavailability, they are estimated on the basis of the ration of foreign to total sales, the ratio of foreign to total employment, or similar ratios.

Reasons for Corporations Becoming Transnational

1. *Cost-Related Reasons*

    a. To take advantage of differences in technological development, labor potential, productivity and mentality, capital market, and local taxes
    b. Reduction of transport costs
    c. Avoidance of high tariff barriers
    d. To take advantage of local talents when establishing R&D overseas

2. Sales Volume Reasons

    a. Foreign middlemen unable to meet financial demands of expanded marketing
    b. For quicker adaptation to local market changes and better adaptation to local conditions
    c. Following important customers abroad
    d. Keeping up with competitors
    e. Persuasion and coercion of foreign governments
    f. To obtain a better international division of labor, larger production runs, and better utilization of available economies of scale
    g. To avoid home country regulations, e.g., fiscal and antitrust legislation

3. Reasons Related to Risk Factors

    a. To avoid exclusion from customers' and suppliers' markets, promoting forward and backward integration
    b. To counter inflexibility and avoid country-specific recessions
    c. To reduce risks of social and political disruption by establishing operations in a number of host countries

Table 3

SOURCE: Taylor and Thrift (1982), p. 21.

ment. Historically, there have been several distinct strategies: (1) expansion in the size of operations to achieve economies of scale, (2) horizontal integration, or the merging of similar firms to increase market share, (3) vertical integration, or the acquiring of firms that either supply raw materials (backward integration) or handle output (forward integration) to attain greater control, (4) spatial dispersion or regional relocation to expand markets, (5) product diversification to develop new markets, and (6) conglomeration or mergers with companies on the basis of their financial performance rather than what they produce (Chandler 1962, 1990; Fligstein 1990). Establishing an integrated TNC simply represents a new strategy in this evolutionary chain. Furthermore, depending on how a corporation is set up and with recent innovations in communications and information technology, a TNC can incorporate all these strategies so that the newly structured enterprise has far

greater control and a much less restricted market than it had previously.

Table 3 presents a list of reasons why it may be profitable for an organization to become transnational. First, direct costs for raw materials, labor, and transportation as well as indirect cost considerations such as tariff barriers and trade restrictions, local tax structures, and various government inducements obviously loom large in the decision to establish operations transnationally. Second, market factors may be equally important in that decision. Direct and easy access to local markets unfettered by foreign trade quotas and other legislative restraints can give TNCs an edge over their nontransnational competitors. Finally, the decision to become transnational may hinge on factors related to organizational control. Control over raw materials (backward integration) and markets (forward integration) and achieving sufficient regional and product diversification to withstand temporary economic downturns are other reasons for transnational relocation.

TNCS, NATION-STATES, AND GLOBALIZATION

Integrated TNCs traversing real-time electronic networks that span the global economy have produced a "borderless world" (Ohmae 1991). These technologically enhanced corporations also operate in the nonnationally controlled interstices of the planet (i.e., oceans, seabeds, airwaves, sky, and space), sometimes leaving toxic, life-threatening indicators of their presence. Existing in a sort of parallel world, they are responsible only to amorphous groups of shareholders. Gill and Law (1988, pp. 364–365) state that there is a "growing lack of congruence between the 'world economy,' with its tendencies to promote ever-greater levels of economic integration, and an 'international political system' comprised of many rival states." The rivalry between these two systems of world organization is revealed by the fact that 51 of the 100 largest economies in the world are TNCs (Karliner 1997).

The increasing domination of the world economy by TNCs directly challenges national sovereignty. Historically, the sovereignty and therefore the power of a nation-state lay in its ability to achieve compliance with whatever it commanded its territorially defined space. Borderlines physically defined what was territorially sovereign and what was not. If a state's sovereignty was challenged from outside its territory, it could resort to force to maintain control. However, as a result of various technological developments, the idea of a physically bounded and sealed state is now open to question. These developments underlie the transnational corporate threat to state sovereignty along the following three dimensions:

1. *Permeability of borders.* Borderlines between nation-states have been rendered permeable and porous in a number of innovative ways, erasing many of the traditional distinctions between "inside" and "outside." For example, what borders do electronic communications and atmospheric pollutants observe? Under whose borders do oil and gas reserves lie? Do space satellites invade territorial integrity? The new permeability of borders diminishes the capacity of nation-states to distinguish and determine what occurs "inside" their territory.

2. *Mobility across borders.* Developments in transportation, communication, and information technology not only have increased the rate of cross-border mobility among TNCs but also have increased the speed or velocity with which cross-border transactions take place. Concurrently measuring both the location and the velocity of TNC activity often produces "uncertain" results, generating "inderminacy" for a state.

3. *Border straddling.* To the extent that TNCs operate simultaneously in different sovereign jurisdictions, which jurisdiction has precedence over which corporate activities at what time? This complex issue blurs the legal boundaries between states. It also confuses the notion of "citizenship" and its attendant rights and responsibilities.

Through the use of these and other innovative strategies, TNCs have manipulated the concept of borders to their advantage. What exactly is the advantage that TNCs achieve through their cross-border flexibility? They gain between-border variability. The fact that different states have different laws and standards regarding all aspects of economic activity contributes to the power of TNCs that strategically play off one country's set of rules against another's. For example, variations in national laws on tariffs, financing, competition, labor, environmental protection, consumer rights, taxation, and transfer of profits are all carefully weighed by TNCs in deciding where and how to conduct business. Together, these considerations form what has come to be known as "the policy environment" (UNCTAD 1993, pp. 173–175). In the internation competition to attract foreign investment by creating a "favorable policy environment," between-border variability encourages a "race to the bottom" (Chamberlain 1982, p. 126), resulting in a continuing erosion of sovereignty. Whereas TNCs operate in a de facto borderless world created by technological ingenuity, de jure political and legal distinctions still mark the boundaries on a world map composed of nation-states. This represents the crux of the inherent conflict between TNCs and nation-states as they are currently structured.

Never before has there been a situation in which foreign organizations have been granted license almost as a matter of course to operate freely within the legally defined boundaries of a sovereign state. This, together with the fact that TNCs and nation-states are different organizational forms, established for different purposes, administered by different principles, and loyal to different constituencies, means that structural problems are bound to arise.

TNCS AND WORLD DEVELOPMENT

Although only 30 percent of FDI stock is in developing countries (UNCTAD 1998, p. 373), because of the immense power of many TNCs, great concern has arisen about the impact of TNCs on world development. Because the goals of transnational capitalist enterprise and indigenous national government are fundamentally different, many scholars have debated whether TNCs are an aid or a hindrance to world development. According to Biersteker (1978), the major points of contention in this debate are the degrees to which TNCs (1) are responsible for a net outflow of capital from developing countries, (2) displace indigenous production, (3) engage in technology transfer, (4) introduce capital-intensive, labor-displacing technologies, (5) encourage elite-oriented patterns of consumption, (6) produce divisiveness within local social structures owing to competing loyalties to TNCs and nation-states, and (7) exacerbate unequal distributions of income.

In a study of many of these issues, Kentor (1998, p. 1025) analyzed a fifty-year data set consisting of seventy-five developing countries to determine whether the modernization thesis (i.e., FDI in developing countries promotes "economic growth by creating industries, transferring technology, and fostering a 'modern' perspective in the local population") or dependency theory (i.e., FDI results in disarticulated economic growth, repatriation of profits, increased income inequality, and stagnation) better explains the long-term results of foreign direct investment. Kentor (p. 1042) summarizes his findings as follows:

> *The results of this study confirm that peripheral countries with relatively high dependence on foreign capital exhibit slower economic growth than those less dependent peripheral countries. These findings have been replicated using different measures of foreign investment dependence, GDP data, countries, time periods, and statistical methods. This is a significant and persistent negative effect, lasting for decades. Further, a structure of dependency is created that perpetuates these effects. The consequences of these effects, as described in the literature, are pervasive: unemployment, overurbanization, income inequality, and social unrest, to name a few.*

Given current conditions, it would appear that overreliance on foreign investment by developing countries will widen the already huge global rift between rich and poor nations.

TNCS AND REGULATION

In the late 1960s, the United Nations (UN) reached the opinion that "transnational corporations had come to play a central role in the world economy and that their role, with its transnational character, was not matched by a corresponding understanding or an international framework covering their activities" (UNCTC 1990, p. 3). In the 1970s, the UN produced a draft "Code of Conduct on Transnational Corporations." However, twenty years later, after much political wrangling, UN delegates concluded in 1992 that "no consensus was possible on the draft Code," and thus the process of trying to achieve some effective legal

reconciliation between the goals of TNCs and those of host governments was brought to "a formal end" (UNCTAD 1993, p. 33).

Currently, although several international voluntary guidelines monitor the activities of TNCs, generally they have not been very successful (Hedley 1999). As of 1997, 143 countries had legislation in effect that specifically governs foreign direct investment (UNCTAD 1998, p. 53). Although initially most of those laws were framed to control the entry and regulate the activities of TNCs, legislative changes increasingly have become *more* favorable to foreign investment. For example, from 1991 to 1997, of the 750 changes to foreign investment policy made by countries worldwide, 94 percent were in the direction of liberalization (UNCTAD 1998, 57). In 1997, in attempts to ease high debt loads and survive a worldwide economic downturn, seventy-six developed and developing countries introduced 135 legislative inducements along the following lines: more liberal operational conditions and frameworks (61), more incentives (41), more sectoral liberalization (17), more promotion (other than incentives) (8), more guarantees and protection (5), and more liberal entry conditions and procedures (3) (UNCTAD 1998, p. 57). In their competition to attract foreign investment by creating favorable policy environments, these countries are yielding ever more control to TNCs.

Given the increasing dominance of TNCs in the global economy, the reasons why corporations become transnational, the diminishing sovereignty of nation-states, and the long-term effects of FDI on world development, one may question whether the move toward liberalization is in the interests of the countries and people who are encouraging it. What is called for is nothing short of a revolution in world governance. To regulate *trans*national corporations, it is necessary to introduce *trans*- or *supra*national legislation. To maintain national sovereignty in a global economy, authority must be coordinated and shared across borders. Legislative harmonization, although entailing an initial loss of sovereignty for participating states, can restore their authority over TNCs operating within their jurisdictions. By these means, corporate accountability can be imposed according to the needs and wishes of civil society. Whether or when such legislative harmonization will occur is open to question. However, in the view of the U.S. Tariff

Commission, "It is beyond dispute that the spread of multinational business ranks with the development of the steam engine, electric power, and the automobile as one of the major events of economic history" (cited in Lall and Streeton 1977, p. 15).

REFERENCES

Biersteker, Thomas J. 1978 *Distortion of Development? Contending Perspectives on the Multinational Corporation*. Cambridge, Mass.: MIT Press.

Buckley, Peter J. 1985 "Testing Theories of the Multinational Enterprise." In Peter J. Buckley and Mark Casson, eds., *The Economic Theory of the Multinational Enterprise*. London: Macmillan.

Chamberlain, Neil W. 1982 *Social Strategy and Corporate Structure*. New York: Macmillan.

Chandler, Alfred D., Jr. 1962 *Strategy and Structure: Chapters in the History of Industrial Enterprise*. Cambridge, Mass.: MIT Press.

—— 1990 *Scale and Scope: The Dynamics of Industrial Capitalism*. Cambridge, Mass.: Belknap Press of Harvard University Press.

Fligstein, Neil 1990 *The Transformation of Corporate Control*. Cambridge, Mass.: Harvard University Press.

Gill, Stephen, and David Law 1988 *The Global Political Economy*. Baltimore: Johns Hopkins University Press.

Hedley, R. Alan 1999 "Transnational Corporations and Their Regulation: Issues and Strategies." *International Journal of Comparative Sociology* 40(2):215–230.

Karliner, Joshua 1997 *The Corporate Planet: Ecology and Politics in the Age of Globalization*. Sierra Club Books. Available at http://www.sierraclub.org/books/.

Kentor, Jeffrey 1998 "The Long-Term Effects of Foreign Investment Dependence on Economic Growth, 1940–1990." *American Journal of Sociology* 103(4):1024–1046.

Lall, Sanjaya, and P. Streeton 1977 *Foreign Investment, Transnationals, and Developing Countries*. London: Macmillan.

Ohmae, Kenichi 1991 *The Borderless World: Power and Strategy in the Interlinked Economy*. Hammersmith, UK: Fontana.

Taylor, M. J., and N. J. Thrift 1982 *The Geography of Multinationals: Studies in the Spatial Development and Economic Consequences of Multinational Corporations*. London: Croom Helm.

UNCTAD 1993 *World Investment Report 1993: Transnational Corporations and Integrated International Production*. New York: United Nations Conference on Trade and Development.

—— 1998 *World Investment Report 1997: Trends and Determinants*. New York: United Nations Conference on Trade and Development.

UNCTC 1990 *The New Code Environment*, Series A, No. 16. New York: United Nations Centre on Transnational Corporations.

Wilkins, Mira 1974 *The Maturing of Multinational Enterprise: American Business Abroad from 1914 to 1970*. Cambridge, Mass.: Harvard University Press.

World Bank 1987 *World Development Report 1987*. New York: Oxford University Press.

R. ALAN HEDLEY

TRANSSEXUALS

See Sexual Orientation.

TRANSVESTITISM

See Sexual Orientation.

TRIBES

See Indigenous Peoples.

TYPOLOGIES

A typology is a multidimensional classification. The study of typological procedures is impeded by the use of a plethora of terms, some of which are used interchangeably. "Classification" can be defined as the grouping of entities on the basis of similarity. For example, humans can be classified into female and male. A related term is "taxonomy." According to Simpson (1961, p. 11), taxonomy "is the theoretical study of classification, including its bases, principles, procedures, and rules." Interestingly, the term "classification" has two meanings: One can speak of both the process of classification and its end product, a classification. The terms "classification," "typology," and "taxonomy" are all used widely and somewhat interchangeably in sociology.

Any classification must be mutually exclusive and exhaustive. This requires that there be only one cell for each case. For example, if humans are being classified by sex, this requires that every case be placed in a cell (either male or female) but that *no* case be placed in more than one cell (no intermediate cases are allowed). It is assumed that the bases or dimensions for classification (such as sex) are clear and important (see Tiryakian 1968).

A type is one cell in a full typology. In sociology, emphasis often has been placed on one or a few types rather than on the full typology. The study of types developed largely as a verbal tradition in sociology and lately has been merged with a more recently developed quantitative approach.

In the verbal tradition, types were often defined as mental constructs or concepts, in contrast to empirically derived entities. Stinchcombe (1968, p. 43, original emphasis) says that "a *type concept* in scientific discourse is a concept which is constructed out of a *combination of the values of several variables.*" Lazarsfeld (1937, p. 120) says that "one is safe in saying that the concept of type is always used in referring to special compounds of attributes." The variables that combine to form a type must be correlated or "connected to each other" (Stinchcombe 1968, pp. 44–45).

An important function of a type is to serve as a criterion point (for comparative purposes) for the study of other types or empirical phenomena. In this case, only a single type is formulated. The most famous single-type formulation is Weber's ideal type:

> *An ideal type is formed by the one-sided* accentuation *of one or more points of view. . . In its conceptual purity, this mental construct* [Gedankenbild] *cannot be found empirically anywhere in reality. It is a utopia. Historical research faces the task of determining in each individual case the extent to which this ideal-construct approximates to or diverges from reality, to what extent for example, the economic structure of a certain city is to be classified as a "city economy."* (1947, p. 90, original emphasis)

This strategy has been criticized. Martindale is startled by the suggestion that "we compare actual individuals with the (admittedly imaginary) ideal typical individuals to see how much they deviate from them. This is nothing but a form of intellectual acrobatics, for actual individuals ought to deviate from the ideal type just as much as one made them deviate in the first place" (1960, p. 382).

Seizing on Weber's statement that the pure ideal type "cannot be found empirically anywhere in reality," critics view the ideal type as hypothetical and thus without a fixed position, rendering it useless as a criterion point. A more realistic interpretation is that the ideal type represents a type that *could* be found empirically; it is simply that the purest case is the one most useful as a criterion, and this case is unlikely to be found empirically. As an example, a proof specimen of a coin is the best criterion for classifying or grading other coins, but it is not found empirically in the sense of being in circulation. If it were circulated, its features soon would be worn to the extent that its value for comparison with other coins would be greatly diminished.

The strategy of the ideal type is a sound one. Its logic is simple, and the confusion surrounding it is unfortunate, perhaps being due in part to the translation of Weber's work. The genius of the ideal type lies in its parsimony. Instead of using a large full typology (say, of 144 cells, many of which may turn out to be empirically null or empty), a researcher can utilize a single ideal type. Then, instead of dealing needlessly with many null cells, the researcher need only fill in cells for which there are actual empirical cases and only as those cases are encountered. The ideal type is an accentuated or magnified version (or purest form) of the type. Although rarely found empirically in this pure form, the ideal type serves as a good comparison point. It usually represents the highest value on each of the intercorrelated variables or the end point of the continuum. While one could use the middle of the continuum as a referent (just as one uses the mean or median), it is convenient and perhaps clearer to use the end point (just as one measures from the end of a ruler rather than from its middle or another intermediate point).

Another single type that is used as a criterion is the constructed type. McKinney (1966, p. 3, original emphasis) defines the constructed type as "a *purposive, planned selection, abstraction, combination, and (sometimes) accentuation of a set of criteria with empirical referents that serves as a basis for comparison of empirical cases.*" The constructed type is a more general form of the ideal type.

In addition to formulations that use a single type, there are formulations that use two or more types. One strategy involves the use of two "polar" types (as in the North and South poles). These types serve as two bracketing criteria for the comparison of cases. A famous set of types is Tönnies's (1957) *Gemeinschaft* and *Gesellschaft* ("community" and "society"). Another is introvert and extrovert. Still others are primary and secondary groups and localistic and cosmopolitan communities (see McKinney 1966, p. 101, for these and other examples).

SUBSTRUCTION

One problem with the common practice of using only a single type or a few types is that the underlying correlated dimensions on which they are based may not be clear. In some cases, it is possible to make these dimensions clear and extend them all to form a property space or attribute space; a set of axes representing the full range of values on each dimension. Then the existence of other potential related types that were not originally formulated, can be discerned. This process of extending the full property space and the resulting full typology from a single type or a few types is called *substruction* and was developed by Lazarsfeld (1937; Barton 1955). As an example, Barton (1955, pp. 51–52) performed a substruction in which the attributes underlying the four types of folkways, mores, law, and custom were extended to form a full property space. Barton found three underlying dimensions of the four types ("how originated," "how enforced," and "strength of group feeling") and combined them to form the property space.

REDUCTION

The opposite of substruction is *reduction*. Reduction is used when one has a full typology that is unmanageable because of its size. The three basic forms of reduction presented by Lazarsfeld (1937, p. 127) are functional, arbitrary numerical, and pragmatic. Lazarsfeld's functional reduction consists of discarding from the typology all empirically null and thus unnecessary cells.

The second form of reduction is arbitrary numerical. Lazarsfeld (1937, p. 128) provides an example: In constructing an index of housing conditions, one might weight plumbing without central heat or a refrigerator as being equal to the other two without plumbing. Coding the existence of an attribute by 1 and the lack of it by 0 and taking variables in this order (plumbing, central heat, refrigerator), Lazarsfeld is saying that (1, 0, 0) = (0, 1, 1). Thus, two previously different three-dimensional cells are equated and reduced to one.

Lazarsfeld's third form of reduction is pragmatic reduction. It consists of collapsing contiguous cells together to make one larger (but generally more heterogeneous) cell. As Lazarsfeld (1937, p. 128) says, "in the case of pragmatic reduction, certain groups of combinations are contracted to one class in view of the research purpose." For examples of these three forms of reduction, see Bailey (1973).

With Lazarsfeld's rigorous work as a notable exception, it can be said that most work in the typological tradition has been qualitative. Blalock, commenting on McKinney's (1966) constructive typology, says:

> He [McKinney] also claims that there is nothing inherently anti-quantitative in the use of typologies. He notes that historically, however, researchers skilled in the use of typologies have not been statistically or mathematically inclined, and vice-versa. This may be one of the reasons for the existing gap between sociological theory and research. (1969, p. 33)

A persistent problem in the qualitative typological tradition has been the confusion over the status of the type as a heuristic device, a mental construct, or an empirical entity. Winch (1947) distinguished between heuristic and empirical types. He said that heuristic types are conceptually derived and may not have empirical examples. Empirical types, in contrast, result solely from data analysis, without prior conceptualization. A persistent problem with the conceptual types, such as the ideal type, has been the problem of inappropriate reification. If a type is a construct, concept, or model, it may not be found empirically but is designed only to be heuristically used in developing theory. However, there is often a tendency over time to reify the type or act as though it were actually found empirically. Figure 1 shows that the qualitative tradition has both heuristic and empirical types, while the quantitative tradition (discussed below) has primarily empirical types, as its types are derived from data analysis.

In other cases in the qualitative typological tradition, types are meant as empirical phenom-

	Qualitative	Quantitative
Heuristic	Ideal type	Probably null
Empirical	Ethnographic types	Types derived from cluster analysis or numerical taxonomy

Figure 1. A Typology of Typologies

ena rather than heuristic devices. This is particularly true in the area of social ethnography or field research, where researchers eschew statistical analysis but analyze data resulting from field studies by developing typologies based on observations recorded in their field notes (see Spradley and McCurdy 1972). Typologies in this case take the form of tables with names or labels in the cells rather than frequencies of occurrence as in statistical tables. Here the labels or types are generally inductively or empirically derived through intensive study of groups in the field. However, even here there may be a distinction between the types derived by the researcher and the types actually used by the people being studied. For example, the types that tramps identify among themselves (mission stiff, bindle stiff) may be different from the types identified by researchers or the lay public (bums, winos, homeless persons). For a discussion of taxonomies in ethnographic research and a number of examples of actual taxonomies (inducting the tramp example), see Spradley and McCurdy (1972).

EMPIRICAL DERIVATION

Computerization has brought on a new era of quantitative typology construction, which now coexists with the older qualitative tradition. This new approach often is called numerical taxonomy, cluster analysis, or pattern recognition (see Sneath and Sokal 1973; Bailey 1974). In contrast to the earlier verbal approach, which largely dealt with concepts and mental constructs, the newer quantitative approach is largely empirical and inductive. It begins with a data set and derives empirical types from the data through a variety of quantitative procedures, many of them computerized.

This newer statistical approach to classification can be elucidated through the monothetic-polythetic distinction. A typology is monothetic if the possession of a unique set of features is both necessary and sufficient for identifying a specimen as belonging to a particular cell in the typology. That is, each feature is necessary and the set is sufficient. Thus, no specimen can be assigned to a particular type unless it possesses all the features (and no others) required of that type. This means that all the specimens in a given type are identical in every way (at least in all the features specified).

In contrast, a polythetic typology is constructed by grouping together the individuals within a sample that have the greatest number of shared features. No single feature is either necessary or sufficient (Sokal and Sneath 1963, p. 14). The objects or specimens are grouped to maximize overall similarity within each group. In a polythetic type, each individual possesses a large number of the classifying properties and each property is possessed by a large number of individuals. In the case where *no* single property is possessed by every individual in the group, the type is said to be fully polythetic.

While a verbal type (such as the ideal type) may be purely homogeneous (i.e., monothetic), it is unlikely that an empirically constructed type will be monothetic (except for some divisively derived types), especially if it contains a large number of cases grouped on a large number of variables. Thus, most empirically constructed types are polythetic, and some may be fully polythetic, without even a single feature being common to all the members of the group.

A basic distinction for all empirical classification techniques is whether one groups objects or variables. The former is known as Q-analysis, and the latter as R-analysis (Sokal and Sneath 1963, p. 124). In R-analysis, one computes coefficients (either similarity or distance coefficients) down the columns of the basic score matrix, which includes objects and variables (see Table 1 in Bailey 1972). In Q-analysis, one correlates rows. The interior data cells are the same in any case, and one form is the simple matrix transposition of the other. The difference is that Q-analysis correlates the objects (e.g., persons), while R-analysis correlates the variables (e.g., age). While Q-analysis is the most common form in biology (see Sneath and Sokal 1973), it rarely is used in sociology (for an example, see Butler and Adams 1966). One problem is that Q-analysis requires a small sample of cases measured on a large number of variables, while R-analysis requires a large sample of cases with a smaller number of variables. Biology has the former sort of data; sociology, the latter.

Most sociologists have had little experience with Q-analysis. Most statistical analysis in sociology is concerned with relationships between two or more variables, with few studies making inferences concerning individuals rather than variables. Thus, the very notion of correlating individuals is alien to many sociologists.

Once the researcher has decided whether to pursue Q-analysis or R-analysis, the next step is to decide which measure of similarity to use. A researcher can measure similarity either directly, with a correlation coefficient, or indirectly, with a distance coefficient. While similarity coefficients show how close together two objects or variables are in the property space, distance coefficients show how far apart they are in that space. For a discussion of these measures, see Bailey (1974).

The next task of empirical typology construction is to parsimoniously group the cases into homogeneous types. There are two chief ways to proceed. One can envision all N cases as forming a single type. This is maximally parsimonious but maximizes within-group or internal variance. Grouping proceeds "from above" by dividing the cases into smaller groups that are more homogeneous. This is called the *divisive strategy*. Divisive classification generally proceeds by dividing the group on the basis of similarity on one or more variables, either simultaneously or sequentially. According to Sokal and Sneath (1963, p. 16), divisive classification is "inevitably largely monothetic."

The alternative strategy (the *agglomerative strategy*) is to envision the N cases as forming N separate groups of one case each. Then each group is homogeneous (including only a single case), but parsimony is minimal. The strategy here is "classification from below" by agglomerating or grouping the most similar cases together, yielding some loss of internal homogeneity but gaining parsimony (as N groups are generally too unwieldy).

Unlike divisively formed types, agglomeratively formed types are generally polythetic and often fully polythetic.

The basic typological strategy is very straightforward and logically simple for divisive methods. All one must do is partition the set of cases in all possible ways and choose the grouping that maximizes internal homogeneity in a sufficiently small number of clusters. The problem is that the computation is prohibitive even for a modest number of cases measured on a modest number of variables.

A basic problem with empirically derived typologies is that they are generally static because the measures of similarity or distance that are used are synchronic rather than diachronic. While this is a problem, it is not a problem unique to classification but is shared by almost all forms of sociological analysis. Further, it is possible to deal with this issue by using diachronic data such as change coefficients or time series data.

Despite procedural differences, there are clear congruences between the qualitative and quantitative typological approaches. The ideal type is essentially monothetic, as are some types produced by quantitative divisive procedures. Quantitative procedures produce types that are polythetic, even fully polythetic. The results of quantitative procedures are generally not full typologies but reduced form that include fewer than the potential maximum number of types. Such polythetic types can be seen as analogous to the result of subjecting full monothetic typologies to reduction (either pragmatic or arbitrary numerical). Thus, contemporary typologists meet the need for reduction by using quantitative methods. Any correlational method of typology construction is by definition a method of functional reduction.

Further, the method usually will perform pragmatic reduction along with the functional reduction. Remember that pragmatic reduction collapses monothetic cells. The correlation coefficients utilized in typological methods are never perfect. The lower the correlations are, the more diverse the individuals in a group are. Placing diverse individuals in one group is tantamount to collapsing monothetic cells by means of pragmatic reduction. Thus, there are two basic avenues for constructing reduced types: Begin with monothetic types (such as ideal types) and subject them to the various forms of reduction to yield polythetic types or construct polythetic types directly by using quantitative methods. Thus, the qualitative and quantitative procedures can produce similar results.

Given the breadth and diversity of sociological typologies (for example, from quantitative to qualitative procedures and from heuristic to empirical types), it is not surprising that there have been a number of criticisms of typologies. Some alleged problems are that typologies are not mutually exclusive and exhaustive, are treated as ends in themselves rather than as means to an end, are not parsimonious, are based on arbitrary and ad hoc criteria, are essentially static, rely on dichotomized rather than internally measured variables, yield types that are subject to reification, and are basically descriptive rather than explanatory or predictive. All these factors can be problems but are relatively easy for a knowledgeable typologist to avoid. The ones that cannot be easily avoided (such as the problem of cross-sectional data) often are seen as general problems for sociology as a whole and are not specific to typology construction.

MERITS

Even if pitfalls remain, the merits of carefully constructed typologies make them well worth the effort. One of the chief merits of a typology is parsimony. A researcher who is overwhelmed by thousands or even millions of individual cases can work comfortably with those cases when they are grouped into a few main types. A related merit is the emphasis on bringing simplicity and order out of complexity and chaos. A focus on the relative homogeneity of types provides an emphasis on order in contrast to the emphasis on diversity and complexity that is paramount in untyped phenomena. A third merit of a full typology is its comprehensiveness. There is no other tool available that can show not only all relevant dimensions but also the relationships between them and the categories created by the intersections. Such a typology shows the entire range of every variable and all their confluences. A fourth merit (as was noted above) is a typology's use of a type or types for comparative purposes. A fifth merit is a typology's use as a heuristic tool to highlight the relevant theoretical dimensions of a type. A sixth is a typology's ability to show which cells have empirical examples and which are empirically null. This can aid in hypothesis testing, especially when a large number of variables have a small number of values that actually occur (Stinchcombe 1968, p. 47). A seventh merit is a typology's ability to combine two or more variables in such a way that interaction effects can be analyzed (Stinchcombe 1968, pp. 46–47).

TYPOLOGIES AND CONTINUOUS DATA

A clear but sometimes unstated goal of scientific development is to move past simple, nominal-variable analysis to the use of complex continuous-data models by employing ratio or interval variables. This has clearly been the case in sociology, which now depends on sophisticated regression models that work best with ratio (or at least interval) variables. Thus, some might argue that as science moves away from types toward the use of variables, typology construction becomes secondary.

Although the logic of moving from a reliance on types to a reliance on interval and ratio variables may seem irrefutable, this transition is not as smooth as some might wish. In fact, a number of obstacles to the transition from types to variables have arisen. Some researchers feel that once they have adopted sophisticated statistical techniques that use ratio variables, typologies are no longer needed. The reasoning here is that typologies are chiefly descriptive, arise at an early level of scientific analysis, and are essentially crude or unsophisticated formulations. In contrast, later models focus on explanation and prediction rather than description.

This notion belies the fact that science must constantly develop new ideas and theories to regenerate itself. As it does so, it must repeat the process of providing sound typologies that facilitate research by aiding in concept development and clarification and provide a comprehensive overview. Thus, it is a dangerous myth to think that sociology has "outgrown" the need for typologies. In fact, new ideas, theories, and sociological areas of research continually require new typologies. Even researchers in older, more mature sociological areas that have based their theory and research on inadequate typologies may find that the foundations of their field are crumbling, requiring new attempts to provide sound typological reinforcements.

In addition to the constant need for typological renewal and rejuvenation, some sociologists find that attempts to move past types to sophisticated statistical analyses of ratio variables are confronted with a bewildering array of obstacles. Contemporary sociological statisticians who wish to rely on ratio variables are faced with a classic paradox. On the one hand, their regression models assume (or even demand) at least interval, or ideally ratio, variables. On the other hand, sociological theory is dependent on empirically important concepts, many of which are found to be essentially nominal or ordinal in their measurement levels. These include central ascribed or achieved statuses such as gender, race, religion, geographic region, nationality, occupation, and political affiliation.

Other important variables, such as income, education, and age, are more suitable for sophisticated statistical models. However, even these variables often are utilized theoretically in a limited ordinal form (young–old, high income–low income, etc.). Thus, there may be an empirical disjuncture between the type of variable needed for regression analysis (or other modern statistical techniques) and the type required by empirical sociological theory. Theory needs concepts such as race, gender, and religion, and these concepts are more suited for typological analysis than for regression analysis.

This suggests two areas of future research. One is to modify regression models to accommodate categorical variables, and this has been done (Aldrich and Nelson 1984). However, such accommodation may be costly, as it is unclear whether modified models operate efficiently or significantly underestimate the degree of explained variance. The second avenue is to rely more heavily on typological analysis. Although this may not seem as "sophisticated," it may prove more compatible with theory and thus facilitate theoretical development more than statistical models do.

TYPOLOGIES IN THE AGE OF STATISTICS

If one has to choose between a sophisticated statistical analysis with variables that are not central to sociological theory and a typological analysis that accommodates theoretically important variables, it is foolish to rule out the latter in the name of scientific progress. Such progress would be false if the use of sophisticated techniques proved theo-

retically vacuous. This would be a classic case of the statistical tale wagging the theoretical dog. A wiser course is to recognize the complementarity between typologies and statistics. Statistics need not be viewed as necessarily or inevitably supplanting typologies; instead, each can be used when it proves valuable.

The conclusion to this point is that sociological progress has not rendered typological analysis obsolete by emphasizing statistical techniques such as multiple regression analysis. Thus, it may prove useful to look further at the epistemological foundations of contemporary sociology to see what the role of typologies is in an era when statistical analysis dominates. Consider the gap between the language of theory construction and the language of statistical data analysis. Imagine that a sociologist is interested in the type concept of "underachiever" and defines it as a person who has the ability to achieve at a higher level than is actualized.

When one substructs this type, it is clear that it is formed from two dimensions: (1) individual ability and (2) individual achievement. The sociologist can then theorize that an affluent childhood results in a particular type of personality. Individuals with that personality feel no pressing psychological need to achieve at a high level, since their needs continue to be met. This is an intriguing and ideographically rich sociological hypothesis. It involves images of a living person who has a particular type of childhood that leads to a particular type of adulthood. Thus, an earlier type concept ("the rich kid") evolves into a later type concept ("the underachiever"). Conversely, one could hypothesize that the type concept of "impoverished youth" leads to the subsequent adult concept of "overachiever."

The most direct way to test the hypothesis that the rich kid evolves into the adult underachiever is to identify a group of rich kids, follow them until adulthood, and then measure their subsequent achievement rates over a period of time. However, this is both tedious and time-consuming and is not the typical approach in social science. The most common approach is to gather cross-sectional survey data and then conduct a statistical analysis on the data. It is simple to select the two salient variables of parental wealth and adult achievement. Suppose one finds a negative correlation between parental wealth and adult achievement.

Since a negative correlation of achievement with wealth is not synonymous with the type concept of underachievement, the data analysis is not adequate to test the hypothesis.

Even if the statistical analysis were sufficient to test the hypothesis, a mere correlation value (e.g., r = .43) is very sterile and is isolated from both sociological reality and the richness of sociological theory. It fails to convey the richness of the type-concept description. While the type referent for the type concept of "underachiever" is the holistic, living human individual, the referents for the statistical analysis are the variables of wealth and achievement, which seem artificially separated from the sociological reality the theory refers to and the type concept manages to capture.

The unfortunate aspect of this for sociological development is that it leaves theory construction and statistical analysis as two juxtaposed but separate entities with a clear disjuncture between them. This disjuncture results from the fact that theorizing is largely a conceptual undertaking. It involves both deductive and inductive reasoning, and its language is the holistic language of the individual actor. The prime theoretical referent is the object, not the variable. This object is usually the human individual but can be an alternative object, such as a group, city, or country. In any event, the primary focus is on the object, with variables receiving a secondary focus. However, even if variables have the primary focus, the focus remains on both object and the variables.

In statistics using R-analysis such as multiple regression, the epistemological focus is quite different. Here objects such as persons enter the analysis only as data carriers in the sample. As soon as the R-matrix of correlations among variables is established, it suffices for the remainder of the analysis. The result is that the individuals virtually disappear from the picture except in those rare instances in sociology where Q-correlations are used.

Thus, theory and statistical analysis remain two separate paradigms within sociology rather than two aspects of the same research process. This obviously hinders scientific progress sociology and stands in stark contrast to the physical sciences, where theory and method are not separated processes but are well integrated, enabling much swifter progress.

INTEGRATING TYPES AND TAXA

One way to bridge the dichotomy between theory and statistical method is to link qualitative type concepts with the empirical clusters derived quantitatively through methods of numerical taxonomy. Following the lead of Bailey (1994), these are called taxa. As was noted above, types are generally conceptual, monothetic, and based on underlying R-dimensions (although the cell entries are empirical objects). In contrast, taxa tend to be empirical, polythetic, and Q-analytic (based on individuals). While the differences may seem to mimic the differences between theory and statistics discussed above, both types and taxa can be seen primarily as mirror images of each other and thus as having structural similarities that allow a bridge to be built from one to the other.

Since much theorizing is done in terms of types, a needed first step is to move from the realm of type concepts to the realm of empirical data analysis. While this traditionally is accomplished by turning from theory to statistical analysis, an alternative is to link conceptually formed types with statistically derived taxa.

The first task is to move from the conceptual to the empirical. As outlined in Bailey (1994, p. 66), this is rather straightforward and merely involves the identification of empirical cases for each conceptual cell. An example would be to locate an actual ethnographic type such as "bindle stiff" (Spradley and McCurdy, 1972). The empirical cases found for each cell in a typology (such as Figure 1) are equivalent to the taxa formed through cluster analysis. The second task in bridging the gap between types and taxa is converting from monothetic to polythetic As was discussed above, this can be achieved in various ways, such as Lazarfeld's (1937) process of pragmatic reduction. The third task is to connect the R-analysis of types with the Q-analysis of taxa. The easiest way to accomplish this is to use R-analysis for clustering.

In the other direction—from taxa to types—all the tasks are reversed and involve going from empirical to conceptual, from poythetic to monothetic, and from Q-analysis to R-analysis. Going from empirical to conceptual entails finding a concept to represent the statistically constructed group. For example, if the cluster analysis yields an empirical cluster composed primarily of people who scored very high on an exam, one could formulate the type concept of "high achievers" to represent it.

The second task involves going from polythetic to monothetic. Technically speaking, this entails changing a heterogeneous empirical grouping to a homogeneous grouping and cannot be accomplished empirically except somewhat artificially. For example, Lockhart and Hartman (1963) constructed monothetic clusters by discarding all the characters that varied within the group. This is compensated for by the prior step, in which the conceptual type concept monothetically represents the empirical polythetic taxa. The third task is to achieve R-analytic clustering by using R-correlations rather than Q-correlations in the cluster analysis.

CONCLUSION

A well-constructed typology can bring order out of chaos. It can transform the overwhelming complexity of an apparently eclectic congeries of numerous apparently diverse cases into a well-ordered set of a few homogeneous types clearly situated in a property space of a few important dimensions. A sound typology forms a firm foundation and provides direction for both theorizing and empirical research. No other tool has as much power to simplify life for a sociologist.

The task for the future is the further elaboration of this crucial nexus between the qualitative and statistical approaches. This requires effort from sociologists with both theoretical and statistical talents. McKinney (1966, p. 49) recognizes the "complementary relationship of quantitative and typological procedures" and advocates "the emergence of a number of social scientists who are procedurally competent in both typology and statistical techniques." Costner (1972, p. xi) also recognizes the basic unity of the qualitative and quantitative approaches to typology construction.

For further information on typologies, see Capecchi (1966), Sokal and Sneath, (1963), Sneath and Sokal (1973), Bailey (1973, 1974, 1983, 1989, 1993, 1994), Hudson et al. (1982), Aldenderfer and Blashfield (1984), and Kreps (1989).

(SEE ALSO: *Levels of Analysis; Tabular Analysis*)

REFERENCES

Aldenderfer, Mark S., and Roger K. Blashfield 1984 *Cluster Analysis*. Thousandd Oaks, Calif.: Sage.

Aldrich, John H., and Forrest D. Nelson 1984 *Cluster Analysis*. Thousand Oaks, Calif.: Sage.

Bailey, Kenneth D. 1972 "Polythetic Reduction of Monothetic Property Space." In Herbert L. Costner, ed., *Sociological Methodology 1972*. San Francisco: Jossey-Bass.

—— 1973 "Monothetic and Polythetic Typologies and Their Relationship to Conceptualization, Measurement, and Scaling." *American Sociological Review* 38:18–33.

—— 1974 "Cluster Analysis." In David R. Heise, ed., *Sociological Methodology 1975*. San Francisco: Jossey-Bass.

—— 1983 "Sociological Classification and Cluster Analysis." *Quality and Quantity* 17:251–268.

—— 1989 "Taxonomy and Disaster: Prospects and Problems." *International Journal of Mass Emergencies and Disasters* 7:419–431.

—— 1993 "Strategies of Nucleus Formation in Agglomerative Clustering Techniques." *Bulletin De Methodologie Sociologique* 38:38–51.

—— 1994 *Typologies and Taxonomies: An Introduction to Classification Techniques*. Thousand Oaks, Calif.: Sage.

Barton, Allen H. 1955 "The Concept of Property Space in Social Research." In Paul F. Lazarsfeld and Morris Rosenberg, eds., *The Language of Social Research*. New York: Free Press.

Blalock, Herbert M. 1969 *Theory Construction: From Verbal to Mathematical Formulations*. Englewood Cliffs, N.J.: Prentice-Hall.

Butler, Edgar W., and Stuart N. Adams 1966 "Typologies of Delinquent Girls: Some Alternative Approaches." *Social Forces* 44:401–407.

Capecchi, Vittorio 1966 "Typologies in Relation to Mathematical Models." *Ikon* Suppl. No. 58:1–62.

Costner, Herbert L. 1972 "Prologue." In Herbert L. Costner, ed., *Sociological Methodology 1972*. San Francisco: Jossey-Bass.

Hudson, Herschel C., and associates (eds.) 1982 *Classifying Social Data*. San Francisco: Jossey-Bass.

Kreps, Gary A. (ed.) 1989 "The Boundaries of Disaster Research: Taxonomy and Comparative Research" (Special Issue). *International Journal of Mass Emergencies and Disasters* 7:213–431.

Lazarsfeld, Paul F. 1937 "Some Remarks on the Typological Procedures in Social Research." *Zeitschrift für Sozialforschung* 6:119–139.

Lockhart, W. R., and P. A. Hartman 1963 "Formation of Monothetic Groups in Quantitative Bacterial Taxonomy." *Journal of Bacteriology* 85:68–77.

Martindale, Don 1960 *The Nature and Types of Sociological Theory*. Boston: Houghton Mifflin.

McKinney, John C. 1966 *Constructive Typology and Social Theory*. New York: Appleton, Century, Crofts.

Simpson, George G. 1961 *Principles of Animal Taxonomy*. New York: Columbia University Press.

Sneath, Peter H. A., and Robert R. Sokal 1973 *Numerical Taxonomy: The Principles and Practice of Numerical Classification*. San Francisco: Freeman.

Sokal, Robert R., and Peter H. A. Sneath 1963 *Principles of Numerical Taxonomy*. San Francisco: Freeman.

Spradley, James P., and David W. McCurdy 1972 *The Cultural Experience: Ethnography in Complex Society*. Chicago: Science Research Associates.

Stinchcombe, Arthur L. 1968 *Constructing Social Theories*. New York: Harcourt, Brace, and World.

Tiryakian, Edward A. 1968 "Typologies." In David L. Sills, ed., *International Encyclopedia of the Social Sciences*. New York: Macmillan and Free Press.

Tönnies, Ferdinand 1957 *Gemeinschaft und Gesellschaft*, trans. and ed. C. P. Loomis. East Lansing: Michigan State University Press.

Weber, Max 1947 *Theory of Social and Economic Organization*. A. R. Henderson and Talcott Parsons, trans., and Talcott Parsons, ed. New York: Free Press.

Winch, Robert F. 1947 "Heuristic and Empirical Typologies: A Job for Factor Analysis." *American Sociological Review* 12:68–75.

KENNETH D. BAILEY

U

UNIONS

See Labor Movements and Unions; Industrial Sociology.

URBAN SOCIOLOGY

Urban sociology studies human groups in a territorial frame of reference. In this field, social organization is the major focus of inquiry, with an emphasis on the interplay between social and spatial organization and the ways in which changes in spatial organization affect social and psychological well being. A wide variety of interests are tied together by a common curiosity about the changing dynamics, determinants, and consequences of urban society's most characteristic form of settlement: the city.

Scholars recognized early that urbanization is accompanied by dramatic structural, cognitive, and behavioral changes. Classic sociologists (Durkheim, Weber, Toinnes, Marx) delineated the differences in institutional forms that seemed to accompany the dual processes of urbanization and industrialization as rural-agrarian societies were transformed into urban-industrial societies (see Table 1).

Several key questions that guide contemporary research are derived from this tradition: How are human communities organized? What forces produce revolutionary transformations in human settlement patterns? What organizational forms accompany these transformations? What differences do urban living make, and why do those differences exist? What consequences does the increasing size of human concentrations have for human beings, their social worlds, and their environment?

Students of the urban scene have long been interested in the emergence of cities (Childe 1950), how cities grow and change (Weber 1899), and unique ways of life associated with city living (Wirth 1938). These classic treatments have historical value for understanding the nature of pre-twentieth-century cities, their determinants, and their human consequences, but comparative analysis of contemporary urbanization processes leads Berry (1981, p. xv) to conclude that "what is apparent is an accelerating change in the nature of change itself, speedily rendering not-yet-conventional wisdom inappropriate at best."

Urban sociologists use several different approaches to the notion of community to capture changes in how individual urbanites are tied together into meaningful social groups and how those groups are tied to other social groups in the broader territory they occupy. An interactional community is indicated by networks of routine, face-to-face primary interaction among the members of a group. This is most evident among close friends and in families, tribes, and closely knit locality groups. An ecological community is delimited by routine patterns of activity that its members engage in to meet the basic requirements of daily life. It corresponds with the territory over which the group ranges in performing necessary activities such as work, sleep, shopping, education,

Classic Contrasts Between Urban and Rural Societies

Institution	Urban-Industrial	Rural-Agrarian
Agreements	Contractual	Personal
Authority	Bureaucratic	Paternalistic
Communication	Secondary	Primary
Integrative mechanism	Specialization	Common experience
Normative standards	Universalistic	Particularistic
Normative structure	Anomic	Integrated
Problem solution	Rational	Traditional
Production	Manufacturing	Agriculture
Social control	Restitutive	Repressive
Social relations	Segmentalized	All encompassing
Socialization	Formal	Informal
Stratification	Achieved status	Ascribed status
Values	Money and power	Family
World views	Secular	Sacred

Table 1

and recreation. Compositional communities are clusters of people who share common social characteristics. People of similar race, social status, or family characteristics, for example, form a compositional community. A symbolic community is defined by a commonality of beliefs and attitudes among its members. Its members view themselves as belonging to the group and are committed to it.

Research on the general issue of how these forms of organization change as cities grow has spawned a voluminous literature. An ecological perspective and a sociocultural perspective guide two major research traditions. Ecological studies focus on the role of economic competition in shaping the urban environment. Ecological and compositional communities are analyzed in an attempt to describe and generalize about urban forms and the processes of urban growth (Hawley 1981).

Sociocultural studies emphasize the importance of cultural, psychological, and other social dimensions of urban life. These studies focus on the interactional and symbolic communities that characterize the urban setting (Wellman and Leighton 1979; Suttles 1972).

Early theoretical work suggested that the most evident consequence of the increasing size, density, and heterogeneity of human settlements was a breakdown of social ties, a decline in the family, alienation, an erosion of moral codes, and social disorganization (Wirth 1938). Later empirical research has clearly shown that in general, urbanites

are integrated into meaningful social groups (Fischer 1984).

The sociocultural tradition suggests that cultural values derive from socialization into a variety of subcultures and are relatively undisturbed by changes in ecological processes. Different subcultures select, are forced into, or unwittingly drift into different areas that come to exhibit the characteristics of a particular subculture (Gans 1962). Fischer (1975) combines the ecological and subcultural perspectives by suggesting that size, density, and heterogeneity are important but that they produce integrated subcultures rather than fostering alienation and community disorganization. Size provides the critical masses necessary for viable unconventional subcultures to form. With increased variability in the subcultural mix in urban areas, subcultures become more intensified as they defend their ways of life against the broad array of others in the environment. The more subcultures, the more diffusion of cultural elements, and the greater the likelihood of new subcultures emerging, creating the ever-changing mosaic of unconventional subcultures that most distinguishes large places from small ones.

Empirical approaches to urban organization vary according to the unit of analysis and what is being observed. Patterns of activity (e.g., commuting, retail sales, crime) and characteristics of people (e.g., age, race, income, household composition) most commonly are derived from government reports for units of analysis as small as city blocks and as large as metropolitan areas. These types of data are used to develop general principles of organization and change in urban systems. General questions range from how certain activities and characteristics come to be organized in particular ways in space to why certain locales exhibit particular characteristics and activities. Territorial frameworks for the analysis of urban systems include neighborhoods, community areas, cities, urban areas, metropolitan regions, nations, and the world.

Observations of networks of interaction (e.g., visiting patterns, helping networks) and symbolic meanings of people (e.g., alienation, values, worldviews) are less systematically available because social surveys are more appropriate for obtaining this kind of information. Consequently, less is known about these dimensions of community than is desirable.

It is clear that territoriality has waned as an integrative force and that new forms of extralocal community have emerged. High mobility, an expanded scale of organization, and an increased range and volume of communication flow coalesce to alter the forms of social groups and their organization in space (Greer 1962). With modern communication and transportation technology, as exists in the United States today, space becomes less of an organizing principle and new forms of territorial organization emerge that reflect the power of large-scale corporate organization and the federal government in shaping urban social and spatial organization (Gottdiener 1985).

Hawley's (1950, 1981) ecological approach to the study of urban communities serves as the major paradigm in contemporary research. This approach views social organization as developing in response to basic problems of existence that all populations face in adapting to their environments. The urban community is conceptualized as the complex system of interdependence that develops as a population collectively adapts to an environment, using whatever technology is available. Population, environment, technology, and social organization interact to produce various forms of human communities at different times and in different places (Table 2). Population is conceptualized as an organized group of humans that function routinely as a unit; the environment is defined as everything that is external to the population, including other organized social groups.

Technological advances allow people to expand and redefine the nature of the relevant environment and therefore influence the forms of community organization that populations develop (Duncan 1973).

In the last half of the twentieth century, there were revolutionary transformations in the size and nature of human settlements and the nature of the interrelationships among them (Table 3). The global population "explosion" created by an unprecedented rapid decline in human mortality in less developed regions of the world after 1950 provided the additional people necessary for this population "implosion:" the rapid increase in the size and number of human agglomerations of unprecedented size. Urban sociology attempts to understand the determinants and consequences of this transformation.

The urbanization process involves an expansion in the entire system of interrelationships by which a population maintains itself in its habitat (Hawley 1981, p. 12). The most evident consequences of the process and the most common measures of it are an increase in the number of people at points of population concentration, an increase in the number of points at which population is concentrated, or both (Eldridge 1956). Theories of urbanization attempt to understand how human settlement patterns change as technology expands the scale of social systems.

Because technological regimes, population growth mechanisms, and environmental contingencies change over time and vary in different regions of the world, variations in the pattern of distribution of human settlements generally can be understood by attending to these related processes. In the literature on urbanization, an interest in the organizational forms of systems of cities is complemented by an interest in how growth is accommodated in cities through changes in density gradients, the location of socially meaningful population subgroups, and patterns of urban activities. Although the expansion of cities has been the historical focus in describing the urbanization process, revolutionary developments in transportation, communication, and information technology in the last fifty years expanded the scale of urban systems and directed attention toward the broader system of the form of organization in which cities emerge and grow.

Comparative Urban Features of Major World Regions

Basic Feature	Nineteenth Century North America	Twentieth Century North America	Third World	Postwar Europe
Summary	Concentrated	Spread out	Constrained	Planned
Size	1–2 million	14 million	19 million	8 million
Density	High	Low	Medium	High
Timing	250 years long period	Emergent no pressure	Very rapid since 1950s	Very slow stationary
Scale	Regional and local	Inter-metro and global	Global and local	National and local
City system	Rank size regional	Daily urban national	Primate national	Rank size national
Occupations	Secondary manufacture	Tertiary services	Family and corporate	Diverse mixture
Spatial mix	Zone-sector core focus	Mutlinodal mosaic	Reverse zonal	Overlayed mixed use
Rural–urban differences	Great in all areas	Narrow and declining	Medium and growing	Narrow except work
Status mix	Diverse hierarchical	High overall poor pockets	Bifurcated high % poor	Medium compacted
Migration	Heavy rural-urban and foreign	Inter-metro and foreign	Heavy rural-urban circulation	Foreign skilled
Planning	Laissez-faire capitalism	Decentral, ineffective	Centralized, ineffective	Decentral, effective

Table 2

SOURCE: Abstracted from Berry 1981.

Much research on the urbanization process is descriptive in nature, with an emphasis on identifying and measuring patterns of change in demographic and social organization in a territorial frame of reference. Territorially circumscribed environments employed as units of analysis include administrative units (villages, cities, counties, states, nations), population concentrations (places, agglomerations, urbanized areas), and networks of interdependency (neighborhoods, metropolitan areas, daily urban systems, city systems, the earth).

The American urban system is suburbanizing and deconcentrating. One measure of suburbanization is the ratio of the rate of growth in the ring to that in the central city over a decade (Schnore 1959). While some Metropolitan Statistical Areas (MSAs) began suburbanizing in the late 1800s, the greatest rates for the majority of places occurred in the 1950s and 1960s. Widespread use of the automobile, inexpensive energy, the efficient production of materials for residential infrastructure, and federal housing policy allowed metropolitan growth to be absorbed by sprawl instead of by increased congestion at the center.

As the scale of territorial organization increased, so did the physical distances between black and white, rich and poor, young and old, and other meaningful population subgroups. The Index of Dissimilarity measures the degree of segregation between two groups by computing the percentage of one group that would have to reside on a different city block for it to have the same proportional distribution across urban space as the group to which it is being compared (Taeuber and Taeuber 1965). Although there has been some decline in indices of dissimilarity between black and white Americans since the 1960s, partly as a result of increasing black suburbanization, the index for the fifteen most segregated MSAs in 1990 remained at or above 80, meaning that 80 percent or more of the blacks would have had to live on different city blocks to have the same distribution in space as whites; thus, a very high

**Population of World's Largest Metropolises
(in millions), 1950–2000 and Percent Change, 1950–2000**

Metropolis	1950	2000	% Change
Mexico City, Mexico	3.1	26.3	748
Sao Paulo, Brazil	2.8	24.0	757
Tokyo/Yokohama, Japan	6.7	17.1	155
Calcutta, India	4.4	16.6	277
Greater Bombay, India	2.9	16.0	452
New York/northeastern N.J., USA	12.4	15.5	25
Seoul, Republic of Korea	1.1	13.5	113
Shanghai, China	10.3	13.5	31
Rio de Janeiro, Brazil	3.5	13.3	280
Delhi, India	1.4	13.2	843
Greater Buenos Aires, Argentina	5.3	13.2	149
Cairo/Giza/Imbaba, Egypt	2.5	13.2	428
Jakarta, Indonesia	1.8	12.8	611
Baghdad, Iraq	0.6	12.8	2033
Teheran, Iran	0.9	12.7	1311
Karachi, Pakistan	1.0	12.1	1110
Istanbul, Turkey	1.0	11.9	1090
Los Angeles/Long Beach, Cailf., USA	4.1	11.2	173
Dacca, Bangladesh	0.4	11.2	2700
Manila, Philippines	1.6	11.1	594
Beijing (Peking), China	6.7	10.8	61
Moscow, USSR	4.8	10.1	110
Total world population	2,500	6,300	152

Table 3

SOURCE: Adapted from Dogan and Kasarda (1988b) Table 1.2.

degree of residential segregation remains. Although there is great social status diversity in central cities and increasing diversity in suburban rings, disadvantaged and minority populations are overrepresented in central cities, while the better educated and more affluent are overrepresented in suburban rings.

A related process—deconcentration—involves a shedding of urban activities at the center and is indicated by greater growth in employment and office space in the ring than in the central city. This process was under way by the mid-1970s and continued unabated through the 1980s. A surprising turn of events in the late 1970s was signaled by mounting evidence that nonmetropolitan counties were, for the first time since the Depression of the 1930s, growing more rapidly than were metropolitan counties (Lichter and Fuguitt 1982). This process has been referred to as "deurbanization" and "the nonmetropolitan turnaround." It is unclear whether this trend represents an enlargement of the scale of metropolitan organization to encompass more remote counties or whether new growth nodes are developing in nonmetropolitan areas.

The American urban system is undergoing major changes as a result of shifts from a manufacturing economy to a service economy, the aging of the population, and an expansion of organizational scale from regional and national to global decision making. Older industrial cities in the Northeast and Midwest lost population as the locus of economic activity shifted from heavy manufacturing to information and residentiary services. Cities in Florida, Arizona, California, and the Northwest have received growing numbers of retirees seeking environmental, recreational, and medical amenities that are not tied to economic production. Investment decisions regarding the location of office complexes, the factories of the future, are made more on the basis of the availability of an educated labor pool, favorable tax treatment, and the availability of amenities than on the basis of the access to raw materials that underpinned the urbanization process through the middle of the twentieth century.

The same shifts are reflected in the internal reorganization of American cities. The scale of local communities has expanded from the central business district–oriented city to the multinodal metropolis. Daily commuting patterns are shifting from radial trips between bedroom suburbs and workplaces in the central city to lateral trips among highly differentiated subareas throughout urban regions. Urban villages with affluent residences, high-end retail minimalls, and office complexes are emerging in nonmetropolitan counties beyond the reach of metropolitan political constraints, creating even greater segregation between the most and least affluent Americans

Deteriorating residential and warehousing districts adjacent to new downtown office complexes are being rehabilitated for residential use by childless professionals, or "gentry." The process of gentrification, or the invasion of lower-status deteriorating neighborhoods of absentee-owned rental housing by middle- to upper-status home or condominium owners, is driven by a desire for accessibility to nearby white-collar jobs and cultural amenities as well as by the relatively high costs of suburban housing, which have been pushed up by competing demand in these rapidly growing metropolitan areas. Although the number of people involved in gentrification is too small to have reversed the overall decline of central cities, the return of affluent middle-class residents has reduced segregation to some extent. Gentrification reclaims deteriorated neighborhoods, but it also results in the displacement of the poor, who have no place else to live at rents they can afford (Feagin and Parker 1990).

The extent to which dispersed population is involved in urban systems is quite variable. An estimated 90 percent of the American population now lives in a daily urban system (DUS). These units are constructed from counties that are allocated to economic centers on the basis of commuting patterns and economic interdependence. The residents of a DUS are closely tied together by efficient transportation and communication technology. Each DUS has a minimum population of 200,000 in its labor shed and constitutes "a multinode, multiconnective system [which] has replaced the core dominated metropolis as the basic urban unit" (Berry and Kasarda 1977, p. 304). Less than 4 percent of the American labor force is engaged in agricultural occupations. Even

the residents of remote rural areas are mostly "urban" in their activities and outlook.

In contrast, many residents of uncontrolled developments on the fringes of emerging megacities in less developed countries are practically isolated from the urban center and live much as they have for generations. Over a third of the people in the largest cities in India were born elsewhere, and the maintenance of rural ways of life in those cities is common because of a lack of urban employment, the persistence of village kinship ties, and seasonal circulatory migration to rural areas. Although India has three of the ten largest cities in the world, it remains decidedly rural, with 75 percent of the population residing in agriculturally oriented villages (Nagpaul 1988).

The pace and direction of the urbanization process are closely tied to technological advances. As industrialization proceeded in western Europe and the United States over a 300-year period, an urban system emerged that reflected the interplay between the development of city-centered heavy industry and requirements for energy and raw materials from regional hinterlands. The form of city systems that emerged has been described as rank-size. Cities in that type of system form a hierarchy of places from large to small in which the number of places of a given size decreases proportionally to the size of the place. Larger places are fewer in number, are more widely spaced, and offer more specialized goods and services than do smaller places (Christaller 1933).

City systems that emerged in less industrialized nations are primate in character. In a primate system, the largest cities absorb far more than their share of societal population growth. Sharp breaks exist in the size hierarchy of places, with one or two very large, several medium-sized, and many very small places. Rapid declines in mortality beginning in the 1950s, coupled with traditionally high fertility, created unprecedented rates of population growth. Primate city systems developed with an orientation toward the exportation of raw materials to the industrialized world rather than manufacturing and the development of local markets. As economic development proceeds, it occurs primarily in the large primate cities, with very low rates of economic growth in rural areas. Consequently, nearly all the excess of births over deaths in the nation is absorbed by the large cities, which are more integrated into the emerging global urban system (Dogan and Kasarda 1988a).

Megacities of over 10 million population are a very recent phenomenon, and their number is increasing rapidly. Their emergence can be understood only in the context of a globally interdependent system of relationships. The territorial bounds of the relevant environment to which population collectively adapts have expanded from the immediate hinterland to the entire world in only half a century.

Convergence theory suggests that cities throughout the would will come to exhibit organizational forms increasingly similar to one another, converging on the North American pattern, as technology becomes more accessible globally (Young and Young 1962). Divergence theory suggests that increasingly divergent forms of urban organization are likely to emerge as a result of differences in the timing and pace of the urbanization process, differences in the positions of cities in the global system, and the increasing effectiveness of deliberate planning of the urbanization process by centralized governments holding differing values and therefore pursuing a variety of goals for the future (Berry 1981).

The importance of understanding this process is suggested by Hawley (1981, p. 13): "Urbanization is a transformation of society, the effects of which penetrate every sphere of personal and collective life. It affects the status of the individual and opportunities for advancement, it alters the types of social units in which people group themselves, and it sorts people into new and shifting patterns of stratification. The distribution of power is altered, normal social processes are reconstituted, and the rules and norms by which behavior is guided are redesigned."

REFERENCES

Berry, Brian J. L. 1981. *Comparative Urbanization: Divergent Paths in the Twentieth Century*. New York: St. Martins.

——, and John D. Kasarda 1977 *Contemporary Urban Ecology*. New York: Macmillan.

Childe, V. Gordon 1950 "The Urban Revolution." *Town Planning Review* 21:4–7.

Christaller, W. 1933 *Central Places in Southern Germany*, transl. C. W. Baskin. Englewood Cliffs, N.J.: Prentice-Hall.

Dogan, Mattei, and John D. Kasarda 1988a *The Metropolis Era: A World of Giant Cities*, vol. 1. Newbury Park, Calif.: Sage.

—— 1988b. "Introduction: How Giant Cities Will Multiply and Grow." In Mattei Dogan and John D. Kasarda, eds., *The Metropolis Era: A World of Giant Cities*, vol. 1. Newbury Park, Calif.: Sage.

Duncan, Otis Dudley 1973 "From Social System to Ecosystem." In Michael Micklin, ed., *Population, Environment, and Social Organization: Current Issues in Human Ecology* Hinsdale, Ill.: Dryden.

Eldridge, Hope Tisdale 1956 "The Process of Urbanization." In J. J. Spengler and O. D. Duncan, eds., *Demographic Analysis*. Glencoe, Ill.: Free Press.

Feagin, Joe R., and Robert Parker 1990 *Building American Cities: The Urban Real Estate Game*, 2nd ed. Englewood Cliffs, N.J.: Prentice-Hall.

Fischer, Claude S. 1975 "Toward a Subcultural Theory of Urbanism." *American Journal of Sociology* 80:1319–1341.

—— 1984 *The Urban Experience*. San Diego: Harcourt Brace Jovanovich.

Gans, Herbert J. 1962 "Urbanism and Suburbanism as Ways of life: A Reevaluation of Definitions." In A. M. Rose, ed., *Human Behavior and Social Processes*. Boston: Houghton Mifflin.

Gottdiener, Mark 1985 *The Social Production of Urban Space*. Austin: University of Texas Press.

Greer, Scott 1962 *The Emerging City*. New York: Free Press.

Hawley, Amos H. 1950 *Human Ecology: A Theory of Community Structure*. New York: Ronald.

—— 1981 *Urban Society: An Ecological Approach*. New York: Wiley.

Kleniewski, Nancy 1997 *Cities, Change, and Conflict: A Political Economy of Urban Life*. Belmont, Calif.: Wadsworth.

Lichter, Daniel T., and Glenn V. Fuguitt 1982 "The Transition to Nonmetropolitan Population Deconcentration." *Demography* 19:211–221.

Nagpaul, Hans 1988 "India's Giant Cities." In Mattei Dogan and John D. Kasarda, eds., *The Metropolis Era: A World of Giant Cities*, vol. 1. Newbury Park, Calif.: Sage.

Palen, J. John 1997 *The Urban World*. New York: McGraw-Hill.

Schnore, Leo F. 1959 "The Timing of Metropolitan Decentralization." *Journal of the American Institute of Planners* 25:200–206.

Suttles, Gerald 1972 *The Social Construction of Communities*. Chicago: University of Chicago Press.

Taeuber, Karl E., and Alma F. Taeuber 1965 *Negroes in Cities: Residential Segregation and Neighborhood Change*. Chicago: Aldine.

Weber, Adna F. 1899 *The Growth of Cities in the Nineteenth Century*. New York: Columbia University Press.

Wellman, B., and B. Leighton 1979 "Networks, Neighborhoods and Communities: Approaches to the Study of the Community Question." *Urban Affairs Quarterly* 15:369–393.

Wirth, Louis 1938 "Urbanism as a Way of Life." *American Journal of Sociology* 44:1–24.

Young, Frank, and Ruth Young 1962 "The Sequence and Direction of Community Growth: A Cross-Cultural Generalization." *Rural Sociology* 27:374–386.

LEE J. HAGGERTY

URBAN UNDERCLASS

No social science concept has generated more discussion and controversy in recent years than that of the urban underclass. Some argue that it is little more than a pithy and stigmatizing term for the poor people who have always existed in stratified societies (Gans 1990; Jencks 1989; Katz 1989; McGahey 1982). Others contend that the underclass is a distinct and recent phenomenon, reflecting extreme marginalization from mainstream economic institutions and aberrant behavior (drug abuse, violent crime, out-of-wedlock births), that reached catastrophic proportions in the inner cities by the early 1980s (Glasow 1980; Auletta 1982; Reischauer 1987; Nathan 1987; Wilson 1987, 1996). Among the multifaceted, subjective, and often ambiguous definitions of the urban underclass, most all include the notions of weak labor-force attachment and persistently low income (Jencks and Peterson 1991; Sjoquist 1990). Indeed, the first scholar who introduced the term "underclass" in literature characterized its members as an emergent substratum of the permanently unemployed, the unemployable and the underemployed (Myrdal 1962).

Widely differing interpretations of the causes of the presence of an underclass have been offered, ranging from Marxist to social Darwinist. The most influential contemporary analysis of the urban underclass is Wilson's (1996) *When Work Disappears*. Building on his earlier treatise *The Truly Disadvantaged* (1987), Wilson links the origins and growth of the urban underclass to the structure of opportunities and constraints in American society. Its roots are hypothesized to lie in historical discrimination and the mass migration of African-Americans to northern cities in the first half of the twentieth century. Its more recent growth and experiences are posited to have resulted from industrial restructuring and geographic changes in metropolitan economies since the 1960s, in particular the economic transformation of major cities from centers of goods processing to centers of information processing and the relocation of blue-collar jobs to the suburbs. These changes led to sharp increases in joblessness among racially and economically segregated African-Americans who had neither the skills to participate in new urban growth industries nor the transportation or financial means to commute or relocate to the suburbs. Rapidly rising joblessness among inner-city African-Americans, together with selective outmigration of the nonpoor, in turn caused the high concentrations of poverty and related social problems that characterize the urban underclass (see also Kasarda 1985, 1989; Wilson 1991; Hughes, 1993).

Alternative views on the cause of the underclass appear in the works of Murray (1984), Mead (1988), and Magnet (1993). These conservative scholars view underclass behaviors as rational adaptations to the perverse incentives offered by government welfare programs that discourage work and a lack of personal responsibility among many for actions harmful to themselves and others. Abetted by well-intentioned but misguided public programs, joblessness and persistent poverty are seen more as the consequences of deviant behaviors than as the causes of those behaviors. For an elaboration of these competing views and a partial empirical assessment, see Kasarda and Ting (1996).

Measurement of the size of the underclass varies as much as explanations of its causes. A number of researchers have focused on individual-level indicators of persistent poverty, defined as those who are poor for spells from n to n + x years (Levy 1977; Duncan et al. 1984; Bane and Ellwood 1986) and long-term Aid to Families with Dependent Children (AFDC) recipients (Gottschalk and Danziger 1987). In an empirical study, Levy (1977) estimated that approximately eleven million Americans were persistently poor for at least five years. When the underclass was defined as those who were not need persistently poor for eight or more years, six million people were found in that category (Duncan et al. 1984). This represented approximately one-fifth of the thirty-two million Americans living in poor households in 1988 (Mincy et al. 1990).

Another measurement strategy focuses on the geographic concentration of the poor. Using the U.S. Bureau of the Census tract-level definitions of local poverty areas, Reischauer (1987) reported that among the population living in such poverty areas, the central cities housed over half in 1985, up from one-third in 1972. Jargowsky (1997) documented that along with the growth of poverty populations in metropolitan areas, the number of high poverty areas (defined as census tracts containing at least 40 percent poor people) more than doubled between 1970 and 1990. The number of African-Americans living in high-poverty areas, mostly segregated ghettos, climbed from 2.4 million to 4.2 million in that period, far outpacing other minority groups. By 1990, 34 percent of poor African-Americans in metropolitan areas resided in high-poverty census tracts (see also Kasarda 1993).

Massey and Denton (1993) present an analysis and simulations that lead them to conclude that concentrated poverty can be explained largely by two basic factors: the degree of spatial segregation of a racial group and the group's overall poverty rate. Their analysis and conclusion sparked heated debates over racial versus economic segregation explanations (Jargowsky 1997).

As was noted above, the concept of the underclass typically is considered to entail more than poverty. It also is posited to incorporate geographically concentrated behavioral characteristics that conflict with mainstream values: joblessness, out-of-wedlock births, welfare dependency, dropping out of school, drug abuse, and illicit activities.

While considerable debate continues to surround definitions and even the existence of the underclass, attempts have been made to measure its size by using aggregated "behavioral" indicators derived from census tract data. Ricketts and Sawhill (1988) measured the underclass as people living in neighborhoods whose residents in 1980 exhibited disproportionately high rates of school dropout, joblessness, female-headed families, and welfare dependency. Using a composite definition in which tracts must fall at least one standard deviation above the national mean on all four characteristics, they found that approximately 2.5 million people lived in those tracts in 1980 and that those tracts were disproportionately located in major cities in the Northeast and Midwest. They reported that in underclass tracts, on average, 63 percent of the resident adults had less than a high school education, 60 percent of the families with children were headed by women, 56 percent of the adult men were not regularly employed, and 34 percent of the households received public assistance. Their research also revealed that although the total poverty population grew only 8 percent between 1970 and 1980, the number of people living in underclass areas grew 230 percent, from 752,000 to 2,484,000.

Mincy and Wiener (1993) and Kasarda (1993) updated Ricketts and Sawhill's analysis by using 1990 census tract data. Both found that the number and concentration of persons living in tracts with disproportionately high rates of problem attributes continued to rise in the 1980s, although not nearly as much as it did in the 1970s.

These location-based aggregate measures of underclass populations have been criticized on the grounds that aside from race, most urban census tracts are quite heterogeneous along economic and social dimensions. Jencks (1989; Jencks and Peterson 1991), for example, observes that with the exception of tracts made up of public housing projects, there is considerable diversity in residents' income and education levels, joblessness, and public assistance recipiency in even the poorest urban neighborhoods. Conversely, considerable numbers of urban residents who are poor, jobless, and welfare-dependent live in census tracts where fewer than 20 percent of the families fall below the poverty line.

Nevertheless, while most scholars concur that behaviors linked to underclass definitions and measurements are found throughout society, it is the concentration of these behaviors in economically declining inner-city areas that is said to distinguish the underclass from previously impoverished urban subgroups. Geographic concentration is argued to magnify social problems and accelerate their spread to *nearby households* through social contagion, peer pressure, and imitative behavior (Wilson 1987, 1996). The members of economically stable households selectively flee the neighborhood to avoid these problems. Left behind in increasingly isolated concentrations are those with the least to offer in terms of marketable skills, role models, and familial stability. The result is a spiral of negative social and economic outcomes for those neighborhoods and the households that remain.

Incorporating the effects of neighborhoods and social transmission processes means that the future research agenda on the urban underclass will be qualitative as well as quantitative in approach. Ethnographic studies of underclass neighborhoods, family structures, and individual behaviors will complement growing numbers of surveys on and sophisticated statistical analyses of the persistence and intergenerational transfer of urban poverty (see Anderson 1990, 1994; Furstenberg et al. 1999). Additionally more comparative studies will assess similarities to and differences from the American case in European, Latin American, and Asian cities. The root of this work stretches deep, building on classic culture of poverty (Lewis 1966) and social and economic marginalization theses (Clark 1965).

(SEE ALSO: *Cities; Community; Poverty; Segregation and Desegregation; Urbanization; Urban Sociology*)

REFERENCES

Anderson, Elijah 1990 *Street Wise: Race, Class, and Change in an Urban Community*. Chicago: University of Chicago Press.

—— 1994 "The Code on the Streets." *Atlantic Monthly*, May, pp. 81–94.

Auletta, Ken 1982 *The Underclass*. New York: Random House.

Bane, Mary Jo, and David Ellwood 1986 "Slipping into and out of Poverty: The Dynamics of Spells." *Journal of Human Resources* 21:1–23.

Clark, Kenneth B. 1965 *Dark Ghetto: Dilemmas of Social Power*. New York: Harper & Row.

Duncan, G. J., R. D. Coc, and M. S. Hill 1984 In *Years of Poverty, Years of Plenty*. Ann Arbor: Institute of Social Research, University of Michigan.

Furstenberg, Frank F., Jr., Thomas D Cook, Jacquelynne Eccles, Glen H. Elder, Jr., and Arnold Sameroff 1999 *Managing to Make It: Urban Families an Adolescent*

Success. Chicago and London: University of Chicago Press.

Gans, Herbert J. 1990 "Deconstructing the Underclass: The Term's Danger as a Planning Concept." *Journal of the American Planning Association*, pp. 271–277.

Glasgow, Douglas G. 1980 *The Black Underclass: Poverty, Unemployment, and Entrapment of Ghetto Youth*. San Francisco: Jossey-Bass.

Gottschalk, P., and S. Danziger 1987 Testimony on poverty, hunger, and the welfare system, August 5, 1986. *Hearing before the Select Committee on Hunger, House of Representatives*, 99th Cong., 2nd Sess., Ser. No. 23. Washington, D.C.: U.S. Government Printing Office.

Hughes, Mark Alan 1993 *Over the Horizon: Jobs in the Suburbs of Major Metropolitan Areas*. Philadelphia: Public/Private Ventures.

Jargowsky, Paul A. 1997 *Poverty and Place: Ghettos, Barrios, and the American City*. New York: Russell Sage Foundation.

Jencks, Christopher 1989 "What Is the Underclass—and Is It Growing?" *Focus* 12:14–31.

——, and Paul Peterson, eds. 1991 *The Urban Underclass*. Washington, D.C.: Brookings Institution.

Kasarda, John D. 1985 "Urban Change and Minority Opportunities." In Paul Peterson, ed., *The New Urban Reality*. Washington, D.C.: Brookings Institution.

—— 1989 "Urban Industrial Transition and the Underclass." *Annals of the American Academy of Political and Social Sciences* 501:26–47.

—— 1993 "Inner City Concentrated Poverty and Neighborhood Distress: 1970 to 1990." *Housing Policy Debate* 4(3):253–302.

——, and Kwok-Fai Ting 1996 "Joblessness and Poverty in America's Central Cities: Causes and Policy Prescriptions." *Housing Policy Debate* 7(2):387–419.

Katz, Michael 1989 *The Undeserving Poor: From the War on Poverty to the War on Welfare*. New York: Pantheon.

Levy, Frank 1977 "How Big Is the American Underclass?" Washington, D.C.: Urban Institute.

Lewis, Oscar 1966 *La Vida: A Puerto Rican Family in the Culture of Poverty–San Juan and New York*. New York: Random House.

Magnet, Myron 1993 *The Dream and the Nightmare: The Sixties' Legacy to the Underclass*. New York: Morrow.

Massey, Douglas S., and Nancy Denton 1993 *American Apartheid: Segregation and the Making of the Underclass*. Cambridge, Mass.: Harvard University Press.

McGahay, R. 1982 "Poverty's Voguish Stigma." *New York Times*, March 12:29.

Mead, Lawrence M. 1988 "The Hidden Jobs Debate." *Public Interest*, spring: 40–59.

Mincy, Ronald B., Isabel V. Sawhill, and Douglas A. Wolf 1990 "The Underclass: Definition and Measurement." *Science* 248:450–453.

——, and Susan J. Wiener 1993 *The Under Class in the 1980s: Changing Concepts, Changing Realty*. Washington, D.C.: Urban Institute.

Murray, Charles A. 1984. *Losing Ground: American Social Policy, 1950–1980*. New York: Basic Books

Myrdal, Gunner 1962 *Challenge to Affluence*. New York: Pantheon.

Nathan, Richard P. 1987 "Will the Underclass Always Be with Us?" *Society* 24:57–62.

Reischauer, Robert D. 1987 *The Geographic Concentration of Poverty: What Do We Know?* Washington, D.C.: Brookings Institution.

Ricketts, Erol, and Isabel Sawhill 1988 "Defining and Measuring the Underclass." *Journal of Policy Analysis and Management* 7:316–325.

Sjoquist, David 1990 "Concepts, Measurements, and Analysis of the Underclass: A Review of the Literature." Atlanta: Georgia State University, typescript.

Wilson, William Julius 1996 *When Work Disappears: The World of the New Urban Poor*. New York: Knopf.

—— 1991 "Studying Inner-City Social Dislocations." *American Sociological Review* 56:1–14.

—— 1987 *The Truly Disadvantaged: The Inner City, the Underclass, and Public Policy*. Chicago: University of Chicago Press.

JOHN D. KASARDA

UTILITY THEORY

See Decision-Making Theory and Research; Rational Choice Theory.

UTOPIAN ANALYSIS AND DESIGN

NOTE: *Although the following article has not been revised for this edition of the Encyclopedia, the substantive coverage is currently appropriate. The editors have provided a list of recent works at the end of the article to facilitate research and exploration of the topic.*

"From the time of its first discovery, the island of King Utopus has been shrouded in ambiguity, and no latter-day scholars should presume to dispel the fog, polluting utopia's natural environment with an excess of clarity and definition" (Manuel and Manuel 1979, p. 5).

But this ambiguity extends well beyond simple obscurity or murkiness; it reaches to unqualified contradiction. Many utopian visionaries have been denounced for their meticulous delineation of details as they constructed models of social worlds bearing no resemblance to existing, potential, or possible reality. Utopias, it would seem, suffer from the twin infirmities of ambiguity and excessive efforts to achieve clarity and definition. Our dictionaries tell us they are, on the one hand, ideally perfect places but, on the other hand, are simply impractical thought or theory. Utopians are customarily viewed as zealous but quixotic reformers. The books in which they describe their societies may be praised as fascinating, fanciful literature but not as scientific tomes.

It is quite possible as well as reasonable to view utopians as model builders. Models are quite different objects from what is being modeled and have properties not shared by their counterparts. "The aim of a model is precisely not to reproduce reality in all its complexity. It is, rather, to capture in a vivid, often formal way what is essential to understanding some aspect of its structure or behavior" (Weizenbaum 1976, pp. 149–150).

One occupational disability of model builders everywhere is a sort of pathological obsession with a single element, or at most a strictly circumscribed set of elements, of reality, along with an unwavering refusal to examine the larger milieu in which they are found.

In Sir Thomas More's *Utopia* (1965), a central value or societal goal is the concept of economic equality; but this does not include the notion of social equality. There exists in Utopia a large underclass of slaves who are assigned the more distasteful but necessary tasks of the society. This class is composed of war prisoners (More's society is not free of war), persons born into slavery (it is not free of slavery), condemned criminals from other countries who are purchased from foreign slave markets (crime has not been eliminated), and working-class foreigners (class distinctions persist) who volunteer for slavery in Utopia rather than suffer the unpleasant conditions in their home countries (ethnic and immigration difficulties continue to exist). All able-bodied persons in Utopia become part of its work force—slaves, male nonslaves, and even women! This is seen as an enormous augmentation of the work force. Within each household, however, male dominance prevails. Households are under the authority of the oldest free male. Women are specifically designated as "subordinate" to their husbands, as children are to their parents and younger people generally are to their elders. In Utopia, the applicability of equality is severely restricted.

In discussing utopias it is important to distinguish between analytic and design models. Analytic models purport to be summaries of existing empirical reality; design models are summaries or sketches of future, past, or alternative societies, social structures, or worlds.

Characteristically, utopian literature contains a critique of existing society along with a model of a different one. Frequently the design model incorporates a more or less indirect critique of an existing state of affairs. Plato's *Republic* (1941), the work that seems to have been the prototype of More's *Utopia*, was greatly influenced by the social conditions observed and experienced by Plato. He saw the Athens in which he lived as a very corrupt democracy and felt that in such a system politicians inevitably pandered to mobs. If the mob insisted upon venal demands, politicians found it necessary to agree with them or lose their own positions. Reform, he felt, was not possible in a corrupt society. In the *Republic* Socrates, voicing Plato's sentiments, concludes that "the multitude can never be philosophical. Accordingly, it is bound to disapprove of all who pursue wisdom; and so also, of course, are those individuals who associate with the mob and set their hearts on pleasing it" (1941, p. 201).

Interestingly, it has been suggested that Plato's hostility to democracy was, at least to some extent, shaped by his economic and social background. Members of his family were large landholders who, along with others in a similar position, saw the rise of commerce as a threat to their economic positions. Democratic government undermined their political preeminence, as did militant foreign policies. They had a great deal to lose through war because they were subject to heavy war taxes. Moreover, some had had their lands ravaged by Spartans during the Peloponnesian War; others

had retreated behind the walls of Athens. These conservative elements were not above attempting to subvert the democratic system (Klosko 1986, p. 10).

In any event, Plato's utopia is clearly elitist in nature. For a variety of reasons most utopian schemes seem to be controlled by elites of some sort. As one writer explains it:

> *They begin with the proposition that things are bad; things must become better, perhaps perfect here on earth; things will not improve by themselves; a plan must be developed and carried out; this implies the existence of an enlightened individual, or a few, who will think and act in a way that many by themselves cannot think and act.* (Brinton 1965, p. 50)

For Plato, the elites were what he called philosophers. In a sense these were the theoreticians or model makers. The problem he saw was converting their models—their ideal worlds—into reality. Plato was very realistic about this matter of convertibility. He has Socrates ask, "Is it not in the nature of things that action should come less close to truth than thought?" (1941, p. 178). He is, however, concerned about trying to come as close as possible to having the real world correspond to the ideal one. The solution? To have philosophers become rulers or to have rulers become philosophers. In either case enormous, if not complete, power is to be held by a caste of elites.

In effect, social inequality is found even in the work of the triumvirate usually referred to as the "utopian socialists": Claude Henri de Rouvroy de Saint Simon (1760–1825), Charles Fourier (1772–1837), and Robert Owen (1771–1858).

In his early work Saint Simon's elites were scientists, but later he tended to subordinate them or at least to keep them on a par with industrial chiefs. He evaded the problem of social equality by saying that each member of society would be paid in accordance with his or her "investment." This referred to the contribution each made to the productive process. Since different people had different talents, these contributions would differ. Some people's contributions would be more important than others', and accordingly those people would be paid more. But although the rewards of different people would differ, there would not be wide discrepancies between the rewards of the lowest- and highest-paid workers (Manuel and Manuel 1979, pp. 590–614).

Unlike Saint Simon, who never wrote a detailed description of a utopian society, Charles Fourier wrote thousands of pages of detailed descriptions of his "Phalanx," including architectural specifications, work schedules and countless other details. The Phalanx was to be organized essentially as a shareholding corporation. Members were free to buy as many shares as they wished or could afford. Fourier stressed the fact that in his utopia there would be three social classes: the rich, the poor, and the middle. The condition of the poor would be enormously better than their condition in existing society, but the rich or upper class would be entitled to more lavish living quarters, more sumptuous food, and, in general, a more luxurious life-style than the others. During the last fifteen years or so of his life, most of Fourier's efforts were devoted to the search for a wealthy person to subsidize a trial of his Phalanx (Beecher 1986).

Robert Owen insisted on what he regarded to be complete equality. Conceding that people were born with differing abilities, he contended that these abilities were provided by God and should not be the basis for differential rewards. Nevertheless, as a self-made man who became extremely successful and managed the most important cotton-spinning factory in Britain, he never seemed to lose the self-assurance that he knew best how to manage a community and that all members would understand the wisdom of his decisions. He has been characterized as a benevolent autocrat who acted somewhat like a military commander who has little direct contact with his troops (Cole 1969; Manuel and Manuel 1979, pp. 676–693).

In the United States, the most widely read utopian novel based on the assumption of absolute economic equality is undoubtedly Edward Bellamy's *Looking Backward* (1887). Bellamy (1850–1898), influenced by the development of the large economic trusts in the United States, postulated that by the year 2000 only one enormous trust would remain: the United States government. He went to great pains to make it clear that his utopia was devoid of Marxist or other European influences. The principle of income or reward on which it was based was neither "From each according to his investment or product" nor the classic "From each according to his ability, to each according to his need," although it was much closer to the latter than to the former.

In Bellamy's vision of the United States in the year 2000, each person received an equal share of the total national product. In effect, every inhabitant received a credit card showing his or her share of the product. The share could be spent in any manner. If too many individuals decided to buy a particular product, the price of that product would be raised. The point, however, is that people were entitled to a share of the national product *not* on the basis of their individual productivity but simply because they existed as human beings. In some telling passages Bellamy's characters observe that members of families do not deny food or other needs to other family members because they have been unproductive. In effect, the entire country (and, presumably, ultimately the entire world) would resemble our more primitive notion of one family.

Bellamy's work received widespread attention throughout the world. In England, William Morris (1834–1896) objected strenuously to the centralized control and bureaucratic form of organization in *Looking Backward*. Morris wrote his own utopian novel, *News from Nowhere* (1866). Unlike Bellamy's utopia, which came into being through a process of evolution, a violent revolution has occurred in *Nowhere*. London has become a series of relatively small villages separated by flowers and wooded areas. There is no centralized government—no government at all—as we normally understand it. With the end of private property and domestic arrangements in which women are essentially the property of men, the underlying reasons for criminal behavior have been eliminated. Random acts of violence are regarded as transitory diseases and are dealt with by nurses and doctors rather than by jailers.

It has been argued that Morris was essentially an anarchist theorist, although Morris himself vigorously objected to such characterization of his work. It has been suggested that anarchism has two major forms: collectivist and individualist. Morris is seen as essentially a collectivist anarchist, although not an anarchosyndicalist—the form that stresses trade-union activity. He ridiculed conventional forms of individualism. Anarchism itself is defined as a social theory that advocates a community-centered life with great amounts of personal liberty. It opposes coercion of its population (Sargent 1990, pp. 61–64).

Other commentators see *News from Nowhere* as an effort by Morris to present his arguments against anarchism (Holzman 1990, p. 99). It seems clear that his work does not fit neatly into any prefabricated ideological cubbyhole. Morris cherished aesthetic over intellectual values (he was an architect, artist, poet, designer, and craftsman). When one of his characters in *News from Nowhere* is asked how labor is rewarded, the reply is quite predictable: it is *not* rewarded. Work has become a pleasure—not a hardship. Each person does what he or she can do best; the quandary of extrinsic motivation has substantially disappeared.

Motivation, however, is the central concern in B. F. Skinner's *Walden Two* (1948). Burrhus Frederic Skinner (1904–1990) was a professional psychologist whose utopia was a product of his interest in behavioral engineering. His ideal community has been described as one of means rather than of ends—one in which technique has been elevated to utopian status (Kumar 1987, p. 349).

This is not completely accurate. It does capture the essence of how Skinner himself saw his utopia, but it omits direct consideration of the implicit values held by its designer.

Skinner himself was unquestionably a well-motivated, humanistic scientist, but he neglected his customary penetrating analysis when approaching the area of values held by the boss scientist. At one point in *Walden Two*, however, he does seem to have some insight into this difficulty. Frazier, the founder of the community, voices the unspoken criticism of one of the other characters by pointing to his own insensitivity to the effect he has on others, except when the effect is calculated; his lack of the personal warmth responsible in part for the success of the community; the ulterior and devious nature of his own motives. He then cries out, "But God *damn* it Burris ... can't you see? *I'm–not–a–product–of–Walden–Two!*" (Skinner 1948, p. 233).

Economic and basic social equality exist in this community, but effective control is exercised through the built-in reinforcement techniques of its designer. When Frazier is challenged on this by one of the characters who observes that Frazier, looking at the world from the middle of the twentieth century, assumes he knows the best course for humanity forever, Frazier essentially agrees. His defense is that the techniques of behavioral engineering currently exist (and presumably will continue to be used), but they are in the wrong hands—those of charlatans, salespeople, ward heelers, bullies, cheats, educators, priests, and others. Ultimately, Skinner's designer insists, human beings are never free—their behavior is determined by prior conditioning in the society in which they were raised. The belief in their own freedom is what allows human beings unwittingly to become conditioned by reinforcers in their existing environments.

Thus, in effect, *Walden Two* achieves its effects by changing the psychological characteristics of its inhabitants through environmental modification. Its final form is presumably an experimental question. The queries are simple enough and are stated explicitly at one point: What is the best behavior for the individual as far as the group is concerned? How can an individual be induced to behave in that way? The answer presumably can change over time, on the basis of experimental experience. The entire edifice would seem to depend upon the continuing moral superiority of the reinforcement designers over the charlatans they replace.

Quite a different sort of utopia has been proposed by the philosopher Robert Nozick, who outlines what he calls the framework for a utopia. In a word (or two), this framework is equivalent to what Nozick calls the minimal state (Nozick 1974, pp. 297–334). This is a state "limited to the narrow functions of protection against force, theft, fraud, enforcement of contracts, and so on ... any more extensive state will violate persons' rights not to be forced to do certain things and is unjustified ..." (Nozick 1974, p. ix).

Nozick is not concerned with modifying behavior or specifying social structures beyond this minimum state. He begins with the assumption that individual persons have certain rights that may never be violated by any other person or the state. These include the right *not* to be killed or attacked if you are not doing any harm; *not* to be coerced or imprisoned; *not* to be limited in the use of your property if that use does not violate the rights of others.

In arguing for a minimal state, Nozick, on the one hand, is arguing against anarchism (in which there is no state at all). On the other hand, he argues against all forms of the welfare state (in which some people with excessive wealth may be required to surrender some of their property to help others who are less fortunate) (Paul 1981).

As Nozick sees it, rights define a moral boundary around individual persons. The sanctity of this boundary takes priority over all other possible goals. Thus, it becomes readily understandable why he feels that nonvoluntary redistribution of income is morally indefensible:

> It is an extraordinary but apparent consequence of this view that for a government to tax each of its able-bodied citizens five dollars a year to support cripples and orphans would violate the rights of the able-bodied and would be morally impermissible, whereas to refrain from taxation even if it meant allowing the cripples and orphans to starve to death would be the morally required governmental policy. (Scheffler 1981, p. 151)

Here again we see the clash of values that lie at the heart of utopian schemes and their critics. A serious and widely discussed effort to resolve these clashes was made late in the twentieth century by another social philosopher, John Rawls. *A Theory of Justice* (Rawls 1971) was not a utopian novel but a meticulously argued tome that has been compared with John Locke's *Second Treatise of Civil Government* and John Stuart Mill's *On Liberty*. The central question confronting his work has been expressed thus: "Is it possible to satisfy the legitimate 'leftist', 'socialist' critics of Western capitalism within a broadly liberal, capitalist and democratic framework?" (Goldman 1980, p. 431).

Unfortunately, Rawls has found himself increasingly caught between attacks from both the left and the right. The left feels he has not gone far enough in constraining property rights; the right feels he places too great an emphasis upon the value of equality, especially at the expense of the right to property (Goldman 1980, pp. 431–432).

A central point argued by Rawls is that there is no injustice if greater benefits are earned by a few, provided the situation of people not so fortunate is thereby improved (Rawls 1971, pp. 14–15).

As one commentator expressed it, for Rawls equality comes first. Goods are to be distributed equally unless it can be shown that an unequal distribution is to the advantage of the least advantaged. This would be a "just" distribution (Schaar 1980). One might add, parenthetically, that this justice would depend substantially upon the nature of the existing social and economic arrangements under which this inequality occurs. Would a different set of arrangements allow greater equality? For example, is capital available only through private sources? Would public sources serve similar ends with less inequality?

The central issue for utopian analysts from Plato through twentieth-century philosophers is how one constructs a "just" society. But there is no single definition of "just"; it all depends on what you consider to be important. Are you concerned exclusively with yourself? your immediate family? others in your community? in your country? in the world?

And so it is that utopian analysis and design ultimately begin with an implicit, if not explicit, value orientation. One school of thought begins with an overwhelming belief that elites of one sort or another must be favored in the new society. Elite status may be gained through existing wealth, birth, talent, skill, intelligence, or physical strength. Another school begins with what is, broadly speaking, the concept of equality. Here the implicit notion is not unlike Western ideas of the family: to each equally, irrespective of either productivity or need. Between these two polar positions lie a range of intermediate proposals that may provide greater amounts of compensation based upon some definition of need or elite status. In turn, compensation may or may not be linked directly to political or other forms of power.

Issues relating to the nation-state (its form, its powers, and even its very existence), ethnicity, and inequality became acute in the final decade of the twentieth century. Ethnic groups throughout the world grew militant in their demands for their own national entities. Many saw this as a path to a solution for their own problems of inequality. With the apparent easing, if not the elimination, of Cold War tensions between the Soviet Union and the United States, widespread controversies began relative to the shape of a "new world order." This posed unprecedented challenges to utopian thought.

To deal with these challenges, social scientists, as well as imaginative novelists and others, were confronted with the task of integrating value configurations, social structures, and psychological sets on levels that may well make all previous efforts at utopian analysis and design resemble the stumbling steps of a child just learning to walk.

(SEE ALSO: *Equity Theory; Social Philosophy*)

REFERENCES

Beecher, Jonathan 1986 *Charles Fourier: The Visionary and His World.* Berkeley: University of California Press.

Brinton, Crane 1965 "Utopia and Democracy." In Frank E. Manuel, ed., *Utopias and Utopian Thought.* Boston: Beacon Press.

Cole, Margaret 1969 *Robert Owen of New Lanark 1771–1858.* New York: August M. Kelley.

Gil, Efraim 1996 "The Individual within the Collective: A New Perspective." *Journal of Rural Cooperation* 24:5–15.

Goldman, Alan H. 1980 "Responses to Rawls from the Political Right." In H. Gene Blocker and Elizabeth H. Smith, eds., *John Rawls' Theory of Social Justice.* Athens: Ohio University Press.

Hacohen, Malachi-Haim 1996 "Karl Popper in Exile: The Viennese Progressive Imagination and the Making of The Open Society." *Philosophy of the Social Sciences* 26:452–492.

Hodgson, Geoffrey M. 1995 "The Political Economy of Utopia." *Review of Social Economy* 53:195–213.

Holzman, Michael 1990 "The Encouragement and Warning of History: William Morris's *A Dream of John Ball.*" In Florence S. Boos and Carole G. Silver, eds., *Socialism and the Literary Artistry of William Morris.* Columbia: University of Missouri Press.

Klosko, George 1986 *The Development of Plato's Political Theory.* New York: Methuen.

Kumar, Krishan 1987 *Utopia and Anti-Utopia in Modern Times.* New York: Basil Blackwell.

Lowy, Michael 1997 "The Romantic Utopia of Walter Benjamin" (L'Utopie romantique de Walter Benjamin) *Raison Presente* 121:19–27.

Maler, Henri. 1998. "An Pocryphal Testament: Socialism, Utopian and Scientific." *Science and Society* 62:48–61.

Manuel, Frank E., and Fritzie P. Manuel 1979 *Utopian Thought in the Western World.* Cambridge, Mass.: Harvard University Press.

Martensson, Bertil 1991 "The Paradoxes of Utopia: A Study in Utopian Rationalism." *Philosophy of the Social Sciences* 21:476–514.

More, Sir Thomas (1516) 1965 *Utopia.* Paul Turner, trans. London: Penguin.

Morris, William 1966 *News from Nowhere.* In *The Collected Works of William Morris,* vol. 16, pp. 3–211. New York: Russell and Russell.

Nozick, Robert 1974 *Anarchy, State and Utopia.* New York: Basic Books.

Oyzerman, Teodor Il ich. 1998 "Marxism and Utopianism. Marxisms's Overcoming of Utopianism as an Unfinished Historical Process" (Marksizm i utopiszm. Preodolenie marksizmom utopizma kak nezavershennyi istoricheskiy protsess) *Svobodnya-Mysl* 2:76–83.

Paul, Jeffrey (ed.) 1981 *Reading Nozick.* Totowa, N.J.: Rowan and Littlefield.

Plato 1941 *The Republic of Plato,* Francis MacDonald Cornford, trans. and ed. New York and London: Oxford University Press.

Prat, Jean-Louis 1995 "Utopian Utilitarianism" (L'Utiliarisme utopique) *Revue du MAUSS* 6:53–60.

Rawls, John 1971 *A Theory of Justice.* Cambridge, Mass.: Harvard University Press.

Sargent, Lyman Tower 1990 "William Morris and the Anarchist Tradition." In F. S. Boos and C. G. Silver, eds., *Socialism and the Literary Artistry of William Morris.* Columbia: University of Missouri Press.

Schaar, John H. 1980 "Equality of Opportunity and the Just Society." In H. G. Blocker and E. H. Smith, eds., *John Rawls' Theory of Social Justice.* Athens: Ohio University Press.

Scheffler, Samuel 1981 "Natural Rights, Equality and the Minimal State." In Jeffrey Paul, ed., *Reading Nozick.* Totowa, N.J.: Rowan and Littlefield.

Skinner, B. F. 1948 *Walden Two.* New York: Macmillan.

ROBERT BOGUSLAW

V

VALIDITY

In the simplest sense, a measure is said to be valid to the degree that it measures what it is hypothesized to measure (Nunnally 1967, p. 75). More precisely, validity has been defined as the degree to which a score derived from a measurement procedure reflects a point on the underlying construct it is hypothesized to reflect (Bohrnstedt 1983). In the most recent *Standards for Educational and Psychological Testing* (American Psychological Association 1985), it is stated that validity "refers to the appropriateness, meaningfulness, and usefulness of the specific inferences made from . . . scores." The emphasis is clear: Validity refers to the degree to which evidence supports the *inferences* drawn from a score rather than the scores or the instruments that produce the scores. Inferences drawn for a given measure with one population may be valid but may not be valid for other measures. As will be shown below, evidence for inferences about validity can be accumulated in a variety of ways. In spite of this variety, validity is a unitary concept. The varied types of inferential evidence relate to the validity of a particular measure under investigation.

Several important points related to validity should be noted:

1. Validity is a matter of degree rather than an all-or-none matter (Nunnally 1967, p. 75; Messick 1989).

2. Since the constructs of interest in sociology (normlessness, religiosity, economic conservatism, etc.) generally are not amenable to direct observation, validity can be ascertained only indirectly.

3. Validation is a dynamic process; the evidence for or against the validity of the inferences that can be drawn from a measure may change with accumulating evidence. Validity in this sense is always a continuing and evolving matter rather than something that is fixed once and for all (Messick 1989).

4. Validity is the sine qua non of measurement; without it, measurement is meaningless.

In spite of the clear importance of validity in making defensible inferences about the reasonableness of theoretical formulations, the construct more often than not is given little more than lip service in sociological research. Measures are assumed to be valid because they "look valid," not because they have been evaluated as a way to get statistical estimates of validity. In this article, the different meanings of validity are introduced and methods for estimating the various types of validity are discussed.

TYPES OF VALIDITY

The *Standards* produced jointly by the American Psychological Association, the American Educational Research Association, and the National Council on Measurement in Education distinguish between and among three types of evidence related to validity: (1) *criterion-related*, (2) *content*, and (3) *construct evidence* (American Psychological Association 1985).

Criterion-Related Evidence for Validity. Criterion-related evidence for validity is assessed by the correlation between a measure and a criterion variable of interest. The criterion varies with the purpose of the researcher and/or the client for the research. Thus, in a study to determine the effect of early childhood education, a criterion of interest might be how well children perform on a standardized reading test at the end of the third grade. In a study for an industrial client, it might be the number of years it takes to reach a certain job level. The question that is always asked when one is accumulating evidence for criterion-related validity is: How accurately can the criterion be predicted from the scores on a measure? (American Psychological Association 1985).

Since the criterion variable may be one that exists in the present or one that a researcher may want to predict in the future, evidence for criterion-related validity is classified into two major types: predictive and concurrent.

Evidence for *predictive validity* is assessed by examining the future standing on a criterion variable as predicted from the present standing on a measure of interest. For example, if one constructs a measure of work orientation, evidence of its predictive validity for job performance might be ascertained by administering that measure to a group of new hires and correlating it with a criterion of success (supervisors' ratings, regular advances within the organization, etc.) at a later point in time. The evidence for the validity of a measure is not limited to a single criterion. There are as many validities as there are criterion variables to be predicted from that measure. The preceding example makes this clear. In addition, the example shows that the evidence for the validity of a measure varies depending on the time at which the criterion is assessed. Generally, the closer in time the measure and the criterion are assessed, the higher the validity, but this is not always true.

Evidence for *concurrent validity* is assessed by correlating a measure and a criterion of interest at the *same* point in time. A measure of the concurrent validity of a measure of religious belief, for example, is its correlation with concurrent attendance at religious services. Just as is the case for predictive validity, there are as many concurrent validities as there are criteria to be explained; there is no single concurrent validity for a measure.

Concurrent validation also can be evaluated by correlating a measure of X with extant measures of X, for instance, correlating one measure of self-esteem with a second one. It is assumed that the two measures reflect the same underlying construct. Two measures may both be labeled self-esteem, but if one contains items that deal with one's social competence and the other contains items that deal with how one feels and evaluates oneself, it will not be surprising to find no more than a modest correlation between the two.

Evidence for validity based on concurrent studies may not square with evidence for validity based on predictive studies. For example, a measure of an attitude toward a political issue may correlate highly in August in terms of which political party one *believes* one will vote for in November but may correlate rather poorly with the *actual* vote in November.

Many of the constructs of interest to sociologists do not have criteria against which the validity of a measure can be ascertained easily. When they do, the criteria may be so poorly measured that the validity coefficients are badly attenuated by measurement error. For these reasons, sociological researchers have rarely computed criterion-related validities.

Content Validity. One can imagine a *domain of meaning* that a construct is intended to measure. *Content validity* provides evidence for the degree to which one has representatively sampled from that domain of meaning. (Bohrnstedt 1983). One also can think of a domain as having various facets (Guttman 1959), and just as one can use stratification to obtain a sample of persons, one can use stratification principles to improve the evidence for content validity.

While content validity has received close attention in the construction of achievement and proficiency measures psychology and educational psychology, it usually has been ignored by sociologists. Many sociological researchers have instead been satisfied to construct a few items on an ad hoc, one-shot basis in the apparent belief that they are measuring what they intended to measure. In fact, the construction of good measures is a tedious, arduous, and time-consuming task.

Because domains of interest cannot be enumerated in the same way that a population of persons or objects can, the task of assuring the content validity of one's measures is less rigorous than one would hope. While an educational psychologist can sample four-, five-, or six-letter words in constructing a spelling test, no such clear criteria exist for a sociologist who engages in social measurement. However, some guidelines can be provided. First, the researcher should search the literature carefully to determine how various authors have used the concept that is to be measured. There are several excellent handbooks that summarize social measures in use, including Robinson and Shaver's *Measures of Social Psychological Attitudes* (1973); Robinson et al.'s *Measures of Political Attitudes* (1968); Robinson et al.'s *Measures of Occupational Attitudes and Occupational Characteristics* (1969); Shaw and Wright's *Scales for the Measurement of Attitudes* (1967); and Miller's *Handbook of Research Design and Social Measurement* (1977). These volumes not only contain lists of measures but provide existing data on the reliability and validity of those measures. However, since these books are out of date as soon as they go to press, researchers developing their own methods must do additional literature searches. Second, sociological researchers should rely on their own observations and insights and ask whether they yield additional facets to the construct under consideration.

Using these two approaches, one develops *sets* of items, one to capture each of the various facets or strata within the domain of meaning. There is no simple criterion by which one can judge whether a domain of meaning has been sampled properly. However, a few precautions can be taken to help ensure the representation of the various facets within the domain.

First, the domain can be stratified into its major facets. One first notes the most central meanings of the construct, making certain that the stratification is exhaustive, that is, that all major meaning facets are represented. If a facet appears to involve a complex of meanings, it should be subdivided further into substrata. *The more one refines the strata and substrata the easier it is to construct the items later and the more complete the coverage of meanings associated with the construct will be.* Second, one should write several items or locate several extant indicators to reflect the meanings associated with each stratum and substratum. Third, after the items have been written, they should tried out on very small samples composed of persons of the type the items will eventually be used with, using cognitive interviewing techniques, in which subjects are asked to "think aloud" as they respond to the items. This technique for the improvement of items, while quite new in survey research, is very useful for improving the validity of items (Sudman et al. 1995). For example, Levine et al. (1997) have shown how cognitive interviewing helped in the improvement of school staffing resources, as did Levine (1996) in describing the development of background questionnaires for use with the large-scale cognitive assessments. Fourth, after the items have been refined through the use of cognitive laboratory techniques, the newly developed items should be field-tested on a sample similar to that with which one intends to examine the main research questions. The field-test sample should be large enough to examine whether the items are operating as planned vis-à-vis the constructs they are putatively measuring, using multivariate tools such as confirmatory factor analysis (Joreskog 1969) and item response theory methods (Hambleton and Swaminathan 1985).

Finally, after the items are developed, the main study should employ a sampling design that takes into account the characteristics of the population about which generalizations are to be made (ethnicity, gender, region of country, etc.). The study also should be large enough to generate stable parameter estimates when one is using multivariate techniques such as multiple regression (Bohrnstedt and Knoke 1988) and structural equation techniques (Bollen 1989).

It can be argued that what the *Standards* call content validity is not a separate method for assessing validity. Instead, it is a set of procedures for sampling content domains that, if followed, can help provide evidence for *construct validity* (see the discussion of construct validity below). Messick (1989), in a similar stance, states that so-called content validity does not meet the definition of validity given above, since it does not deal directly with scores or their interpretation. This position can be better understood in the context of construct validity.

Construct Validity. The 1974 *Standards* state: "A construct is. . . a theoretical idea developed to explain and to organize some aspects of existing knowledge. . . It is a dimension understood or inferred from its network of interrelationships" (American Psychological Association 1985). The *Standards* further indicate that in developing evidence for construct validity,

the investigator begins by formulating hypotheses about the characteristics of those who have high scores on the [measure] in contrast to those who have low scores. Taken together, such hypotheses form at least a tentative theory about the nature of the construct the [measure] is believed to be measuring.

Such hypotheses or theoretical formulations lead to certain predictions about how people. . . will behave. . . in certain defined situations. If the investigator's theory. . . is correct, most predictions should be confirmed. (p. 30)

The notion of a construct implies hypotheses of two types. First, it implies that items from one stratum within the domain of meaning correlate together because they all reflect the same underlying construct or "true" score. Second, whereas items from one domain may correlate with items from another domain, the implication is that they do so only because the constructs themselves are correlated. Furthermore, it is assumed that there are *hypotheses* about how measures of different domains correlate with one another. To repeat, construct validation involves two types of evidence. The first is evidence for *theoretical validity* (Lord and Novick 1968): an assessment of the relationship between items and an underlying, latent unobserved construct. The second involves evidence that the underlying latent variables correlate as hypothesized. If either or both sets of these hypotheses fail, evidence for construct validation is absent. If one can show evidence for theoretical validity but evidence about the interrelations among those constructs is missing, that suggests that one is not measuring the intended construct or that the theory is wrong or inadequate. The more unconfirmed hypotheses one has involving the constructs, the more one is likely to assume the former rather than the latter.

The discussion above makes clear the close relationship between construct validation and the-ory validation. To be able to show construct validity assumes that the researcher has a clearly stated set of interrelated hypotheses between important theoretical constructs, which in turn can be measured by sets of indicators. Too often in sociology, one or both of these components are missing.

Campbell (1953, 1956) uses a *multitrait–multimethod matrix*, a useful tool for assessing the construct validity of a set of measures collected using differing methods. Thus, for example, one might collect data using multiple indicators of three constructs, say, prejudice, alienation, and anomie, using three different data collection methods: a face-to-face interview, a telephone interview, and a questionnaire. To the degree that different methods yield the same or a very similar result, the construct demonstrates what Campbell (1954) calls *convergent validity*. Campbell argues that in addition, the constructs must not correlate too highly with each other; that is, to use Campbell and Fiske's (1959) term, they must also exhibit *discriminant validity*. Measures that meet both criteria provide evidence for construct validity.

VALIDITY GENERALIZATION

An important issue for work in educational and industrial settings is the degree to which the criterion-related evidence for validity obtained in one setting generalizes to other settings (American Psychological Association 1985). The point is that evidence for the validity of an instrument in one setting in no ways guarantees its validity in any other setting. By contrast, the more evidence there is of consistency of findings across settings that are maximally different, the stronger the evidence for *validity generalization is*.

Evidence for validity generalization generally is garnered in one of two ways. The usual way is simply to do a nonquantitative review of the relevant literature; then, on the basis of that review, a conclusion about the generalizability of the measure across a variety of settings is made. More recently, however, meta-analytic techniques (Hedges and Olkin 1985) have been employed to provide quantitative evidence for validity generalization.

Variables that may affect validity generalization include the particular criterion measure used, the sample to which the instrument is administered, the time period during which the instrument was used, and the setting in which the assessment is done.

Differential predication. In using a measure in different demographic groups that differ in experience or that have received different treatments (e.g., different instructional programs), the possibility exists that the relationship between the criterion measure and the predictor will vary across groups. To the degree that this is true, a measure is said to display *differential prediction*.

Closely related is the notion of *predictive bias*. While there is some dispute about the best definition, the most commonly accepted definition states that predictive bias exists if different regression equations are needed for different groups and if predictions result in decisions for those groups that are different from the decisions that would be made based on a pooled groups regression analysis (American Psychological Association 1985). Perhaps the best example to differentiate the two concepts is drawn from examining the relationship between education and income. It has been shown that that relationship is stronger for whites than it is for blacks; that is, education differentially predicts income. If education were then used as a basis for selection into jobs at a given income level, education would be said to have a predictive bias against blacks because they would have to have a greater number of years of education to be selected for a given job level compared to whites.

Differential prediction should not be confused with *differential validity*, a term used in the context of job placement and classification. Differential validity refers to the ability of a measure or, more commonly, a battery of measures to differentially predict success or failure in one job compared to another. Thus, the armed services use the battery of subtests in the Armed Services Vocational Aptitude Battery (U.S. Government Printing Office 1989; McLaughlin et al. 1984) in making the initial assignment of enlistees to military occupational specialties.

MORE RECENT FORMULATIONS OF VALIDITY

More recent definitions of validity have been even broader than that used in the 1985 *Standards*.

Messick (1989) defines validity as an evaluative judgment about the degree to which "empirical and theoretical rationales support the *adequacy* and *appropriateness* of *inferences* and *actions* based on . . . scores or other modes of assessment" (p. 13). For Messick, validity is more than a statement of the existing empirical evidence linking a score to a latent construct; it is also a statement about the evidence for the appropriateness of using and interpreting the scores. While most measurement specialists separate the use of scores from their interpretation, Messick (1989) argues that the value implications and social consequences of testing are inextricably bound to the issue of validity:

> [A] social consequence of testing, such as adverse impact against females in the use of a quantitative test, either stems from a source of test invalidity or a valid property of the construct assessed, or both. In the former case, this adverse consequence bears on the meaning of the test scores and, in the later case, on the meaning of the construct. In both cases, therefore, construct validity binds social consequences to the evidential basis of test interpretation and use." (p. 21)

Whether the interpretation and social consequences of the uses of measures become widely adopted (i.e., are adopted in the next edition of the *Standards*) remains to be seen. Messick's (1989) definition does reinforce, the idea that although there are many facets to and methods for garnering evidence for inferences about validity, it remains a unitary concept; evidence bears on inferences about a single measure or instrument.

REFERENCES

American Psychological Association 1985 *Standards for Educational and Psychological Testing*. Washington, D.C.: American Psychological Association.

Bohrnstedt, G. W. 1983 "Measurement." In Rossi, P. H., J. D. Wright, and A. B. Anderson, eds., *Handbook of Survey Research*. New York: Academic Press

Bohrnstedt, G. W., and D. Knoke 1988, *Statistics for Social Data Analysis*. Itasca, Ill.: F.E. Peacock.

Bohrnstedt, G. W. 1992 "Reliability." In E. F. Borgatta (ed.) *Encyclopedia of Sociology*. 1st ed., New York: Macmillan.

Bollen, K. A. 1989 *Structural Equations with Latent Variables*. New York: Wiley.

Campbell, D. T. 1953 *A Study of Leadership among Submarine Officers.* Columbus: Ohio State University Research Foundation.

—— 1954 "Operational Delineation of What Is Learned' via the Transportation Experiment." *Psychological Review* 61:167–174.

—— 1956 *Leadership and Its Effects upon the Group.* Monograph no. 83. Columbus: Ohio State University Bureau of Business Research.

——, and D.W. Fiske 1959 "Convergent and Discriminant Validation by the Multitrait-Multimethod Matrix." *Psychological Bulletin* 56:81–105.

Guttman, L. 1959 "A Structural Theory for Intergroup Beliefs and Action." *American Sociological Review* 24:318–328.

Hambleton, R., and H. Swaminathan 1985 *Item Response Theory: Principles and Applications.* Norwell, Mass.: Kluwer Academic.

Hedges, L. V., and I. Olkin 1985 *Statistical Methods for Meta-Analysis.* Orlando, Fla.: Academic Press.

Jöreskog, K. G. 1969 "A general approach to confirmatory maximum likelihood factor analysis." *Psyclometrika* 36:409–426.

Levine, R. 1998 "What Do Cognitive Labs Tell Us about Student Knowledge?" Paper presented at the 28th Annual Conference on Large Scale Assessment sponsored by the Council of Chief State School Officers, Colorado Springs, Colo. Palo Alto, Calif.: American Institutes for Research

Levine, R., J. Chambers, I. Duenas, and C. Hikido 1997 *Improving the Measurement of Staffing Resources at the School Level: The Development of Recommendations for NCES for the Schools and Staffing Surveys (SASS).* Palo Alto, Calif.: American Institutes for Research

Lord, F. M., and M. R. Novick 1968 *Statistical Theories of Mental Test Scores.* Reading, Mass.: Addison-Wesley.

McLaughlin, D. H., P. G. Rossmeissl, L. L. Wise, D. A. Brandt, and M. Wang 1984 *Validation of Current and Alternative Armed Services Vocational Aptitude Battery (ASVAB) Area Composites.* Washington, D.C.: U.S. Army Research Institute for the Behavioral and Social Sciences.

Messick, S. 1989 "Validity." In L. Linn, ed., *Educational Measurement,* 3rd ed. New York: Macmillan.

Miller, D. 1977 *Handbook of Research Design and Social Measurement,* 3rd ed. New York: David McKay.

Nunnally, J. C. 1967 *Psychometric Theory.* New York: McGraw-Hill.

Robinson, J. P., R. Athanasiou, and K. B. Head 1969 Measures of Occupational Attitudes and Occupational Characteristics. Ann Arbor: Institute for Social Research.

——, J. G. Rusk, and K. B. Head 1968 *Measures of Political Attitudes.* Ann Arbor, Mich.: Institute for Social Research.

Robinson, J. P. and P. R. Shaver 1973 *Measures of Social Psychological Attitudes.* Ann Arbor, Mich.: Institute for Social Research.

Shaw, M., and J. Wright 1967 *Scales for the Measurement of Attitudes.* New York: McGraw-Hill.

Sudburn, S., N. Bradburn, and N. Schwarz 1995 *Thinking about Answers, The Application of Cognitive Processes to Survey Methodology.* San Francisco: Jossey-Bass.

U.S. Government Printing Office 1989 *A Brief Guide: ASVAB for Counselors and Educators.* Washington, D. C.: U.S. Government Printing Office.

GEORGE W. BOHRNSTEDT

VALUE-FREE ANALYSIS

See Epistemology; Positivism; Scientific Explanation.

VALUES THEORY AND RESEARCH

The study of values covers a broad multidisciplinary terrain. Different disciplines have pursued this topic with unique orientations to the concept of values. The classic conception of values in anthropology was introduced by Kluckhohn and Strodtbeck (1961). In this view, values answer basic existential questions, helping to provide meaning in people's lives. For example, Kluckhohn and Strodtbeck argue that Americans value individual effort and reward because of their fundamental belief in the inherent goodness of human nature and the capacity of individuals to obtain desired ends. Economists have considered values not in terms of the meaning they provide but as a quality of the objects used in social exchange (Stigler 1950). For economists, objects have value but people have preferences, and those preferences establish hierarchies of goods. It is the goods that have value, with those which are both scarce and highly desirable being the most highly valued.

Sociologists, particularly Parsons, have emphasized a different conception of values (see

Parsons and Shils 1951). In sociology, values are believed to help ease the conflict between individual and collective interests. Values serve an important function by enabling individuals to work together to realize collectively desirable goals. For example, while all the individual members of society may believe that public education is a good idea for themselves, their children, and/or the well-being of society in general, none of them is excited by the prospect of paying taxes to build schools and pay teachers. Even when people believe in the collective good, their private interest (keeping one's money for one's own use) conflicts with the necessities for keeping a society organized. Values such as being socially responsible, showing concern for others, and education encourage people to sidestep their own desires and commit themselves to the more difficult task of social cooperation. As Grube et al. (1994, p. 155) argue, "values play a particularly important role because they are cognitive representations of individual needs and desires, on the one hand, and of societal demands on the other."

Another way to understand the sociological conception of values is to examine when values become vital in social life. They do not matter much when everyone is in full agreement. For example, everyone values breathing over asphyxiation. Even though this value may be of life-and-death importance, it is not a particularly important object of social inquiry because no one disagrees about whether one should hold one's breath. The situation has been quite different with regard to abortion, affirmative action, the death penalty, same-sex marriage, environmental protection, and many other social issues that elicit conflicts in personal values. Values are important to understand when they conflict between individuals, groups, or whole societies. They provide a window through which one can view conflicts and variations within and between societies.

Although many formal definitions of values have been advanced by sociologists, one definition in particular captures the concept's core features well. Smith and Schwartz (1997, p. 80) observe five features:

1. Values are beliefs. But they are not objective, cold ideas. Rather, when values are activated, they become infused with feeling.

2. Values refer to desirable goals (e.g., equality) and to the modes of conduct that promote these goals (e.g., fairness, helpfulness).

3. Values transcend specific actions and situations. Obedience, for example, is relevant at work or in school, in sports or in business, with family, friends or strangers.

4. Values serve as standards to guide the selection or evaluation of behavior, people, and events.

5. Values are ordered by importance relative to one another. The ordered set of values forms a system of value priorities. Cultures and individuals can be characterized by their systems of value priorities.

Smith and Schwartz's conceptualization is consistent with the sociological view that values are abstract concepts, but not so abstract that they cannot motivate behavior. Hence, an important theme of values research has been to assess how well one can predict specific behavior by knowing something about a person's values. If someone claims to believe in protecting the environment, for example, how confidently can one assume that that person recyles, contributes to the Sierra Club, or supports proenvironmental legislation? Below, several empirical efforts to measure the link between values and behavior are discussed. However, some scholars are skeptical that such a link can be drawn (Hechter 1992, 1993).

The definition given above emphasizes the link between values and desired goals. In an earlier discussion, Schwartz (1992, p. 4) argued that values, when defined in this way, reflect three basic requirements of human existence: "needs of individuals as biological organisms, requisites of coordinated social interaction, and survival and welfare needs of groups." By understanding values, one can learn about the needs of both individuals and societies. Sociologists are especially concerned with how values facilitate action toward ends that enhance individual and collective outcomes or are perceived to do so by society's members. Research on values does not presuppose which values are best (social scientists are not preachers) but tries to discover what people believe in and how their beliefs motivate their behavior. A major part of the enterprise is concerned with strategies to measure values: which ones people hold, how strongly they hold them, how their value priorities compare with those of others, how the value priorities of different groups or societies compare with one another.

Values research has a long and varied history in sociology. Important theoretical and empirical studies of values have been made by Parsons and Shils (1951), Kluckhohn (1951), Williams (1960), Allport et al. (1960), Scott (1965), Smith (1969), and Kohn (1969). Because the field is so broad, this article cannot cover all the ground but concentrates on recent empirical endeavors. Other reviews summarize the early studies in detail, such as Blake and Davis (1964), Williams (1968), Zavalloni (1980), Spates (1983), and Ball-Rokeach and Loges (1992).

Contemporary areas of research in values are not well integrated; each represents an active arena of social research that is empirically driven and theoretically informed. Below, will be summarized these areas, noting the unique contributions and insights of each one. The research reviewed here has been conducted by psychologists and political scientists as well as sociologists. However, all of it is premised on the sociological conceptual framework of values inherent in the definition given above.

THE ROKEACH TRADITION

The most influential researcher on values in the last three decades is Rokeach. The focus of his work has been the development of an instrument to measure values that he believes are universal and transsituational (see especially Rokeach 1973). That is, Rokeach has tried to develop an instrument that can be used to compare individual commitment to a set of values wherever the researchers live and whenever they complete a survey. This instrument has been widely used in the measurement of values (Mayton et al. 1994).

The Rokeach Value Survey is an instrument made up of thirty-six value items that are ranked by survey subjects. The items are divided into two sets. The first ones are termed "instrumental values" and refer to values that reflect modes of conduct, such as politeness, honesty, and obedience. The second set refers to "terminal values" that reflect desired end states, such as freedom, equality, peace, and salvation. Each set of eighteen value items is ranked by subjects according to the items' importance as guiding principles in their lives. The purpose of the procedure is to force subjects to identify priorities among competing values. In this model, the values are assumed to be universal; therefore, to some extent, each value is supported by every subject. The question is how subjects adjudicate between value conflicts. For example, the instrumental value "broad-minded" may conflict with the value "obedience." How would a person who is trying to conform to the expectations of racist parents maintain a broad-minded commitment to diversity? By requiring that values be rank-ordered, the Rokeach Values Survey helps disclose a person's value priorities.

One of the distinct advantages of the Rokeach Value Survey is that it is a fairly simple instrument that can be used by researchers in a variety of settings. Thus, it was possible to see if the value priorities of Michigan college students were similar to those of other subsamples of Americans, allowing comparisons of those with different demographic characteristics, such as age, sex, race, religion, and education. For example, in a national sample, Rokeach found that men and women tended to prioritize "a world at peace," "family security," and "freedom; however, men strongly valued "a comfortable life" while women did not, and women strongly valued "salvation" while men did not. Value priorities have been shown to be linked to a variety of attitudes about contemporary social issues. For example, as would be predicted, concern for the welfare of blacks and the poor is stronger among those who value equality.

The Rokeach Value Survey has been used by numerous researchers to explore many facets of values, such as the relationship between values and behavior, the role of values in justifying attitudes, and the extent to which people remain committed to particular values over time. An important early study of values employing the Rokeach model was conducted by Feather (1975), who measured the values of Australian high school and college students as well as those of their parents. One central finding demonstrated the importance of a close fit between the person and the environment in which that person is situated: Students were happiest when their values were congruent with those articulated by the schools they attended or the subjects they studied. Another finding was that parents were consistently more conservative, emphasizing values such as national security, responsibility, and politeness, while their children where more likely to emphasize excitement and pleasure, equality and freedom, a world of beauty, friendship, and broad-mindedness. It also was found that student activists were distinctive in their emphasis on humanitarianism, nonmaterialism, and social and political goals.

The Rokeach model underscores the potential conflicts between individuals with different value priorities. Different positions on important social issues may be traced to differential commitments to particular values. For example, Kristiansen and Zanna (1994) report that supporters of abortion rights emphasize values such as freedom and a comfortable life, whereas opponents place a high priority on religious salvation. Moreover, as they defend their positions, each group will justify its position by referring to its own value priorities; this, of course, may not be very convincing to people who do not share them. This may be one reason why the abortion debate seems intractable. Individuals also may be ambivalent about particular social issues because of their pluralistic commitment to two or more values that conflict in the public policy domain. This is the essence of Tetlock's (1986) "value pluralism model of ideological reasoning." For example, liberals tend to weight equality and freedom fairly equally, causing them to feel ambivalently about affirmative action policies (Peterson 1994).

Rokeach and Rokeach (1980) argue that values are not simply hierarchically prioritized but that each is interrelated in a complex system of beliefs and attitudes. Thus, a belief system may be relatively enduring, but changes in one value may lead to changes in others and in the whole system. When are personal values likely to endure, and when are they likely to change? Rokeach argues that individuals try to maintain a consistent conception of themselves that reflects their morality and competence. When their actions or beliefs contradict this self-conception, they feel dissatisfied and change is likely to occur to bring their actions or beliefs into line. Grube et al. (1994) review a number of studies in which researchers attempted to uncover contradictions in subjects'

values with the prediction that this conflict would lead to value change. These works have been called "self-confrontation" studies; they have found a significant degree of value change as a result of the method, even over long periods. However, the method is much less effective at inducing specific behavioral changes.

The central claim of values researchers is consistent with a commonsense understanding of values. Values are important because they guide people's behavior. At times they may be an even stronger motivation than is self-interest. For example, fear of arrest may not be as good an explanation for one's choice not to shoplift as is the more straightforward commitment to the value of right conduct. However, this central claim has been the most controversial in values research. The robust finding that values directly affect behavior has never surfaced in values research. The link does not exist, or several links in a long chain of causes intervene between these two crucial variables. This ambiguity has led Hechter (1992), for example, to suggest that social scientists stop using the term "values." Kristiansen and Hotte (1996, p. 79) observed that "although values, attitudes, and behavior are related, these relations are often small . . . one wonders why people do not express attitudes and actions that are more strongly in line with their values." Many people also wonder whether current measures of values are adequate. The Rokeach Value Survey, for example, may not be sufficiently complete or its definitions of values may be too abstract or vague to predict behavior accurately.

Kristiansen and Hotte (1996) argue that values researchers must pay much closer attention to the intervening factors in the values–behavior relationship. For example, those factors may include the way in which individuals engage in moral reasoning. Making a behavioral choice requires the direct application of very general values. How is this done? What do people consider in trying to make such a decision? Do they rely on ideological commitments to moral principles? Do they take into consideration the immediate context or circumstances? How much are they influenced by social norms? These questions are likely to guide research on the values–behavior connection in the future.

THE SCHWARTZ SCALE OF VALUES

A major evolution of the Rokeach Values Survey is found in the cross-cultural values research of Schwartz (see especially Schwartz 1992 and Smith and Schwartz 1997). Like Rokeach, Schwartz has focused on the measurement of values that are assumed to be universal. To that end, Schwartz has modified and expanded the Rokeach instrument. He also has proposed a new conceptual model that is based on the use of the new instrument in more than fifty countries around the world and more than 44,000 subjects (Smith and Schwartz 1997).

According to Schwartz (1992), values are arrayed along two general dimensions (Figure 1). In any culture, individual values fall along a dimension ranging from "self-enhancement" to "self-transcendence." This dimension reflects the distinction between values oriented toward the pursuit of self-interest and values related to a concern for the welfare of others: "It arrays values in terms of the extent to which they motivate people to enhance their own personal interests (even at the expense of others) versus the extent to which they motivate people to transcend selfish concerns and promote the welfare of others, close and distant, and of nature" (1992, p. 43). The second dimension contrasts "openness to change" with "conservation": "It arrays values in terms of the extent to which they motivate people to follow their own intellectual and emotional interests in unpredictable and uncertain directions versus to preserve the status quo and the certainty it provides in relationships with close others, institutions, and traditions" (1992, p. 43). This dimension indicates the degree to which individuals are motivated to engage in independent action and are willing to challenge themselves for both intellectual and emotional realization. Schwartz (1992, pp. 5–12) further postulates that within these two dimensions, there are ten motivational value types:

1. *Universalism*: "understanding, appreciation, tolerance, and protection for the welfare of all people and for nature"

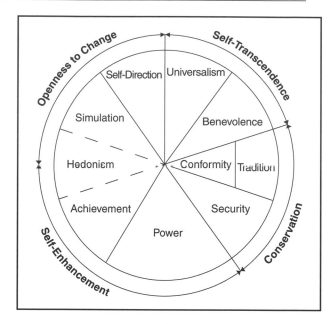

Figure 1. Structural relations among ten motivational types of values

SOURCE: Schwartz (1997), p. 87.

2. *Benevolence*: "preservation and enhancement of the welfare of people with whom one is in frequent personal contact"

3. *Conformity*: "restraint of actions, inclinations, and impulses likely to upset or harm others and violate social expectations or norms"

4. *Tradition*: "respect, commitment, and acceptance of the customs and ideas that one's culture or religion imposes on the individual"

5. *Security*: "safety, harmony, and stability of society, of relationships, and of self"

6. *Power*: "attainment of social status and prestige, and control or dominance over people and resources"

7. *Achievement*: "personal success through demonstrating competence according to social standards"

8. *Hedonism*: "pleasure or sensuous gratification for oneself"

9. *Stimulation*: "excitement, novelty, and challenge in life"

10. *Self-direction*: "independent thought and action—choosing, creating, exploring"

Like Rokeach, Schwartz conceptualizes these motivational types as being dynamically interrelated, with those closest together being conceptually linked and having the greatest influence on one another. This model was not developed deductively but was derived from an empirical project of data collection in which the Schwartz Scale of Values was used. This instrument, which includes fifty-six Rokeach-style values items, is completed by subjects who rate each item on a ten-point scale of personal importance. Unlike the Rokeach instrument, this scale does not require the respondents to rank-order the items. Through the use of a multidimensional scaling technique (smallest-space analysis), statistical correlations of individual items in a survey sample are mapped in a two-dimensional space. Thus, each item is plotted on a graph, and clusters of those items constitute the domains identified in Figure 1. The major finding of the Schwartz project is that this basic visual model reappears in culture after culture. The system of values is essentially the same worldwide, although the emphasis given to particular domains varies from place to place.

Schwartz's dynamic model provides new insight into the values–behavior debate. Schwartz argues that the relationship of values to behavior (or any other variable) must be understood in the context of a multidimensional system. Voting for a particular political platform, for example, can be predicted on the basis of a person's value priorities. Given the interrelatedness of values in Schwartz's model, a person's values form a system: For example, a person who strongly endorses universalism is unlikely to endorse its distal correlate power while moderately endorsing values that are in closer proximity. Schwartz (1996) has used data from these values systems to predict political behavior.

Schwartz's research is especially important for distinguishing values at the individual and cultural levels. Individuals may differ in their values, but so too do cultures, with the members of one culture tending toward one set of priorities and the members of another culture tending toward a different set. Cultural variation in values is of special interest to sociologists, while individual-level values are closer to the interests of social psychologists. Cultural values are important to sociologists because they reflect ways in which society balances conflicting concerns between individuals and groups and the dominant themes around which individuals are socialized. One issue is the provision of public goods; another is the extent to which individuals profess autonomy from the collectivity rather than identifying with it.

To obtain cultural-level values, Schwartz (1994) used the mean scores of values for each culture sample as the basis for plotting a new two-dimensional model. The data points thus are cultures rather than individual respondents. Among other findings, Schwartz discovered that east Asian nations emphasize hierarchy and conservatism, whereas west European nations emphasize egalitarianism and individual autonomy. Anglo nations, including the United States, fall between these extremes, emphasizing mastery and autonomy but also hierarchy; this may explain the greater tolerance for income inequality in countries such as the United States (Smith and Schwartz 1997).

Smith and Schwartz (1997) argue that values research should take two trajectories in the future. First, most studies now ask the respondents to report their own value priorities, whereas, especially for culture-level analyses, it would be useful to ask the respondents to report what they believe are the prevailing values of their culture. This may provide a better account of the normative milieu in which people evaluate their values and decisions. Second, most studies have examined the strength of individual commitment to particular values, but little research has dealt with the degree of value consensus in a culture. Because of the sociological concern about linking cultural values and the organization of societies, this is a crucial topic. One intriguing hypothesis is that socioeconomic development may enhance value consensus, while democratization may decrease it. These tendencies have broad implications for social stability and change in the future as countries pursue these goals.

INDIVIDUALISM AND COLLECTIVISM

In cross-cultural research on values, no concepts have been explored in as much detail as individualism and collectivism. Consistent with the underlying theme of values research that private and communal interests may conflict, individualism and collectivism speak directly to the various ways in which cultures have balanced these competing goals.

The concept of individualism as a cultural construct has received much empirical attention, particularly since the publication of Hofstede's (1980) study of 117,000 IBM employees worldwide. In that study, fifteen items related to employment goals were subdivided into related clusters by using factor analysis, one of which Hofstede labeled individualism, inspiring this line of research. Theory and measurement in individualism and collectivism are associated primarily with Triandis (see especially Triandis 1989, 1995 and a review by Kagitcibasi 1997). In this tradition, the individualistic cultures of the West are typically contrasted with the collectivistic cultures of the East and Latin America. For example, Kim et al. (1994, pp. 6–7) argue that an individualistic ethos encourages individuals to be "autonomous, self-directing, unique, assertive, and to value privacy and freedom of choice." In contrast, "interdependency, succor, nurturance, common fate, and compliance" characterize a collectivistic ethos.

Triandis (1989, p. 52) defines collectivism in terms of in-groups and out-groups: "Collectivism means greater emphasis on (a) the views, needs, and goals of the in-group rather than oneself; (b) social norms and duty defined by the in-group rather than behavior to get pleasure; (c) beliefs shared with the in-group rather than beliefs that distinguish self from in-group; and (d) great readiness to cooperate with in-group members." Collectivism is characterized by two major themes that are consistent with the values dimensions of Schwartz's theory. First, collectivism is defined by conservation values: conformity, tradition, and security. The Japanese proverb "The nail that sticks up gets hammered down" illustrates the demand for conformity in the collectivistic Japanese society. Second, collectivism is characterized by self-transcendent values. Individuals demonstrate a great willingness to cooperate in the pursuit of collective benefits, sacrificing their self-interest to do so. In conflicts between individual and collective interests, collectivists will subsume their individual interests in favor of those of the in-group. However, collectivists are not universally self-transcendent. Cooperation and self-sacrifice extend only to the boundaries of the in-group.

Individualism and collectivism are cultural constructs that define the values of societies, not those of individuals. Triandis argues that individuals vary in their adoption of the cultural ethos. To distinguish individualistic cultures from individualistic individuals, he uses the terms "idiocentrism" for the individual-level correlates of individualism and "allocentrism" for the individual-level correlates of collectivism. An individualistic culture is defined by having a majority of idiocentrics. These individuals identify primarily with the values of individualism, but not in every situation. Thus, individualistic cultures have both idiocentrics and allocentrics, and idiocentrics are collectivistic on occasion.

Triandis has developed a fifty-item scale to measure the various elements of individualism and collectivism. In addition, he advocates a multimethod approach to their study. For example, Triandis et al. (1990) used several measures, including the Schwartz Scale of Values. One of the measures is the Twenty Statements Test (Kuhn and McPartland 1954), which asks respondents to finish twenty sentences that begin with the words "I am . . ." This test is used to measure the degree of social identification or the "social content of the self" by disclosing the number and ordinal position of group membership references to the self relative to the number and ordinal position of individual references to the self. For example, "I am white" refers to group membership, whereas "I am kind" refers to a character trait. Collectivists are predicted to identify more closely with groups than are individualists. In Triandis et al.'s study, less than one-fifth of a U.S. sample's responses were social, whereas more than half of a mainland Chinese sample's responses were social. Using another measure, individualists and collectivists were distinguished by attitude scales measuring the perceived social distance between in-group members and out-group members. Collectivists perceived in-group members as being more homogeneous than did individualist and also perceived out-group members as being more different from in-group members than did individualists.

Among the numerous findings of studies of the values–behavior relationship, one theme is particularly apparent. Individualists tend to emphasize competition, self-interest, and "free riding," whereas collectivists tend to emphasize cooperation, conflict avoidance, group harmony, and group enhancement. Thus, in balancing individual and collective needs, collectivists favor the group more readily than do individualists. Collectivists also have been shown to favor equality in distributive outcomes, whereas individualists favor equity (Kagitcibasi 1997). Because this adjudication between the self and the collective is central to values research, this theme is replayed across research programs. Below, a line of research—"social values"—that provides a unique methodology for understanding these values will be examined.

Sociological research on values has long considered the relationship between values and social progress. For example, Weber ([1905] 1958) argued that an important factor in the rise of capitalism was the emergence of the Protestant Ethic, which encouraged hard work and self-control as a means of salvation. Thus, individuals were guided less by economic necessities or external coercion than by religious commitment. In values research, establishing a causal relationship between cultural values and social arrangements and outcomes is an ongoing endeavor. Triandis (1989), for example, suggests that individualism has two important structural antecedents: economic independence and cultural complexity. Independence enables individuals to pursue their own interests without fearing the economic consequences of deviation from the group. Cultural complexity, such as ethnic diversity and occupational specialization, fosters divergent interests and perspectives within a culture, increasing individualistic orientations. Another strand in values research has examined the

issues of cultural values and economic development. This line of research, which was initiated by Inglehart, is summarized below.

Future research on individualistic and collectivistic values is likely to proceed along three lines. First, these concepts may become more closely integrated with Schwartz's general theory of values. Schwartz (1990, 1994) makes a case for this, and researchers are beginning to use measures of individualism/collectivism concurrently with the Schwartz Scale of Values (Triandis et al. 1990). Second, the overarching concepts of individualism and collectivism are becoming increasingly refined as specific relationships between values and other variables are examined. Triandis (1995) proposes that individualism and collectivism be further distinguished by horizontal and vertical dimensions in which "horizontal" refers to egalitarian social commitments and "vertical" refers to social hierarchies. Vertical collectivism may characterize the value structure of rural India, vertical individualism may characterize the structure of the United States, horizontal collectivism may characterize an Israeli kibbutz, and horizontal individualism may characterize Sweden's value structure (Singelis et al. 1995). Third, another refinement has been proposed by Kagitcibasi (1997), who argues that "relational" individualism/collectivism be distinguished from "normative" individualism/collectivism. The normative approach emphasizes cultural ideals, such as an individualistic culture's prioritization of rights and a collectivistic culture's stress on group harmony and loyalty. The relational approach emphasizes differing concepts of the self in individualism and collectivism. In individualistic cultures, the self is perceived to be autonomous, with clear boundaries drawn between the self and others. In collectivist cultures, the self is perceived as more interdependent, with greater self-identification with the group.

SOCIAL VALUES

The measurement of social values constitutes a unique approach in values research. More than any other approach, this one directly addresses the adjudication between individual and collective interests. The basic issue in this research is how individuals prioritize allocations between themselves and anonymous others. How much are individuals willing to sacrifice their own interests for the good of the group?

Social values research is grounded in a larger paradigm of experimental gaming, the most famous example of which is the "prisoner's dilemma." Although game theory is quite complex, most experimental games have as a central theme the conflict between individual and collective outcomes. This is particularly true in "*n*-person" prisoner's dilemma games and "commons" games, both of which are more generally called social dilemma games (for a general review of social dilemmas research, see Yamagishi 1994). The social values measure is a slight variation of these games, which always involve decisions that result in various payoffs to the self and others. These games are laboratory analogues of real-world situations in which values may play a significant role in behavioral choices. The example of supporting a tax levy for public education discussed at the beginning of the article constitutes a social dilemma because individual interests are in direct conflict with the common good. Another example is proenvironmental behavior such as not littering and recycling. The classic prisoner's dilemma refers to a hypothetical situation involving the choice between exposing a coconspirator of a crime to obtain a lenient sentence and remaining loyal in spite of the greater personal risk in doing so.

In this research tradition, social values are measured through the administration of "decomposed games" to college students participating in social psychology experiments (Messick and McClintock 1968). Essentially, the subjects are presented with a series of payoffs that vary in consequence for both the self and a paired player. The subjects are asked to choose between two and sometimes three outcomes. For example, a subject may be asked which of the following outcomes would be preferable: receiving $8 while the other person receives $2 and receiving $5 while the other person also receives $5. The constellation of several choices with varying outcomes determines the subject's social values. Primarily, the technique

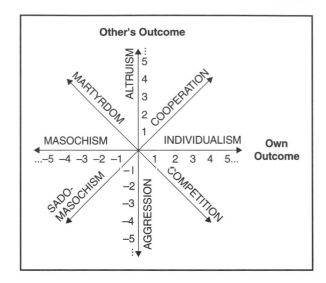

Figure 2. Vectors that define a subset of social values (Given a particular value orientation, an actor should select that combination of available own and others outcomes that has the greatest projection on the correspondent vector)

SOURCE: McClintock and Van Avermaet (1982), p. 49.

distinguishes between altruists, cooperators, individualists, and competitors, the most common classifications.

Each orientation is an indication of the preference that is given for the outcomes for both the self and the other. Subjects may attempt to maximize or minimize their own or others' outcomes or may be indifferent to one or the other. Figure 2 displays the universe of social values in a two-dimensional representation of preferences for the self and the other. Altruists are defined by indifference to their own outcomes and a preference for maximizing others' outcomes. Cooperators attempt to maximize both their own and others' outcomes. Individualists maximize their own outcomes but are indifferent to those of others. Competitors are concerned with maximizing their own outcomes while minimizing others' outcomes; that is, they attempt to maximize the difference between their own and others' outcomes. Theoretically, other social values may exist, such as aggressors, who are indifferent to the self while minimizing others' outcomes; sadomasochists, who minimize both self and others' outcomes; masochists, who minimize their own outcomes but are indifferent to others', and martyrs, who minimize their own outcomes while maximizing those of others. Except for occasional aggressors, these orientations have not been found empirically. Subjects who show no consistent pattern of choice are treated as unclassifiable.

Kuhlman and Marshello (1975) have shown that social values influence choices in prisoner's dilemma games, Liebrand (1986) and McClintock and Liebrand (1988) have demonstrated their influence in a variety of n-person games, and Kramer et al. (1986) have done the same thing in regard to a commons dilemma. In other words, values have been demonstrated to clearly affect behavioral choices in these laboratory situations.

Altruists and cooperators tend to cooperate, while individualists and competitors tend to defect (not cooperate). The essence of social values is the identification of individual differences regarding preferred outcomes in interdependent situations. One interpretation of social values is that "cooperators have internalized a value system in which satisfaction with interdependent relationships is directly proportional to the level of collective welfare they produce; competitors' rewards are directly proportional to how much more they receive than others; and individualists are relatively indifferent to others' outcomes, making them most similar to the traditionally conceived 'economic person'" (Kuhlman et al. 1986, p. 164).

Studies of social values have found that cooperators and noncooperators view social dilemmas differently. In general, decisions in social dilemmas are evaluated in terms of intelligence and morality. Players often are seen as making either "smart" or "good" decisions. Intelligence conforms to a player's social values. Cooperators tend to view cooperation as the intelligent choice, predicting that unintelligent others will defect. Noncooperators tend to view defection as the intelligent choice, predicting that unintelligent others will cooperate. This self-serving reversal does not occur with morality, however. Van Lange (1993) found that both cooperators and noncooperators view cooperation as moral. Both groups expect more cooperation from highly moral others than from less moral others.

Although noncooperators see a link between morality and cooperation, they do not tend to view the social dilemma situation as being primarily moral. Cooperators are more likely to view cooperation as a moral act. Noncooperators frame the problem not in terms of morality but in terms of power: Cooperation is viewed as weak rather than moral. This is called the "might over morality hypothesis" (Liebrand et al. 1986). Viewing cooperation as both weak and unintelligent may provide the self-justification necessary for pursuing an egoistic goal ("Van Lange 1993). The might over morality hypothesis may overstate the case for noncooperators. Defectors have been found to assign more moral attributions to defection than do cooperators (Van Lange et al. 1990). The difference may be not only that cooperators view the dilemma as a moral situation more than defectors do but also that defectors may view their moral obligations differently. Both groups are likely to view self-enhancement as an important value.

Despite the fact that cooperators view social dilemmas as highly moral, their cooperation is not a matter of pure altruism. They are concerned with joint outcomes, with the self included. When they are exploited by noncooperators, they quickly defect (Kuhlman and Marshello 1975). In a study by Kuhlman et al. (1993), cooperators viewed cooperation as a partially self-interested act. That is, they recognized the self-beneficial outcomes of collective cooperation. By contrast, competitors and individualists did not do this. For cooperators and competitors, the difference may be explained by trust. Cooperators are high trusters, assuming that others will be cooperative. Competitors are low trusters, expecting others to defect as they themselves do (Kelley and Stahelski 1970). Competition therefore may be a result of a fear of exploitation or of losing in a competitive social arena. Individualists were found to be high trusters (expecting others to cooperate), unlike competitors. In this case, defection may be motivated more by greed than by fear.

Two studies suggest that social values discovered in the laboratory may have ecological validity, that is, be relevant to real-world situations. Bem and Lord (1979) created a three-part strategy: First, they had experts list the personality characteristics of cooperators, competitors, and individualists. Second, they used decomposed games to measure the subjects' values. Third, they had the subjects' dormitory roommates describe the personality of the subjects. The personal descriptions of specific individuals correlated with both the personality templates created by the experts and subjects' social values as measured by the games. McClintock and Allison (1989) assessed the social values of subjects and, after several months, mailed them a request to donate their time to a charitable cause. Cooperators were more willing to donate time than were competitors and individualists.

Social values research describes differing motivational preferences and behaviors in social dilemmas. This line of research is fascinating because it has adopted the methodology (experimental games) of "rational choice" theorists, who argue that prosocial values always will be trumped by considerations of self-interest. Although the experimental paradigm is clearly artificial and perhaps contrived, it has fostered an accumulation of controlled evidence that supports the basic thesis of values research: Values are important determinants of behavioral choice.

INGLEHART'S POSTMODERN THESIS

Values research as it is described in this article has followed two distinct strands represented by several schools of theory and research. The first is the micro-level strand. Values research at the microlevel has focused on individual values: what they are, how they are measured, how they vary, and how they affect behavior. The various methodologies for measuring values, from Rokeach's value survey, to the Schwartz scale, to Messick and McClintock's decomposed games, represent this strand. The second strand operates at the macro level, the level of cultures or societies. In this strand, one question concerns the distinct cultural variations in values priorities, such as Triandis's individualism versus collectivism. Another question follows from

Weber's work drawing a link between cultural values (Protestantism) and socioeconomic change (the emergence of capitalism). The contemporary work of Inglehart is concerned with the association of values and economic development and with how changes in economic conditions are reflected in very different value priorities. Important works in this tradition include Inglehart (1990) and Abramson and Inglehart (1995). A good summary is found in Inglehart (1995).

The starting point for this line of research is Weber's ([1905] 1958) classic association between Protestantism and the rise of capitalism in the West. Protestant Europe created a new value system that replaced several dogmatic restraints on the development of medieval European society. Weber was principally interested in the shift from traditional authority, best represented by the church, to what he called "rational-legal" authority, which endorsed individual achievement over ascriptive status and the preeminence of the impersonal state as an arbiter of conflicts. Crucial to modernization was secularization, which was reflected in an emerging scientific worldview, and bureaucratization, which was reflected in the rise of organizations driven by attempts at efficiency and explicit goal setting.

Inglehart argues that modernization has followed a fairly straightforward trajectory with economic growth and security at its epicenter. Correlated with modernization has been a coherent set of values such as industriousness, equity, thrift, and security. However, the achievement of economic security in the last twenty-five years in many countries around the world is fostering a change in the dominant values paradigm. Inglehart suggests that people may be experiencing a turn toward postmodern values that emphasize individualistic concerns such as friendship, leisure, self-expression, and the desire for meaningful, not just wealth-creating, work. In key ways, postmodern values follow a path similar to that of modernization values, especially in regard to secularization and individuation. However, they branch in other directions on several points. In societies in which major proportions of the members are economically secure, individuals seek to fulfill postmaterialistic aims such as environmental protection and relational satisfaction. Individuals reject large institutions, whether religious or state-based, focusing instead on more private concerns. They seek new outlets for self-expression and political participation, particularly through local activism.

Some evidence for the postmodern shift comes from Inglehart and Abramson's (1994) analyses of the Euro-Barometer Surveys, which have measured values at frequent intervals since 1970 in all the European Community nations. These surveys have shown a general increase in postmaterialistic values.

Other evidence regarding the postmodern thesis is drawn from the 1990–1991 World Values Survey, which included data from representative samples from forty-three countries and more than 56,000 respondents. Using multiple indicators for the identification of modern and postmodern values, Inglehart tabulated mean scores for each country for forty-seven values. Those scores were employed in a factor analysis that disclosed two important dimensions. The first dimension contrasts traditional authority with rational-legal authority, and the second contrasts values guided by scarcity conditions with those guided by postmodern or security conditions. The distribution of these values in a two-dimensional space is illustrated in Figure 3. These distributions of values also correspond to countries, and so they can be plotted in a two-dimensional space (Inglehart 1995). For example, Inglehart places the United States, Great Britain, and Canada as well as the Scandinavian countries in the postmodern end of this dimension. China, Russia, and Germany ranked highest in the rational-legal domain. Nigeria stood out in its emphasis on traditional authority, while India, South Africa, and Poland fell between an emphasis on traditional authority and an emphasis on scarcity values.

These data do not suggest that once a country achieves a certain level of economic security, a sweeping change in values follows. The process is gradual, with segments of the population shifting from generation to generation. Hence, even in "postmodern" societies, many, if not most, of the members are likely to emphasize "modernist" val-

ues (Kidd and Lee 1997). These data do not suggest that those who adopt postmodern values score higher on various indicators of subjective well-being (Inglehart 1995). What changes is not their level of happiness per se but the criteria by which they evaluate their happiness.

Two issues will continue to receive attention in this line of research. First, there has been some debate about the role of environmentalism as a postmodern value. Does it indicate postmodern commitments, suggesting that it will be valued only by economically secure societies, or is it a more inclusive phenomenon? For a discussion of this issue, see Kidd and Lee (1997) and Brechin and Kempton (1997) along with other articles in that issue of Social Science Quarterly. More generally, the postmodern thesis must be tested with cross-national time-series data to identify values changes over time. These data also will provide insight into questions of causality (Granato et al. 1996): Do values affect economic development, or vice versa?

CONCLUSION

Values research has been of interest to sociologists throughout the history of the discipline. Recently, the study of values has produced novel empirical research programs that carefully address core questions in this field of inquiry. Most fundamentally, values researchers ask what motivates behavior: Is it self-interest alone, self-interest and external coercion, or a combination of self-interest, coercion, and internalized values? A central issue in this line of questioning is the role of values in adjudicating conflicts between individual and collective pursuits.

Values researchers begin with the task of values measurement. What values to people hold? Which ones do they prioritize? How do values differ between members of society and between different cultures? Rokeach supplied the most common measure of values, and Schwartz expanded that measure. Messick and McClintock supplied a very different and innovative measure of social values within the paradigm of game theory research. Schwartz, Triandis, and Inglehart have

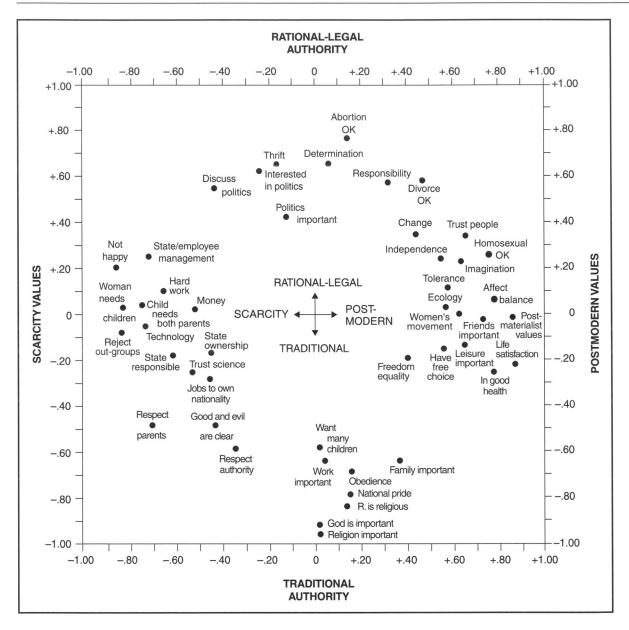

Figure 3. Variation in the values emphasized by different societies: traditional authority versus rational-legal authority and scarcity values versus postmodern values

SOURCE: Source: Inglehart (1995), p. 389.

made valuable contributions to the understanding of values cross-culturally. Of particular note is the apparent universality in the conceptual organization of values worldwide, while much variation in the cultural commitment to particular values has been observed.

Beyond measurement, values researchers have been concerned with the role of values in social interaction. Do values motivate behavior? How are values related to other motivators of behavior? How do individuals increase or decrease their commitment to particular values? How do societies undergo values changes? How are conflicts between values adjudicated between individuals, between individuals and their communities, and between different cultures? Each of the research traditions described in this article has made a contribution to an understanding of the complex values–behavior relationship. Rarely, however, has the question of values acquisition and retention been addressed. Given the enormous progress in cross-cultural values research, it is likely that this domain will garner a great deal of research attention in the next few years.

REFERENCES

Abramson, Paul R., and Ronald Inglehart 1995 *Value Change in Global Perspective*. Ann Arbor: University of Michigan Press.

Allport, G. W., P. E. Vernon, and G. Lindsey 1960 *A Study of Values*. Boston: Houghton Mifflin.

Ball-Rokeach, Sandra J., and William E. Loges 1992 "Value Theory and Research." In E. F. Borgatta and M. L. Borgatta, eds., *Encyclopedia of Sociology*, vol. 1. New York: MacMillan

Bem, Daryl J., and Charles G. Lord 1979 "Template Matching: A Proposal for Probing the Ecological Validity of Experimental Settings in Social Psychology." *Journal of Personality and Social Psychology* 37:833–846.

Blake, Judith, and Kingsley Davis 1964 "Norms, Values, and Sanctions." In R. E. L. Faris, ed., *Handbook of Modern Sociology*, Boston: Rand McNally.

Brechin, Steven R., and Willett Kempton 1997 "Beyond Postmaterialist Values: National versus Individual Explanations of Global Environmentalism." *Social Science Quarterly* 78:16–20.

Feather, Norman T. 1975 *Values in Education and Society*. New York: Free Press.

Granato, Jim, Ronald Inglehart, and David Leblang 1996 "The Effect of Cultural Values on Economic Development: Theory, Hypotheses, and Some Empirical Tests." *American Journal of Political Science* 40:607–631.

Grube, Joel W., Daniel M. Mayton, and Sandra J. Ball-Rokeach 1994 "Inducing Change in Values, Attitudes, and Behaviors: Belief System Theory and the Method of Value Self-Confrontation." *Journal of Social Issues* 50:153–174.

Hechter, Michael 1992 "Should Values Be Written Out of the Social Scientist's Lexicon?" *Sociological Theory* 10:214–230.

—— 1993 "Values Research in the Social and Behavioral Sciences." In M. Hechter, L. Nadel, and R. E.

Michod, ed., *The Origin of Values*. New York: Aldine de Gruyter.

Hofstede, G. 1980 *Culture's Consequences: International Differences in Work-Related Values*. Thousand Oaks, Calif.: Sage.

Inglehart, Ronald 1990 *Culture Shift in Advanced Industrial Society*. Princeton, N. J.: Princeton University Press.

—— 1995 "Changing Values, Economic Development, and Political Change." *International Social Science Journal* 145:379–403.

—— and Paul R. Abramson 1994 "Economic Security and Value Change." *American Political Science Review* 88:336–354.

Kagitcibasi, Cigdem 1997 "Individualism and Collectivism." In J. W. Berry, M. H. Segall, and C. Kagitcibasi, eds. *Handbook of Cross-Cultural Psychology*, vol. 3. Boston: Allyn and Bacon.

Kelley, Harold H., and A. J. Stahelski 1970 "Social Interaction Basis of Cooperators' and Competitors' Beliefs about Others." *Journal of Personality and Social Psychology* 16:66–91.

Kidd, Quentin, and Aie-Rie Lee 1997 "Postmaterialist Values and the Environment: A Critique and Reappraisal." *Social Science Quarterly* 78:1–15.

Kim, Uichol, Harry C. Triandis, Cigdem Kagitcibasi, Sang-Chin Choi, and Gene Yoon 1994. "Introduction." In U. Kim, H. C. Triandis, C. Kagitcibasi S.-C. Choi, and G. Yoon, eds., *Individualism and Collectivism: Theory, Method and Applications*. Thousand Oaks, Calif.: Sage.

Kluckhohn, Clyde 1951 "Values and Value Orientation in the Theory of Action." In T. Parsons and E. A. Shils, eds., *Toward a General Theory of Action*. Cambridge, Mass.: Harvard University Press.

Kluckhohn, Florence R., and Fred L. Strodtbeck 1961 *Variations in Value Orientations*. Westport, Conn.: Greenwood Press.

Kohn, Melvin L. 1969 *Class and Conformity: A Study in Values*. Homewood, Ill.: Dorsey.

Kristiansen, Connie M., and Alan M. Hotte 1996 "Morality and the Self: Implications for the When and How of Value-Attitude-Behavior Relations." In C. Seligman, J. M. Olson, and M. P. Zanna, eds., *The Psychology of Values: The Ontario Symposium*, vol. 8. Mahwah, N.J.: Erlbaum.

——, and Mark P. Zanna 1994 "The Rhetorical Use of Values to Justify Social and Intergroup Attitudes." *Journal of Social Issues* 50:47–66.

Kuhlman, D. Michael, Clifford Brown, and Paul Teta 1993 "Judgments of Cooperation and Defection in

Social Dilemmas: The Moderating Role of Judges' Social Orientation." In W. B. G. Liebrand, D. M. Messick, and H. A. M. Wilke, eds., *Social Dilemmas: Theoretical Issues and Research Findings*. New York: Pergamon.

——, Curt R. Camac, and Denise A. Cunha 1986 "Individual Differences in Social Orientation." In H. A. M. Wilke, D. M. Messick, and C. G. Rutte, eds., *Experimental Social Dilemmas*. Franfurt: Verlag Peter Lang.

——, and Alfred F. J. Marshello 1975 "Individual Differences in Game Motivation as Moderators of Preprogrammed Strategy Effects in Prisoner's Dilemma." *Journal of Personality and Social Psychology* 32:922–931.

Kuhn, M. H., and R. McPartland 1954 "An Empirical Investigation of Self Attitudes." *American Sociological Review* 19:68–76.

Liebrand, Wim B. G. 1986 "The Ubiquity of Social Values in Social Dilemmas." In H. A. M. Wilke, D. M. Messick, and C. G. Rutte, eds., *Experimental Social Dilemmas*. Franfurt: Verlag Peter Lang.

——, Ronald W. T. L. Jansen, Victor M. Rijken, and Cor J. M. Suhre 1986 "Might Over Morality: Social Values and the Perception of Other Players in Experimental Games." *Journal of Experimental Social Psychology* 22:203–215.

Mayton, Daniel M., Sandra J. Ball-Rokeach, and William E. Loges 1994 "Human Values and Social Issues: An Introduction." *Journal of Social Issues* 50:1–8.

McClintock, Charles G., and Scott T. Allison 1989 "Social Value Orientation and Helping Behavior." *Journal of Applied Social Psychology* 19:353–362.

——, and Wim B. G. Liebrand 1988 "Role of Interdependence Structure, Individual Value Orientation, and Another's Strategy in Social Decision Making: A Transformational Analysis." *Journal of Personality and Social Psychology* 55:396–409.

Messick, David M., and Charles G. McClintock 1968 "Motivational Bases of Choice in Experimental Games." *Journal of Experimental Social Psychology* 4:1–25.

Parsons, Talcott, and Edward A. Shils 1951 "Values, Motives, and Systems of Action." In T. Parsons and E. A. Shils, eds., *Toward a General Theory of Action*. Cambridge, Mass., Harvard University Press.

Peterson, Randall S. 1994 "The Role of Values in Predicting Fairness Judgments and Support of Affirmative Action." *Journal of Social Issues* 50:95–116.

Rokeach, Milton 1973 *The Nature of Human Values*. New York: Free Press.

——, and Sandra J. Ball-Rokeach 1980 "Stability and Change in American Value Priorities, 1968–1981." *American Psychologist* 44:775–784.

Schwartz, Shalom H. 1990 "Individualism-Collectivism: Critique and Proposed Refinements." *Journal of Cross-Cultural Psychology* 21:139–157.

——, 1992 "Universals in the Content and Structure of Values: Theoretical Advances and Empirical Tests in 20 Countries." *Advances in Experimental Social Psychology* 25:1 65.

—— 1994 "Beyond Individualism/Collectivism: New Cultural Dimensions of Values." In U. Kim, H. C. Triandis, C. Kagitcibasi, S.-C. Choi, and G. Yoon, eds., *Individualism and Collectivism: Theory, Method, and Applications*. Thousand Oaks, Calif., Sage.

—— 1996 "Value Priorities and Behavior: Applying a Theory of Integrated Value Systems." In C. Seligman, J. M. Olson, and M. P. Zanna, eds., *The Psychology of Values: The Ontario Symposium*, vol. 8. Mahwah, N. J.: Erlbaum.

Scott, W. A. 1965 *Values and Organizations*. Chicago: Rand McNally.

Singelis, T. M, H. C. Triandis, D. S. Bhawuk, and M. Gelfand 1995 "Horizontal and Vertical Dimensions of Individualism and Collectivism: A Theoretical and Measurement Refinement." *Cross-Cultural Research* 29:240–275.

Smith, M. Brewster 1969 *Social Psychology and Human Values: Selected Essays*. Chicago: Aldine.

Smith, Peter B., and Shalom Schwartz 1997 "Values." In J. W. Berry, M. H. Segall, and C. Kagitcibasi, eds., *Handbook of Cross-Cultural Psychology*, vol. 3. Boston: Allyn and Bacon.

Spates, James L. 1983 "The Sociology of Values." *Annual Review of Sociology* 9:27–49.

Stigler, George J. 1950 "The Development of Utility Theory (I)." *Journal of Political Economy* 58:307–327.

Tetlock, Philip E. 1986. "A Value Pluralism Model of Ideological Reasoning." *Journal of Personality and Social Psychology* 50:819–827.

Triandis, Harry C. 1989 "Cross-Cultural Studies of Individualism and Collectivism." In J. J. Berman, ed., *Nebraska Symposium of Motivation: Cross-Cultural Perspectives*. Nebraska: University of Nebraska Press.

—— 1995 *Individualism and Collectivism*. Boulder, C Col.: Westview.

——, Christopher McCusker, and C. Harry Hui 1990 "Multimethod Probes of Individualism and Collectivism." *Journal of Personality and Social Psychology* 59:1006–1020.

Van Lange, Paul A. M. 1993 "Rationality and Morality in Social Dilemmas: The Influence of Social Value Orientations." In W. B. G. Liebrand, D. M. Messick, and H. A. M. Wilke, eds., *Social Dilemmas: Theoretical Issues and Research Findings*. New York: Pergamon.

——, B. G. Liebrand, and D. Michael Kuhlman 1990 "Causal Attribution of Choice Behavior in Three N-Person Prisoners Dilemmas." *Journal of Experimental Social Psychology* 26:34–48.

Weber, Max 1958 [1905] *The Protestant Ethic and the Spirit of Capitalism*. New York: Scribner's.

Williams, Robin M. 1960 *American Society: A Sociological Interpretation*. New York: Knopf.

—— 1968 "The Concept of Values." In D. L. Shils, ed., *International Encyclopedia of the Social Sciences*, vol. 16. New York: Free Press.

Yamagishi, Toshio 1994 "Social Dilemmas." In K. S. Cook, G. A. Fine, and J. House, eds., *Sociological Perspectives on Social Psychology*. Boston: Allyn and Bacon.

Zavalloni, M. 1980 "Values." In H. C. Triandis and R. W. Brishan, eds., *Handbook of Cross-Cultural Psychology*, vol. 5. Boston: Allyn and Bacon.

DAVID R. KARP

VIOLENCE

See Crime Rates; Criminology; Crowds and Riots; Family Violence; Sexual Violence and Exploitation; Terrorism.

VOLUNTARY ASSOCIATIONS

The 1990s saw renewed interest in and concerns about voluntary associations and their roles in society. On the international level, countries that had been part of the Soviet Union and its power bloc continued to form and experiment with what they called "informal groups," which had the essential characteristics of voluntary associations. That is, those groups were independent of control from outside sources, people were free to join or leave them, and members established their own objectives and goals and developed means that might achieve them. Among the most important developments arising from these informal groups was the emergence of political parties as part of the struggle to establish democratic governments.

ORIGIN OF THE IDEA OF VOLUNTARY ASSOCIATIONS

It is generally acknowledged that the origins of voluntary associations are in the writings of early Reformation leaders such as Martin Luther and John Calvin (Hooker 1997). Calvin taught that all believers should participate equally in church decisions. The way to accomplish this equality was to see the church as a free and voluntary association of members; at the same time, to become a member, an individual had to be approved by the congregation. An early expression of this democratic church model developed in New England towns, with the local Congregationalist church as the prototypical voluntary association.

When Alexis de Tocqueville based *Democracy in America* on his tour of the United States in the 1830s, he took particular note of the degree to which Americans formed groups to serve personal interests and solve problems from the mundane to the profound. Tocqueville (1956) was particularly impressed by New England small towns with their autonomous local church congregations, whose citizens gathered in "town meetings" and voted on projects, from building schools and roads to caring for the poor. Current American nostalgia for local control to preserve the moral order may owe much to the almost sacred aura given to the reading of Tocqueville's description of early American society.

CHARACTERISTICS AND OBJECTIVES OF VOLUNTARY ASSOCIATIONS

Research on voluntary associations was limited until recently, with most people accepting their importance to a free society and concentrating on questions of demographic characteristics and the contributions they made to local communities (Irwin et al. 1997).

One of the most consistent findings about voluntary associations (Cutler 1976) was that individuals with higher socioeconomic status (SES) were more likely to participate in voluntary associations. Age, race, and gender (while influenced strongly by SES) also were identified as important factors in membership, with middle-aged persons, whites, and males more likely to be members.

Gender differences in voluntary association membership have been studied in terms of rates of participation as well as differences in the types of organizations to which each sex belongs. Historically, women's participation rates in voluntary associations (McPherson and Smith-Lowin 1986) were lower than men's. Furthermore, the groups to which women belonged tended to be smaller, single-sex, and expressive rather than instrumental. Still, in the 1980s, Knoke (1986) reported that the gender gap was narrowing as more women entered the professional ranks.

Studies of the effect of race on voluntary association membership provided inconsistent findings. For example, Hyman and Wright (1971) documented a sharp increase in membership among blacks between 1955 and 1962 (sharper than that among whites). However, blacks continued to be less likely to belong to a voluntary association other than the local church congregation and its Bible study groups. Knoke (1986, p.4) summarized more recent research with the statement that "researchers generally found that blacks' participation rates fell below whites' but disagreed on whether the gap could be traced to black SES disadvantages."

Researchers interested in the way nonpolitical voluntary associations influence political participation have found that individuals who are members of such organizations are more likely to vote and participate in politics (Sigelman et al. 1985; Wolfinger and Rosenstone 1980; Milbrath and Goel 1977; Rogers et al. 1975).

Voluntary associations range in size from groups of four or five persons to those with hundreds of thousands of members worldwide; structures vary from very informal with little leadership and few norms or guiding rules to highly structured with formal leadership, codes of conduct, and elected and appointed offices. These differences reflect different goals and the ability to influence civic and political affairs.

Some associations, such as the American Medical Association, labor unions, and churches that are hierarchic in structure or practice infant baptism, may have some of the characteristics of voluntary associations, but they are not seen as such in the definition adopted here.

CURRENT RESEARCH

In the United States, Putnam (1996) developed the hypothesis that voluntary associations might well have run their course as he recounted the tale of "Bowling Alone," suggesting that the decline of voluntary associations was bringing with it a decline in the country's civic health. His hypothesis sparked renewed interest in voluntary associations and their place in American society.

While Putnam was suggesting the decline of voluntary associations, Wuthnow (1994) was reporting on the large and apparently growing number of Americans who were joining small groups that seemed to have the characteristics of voluntary associations. Wuthnow's national survey of American adults found that "exactly forty percent of the adult population of the United States claims to be involved in a small group that meets regularly and provides caring and support for those who participate in it"(1994, p. 45). Assuming that an American adult belonged only to one small group, Wuthnow estimated that at the time of his study, there were at least three million small groups active in the United States, with approximately one group for every eighty people, assuming group size averages of close to twenty-five. Drawing on a variety of sources, Wuthnow subdivided these small groups as follows:

Bible study and related religious groups: 1.7 million

Self-help groups: 500,000

Special-interest groups (political, sports, book and/or discussion): 750,000
(1994, p.76)

These figures contrast sharply with earlier attempts to estimate the number of voluntary associations active in American society. Rose (1967) estimated that there were over 100,000 such associations in the United States, and Hyman and Wright (1971) reported that 57 percent of the American adult population did *not* belong to a voluntary association. However, local and regional studies found higher participation rates. For example, Babchuk and Booth's Nebraska study (1969) found that 80 percent of the adult population belonged to at least one voluntary association. More recently, Knoke observed that "perhaps one third of U.S. adults belong to no formal voluntary organizations and only a third hold membership in more than one (not including churches)" (1986, p. 3). Excluding churches may help account for much of the discrepancy in the figures provided by various scholars.

The highest figure provided for membership in voluntary associations among adult Americans came from the 1990–1991 World Values survey. Galston and Levine (1997, p. 2) reported that that survey showed that "82 percent of Americans belonged to at least one voluntary association, a rate exceeded only by Iceland, Sweden and the Netherlands." This survey was carried out as Wuthnow was doing his study of small groups and Putnam was bemoaning the decline of at least some kinds of voluntary associations.

Evidence of concerns about growth and decline in voluntary associations can be found in events such as the agreement between Lions Clubs International and the Junior Chamber International (JCs) to form a global partnership to boost membership and encourage lifelong service to the community. Lions International (1998) reported 1.4 million members representing 43,700 clubs in 185 countries, while the Junior Chamber reported 322,000 members in 9,000 chapters in 123 nations. The members of JCs typically have been in the under-40 age bracket; the intent of the new collaboration is to have them join Lions Clubs as they move up the age ladder. Both groups would be encouraged to work more closely together in community service. In this way, they hope to stem the age creep that has brought stagnation and decline to many voluntary associations.

Skocpol and her colleagues in the Harvard Civic Engagement Project have begun to document the local, state, and national linkages of voluntary associations, in the process challenging the assumption that the strength of American civic life ever lay in the local focus of voluntary associations. In her historical overview, Skocpol (1997) identified events such as the Revolutionary War and the subsequent electoral politics, along with the development of an extraordinarily extensive and efficient national postal system, as key factors encouraging the activities of thousands of local and extralocal voluntary associations. Major growth spurts occurred between 1820 and 1840, from after the Civil War to the end of the century, and in the 1930s. These growth spurts seem to be related to the great issues of the time: slavery and its moral dilemmas, industrialization, and economic crisis.

The Harvard group has so far tracked detailed life histories of some fifty-five voluntary associations that have enrolled 1 percent or more of American adults at some point in their history. Four-fifths of these associations still exist, with most of them paralleling the three-tiered government structure with local, state, and national branches. Although many groups have come and gone at the local level, a more balanced historical view sees voluntary associations as vital links between local and national civil life. The social historian Alexander Hoffman was cited as stating that "local institutions and organizations may best be understood as branch offices and local chapters . . . the building blocks of a 'nation of joiners.'. . . Americans enlisted in local church groups, fraternal lodges, clubs, and other organizations that belonged to nationwide networks" (Skocpol 1997, p. 3).

There is evidence of a decline in some types of voluntary associations even as new small groups emerge. For example, Skocpol (1996) noted that since the 1960s, the Christian Coalition has been one of the few cases of local to national federations growing, while some, such as the Lions, Rotary, and the Junior Chamber, have found themselves with an aging population and in a process of slow decline or even death. Thus, the new alliance between the Lions and the Junior Chambers mentioned above may be seen as an effort at revitalization.

Current research about voluntary associations has revealed a decline of same-sex organizations, growing numbers of college-educated and professional women members, and the replacement of family-oriented by professional associations. As Skocpol put it, "the best educated people are still participating in more groups overall, but not in the same groups as their less well-educated fellow citizens" (1997, p. 5).

At least in the short run, the educational gap, which is reflected in the occupational and income gaps, seems more of a threat to the well-being of civil society than does the so-called loss of the local group. Indeed, Wuthnow's data, supported by recent research on small faith communities in the U.S. Catholic Church (D'Antonio 1997), suggests the opposite: Small associations are alive and booming at the local level, with more than a little support from national organizations that provide regional gatherings, bring together diverse racial and ethnic groups, and provide a wide range of literature that urges outreach as a part of their mission. Their members may be spending more time working in soup kitchens and other service activities. Meanwhile, other small groups are supporting local teenage sports clubs rather than participating in union-style bowling leagues.

Among Wuthnow's findings was that social support in these small groups tends to focus on the individual; the groups themselves revealed tendencies to see political and social issues in a conservative vein. Outreach seldom got beyond the soup kitchen state of concern for others.

To the extent that these new groups cut across class, gender, and age lines, they may be fulfilling the hope expressed by Skocpol (1997, p. 5) that Americans will find new ways to work together, "not just on 'helping the poor' but 'doing with' rather than 'doing for' if we want to revitalize the best traditions of American voluntarism."

NEW DIRECTIONS

Among the new directions in voluntary association activity is the development of an interdisciplinary relationship between social work and veterinary medicine. Built on the premise that "democracies are based on the value of the worth and dignity of each person, and the empowering of persons to take action in their own lives" (Granger and Granger 1998), Colorado State University has established a Human-Animal Bond Center (HABIC). Its goal is to provide animal-assisted therapy and activities in partnership with community health, mental health, education, and human service programs. The founders of this program extend the respect for humans to animals and to the environment as a crucial element in the survival of a democratic society. The essential factor in their vision is the linkage of voluntary associations with formal groups such as social work agencies and veterinary medicine societies.

At the international level, scholars in Finland are going beyond studying the functional role of voluntary associations in the stability and growth of democratic societies. They propose that "from the point of view of social constructionism voluntary associations can be seen as forums for the production and transmitting of social meanings. This is an intersubjective process which may yield objectivated and taken-for-granted meanings. If internalized, these meanings become the source of personal identity and goal-formation of the association. Thus voluntary associations can be seen not only as part of the western culture heritage but also as cultures in themselves" (Raivio and Heikkala 1998, p. 1).

CONCLUSION

Voluntary associations generally are seen as central ingredients of a pluralist democratic society. Millions of Americans belong to hundreds of thousands of these associations, as do growing numbers of people worldwide. Among the more important research findings has been the multifaceted nature of voluntary associations' growth and impact: Some associations have remained strictly local; some have grown from local to state, national, and international levels; and not a few have grown from the top down, such as the American Legion and the PTA. Their influence on local, state, and national governments has led to much important legislation, such as the GI Bill fostered by the American Legion.

A review of the literature and current research challenges the nostalgic view that what is needed to restore vitality to American democracy is a return to localism and a shrinking national government. Instead, these findings suggest that the current trend toward the growth of a variety of types of voluntary associations, within and across national boundaries and working with rather than apart from governments, is the best formula for the revitalization of American political democracy. The limited evidence from other societies suggests that that same formula applies to all societies seeking to model Western democracies.

REFERENCES

1998 "Joining Forces to Promote Volunteerism, Membership Growth." *Association Management* 50:24.

Babchuk, Nicholas, and Alan Booth 1969 "Voluntary Association Membership: A Longitudinal Analysis." *American Sociological Review* 34:31–45.

Cutler, Stephen J. 1976 "Age Differences in Voluntary Association Membership." *Social Forces* 55:43–58.

D'Antonio, William V. 1997 "Small Christian Communities in the Catholic Church: A Study in Progress" In Robert S. Pelton, ed., *Small Christian Communities: Imagining Future Church*. Notre Dame, Ind.: University of Notre Dame Press.

Galston, William A., and Peter Levine 1997 "America's Civic Condition: A Glance at the Evidence." *Brookings Review*. 15:23–26.

Granger, Ben P., and Georgia V. Granger 1998 "Voluntary Association Development and the Human-Animal Bond." http://www/friends-partners.org/friends/audem/audem93/granger.htmlopt-other-unix-english.

Hooker, Richard 1997 "Voluntary Associations." World Cultures Home Page: http://www.wsu.edu:8080/dee/GLOSSARY/VOLUNTA.HTM.

Hyman, Herbert H., and Charles R. Wright 1971 "American Adults: Replication Based on Secondary Analyses of National Sample Surveys." *American Sociological Review* 36:191–206.

Irwin, Michael, Charles Tolbert, and Thomas Lyson 1997 "How to Build Strong Home Towns." *American Demographics* N.Y. Vol 19:42–47.

Knoke, David 1986 "Associations and Interest Groups." *Annual Review of Sociology* 12:1–21.

McPherson, J. Miller, and Lynn Smith-Lowin 1986 "Sex Segregation in Voluntary Associations." *American Sociological Review* 51:61–79.

Milbrath, Lester W., and M. L. Goel 1977 *Political Participation*. Chicago: Rand McNally.

Morgan, Patrick 1997 "Renovating Civil Society." *IPA Review*, March, pp. 29–30.

Putnam, Robert D. 1996 "The Strange Disappearance of Civic America." *American Prospect* 24:34–49.

Raivio, Risto, and Juha Heikkala 1998 "Voluntary Associations as Cultures." http://www.uta.fi/laitokset/sosio/culture/firstassociat.htm.

Rogers, David L., Gordon L. Bultena, and Ken H. Barb 1975 "Voluntary Association Membership and Political Participation: An Exploration of the Mobilization Hypothesis." *Sociological Quarterly* 16:305–318.

Rose, Arnold M. 1967 *The Power Structure*. New York: Oxford University Press.

Sigelman, Lee, Philip W. Roeder, Malcolm E. Jewell, and Michael A. Baer 1985 "Voting and Nonvoting": A Multi-Election Perspective." *American Journal of Political Science* 29:749–765.

Skocpol, Theda 1996 "Unravelling from Above." *American Prospect*. 25:20–25.

—— 1997 "Building Community Top-Down or Bottom-Up? America's Voluntary Groups Thrive in a National Network." *Brookings Review* 15:16–19.

Tocqueville, Alexis de [1836] 1956 *Democracy in America*, ed. and abridged by Richard D. Heffner. New York: Mentor.

Wolfinger, Raymond E., and Steven J. Rosenstone 1980 *Who Votes?* New Haven, Conn.: Yale University Press.

Wuthnow, Robert (ed.) 1991 *Between States and Markets: The Voluntary Sector in Comparative Perspective*. Princeton, N. J: Princeton, University Press.

——, 1994 *Sharing the Journey: Support Groups and America's New Quest for Community*. New York: Free Press.

WILLIAM V. D'ANTONIO

VOTING BEHAVIOR

In addition to sociologists, scholars from many different fields, including history, political science, psychology, and geography, have studied elections and voting behavior. In current American sociology, however, these topics are largely neglected. Major advances have been made in related disciplines, yet as of one of the pioneers, the sociologist Rice (1928, p. p.vii) stated: "The phenomena of politics are functions of group life. The study of group life per se is a task of sociology." In general terms, despite variations in emphasis between different approaches, the sociological study of voting behavior is concerned with the way individuals obtain, select, and process information related to the political arena; the various forces that shape this process; the relevance individuals attribute to the political sphere; and how they decide to participate in or refrain from specific political actions. Elections provide a convenient focus, a point where the often elusive and latent processing of political information manifests behavioral correlates such as voting or abstaining and supporting one candidate or the other. In contrast, forecasting election returns is not a primary goal of the sociological study of voting behavior, although the general public, parties, and politicians are interested mostly in this aspect. Much applied research served these immediate needs and interests in the past and continues to do so. Still, in the field of voting behavior, pure (academic) and applied research peacefully coexist; cross-fertilization rather than mutual irreverence characterizes their relationship.

The study of voting behavior began in the late eighteenth century (Jensen 1969), although most of the very early work does not meet strict scholarly standards. In the course of its development as an academic discipline, two different strands that are still discernible have emerged. The first strand—*aggregate data analysis*—is characterized by the use of actual election returns compiled for geopolitical units such as wards, districts, and counties. Those returns are compared with census data, providing a sociodemographic profile of those areal units. Starting in the late nineteenth century, there developed a school of quantitative historiography that made extensive use of maps representing voting and/or census information by using different shades and colors (Frederick Jackson Turner in the United States and André Siegfried in France). The mere visual inspection and somewhat subjective interpretation of those maps by the Turner school were supplemented and then replaced by more vigorous statistical techniques, in particular correlation analysis, inspired by the sociologist Franklin Giddins at Columbia. One of Giddins's students, Rice (1928), demonstrated the utility of quantitative methods in politics. At the University of Chicago, interdisciplinary cooperation in the social sciences produced some of the most outstanding work of that time (e.g., Gosnell 1930). The advent of modern survey research in the 1930s and 1940s, however, obscured the aggregate approach for quite some time.

The second strand in the study of voting behavior—*analysis of survey data*—also had some early forerunners. Polling individuals about their voting intentions ("straw polls") or past voting decisions started in the late nineteenth century. In one of the most extensive efforts, more than a quarter million returns from twelve midwestern states were tabulated by a Chicago newspaper for the 1896 presidential contest between McKinley and Bryant. In the 1920s, straw polls conducted by newspapers and other periodicals were quite common and popular. Their reputation was ruined, though, by the failure of the *Literary Digest* poll to foresee the landslide victory of Franklin D. Roosevelt in the 1936 election. By that time, however, pioneers of modern public opinion research such as George Gallup, Archibald Crossley, and Elmo Roper had started to use more rigorous sampling methods as well as trained interviewers to ensure a proper representation of all strata of the electorate (Gallup [1944] 1948).

Interest in voting and political behavior and concern with mass communication, marketing strategies, and the public's attitude toward World War II stimulated the rapid development of modern survey research from about the mid-1930s through the 1940s and the establishment of survey research centers in both the academic and commercial sectors (Converse 1986). These centers include the Survey Research Center/Institute for Social Research (ISR) at the University of Michigan and the National Opinion Research Center (NORC) at the University of Chicago on the academic side and Gallup's American Institute of Public Opinion on the commercial side, to name just a few early organizations that are still leaders in the field.

Modern voting research based on the survey method typically uses small but randomly selected samples of about 1,000 (rarely more than 2,000) eligible voters. Information is collected through the use of standardized questionnaires that are administered by trained interviewers in person or increasingly over the telephone. Advances in modern communication technology such as the Internet are likely to change the face of scholarly survey research even more drastically in the very near future. "Standardized" means that a question's wording is predetermined by the researcher and that the interviewer is supposed to read questions exactly as stated and in the prearranged order. For the most part, the response alternatives also are predetermined ("closed questions"); sometimes, for select questions, verbatim answers are recorded ("open questions") and subsequently sorted into a categorical scheme. In contrast to aggregate-level analysis and the use of official election returns, survey-based research on voting behavior relies on self-reports by individual citizens. Thus, it is subject to bias and distortion resulting from question wording, dishonest answers, memory failure, and unstable attitudes even if the sample is properly drawn. Its major advantage is the unequivocal linkage of demographic traits (e.g., age, sex, ethnicity, and social class) and political attitudes and behavior on the level of the individual.

AGGREGATE DATA ANALYSIS

The use of aggregate data in studying voting behavior poses formidable methodological problems, yet it is the only approach available to study voting behavior before the mid-1930s. For example, the Germans voted Hitler into power in genuinely democratic elections in the late 1920s and early 1930s. The voting behavior of Germans in the Weimar Republic has been subject to much debate and controversy in political sociology. The earlier consensus that Hitler's support came predominantly from the lower middle classes was challenged by later studies (e.g., Childers 1983; Falter 1991) that contended that his support had a much wider base cutting across all social groups.

Findings based on aggregate data analysis often depend heavily on seemingly technical details of preparing the database and the choice of specific statistical techniques. As a rule, findings are more reliable if the geopolitical units are small. However, even if the greatest care is exercised, there is always the danger of an "ecological fallacy." To use a contemporary example, if the vote for a white candidate increases with a rising percentage of white voters across voting districts, it is plausible to assume that people have voted along racial lines, yet this need not be the case. Perhaps ethnic minorities in predominantly white districts are more likely to vote for a white candidate than they are elsewhere. Therefore, they, not the white voters, may be responsible for the increased share of the white candidate.

A solution to the ecological inference problem has been proclaimed (King 1997), but despite some progress, that claim appears to be overstated. In spite of all the remaining shortcomings, though, aggregate data analysis is an indispensable tool for tracing patterns of voting behavior over time in a sociohistorical analysis (e.g., Silbey et al. 1978) or analyzing contemporary voting behavior when sufficiently detailed and reliable survey data are not available. Particularly for local or regional studies, there may not be sufficient funds to conduct appropriate surveys or the research interest may develop only after the elections have taken place.

SURVEY-BASED VOTING RESEARCH

The Columbia School. Four landmark studies connected with the presidential elections of 1940, 1948, 1952, and 1956 mark the establishment of scholarly survey-based research on voting behavior (Rossi 1959). In essence, those studies provided the core concepts and models used in contemporary voting research. Reviewing those studies provides an introduction to present-day theories of voting behavior in U.S. presidential elections,

while congressional elections typically follow a very simple pattern: Incumbents are rarely defeated.

The first two studies were conducted by Lazarsfeld and his associates at Columbia University. Their main intention was to "relate preceding attitudes, expectations, personal contacts, group affiliations and similar data to the final decision" (Berelson et al. 1954, p.viii) and trace changes of opinion over the course of a campaign. Emphasizing the particular set of political and social conditions and its importance for this process, the Columbia group restricted its studies to one community (Erie County, Ohio, in 1940 and Elmira, New York, in 1948) and interviewed the same respondents repeatedly: up to seven times in 1940 and four times in 1948. Repeated interviews, or a "panel design," became a standard feature of more sophisticated voting studies, while the major studies to come abandoned the focus on one community in favor of nationwide representation.

Several major findings emerged from the Erie County study (Lazarsfeld et al. [1944] 1968). First, people tend to vote as they always have, in fact as their families have. In the Michigan school of voting behavior (see below), this attitude stability was conceptualized as "party identification," a stable inclination toward a particular party that for the most part develops during adolescence and early adulthood.

Second, attitudes are formed and reinforced by individuals' membership in social groups such as their social class, ethnic group, and religious group and by the associations they belong to. More concretely, the research team found that people of lower social status, people in urban areas, and Catholics tended to be Democrats while people of higher social class, people in rural areas, and Protestants were more likely to be Republicans. Subsequently, the alliance of particular segments of the population with specific parties was amply documented despite modifications in its particular form. More so than in the United States, voting behavior in the major European democracies (notably Britain and West Germany) could be explained largely by the links between social groups and particular parties (Lipset and Rokkan 1967), although those links have been weakening.

Third, change does occur, and people under cross-pressures are the most likely to change. A cross-pressure occurs when the set of different group memberships provides conflicting stimuli. For example, in 1940, Protestant blue-collar workers experienced a pull toward the Republicans on the basis of their religious affiliation and a pull toward the Democrats because of their class position. In the United States today, the impact of religious affiliation is more complicated, but the general notion of cross-pressure remains important.

Fourth, Lazarsfeld and colleagues developed the concept of a "two-step flow of information." According to this concept, most people are not directly persuaded by the mass media even if they are susceptible to change. Instead, they tend to follow opinion leaders, who are the informal leaders in the various social networks (family, friends, associates at the workplace) in which individuals are involved. These leaders pay close attention to the media; they redisseminate and validate media messages. With the ever-increasing impact of mass media (television and more recently the Internet) over the last fifty years, this result of the 1940 study may not reflect the situation today. Unfortunately, it is very difficult to prove media effects conclusively, and the cumulative empirical evidence has not been able to settle a long-standing controversy about the extent of media effects.

The 1948 Elmira study was designed to test further and if necessary modify the findings of the earlier study and integrate the results into the body of existing knowledge (see Berelson et al. 1954, pp. 327–347, for a comparative synopsis of several major studies). As a matter of fact, its main contribution lies in the refinement of several aspects that were not covered sufficiently in the Erie County study. However, the Elmira study still failed to show systematically the links between the efforts of the various institutions in the community and the decisions of the voters. The focus on those links was the key rationale for limiting these studies to one community, a feature that invites doubt whether the findings can be generalized to all American voters.

The Michigan School. The sociological approach of the Columbia school was subsequently overshadowed by the social psychological model of the Michigan school that came to dominate survey-based voting research for many years. After a smaller study in 1948 (Campbell and Kahn 1952), the Michigan team, led by Campbell, conducted major studies in 1952 and 1956 (Campbell et al.

1954; Campbell et al. 1960). In contrast to Lazarsfeld and associates, their studies used national samples, thus expanding the geographic coverage, but only two interviews, one shortly before and one shortly after the elections. In addition, the Michigan group introduced far-reaching changes in the conceptualization of the voting process. On the basis of its national study of 1948, those researchers felt that social group memberships have little direct impact on the voting decision. Instead, they focused on "the psychological variables which intervene between the external events of the voter's world and his ultimate behavior" (Campbell et al. 1954, pp. 85–86). In particular, they considered three concepts: party identification, issue orientation, and candidate orientation. *Party identification* refers to the sense of personal attachment an individual feels toward a party irrespective of formal membership or direct involvement in that party's activities. It is thought of as a stable attitude that develops early in life. In contrast, both issue orientation and candidate orientation depend on the context of a particular election. *Issue orientation* refers to individuals' involvement in issues they perceive as being affected by the outcome of an election. For example, if individuals are concerned about the economy and feel that it makes a difference whether the country has a Democratic or a Republican president, this will have an impact on their voting decisions. Similarly, *candidate orientation* refers to individuals' interest in the personality of the candidates and to a possible preference that derives from the personal traits of the candidates. For example, Ronald Reagan portrayed himself as a firm and determined leader but also as a caring and understanding father. In that way, he was able to attract many voters otherwise attached to the Democrats.

The Michigan model posits a "funnel of causality." The social factors emphasized by the Columbia school are not dismissed outright but are viewed as being at the mouth of the funnel, having an indirect effect only through the three central psychological variables, particularly party identification. Party identification in turn affects issue orientation and candidate orientation as well as having a direct effect on the voting decision. The simplicity of this model is both its strength and its weakness. It clearly marks the shift of emphasis to psychological processes of individual perception and evaluation, but it does not explicitly address the social and political context. However, in *The American Voter* (Campbell et al. 1960), the Michigan group presents a much more comprehensive analysis of the 1956 elections, addressing topics such as the role of group membership, social class, and the political system without, however, explicitly expanding the basic model.

Additional concepts that have been used widely in subsequent research include the concept of a *normal vote* and the typology of elections as *maintaining, deviating,* or *realigning* (Campbell et al. 1966) and an assessment of mass belief systems (Converse 1964). The concept of a normal vote follows directly from the basic model: If all voters follow their long-standing inclinations (vote according to party identification), they produce a normal vote. Comparing actual election returns with the (hypothetical) normal vote allows one to assess the impact of contemporaneous, mostly short-term factors. In a maintaining election, the party with the larger number of partisans wins, but its vote share may be somewhat different from its normal share as a result of short-term factors. If short-term factors lead to the defeat of that party, the elections are considered deviating. Realigning elections mark a major shift in basic allegiances. Such shifts are rare and typically are not accomplished in a single election. In the 1930s, the American electorate shifted toward the Democrats as a consequence of economic depression and Roosevelt's New Deal, which promised a way out. However, given their long-term nature, processes of dealignment and realignment are difficult to determine in strict empirical terms (Dalton et al. 1984; Lawrence 1996).

With respect to the nature of mass belief systems, Converse's (1964) article triggered a long-lasting debate that has been settled. Converse asserted that the vast majority of the American people have little interest in politics, that their opinions on issues lack consistency and stability over time, and that those opinions are mostly "non-attitudes." Consequently, a large portion of the electorate does not vote at all; if those people do vote, their vote is based mostly on partisanship and/or a candidate's personality, not on an independent and careful evaluation of the issues.

Critique of *The American Voter* and subsequent refinements. Like other landmark empirical studies, *The American Voter* was not exempt from sometimes radical critiques that can be grouped into three categories: challenges to the allegedly derogatory image of the American electorate and its implications for the democratic process, assertions that the findings are valid only for the 1950s, and a methodological critique of operationalization, measurement, and model specification. Most of the methodological critique is too technical to be discussed in this article (see, Asher 1983).

One of the earliest and most vocal critics was Key (1966). Using a reanalysis of Gallup data from 1936 to 1960, he developed a typology of "standpatters," "switchers," and "new voters" and asserted that the global outcome of those elections followed a rational pattern derived from an appraisal of past government performance. Hence, as a whole, the electorate acts responsibly despite the fact "that many individual voters act in odd ways indeed" (Key 1966, p. 7).

The most comprehensive effort to review American voting behavior over time, a critique of the second type, was presented by Nie et al. (1976), based on the series of Michigan election studies from 1952 to 1972. Still working within the framework of the Michigan model, those authors found significant changes in the relative importance of its three central factors: a steady decrease in the level of party identification, particularly among younger groups, and a much stronger relative weight of issue orientation and candidate orientation. In a turbulent period of internal strife and social change (civil rights, the Vietnam War, Watergate), the electorate became more aware of issues and much more critical of parties and the established political process. Nie et al. (1976) found a decomposition of the traditional support bases for both Democrats and Republicans, all adding up to an "'individuation' of American political life" (p. 347).

Still largely following the path of the Michigan school, much research in the 1980s was directed toward issue voting, which reflects a continuing decline in stable party attachments through political socialization and/or group memberships. In particular, the impact of economic conditions on electoral outcomes was investigated both in the United States and in other major Western democracies (Eulau and Lewis-Beck 1985; Lewis-Beck 1988; Norpoth et al. 1991). The findings were diverse, contingent on the specification of the research question and the national context, yet one general pattern emerged and was confirmed beyond the United States in many national elections in the 1990s: Political actors perceived as better able to handle economic matters than their competitors have a significant advantage, and perceived economic competence is strongly related to an individual's voting decision.

Fiorina's (1981) concept of *retrospective voting* can be seen as a bridge between the classic Michigan model and the newer directions that have emerged in the last two decades. Fierina posits that both party identification and issue orientation are largely dependent on the evaluation of past government performance. Party identification thus represents a sort of running tally of past experience. It is still a long-term influence, but it is subject to gradual change and is based more on cognition than on affection.

More Recent Approaches. With some simplification, one can discern three major directions in voting research in the last fifteen to twenty years, each anchored in a different discipline: Rooted in economic theory, rational choice models have been applied to voting (as well as to many other forms of social behavior); drawing on more general psychological theories, the subfield of political psychology studies in a comprehensive way how the individual perceives and processes political information, with voting being only one specific aspect; and the focus on reference groups on both the macro level such as class or religion (an important strand in European research on voting) and the micro level (social networks) has reemphasized the sociological perspective.

Rational choice models see the voter as carefully evaluating the pros and cons of each party or candidate, assessing its utility (consumer models as in Himmelweit et al. 1985) and proximity to the voter's own position (spatial models as in Enelow and Hinich 1984, 1990; directional models as in Rabinowitz and MacDonald 1989), and then voting for the closest or most useful party and/or candidate. It is doubtful, however, whether such models adequately portray the actual process of reaching a voting decision except among the small segment of highly informed and highly motivated citizens. The rational choice approach has been critized more generally as conceptually inadequate

for the analysis of mass political behavior (e.g., Green and Shapiro 1994). Other criticism has come from within the rational choice camp, leading, for example, to an "expressive model of voting" (Brennan and Lomasky 1993) that shifts the focus away from the instrumental aspect of voting but maintains the conceptual and terminological framework.

The literature in political psychology is too extensive to be discussed in detail here; overviews are provided by Lau and Sears (1986), Sniderman et al. (1991), and Mutz et al. (1996), among others. However, the contribution of this approach to the discussion of two long-standing controversial topics must be mentioned explicitly: media effects and political belief systems. In regard to media effects, a number of studies using more refined concepts (agenda setting, framing, priming) have suggested a more direct and stronger impact of media than previously had been assumed (see Kinder 1998; Zaller 1996), but a generally accepted model of how the mass media influence the political process has not emerged. In regard to political belief systems or the lack thereof, the notion of a politically uninformed or ignorant and irrational electorate has strong implications for normative theories of democracy and, on a practically level, campaign strategists. There continues to be strong and largely undisputed empirical evidence that many Americans have rather limited factual knowledge of specific bills and policies, the makeup of political institutions, and even their elected representatives. However, it is controversial whether that lack of specific knowledge matters and whether voters are nevertheless able to make "correct" or "reasonable" choices on the basis of more implicit forms of information processing (Delli Carpini and Keeter 1996, Lau and Redlawsk 1997). In both areas, political psychology has not settled the controversy, but it has provided enhanced conceptualizations to guide more productive empirical analyses.

In regard to sociological perspectives, community studies (as in the Columbia school) have attempted to assess the impact of the local context on the decision making of the individual. Context information is gathered by using block-level census data or tracing and interviewing members of the social network of the primary respondents (Huckfeldt 1986; Huckfeldt and Sprague 1995).

On the macro level, the social cleavage approach, long dominant in European voting research (see below), has gained some attention in the United States (see Brooks and Manza 1997).

Voting Behavior in Other National Contexts.
The Michigan school of voting behavior has continued to have a major impact on the emergence of survey-based voting research in other Western democracies (see Beyme and Kaase 1978; Butler and Stokes 1976; Heath et al. 1985; Rose 1974) and electoral research today (e.g., Kaase and Klingemann 1998). A strict replication of the basic model, however, has rarely been feasible because of considerable differences in political systems, party organizations, and electoral rules. In particular, attempts to devise valid measures of the key concept of party identification have produced mixed results at best (e.g., Budge et al. 1976).

Despite considerable variation across European democracies and within specific countries, political parties articulate specific programmatic positions derived from basic ideological beliefs that bind all party members, and parliamentary votes typically follow party lines. Political parties, then, dominate the political contest, and most major parties have their roots in social cleavages relating to class, religion, region, or ethnicity. Consequently, such social group memberships have been powerful determinants of voting behavior (Lipset and Rokkan 1967). Much of the European debate in the last twenty years, however, has focused on evolving changes in the electorate that result in more volatile voters. First, the impact of social (class) origin on the individual life course in general (educational attainment, occupational opportunities, marriage and family, etc.) has declined, leading to a more idiosyncratic definition of self-interest and as a consequence a less predetermined voting pattern. Second, a growing disenchantment with established political parties and politicians in general has weakened the once highly internalized norm of political participation through voting and increased the propensity to vote for new and often extremist parties as a token of protest. Thus, the once stable alliances between parties and certain segments in the electorate along social cleavages have weakened (Crewe and Denver 1985; Franklin et al. 1991; Miller et al. 1990), though there is no consensus whether "class voting" has ended (e.g., Manza et al. 1995).

The emergence of new democracies after the demise of the Communist bloc in eastern Europe in the late 1980s and the continuing process of European integration, including the creation of European Union as a single political and not just economic entity, have created new challenges and opportunities for voting research in Europe. With the introduction of a common currency in 1999, a continuing reduction of national sovereignty, and a generally strengthened position of the European Parliament in exercising control over the executive branch (European Commission), European elections will lose their stigma as second-order elections. Studies of European elections in 1974, 1979, and 1994 suffered from limited funding and broke no new conceptual ground. However, they did establish the fact that national rather than pan-European issues dominated voting choices (Schmitt and Mannheimer 1990; Van der Eijk and Franklin 1996). This is likely to change, but it is too early to tell the role these elections will play in the further process of European unification and whether voting behavior in those elections will follow patterns different from those in national elections.

The methodological problems of the European election studies in achieving functional equivalence of the instruments (questions) and ensuring uniform quality standards in sampling and interviewing are even more formidable in the new eastern European democracies. Apart from the technical aspects of conducting valid and reliable surveys, there may be inherent limits to exporting the survey method (Bulmer 1998). Rather than relying solely on survey data and taking them at face value, analysts must employ a more comprehensive approach that integrates quantitative and qualitative research, such as the one used by White et al. (1997) in their study of Russian voters. In the absence of a stable party structure and stable political institutions more generally and with the relative novelty of voting in free elections, it is unrealistic to expect the Michigan model or any other "reductionist" model to provide an adequate description of voting behavior in eastern Europe.

Beyond Europe, it is doubtful whether the concept of voting is functionally equivalent to voting in the United States or western Europe because of systemic differences and traditions. For example, even if one accepts the premise that Japan is a pluralist democracy (Richardson 1997), an intricate net of mutual obligations governs much social behavior, including voting, and for many years relevant electoral competition occurred only within one dominant party. Still, the Michigan model has guided much Western research on Japanese voting behavior (Flanagan et al. 1991).

OUTLOOK

Compared to the United States, research on voting behavior in western Europe has been tied more closely to the study of mass political behavior in general, satisfaction with democracy, the parties, the politicians, and, the stability of the political system despite a continuing orientation toward the Michigan model and its variants. What European research has to offer are not better micro models of voting behavior but detailed trend analyses of cross-national comparative data that put voting into a broader context of political behavior (e.g., Klingemann and Fuchs 1995). As a result of the systemic differences within Europe and the methodological limitations of the database, no unified theory of voting behavior has emerged. For each individual (national) election, there is a plausible explanation, at least in retrospect, drawing on well-recognized factors such as perceived economic competence and leadership image, but the relative weight of each factor varies from one election to the next. As information and communication behavior is undergoing drastic changes as a result of technological advances (Internet) and the ever-increasing presence of the media, it will become even more difficult to determine the relative weight of each factor in a voter's choice. The Columbia studies dealt with voters in a relatively contained world in which the amount of information and the number of transmission channels were limited; voters in the twenty-first century will be faced with an overload of information and will be as closely connected to the political world (or its competing representations) as they want to be. At best, more knowlegeable voters will be able to make better informed choices; at worst, more perplexed voters will succumb to the most skillful public relations managers. Somehow voters will have to reduce this complexity, and turning to social groups for guidance is a likely strategy. While it will be important to continue to study the processes of cognition and information processing, the real key to voters' "rationality" may lie in their social relations. More than ever, the study of voting behavior will have to build bridges between the various disciplines and incorporate the sociological perspective.

REFERENCES

Asher, Herbert B. 1983 "Voting Behavior Research in the 1980s." In Ada W. Finifter, ed., *Political Science*. Washington, D.C.: American Political Science Association.

Berelson, Bernard, Paul F. Lazarsfeld, and William N. McPhee 1954 *Voting: A Study of Opinion Formation in a Presidential Campaign*. Chicago: University of Chicago Press.

Beyme, Klaus von, and Max Kaase (eds.) 1978 *Elections and Parties*. London: Sage.

Brennan, Geoffrey, and Loren Lomasky 1993 *Democracy and Decision: The Pure Theory of Electoral Preference*. New York: Cambridge University Press.

Brooks, Clem, and Jeff Manza 1997 "Social Cleavages and Political Alignments: U.S. Presidential Elections, 1960 to 1992." *American Sociological Review* 62:937–946.

Budge, Ian, Ivor Crewe, and Dennis Fairlie, eds. 1976 *Party Identification and Beyond*. London: Wiley.

Bulmer, Martin (ed.) 1998 "Exporting Social Survey Research." *American Behavioral Scientist* (special issue) 42(2).

Butler, David, and Donald Stokes 1976 *Political Change in Britain*, 2nd ed. New York: St. Martin's.

Campbell, Angus, Philip E. Converse, Warren E. Miller, and Donald E. Stokes 1966 *Elections and the Political Order*. New York: Wiley.

—— 1960 *The American Voter*. New York: Wiley.

——, Gerald Gurin, and Warren E. Miller 1954 *The Voter Decides*. Evanston, Ill.: Row, Peterson.

——, and Robert L. Kahn 1952 *The People Elect a President*. Ann Arbor, Mich.: Institute for Social Research.

Childers, Thomas 1983 *The Nazi Voter*. Chapel Hill: University of North Carolina Press.

Converse, Jean M. 1986 *Survey Research in the United States: Roots and Emergence*. Berkeley: University of California Press.

Converse, Philip 1964 "The Nature of Belief Systems in Mass Publics." In David Apter, ed., *Ideology and Discontent*. New York: Free Press.

Crewe, Ivor, and David Denver (eds.) 1985 *Electoral Change in Western Democracies: Patterns and Sources of Electoral Volatility*. New York: St. Martin's.

Dalton, Russell J., Scott C. Flanagan, and Paul Allen Beck, eds. 1984 *Electoral Change in Advanced Industrial Democracies: Realignment or Dealignment?* Princeton, N.J.: Princeton University Press.

Delli Carpini, Michael X., and Scott Keeter 1996 *What Americans Know about Politics and Why it Matters*. New Haven, Conn.: Yale University Press.

Enelow, James M., and Melvin J. Hinich 1984 *The Spatial Theory of Voting*. New York: Cambridge University Press.

——1990 *Advances in the Spatial Theory of Voting*. New York: Cambridge University Press.

Eulau, Heinz, and Michael Lewis-Beck (eds.) 1985 *Economic Conditions and Electoral Outcomes: The United States and Western Europe*. New York: Agathon Press.

Falter, Jürgen W. 1991 *Hitler's Wähler*. Munich: Beck.

Fiorina, Morris P. 1981 *Retrospective Voting in American National Elections*. New Haven, Conn.: Yale University Press.

Flanagan, Scott C., Shinsaku Kohei, Ichiro Miyake, Bradley M. Richardson, and Joji Watanuki 1991 *The Japanese Voter*. New Haven, Conn.: Yale University Press.

Franklin, Mark, Tom Mackie, and Henry Valen, eds. 1991. *Electoral Change: Responses to Evolving Social and Attitudinal Structures in Seventeen Democracies*. Cambridge, UK: Cambridge University Press.

Gallup, George (1944) 1948 *A Guide to Public Opinion Polls*. Princeton, N.J. Princeton University Press.

Gosnell, Harold 1930 *Why Europe Votes*. Chicago: University of Chicago Press.

Green, Donald P., and Ian Shapiro 1994 *Pathologies of Rational Choice Theory*. New Haven, Conn.: Yale University Press.

Heath, Anthony, Roger Jowell, and John Curtice 1985 *How Britain Votes*. New York: Pergamon Press.

Himmelweit, Hilde, Patrick Humphreys, and Marianne Jaeger 1985 *How Voters Decide*. Milton Keynes, UK: Open University Press.

Huckfeldt, Robert 1986 *Politics in Context: Assimilation and Conflict in Urban Neighborhoods*. New York: Agathon Press.

——, and John Sprague 1995 *Citizens, Politics, and Social Communication*. New York: Cambridge University Press.

Jensen, Richard 1969 "American Election Analysis: A Case History of Methodological Innovation and Diffusion." In Seymour M. Lipset, ed., *Politics and the Social Sciences*. New York: Oxford University Press.

Kaase, Max, and Hans-Dieter Klingemann (eds.) 1998. *Wahlen und Wähler: Analysen aus Anlass der Bundestagswahl 1994*. Opladen, Germany: Westdeutscher Verlag.

Key, Valdimer Orlando, Jr. 1966 *The Responsible Electorate*. Cambridge, Mass.: Belknap Press, Harvard University Press.

Kinder, Donald 1998 "Communication and Opinion." *Annual Review of Political Science* 1:167–197.

King, Gary S. 1997 *A Solution to the Ecological Inference Problem*. Princeton, N.J. Princeton University Press.

Klingemann, Hans-Dieter, and Dieter Fuchs 1995 *Citizens and the State* (vol. 1 of Max Kaase and Kenneth Newton, eds., *Beliefs in Government*). Oxford, UK: Oxford University Press.

Lau, Richard, and David P. Redlawsk 1997 "Voting Correctly." *American Political Science Review* 91:585–598.

——, and David Sears 1986 *Political Cognition*. Hillsdale, N.J.: Erlbaum.

Lawrence, David G. 1996 *The Collapse of the Democratic Presidential Majority*. Boulder, Colo.: Westview.

Lazarsfeld, Paul F., Bernard Berelson, and Hazel Gaudet (1944) 1968 *The People's Choice*. 3rd ed. New York: Columbia University Press.

Lewis-Beck, Michael 1988 *Economics and Elections: The Major Western Democracies*. Ann Arbor: University of Michigan Press.

Lipset, Seymour Martin, and Stein Rokkan (eds.) 1967 *Party Systems and Voter Alignments*. New York: Free Press.

Manza, Jeff, Michael Hout, and Clem Brooks 1995 "Class Voting in Capitalist Democracies since World War II." *Annual Review of Sociology* 21:137–162.

Miller, William L., Harold D, Clarke, Lawrence Leduc, and Paul Whiteley 1990 *How Voters Change*. New York: Oxford University Press.

Mutz, Diana C., Paul M. Sniderman, and Richard A. Brody (eds.) 1996 *Political Persuasion and Attitude Change*. Ann Arbor: University of Michigan Press.

Nie, Norman H, Sidney Verba, and John R. Petrocik 1976 *The Changing American Voter*. Cambridge, Mass.: Harvard University Press.

Norpoth, Helmut, Michael Lewis-Beck, and Jean-Dominique Lafay (eds.) 1991 *Making Governments Pay*. Ann Arbor: University of Michigan Press.

Rabinowitz, George, and Stuart Elaine MacDonald 1989 "A Directional Theory of Issue Voting." *American Political Science Review* 83:93–121.

Rice, Stuart A. 1928 *Quantitative Methods in Politics*. New York: Knopf.

Richardson, Bradley 1997 *Japanese Democracy*. New Haven, Conn.: Yale University Press.

Rose, Richard (ed.) 1974 *Electoral Behavior: A Comparative Handbook*. New York: Free Press.

Rossi, Peter A. 1959 "Four Landmarks in Voting Research." In Eugene Burdick and Arthur Brodbeck, eds., *American Voting Bahavior*. Glencoe, Ill.: Free Press.

Schmitt, Hermann, and Renato Mannheimer (eds.) 1990. "The European Elections of 1989." *European Journal of Political Research* (special issue) 19(1).

Silbey, Joel H., Allan G. Bogue, and William H. Flanigan, eds. 1978 *The History of American Electoral Behavior*. Princeton, N.J.: Princeton University Press.

Snidermann, Paul M., Richard A. Brody, and Philip E. Tetlock 1991 *Reasoning and Choice*. New York: Cambridge University Press.

Van der Eijk, Cees, and Mark N. Franklin 1996 *Choosing Europe?* Ann Arbor: University of Michigan Press.

White, Stephen, Richard Rose, and Ian McAllister 1997 *How Russia Votes*. Chatham, N.J.: Chatham House.

Zaller, John 1996 "The Myth of Massive Media Impact Revived: New Support for a Discredited Idea." In Diana C. Mutz, Paul M. Sniderman, and Richard A. Brody, eds., *Political Persuasion and Attitude Change*. Ann Arbor: University of Michigan Press.

MANFRED KUECHLER

W

WAR

The ubiquity and importance of war have made analyses of its causes a central concern of scholars for over two millennia. Many of the fundamental questions about the causes of war were raised by Thucydides in the fifth century B.C., but the vast amount of work on the topic since that time has produced ongoing debates instead of generally accepted answers. Studies of war can be divided into three broad categories (reviews of the literature using similar frameworks are provided by Waltz 1959; Bueno de Mesquita 1980; and Levy 1989). The first type takes the system as whole as the unit of analysis and focuses on how characteristics of the interstate system affect the frequency of war. States are the unit of analysis in the second type, which explores the relationships among the political, economic, and cultural features of particular states and the propensity of states to initiate wars. The third type analyzes war as an outcome of choices resulting from small group decision making.

Some debates focus on characteristics of the interstate system that are thought to increase or decrease the chance of war. Are wars more likely during a period of economic prosperity or one of economic contraction? Which is more likely to maintain peace, a balance of power in the international system or a situation in which one state is hegemonic? Has the increasing power of transnational organizations such as the United Nations changed the likelihood of war in the contemporary world?

Social scientists also disagree about the effects of political and economic factors within a state on the possibility of war. Does a capitalist economy make a state more or less likely to initiate wars? Do democratic states start wars less often than autocracies do? Is increasing nationalism likely to cause more wars? Is the ethnic composition within and between states an important determinant of war?

There is also no consensus on which model of individual decision making is most appropriate for the study of war. Is the decision to go to war based on a rational calculation of economic costs and benefits, or is it an irrational outcome of distortion in decision making in small groups and bureaucracies? Are wars based on nationalist, ethnic, or religious conflicts generated more by emotions or values than by rational choices?

THE INTERSTATE SYSTEM AND WAR

Most studies of war that use the interstate system as the unit of analysis begin with assumptions from the "realist" paradigm. States are seen as unitary actors in realist theories, and their actions are explained in terms of the structural characteristics of the system. The most important feature of the interstate system is that it is anarchic. Unlike politics within states, relations between states take place in a Hobbesian state of nature. Since an anarchic system is one in which all states constantly face actual or potential threats, their main goal is security. Security can be achieved in such a system only by maintaining power. In realist theories, the distribution of power in the interstate system is the main determinant of the frequency of war.

Although all realist theories agree on the importance of power distribution in determining war, they disagree about which types of power distributions make war more likely. Balance-of-power theories (Morgenthau 1967) suggest that an equal distribution of power in the system facilitates peace and that an unequal distribution leads to war. They argue that parity deters all states from aggression and that an unequal power distribution generally will result in the strong using force against the weak. When one state begins to gain a preponderance of power, a coalition of weaker states will from to maintain their security by blocking the further expansion of the powerful state. The coalitions that formed against Louis XIV, Napoleon, and Hitler seem to fit this pattern.

Hegemonic stability theory (Gilpin 1981) suggests exactly the opposite: that unequal power in the system produces peace while parity results in war. When one state has hegemony in the world system, it has both the incentive and the means to maintain order. It is not necessary for the most powerful state to fight wars, since its objectives can be achieved in less costly ways, and it is not rational for other states to challenge a state with overwhelming power. Gilpin notes that the periods of British and U.S. hegemony were relatively peaceful and that World Wars I and II occurred during intervening periods in which power was distributed more equally. Since balance-of-power and hegemonic stability theories seem to explain some but not all of the cases, what is needed is a theory specifying the conditions under which either parity or hegemony leads to war.

Balance-of-power and hegemonic stability arguments are not applicable to all wars, only those between great powers. A third attempt to explain great-power war is power transition theory (Organski 1968). This theory suggests that differential rates of economic growth create situations in which rising states rapidly catch up with the hegemonic state in the system and that this change in relative power leads to war. Organiski argues that the rising state will initiate a war to displace the hegemonic state. This final part of the argument is questionable, since it seems at least as plausible that the hegemonic state will initiate the war against the rising challenger to keep the small advantage it still has (Levy 1989, p. 253).

Debates about power transitions and hegemonic stability are of much more than theoretical interest in the contemporary world. Although the demise of the Soviet Union has left the United States as an unchallenged military hegemon, American economic superiority is being challenged by the European Union (EU) and emerging Asian states (Japan in the short run, perhaps China in the long run). If power transition and hegemonic stability theories are correct, this shift of economic power could lead to great-power wars in the near future. If the main challenge is from the EU (the most likely scenario), it will be interesting to see if the cultural heritage of cooperation between the United States and most of Europe will be sufficient to prevent the great-power war that some theories predict.

Another ongoing debate about systemic causes of war concerns the effects of long cycles of economic expansion and contraction. Some scholars argue that economic contraction increases the chance of war, since the increased scarcity of resources leads to more conflict. Others have suggested the opposite: Major wars are more common in periods of economic expansion because only then do states have the resources necessary to fight. Goldstein's (1988) research suggests that economic expansion tends to increase the severity of great-power wars but that economic cycles have no effect on the frequency of war.

Two important changes in the last fifty years may make many systemic theories of war obsolete (or at least require major revisions). The first is technology. Throughout history, technological changes have determined the general nature of warfare. By far the most significant recent development has been the availability of nuclear weapons. Since the use of these weapons would result in "mutually assured destruction," they may have made war much less likely by making it irrational for both parties. Of course, the broadening proliferation of nuclear weapons raises serious problems, as does their existence in currently unstable states such as the Russian federation. A second technological change that may alter the nature of war is increasing dependence on computers. Although computers have increased the accuracy and precision of many types of military technology, they also leave the countries using them vulnerable to new kinds of attacks by "hackers" who could not only disarm military operations but bring whole economies to a halt by disrupting the computer systems necessary for their operation.

The second significant change in the last half of the twentieth century has been the development and increasing power of transnational organizations such as the United Nations. Most theories of war begin with the assumption that the interstate system is anarchic, but this is no longer valid. If the military power of the United Nations continues to grow, that organization could become more and more effective at preventing wars and suppressing them quickly when they start. Of course, it remains to be seen whether powerful existing states will cede more power to such institutions.

Theoretical debates about the systemic causes of war have not been resolved, in part because the results of empirical research have been inconclusive. To take one example, equality of power in the interstate system decreased the number of wars in the nineteenth century and increased the number in the twentieth century. Proponents of each theory can point to specific cases that seem to fit its predictions, but they must admit that there are many cases it cannot explain. At least part of the problem is that systemic theories have not incorporated causal factors at lower levels of analysis, such as the internal economic and political characteristics of states. Since the effects of system-level factors on war are not direct but always are mediated by the internal political economy of states and the decisions made by individual leaders, complete theories of the causes of war must include these factors as well.

CAPITALISM, DEMOCRACY, AND WAR

One of the longest and most heated debates about the causes of war concerns the effects of capitalism. Beginning with Adam Smith, liberal economists have argued that capitalism promotes peace. Marxists, by contrast, suggest that capitalism leads to frequent imperialist wars.

Liberal economic theories point to the wealth generated by laissez-faire capitalist economies, the interdependence produced by trade, and the death and destruction of assets caused by war. Since capitalism has increased both the benefits of peace (by increasing productivity and trade) and the costs of war (by producing new and better instru-

ments of destruction), it is no longer rational for states to wage war. The long period of relative peace that followed the triumph of capitalism in the nineteenth century and the two world wars that came after the rise of protectionist barriers to free trade often are cited in support of liberal economic theories, but those facts can be explained by hegemonic stability theorists as a consequence of the rise and decline of British hegemony.

In contrast to the sanguine views of capitalism presented by liberal economic theories, Marxists argue that economic problems inherent in advanced capitalist economies create incentives for war. First, the high productivity of industrial capitalism and a limited home market resulting from the poverty of the working class result in chronic "underconsumption" (Hobson [1902] 1954). Capitalists thus seek imperial expansion to control new markets for their goods. Second, Lenin ([1917] 1939) argued that capitalists fight imperialist wars to gain access to more raw materials and find more profitable outlets for their capital. These pressures lead first to wars between powerful capitalist states and weaker peripheral states and then to wars between great powers over which of them will get to exploit the periphery.

In contrast to the stress on the political causes (power and security) of war in most theories, the Marxist theory of imperialism has the virtue of drawing attention to economic causes. However, there are several problems with the economic causes posited in theories of imperialism. Like most Marxist arguments about politics, theories of imperialism assume that states are controlled directly or indirectly by dominant economic classes and thus that state policies reflect dominant class interests. Since states are often free of dominant class control and since many groups other than capitalists often influence state policies, it is simplistic to view war as a reflection of the interests of capitalists. Moreover, in light of the arguments made by liberal economists, it is far from clear that capitalists prefer war to other means of expanding markets and increasing profits.

With the increasing globalization of economies and the transition of more states to capitalist economies, the debates about the effects of capitalism, trade, and imperialism on war have become increasingly significant. If Adam Smith is right, the future is likely to be more peaceful than the past, but if Marxist theorists are right, there will be an unprecedented increase in economically based warfare.

The form of government in a country also may determine how often that country initiates wars. Kant ([1795] 1949) argued that democratic states (with constitutions and separation of powers) initiate wars less often than do autocratic states. This conclusion follows from an analysis of who pays the costs of war and who gets the benefits. Since citizens are required to pay for war with high taxes and their lives, they will rarely support war initiation. Rulers of states, by contrast, have much to gain from war and can pass on most of the costs to their subjects. Therefore, when decisions about war are made only by rulers (in autocracies), war will be frequent, and when citizens have more control of the decision (in democracies), peace generally will be the result.

Empirical research indicates that democratic states are less likely than are nondemocratic states to initiate wars, but the relationship is not strong (Levy 1989, p. 270). Perhaps one reason for the weakness of the relationship is that the assumption that citizens will oppose war initiation is not always correct. Many historical examples indicate that in at least some conditions citizens will support war even though it is not in their economic interest to do so. Nationalism, religion, ethnicity, and other cultural factors often are cited as important causes of particular wars in journalistic and historical accounts, but there still is no general theory of the conditions in which these factors modify or even override economic interests. Many classical sociological arguments suggested that these "premodern" and "irrational" sources of war would decline over time, but the late twentieth century has demonstrated the opposite. Nationalist and ethnic wars have become more common and intense. This raises the general issue of the factors affecting the choices individuals make about war initiation: Can these factors be modeled as rational maximization of interests, or is the process more complex?

DECISION MAKING AND WAR

Although the assumptions may be only implicit or undeveloped, all theories of war must contain some assumptions about individual decision making. However, few theories of war focus on the individual level of analysis. One notable exception is the rational-choice theory of war developed and tested by Bueno do Mesquita (1981).

Bueno de Mesquita begins by assuming that the decision to initiate war is made by a single dominant ruler who is a rational expected-utility maximizer. Utilities are defined in terms of state policies. Rulers fight wars to affect the policies of other states, essentially to make other states' policies more similar to their interests. Rulers calculate the costs and benefits of initiating war and the probability of victory. War is initiated only when rulers expect a net gain from it.

This parsimonious set of assumptions has been used to generate several counterintuitive propositions. For example, common sense might suggest that states would fight their enemies and not their allies, but Bueno de Mesquita argues that war will be more common between allies than between enemies. Wars between allies are caused by actual or anticipated policy changes that threaten the existing relationship. The interventions of the United States in Latin America and of the Soviet Union in eastern Europe after World War II illustrate the process. Other counterintuitive propositions suggest that under some conditions a state may rationally choose to attack the stronger of two allied states instead of the weaker, and under some conditions it is rational for a state with no allies to initiate a war against a stronger state with allies (if the distance between the two is great, the weaker state will be unable to aid the stronger). Although these propositions and others derived from the theory have received strong empirical support, many have argued that the basic rational-choice assumptions of the theory are unrealistic and have rejected Bueno de Mesquita's work on those grounds.

Other analyses of the decision to initiate war focus on how the social features of the decision-making process lead to deviations from rational choice. Allison (1971) notes that all political decisions are made within organizations and that this setting often influences the content of decisions. He argues that standard operating procedures and repertoires tend to limit the flexibility of decision makers and make it difficult to respond adequately to novel situations. Janis (1972) focuses on the small groups within political organizations (such as executives and their cabinet advisers) that actually make decisions about war. He suggests that the cohesiveness of these small groups often leads to a striving for unanimity that prevents a full debate about options and produces a premature consensus. Other scholars have discussed common misperceptions that distort decisions about war, such as the tendency to underestimate the capabilities of one's enemies and overestimate one's own. In spite of these promising studies, work on deviations from rational choice is just beginning, and there still is no general theoretical model of the decision to initiate war.

CONCLUSION

The failure to develop a convincing general theory of the causes of war has convinced some scholars that no such theory is possible, that all one can do is describe the causes of particular wars. This pessimistic conclusion is premature. The existing literature on the causes of war provides several fragments of a general theory, many of which have some empirical support. The goal of theory and research on war in the future will be to combine aspects of arguments at all three levels of analysis to create a general theory of the causes of war.

(SEE ALSO: *Global Systems Analysis; Peace; Revolutions; Terrorism*)

REFERENCES

Allison, Graham 1971 *Essence of Decision.* Boston: Little, Brown.

Bueno de Mesquita, Bruce 1980 "Theories of International Conflict: An Analysis and Appraisal." In Ted Robert Gurr, ed., *Handbook of Political Conflict.* New York: Free Press.

—— 1981 *The War Trap.* New Haven, Conn.: Yale University Press.

Gilpin, Robert 1981 *War and Change in World Politics.* Cambridge, UK: Cambridge University Press.

Golstein, Joshua 1988 *Long Cycles.* New Haven, Conn.: Yale University Press.

Hobson, J. A. (1902) 1954 *Imperialism.* London: Allen and Unwin.

Janis, Irving 1972 *Victims of Groupthink.* Boston: Houghton Mifflin.

Kant, Immanuel (1795) 1949 "Eternal Peace." In C. J. Friedrich, ed., *The Philosophy of Kant.* New York: Modern Library.

Lenin, V. I. (1917) 1939 *Imperialism.* New York: International.

Levy, Jack S. 1989 "The Causes of War: A Review of Theories and Evidence." In Philip E. Tetlock, Robert Jarvis, Paul Stern, and Charles Tilly, eds., *Behavior, Society and Nuclear War.* Oxford, UK: Oxford University Press.

Morgenthau, Hans 1967 *Politics among Nations.* New York: Knopf.

Organski, J. F. K. 1968 *World Politics.* New York: Knopf.

Waltz, Kenneth 1959 *Man, the State, and War.* New York: Columbia University Press.

EDGAR KISER

WELFARE

See Poverty; Public Policy Analysis; Social Security Systems.

WELL-BEING

See Quality of Life.

WHITE-COLLAR CRIME

In his 1939 presidential address at the annual meeting of the American Sociological Society, Edward H. Sutherland used, with great effect, the term "white-collar crime." In an interesting introduction to his discussion of Sutherland, Green (1990) noted that in 1901, 1907, and 1935, respectively, Charles Henderson, Edward Alsworth Ross, and Albert Morris had "anticipated" the ideas Sutherland had presented, after conducting much research, in 1939. Sutherland depicted a white-collar criminal as any person of high socioeconomic status who commits a legal violation in the course of his or her occupation (Green 1990). Later he defined white-collar crime as criminal acts committed by persons in the middle or upper socioeconomic groups in connection with their occupations (Sutherland 1949). Since that time, the concept has undergone some modification and "has gained widespread popularity among the public" but "remains ambiguous and controversial in criminology" (Vold and Bernard 1986). More specifically, some definitions have deleted the class of the offender as a consideration.

Edelhertz (1970) defines white-collar crime as an "illegal act or series of illegal acts committed by nonphysical means and by concealment or guile, to obtain money or property, to avoid payment or loss of money or property, or to obtain business or personal advantage."

Others have attempted to refine the definition by differentiating between occupational and corporate contexts (Clinard and Quinney 1973: Clinard and Yeager 1980), clarifying the difference between and among government, corporate, organizational, and occupational crimes (Coleman 1994; Green 1990; Punch 1996) and avoiding the use of the term "crime" by substituting "law violations" that involve the violator's position of power (Biderman and Reiss, 1980). Tappan (1947) said that white-collar crimes are not "crimes" if they are not included in legal definitions.

While various writers measure the extent of white-collar crimes in terms of the number of "violations" (Clinard and Yeager 1980) or the extent of harm done to the public, business, or the environment (Punch 1996), others focus on dollar costs. Reiman (1995) modified the cost estimates of white-collar crimes by the U.S. Chamber of Commerce (1974) and made those figures applicable to 1991. Among his categories were consumer fraud, credit card and check fraud, embezzlement and pilferage, insurance fraud, receiving stolen property, and securities theft and fraud. His total amounted to $197.76 billion for 1991. Reiman noted that those figures compared favorably with Clinard's estimate of $200 billion for one year (1990) and with a similar figure reported in *U.S. News and World Report* (1985). Reiman notes that his own estimate, is on the conservative side but that it is "almost 6000 times the total amount taken in all bank-robberies in the US in 1991 and more than eleven times the total amount stolen in all thefts reported in the FBI Uniform Crime Reports for that year" (1995, p.111). Reiman's figures apparently do not include any of the vast amounts of money lost in the savings and loan scandal. These issues are elaborated on below.

Green (1990) states that Sutherland's three main objectives were to show that: (1) white-collar crime is real criminality because it is law-violative behavior (Sutherland asserted that civil lawsuits resulting in decisions against persons or corporations should be considered convictions and are

proof of violations of law), (2) poor people are not the only ones who commit crime, and (3) his theory of differential association constituted an approach that could explain a general process characteristic of all criminality.

Sutherland held that typical crime "statistics" picturing the criminal population as made up largely of lower-class, economically underprivileged people give a false impression of noncriminality on the part of the upper classes, including respected and highly placed business and political persons (Sutherland 1949). His white-collar criminality included some of the following: misinterpretation of the financial statements of corporations, manipulation of the stock exchange, bribery of public officials to obtain desirable contracts, misrepresentation in advertising and salesmanship, embezzlement and misuse of trust funds, dishonest bankruptcies, and price-fixing. He quoted the Chicago gangster Al Capone calling such practices "legitimate rackets" (Sutherland 1949) to differentiate them from the more violent rackets of the underworld.

Sutherland held that white-collar criminals are relatively immune because of the class bias of the courts and the power of their class to influence the administration of the law. As a result of this class bias, the crimes of the "respectable" upper class generally are handled differently than are the crimes of the lower class. To compensate for this class bias, Sutherland argued that official conviction statistics must be supplemented by evidence of criminal violations from other sources, such as hearings before regulatory commissions, civil suits for damages, administrative hearings, and various other procedures outside criminal court prosecutions (Vold and Bernard, 1986).

Coleman (1994) says that because "Sutherland's work focused almost exclusively on business crimes and especially violations of federal economic regulations" and because he failed "to devote more attention to violent white-collar crimes," a debate sprang up about whether white-collar crime is really crime. Since business offenses were handled as civil or administrative matters, Sutherland's detractors suggested that white-collar criminals were not "real" criminals. Coleman states, "Had the argument focused on flammable clothes that burned helpless children," Sutherland would have been in a stronger position. Still, Coleman suggests, Sutherland would have encountered resistance. When he made his address in 1939, crime was seen as something that happened primarily among immigrants and poor people. The idea that business leaders should be considered criminals had an un-American sound to it. Moreover, corporate executives were not likely to support such ideas. Coleman holds, however, that Sutherland won the first round of this debate with the scholars who criticized him.

Tappan was one of the first to criticize Sutherland's position. Tappan, who was trained as both a lawyer and a sociologist, asserted that crime, if legally defined, was an appropriate topic of study for sociologists (1947). Accordingly, he felt that actions that were not against the law were not crimes and that persons who had not been convicted of criminal charges were not criminals. Sutherland, following Sellin (1951), held that Tappan's criterion of legal conviction was too far removed from the offense, which may go undetected, unprosecuted, and/or unconvicted (Green 1990). Burgess (1950) agreed with Tappan that Sutherland erred in failing to distinguish between civil and criminal law. However, Vold and Bernard (1986) suggest that a scientifically adequate theory of crime must explain all behaviors that have the same essential characteristics, whether or not the behavior has been defined as a crime by criminal justice agencies. Sutherland initiated his attempt to develop such a theory with his theory of differential association, which he felt could explain both lower-class and white-collar crime.

Biderman and Reiss (1980) considered white-collar crime to consist of "violations of law, to which penalties are attached, and that involve the use of a violator's position of significant power, influence, or trust in the legitimate economic or political institutional order for the purpose of illegal gain, or to commit an illegal act for personal or organizational gain." Coleman (1994) defines white-collar crime as a "violation of the law committed by a person or group of persons in the course of their otherwise respected and legitimate occupational or financial activity." Green (1990) points out that the terms "respectable" and "significant power or influence" employed in these definitions do not represent an improvement of Sutherland's definition because they are relative terms. Because of such problems, Green seems to suggest that pinpointing the white-collar criminal

(person) is considerably more problematic than delineating white-collar crime. He agrees with Sutherland that white-collar crime is inexorably limited to occupational opportunity.

In their analysis of corporate violations, Clinard and Yeager (1980) say that while corporate crime is white-collar crime, occupational crime is a different type of white-collar crime. Building on earlier work by Clinard and Quinney (1973), they suggest that "occupational crime is committed largely by individuals or by small groups of individuals in connection with their occupations." They include under this type "businessmen, politicians, labor union leaders, lawyers, doctors, pharmacists, and employees who embezzle money from their employers or steal merchandise and tools. Occupational crimes encompass income tax evasion; manipulation in the sale of used cars and other products; fraudulent repairs of automobiles, television sets, and appliances; embezzlement; check-kiting; and violations in the sale of securities" (1980, p. 18).

Clinard and Yeager, in agreement with Sutherland's opinion of what constitutes law violation, say that "a corporate crime is any act committed by corporations that is punished by the state, regardless of whether it is punished under administrative, civil, or criminal law" (1980, p. 16). They also state that Sutherland conducted the first research in this area and that his book *White Collar Crime* (1949) should have had the title of their book: *Corporate Crime*.

Green has extended the work of Clinard and Quinney and Clinard and Yeager and that of others in *Occupational Crime* (1990). He claims that corporate crime almost always occurs within the course of one's occupation, and thus the term "occupational crime" encompasses corporate offenses. To Green, occupational crime refers to any act punishable by law that is committed through an opportunity created in the course of an occupation that is legal. Green goes on to say that the criterion of a legal occupation is necessary, since otherwise the term could include all crimes. A legal occupation, he indicates, is one that does not in itself violate any laws. Thus, the term would exclude persons with occupations that are illegal to begin with, such as bank robbers and professional con men. He lists four types of occupational crime: (1) crimes for the benefit of an employing organization, (2) crimes by officials through their state-based authority, (3) crimes by professionals in their capacity as professionals, and (4) crimes by individuals as individuals.

Coleman (1994) has noted both the tendency to redefine the concept of white-collar crime to include any nonviolent crime based on concealment or guile (Webster 1980) and the tendency to impose new terms such as "occupational crime," "corporate crime" (discussed above), "elite deviance," "corporate deviance," and "organizational crime" (not to be confused with "organized crime"). Coleman states that "the whole point behind most criminologists' concern with white collar crime is to give the same kind of attention to the crimes of the powerful and privileged that is given to common offenders." He states that the term "white-collar crime" best serves this purpose or goal and is too useful a conceptual tool to be thrown out: "Because it clearly identifies a specific problem of great concern to people around the world, 'white collar crime' has become one of the most popular phrases ever to come out of sociological research" (Coleman 1994, p. 5).

Coleman (1994) clearly acknowledges that some of the criticisms of Sutherland's original definition are valid; for example, (1) responsibility for some white-collar offenses is attributable to groups, and (2) many white-collar offenses are committed by persons from the middle levels of the status hierarchy. Coleman (1994) states that in a major respect, however, Sutherland's views seem relevant. One of the central issues in early debates about the definition of white-collar crime was whether the term should include violations of civil as well as criminal law. As the study of white-collar crime has developed over the last fifty years, many criminologists have sided with Sutherland's view that it should include both civil and criminal violations (Wheeler 1976; Schrager and Short 1978; Braithewaite 1979; Clinard and Yeager 1980; Hagar and Parker 1985).

Following the lines of other students, Coleman states that a typology of white-collar crimes is needed (1994, p. 10). He suggests that while a humanistic perspective might focus on the consequences of white-collar crimes for victims (property losses versus physical injury), a more useful typology might center on differences between offenders. Thus, he suggests a dichotomy between occupational crimes (consisting of offenses by individuals, whether employee or employer) and organizational crimes, which include both corporate and government crimes.

Poveda (1994, p. 70) asserts with some justification that the design of a typology depends on the theoretical biases of the researcher. He says that scholars need to be aware of the diversity of white-collar crime in considering explanations. Poveda suggests that there are two traditions, both of which can be traced to the initial Sutherland–Tappan debate. One school, the Sutherland school, focuses on the offender as the defining characteristic of white-collar crime. The other school emphasizes the offense as the central criterion of white-collar crime (Poveda 1994, p. 39). Both traditions are alive and well.

TRENDS IN RESEARCH: CORPORATE, OCCUPATIONAL, AND ORGANIZATIONAL CASES

Punch, Reiman, Clinard and Yeager, Green, and Coleman are unanimous that interest in white-collar crime emerged or gathered speed after the Watergate scandal in the 1970s. It does seem that while there was early excitement over Sutherland's initial 1939 address, interest quickly waned. In the late 1940s, interest in social order seemed to predominate. Clinard and Yeager (1980) reviewed the events of the 1960s and 1970s, describing the occasional corporate conspiracies and environmental abuses that came to the public's attention. They noted how the short and suspended sentences given to Watergate offenders contrasted "sharply with the 10-, 20-, 50-, and even 150-year sentences given to burglars and robbers." Reiman, beginning with the first edition *The Rich Get Richer and the Poor Get Prison* (1979), has been a consistent critic of the different ways in which justice has been meted out to the poor and the well to do.

Clinard and Yeager (1980), in what Punch (1996) calls the piece of research that is closest to Sutherland's legacy, conducted the first large-scale comprehensive investigation of the law violations of major firms since Sutherland's pioneering work. Sutherland (1949) conducted his study on seventy of the two-hundred largest U.S. nonfinancial corporations. The study of Clinard and Yeager (1980) involved a systematic analysis of federal administrative, civil, and criminal actions initiated or completed by twenty-five federal agencies against the 477 largest publicly owned manufacturing (Fortune 500) corporations and 105 of the largest wholesale, retail, and service corporations in the United States in the period 1975–1976. Thus, they had a total sample of 582 corporations. Clinard and Yeager found the following:

> A total of 1,553 federal cases were begun against all 582 corporations during 1975 and 1976 or an average of 2.7 federal cases of violation each. Of the 582 corporations, 350 (60.1 percent) had at least one federal action brought against them, and for those firms that had at least one actions brought against them, the average was 4.4 cases. (1980, p. 113)

Six main types of violations were reported by Clinard and Yeager (1980): administrative, environmental, financial, labor, manufacturing, and unfair trade practices. Their evidence shows that "often decisions on malpractice were taken at the highest corporate levels, that records were destroyed or ingeniously doctored by executives and their accountants and that the outcomes of these decisions can have serious economic, financial, political, personal, and even physical consequences" (Punch 1996, p. 52).

Punch (1996) focused on selected cases, mainly from other countries, that bear on his hypothesis that business is crimogenic, i.e., it justifies or tolerates illegal behavior. This parallels Clarke's (1990) contention that crime and misconduct are endemic to business and that the key to understanding them lies in recognizing the structure that the business environment gives to misconduct both in terms of opportunities and in terms of how misconduct is managed. Punch states that his underlying purpose is to use his cases to "unmask the underlying logic of business and the submerged social world of the manager" (1991, p. 213). Punch states, however, that he is not asserting that most companies are guilty of criminal behavior. Indeed, he says that "there are companies which explicitly set out to conform to the law; they maintain a record of no transgressions" (p. 214). In short, Punch focuses on companies that engage in corporate deviance.

If after reviewing the works of Clinard and Yeager (1980) and Sutherland (1949), a student of crime still is inclined to conclude that the term "white-collar crime" refers to harmless or small mistakes in judgment rather than to harmful, selfish, profit-oriented motives followed by an intentional cover-up of brutal consequences, Punch sets the record straight. One of the most chilling of his cases is the Three Mile Island nuclear accident in Pennsylvania in March 1979. A series of incidents involved (1) a leaking seal, (2) leading to feedwater pumps that failed to come into operation and remove heat from the core (3) because of blocked pipes stemming from (4) valves having been left in the wrong position after routine maintenance some days earlier and (5) that could not be seen because the control switch indicator was obscured. Through further accidents, mounting tension, and delays, danger increased and a complete meltdown loomed. Then, "almost by coincidence, and perhaps because of a new shift supervisor checking the PORV [pilot-operated relief valve], the stuck relief valve was discovered. More as an act of desperation than understanding. . . the valve was shut" (p. 126). Punch then quotes Perrow (1984, p. 29):

> It was fortunate that it occurred when it did; incredible damage had been done with substantial parts of the core melting, but had it remained open for another thirty minutes or so, and HPI [high-pressure injector] remained throttled back, there would have been a complete meltdown, with the fissioning material threatening to breach containment.

What Punch (1996) describes in his recounting of this case and others includes the following:

1. Earlier warnings by an efficient inspector about the inherent dangers in nuclear plant procedures had been brushed aside; the inspector then had been subjected to strong informal control in an attempt to deflect his message.

2. Profitability (based on the productivity of privately run industry) was the top priority, and this is a problem in most corporations.

3. Management responds to crises such as the one described (by Perrow, Punch, and others) by keeping things running.

4. Regulatory agencies tend to compromise rather than enforce the rules governing safety; indeed, they appear to "have a dual function both to regulate and promote an industry" (p. 255).

Among his conclusions, Punch writes:

When cleared of radioactive debris, Unit Two will remain in quarantine for thirty years until it is dismantled as planned along with Unit One, which will then have reached the end of its working life. Until 2020, then, Unit Two at Three Mile Island in the middle of the Susquehanna River will remain a silent sentinel to a disturbing case of incompetence, dishonesty, complacency, and cover-up. (pp. 134–135).

This conclusion is disturbingly similar to that made earlier by Clinard and Yeager (1980) as they noted the evasion of responsibility by many of the corporate managers in their study and the unethical climates that disregarded the public's welfare (p. 299). Punch (1996) found a similar criminal climate in cases that involved Thalidomide and its effects on pregnancy, originating in Germany; the Guiness affair in England involving illegal financial dealings; the Italian affair involving business, politics, organized crime, and the Vatican Bank; a case in the Netherlands involving deviance in a shipbuilding conglomerate; and the savings and loan scandal in the United States.

The savings and loan scandal, covering the period 1987–1992, represents one of the greatest fraud cases in the twentieth century (Mayer 1990; Pizzo et al. 1989; Thio 1998). Thio stated that this fraud cost taxpayers $1.4 trillion. Coleman (1994) explained that the rise in interest rates in the 1980s created serious economic problems for many savings and loan associations (thrifts) as their inventories of low-interest fixed-rate mortgage loans became increasingly unprofitable. The thrifts had been restricted until then by government regulations and were losing money. Punch (1996) suggests that the election of Ronald Reagan to the presidency accelerated an ideology of deregulation that held that business should be freed from undue rules and restrictions and that market forces should be given free rein to enhance competition. Deregulation of the industry did take place, and this meant that interest rates were not rigid, financing could be offered with no down payment, and loans could be given for consumer and commercial purposes. Those developments opened up opportunities for unscrupulous businesspersons who moved in and exploited the thrifts for devious purposes. Deregulation not only loosened controls but "raised the limit of federal protection on deposits to $100,000; brokers could make commissions on them, investors received higher interest rates and the S&L attracted new funds while enjoying a federal safety net" (Punch 1996, p. 16). As quoted by Punch (1996), the Federal Home Loan Bank-Board reported the following to Congress in 1988:

Individuals in a position of trust in the institution or closely affiliated with it have, in general terms, breached their fiduciary duties; traded on inside information; usurped opportunities for profits; engaged in self-dealing; or otherwise used the institution for personal advantage. Specific examples of insider abuse include loans to insiders in excess of that allowed by regulation; high-risk speculative ventures; payment of exorbitant dividends at times when the institution is at or near insolvency; payment from institutions' funds for personal vacations, automobiles, clothing, and art; payment of unwarranted commissions and fees to companies owned by a shareholder; payment of "consulting fees" to insiders or their companies; use of insiders' companies for association business; and putting friends and relatives on the payroll of the institutions. (U.S. General Accounting Office 1989, p. 22).

Calavita and Pontell (1990) categorized these fraudulent practices as "unlawful risk-taking," "looting," and "covering-up." Their work indicates that this type of corporate crime was unlike that reported by writers such as Clinard and Yeager (1980), which was designed to enhance corporate profits; rather, the savings and loan affair revealed premeditated looting for personal gain. They called this kind of crime "a hybrid of organizational and occupational crime"; this was crime by the corporation against the corporation, encouraged by the state, and with the taxpayer as the ultimate victim (Calavita and Pontell 1991).

Those studies of corporate, organizational, and occupational crimes appear to follow Sutherland's initial focus and concerns and to establish what might be called a Sutherland school of white-collar crime. Other researchers besides those mentioned earlier have made valuable contributions to this growing field, including Geis (1968), Braithewaite (1984), and Vaughn (1983).

OFFENDERS AND OFFENSES

The focus on offenses has been referred to by Poveda (1994) as a second school of thought that follows Tappan's tradition and is distinct from Sutherland's tradition with its emphasis on the offender. Social class, of course, has always been at the center of this debate in terms of its relationship to white-collar crime. While Sutherland emphasized that many violations were committed by respectable persons in the course of their occupations, Tappan argued for the recognition of the law in defining crime. Poveda states that

> the law of course specifies which acts are to be criminalized regardless of who commits them. In this view the defining characteristic of white-collar crime is the offense rather than the offender. The problem of defining white-collar crime from this perspective becomes one of deciding which subset of crimes is "white collar." By separating white-collar crime from the characteristics of the offender, white-collar crime in the legal tradition ceases to be linked to any particular social class. (1994, p. 40)

Edelhertz (1970) objected to Sutherland's assertion that white-collar crimes must occur in the course of the offender's occupation. He argued that that definition excludes offenses such as income tax evasion, receiving illegal Social Security payments, and other similar offenses, that he considered white-collar crime. Edelhertz's work suggests that the class of the offender need not be central to the concept of white-collar crime but that the offense should be the central consideration. In this respect, he reflected Tappan's stance. According to Poveda (1994), criminologists who focus on the offense have come to dominate views among workers in the justice system and have become more numerous among criminologists since Edelhertz modified Sutherland's definition in the 1970s.

Shapiro (1990) also suggests that the analysis of white-collar crime must shift from a focus on the offender to focus on the offense, particularly when violations of trust situations and norms are involved. She argues that the leniency shown to white-collar criminals accused of securities fraud has resulted from the social organization of their offenses and the problems of social control they posed rather than from class biases involving higher status.

It is relevant, then, to ask whether the laws on white-collar crime are applicable to corporations as well as to individuals. After reviewing the historical development of laws creating various white-collar crimes (embezzlement and theft, unfair competition, bribery and corruption, endangerment of consumers and workers, and environmental degradation), Coleman (1994) explained that the laws involving criminal intent have been extended to include corporations, stating that "it is now common for corporations to be charged with criminal violations of the regulatory statutes as well as more serious offenses" (p 125). As will be seen below, conviction and punishment are different matters.

CONVICTIONS AND SENTENCING

In the 1980s, Wheeler directed a series of studies at Yale University that focused on both offenders and offenses as well as on a comparison of white-collar and conventional crimes. Wheeler et al. (1982, 1988) focused on eight white-collar offenses in the federal system, which they clustered into three types organized by complexity: (1) the most organized: antitrust and securities fraud, (2) intermediate: mail fraud, false claims, credit fraud, and bribery, (3) the least organized: tax fraud and bank embezzlement. Their studies included only convicted offenses, not violations of civil or administrative regulations. They found that white-collar criminals are better educated, older, and more likely to be white and well off financially compared with conventional criminals. They also found that female white-collar offenders are more similar to conventional criminals than to their male counterparts. In an analysis of the Yale data, Daly (1989) found substantial differences between male and female white-collar offenders. Daly raised questions about whether the term "white collar" should be applied to women since they seldom committed offenses as part of a group, made less money from their crimes, and were less educated. Box (1983) suggested that female workers had fewer criminal opportunities than men. In another important tangent to their findings, Weisbund et al. (1991) argued that much white-collar crime is engaged in by middle-class individuals, revealing an unexpected source of inequality in the Justice Department.

In the area of sentencing, Wheeler and colleagues (1982) found that higher-status defendants charged with white-collar crimes were more likely to receive jail sentences than were lower-status defendants. In explanation, they suggested that because most cases against high-status defendants were never prosecuted, the few cases that were prosecuted were compelling. They also noted that the research was conducted shortly after the Watergate scandals, when judges were more attentive to misdeeds attributed to greed. In another study of sentencing and status, Hagar and Parker (1985), in an analysis of data on persons charged with criminal and noncriminal acts, observed differential sentencing of employers, managers, and workers. They found that compared with workers, managers were more likely and employers were less likely to be charged under the criminal code. Employers were instead more likely to be charged with Securities Act violations that carried less stigma and a shorter sentence. They noted that employers are in positions of power that allow them to be distanced from criminal events and obscure their involvement. Finally, they stated that Sutherland noted an "obfuscation as to responsibility" that accompanies corporate positions of power. Thus, employers face securities charges rather than criminal charges that require a demonstration of malice.

The Clinard and Yeager study (1980) did not include street criminals. The authors note that there is more leniency for corporate than for other white-collar offenders. In their study, it was found that only 4 percent of sanctions handed out for corporate violations involved criminal cases against individual executives. Of the fifty-six convicted executives in large corporations, 62.5 percent received probation, 21.4 percent had their sentences suspended, and 28.6 percent were incarcerated (p. 287). Among the latter defendants, two received six-month sentences and the remaining fourteen received sentences averaging only nine days (1980).

Relevant here are criticisms of legislation designed to control crime. Geis (1996) points out that legislation dealing with "three strikes" has given a "base on balls" to white-collar offenders and indicates an underlying class, ethnic, and racial bias that seeks to define criminals as "others" rather than confronting the more costly crimes of community leaders and the corporate world.

After reviewing a number of studies of sentencing, including studies by Shapiro, Wheeler and colleagues, Clinard and Yeager, Hagar and Parker, and Mann, Coleman concludes that "the evidence leaves little doubt that white collar offenders get off much easier than street offenders who commit crimes of similar severity" (1994, p. 157). He notes, however, that "there is some evidence that the punishment for white-collar offenses has been slowly increasing in recent years"(p. 157). Coleman still maintains that while there is increasing severity of punishment, such prosecutors remain rare. He says that "Leo Barrile [1991] concluded that only 16 cases of corporate homicide have [ever] been charged, only 9 of those made it to trial, and in only three cases were corporate agents sentenced to prison" (p. 157).

IMPLICATIONS FOR RESEARCH AND THEORY

Poveda (1994) notes that "in spite of the recent work on white collar offenses, our knowledge of white-collar crime is much more circumscribed than that of conventional crime and draws more heavily upon official crime statistics" (p. 79). He says that Wheeler and associates concluded that the vast majority of white-collar offenders are nonelite offenders who look like average Americans. Wheeler and colleagues argued that Sutherland's definition was narrowly focused on the upper class and ignored the middle group of offenders. Poveda suggests that "it is time to consider alternate approaches to gaining knowledge about white-collar crime, approaches that circumvent the official statistics." (1994, p. 79) because of the need to gather more information about crimes in large organizations. Poveda states that "large organizations have the power and resources to control public information about themselves to a much greater extent than other kinds of offenders" (1994, p. 79). He asserts that researchers will have to penetrate the curtain of secrecy that may enclose illegal behavior.

Poveda proposes that there is a need to study accidents and scandals. He cites the suggestions of Molotch and Lester (1974), who showed how routine news events are managed by political actors in society: corporations, labor unions, the president, members of Congress, and so on. These actors define issues for the public construct the news. Only accidents and scandals "penetrate this constructed reality of the news by catching these major actors off guard. While accidents are unplanned, scandals involve planned events but they must typically be disclosed by an inside informer to an organization because they involve sensitive information (Poveda 1994, p. 80). Poveda suggests that these events often reveal the incidence of white-collar crime. He says that the *Challenger* disaster was an "'accident' that led to disclosures of questionable judgment by the National Aeronautics and Space Administration and the Morton Thiokol Corporation" (p. 81). Punch (1996) has undertaken research that focused on accidents and scandals. This research involved case studies of the savings and loan scandal, the Three-Mile Island nuclear accident, and many others. Braithwaite has written about the drug companies and their record of fraud in testing, price-fixing, and the provision of perks for medical practitioners (Braithwaite 1984).

It is important to note that research in Britain by Clarke and in Britain, Holland, and the Untied States by Punch and others suggests that corporate, organizational, and occupational crime in the industrial world have more common elements than differences. Moreover, cybercrime, relying heavily on the Internet, has increased greatly according to a report by the British Broadcasting Corporation. Fraud employing stolen credit cards and stolen identities would appear to have worldwide similarities as a result of the growing use of the World Wide Web.

Punch has noted that researchers are increasingly targeting accidents, disasters, and scandals in the business world. He has not noticed any slackening of the calculative nature of business, as evidenced in the transfer of technology and manufacturing to developing nations. Noting the existence of, if not an increase in, the number of shrewd players on the world scene and the growth of unregulated markets, Punch expects fresh scandals not only in the United States but in eastern Europe and the Far East (1996, pp. 268, 269). There is, then, growing agreement that a focus on accidents, disasters, and scandals will provide a growing database on white-collar crime and its various types and that such a database will lead to the development of a more adequate theory of white-collar crime. This would seem to be a prerequisite for the development of an adequate system of deterrence of white-collar crime.

There seems to be agreement that criminologists are some distance away from developing an adequate theory of white-collar crime. Wheeler and associates, Yeager and associates, Poveda, Braithwaite, Coleman, and others have contributed to concept development and theory building in this field. Thus, Reed and Yeager (1996) have emphasized the need to assess how notions of self-interest become merged with corporate interests and the conditions under which these socially constructed interests lead to socially harmful outcomes. Wheeler (1992) has addressed a similar concern with motivational and situational processes that drive individuals to risk involvement in white-collar crime. Coleman also asserts that the related theoretical problems of motivation and opportunity must be understood. He considers the neutralization of ethical standards by which white-collar criminals justify their pursuit of success, the secrecy that shields corporate actions, and the opportunities provided by the legal and judicial systems essential links in the development of an understanding of this type of crime.

Braithwaite (1984) also draws on the structure of opportunity in attempting to understand organizational crime but is perhaps best known for his concept of reintegrative shaming. In his approach, he utilizes control theory, specifying the processes by which corporate offenders are encouraged to strengthen their stake in conformity. He asserts that the other kind of shaming—stigmatization—has the effect of reinforcing offenders in their criminality.

There is an apparent need for a continued focus on occupational and corporate deviance and on individual and organizational offenders in the field of white-collar crime. Interest has been growing in the field, and there is reason to believe that academic researchers, government agencies, and legislatures must communicate with one another more if progress is to be made in the important matter of constructing better deterrents to white-collar crime. However, as suggested by Punch and others, investigators must search more closely for the dark, irrational side of organizations—incompetence, neglect, ambition, greed, power—as well as for motives and structures that allow managers to practice deviance against the organization. It is clear that while many researchers argue for a focus on the organization and others emphasize the need to study individual offenders, there is a growing acceptance of the need to explore all avenues that lead to white-collar crime. Indeed, there seems to be a clamor among researchers that not only must motivation and opportunity be studied but that the subcultures that facilitate immoral behavioral structures should be analyzed to understand white-collar or any other type of crime.

REFERENCES

Barrile, Leo 1991 "Determining Criminal Responsibility of Corporations." Paper presented at the American Society of Criminology, San Francisco, November.

Biderman, Albert, and Albert J. Reiss 1980 *Data Sources on White Collar Lawbreaking.* Washington D.C.: National Institute of Justice.

Box, Steven 1983 *Power, Crime, and Mystification.* New York: Tavistock.

Braithwaite, John 1979 *Inequality Crime and Public Policy.* London: Routledge and Kegan Paul.

—— 1984 *Corporate Crime in the Pharmaceutical Industry.* London: Routledge & Kegan Paul.

Burgess, Ernest W. 1950 "Comment to Harting." *American Journal of Sociology* 56:25–34.

Calavita, Kitty and Henry Pontell 1991 "Other People's Money Revisited: Collective Embezzlement in the Savings and Loan and Insurance Industries." *Social Problems* 38: 94–112.

—— 1990 "Heads I Win, Tails You Lose: Dergulation, Crime, and Crisis in the Savings and Loan Industry." *Crime and Delinquency* 36:309–341.

Chamber of Commerce of the United States 1974 *A Handbook on White Collar Crime.* Washington, D.C.: Chamber of Commerce of the United States.

Clarke, M. 1990 *Business Crime* Cambridge, U.K.: Polity Press.

Clinard, Marshall B., and Richard Quinney 1973 *Criminal Behavior Systems,* 2nd; ed. New York: Holt, Rinehart & Winston.

——, and Peter C. Yeager. 1980 *Corporate Crime.* New York: Free Press.

Coleman, James 1994 *The Criminal Elite: The Sociology of White Collar Crime,* 3rd; ed. New York: St. Martin's.

Daly, Kathleen 1989. "Gender and Varieties of White Collar-Crime." *Criminology* 27: 269–294.

Edelhertz, Herbert 1970. *The Nature, Impact and Prosecution of White Collar Crime.* Washington D.C.: U.S. Government Printing Office.

—— 1996 "A Base on Balls for White Collar Criminals." In David Shicor and Dale Seckrest, eds., *Three Strikes and You're Out: Vengeance as Public Policy.* Thousand Oaks, Calif.: Sage.

Geis, Gilbert, ed. 1968 *White Collar Crime.* New York: Atherton Press.

Green, Gary S. 1990 *Occupational Crime.* Chicago: Nelson Hall.

Hagar, John, and Patricia Parker 1985 "White Collar Crime and Punishment: The Class Structure and Legal Sanctioning of Securities Violations." *American Sociological Review* 50:302–916.

Mayer, Martin 1990 *The Greatest Ever Bank Robbery: The Collapse of the Savings and Loan Industry.* New York: Scribner.

Molotch, Harvey, and Marilyn Lester 1974 "News as Purposive Behavior: On the Strategic Use of Routine Events, Accidents, and Scandals." *American Sociological Review* 39:101–112.

Pizzo, S., M. Fricker, and P. Muolo 1989 *Inside Job: The Looting of America's Savings and Loans.* New York: McGraw-Hill.

Poveda, Tony 1994 *Rethinking White-Collar Crime.* Westport, Conn.: Praeger.

Perrow, Charles 1984 *Normal Accidents.* New York: Basis Books.

Punch, Maurice 1996 *Dirty Business: Exploring Corporate Misconduct.* London: Sage.

Reed, Gary E., and Peter Cleary Yeager 1996 "Organizational Offending and Neoclassical Criminology: Challenging the Reach of a General Theory of Crime." *Criminology* 34:357–382.

Reiman, Jeffrey 1995 *The Rich Get Rich and the Poor Get Prison,* 4th ed. Boston: Allyn & Bacon.

Sellin, Thorsten 1951 "The Significance of Records of Crime." *Law Quarterly Review* 67:489–504.

Schrager, Laura S., and James P. Short 1978 "Toward a Sociology of Organizational Crime." *Social Problems* 25:407–419.

Shapiro, Susan 1990 "Collaring the Crime, Not the Criminal: Reconsidering the Concept of White Collar Crime." *American Sociological Review* 55: 346–365.

Sutherland, Edwin H. 1949 *White Collar Crime.* New York: Dryden Press.

Tappan, Paul 1947 "Who Is the Criminal." *American Sociological Review* 12:96–102.

Thio, Alex 1998 *Deviant Behavior,* 5th ed. New York: Addison-Wesley. *US News & World Report* 1985 May 20.

Vaughn, Diane 1983 *Controlling Unlawful Organizational Behavior: Social Structure and Corporate Misconduct.* Chicago: University of Chicago Press.

Vold, George, and Thomas J. Bernard 1986 *Theoretical Criminology*, 3rd ed. New York: Oxford University Press.

Webster, Wilham 1980. "An Examination of FBI Theory and Methodology Regarding White Collar Crime Investigation and Prevention." *American Criminal Law Review* 17:275–286.

Weisbund, D., S. Wheeler, E. Waring, and N. Bode 1991 *Crimes of the Middle Classes: White Collar Offenders in the Federal Courts*. New Haven, Conn.: Yale University Press.

Wheeler, Stanton 1992 "The Problem of White Collar Crime Motivation." In Kip Schlegel and David Weisbund, eds., *White Collar Crime Reconsidered*. Boston: Northeastern University Press.

——, and E. Waring. 1988 "White Collar Crimes and Criminals." *American Criminal Law Review* 25:331–357.

——, D. Weisbund, and N. Bode 1982 "Sentencing the White-Collar Offenses." *American Sociological Review* 47:641–659.

—— 1976 "Trends and Problems in the Sociological Study of Crime." *Social Problems.* 23:523–534

James E. Teele

WIDOWHOOD

Marriages that do not end in divorce eventually dissolve through the death of a spouse. The stress of bereavement derives largely from the disorganization caused by the loss of the deceased from the social support system of the survivor. The death of a marital partner requircs the development of alternative patterns of behavior so that the survivor can maintain satisfactory relations with the family, the kin group, and the community and sustain his or her personal equilibrium. Families exhibit considerable diversity in their attempts to accomplish these transitions. The difficult and sometimes devastating transition to widowhood or widowerhood necessitates a reintegration of roles suitable to a new status. If children are present, parental death precipitates a reorganization of the family as a social system. Roles and status positions must be shifted, values reoriented, and personal and family time restructured. The potential for role strains and interpersonal conflicts becomes evident as relationships are lost, added, or redefined (Pitcher and Larson 1989). Loneliness becomes a major problem. In many modern societies, this adaptive process proceeds with few or no guidelines because the widowed person tends to be "roleless," lacking clear norms or prescriptions for behavior (Hiltz 1979).

WIDOWHOOD ACROSS CULTURES

Human behaviors generally are guided by the dominant prescriptions and proscriptions embedded in particular societies, and this is reflected in wide cross-cultural variations among those who have lost a spouse through death (Lopata 1996). For example, the situation of Hindu widows in India has undergone numerous changes, ranging from extremely harsh treatment in the past to slow but steady improvement in the modern era. The custom of *suttee*–the wife's self-immolation on her husband's funeral pyre–has long been outlawed but periodically reappears, especially in rural areas. Even today, widows in that highly patriarchal, patrilineal, and patrilocal society experience isolation and a loss of status. Their remarriage rate is very low. Widows often face a difficult life that is influenced by vestiges of patriarchal and religious dogma and exacerbated by economic problems that force them to become dependent on sons, in-laws, and others. Widowers, by contrast, are encouraged to remarry soon and add progeny to the patriarchal line. Israel is another place where the society and religion are strongly patriarchal and women lose status in widowhood. Jewish mourning rituals "tend to isolate the widow and tie her to the past rather than providing means of creating a new life" (Lopata 1996). Moreover, women who lose husbands through civilian causes of death encounter greater difficulties than do those whose husbands are killed in the military. War widows and their families receive preferential treatment through government policies that give them special recognition, numerous benefits, and many more alternatives for improving their status and prestige than is possible in more traditional societies. Remarriage, for example, is is a much more acceptable alternative for women in Israel than it is in India.

All societies are undergoing various degrees of transition. Korea is a society whose transitional problems are dramatically reflected in the situation of widows. Earlier in Korean history, widowhood resulted in a loss of status and remarriage generally was prohibited. Husbands tended to be much older than their wives and to have a higher mortality rate, and a large number were killed in wars. Moreover, widowers remarried, whereas most widows remained single. All these factors contributed to a widening ratio of widows to widowers over the years. Under the impact of modernization, including increased urbanization and industrialization, Korean society is being transformed, and with it the conditions surrounding the status of widowhood. This transformation includes a shift from authoritarian societal and familial system in a primarily rural environment toward systems based on more equalitarian norms. Widows began to move to the cities, and this had advantages and disadvantages. On the one hand, they could accompany their sons and take advantage of urban services and the possibility of new friendships. On the other hand, the move removed them from their extended families and neighborhood friends and the communal supports in their rural villages. Living with a son in the city often strained the daughter-in-law relationship. In addition, being distanced from the relatively stable and integrated life of their villages and lacking friendship networks in their new environment often left them vulnerable to loneliness, especially in the case of the elderly widowed. Presumably, succeeding generations with greater personal resources will encounter fewer adaptational requirements.

While survivors face certain common problems and role strains both within and outside the immediate family, it is difficult to specify a normative course of adjustment. This is the case because the widowed are a heterogeneous group characterized by wide differences in social and psychological characteristics. It also is due to the fact that spousal loss evokes a panorama of emotional and behavioral responses from the survivors, depending on factors such as the timing and circumstances of the spouse's death. For example, a wife whose husband was killed in a military battle will respond differently than she would if he had committed suicide or suffered a long terminal illness. Many other antecedent conditions, such as the quality of the marital relationship, affect the bereavement reactions and coping strategies of survivors.

THE DEMOGRAPHICS OF WIDOWHOOD

Census data for the United States show that at the end of the 1990s there were more than 13.5 million widowed persons, 85 percent of whom were women. However, people in the widowed category may leave it through remarriage. Hence, the number of people who have ever experienced spousal loss is much greater than is indicated by these data.

For some decades, the widowed female has outnumbered her male counterpart by an ever widening margin. Three factors account for this: (1) Mortality among females is lower than it is among males, and therefore, greater numbers of women survive to advanced years, (2) wives are typically younger than their husbands and consequently have a greater probability of outliving them, and (3) among the widowed, remarriage rates are significantly lower for women than for men. Other factors that contribute to the preponderance of widows include war, depressions, and disease pandemics.

For several reasons, widowhood has become largely a problem of aged women. Each year in the United States, deaths of spouses create nearly a million new widows and widowers. Among people 65 years of age or over, roughly half the women compared with about 14 percent of the men are widowed. (U.S. Bureau of the Census 1997). Advances in medical technology and the pervasiveness health programs have extended life expectancy. The probability of mortality before middle age has decreased, and for the most part widowhood has been postponed to the later stages of the life cycle. Gains in longevity have been more rapid for women than for men. Thus, the growing proportion of elderly females accents their higher rates of widowhood. About one-fourth of all married women will become widows by age 65, and one-half of the remaining women will be widowed by age 75. During that age span, only one-fifth of men will lose their wives. It is projected that the ratio of widows to widowers will increase dramatically from nearly six to one currently to ten to one over the next quarter century.

Because the large majority of the widowed are women, most studies have concentrated on them, while the social consequences for men who lose their spouses has remained a comparatively unexplored area since Berardo (1970) called attention to this gap three decades ago. Widowers, although fewer in number, face many of the same adjustments that confront their female counterparts. At the same time, there is ambiguous evidence that suggests that widowers have greater vulnerability compared to their female counterparts, while other studies present the situation of widows as more problematic. This disagreement in findings results in part from the failure of many studies to control for the confounding influences of factors such as age, social class, income, health, and retirement.

RESEARCH FINDINGS ON WIDOWHOOD

In making the transition from marriage to widowedhood, the bereaved often are confronted with a variety of personal and familial problems and are not always successful in adapting to those circumstances. This is reflected in the findings that compared with married persons, the widowed consistently have higher rates of mortality, mental disorders, and suicide (Balkwell 1981; Smith et al. 1988). While there is a consensus that bereavement is stressful, research on its effects on physical health has yielded inconsistent results. The evidence shows that the widowed experience poorer health than do the married, but the reasons for this difference are unclear.

Because widowhood is most likely to occur in the elderly, research has focused on that population. However, there is some evidence that the transition to widowhood varies by developmental stage. Older widows adapt more readily because losing a spouse at an advanced age is more the norm, making acceptance of the loss easier than it is for those who are young when widowed. Grieving over the death of a husband or wife at older ages can be exacerbated if additional significant others also die, requiring multiple grieving. This can cause *bereavement overload*, which makes it difficult for the survivor to complete the grief work and bring closure to the bereavement process (Berardo 1988). There is a consensus that the distress associated with conjugal bereavement diminishes over time. Grief becomes less intense as the years pass, but this is not a simple, linear process. The emotional and psychological traumas of grief and mourning may recur sporadically long after a spouse has died.

Gender differences in adaptation to widowhood have been widely debated. The evidence suggests a somewhat greater vulnerability for widowers (Stroebe and Stroebe 1983). Men are less likely to have same-sex widowed friends, are more likely to be older and less healthy, have fewer family and social ties, and experience greater difficulty in becoming proficient in domestic roles (Berardo 1968, 1970). Higher mortality and suicide rates also suggest greater distress among widowers.

Continuous widowhood has been associated with a loss of income and an increased risk of poverty. Two-fifths of widows fall into poverty at some time during the five years after the death of their husbands. Female survivors, for example, have dramatically higher proportions in poverty than do their divorced counterparts, although both groups experience economic risk resulting from the ending of their marriages that may impede their and their families' adjustment to a new lifestyle (Morgan 1989). There is some evidence that widowers also suffer a decline in economic well-being, although to a lesser degree than do their female counterparts (Zick and Smith 1988). Poor adjustment to widowhood thus may be related to a lack of finances. Elderly individuals often have below-average incomes before the death of a spouse. They may be unwilling or unable to seek employment and are likely to face discrimination in the labor market (Morgan 1989). The younger widowed are more likely to have lost a spouse suddenly and therefore may be unprepared to cope with a lower financial status.

Life insurance has become a principal defense against the insecurity and risk of widowhood in urban industrial society with its nuclear family system. It is a concrete form of security that may help a bereaved family avoid an embarrassing dependence on relatives and the state in the case of an untimely death. However, the amount of insurance obtained is often insufficient to meet the needs of the survivors. Even in instances in which adequate assets have been accumulated, many surviving wives are not prepared to handle the economic responsibilities brought about by a husband's death (Nye and Berardo 1973). Presumably, in the future, a better educated and occupationally experienced population of widows, especially those who were involved in a more equalitarian marital relationship of shared responsibilities, will be better able to cope with their new single status.

Widowhood often leads to changes in living arrangements. Reduced income may force surviving spouses to seek more affordable housing. They also may choose to relocate for other reasons, such as future financial and health concerns, a desire to divest themselves of possessions, and a desire to be near relatives or friends (Hartwigsen 1987). Most often, survivors living alone are women, usually elderly widows. Isolation and lack of social support can lead to deterioration in their physical and mental well-being. Compared with elderly couples, they are much more likely to live in poverty and less likely to receive medical care when it is needed (Kasper 1988).

WIDOWHOOD AND DIVORCE

Similarities and Differences. Early epidemiological analyses suggested that more deleterious effects were associated with separation and divorce than with widowhood. However, later surveys found higher levels of physical and psychological distress among the widowed than among the divorced. (Kitson et al. 1989). These contradictory findings have not been reconciled. However, for many decades, researchers also have perceived a number of similarities in adjustment between the two groups. For both, there are accompanying disruptions in lifestyle related to changes in income, social interactions, definitions of self, lost emotional attachment, and general psychological well-being. For example, similarities in adjustment have been noted with respect to mode of death or cause of divorce, including the amount of prior warning or preparation a person has before either event, the degree of responsibility felt, and the cause of the event. The more unexpected the loss is, the more responsibility one feels for the loss and wonders whether he or she could have prevented it or helped the spouse and the more difficult the adjustment is.

Another similarity is that whether a spouse is lost through divorce or widowhood, the length of time for adjustment shows considerable variability. The degree of emotional attachment affects the degree of anxiety and depression associated with the loss of a partner, and in both cases the attachment declines as time passes. Emotional attachment is a normal outcome of the tendency for people to form strong affectional bonds to significant others and is not pathological. However, the accumulative changes that occur with the loss of a partner make those who are divorced or widowed more vulnerable to psychological and physical illness, suicide, accidents, and death. While most partners return to their former level of functioning within a couple of years after the loss of a spouse, some never recover and continue to have poor levels of functioning.

There are also specific factors that make adjustment in widowhood or divorce more difficult, including age, gender, race, and socioeconomic status. Adjustment to the loss of a spouse in either case appears to be more difficult for younger women. Some analysts argue that age is a confounding factor because younger women are more studied as divorcees and older women more studied as widows and because divorce is more common among the young and widowhood more common among the old. The latter factor means that one's adjustment is somewhat dependent on those who have gone before and can help socialize a person to the new role. However, more recent research suggests that younger women still face more adjustment problems (Kitson et al. 1989; Gove and Shin 1989). Analyses suggest that the young and the old bereaved differ in both the intensity of grief and patterns of grief reactions, especially with respect to adverse health and psychological outcomes within the first two years after the demise of a husband (Sanders 1988). It appears that younger widows experience a different adjustment than do older widows, in part because they have fewer cohort friends who are also widows.

Younger survivors are developmentally "out of sync" with their cohorts, and this exacerbates their sense of loneliness and need for companionship (Levinson 1997) Their expectations may be different because they have more years ahead and more potentially eligible marital partners in the future than do older widows. Blacks appear to have an easier time adjusting to the loss of a spouse through divorce than do whites, and black females, who may receive more familial support than whites do, appear to adjust more easily than do white females. Finally, income and financial security play a major role in adjustment: Those near poverty have the most difficult time coping with the loss of a spouse. Female survivors have more problems coping with the loss of income than do their male counterparts, often because their incomes are tied to health insurance, retirement, and other benefits that accompanied the husband's occupation. Men have more difficulty than do women handling the household chores that were often the responsibility of their wives. Future male cohorts may have less difficulty with this because of changes in the socialization of male children and the rising age at first marriage, and the fact that young men have to cope with household responsibilities on their own before marriage.

WIDOWHOOD AND REMARRIAGE

The probability of remarriage is significantly lower for widows than for widowers, especially at the older ages. It appears that while a large majority of older widows remain attracted to and interested in men in terms of companionship, for a variety of reasons only a small minority report a favorable attitude toward remarriage (Talbott 1998). Some may feel they are committing psychological bigamy and therefore reject remarriage as an option (DiGiulio 1989). There is also a tendency to idealize the former partner, a process known as sanctification (Lopata 1979). This makes it difficult for widows to find a new partner who can compare favorably with the idealized image of the deceased (Berardo 1982). Widows also remarry less frequently than do widowers because of the lack of eligible men and the existence of cultural norms that degrade the sexuality of older women and discourage them from selecting younger mates. Many women manage to develop and value a new and independent identity after being widowed, leading them to be less interested in reentering the marriage market.

There are other barriers to remarriage for the widowed. Dependent children limit the opportunities of their widowed parents to meet potential mates or develop relationships with them. Older children may oppose remarriage out of concern for their inheritance. Widowed persons who cared for a dependent spouse through a lengthy terminal illness may be unwilling to risk bearing that burden again.

WIDOWHOOD AND MORTALITY

The increased risk of mortality for widowed persons has been widely reported. Men are at a greater risk than women after bereavement. The causes of these differences are unknown. Marital selection theory posits that healthy widowers remarry quickly, leaving a less healthy subset that experiences premature mortality. Other factors, such as common infection, shared environment, and lack of adequate daily care, also may influence the higher mortality rates of the widowed.

Studies of whether anticipatory grief or forewarning of the pending death of a spouse contributes to adjustment to bereavement have yielded conflicting results (Roach and Kitson 1989). Some suggest that anticipation is important because it allows the survivor to begin the process of role redefinition before the death, whereas unanticipated death produces more severe grief reactions. Survivors who have experienced unexpected deaths of their spouses report more somatic problems and longer adjustment periods than do those who anticipated the loss. Anticipatory role rehearsal does not consistently produce smoother or more positive adjustment among the bereaved. It appears that the coping strategies employed by survivors vary with the timing and mode of death, which in turn influence the bereavement outcome.

SOCIAL SUPPORT AND REINTEGRATION

It has been suggested that social support plays an important role in the bereavement outcome and acts as a buffer for stressful life events, but the research is somewhat inconclusive, partly as a result of difficulties identifying those support efforts which produce positive outcomes and those which do not and the fact that support needs change over time. Nevertheless, there is evidence that the extent to which members of the social network provide various types of support to the bereaved is important in the pattern of recovery and adaptation (Vachon and Stanley 1988). Available confidants and access to self-help groups to assist with emotional management can help counter loneliness and promote a survivor's reintegration into society. The social resources of finances and education have been found to be particularly influential in countering the stresses associated with the death of a spouse. Community programs that provide education, counseling, and financial services can facilitate the efforts of the widowed and their families to restructure their lives.

For many older widows, a substantial period of future living alone remains: on average, another fourteen years or more. Borrowing from occupational career models, some researchers have suggested that adopting a "career of widowhood" orientation may facilitate the recovery and well-being of these survivors: "That is, for most persons, widowhood need not be considered the end of productive life, but rather the beginning of a major segment of the life course, and one that should be pursued vigorously in order for it to be successful and fulfilling" (Hansson and Remondet 1988). In this perspective, the widowed are encouraged to seek control over their existence by actively construing their own life courses. The assumption is that they will adapt better if they plan for where they want to be at different potential stages during the entire course of widowhood. This plan might include the following phases: "a time for emotional recovery; a time for taking stock, reestablishing or restructuring support relationships, and formulating personal directions for the future; a time for discovering a comfortable and satisfying independent lifestyle, and for determining an approach to maintaining economic, psychological, and social functioning; perhaps a time for personal growth and change; and a time for reasoned consideration of one's last years and assertion of a degree of control over the arrangements surrounding one's own decline and death."

There is considerable heterogeneity among the survivor population and thus in their ability to implement a successful "career in widowhood." They differ, for example, in *relational competence*, that is, characteristics that help them acquire, develop, and maintain personal relationships that are essential for social support (Hansson and Remondet 1988). Establishing a new and satisfying autonomous identity after the loss of a spouse is never easy. The probability of achieving that goal can, however, be enhanced through counseling strategies designed for individual circumstances and programs that help survivors avoid desolation coupled with meaningful social and familial support systems.

(SEE ALSO: *Death and Dying; Filial Responsibility; Remarriage; Social Gerontology*)

REFERENCES

Arbuckle, Nancy Weber, and Brian de Vries 1995 "The Long-Term Effects of Later Life Spousal and Parental Bereavement on Personal Functioning." *The Gerontologist* 35:637–647.

Aquilino, William S. 1994 "Later Life Parental Divorce and Widowhood: Impact on Young Adults' Assessment of Parent Child Relations." *Journal of Marriage and the Family* 56:908–922.

Balkwell, Carolyn 1981 "Transition to Widowhood: A Review of the Literature." *Family Relations* 30:117–127.

Bennett, Kate Mary 1997 "Longitudinal Study of Well-being in Widowed Women." *International Journal of Geriatric Psychiatry* 12:61–66.

Berardo, Donna H. 1982 "Divorce and Remarriage at Middle-Age and Beyond." *Annals of the American Academy of Political and Social Science* 464:132–139.

—— 1988 "Bereavement and Mourning." In Hannelore Wass, Felix M. Berardo, and Robert A. Neimeyer, eds., *Dying: Facing the Facts*, 2nd ed. New York: Hemisphere.

Berardo, Felix M. 1968 "Widowhood Status in the United States: A Neglected Aspect of the Family Life-Cycle." *Family Coordinator* 17:191–203.

—— 1970 "Survivorship and Social Isolation: The Case of the Aged Widower." *Family Coordinator* 19:11–25.

—— 1992 "Widowhood." In Edgar F. Borgatta and Marie L. Borgatta, eds., *Encyclopedia of Sociology*. New York: Macmillan.

—— 1995 "Widowhood." In David Levinson, ed., *Encyclopedia of Marriage and the Family*. New York: Simon & Schuster, Macmillan.

Campbell, Scott, and Phyllis R. Silverman 1996 *Widower: When Men Are Left Alone*. Amityville, New York: Baywood Publishing Company.

Clark, Philip G., Robert W. Siviski, and Ruth Weiner 1986 "Coping Strategies of Widowers in the First Year." *Family Relations* 35:425–430.

DiGiulio, R. C. 1989 *Beyond Widowhood*. New York: Free Press.

Dimond, Margaret, Dale A. Lund, and Michael S. Caserta 1987 "The Role of Social Support in the First Two Years of Bereavement in an Elderly Sample." *Gerontologist* 27:599–604.

Dykstra, Pearl A. 1995 "Loneliness Among the Never and Formerly Married: The Importance of Supportive Friendships." *Journal of Gerontology* 50B: S321–S329.

Gove, Walter R., and Hee-Choon Shin. 1989 "The Psychological Well-Being of Divorced and Widowed Men and Women." *Journal of Family Issues* 10:122–144.

Hansson, Robert O., and Jacquline H. Remondet 1988 "Old Age and Widowhood: Issues of Personal Control and Independence." *Journal of Social Issues* 44:159–174.

Hartwigsen, G. 1987 "Older Widows and the Transference of Home." *International Journal of Aging and Human Development* 25:195–207.

Hiltz, Starr R. 1979 "Widowhood: A Roleless Role." In Marvin B. Sussman, ed., *Marriage and Family.* Collected Essay Series. New York: Hayworth Press.

Hong, Lawrence K., and Robert W. Duff 1994 "Widows in Retirement Communities: The Social Context of Subjective Well-being." *The Gerontologist* 34:347–352.

Kasper, Judith D. 1988 *Aging Alone–Profiles and Projections.* Baltimore: Commonwealth Fund.

Kitson, Gay C., Karen Benson Babri, Mary Joan Roach, and Kathleen S. Placidi 1989 "Adjustment to Widowhood and Divorce." *Journal of Family Issue* 10:5–32.

Levinson, Deborah S. 1997 "Young Widowhood: A Life Change Journay." *Journal of Personal and Interpersonal Loss* 2:277–291.

Littlewood, Jane 1994 "Widows' Weeds and Women's Needs: The Re-feminization of Death, Dying and Bereavement." In Sue Wilkonson and Celia Kitzinger, eds., *Women and Health: Feminist Perspective.* New York: Taylor and Francis.

Lopata, Helen Z. 1973 *Widowhood in an American City.* Cambridge, Mass.: Schenkman.

—— 1979 *Women as Widows.* New York: Elsevier.

—— 1996 *Current Widowhood.* Thousand Oaks, Calif.: Sage.

Morgan, Leslie 1989 "Economic Well-Being Following Marital Termination: A Comparison of Widowed and Divorced Women." *Journal of Family Issues* 10:86–101.

Murdock, Melissa E. et al. 1998 "Contribution of Small Life Events to the Psychological Distress of Married and Widowed Older Women." *Journal of Women and Aging* 10:3–22.

Nye, F. Ivan, and Felix M. Berardo 1973 *The Family: Its Structure and Interaction.* New York: Macmillan

Pitcher, Brian L., and Don C. Larson 1989 "Elderly Widowhood." In Stephen J. Bahr and Evan T. Peterson, eds., *Aging and the Family.* Lexington, Mass.: Heath.

Roach, Mary J., and Gay T. Kitson 1989 "Impact of Forewarning and Adjustment to Widowhood and Divorce." In Dale A. Lund, ed., *Older Bereaved Spouses.* New York: Hemisphere.

Sandell, Steven B., and Howard M. Iams 1997 "Reducing Women's Poverty by Shifting Social Security Benefits from Retired Couples to Widows." *Journal of Policy Analysis and Management* 16:279–297.

Sanders, Catherine M. 1988 "Risk Factors in Bereavement Outcomes." *Journal of Social Issues* 44:97–11.

Smith, Jack C., James A. Mercy, and Judith A. Conn 1988 "Marital Status and the Risk of Suicide." *American Journal of Public Health* 78:78–80.

Stroebe, Margaret S., and Wolfgang Stroebe 1983 "Who Suffers More: Sex Differences in Health Risks of the Widowed." *Psychological Bulletin* 93:279–299.

Talbott, Maria M. 1998 "Older Widows' Attitudes towards Men and Remarriage." *Journal of Aging Studies.*" 12:429–449.

U.S. Bureau of the Census 1997 "Marital Status of the Population, by Sex and Age, 1996." *Current Population Reports.* Series P20–491.

Vachon, Mary L.S., and Stanley K. Stylianos, 1988 "The Role of Social Support in Bereavement." *Journal of Social Issues* 44:175–190.

Zick, Cathleen D., and Ken R. Smith 1988 "Recent Widowhood, Remarriage, and Changes in Economic Well-Being." *Journal of Marriage and the Family* 50:233–244.

FELIX M. BERARDO
DONNA H. BERARDO

WORK AND OCCUPATIONS

Work is the defining activity in people's lives. In most of the world, it is a matter of survival, but work also places people in stratification systems, shapes their physical and emotional well-being, and influences their chances for social mobility. Although the term "work" generally is used to denote the exertion of effort toward some end, economically it refers to activities oriented toward producing goods and services for one's own use or for pay. The conception of work as a means of generating income underlies most sociological scholarship on work and most of the available statistics. Unpaid productive work, including that done in the home (indeed, homemaking is the largest occupation in the United States) and volunteer work, tends to be invisible. This article focuses primarily on paid work.

EVOLUTION OF WORK

Although contemporary work differs dramatically from work in the past, the evolution of the organization of production and people's attitudes toward work have important legacies for workers today. For much of human history, work and home lives were integrated: Most work was done at or near the home, and people consumed the products of their labor. The predecessors of the modern labor force were nonagricultural workers, including servants and skilled artisans who made and sold products. The development of industrial work supplemented human effort with machines, introduced a division of labor that assigned specialized tasks to different workers, and ushered in a wage economy. In Europe, industrial work began as cottage industry, in which middlemen brought unfinished goods to cottagers—often women and children—who manufactured products. However, the exploitation of energy sources that could fuel large machines, the growing number of displaced peasants forced to sell their labor, and the expansion of markets for industrial goods made it more economical to shift industrial work to factories. The ensuing Industrial Revolution in the West laid the foundation for modern work and created the modern labor force. Some workers in developing countries continue to do agricultural or other subsistence work; others work in industrialized sectors, although seldom with the protections advanced industrial countries afford their workers.

THE LABOR FORCE

In developed societies, the labor force—people who are employed or are seeking paid work—includes most adults. In Western industrialized nations, it ranged in the middle 1990s from less than half the adults in Ireland, Italy, and several Middle Eastern and north African countries to around 80 percent in Denmark, Cambodia, China, Iceland, Rwanda, Solvenia, and Burundi (United Nations 1999).

The composition of the labor force is in a continual flux. Although women and children were well represented in the earliest labor force in Western countries, as industrial labor replaced agricultural work, wage workers became increasingly male. However, as the growth of jobs labeled "women's work" has drawn increasing numbers of women into the labor force worldwide, the labor force has become more sex-balanced. Women's participation in the formal labor force varies cross-nationally, however. In the 1990s, according to the United Nations, women's share of the labor force ranged from one in nine (Iran) to one in four workers (Turkey) in the Middle East and in north African countries. In Latin American countries, three to four in ten workers were female; as were 38 (Indonesia) to 48 percent (Cambodia) in southeast Asia, 38 (South Africa) to 50 percent (Burundi)

in sub-Saharan Africa, and 38 (Italy, Spain, Japan) to 48 percent (Norway, Denmark, Sweden) in the advanced industrial countries.

In the United States, more than 46 percent of the labor force was female in 1998. Just as the U.S. labor force has become more diverse in gender, it has become more diverse in its racial and ethnic composition. As the "baby bust" cohorts replace the baby boom cohorts, the U.S. labor force is aging. Smaller cohorts of young workers will lead employers to turn to other labor sources, such as immigrants, to fill low-wage, entry-level jobs.

Although child labor has all but disappeared in advanced industrial nations, children are a significant presence in the labor force in many developing countries. According to the International Labour Organization (ILO) (1996, number 16), in the mid-1990s, three to four of every ten sub-Saharan African children between ages 10 and 14 worked to help support themselves and their families. In some Asian countries, more than three children in ten are in the labor force (Bangladesh, Bhutan, East Timor, Nepal), and in several Latin American countries, at least one child in four works for pay (Bolivia, Brazil, Dominican Republic, Guatemala, Haiti, and Nicaragua). Child labor in Third World countries is partly a product of a global economy that makes impoverished children particularly attractive to Western-based multinational corporations in their worldwide search for cheap and docile workers.

Extent of paid work. The amount of time people spend at paid work has changed through the centuries. In the early decades of industrialization, adults and children often worked fourteen-hour days, six days a week. After labor organizations won maximum-hours laws and overtime pay, the average workweek shrank for European and American workers, although in some countries hours are increasing for some workers. In 1997, Japan's workers logged more hours of work than did those in other countries for which records are available, averaging 1,990 hours annually, with U.S. workers second at 1,904 hours. Germany's and Denmark's workers average the fewest hours of paid work per year: 1,573 and 1,665, respectively (ILO 1998, number 25, p. 31). Declines in work hours mask a division in the extent of paid work, with growing numbers either putting in very long workweeks or working part-time. In many industrialized countries, the proportion of workers employed part-time has doubled since the 1970s; indeed, the growth in part-time jobs almost entirely accounts for the growth of total employment in industrialized countries (ILO 1996, number 17, p. 28). This growth reflects both demand-side and supply-side forces. Teenagers and women with children disproportionately opt for part-time jobs to leave time for school or unpaid family work, and employers structure some jobs as part-time to avoid paying fringe benefits. The increased number of jobs structured as part-time has caused growth in the number of persons who work part-time involuntarily.

Unemployment and underemployment. Throughout history, people seeking adequately paid employment usually have outnumbered jobs, leaving some would-be workers unemployed or underemployed. According to the ILO (1998, number 27, p. 6), one-third of the world's workers are underemployed (850 million persons) or unemployed (150 million persons), and unemployment is in the double digits in several countries, including Botswana, Spain, Finland, Puerto Rico, Barbados, and Poland (United Nations 1999). Globalization contributes to unemployment as multinational companies draw people in developing countries into the labor force and then put them out of work when they close plants in pursuit of cheaper labor (Dickinson 1997). In 1996, unemployment in the industrialized countries ranged from 4 percent in Norway to over 11 percent in Germany, with intermediate levels in Sweden, the United Kingdom, and the United States. (At the end of 1998, U.S. unemployment had fallen to 4.3 percent, although the rates for racial and ethnic minorities and youth were much higher.) In general, official statistics in industrialized countries underestimate unemployment by excluding "discouraged workers" who have stopped looking because they cannot find jobs for which they qualify.

Preparing for jobs. Workers' education and training affect the jobs they obtain. Schools teach vocational skills (including literacy and numeracy), inculcate traits that employers value (e.g., punctuality, ability to deal with bureaucracies), and provide credentials that signal the ability to acquire new skills. Vocational education provides skills and certification. In Germany, for example, vocational training is a major source of workers' skills. In the United States, in contrast, many workers—especially those in traditionally male blue-collar jobs—acquire most of their skills on the job, whereas professionals and clerical workers acquire their skills largely before beginning employment. Jobs in advanced industrial societies—especially high-technology jobs—tend to require both more and different kinds of skills, such as precision and flexibility, as well as formal knowledge (Hodson and Parker 1988). In postindustrial societies, knowledge and technical expertise have become increasingly important for good jobs. As a growing number of jobs require at least some college, workers without a high school diploma face difficulties finding jobs that pay well and provide advancement opportunities. Moreover, workers displaced from production jobs need new skills for reemployment, and so refraining has become increasingly important.

Job outcomes. The processes that allocate workers to occupations, employers, and jobs are important because those elements strongly affect workers' earnings. Although thousands of distinct labor markets serve different locales and occupations, to understand the job-allocation process, it is necessary to distinguish primary markets that fill jobs characterized by high wages, pleasant working conditions, the chance to acquire skills, job security, and opportunities to advance from secondary markets that fill low-paid, dead-end, low-security jobs. Firms in the primary sector fill non-entry-level jobs through internal labor markets that provide employees with "ladders" that connect their jobs to related jobs higher in the organization. The failure of secondary-market jobs to provide job ladders that reward seniority, along with low pay and poor working conditions, encourage turnover (Gordon 1972). Both statistical discrimination and prejudice disproportionately relegate certain workers—the young, inexperienced, and poorly educated; racial and ethnic minorities; immigrants; and women—to jobs filled through secondary labor markets.

WORK STRUCTURES

In classifying the paid work people do, social scientists refer to industries, occupations, establishments, and jobs. An industry is a branch of economic activity that produces specific goods or services. An establishment is a place where employees report for work, such as a firm or plant. An occupation refers to a collection of jobs involving similar activities across establishments, whereas a job is a set of similar work activities performed at a specific establishment. In 1990, the U.S. Census Bureau distinguished 503 "detailed" occupations (for example, funeral director, meter reader, x-ray technician) that it grouped into six broad categories: managerial and professional specialties; technical, sales, and administrative-support occupations; service occupations; precision production, craft, and repair occupations; operators, fabricators, and laborers; and farming, forestry, and fishing occupations. The steady growth in the number of occupations since the Industrial Revolution reflects the increasing division of labor in complex societies. This elaboration of the division of labor is more visible at the job level. The U.S. Department of Labor's *Dictionary of Occupational Titles* lists several thousand job titles, and the approximately 130 million employed Americans hold about a million different jobs.

Occupational structure. The distribution of workers across occupations in a society provides a snapshot of that society's occupational structure. Comparing societies' occupational and industrial structures at different times or across nations reveals a lot about their economic and technological development and the job opportunities available to their members. For example, in 1870, agriculture employed half of all American workers; in the 1990s, it provided jobs for about 2 percent. The effects of changing occupational and industrial structures—driven largely by the disappearance of smokestack industries and the explosion of service jobs in the United States—are expressed in the sharp decline in a worker's chances of getting a unionized skilled production job. Hit hardest by the dwindling number of these jobs are the white men who once monopolized them. In contrast, the growing number of management jobs in the United States created a record number of managerial positions in the 1990s. This growth has helped to integrate managerial jobs by sex and race.

Job segregation by sex and race. One of the most enduring features of paid work is the differential distribution of male and female and white and minority workers across lines of work and places of employment, with minorities and white women concentrated in the less desirable jobs (Carrington and Troske 1998a, 1998b). In 1990, among all gainfully employed women in the United States, 28 percent were concentrated in just 5 of the 503 detailed occupational categories—secretary, bookkeeper, manager, clerk, and registered nurse—and over half worked in just 19 of the 503 occupations distinguished by the Census Bureau. Men, in contrast, are spread more evenly across occupations: The top five—manager/administrator, production supervisor, truck driver, sales supervisor, and wholesale sales representative—accounted for 19 percent of all employed men. However, within-occupation sex segregation (many jobs share a single occupational title) means that job segregation is considerably more pervasive than is occupational segregation.

In every country, the sexes are segregated into different jobs, although the extent of occupational sex segregation varies sharply across nations: It is highest in Middle Eastern and African nations and lowest in Asian/Pacific nations (Anker 1998). In advanced industrial nations, it correlates positively with women's labor force participation, paid maternity leave, and the size of the wage gap (Rosenfeld and Kalleberg 1990). Levels of sex segregation in European countries reflect both postindustrial economic structures that concentrate women in sales and service jobs and adherence to norms of gender equality. Independent of these forces, customarily male production jobs remain outside the reach of most women, and women continue to dominate clerical occupations (Charles 1998).

The last thirty years has witnessed worldwide declines in occupational sex segregation (Anker 1998). Integration occurs primarily through women's entry into customarily male occupations rather than the reverse. Falling levels of occupational sex segregation can mask ongoing job-level segregation (Reskin and Roos 1990). Training workers for nontraditional jobs and enforcing antidiscrimination laws and affirmative-action regulations appear to be the most effective remedies for reducing sex segregation.

Occupations and jobs also are segregated by race. For example, before World War II, American blacks were concentrated in farming, service, and unskilled-labor jobs in the secondary sector of the economy, such as domestic worker, porter, and orderly. War-induced labor shortages opened the door to a wider range of jobs for blacks, and antidiscrimination regulations (especially Title VII of 1964 Civil Rights Act) further expanded blacks' opportunities. As a result, racial segregation across occupations has declined sharply in the United States since 1940, especially among women. There is little systematic cross-national research on job segregation or job discrimination by race, although scattered studies document both around the world. For example, Moroccans are excluded from semi-skilled jobs in the Netherlands, West Indians face discrimination in Canada, and Vietnamese and the aboriginal populations encounter it in Australia (ILO 1995, number 12, pp. 29–30).

Workers' experience and preferences influence where they work and what they do, but at least as important are the operation of labor markets—the mechanisms that match workers to jobs and set wages—and employers' preferences and personnel practices. Sociologists have documented the importance of personal networks for workers' employment outcomes (e.g., Fernandez and Weinberg 1997). Employers favor the use of social networks to recruit workers because of their efficiency, low cost, and ability to provide information unavailable through formal sources. However, because people's acquaintances tend to be of the same sex and race, recruiting through employees' networks effectively excludes sex- and race-atypical workers.

Layoffs and Displacement. U.S. data for the 1980s and 1990s indicate that trends in job displacement rates roughly parallel those for unemployment. Between 1993 and 1995, 12 to 15 percent of workers lost a job because their companies closed, their jobs were cut, or work was slack. Depending on economic conditions, between 25 and 40 percent of displaced workers remain jobless one to three years later, and reemployed workers typically earn less than they did in their previous jobs (Economic Report of the President 1999).

REWARDS FOR EMPLOYMENT

People seek jobs that maximize extrinsic rewards—income, prestige, the chance for promotion, and job security (Jencks et al. 1988)—as well as intrinsic rewards—satisfaction and autonomy. Earnings are the primary incentive for most workers. However, pay differs sharply across individuals and social groups. Substantial racial, sex, and ethnic inequality in pay characterize all industrial societies, although their extent depends on whether

countries permit unequal pay for equal work and the degree to which workers are segregated into unequally paying jobs on the basis of sex, race, or ethnicity. In the United States, the 1963 Equal Pay Act that outlawed wage discrimination by race, national origin, and sex and declining occupational segregation by race have reduced the racial gap in earnings among men and almost eliminated it among women. The disparity in earnings between the sexes has declined more slowly because of the resilience of sex segregation. Hence, in 1998, women employed full-time year-round earned 74 percent of the annual earnings of their male counterparts. The wage gap varies across nations (and across occupations and industries within countries). In the first half of the 1990s, pay inequality was lowest in Australia, Egypt, Kenya, Jordan, and New Zealand, where women averaged about 80 percent of what men earned, compared to a low of just 60 percent in Korea (ILO 1997, number 22). Factors that can reduce the wage gap among full-time workers include equalizing the sexes' educational attainment and labor-market experience, creating sex-integrated jobs, and implementing pay systems that compensate workers for the worth of a job without regard to its sex composition.

Occupational prestige. Social standing is conferred on persons partly on the basis of their jobs. In fact, social scientists have treated the distinction between blue-collar and white-collar jobs as a rough proxy for workers' social status. However, to capture the effects of one's type of work on one's social status, more sophisticated ways to measure occupational prestige are needed. The most commonly used is the Duncan Socioeconomic Index (SEI)(Duncan 1961), which assigns a score to each occupation on the basis of its incumbents' average educational and income levels. The occupational status hierarchy is quite stable over time and across cultures (Treiman 1977). Within societies, the occupational standing of workers is highly stratified. In the United States, for example, most workers have occupations with relatively low SEI scores.

Intrinsic rewards: job satisfaction. In advanced industrialized countries, many workers see a job as a place to find fulfillment, self-expression, and satisfaction. Workers in routine jobs try to imbue them with challenge or meaning, in part by creating a workplace culture. These adaptations contribute to the high levels of satisfaction Americans report with their jobs. Nonetheless, not all jobs are satisfying, and not all workers are satisfied. On the assumption that dissatisfied workers are less productive, employers in the United States and other advanced industrialized countries have devised strategies such as workplace democracy, job-enrichment programs, and "quality circles" to enhance job satisfaction. According to Lincoln and Kalleberg (1990), however, Japanese and German workers, who show the lowest levels of satisfaction, are among the world's most productive.

WORK AND FAMILY

In expanding the factory system, the Industrial Revolution separated work and family, creating a division of labor that mandated domestic work for women and market work for men. Although women increasingly hold paid jobs, paid employment has not exempted them from primary responsibility for domestic work. Role overload and its concomitant stresses are risks for all workers, but especially for employed mothers, who accounted for 70 percent of married mothers and 60 percent of single mothers in the United States in 1996. Women have adapted by working part-time, sacrificing leisure time, renegotiating the domestic division of labor in their families, cutting out some domestic tasks, and purchasing more services. (The trend toward purchasing more services has fueled the growth of service jobs in fast-food chains, child care, and cleaning services and thus has increased the demand for low-wage workers.) What employed parents want most is flexible scheduling (Glass and Estes 1997), although organizational pressure prevents some from taking advantage of it when it is available (Hochschild 1997).

Just as paid work competes with workers' domestic obligations, the demands of family life interfere with workers' ability to devote themselves entirely to their jobs. Thus, employers have two incentives to reduce work–family conflicts: reducing absenteeism and turnover and increasing workers' productivity and organizational commitment (Glass and Estes 1997). Many employers in advanced industrial societies have provided some of their employees with assistance with child care. The governments of most advanced industrialized countries have mandated programs such as parental leave, state-run nurseries, and guaranteed benefits for part-time workers. Among the 152 member nations of the ILO, only two advanced industrial countries provide no paid maternity leave: New Zealand and the United States (ILO 1998, number 24, pp. 18–19). Employers' increasing reliance on female workers and politicians' desire for women's support should bring more family-friendly policies and practices in the twenty-first century.

TRENDS IN WORK

Control of work. As Marx recognized, whenever different actors control the tools of production and perform work, control over the work process is potentially a matter of contention. Employers have relied on a variety of tactics to control the labor process: paternalism, close supervision, embedding control into the technology of work, deskilling work, and bureaucratic procedures such as career ladders (Edwards 1979). Workers have resisted more or less effectively through collective action, including attempts to create a monopoly of their skills or the supply of labor. At the end of the twentieth century, several factors had given employers the upper hand in the struggle for control, including the decline of labor unions in Western industrialized societies (ILO 1997, number 22, p. 7), the disappearance of lifetime job protection in formerly communist societies, an increasing technological capacity to monitor workers electronically, access to a global "reserve labor army," and the use of nonstandard employment relationships (see below).

Technological change. The history of work is a chronicle of technological innovation and its transformation of the production of goods and services. Employers invest in technology to increase productivity, contain labor costs, and control how work is done. According to some observers (e.g., Braverman 1974), employers seek technical advances in order to reduce workers' control over the labor process and employ less skilled and thus cheaper labor. Some analysts see technological change as a threat to skilled jobs; others see technology as creating more of those jobs. The development of microelectronic technology has brought this debate to the fore.

Innovations in microprocessor technology have permitted advances in information processing and robotics that are revolutionizing the production of goods and services. Robots work around the clock, perform hazardous tasks, and have low operating costs. Although technical advances enhance jobs, they also subject workers to technological control (an estimated 80 percent of U.S. workers are electronically monitored, for example [ILO 1998, no. 24, p. 25]) and, by improving productivity, lead to job losses. In industrialized nations, for example, microelectronic technology has eliminated some unskilled jobs and facilitated work transfers that shift tasks from paid workers to consumers such as banking transactions. By making it possible to export jobs to cheaper labor markets, technology has reallocated jobs from the workers who once performed them to lower-paid workers in other parts of the world. Although technological change has created jobs, it has eliminated more job—particularly less-skilled ones—than it has created and has eroded skills in middle- to low-skill jobs such as clerical work (Hodson and Parker 1988). Its creation of new highly skilled jobs has contributed to the economic polarization of workers and spurred the migration of well-educated workers from developing to advanced industrial countries (Hodson 1997).

The globalization of work. Although segments of the economy such as service work are organized locally, production work increasingly is organized in a global assembly line (Dickinson 1997). For jobs in which technology preempts skill, multinational corporations' worldwide pursuit of low-wage docile labor and microelectronic technology and cheap transportation reduce the friction associated with moving production around the globe. As a result, there has been a steady exportation of jobs from industrialized countries to the Pacific Rim, Latin America, and the Caribbean, where labor is cheap and tractable and labor laws are lenient. This redistribution of manufacturing jobs from advanced industrial nations to developing nations—fueled by the growth of multinational corporations—has given birth to an international division of labor in which the United States and other advanced industrial nations have become postindustrial societies that specialize in producing services rather than goods, while workers in less developed countries manufacture products, often under unsafe conditions. For example, between 1980 and 1993, semi-industrialized and industrialized countries in the Americas and Europe lost 30 to 70 percent of their jobs in the textile and footwear industries, while African and Asian countries have experienced astronomical job growth in those industries (ILO 1996, vol. number 18). Be-

tween 1970 and 1990, the number of textile and footwear jobs doubled, tripled, or more in Korea, Indonesia, Sri Lanka, Bangladesh, and Malaysia where production workers earn from one-fifth to one-half as much as do their counterparts in advanced industrial countries. Meanwhile job growth in developing countries leads to the disproportionate employment of teenagers and young adult women, who work for lower pay than do adult men.

Just as jobs move in search of cheaper workers, workers move in search of better-paying jobs. Often, however, the outcome of this migration is low-skilled, low-paid employment in domestic or service work. However, skilled technical and professional jobs also draw workers in global migration streams. In the mid-1990s, according to the ILO (1995, number 13), 70 million immigrants—most from the Third World—resided in countries other than their nations of birth. The globalization of competition among employers has made workers on different continents into competitors for jobs, held down wages, and militated against campaigns to improve working conditions in Third World establishments while eroding job security in First World production facilities (Hodson and Parker 1988; Dickinson 1997).

The externalization of work and the erosion of jobs. By the middle of the twentieth century, the normative employment relationship between employers and workers had become standardized in many industrialized societies. This standard employment arrangement typically involves the exchange of labor by a worker for a fixed rate of pay (hourly wages or a weekly, monthly, or annual salary) from an employer, with the labor performed on a preset schedule—usually full-time—at the employer's place of business, under the employer's control, and often with the shared expectation of continued employment. However, to cut costs and enhance flexibility, employers are increasingly "externalizing" work in terms of physical location administrative control and the duration of employment (Pfeffer and Baron 1988).

This externalization is seen in the increasing number of persons working for pay at home and the growth of nonstandard employment relationships (Barker and Christensen 1998). Neither homework nor nonstandard employment relations are new. Only after unions won the right to bargain collectively and statutory rights protecting workers did homework and nonstandard employment relations give way to standard employment relationship in advanced industrialized countries. In the 1990s, however, the trend seemed to have reversed. In 1995, for example, eight million Americans, at least two million Europeans, six million Filipinos, and one million Japanese worked for pay at home. Millions of these homeworkers telecommute (ILO 1998, number 27, p. 23). Many workers, especially women, opt for homework as a way to earn wages while supervising their children (Jurik 1998). However, part of the price of this flexibility is a lack of protection by health and safety regulations or maximum-hours rules, and these workers are outside the reach of organizing efforts. In addition, whether homework involves children is difficult to monitor even in countries strongly opposed to child labor (ILO 1995).

Work is externalized in a second way: Firms contract with individuals for specific duties (independent contractors) or with intermediary organizations that employ workers rather than directly employing all the persons who do work for them. Although contracting has long been common for some forms of work (e.g., agricultural labor), employers around the world are increasingly contracting out jobs formerly done by their own employees in everything from construction and manufacturing to human resources and security. Worldwide, more than one in four service workers are contract laborers. By outsourcing these functions to contract workers or independent contractors, employers avoid the obligation to provide long-term employment and short-circuit protective labor laws that apply to employees. Other nonstandard employment relationships include temporary work and part-time work, both of which disproportionately employ women, members of racial and ethnic minorities, and young workers.

The growth of nonstandard employment relationships has led some observers to predict an end to work organized through standard employment relations or the bifurcation of employment relations, with firms hiring core workers who enjoy the benefits of standard employment and creating explicitly temporary connections with peripheral workers who lack benefits and job security (Smith 1997; Leicht 1998). According to the U.S. Bureau of Labor Statistics, the proportion of U.S. workers in nonstandard work is slowly increasing (Barker and Christensen 1998). In summary, employment relations must be seen as falling on a continuum from long-term attachments under bureaucratic control to weak connections of uncertain duration (Pfeiser and Baron 1988). Most research on work and occupations in industrial societies has dealt with the former end of the continuum. Technological change and globalization are shifting jobs—even in industrial countries—toward the latter end.

REFERENCES

Anker, Richard 1998 *Gender and Jobs: Sex Segregation of Occupations in the World*. Geneva: International Labour Office.

Barker, Kathleen, and Kathleen Christensen 1998 *Contingent Work: American Employment Relations in Transition*. Ithaca, N.Y.: Cornell University Press.

Carrington, William J., and Kenneth R. Troske 1998a "Sex Segregation across U.S. Manufacturing Firms." *Industrial and Labor Relations Review* 51:445–464.

——, and Kenneth R. Troske 1998b "Interfirm Segregation and the Black/White Wage Gap." *Journal of Labor Economics* 16:231–260.

Charles, Maria 1998 "Structure, Culture, and Sex Segregation in Europe." *Research in Social Stratification and Mobility* 16:89–116.

Dickinson, Torry D. 1997 "Selective Globalization: The Relocation of Industrial Production and the Shaping of Women's Work." In Randy Hodson, ed., *Research in the Sociology of Work–Globalization of Work*, vol. 6. Greenwich Conn.: JAI Press.

Duncan, Otis Dudley 1961 "A Socioeconomic Index for All Occupations." In Albert J. Reiss, Otis Dudley Duncan, Paul K. Hatt, and Cecil C. North, eds., *Occupations and Social Status* New York: Free Press.

Economic Report of the President 1999 Washington, D.C.: U.S. Government Printing Office.

Edwards, Richard 1979 *Contested Terrain: The Transformation of the Workplace in the Twentieth Century*. New York: Basic Books.

Fernandez, Roberto M., and Nancy Weinberg 1997 "Sifting and Sorting: Personal Contacts and Hiring in a Retail Bank." *American Sociological Review* 62:883–902.

Glass, Jennifer L., and Sarah Beth Estes 1997 "The Family Responsive Workplace." *Annual Review of Sociology* 21:289–313.

Gordon, David M. 1972 *Theories of Poverty and Unemployment*. Lexington, Mass.: Lexington Books.

Hochschild, Arlie 1997 *The Time Bind: When Work Becomes Home and Home Becomes Work*. New York: Metropolitan.

Hodson, Randy 1997 "Introduction: Work from a Global Perspective." In Randy Hodson, ed., *Research in the Sociology of Work–Globalization of Work*, vol. 6. Greenwich Conn.: JAI Press.

——, and Robert E. Parker 1988 "Work in High Tech Settings—A Literature Review." In Richard L. Simpson and Ida Harper Simpson, eds., Research in the Sociology of Work, vol 4. Greenwich Conn.: JAI Press.

International Labor Organization 1995 *Homework*. Report for the eighty-two seconnd Session of the International Labour Conference, ILO, Geneva, Switzerland.

—— 1995–1998 *World of Work: The Magazine of the ILO*. Selected issues as noted: Geneva, Switzerland.

Jencks, Christopher, Lauri Perman, and Lee Rainwater 1988. "What Is a Good Job? A New Measure of Labor-Market Success." *American Journal of Sociology* 93:1322–57.

Jurik, Nancy 1998 "Getting Away and Getting By: The Experiences of Self-Employed Homeworkers." *Work and Occupations* 25:7–35.

Leicht, Kevin 1998 "Work (If You Can Get It) and Occupations (If There Are Any)? What Social Scientists Can Learn from Predictions of the End of Work and Radical Workplace Change." *Work and Occupations* 25:36–48.

Lincoln, James R., and Arne L. Kalleberg 1990 *Culture, Control and Commitment: A Study of Work Organization and Work Attitudes in the U.S. and Japan*. New York: Cambridge University Press.

Pfeffer, Jeffrey, and James N. Baron 1988 "Taking the Workers Back Out: Recent Trends in the Structuring of Employment." *Research in Organizational Behavior* 10:257–303.

Reskin, Barbara F., and Patricia A. Roos 1990 *Job Queues, Gender Queues: Explaining Women's Inroads into Male Occupations*. Philadelphia: Temple University Press.

Rosenfeld, Rachel A., and Arne L. Kalleberg 1990 "A Cross-National Comparison of the Gender Gap in Income." *American Journal of Sociology* 96:69–106.

Smith, Vickie 1997 "New Forms of Work Organization." *Annual Review of Sociology* 21:315–339.

Treiman, Donald J. 1977 *Occupational Prestige in Comparative Perspective*. New York: Academic Press.

United Nations 1999 Statistics Division Home Page, Social Indicators Home Page. wwww.un.org/depts/unsd/social.

BARBARA F. RESKIN

WORK ORIENTATION

The sociology of work emerged as a specialty area in the 1980s, when the American Sociological Association prepared a compendium of course syllabi for the area and a number of textbooks appeared. The name of this sociological subfield is new, but the general area is not. The sociology of work represents an integration of two long-standing specialties: industrial sociology and occupations/professions. It also draws from industrial and organizational psychologists and sociologists' attempts to integrate stratification and organization literatures to better understand the employment relationship.

The study of the employment relationship encompasses a multitude of topics ranging from how the individual is initially matched to a job to all that happens on the job (being paid, becoming satisfied or dissatisfied, forming cliques, etc.) and to turnover (quitting or being dismissed). Considered important to these topics are the orientations employees have toward their work, the topic of this article.

Definitions of work abound, but most include the following features. First, although groups or collectivities may be viewed as actors involved in work (e.g., work groups, task groups, teams, or committees), the focus of attention, and therefore the unit of analysis, is usually the individual. Second, the individual is involved in physical or mental activity. Third, this activity usually involves some form of payment, but pay is not necessary for an activity to be considered work. This allows people involved in housekeeping activities to be included, along with family members who labor to support a family enterprise and volunteer helpers. Fourth, the activity involves the production or creation of something. Fifth, this usually is a good or service. Sixth, this good or service is valued by the individual or others and thus usually is consumed by either or both. Work thus is defined as the mental or physical activity of an individual directed toward the production of goods or services that are valued by that individual or others.

"Orientation to work," unfortunately, is a term without a clear or precise meaning. Generally, it is used to refer to two broad areas: (1) motivation to work and (2) responses to work. The first area covers why people work and for some time has occupied the attention of industrial and organizational psychologists, who analyze need hierarchies, self-actualization, and intrinsic and extrinsic motivations. The second area has more often attracted the attention of sociologists. It takes the activity of work as given and addresses the ways in which individuals react to it. Job satisfaction and commitment have been given the most attention when sociologists study reactions to work.

This article is organized around work motivation and responses to work, but it places those topics the context of the social organization of the workplace. With only a few exceptions, work occurs in a social setting that has been called a "contested terrain" by Edwards (1979). Sociologists want to go beyond strictly individualistic portrayals of human behavior and are especially interested in understanding how this social setting, the workplace, affects an individual's work orientation. The explanations of this influence, often referred to as social control arguments, are discussed here. Finally, gender differences in work orientations need to be addressed. However, because the concept of alienation is related to job dissatisfaction and has been so prevalent in sociological accounts of work, it is considered first.

ALIENATION

Sociologists continue to draw from Marx in referring to an alienated individual as being separated or estranged from certain aspects of work that give meaning and significance to that work and to life as a whole. For Marx, these aspects of work are control over the product, control over the work process, creative activity, and social relations with others. Clearly, a negative side of work is portrayed when alienation is the concept of interest.

A survey of journals and sociology of work texts over the past several decades suggests that sociologists have lost interest in this concept. For example, indexes for 1980s texts (e.g., Kalleberg and Berg 1987) do not include the term "alienation," and the Price and Mueller (1986) handbook on the measurement of major organization concepts does not devote a chapter to alienation. Even in 1990s texts and anthologies (e.g., Hodson and Sullivan 1995; Wharton 1998), alienation is given only limited attention.

This does not mean that interest in alienation is dead. Three things have happened. First, interest has shifted to conceptualizing and measuring positively worded concepts such as like job satisfaction. Second, scholars have moved away from the picture of capitalist work settings universally producing alienated workers and gone on to formulate a picture of multidimensional work settings and multimotivated employees who respond to work in varying ways. Third, out of this more pluralistic image of work, several concepts—for example, work motivation, self-actualization, job satisfaction and commitment—have emerged in an attempt to bring more precision to descriptions of how individuals are oriented to their work. Thus, alienation has been absorbed into several other concepts.

A particular line of research has implications for understanding alienation: Following more a Marxian picture of work, it has been assumed that the more formal and bureaucratic the workplace is, the more alienated (dissatisfied) the workers are. This assumption has been challenged with the argument that formal rules and regulations actually increase satisfaction in the workplace because they provide guidelines that apply to all and thus protect workers from arbitrary and unfair treatment. Although workers may not like the rules, the authority system is perceived as legitimate because all workers are treated according to the same formal rules. Research supports this more positive portrayal of formal rules and regulations.

WORK MOTIVATION

Historically, sociologists have flirted with psychological concepts such as work motivation and work involvement and have disagreed about the relevance of those concepts to the study of social phenomena. For example, among the authors of the sociology of work textbooks in the past two decades, only Hall (1986) gives critical attention to the theoretical and empirical literature on the topic. Any treatment of work orientation must include this material, however, because most current literature is an offshoot of or a reaction to those theories.

Work motivation is the internal force that activates people to do the work associated with their jobs. Two theoretical traditions have been dominant. First, need theories argue that individuals are motivated by internal needs that usually develop early in life and often are not consciously recognized. Maslow (1954) identified a hierarchy of needs and claimed that higher-order needs (goals) cannot be met until lower-order needs are met sequentially. This hierarchy begins at the bottom with basic physiological needs and ends at the top with self-actualization. Others have modified Maslow's hierarchy into a continuum with fewer levels and with the idea that lower-order needs may reemerge at later stages as unmet. Herzberg (1966) was more interested in job satisfaction and argued that individuals are motivated by two types of factors: "Motivators" are the more intrinsic features of work, such as responsibility, advancement, and achievement, whereas "hygiene" factors characterize the workplace and include pay, job security, and working conditions. When motivators are present, employees are satisfied, but if they are absent, employees are not. When the hygiene factors are present, employees are neither dissatisfied nor satisfied, but when they are absent, employees are dissatisfied. McClelland (1961) argued that certain socialization environments produce a need for achievement and that individuals socialized in that manner strive for excellence in whatever they undertake. Management scholars were especially interested in this theory since it suggested who should be hired or promoted. Finally, McGregor (1960) argued that assumptions about human nature and motivation have resulted in two approaches to organizational design. Theory X is based on the assumption that individuals are basically lazy and are motivated primarily by extrinsic rewards such as pay. Theory Y assumes that humans act responsibly and contribute their skills and talents when their intrinsic needs, such as self-actualization, are met. This distinction is not unlike the classic dichotomy between functionalist and Marxian portrayals of society and human nature.

Overall, these need theories have lost favor. The empirical support is weak, the use in applied settings has proved difficult because of problems associated with measuring need levels and attempting to alter personality patterns that have developed in childhood, and the significance of the environment has been neglected.

The second dominant perspective—expectancy theory—comes from organizational and industrial psychologists. It bypasses the issue of needs and emphasizes cognitive and rational processes. The underlying assumption is that motivations to work vary substantially from one individual to the next and are mutable across time and space (Vroom 1964; Lawler 1973). Motivations reflect the interplay of effort, expectations about outcomes, and the importance or value given to those outcomes. Put another way, a person's motivation to behave in a particular way is a function of the expected results and how valuable those results are to that person. Until recently, this theory has been dominant in studying work motivation in industrial and organizational psychology.

Sociologists are generally aware of these motivation theories and, like psychologists, now give less attention to need theories. However, unlike psychologists, they have not been overly interested in the theories per se of work motivation. In fact, psychologists have led the way in developing theories of motivation, and sociologists usually are a generation behind in adopting or rejecting those theories. For example, Smither (1988) mentions equity, behavioral, and goal-setting theories as receiving much attention in the psychological work motivation literature. Although equity theory has been explored for some time experimentally by sociologists, there is no evidence that sociologists have adopted in significant way any of these "newer" approaches to work motivation. What sociologists do in practice matches the expectancy model more closely. The picture is one in which "the fit" of an individual's characteristics and expectations with the actual work conditions forms the basis for whether that individual is motivated.

What sociologists have emphasized instead of motivation theory is socialization to work, that is, how individuals learn their work roles. This is not surprising given the long-standing interest of both sociologists and social psychologists in socialization processes. One stream of thought in this area concerns socialization into professional roles, where a popular strategy is to examine career stages. Another approach is represented by the work of Kohn and Schooler (1982), who not only argue for the intergenerational class-based transmission of work values but also propound and demonstrate reciprocal effects: An individual's work orientations (e.g., self-direction) are affected by job conditions, but those orientations also affect the kinds of jobs with which the individual is associated.

RESPONSE TO WORK: JOB SATISFACTION

Although the wording of definitions for "job satisfaction" has varied dramatically across disciplines and scholars, there is a near consensus on what the concept is. Smith et al. (1969) succinctly define it as the degree to which individuals like their jobs. The common element across definitions like this is the idea of the individual positively responding emotionally or affectively to the job.

The major issues in the study of job satisfaction are (1) What produces job satisfaction? (2) What are the consequences of differing levels of job satisfaction? and (3) Is it a global or unitary concept, or should facets (dimensions) of it be investigated?

Two dominant arguments exist regarding the determinants of job satisfaction. The first is that an individual's job satisfaction is determined by the dispositions or "personality" traits that an employee brings to the workplace. In simple terms, individuals vary along a continuum from a negative to a positive orientation. These dispositions are reflected in a person's responses to work conditions as well as to aspects of life such as family satisfaction and more general life satisfaction. The second argument is considered more "sociological" and emphasizes the importance of the work conditions an employee experiences. This approach is closer to a Marxian perspective in that it is the structural conditions of the workplace that make work rewarding or not rewarding; any individual dispositional differences that exist wane in importance in the face of these structural features.

Although sociologists give lip service to the disposition argument, the literature unequivocally documents a stronger interest in identifying the features of work that affect job satisfaction. Within this perspective, however, there is considerable disagreement about which features of work are important. One major debate concerns whether extrinsic (e.g., pay and fringe benefits) or intrinsic (e.g., self-actualization and task variety) features of work are more important. Following a needs framework or arguments from neoclassical economics about economic rationality leads one to argue that the extrinsic features must exist before the intrinsic features become important. In contrast, an expectancy argument would state that any of these features can be important and that it is the fit of what is found in the workplace with what the individual expects and values that is crucial in determining the satisfaction level. A popular argument that has an expectancy logic associated with it comes from the justice literature. A theme common to all distributive justice theories is that an individual compares his or her actual reward with what is believed to be just or fair. Individuals expect a just reward and are dissatisfied if a reward is unjust. Another frequently used general perspective for understanding the effect of work conditions on job satisfaction is social exchange theory, which also relies on an expectancy logic. As developed initially by Homans (1958) in the study of small groups and extended to the study of organizations by Blau (1964), exchange theory argues that individuals enter social relations in anticipation of rewards or benefits in exchange for their inputs and/or investments in the relationship. Simply put, workers are satisfied with their jobs if the rewards they value and expect are given to them in exchange for their work effort and performance.

It is impossible to summarize here the thousands of studies conducted on the determinants of job satisfaction. Instead, a list of variables that have been found to have some relationship with job satisfaction is provided (the sign indicates the direction of the relationship with regard to satisfaction): variety (+), pay (+), autonomy (+), instrumental communication (+), role conflict (−), role overload (−), work group cohesion (+), work involvement (+), distributive justice (+), promotional opportunities (+), supervisory support (+), task significance (+), and external job opportunities (−). Spector (1997) provides a more complete account of the determinants and correlates of job satisfaction.

The debate over which work conditions affect job satisfaction continues to direct the research of sociologists, but a more interesting question involves the disposition versus situation debate. Sociologists devote much effort to cataloging and operationalizing the objective structural features of work, and little attention is given to identifying and measuring the dispositional traits of individuals. Evidence, however, continues to mount that individuals exhibit basic dispositional traits (e.g., negative and positive affectivity) that are relatively stable throughout their lifetimes and over different employment situations (Watson and Clark 1984). This research strongly suggests that workers with positive dispositions usually are more satisfied with their jobs regardless of the work conditions, while those with negative dispositions seem not to be satisfied with anything.

Another issue concerns the consequences of job satisfaction. Two outcomes have received the most attention, primarily because of their practical significance to any business enterprise: job performance and withdrawal behavior, which includes absenteeism and voluntary turnover. The satisfaction–performance argument is of long-standing interest and thus has generated considerable empirical data. The hypothesis is that satisfaction is positively and causally related to productivity, and support is provided by meta-analyses showing a positive correlation of .25. In short, satisfied workers perform better, but the relationship is not a strong one. The weakness of this relationship could be due to the difficulties associated with measuring job performance, however.

With regard to the satisfaction–withdrawal relationship, the hypothesis is that the most satisfied employees will be the least often absent and the least likely to quit voluntarily. The meta-analyses for the satisfaction–absenteeism relationship suggest that the relationship is between -.10 and -.15, which is weak at best. The findings for the satisfaction–turnover relationship are stronger (meta-analysis correlation of -.25), but the conclusion is that job satisfaction serves more of a mediating function. That is, the structural features of work (e.g., promotional opportunities) and employee characteristics (e.g., education) directly affect job satisfaction (and commitment), which in turn affects turnover.

The final issue here is whether job satisfaction is a unitary concept or is a complex of many facets or dimensions. Since a fairly large number of work features are known to affect job satisfaction, it is logical to expect that individuals can be satisfied with some of these but not others. The data support this logic. In particular, there is evidence that for almost any distinct feature of the work situation—pay, autonomy, variety, work group cohesion, feedback—satisfaction scales can be developed that divide into distinct (but related) factors along these dimensions. This poses not only a theoretical problem but also a scale construction problem. As a simple example, a person may be satisfied with the pay but not satisfied with feed-

back about job performance. Combining scores for these two factors will show the person to be neither satisfied nor dissatisfied for the composite scale. In such situations, the rule of thumb is that scales developed to measure various satisfaction dimensions should not be combined. However, global job satisfaction scales—those which ask more generally about liking one's job—can be used to represent a person's general affective reaction to a job. Sociologists more often use these global scales and assume that work is experienced and responded to globally.

The facet approach clearly becomes more important in applied research. If an employer wishes to alter the work setting to increase job satisfaction, a global scale will be only somewhat helpful; a scale that captures satisfaction with pay, routinization, communication, and the like, will provide the information necessary to implement specific structural changes. Numerous established measures of job satisfaction, both global and facet-based, exist (see Cook et al. 1981; Price and Mueller 1986; Spector 1997).

RESPONSE TO WORK: WORK COMMITMENT

Although some concepts, such as Dubin's (1956) central life interest and Lodahl and Kejner's (1965) job involvement, go back more than three decades, most of the interest in work commitment has emerged fairly recently, to a large extent during a time when interest in job satisfaction has been diminishing. If employee commitment is defined as the level of attachment to some component or aspect of work, the door is opened to a large number of types of commitment. The most common strategy adopted for understanding various types of commitment is to differentiate between the components and the foci of commitment.

There are numerous potential foci of commitment, with those receiving the most attention being commitment to work, the career, the organization, the job, and the union. It is organizational commitment, however, that has received the most theoretical and empirical attention (Mueller et al. 1992). Considerable interest exists in how workers form and manage their commitments to multiple foci (Hunt and Morgan 1994; Lawler 1992; Wallace 1995). For example, if a worker is strongly committed to his or her career, will this translate into a similarly strong commitment to his or her employer (organization)? Although some suggest that commitment is a zero-sum phenomenon by which commitment to an employer must decline if commitment to one's career increases, research consistently shows that most commitments to multiple foci are positively related.

Three components of commitment have received the most attention (Meyer and Allen 1997): affective commitment, continuance commitment, and normative commitment. *Affective* commitment refers to a worker's emotional attachment to an organization. Organizational and industrial psychologists are given credit for initiating interest in this concept. They argue that commitment intervenes between various features of work and individual characteristics and the outcomes of absenteeism and voluntary turnover. Sociologists (e.g., Lincoln and Kalleberg 1990) tend to see the structural conditions of work as the ultimate causes of affective commitment. The evidence generally is consistent with the claims from both disciplines (Hom and Griffeth 1995; Mueller and Price 1990). *Continuance* commitment treats a person's degree of attachment as a function of the costs associated with leaving an organization. In practice, it has been operationalized as the employee's stated intention to stay (or leave). This form of organizational commitment can be traced back to Becker's (1960) side-bet theory. Individuals are portrayed as making investments (e.g., seniority, a pension fund, coworkers as friends) when they are employed in a particular organization. These side bets accumulate with tenure and thus become costs associated with taking employment elsewhere. An employee will discontinue employment only when the rewards associated with another job outweigh the accumulated side bets associated with the current one. Although the evidence for the reasoning behind this theory has not been supported, research has consistently shown a relatively strong negative relationship (meta-analysis correlation of -.50) between intent to stay and voluntary turnover. Much of the literature identifies intentions to stay or leave as intervening between affective commitment and turnover. *Normative* commitment refers to the felt obligation to stay with an employer. Remaining attached to an organization is what one should do even if one is not emotionally attached or has only a limited investment.

Without question, affective organizational commitment has dominated the scholarly interest of those who study organizational commitment. It is strongly positively related to job satisfaction and negatively related to absenteeism and turnover. These relationships indicate the importance of studying and understanding employee commitment not only to address the practical issues confronting human resource managers but also to address classical sociological concerns about the "glue" that holds social groups together.

SOCIAL CONTROL IN THE WORKPLACE

This article began with a description of the workplace as a contested terrain, a social setting in which employer and employee struggle for control. The image that comes from most economists is that monetary rewards are what motivate both employers and employees: Employers want to maximize profits, and workers want high pay for their work. The implication of this for workers is that they will be satisfied and committed if their pay is high, and if it is not, they can quit to take another job. This argument and causal linkage have been challenged both empirically and theoretically in sociology. There are three issues here. First, as was alluded to above, pay is only one of many factors that affect satisfaction and commitment. Second, employers, not workers, historically have had the upper hand in controlling the workplace and establishing the employment relationship. Third, job satisfaction and commitment can and are manipulated by employers to increase productivity and retain employees. There have been several different historical accounts of how this employer control occurs (e.g., Clawson 1980; Edwards 1979; Jacoby 1985; Vallas 1993), but two basic models dominate the literature. They can be differentiated by whether the social control is direct or indirect and by the importance given to worker satisfaction and commitment in the control process.

The historically dominant model of the workplace portrays direct control of workers by the employer. Direct supervisory monitoring, "machine control," and strictly defined divisions of labor are used to control the behavior of employees. In such instances, job satisfaction and organizational commitment may emerge to increase performance, but they are viewed as secondary to the direct control that is essential to maximizing workers' productivity. The other model relies much less on direct supervision and control by the production process and instead argues that high-performance employees are controlled *indirectly* by manipulating work structures that in turn produce satisfied and committed workers. It is the satisfied and committed workers, then, who will be the most productive. Lincoln and Kalleberg (1990) argue for this model (called the "corporatist" model) in their study of U.S. and Japanese workers. Concretely, they find that organizational structures that facilitate participation, integration, individual mobility, and legitimacy result in more satisfied and committed employees. This sociological interest in workplace control has practical implications. The same dichotomy is recognized in human resource management (HRM), where the direct strategy is called the control strategy and the indirect strategy is called the commitment strategy (Arther 1994). Similarly, in education, concern with low achievement scores among U.S. students has resulted in a debate over the organizational design of schools (Rowan 1990). The more direct approach, also called the control strategy, is based on an elaborate system of bureaucratic controls for regulating classroom teaching and standardizing student learning opportunities and outcomes. The more indirect approach, also called the commitment strategy, rejects bureaucratic controls and standards and argues instead for innovative working arrangements that support teachers' decision making and increase their involvement in the tasks of teaching. The claim for the second approach is that satisfied and committed teachers are critical to improving student performance. Without question, then, worker satisfaction and commitment still constitute a major component in the critical debates about social control in the workplace, worker productivity, and societal outcomes such as student achievement.

GENDER DIFFERENCES

Associated with the increase in sociological interest in gender inequalities over the last three decades has been an increased concern with whether the work orientations of women and men are different. Two questions have received considerable attention. One concerns whether women and men have different work values, and the other refers to what is called the gender job satisfaction paradox.

Research consistently has shown that women are just as satisfied (and often more satisfied) with their jobs as their male counterparts are. This is viewed as a paradox because women's jobs are on the average "worse" jobs with lower pay, less autonomy, and fewer advancement opportunities. Several arguments have been offered to account for this paradox (Phelan 1994; Mueller and Wallace 1996). Justice-related arguments center on (1) women accepting their lower rewards because of their lower inputs, (2) women being socialized to accept the idea that lower rewards are all they are entitled to, and (3) women being satisfied because they are comparing their rewards to those of other women, who also receive less. The consensus seems to be that the "other women as referent" explanation best explains the paradox. The major competing explanation is that women and men value different aspects of work. This leads directly to the question of gender differences in work values.

Probably the most popular explanation for the gender satisfaction paradox is that men value extrinsic rewards (e.g., pay, benefits, and authority) more than women do, while women value intrinsic rewards (e.g., social support) more than men do. As a consequence, women are not less satisfied when they receive less pay and are promoted less often than are men. Research findings strongly reject this argument, however. Women and men hold essentially the same workplace values (Hodson 1989; Phelan 1994; Mueller and Wallace 1996; Rowe and Snizek 1995; Ross and Mirowski 1995).

These similar workplace values do not mean, however, that men have the same degree of work–family conflict as do women. Research shows that this conflict is greater for women (Glass and Estes 1997). This finding only adds to the paradox: If women have worse jobs and experience more work–family conflict, why are they so satisfied with their jobs?

THE FUTURE

The last two decades in the United States have witnessed considerable change in the workplace. Organizations have downsized, hired more temporary (contingent) workers, and outsourced production tasks to become more flexible in competing in an increasingly global marketplace. In addition, the income gap between the top and bottom segments of society has grown, labor union membership has declined to an all-time low, and although unemployment continues to be low, job expansion has occurred mainly in the service sector, where many jobs do not have advancement potential. All this suggests that in the future workers can expect to move from employer to employer more often. Also, workers can expect to find that their employers are less concerned with whether employees are satisfied and less interested in gaining a long-term commitment from them. As a consequence, occupational or career commitment may become a more important motivating factor for workers than is organizational commitment or job satisfaction. Without doubt, this changing landscape for the employment relationship will keep sociologists interested in studying and understanding work values, job satisfaction, and commitment.

REFERENCES

Arther, J. B. 1994 "Effects of Human Resource Systems on Manufacturing Performance and Turnover." *Academy of Management Journal* 37:670–687.

Becker, Howard 1960 "Notes on the Concept of Commitment." *American Sociological Review* 66:32–40.

Blau, Peter M. 1964 *Exchange and Power in Social Life.* New York: Wiley.

Clawson, Dan 1980 *Bureaucracy and the Labor Process.* New York: Monthly Review.

Cook, John, Susan Hepworth, Toby Wall and Peter Warr 1981 *The Experience of Work.* New York: Academic Press.

Dubin, Robert 1956 "Industrial Workers' Worlds: A Study of the Central Life Interests of Industrial Workers." *Social Problems* 3:131–142.

Edwards, Richard 1979 *Contested Terrain.* New York: Basic Books.

Glass, Jennifer L., and Sarah Beth Estes 1997 "The Family Responsive Workplace." *Annual Review of Sociology* 23:289–313.

Hall, Richard 1986 *Dimensions of Work.* Beverly Hills, Calif.: Sage.

Herzberg, Frederick 1966 *Work and the Nature of Man.* Cleveland: World.

Hodson, Randy, and Teresa Sullivan 1995 *The Social Organization of Work.* Belmont, Calif.: Wadsworth.

——— 1989 "Gender Differences in Job Satisfaction: Why Aren't Women More Dissatisfied?" *Sociological Quarterly* 30:385–399.

Hom, Peter W., and Rodger W. Griffeth 1995 *Employee Turnover.* Cincinnati: South-Western College Publishing.

Homans, George C. 1958 "Human Behavior as Exchange." *American Journal of Sociology* 63:597–606.

Hunt, Shelby D., and Robert M. Morgan 1994 "Organizational Commitment: One of Many Commitments or Key Mediating Construct?" *Academy of Management Journal* 37:1568–1587.

Jacoby, Sanford 1985 *Employing Bureaucracy.* New York: Columbia University Press.

Kalleberg, Arne, and Ivar Berg 1987 *Work and Industry.* New York: Plenum.

Kohn, Melvin, and Carmi Schooler 1982 "Job Conditions and Personality: A Longitudinal Assessment of Their Reciprocal Effects." *American Journal of Sociology* 87:1257–1286.

Lawler, Edward III. 1973. *Motivation in Work Organizations.* Monterey, Calif.: Brooks/Cole.

Lawler, Edward J. 1992 "Affective Attachments to Nested Groups: A Choice-Process Theory." *American Sociological Review* 57:327–339.

Lincoln, James, and Arne Kalleberg 1990 *Culture, Control and Commitment: A Study of Work Organization and Work Attitudes in the United States and Japan.* Cambridge, UK: Cambridge University Press.

Lodahl, Thomas, and Mathilde Kejner 1965 "The Definition and Measurement of Job Involvement." *Journal of Applied Psychology* 49:24–33.

Maslow, Abraham 1954 *Motivation and Personality.* New York: Van Nostrand Rheinhold.

McClelland, David 1961 *The Achieving Society.* New York: Van Nostrand.

McGregor, Douglas 1960 *The Human Side of Enterprise.* New York: McGraw-Hill.

Meyer, John P., and Natalie J. Allen 1997 *Commitment in the Workplace: Theory, Research and Application.* Thousand Oaks, Calif.: Sage.

Mueller, Charles W., and James Price 1990 "Economic, Psychological, and Sociological Determinants of Voluntary Turnover." *Journal of Behavioral Economics* 26:2181–2199.

———, and Jean E. Wallace 1996 "Justice and the Paradox of the Contented Female Worker." *Social Psychology Quarterly* 59:338–349.

———,———, and James L. Price 1992 "Employee Commitment: Resolving Some Issues." *Work and Occupations* 19:211–236.

Phelan, Jo 1994 "The Paradox of the Contented Female Worker: An Assessment of Alternative Explanations." *Social Psychological Quarterly* 57:95–107.

Price, James, and Charles W. Mueller 1986 *Handbook of Organizational Measurement*. Cambridge, Mass.: Ballinger.

Ross, Catherine, and John Mirowski 1996 "Economic and Interpersonal Work Rewards: Subjective Utilities of Men's and Women's Compensation." *Social Forces* 75:223–246.

Rowan, B. 1990. "Commitment and Control: Alternative Strategies for the Organizational Design of Schools." In C. Cazden, ed., *Review of Research in Education*. Washington, D.C.: American Educational Research Association.

Rowe, Rcba, and William Snizek 1996 "Gender Differences in Work Values: Perpetuating the Myth." *Work and Occupations* 22:215–229.

Smith, Patricia, Lorne Kendall, and Charles Hullin 1969 *The Measurement of Satisfaction in Work and Retirement*. Chicago: Rand McNally.

Smither, Robert 1988 *The Psychology of Work and Human Performance*. New York: Harper and Row.

Spector, Paul E. 1997 *Job Satisfaction: Application, Assessment, Causes, and Consequences*. Thousand Oaks, Calif.: Sage.

Vallas, Steven P. 1993 *Power in the Workplace*. Albany: State University of New York Press.

Vroom, Victor 1964 *Work and Motivation*. New York: Wiley.

Wallace, Jean E. 1995 "Professionals in Bureaucracies: A Case of Proletarianization or Adaptation?" *Administrative Science Quarterly* 40:228–255.

Watson, David, and Lee Clark 1984 "Negative Affectivity: The Disposition to Experience Aversive Emotional States." *Psychological Bulletin* 96:465–490.

Wharton, Amy 1998 *Working in America*. Mountain View, Calif.: Mayfield.

CHARLES W. MUELLER

WORLD RELIGIONS

Religious life throughout the world, regardless of the specific tradition, exhibits both personal-psychological and communal-social aspects. Of course, persons within the diverse religious traditions of the world perceive the spiritual dimension of their faith as transcending both the individual psychological and emotional as well as the corporate and social aspects of their faith's expressions. Nonetheless, two major academic strands of religious studies over the last century have focused primarily on either the psychological (e.g., James 1961; Freud 1928; Jung 1938) or the social (e.g., Weber 1963; Durkheim 1965; Wach 1958) dimensions of religion. An Oglala Lakota's ("Sioux" in Algonquian) vision reveals these two interactive aspects of religion.

The Plains Indians in America were noted for their vision quests, and periods of fasting and life-cycle rituals often were associated with those quests. However, the vision of Black Elk, a Lakota shaman, occurred spontaneously when he was 9 years old and was stricken by fever and other physical maladies (Neidardt 1972, pp. 17–39). His vision began with two men dressed in traditional garb but shaped like slanting arrows coming from the sky to get him. As a little cloud descended around him, the young Black Elk rose into the sky and disappeared into a large cloud bank. He saw an expansive white plain across which he was led by a beautiful bay horse. As he looked in the four directions, he saw twelve black horses in the West, twelve white horses in the North, twelve sorrel horses in the East, and twelve buckskin horses in the South. After the arrival of Black Elk, the horses formed into lines and formations to lead him to the "Grandfathers." As this heavenly equine parade proceeded, horses appeared everywhere, dancing and frolicking and changing into all types of animals, such as buffalo, deer, and wild birds. Ahead lay a large teepee.

As Black Elk entered the rainbow door of the tepee, he saw six old men sitting in a row. As he stood before the seated figures, he was struck by the fact that the old men reminded him of the ancient hills and stars. The oldest spoke, saying, "Your grandfathers all over the world are having a council, and they have called you here to teach you." Black Elk later remarked of the speaker, "His voice was very kind but I shook all over with fear now, for I knew that these were not old men but the Powers of the World and the first was the Power of the West; the second, of the North; the third, of the East; the fourth, of the South; the fifth, of the Sky; the sixth, of the Earth."

The spokesman of the elders gave Black Elk six sacred objects. First, he received a wooden cup full of water, symbolizing the water of the sky that has the power to make things green and alive. Second, he was given a bow that had within it the power to destroy. Third, he was given a sacred name, "Eagle Wing Stretches," which he was to embody in his role as shaman (healer and diviner) for his tribe. Fourth, he was given an herb of power that would allow him to cleanse and heal those who were sick in body or spirit. Fifth, he was given the sacred pipe, which had as its purposes a strengthening of the collective might of the Lakota tribe and a healing of the divisions among the Lakota, to allow them to live in peace and harmony. Finally, Black Elk received a bright red stick that was the "center of the nation's circle" or hoop. This stick symbolized a sacred focusing of the Lakota nation and linked the Lakota to their ancestors as well as to those who would follow them.

Black Elk's vision ended with a flight into a foreboding future in which the Lakota would encounter white-skinned "bluecoats" who would threaten the sacred hoop of the Lakota nation. Many years later, as Black Elk reflected on his vision, he realized that even in the devastating upheaval caused by the wars between his nation and the "bluecoats," his people had been given the sacred objects and rituals that would allow them to rise above mundane exigencies and to heal the nation and restore the hoop in times of trouble.

The vision of Black Elk makes it clear that what sometimes appear to be perfunctory religious rituals, fantastic myths, or arcane ethical injunctions often have their roots in a deep sense of the contact between human beings and that which they have experienced as a divine power. This article emphasizes the social aspects of world religions, but it is important to keep in mind that the religious experiences codified in the social institutions of the world's religions are not fully captured by psychological or sociological explanations alone. There has been a tendency in the academic study of religion to interpret religious experiences and behavior by reducing them to psychological or social causes or antecedents. For example, Sigmund Freud (1928) reduces religious experiences to unconscious projections of human needs that he likens to infantile fantasies that rational humans should grow beyond. A contemporary of Freud, Emile Durkheim (1965, p. 466), has a tendency to reduce religions to their social functions: "If religion has given birth to all that is essential in society, it is because the idea of society is the soul of religion."

While the pioneering work of Max Weber and Durkheim laid the groundwork for much of contemporary social analysis of religion, comparative sociologists of religion such as Joachim Wach (1958) have tempered earlier tendencies toward sociological reductionism. Wach sought to understand the nature of religion by examining traditions throughout the world and noting the primary elements they shared. He identified religious experience as the basic and formative element in the rise of religious traditions around the world and then investigated the expression of this experience in thought, action, and community.

Wach said that there is a symbiotic relationship between religion and society. On the one hand, religion influences the form and character of social organizations or relations in the family, clan, or nation as well as develops new social institutions such as the Christian church, the Buddhist *sangha*, and the "Lakota nation." On the other hand, social factors shape religious experience, expression, and institutions. For example, in Black Elk's vision, the role of the warrior in Lakota society is expressed through the two men who come to escort Black Elk into the sky, and in his later mystical venture into the future, Black Elk as Lakota shaman (*wichash wakan* is one who converses with and transmits the Lakota's ultimate spiritual power, or *Wakan*) becomes the ultimate warrior who battles a "blue man" (perhaps representing personified evil or the dreaded "bluecoats"). Lakota social conventions that name the natural directions as four (North, South, East, West) are modified by Black Elk's vision to include Sky and Earth, making six vision directions that influence the number of elders Black Elk encounters in the heavenly teepee and the number of sacred objects he is given. Here the shaman's vision modifies social conventions even as it creates a social subconvention for other visionaries who also name the directions as six. The objects are conventional implements of Black Elk's culture that are empowered to serve symbolically as multivocal conveyors of sacred knowledge and wisdom. Finally, Black Elk's vision can be viewed sociologically as confirming the corporate sacredness (the sacred hoop) of the nation of the Lakota. For example, a Lakota's vision was powerful and meaningful only to the extent that the tribe accepted it. In this sense one can understand why Durkheim would say that religion, in this case the Lakota's, is society writ large in the sky.

However, for Wach and for scholars, such as Niman Smart (1969), who follow his lead, the forms and expressions of religious life are best understood as emanating from religious experience. Smart identifies six dimensions that all religions share: (1) ritual, (2) mythological, (3) doctrinal, (4) ethical, (5) social, and (6) experiential. The author of this article has provided an interpretative framework for understanding the necessary interdependence of these six elements of religious traditions in *Two Sacred Worlds: Experience and Structure in the World's Religions* (Shinn 1977). These dimensions of the religious life form the structure of this analysis of the social aspect of world religions.

RELIGIOUS EXPERIENCE

Building on the insights of William James and Rudolph Otto (1946), more recent scholars such as Wach, Smart, and Mircea Eliade (1959) seek the origin of religion in the religious experience of a founder or religious community. These scholars assert that genuinely religious experiences include an awareness or an immediate experience of an ultimate reality or sacred power, whether a theistic divinity as in the case of the God(s) of Judaism, Christianity, and Islam or a nontheistic transcendental reality as in the case of the Buddhists' Nirvana or the Hindus' Brahman/Atman. James suggests that transcendental or mystical experiences are immediate apprehensions of the divine that are marked by ineffability, a noetic quality, transiency, and passivity. From one perspective, ineffability can be understood as the inability of language to relay the emotional and cognitive content of a peak religious experience; it also may be described as a failure of language to capture the divine subject of such an experience, that is, the ultimate reality itself. Nonetheless, religious experiences inevitably are understood as providing new states of knowledge that cannot be grasped fully by the discursive intellect. This noetic dimension of religious experience often is described as the revelation of new knowledge (i.e., illumination) that is provided by religious experiences. In fact, it is precisely an awareness of an encounter with a sacred reality in religious experiences that differentiates these experiences from nonreligious peak experiences (e.g., an aesthetic peak experience of a piece of music). Religious experiences also tend to be marked by brevity (i.e., transiency) and the passivity of the person having the experience. While aesthetic, political, and erotic peak experiences may be characterized by ineffability,

transiency, and passivity, only religious experiences bring with them a consciousness of an encounter with a "holy other" sacred reality.

Whether a founding religious experience is immediate and direct, such as the Buddha's nontheistic enlightenment experience of Nirvana, or cumulative and indirect, as was the lengthy exodus journey of the Hebrews, religious experiences are, in Wach's terms, "the most powerful, comprehensive, shattering, and profound experience" of which human beings are capable (1958, p. 35). Wach concludes that a necessary criterion of genuine religious experience "is that it issues in action. It involves imperative; it is the most powerful source of motivation and action" (1958, p. 36). Consequently, religious experiences may be viewed as the wellspring of religion both in the formation of a new religious tradition and in the origin of the faith of the later generations.

Even if one accepts the primacy of religious experience, it is important to note that founding religious experiences are deeply immersed in the social and cultural realities of their time and place. For example, whether immediate and direct or cumulative and indirect, religious experiences inevitably are expressed in the language and concepts of the persons and culture in which they arose. Black Elk's vision of *Wakan* in the form of the six Grandfathers clearly reflects the Lakotas' social and political structure as well as their idealized notions of nation and nature. The Thunder Beings and Grandfathers who are the personifications of *Wakan* Tanka ("Great Power") obviously arise from the natural, linguistic, and social environments of the Lakota. So does the conception of *Wakan* itself as a pervasive power that permeates animal and human life as well as that of nature. A contemporary Lakota has said, "All life is *Wakan*." So also is everything which exhibits power whether in action, as in the winds and drifting clouds, or in passive endurance, as the boulder by the wayside.

Religious experiences occur to persons who have already been socialized. The most obvious social tool is the language used to express even the most profound religious experiences. The ineffable nature of religious experiences requires the use of metaphors or extensions of everyday language, as in the case of Black Elk, and to some extent, the experience itself is shaped by the language in which it is expressed.

Divine names usually are borrowed from the social and linguistic environment of the founder or founding community. For example, the exodus experience of the Hebrew people was interpreted by them as a liberating religious experience fostered by the God of Abraham, Isaac, and Jacob. This God, whose name is given in the Book of Exodus as Yahweh ("I am who I am"), is also called El Elyon ("God most high"), El Shaddai ("God of the mountain"), and Elohim (usually translated as "God"). Moses probably borrowed the name "Yahweh" from the Midianites. El Elyon was the high god of Salem (later called Jerusalem) and was worshiped by King Melchizedek. It also is known that the Canaanite high god of the same period was named El and appears in different cultic sites throughout the ancient Near East. Although it is clear that the Hebraic religious texts understand Yahweh and El quite differently than do their known local counterparts, the Hebrew high god embraced the local deity nomenclatures while modifying their meanings.

In a similar fashion, the divinity of the man Jesus is acknowledged in early Christian texts through references to earlier Jewish apocalyptic language and expectations. In the Jewish apocalyptic literature (e.g., I Enoch), the "Son of Man" appears as a righteous judge who will come to earth to signal the beginning of the heavenly kingdom and God's rule. As an eternal savior, the Son of Man will come to save the righteous followers of God and destroy all those who ignore him. In those linguistic borrowings, however, significant modifications of the original conceptions are made to adjust the titles and expectations to the man Jesus as perceived by his followers. For example, Jesus comes as the Son of Man not primarily as a stern and vengeful judge but as a savior who is himself the sacrifice. This linguistic and conceptual transformation reflects the dependence of language on experience as much as it reveals the social and linguistic dimensions of religious experience.

Similar examples of borrowed—and transformed—god names abound in religious literature and history throughout the world. In Saudi Arabia in the sixth century, Mohammed elevated a local polytheistic Meccan god, Allah, to the status of an international deity. In tenth-century Indian Puranic literature, devotees of the god Vishnu promote his *avatar*, called Krishna, to a supreme theistic position as the god above all gods. Although the *Bhagavata Purana* recounts the *lilas*, or play, of Krishna as though the author were describing historic figure, it is clear to textual scholars that there are two essentially distinct and dynamic story traditions arise from the Brahminical Krishna of *Bhagavad Gita* fame and from the indigenous cowherd Gopala Krishna associated with the western Indian Abhira tribes.

Although devotees of either Allah or Krishna now perceive their divinity and his name as having been "from the beginning," there is little doubt that the local social and linguistic environments provided both content and context for the names of the divinities in these two traditions. Perhaps the most radical example of theistic amalgamation is that of the Indian goddess Kali. Described in medieval Indian texts as being synonymous with literally dozens of local and regional goddess names and traditions, Kali is a latecomer to the Indian theistic scene as one who is given the primary attributes of many gods and goddesses. The mythological tale of the birth of Kali reveals an amalgamation process that gave birth to this great goddess now worshiped by millions in India as the "Supreme Mother." Finally, the concept and expressions of the nontheistic Nirvana experienced by the Buddha were fundamentally shaped by the notion of reincarnation or rebirth and other metaphysical assumptions common to most religious traditions in India in the fifth century B.C.

These examples show that while religious experience of the sacred may be the initiating point of the world's religious traditions or an individual's faith, that experience is given shape and substance by the linguistic and social context out of which it arises. It is also true, however, that life-altering religious experiences such as those described above shape the language and traditions through which they are expressed. This symbiotic relationship occurs in the other dimensions of religious life that are shared by the world's religions.

MYTH AND RITUAL

Formative religious experiences contain within them impulses to expression (myth) and re-creation (ritual) that later become routinized and then institutionalized. Core myths and rituals, therefore, attempt to convey and re-create the experience of the founder or religious community. Both myths and rituals rely on symbols whose content must be shared in order for them to have meaning for the religious group that uses them. Symbols have not only shared cognitive meanings but also common emotional significance and value. That is, symbols do not simply convey intellectual understanding but also engender an emotive response. Furthermore, religious symbols are integrative and transforming agents in that they point to realities that have been encountered but are hidden from everyday vision and experience. Paul Ricoeur (1972) says that symbols yield their meaning in enigma, not through literal or direct translation. Symbols, therefore, suggest rather than explicate; they provide "opaque glimpses" of reality rather than definitive pictures. Understood in this fashion, the journey from symbol to myth is a short one for Ricoeur, who takes myth to be a narrative form of the symbol. Put simply, myths are narratives or stories of the sacred and of human encounters with it.

As stories of sacred powers or beings, myths fall into two basic categories: expressive and reflective. Expressive myths are sacred narratives that attempt to relate the founding or codifying religious experiences of a religious tradition, while reflective mythic narratives are composed subsequently to integrate the sacred experience into everyday life. For example, Black Elk's "re-telling" of his vision experience becomes an expressive myth or sacred narrative for the Oglala Lakota to which they refer again and again in reflective stories of the Thunderbeings or the Grandfathers, wherein the Lakota attempt to extend the lessons of this experience to later problems they encounter. Nearly every extant religious tradition tells and retells its sacred narrative of the founder's or founders' encounter with the sacred reality. Black Elk's vision becomes such a story for the Oglala Lakota.

The story of the exodus of the Hebrews is recounted as a symbolic and founding narrative of God's liberation for Jewish people of all times. The stories of the life, death, and resurrection of Jesus form the core myths of Christians when one understands a myth to mean "sacred narrative" rather than "untrue story." Likewise, the story of the Buddha's arduous meditative journey culminating in the attainment of Nirvana inspires religious thought and behavior throughout all Buddhist

lands even today. Similarly, Muhammad's auditory experience of Allah on Mount Hira, which resulted in his recording of the Qur'an, constitutes the sacred history of millions of Muslims on all the continents. Finally, even though scholars are confident in their judgment that the life of Krishna as told in the tenth-century *Bhagavata Purana* is really an anthology of stories borrowed from earlier Krishna traditions, these *lilas*, or "playful episodes," told as a single life of Krishna have inspired religious experiences, poetry, and rituals that still enliven the lives of millions of Hindus throughout the world. From even this selective set of examples of founding myths, it is clear how deeply they drink from the social, linguistic, and institutional wellsprings of their time and place.

The generative function of core myths is shared by certain rituals that attempt to "represent" in a spatial and physical context the core experience of a religious tradition. From one perspective, core rituals are those that emerge from sacred narratives or myths as their active component. From a second perspective, core rituals represent repetitive, institutionalized behavior and clearly are immersed in the social sphere of religious life. For example, the Christian narrative that relates the Last Supper of Jesus as a sacramental event (e.g., Mark 14:12–26) is physically presented in the early Christian love feast that becomes the Lord's Supper (Eucharistic ritual or Mass) of later Christian churches.

The work of Victor Turner (1969) in a traditional African religious context provides a vocabulary for the religious and social transactions that take place in core myths and rituals. Turner describes three phases in ritual reenactments that attempt to (1) separate or detach the participant from everyday consciousness and social position, (2) provide a moment of *liminality* and *communitas* of shared experience with participants in rituals, and then (3) reintegrate ritual participants back into everyday life with its social roles and structure. *Liminality* is the neutral psychological and social state of transition between one's former social roles and consciousness and the new status one assumes beyond the ritual. *Communitas* for Turner is a mode of social relationship that is marked by an egalitarianism that is uncommon in the stratified roles and relationships of the everyday world. Consequently, Turner would argue that religious rituals may provide an in-between, or liminal, moment of social and psychological experience that religious devotees often assert includes an encounter with their sacred power or reality.

The Passover narrative in the Book of Exodus provides a good example of a core myth that is later enacted, in this case in a Passover meal. In its literal meaning, the Passover myth refers to the tenth plague, when the angel of death killed Egyptian firstborn children while sparing the Hebrew children just before the exodus journey. In its symbolic sense, the Passover story that is "represented" in the Passover sacrificial meal symbolizes Yahweh's power of liberation. To the extent that the story of the exodus reveals the beginning of Yahweh's covenantal relationship to the Hebrew people, the Passover ritual attempts to re-create or revivify that relationship.

Beyond the community's social embodiment of the sacred story of Israel's encounter with Yahweh in a festive and communal sacrificial ritual of the Passover, the social aspects of both the myth and the ritual are evident. Sacrifices were the common mode of worship for the pre-Mosaic tribal religions as well as for the contemporary cults in Moses' day. It is very likely that the Passover ritual described in Exodus 12 derives from a combination of a nomadic animal sacrifice and an agricultural feast of unleavened cakes, both of which predate the exodus event. While the Hebrews' experience of Yahweh in the exodus journey reshapes both the story and the ritual as a liberation event, both the Hebrew myth and the ritual have antecedents in the social and religious world of which they were a part.

Similarly, the baptism and Eucharist rituals in the Christian faith are core rituals that stem from the religious narratives that gave birth to them. Likewise, traditional nontheistic Theravada forms of Buddhist meditation appear to stem directly from the Buddha's spiritual struggle and release but draw on Jain and Hindu forms that predate them. Among the Oglala Lakota, the horse dance ritual was taught by Black Elk to his tribe in a fashion that replicated as closely as possible the vision he received. Therefore, the six old Grandfathers, the horses representing the four cardinal directions, and the various sacred implements he was given all become central elements of the horse dance ritual.

In Islam, the Hajj is one of the five pillars of faith that is incumbent on all Muslims to honor and embody. The Hajj is a pilgrimage that reenacts the spiritual journey of Muhammad with periods of fasting, prayer, and meditation that culminate with ritual circumambulations of the Ka'ba, the black stone in the central mosque of Mecca that is the seat of Allah's throne. In the Hindu devotional traditions, it is common for dramatic performances, stylized ritual dance forms such as Bharata Natyam, and temple dramatic readings to convey episodes of the encounter of devotees with the divine. Consequently, theatrical dramatic productions of the *lilas*, or playful pastimes, of the cowherd god Krishna are enjoyed by villagers throughout India not simply as theatrical events but as representations of Krishna's delightful divine play. The daily ritual reenactment that occurs before the shrines of Krishna, Kali, and other Indian divinities is called *puja* and is a ritual ceremony that probably emanates from the stylized honorific behavior one accords to a royal guest. Here the social precursors to religious ritual are evident, even though they are transformed by the religious narrative and ritual context into which they are placed.

Scholars across a variety of disciplines and perspectives have asserted the interconnection of myth, ritual, and the religious community. Perhaps the most clear summary of this relationship is given by Bronislaw Malinowski, who says, "An intimate connection exists between the word, the mythos, the sacred tales of a tribe, on the one hand and their ritual acts, their moral deeds, their social organization, and even their practical activities on the other" (1954, p. 96). Malinowski indicates that while core myths and rituals may have their origin in founding religious experiences, they also serve as social "warrants" for the primary beliefs of the society out of which they arise and which they help shape. From this perspective, myths and rituals serve primarily as vehicles that legitimate social institutions. Core myths and rituals appear to be charged with the difficult task of representing and re-creating founding religious experiences. They also reflect and embrace their social and cultural contexts. Furthermore, not all myths and rituals serve this primary and essentialist function; certain myths, rituals, and religious behaviors diverge considerably from the impetus the core narrative seems to suggest.

ETHICS

Malinowski and Wach make clear that ethics arise partly as a result of religious experience but also participate fully in social processes. While religious experiences may give rise to immediate expression (core myths) and reenactments (core rituals), they also give impetus to new attitudes and intentions, which are reflected in norms for behavior. In the Christian context, such behavior is claimed to be the mark of a "reborn" person whose conduct manifests the tangible effects of an experience of God. Conversely, the ethical norms and traditions that arise within a religious institution may reflect as much the mores of the surrounding culture and society as they do the experience upon which the institution was founded. Social factors such as language, family roles, and social customs play a role in the process of the externalization of the religious life in ethical laws. James says simply that behavior is the empirical criterion for determining the quality and validity of a religious experience. The distinction he makes between the person who has a religious experience and the person who undergoes a religious conversion is the distinction between having a highly charged peak experience and living a new life born of that experience.

It appears that all religious traditions evidence an interdependent and necessary relationship of conduct to experience so that what is experienced as an ecstatic encounter with the divine is expressed as a new and integrated mode of living. The committed ethical life of a devotee, then, is ideally understood as an active extension of religious experience expressed through communal or shared norms. While an immediate religious experience may provide a core religious impulse (e.g., to love God and one's neighbor in the Christian context or to fear Allah in the Muslim context), that impetus becomes manifest in the concrete situations of social behavior. For example, the nontheistic enlightenment experience of the Buddha resulted in a sense of detachment from the world that was linked to enduring traditions of *metta* and *karuna* (love and compassion) and resulted in "detached compassion" as the complex ethical norm the Buddha modeled for his disciples.

The most obvious intrusion of social norms and processes into the religious life occurs in moral decision making. The natural and social worlds in which people live provide challenges and problems that require an ethical response. Consequently, life in the world poses many situations not anticipated in the religious texts and routinized ethical norms of religious traditions. As a result, over time, ethical systems often come to reflect the surrounding secular culture and social norms as much as they do the basic religious impulse from which they are supposed to derive their direction. This process is mediated during the life of the founder whose authority and behavior provides a model for action. In subsequent generations, however, individuals and institutions such as the Pope, the Buddhist *sangha* (community of elders), and the Lakota tribal council often determine the ethical norms of a community. When ethical statements and positions stray too far from their initial impulses, they are in danger of mirroring the society they intend to make sacred. Put simply, while ethical impulses may originate in religious experiences, the ethical laws, norms, and traditions that are constituted in scriptures and institutional pronouncements often distort the moral imperative by including rationalizations that conform to social, not religious, expectations.

An example of the difference between ethical impulse and moral law can be found in the Hebrew notion of a covenantal relationship with God. Moses and the exodus tribes experienced a compassionate, mighty, jealous, and demanding God. The laws of the early Hebrews, therefore, were viewed not only as commandments arising from a stern leader or group of legalistic lawmakers but also as expressions of an appreciative and liberating relationship with God. The Sinai story of the transmission of the Ten Commandments is intended to reveal the Hebrews' ethical relationship with Yahweh. It was on that holy mountain that the covenant between Yahweh and his people was given concrete expression. However, this relationship was marked by infidelity on the part of Yahweh's people. Therefore, for many of them, the codes of conduct contained in the Ten Commandments and the Levitical Code were experienced as the oppressive laws of a judgmental God.

Jesus summarized the essence of ethical behavior in a twofold commandment to love God and love one's neighbor that was enjoined on all who would count themselves as disciples of God. However, the teachings of Jesus and the commandment of love have led over the centuries to disputes about whether Christians should engage in war, permit abortions, treat homosexuals as equals, and allow divorces. Institutionalized Christian churches in their many forms have decreed what proper ethical conduct is with regard to such issues, and those norms vary and even contradict each other within and across Christian religious traditions. This is the difference between the imperative to love God and love one's "neighbor" and ethical laws that must express divine love in complex and rapidly changing social contexts and situations. Seemingly universal laws such as "Do not kill" mean something quite different to a Lakota warrior who may kill (and sometimes scalp) his enemy (but not a fellow tribesman) than they do to a Muslim who is encouraged to kill an infidel who defames Allah or to a Buddhist who is enjoined not to kill *any* living being.

Even among seemingly similar traditions, such as the Hindu devotional sects, ethical norms can vary immensely. In the Kali goddess tradition, animal sacrifice is still commonly practiced as a way of returning to the goddess the life-giving force she has bestowed on her creation. Some devotees of Kali have interpreted her mythological destruction of demons as a model for their own behaviors and have followed suit as thieves and murderers in the Indian Thuggi tradition. By contrast, Kali devotees such as Rahmakrishnan understand Kali to be a transcendent "ocean of bliss" who engenders peacefulness and nonviolence in her disciples.

What is true of all these religious traditions around the world is that persons usually are taught what constitutes proper or ethical behavior, and in that context, ethics are learned conceptions born of the social process and its experiences. Consequently, ethical norms and their expression often reflect the social environment in which religious traditions arise. A clear expression of this fact is found in the Hindu religious tradition's embrace of the caste system that sacralizes a socially elitist and patriarchal social system that predates Hinduism. Caste distinctions that are sacralized in the mythical and theological texts of the Hindu tradition serve as warrants for social roles and norms that undergird not only the Hindu traditions but also those of the Buddhists and Jains in India.

THEOLOGY AND DOCTRINES

Just as religious experience may result in the formation of a religious movement that tells the founding story of contact with a sacred power (core myth), tries to re-create that experience for the beginning and subsequent communities (core rituals), and impels new believers to act in accordance with this vision or revelation (ethical impulse leading to institutionalized ethics), so it is that even very early in a religious tradition's history questions and criticisms arise that must be answered. Religious reflection takes a variety of forms that touch the total corporate life of a religious community. Sacred scriptures often encompass expressive myths that relate in narrative form the founder's or founders' contact with the sacred core rituals in outline or in full, ethical injunctions and moral codes, and reflective myths, doctrines, and explications that attempt to answer believers' questions and unbelievers' skepticism. Almost inevitably, members of a religious community are provoked from without and within to explain how their sacred reality is related to the origin of the community and perhaps even to the origin of the world. Consequently, reflective myths that represent second-level or posterior reflection are incorporated to explain those beginnings.

Three distinct but interrelated purposes and functions of reflective myths are to (1) explain origins, (2) rationalize aspects of core beliefs, and (3) provide an apologetic defense of the faith to disbelieving insiders or outsiders. A good example of reflective theologizing is the development of the biography of the Buddha. The oldest Pali texts essentially begin the life of the Buddha with his disillusionment with the world at age 29, when he was already a husband and a father. The early texts indicate that his name was Siddhartha and that his father, Suddhodana, ruled a small district in the north Indian republic of the Sakyas. This early story indicates that Siddhartha was married at the age of 16 or 17, had a son, and then became disillusioned with the human suffering he saw around him and renounced the world to seek spiritual liberation while leaving his family behind.

Approximately five hundred years after the death of the Buddha, two separate "biographies" were written that contained accumulated legends not only about the miraculous birth of the Buddha but also about the great renunciation. The birth story describes the descent of the Buddha from the heavens as a white elephant who miraculously enters his mother's side and is born nine months later as a fully functioning adultlike child. These biographies describe the Buddha's physical features (captured in religious images and icons) as including the lengthened ears of an aristocrat, a smoothly shaped conical bump on the top of the head indicating his intelligence, and other marks that foretell his later enlightenment.

These latter-day scriptures recount his renunciation of the world in a full-blown, theologized story of encounters with an ill man, a decrepit old man, a dead man, and a religious ascetic. The story of the Buddha's four visions provides a fuller explication of the reasons for his renunciation. Both the birth story confirming the Buddha's sacred origins and the story of the four visions of the Buddha (a rationalization of his renunciation) represent reflective myths that fill in biographical gaps in earlier stories of his life in light of his later enlightened status.

Parallels to the biographical history of the Buddha can be found in the scriptural stories of the miraculous births of Jesus, Mahavira (founder of the Jains), Krishna, Kali, and Muhammad, among others. A similar genre of reflective myths can be found in the creation stories that often are added dozens of years or even centuries after the founding experience. Good examples of this process are the Hebrew creation stories told in Genesis 1 and Genesis 2. God's creation in seven days is the youngest creation story (the priestly story of the seventh century B.C. that is told in Genesis 1:1–2:4a) and is placed at the beginning of the book of Genesis. It is likely that the Akkadian myth of Tiamat served as a model for this story of the creation of the world out of a watery chaos.

The older Yahwist creation story, found in Genesis 2:4b ff., is set in a desert environment instead of a primeval ocean and very likely goes back to the tenth century B.C. A decidedly more anthropomorphic story, the Yahwist Garden of Eden story, was added at least three to four hundred years after the exodus experience. Neither the priestly story nor the Yahwist story received its present form until the sixth or seventh century B.C., when both were called upon to explicate the creative power of their Hebrew God set against the Canaanites' theology of nature's seasonal birth, death, and rebirth that the Hebrews encountered in Palestine. For the Palestinian farmer, Canaanite or Israelite, the question was, "Is it Yahweh or Baal to whom one should offer sacrifices and give allegiance if one's crops are to prosper?" The two Genesis creation stories explain not only who is responsible for the origin of life on earth but also how one can explain human illness, suffering, and death in the context of the God who led the Hebrews out of Egypt. In Africa and India, the numerous and sometimes contradictory creation stories one finds in a single religious tradition reveal less about the illogical nature of some reflective myths than they do about the human need to have questions of birth, death, suffering, social relationships, and the founding of the tribe placed in the context of a tradition's ultimate reality.

When religious traditions develop full-fledged social institutions, it is common for sacred texts and other interpretive theological texts to explain the necessity of those religious organizations and their officials. Whether it is the early church fathers' explanations of the seat of Peter on which the Pope sits in the Roman Catholic tradition or a Lakota visionary myth that explains the role of the shaman in the community, reflective myths and theologies develop as intellectual and institutional rationalizations for the extension of the founding experiences and tradition into all aspects of life and society. Religious councils, theological traditions, sectarian disputes, and doctrinal formulas all arise as socialized institutions that attempt to explicate, defend, and provide an apology for a religious faith firmly embedded in the personal and social lives of its adherents. For example, Islamic theology extends the influence of the Qur'anic faith into the economic, political, and social lives of the Muslim people. Likewise, from birth and family relationships through wars and death, the Lakota's life was experienced within the sacred hoop.

The extension of religious faith into all aspects of life is justified in scriptures and doctrinal tracts by the reflective process of mythmaking and theologizing. Peter Berger (1969) calls such activity the construction of a *nomos*. A theological *nomos* is essentially a socially constructed worldview that attempts to order all of human experience in the context of a sacred reality, whether theistic (e.g., Krishna or Allah) or nontheistic (e.g., Nirvana). Such theological reflection is determined to a great extent by the social and human circumstances that give rise to the questions that must be answered as well as the language and social conventions through which the reflections are expressed. However, Wach reminds us that the prophetic function of religious traditions often shapes the social environment to a religious vision and not simply vice versa. Puritan society in colonial America is an example of religious faith shaping social mores and institutions.

INSTITUTIONS

Religious institutions arise as the fullest and most obvious social expression of a religious faith. They are equally the home for the core myths and rituals to be enacted and the loci of the religious communities whose individual and collective needs must be met. Religious institutions vary from formal collectivities such as the Christian church, the Muslim mosque, the Hindu temple, and the Buddhist *sangha* to their extended representations in festivals and ceremonial events such as weddings and funerals. It is within the social institution that *communitas* understood as a spiritual leveling of religious adherents exists alongside a religious community in which social differentiation and hierarchies usually persist. Religious institutions are usually the most deeply embedded social aspect of religion, since it is their task to control the external conduct of their members through rites, rituals, and ethical norms while providing an economic and political power base through which they can compete with other social institutions. Simply put, religious institutions are to a great extent socially constructed realities that provide for the habituation and rationalization of religious thought and behavior.

James (1961) viewed the church, synagogue, or other religious organization as a "secondhand" extension of the religious life. In terms of institutional leadership, Abraham Maslow (1970) distinguishes between "prophets" (i.e., those who found the religion) and "legalists" (those who regulate, systematize, and organize religious behavior in institutional forms). Even from this brief discussion of the interrelationships of the primary aspects of the religious life, one can see why Michael Novak says, "Institutions are the normal, natural expression of the human spirit. But that spirit is self-transcending. It is never satisfied with its own finite expressions" (1971, p. 156). According to Novak, the basic conflict is between the human spirit and all institutions.

No religious institution has escaped criticism of its creeds, dogmas, ethics, and authoritative pronouncements from those within the tradition who insist that the essential faith demands revisions of the institution's expressions of that faith. These criticisms give rise not only to reform movements but also to schisms and new sects that emerge as a result of the clash between the received faith in its textual and social forms and the religious experiences and impulses of a reformer or critic within the organization. Martin Luther was a reformer whose critique of his received Roman Catholic heritage was both personal and theological. Similarly, the numerous Buddhist sects that arose in the first hundred years after the death of the Buddha gained their impetus from quarrels over doctrine, lifestyle, and interpretations of the essential nature of the faith. The Sunni and Shi'a (also called Shi'ite) branches of Islam have dozens of contemporary expressions that emanate from a fundamental split in the tradition that occurred shortly after the death of Muhammad and focused on the source of authority for future proclamations in Islam. Typical of other religious traditions, Islam gave early birth to a pietistic mystical tradition, known as Sufism, which has consistently criticized both major theological branches of that religion for their legalistic and worldly focus to the detriment of the nourishment of the spiritual life. The Kabbala is a similar type of mystical reform tradition within Judaism. From one perspective, sectarian and schismatic movements are attempts to recapture the original experience and spirit of a religious tradition in response to institutionalized forms of worship and expression that appear devoid of the core spirit that gave birth to them. Nonetheless, in those cases where the new movement or sect survives its charismatic beginning, it necessarily develops the same institutional forms (religious community, rituals, ethics, etc.) that it rejected in its predecessor and that are experienced by some faithful later generations as too distant from its spiritual foundation and in need of reform. This pattern of dissatisfaction with institutional codifications of religious experience, a time of spiritual innovation or reform, and then institutionalization of the reform is one that continues in all the major religious traditions in the world, producing new sects or, in rare cases, altogether new religious traditions.

NEW RELIGIOUS MOVEMENTS

The attempt to reform a traditional religion in a given cultural setting sometimes has produced a new religious movement (NRM) that threatens the established norms and values of the host society, not just the established religious institution. Often an NRM emanates from an established religion as a reform or even extension of that tradition. An example is early Christianity, which some Jewish and non-Jewish converts saw as fulfilling Jewish prophecy and others regarded as a dangerous and heretical sect that threatened both the Jewish and the Roman institutions of Jesus' time. When the connection with the established tradition is more tenuous, the new revelation and resulting behavior distance themselves almost immediately from traditional institutional forms. For example, Joseph Smith's discovery of lost tablets of scripture not only "completed" the Christian revelation and scriptures but essentially replaced them. Smith's Mormonism promoted theological (e.g., preeminence of the Book of Mormon), ethical (e.g., polygamy), and other views and practices that were at odds not only with traditional Christian norms and institutions but also with those of American society. Such NRMs often generate considerable opposition from both religious and political authorities who perceive a threat to their worldview and the norms that come from that *nomos*. In the first century after the death of Jesus, his followers were martyred by Roman authorities who considered them members of an NRM outside the protection of law afforded Jews in the Roman Empire. Likewise, by the end of the nineteenth century in America, the Mormons not only were attacked by their Christian neighbors asheretical "cult" but were for a time denied the legal right to hold property and to marry.

Approximately one hundred years after groups such as the Mormons, the Seventh-Day Adventists, and the Theosophical Society were considered "cults" to be suppressed, a new wave of NRMs (also called "cults") flooded America. Some of those NRMs were essentially splinter groups of Christians (e.g., Jesus movements) whose evangelical fervor and communitarian lifestyle set them apart from more established Christian churches. Other NRMs, such as Scientology, were the imaginative offspring of idiosyncratic founders such as L. Ron Hubbard, a science fiction writer who promised "total freedom" to all who would practice his strict regimen of psychological and spiritual "clearing." Still other NRMs were imports from Asia with gurus such as Maharishi Mahesh Yogi (Transcendental Meditation) and Guru Maharaj Ji (Divine Light Mission) who taught their own particular Hindu meditational paths to enlightenment. One NRM, the Unification Church of Sung Mung Moon, was essentially a syncretistic blend of Christian missionary and Korean folk religious traditions. The Reverend Moon claims to have had a special revelation on Easter Sunday in 1936, when Jesus appeared to him and asked that Moon complete the messiah's work. Moon's revelation led to a new scripture called *The Divine Principle*, new rituals, and a worldwide mission to unify all Christian and world faiths.

Finally, some of the NRMs of the 1960s in America were not "new" at all but instead were traditional faiths of other cultures seeking converts in an American mission field. One such NRMs was the International Society for Krishna Consciousness (ISKCON), more commonly called the Hare Krishnas. While lumped together with other NRMs, the Hare Krishnas practice what is more properly understood as a traditional form of devotional (*bhakti*) Hinduism centering on the god Krishna. This devotional Hindu faith was brought to America in 1965 by the Hindu sage A. C. Bhaktivedanta Prabhupada. Prabhupada was an *acharya*, or spiritual teacher, whose lineage traces back to the Krishna reformer Chaitanya in the sixteenth century and whose own guru asked him to bring the Hare Krishna faith to English-speaking people. While adapting his teachings to a foreign culture as all missionaries must, Prabhupada taught the same Indian scriptures (e.g., *Bhagavata Purana*), rituals (e.g., worship before Krishna images and chanting Krishna's name), religious dress (e.g., saffron robes), and ethics (e.g., vegetarianism and ritual cleanliness) that had been taught by Indian masters for centuries. While the Krishna faith originated over 2,000 years ago, part of what made this religion seem so new and different to American youths and religious institutions was its evangelical missionary and ecstatic devotional elements (e.g., public chanting and dancing), which were innovations of Chaitinya's reform nearly 400 years ago (see Shinn 1987a).

Whatever the origin or character of NRMs, they represent external challenges to established religions in much the same way that sectarian reforms represent internal challenges. From the point of view of formative religious experiences, NRMs offer alternative spiritual paths to religious seekers who do not find spiritual satisfaction in their natal or traditional religious institutions (Ellwood 1973; Richardson 1985; Shinn 1993). The host society's response to NRMs often reveals the extent to which that society's secular or religious institutions satisfy the needs of its populace (Robbins and Anthony 1981; Barker 1982; Wilson 1981). When religious institutions have stagnated or strayed from their spiritual source, challenges and alternatives arise from within. Likewise, evangelical and missionary ventures from religions around the world take whatever opportunity they are given to provide alternative paths to spiritual fulfillment.

INTERSECTION OF WORLD RELIGIONS

One tendency of insitutionalized religious traditions is to seek to become world religions. The impetus to spread a religion throughout the world sometimes comes from the exclusivistic theological claims that assert the superiority of one faith over another (e.g., Christianity and Islam). Some religious traditions actively seek less to convert others than to assimilate other religions into their own theology and practice (e.g., Hinduism). Still others spread to other lands and cultures after being forced out of their homelands (e.g., Judaism and Buddhism). The broad reach of world religions has resulted in multifaith societies such as India (e.g., Hinduism, Islam, Sikkhism, and Jainism), China (e.g., Confucianism, Buddhism, and Taoism), and the United States (e.g., Christianity, Judaism, and Islam), where different religions have coexisted for centuries. What can one expect of the interaction of world religions as rapid communications and travel bring people and their religious faiths face to face in ever greater numbers in the twenty-first century?

First, it should be expected that wherever religious institutions are interwoven with political and cultural institutions, resistance to or rejection of other world faiths will occur. This tendency will be exacerbated in areas where religious funda-mentalism is the dominant voice. Islamic states such as Pakistan, Iran, and Afghanistan reveal how religious institutions are interwoven with political institutions in ways that suppress tolerance of other faiths. Adding tribal or ethnic loyalties to the mix only increases the difficulty of achieving interreligious tolerance and harmony. The Catholics and Protestants in Northern Ireland, the Bosnian Muslims and Serbian Christians in Bosnia-Herzegovina and the Tamil Hindus and Singhalese Buddhists in Sri Lanka all represent inseparable blends of political, ethnic, and religious exclusivity. Therefore, one mode of interaction of world religions will be intolerance of and sometimes violence toward other faiths created to a great extent by the socialization of religious institutions by the nationalistic and ethnic norms of the people and cultures they intend to save.

Second, in areas where religions have coexisted for a long time, it is common for accommodations and even assimilation to occur that reflect the common home. For example, Hinduism, Buddhism, and Islam have coexisted for more than nine hundred years in India, and in spite of their sometimes violent interactions, remarkable innovations have occurred. Leaders from the Muslim King Akbar to the Hindu sage Gandhi have sought to bring about mutual respect among the religions of India and all the world. Likewise, devotional Hinduism historically has often bridged religious divides by inviting people of all faiths and castes to join in its worship. In the case of Sikhism, Guru Nanck blended devotional Hindu traditions with certain Islamic tenets to form a syncretistic new faith in the sixteenth century. A similar phenomenon occurred in Iran, where Zoroastrian and Islamic roots gave rise in the nineteenth century to the Baha'i faith, which incorporates the scriptures and symbols of all the major world religions into a new syncretistic religion. While the birth of such new syncretistic world religions is rare, what does occur often—and probably will increase—is the adoption of ideas (e.g., reincarnation and impersonal divinity) and practices (e.g., vegetarianism and meditation) from one faith by persons of another faith.

Third, some religious individuals and institutions will continue to seek dialogue with and understanding of persons of other faiths while maintaining their own religious ideas and practices. For example, Mahatma Gandhi was deeply influenced by the Christian and Muslim scriptures and near the end of his life sought peace between Hindus and Muslims when few others could rise above communal loyalties. Still, when shot by an assassin, Gandhi uttered the name of his Hindu family divinity, Rama. Gandhi appreciated the teachings and practices of other world religions but died a Hindu. In a similar fashion, the Buddhist Sarvodaya Movement in Sri Lanka borrows liberally from Gandhi's ideas and disciples even as it embeds its work in Buddhist ideas and practices. So too the Reverend Dr. Martin Luther King, Jr., learned the rudiments of nonviolent action from Gandhi's teachings while situating them within his Christian theology and faith. Thus, even when certain ideas are transferred from one faith to another out of respectful dialogue and interaction, it is common for one's native tradition to remain at the core of one's thought and action.

On a more formal level, there have been many attempts at interfaith dialogue in which the formulation of a common theology (i.e., "perrienal philosophy") or practice for all religions has been sought (see Shinn 1987b). The Christian Trappist monk Thomas Merton spent many of the last years of his life reading about and having a dialogue with persons of other faiths. He was accidentally killed in Bangkok, Thailand, during an interfaith conference with Christian, Buddhist, and other monks from Asia. Most efforts at interfaith dialogue arise when individuals seek to understand their own faith better and to transcend the institutional reflections of a limited time and place. Both formal and informal dialogues are certain to increase as "the global village" becomes a reality and world religions become increasingly familiar in all lands.

CONCLUSION

Clifford Geertz argues that each world religion is essentially "(1) a system of symbols which acts (2) to establish powerful, pervasive, and long-lasting moods and motivation in men by (3) formulating conceptions of a general order of existence and (4) clothing these conceptions with such an aura of factuality that (5) the moods and motivations seem uniquely realistic" (1968, p. 1). This socio-anthropological definition of religion embraces in a clear and simple fashion most of the interpretation of underlying relationships that this article has described. Any religion, whether established or new,

is a system of symbols that simultaneously attempts to express and reveal dimensions of sacred experience beyond that of the everyday by using socially conditioned language and conceptions. Likewise, the general order of existence (*nomos*) that is formulated in the myths, rituals, and ethical norms of a religious tradition emerges from the social consciousness, communal norms, and shared conceptions of the community which give rise to those elements. Finally, what Berger calls "legitimation" and Geertz calls "factuality" represent nothing other than broad-based social acceptance of certain religious beliefs. Consequently, from their inception in religious experience to their full social expression in concrete institutions, religious traditions involve an interplay between personal and social forces. No aspect—experiential, mythical, ritual, ethical, doctrinal, or institutional—of any of the world's religious traditions escapes some social conditioning, and no culture or society is left unchallenged by its religious expressions and lifestyles.

REFERENCES

Barker, Eileen (ed.) 1982 *New Religious Movements: A Perspective for Understanding Society.* New York: Edwin Mellon Press.

Berger, Peter 1969 *The Sacred Canopy: Elements of a Sociological Theory of Religion.* Garden City, N.Y.: Doubleday.

——, and Thomas Luckmann 1967 *The Social Construction of Reality.* New York: Doubleday.

Durkheim, Emile 1965 *The Elementary Forms of the Religious Life,* trans. Joseph Ward Swain. New York: Free Press.

Eliade, Mircea 1959 *The Sacred and the Profane,* trans. Willard R. Trask. New York: Harper and Brothers.

Ellwood, Robert S., Jr. 1973 *Religious and Spiritual Groups in Modern America.* Englewood Cliffs, N.J.: Prentice-Hall.

Freud, Sigmund 1928 *The Future of an Illusion,* trans.W. D. Robson-Scott, Horace Liveright, and the Institute of Psychoanalysis. London: Hogarth Press.

Geertz, Clifford 1968 "Religion as a Cultural System." In Michael Banton, ed., *Anthropological Approaches to the Study of Religion.* London: Tavistock.

James, William 1961 *The Varieties of Religious Experience: A Study in Human Nature.* New York: Collier.

Jung, Carl 1938 *Psychology and Religion.* New Haven, Conn.: Yale University Press.

Malinowski, Bronislaw 1954 "Myth in Primitive Psychology." In Bronislaw Malinowski, *Magic, Science and Religion*. Garden City, N.Y.: Doubleday.

Maslow, Abraham H. 1970 *Religions, Values, and Peak Experiences*. New York: Penguin.

Neidardt, John G. 1972 *Black Elk Speaks*. New York: Pocket Books (from field notes contained in Raymond J. DaMillie 1984 *The Sixth Grandfather: Black Elk's Teachings given to John Neihardt*. Lincoln: University of Nebraska Press).

Novak, Michael 1971 *Ascent of the Mountain, Flight of the Dove*. New York: Harper & Row.

Otto, Rudolph 1946 *The Idea of the Holy*, trans. J. W. Harvey. London: Oxford University Press.

Richardson, James T. 1985 "The Active vs. Passive Convert: Paradigm Conflict in Conversion/Recruitment Research." *Journal for the Scientific Study of Religion* 24:163–179.

Ricoeur, Paul 1972 "The Symbol Gives Rise to Thought." In Walter H. Capps, ed., *Ways of Understanding Religion*. New York: Macmillan.

Robbins, Thomas and Dick Anthony 1981 *In Gods We Trust: New Patterns of Religious Pluralism in America*. New Brunswick: Transaction Books.

Shinn, Larry D 1977 *Two Sacred Worlds: Experience and Structure in the World's Religions*. Nashville, Tenn.: Abingdon.

—— 1987a *The Dark Lord: Cult Images and the Hare Krishnas in America*. Philadelphia: Westminster Press.

—— 1987b "Inside the Mind of the Infinite: Dialogue and Understanding in Interfaith Encounters." In Larry D. Shinn, ed., *In Search of the Divine: Some Unexpected Consequences of Interfaith Dialogue*. New York: Paragon.

—— 1993 "Who Gets to Define Religion? The Conversion/Brainwashing Controversy." *Religious Studies Review* 19(3): 195–207.

Smart, Ninian 1969 *The Religious Experience of Mankind*. New York: Scribners.

Turner, Victor 1969 *The Ritual Process: Structure and Anti-Structure*. Chicago: Aldine.

Wach, Joachim 1958 *The Comparative Study of Religions*. New York: Columbia University Press.

Weber, Max 1963 *The Sociology of Religion*, trans. Ephraim Fischoff. Boston: Beacon.

Wilson, Bryan (ed.) 1981 *The Social Impact of New Religious Movements*. New York: Rose of Sharon Press.

LARRY D. SHINN

Index

G

Gabba, Carlo Francesco, 1464

Gabon, 2133

Gabor, Istvan, 2117

Gagnon, John H., 2539, 2550, 3091

Gaiser, Ted J., 408

Galanter, Marc, 471, 2961

Galbraith, Jay, 2011

Galbraith, John Kenneth, 724, 2921

Gale, Hugh, 3086

Gale Group, 1608

Galen, 1717, 2086

Galileo Galilei, 1781

Gall, Franz Joseph, 528, 529, 1717

Gallagher, John, 1266

Galli, Maria Callari, 1467

Gallier, Xavier, 1587

Gallino, Luciano, 1467

Gallup, George, 3232

Gallup polls. *See* Election polling; Public opinion; Survey research

Galpin, Charles J., 2428

Galston, William A., 356

Galton, Francis, 446–447, 550, 879, 2091–2092, 3005

    eugenics theory, 1272

    intelligence theory, 1360, 1361, 1364

Galton's problem, 550

Galtung, Johan, 639, 1467

Gambler's fallacy, 594–595

Gambling

    and criminalization of deviance, 525

    organized crime operations, 2017, 2019, 2021

    as self-destructive behavior, 3077

Game theory and strategic interaction, **1045–1056**

    altruism and, 118

    characteristic function form, 1046

    coalition formation and, 329–331, 332

    conflict theory and, 414–416

    differential games, 1049

    dynamic games, 1048–1049

    and economic sociology, 735, 2340

    and equity theory, 2700

evolutionary games, 1049

and exchange networks, 2673–2674

experimental studies, 1047–1048

institutional analysis of, 1049–1051

mathematical sociology and, 1791

rational choice theory and, 2335, 2336–2337, 2338, 2419

representational forms of, 2337

and role theory, 2419

and social dynamics, 2666

and social values research, 3220–3222, 3223

solution concepts, 1046–1047

strategic form, 1046

supergames, 1049

theoretic concepts, 1045–1047

typology, 1046

Gamio, Manuel, 1858

Gamson, William A., 101–102, 645–646, 2270

    on social movement successes, 2725

Gandhi, Indira, 2132

Gandhi, Mohandas, 1230, 2269, 3287–3288

Gang rape, 2580

Gangs

    as counterculture, 460, 461

    criminological research, 530, 533

    cultural values and, 2171

    as delinquent subculture, 509, 511, 512–513, 514

    group norms and structure study of, 244, 363, 364, 365, 2611, 2613

    macro-level deviance theories and, 663, 664

    nineteenth-century urban, 1485

Gans, Herbert, 845

Ganzeboom, H. B. G., 2787

García, Carlos, 2131

Gardner, Howard, 1368, 1369

Gardner, John, 1384–1385, 2140

Garelli, Franco, 1473

Garfield, Eugene, 1610

Garfield, James, 2127

Garfinkel, Harold, 226, 856–857, 859, 2756

and conversation analysis, 431, 432

as founder of ethnomethodology, 246, 431

Garment industry, 2333

Garmon, Lance C., 1903

Garth, Bryant G., 1550–1551

Garvey, Marcus, 66

Garza, Gustav O., 1859

Gasparini, Alberto, 1468, 1472, 1473, 2288

Gaston, Berger, 1037

Gates, Bill, 1285

Gates Commission, 1877

GATT (General Agreement on Tariffs and Trade), 794, 1859

Gaulejac, Vincent de, 328

Gauset, Jessie Redmon, 66

Gauss-Markov theorem, 2251

Gaventa, John, 2040

Gay community. *See* Sexual orientation

Gay Liberation Front, 111

Gay rights movement, 315, 2719

Gaza, 1866

Gaze theory

    collective gaze, 3173

    male gaze, 2172

    tourist gaze, 3166–3167, 3172–3173

Gdansk shipyard (Poland), 2268

GDOS (Group Development Observation System), 1979–1980

GDP. *See* Gross Domestic Product

Geddes, Patrick, 1290, 1291

Geen, R. G., 70

Geertz, Clifford, 387, 547, 852, 2855, 2891, 2906

    Indonesian studies, 2976–2977

    on Islamic society, 2941, 2944

    semiotic theory, 2958

    on world religions, 3289

Gehlen, Arnold, 1076, 1077, 1234

Geiger, Theodor, 2450

Geis, Gilbert, 3250, 3252

Gellner, Ernest, 227, 2941, 2942

    theory of Muslim society, 2943–2944, 2945, 2946, 2947

peripheral, 1267–1268

and political party origins, 2154

regional and global influences, 1944–1945, 1948

social constructions of, 1940–1941

in Southeast Asia, 2975, 2978

in Soviet former republics, 1199, 1934

and state development, 3001–3002

state reaction to, 1945–1946

and violence and terrorism, 1199, 1947–1948, 3137

and war, 3244

See also National border relations

Nation-states. *See* National border relations; Nationalism; State

Native American Church, 137

Native American Rights Fund, 1298

Native Americans. *See* American Indian studies

Nativistic movements, 2367

NATO (North Atlantic Treaty Organization), 1944, 1948, 2130, 2143, 2362, 2608, 3003

Natural disasters. *See* Disaster research

Natural Hazards Research Center, 682

Natural law, 1427

Natural Resources Defensc Council, 803

Natural selection

altruism and, 2882

behaviorism and, 209

Darwin's theory of evolution by, 876, 878, 2330, 2334, 2369, 2418, 2880–2881, 2885

and maximization principle, 2881–2882

racial theories and, 2330, 2334

sexual selection and, 2885–2886

Nature vs. nurture, 998

intelligence and, 1369–1373, 2090, 2140, 2330

personality traits and, 2090

sex differences and, 2530

Navajo, 138

Nazism

as authoritarian communitarianism, 356

compliance with authority and, 404

as dictatorship, 3002

divorce laws, 703

and ethnonationalism, 1944

and eugenics, 1272

expansionist policy, 1933

forced labor camps, 2608

Frankfurt School study of, 2169

genocide policy, 1066, 1067, 1070, 1384, 2206

and German families' "legacy of silence," 1512

and German sociology, 1074, 1075

as 1920s protest movement, 2268

party corruption and patronage, 2130

racial views, 1272, 2332

structuralist view of rise of, 2163

Total War concept, 1067

use of judicial discretion by, 477

war crimes trials, 1429

NCHS. *See* National Center for Health Statistics

NCS. *See* National Crime Survey

NCVS. *See* National Crime and Victimization Survey

Neal, A. G., 2346, 2350–2351

Nebbia, Giorgio, 1473

Need-Achievement Dictionary, 1979

Needle (IV) exchange programs, 712, 1642, 2588

Needs, values differentiated from, 2829

Neff, Ronald, 1276

Negative identity, 460

Negative Income Tax, 2213, 2282, 2284

Negative moods. *See* Depression

Negative self-schema, 651

Negotiation of power, **1950–1956**

group conflict resolution, 1111–1117

group decision-making, 597

interpersonal conflict resolution, 1452

and interpersonal power, 1456–1464

pragmatic theory and, 2221

See also State, The

Negritude movement, 66

Neighborhood structure

community studies, 364–366

ethnic succession, 532

and territorial belongings, 3131

and underclass, 2212, 3200

See also Community

Neitz, Mary Jo, 567, 568

Nemeroff, Charles, 652

NEO Personality Inventory, 2079

Neo-Chicago School, 853

Neoclassical economics, 725, 726–727

Neoclassical price theory, 2340

Neoconservatism, 1600–1601, 1603, 1758

Neofunctionalism, 1031, 2484

and feminist theory, 996

Neoliberalism. *See* Neoconservatism

Neolithic period, 2175

Neo-Machiavellians, 2623

Neo-Malthusianism. *See* Malthusian theory

Neo-Marxist theory, 1078, 1214, 2814–2815, 2928

"late capitalism" terminology, 1078–1079

See also Conflict theory

Neo-Nazis, 462

Neo-Weberians, 2815–2816

NEP (new ecological paradigm), 806–807

Nepal

child labor, 3262

poverty, 2216

slavery and slave-like practices, 2605, 2606–2607

time use research, 3161, 3162

Nepotistic favoritism, 2822

Nested games, 330

Nestlé company, 3174

Netherlands

"clean" government reputation, 2130

cohabitation, 109

substruction, 3182

U

U.S. Chamber of Commerce, 2162

U.S. departments and agencies. *See key word*

U.S. Government Document Depositories, 2477

U.S. Health, 1822

U.S. National Academy of Sciences. *See* National Academy of Sciences

U.S. National Surveys, 577

U.S. Surgeon General report, 1762

UCR. *See* Uniform Crime Reports

Udy, Stanley, 232

Uganda, 2133
AIDS/HIV epidemic, 2591, 2592
poverty in, 2216
and Rwandan genocide, 68, 1069
slavery and forced labor in, 2603, 2606

Uighurs, 3001

Ukraine, 2137, 2362, 2982

Ulmer, Jeffrey, 2221–2222

Ulrich's International Periodicals Directory, 1606

"Ultimate" bargaining game, 597

Ultimate judgement, 597

"Ultimatum game," 597

Unconscious, 1713, 1714

Uncover Reveal (journal article-alerting service), 1611

Underclass. *See* Urban underclass

Underdeveloped countries. *See* Dependency theory; Developing countries; Industrialization in less developed countries;

Underemployment. *See* Marginal employment

Underground economy, 1339

Underidentified model, 1916

Understanding Prediction: Essays in Methodology of Social and Behavioral Sciences (Nowak), 2120

Unemployment
global rates, 3263
layoffs and displacement, 3265
programs, 2795, 2798
rate in rural areas, 2430

rate measurement, 1521, 1720
urban underclass and, 3198

UNESCO. *See* United Nations Educational, Scientific and Cultural Organization

Ungaro, Daniele, 1473

UNICEF, 2607

Unification Church, 900, 2379
affinity of religion and family in, 936
as new religious movement, 2366, 3287

Uniform Code of Military Justice, 1881

Uniform Commercial Code, 475, 476

Uniform Crime Reporting Handbook (FBI), 493

Uniform Crime Reports (UCR), 491–500, 530
arrests by race, 1490
Census Bureau survey as supplement, 1489
and family violence, 982
general definitions of offenses, 492
and juvenile crime, 1486–1487, 1489
and sex crimes, 2557

Uniform distribution, shape of, 661

Unikel, Luis, 1859

Unilineal kinship systems, 1502–1503, 1507

Union Carbide, 2877

Unions. *See* Labor movements and unions; Industrial sociology

United Arab Emirates, 1865, 1866, 1867
sociodemographic profile, 2938

United Arab Republic, 1947

United Furniture Workers, 1533

United HealthCare, 1822

United Kingdom
African colonization, 60, 61
colonial racial conflicts, 321
common law system, 465, 474–475, 477–478, 480, 1545
communitarianism, 361, 362
conditions conducive to democracy, 605–606

crime rate surveys, 498–499

divorce reform laws, 703

drug policy, 712, 713

education and status attainment, 3045

Elizabethan Poor Laws, 2840–2841

ethnic immigrants, 636

ethnic status incongruence, 3051

fertility transitions, 2178

first modern police force, 2110–2112, 2113

foreign-controlled pharmaceutical companies, 1827

governmental division of power, 1953

health-care system, 374, 375, 376, 378–379, 380, 1827

juvenile violence, 1487

kinship systems and family type, 1504

labor movement, 1529, 1533

long-term care and care facilities, 1652, 1653, 1655, 1659, 1661

organizational demographics, 395

political party system, 2154, 2164

political scandals, 2130

postcolonial India and, 641

racial discrimination, 692, 693

and rebellion, 3000

retirement patterns, 2407

slave trade suppression by, 2600, 2602, 2607

social anthropology, 2890, 2893

Social Science Data Archive, 575, 576, 580

social security system, 2796, 2797

social surveys, 577

solicitor-barrister distinction, 478

Southeast Asian influences by, 2975

time use research, 3164

tourism in, 3169

transnational corporations, 3175, 3176

unemployment, 3263

utopian literature, 3203–3204

woman suffrage, 703

World War II, 2362

ISBN 0-02-865581-8

90000

9 780028 655819